Huntington Library Publications

IN THE STRONGHOLD.

T. S. ARTHUR, *Woman to the Rescue* [1874], No. 147.

American Fiction
1851-1875

A CONTRIBUTION TOWARD A BIBLIOGRAPHY

BY

LYLE H. WRIGHT

Additions and Corrections Appended

THE HUNTINGTON LIBRARY
SAN MARINO, CALIFORNIA
1965

Z
1231
F4
W92
1965

PRINTED IN U.S.A. BY
KINGSPORT PRESS, INC., KINGSPORT, TENNESSEE

CONTENTS

PREFACE

THE purpose of this bibliography is to list the fiction written for adults by Americans and published in the United States between 1851 and 1875. It includes novels, novelettes, romances, short stories, tall tales, tract-like tales, allegories, and fictitious biographies and travels, in prose. Anonymous works have been retained when it was not readily determined whether they were of foreign or American authorship. The foreign-born authors who are listed claimed the United States as their home.

The momentous events that occurred during this quarter century are reflected in the fiction of the period. The slavery question, pro and con, was the theme of scores of novels, and as many more covered the Civil War, a national catastrophe that induced authors to attempt to be more realistic in their writing. The westward flow of the population was not overlooked, but few authors treated the overland trek as lightly as James Weir in the opening to his *The Winter Lodge* (1854), when he said, "Now, to go to California is an every-day affair, too tame even to produce excitement." During the 1850's the sentimental novel reached its peak in popularity, aided and abetted by the large increase in women writers. And the woman's rights movement gained impetus through the numerous novels and short stories which presented it in a sympathetic vein. Religion, including controversies between denominations, was also a favorite subject with authors.

The majority of the 2,832 numbered titles of fiction recorded herein are entered under 1,193 authors—694 men and 499 women. The remainder are entered under unidentified initials, pseudonyms, or titles. No summation has been made of the additional authors who produced only short stories which were published in collections or appended to works of others.

Only the first or earliest located edition of each title is recorded, except when a subsequent edition contains new material; then it too is listed as a main entry. For examples see numbers 387 and 388. A few of the items included were also issued simultaneously in cities other than that of the original publishers and usually added the name of the local publisher to the imprint. Such imprints are recorded in the notes under the main entry. Examples are numbers 86 and 88. Whenever a novel was found republished under a new title, this title, in addition to being listed in the title index, is given in a note under the original, provided it appeared before 1876. For examples see numbers 19 and 20. Novels published prior to 1850 though reissued between 1851 and 1875 under new titles are not within the scope of this work.

In general the intention has been to omit the same classifications of fiction as were omitted in my *American Fiction 1774-1850*: annuals, gift books, publications of the American Tract Society, Sunday School Unions, and various religious denominations, juveniles, fictitious Indian captivities, jestbooks, folklore, collections of anecdotes, essays, and periodicals, including such numbered runs as *The Novelette* and *The Weekly Novelette*. The dime novels published in numbered series by such houses as Elliot, Thomes & Talbot, S. Tousey, and all of the publications listed in Albert Johannsen's *The House of Beadle and Adams*, except the "Popular Fifty Cent Books," are omitted.

An effort has been made to screen closely the books designed for "young men and women." In the period covered by this bibliography, publishers became aware of the potential market for books suitable for the teen-age group. Not all of them were as certain about the subject as were Lee and Shepard of Boston and New York. They usually advertised titles under the headings "juveniles" or "for youth." Their "Maidenhood Series" was intended for teen-agers and their publicity was explicit. For instance their release covering *Our Helen* by Sophie May, a pseudonym of Rebecca S. Clarke, and *That Queer Girl* by Virginia F. Townsend, stated both "will be welcomed by many a maiden who finds that between grown-up people's books and those for mere children, this series just supplies her wants." Another firm, D. Lothrop & Co. of Boston, published many titles in their "Prize Stories" series for this group of readers.

If the publisher had difficulty in determining the author's intention, he begged the question by advertising that the book will be safe for older boys and girls "but will be enjoyed equally by adults." Even a reviewer occasionally was in a quandary as to whether the book should be considered for the "in-betweens." Whenever I have been unable to determine the classification easily, or have not found any helpful contemporary advertisements or reviews, I include the title. Many authors during this twenty-five-year period produced books for juveniles, teen-agers, and adults. It was the borderline material between the last two categories that proved to be the most difficult to segregate.

To the best of my knowledge, this work represents the initial effort to list all the adult American fiction of the period covered. Various subject bibliographies, biographies, and the catalogues issued by the antiquarian booksellers, supplied, in part, the titles of books which had to be found and examined. In the course of such a search, happy chance played no small part. Without doubt there are the unknowns which are yet to be revealed.

BIBLIOGRAPHICAL COMMENT

The bibliography was compiled to serve as a guide to the books of American fiction rather than as a complete bibliographical description of them. I have examined a large proportion of the items, but rarely have I examined more than one copy of a single edition of a title. Consequently variations between copies are seldom noted, and in only a few cases are distinguishing points of issues brought out. No effort has been made to locate all copies extant, but only those in the eighteen libraries listed on pages xix and xx. Whenever a book was not found in one of these libraries, either a copy is located in some other library or the source of information about the title is supplied.

MECHANICS OF COMPILATION

Entries The books are entered under authors' names when known, or under unidentified pseudonyms or initials, otherwise under titles. Square brackets around an entry indicate that the author's name is not on the title page.

Titles Some titles are shortened, and authors' names and quotations appearing on the title pages are omitted. Omissions are indicated by ellipses. The abbreviation "pseud." following a name that is on the title page as the author, is self-explanatory. To avoid the eccentricities of nineteenth-century printing, punctuation and capitalization are regularized.

Imprints It is intended to list all the printers and publishers as given in the imprints. Their addresses, if included, are also given whenever publication dates had to be supplied. The "published by" so frequently found in an imprint is omitted.

Dates Roman dates in the imprints are converted into Arabic. The dates in the copyright notices, if any, are used for the undated books, providing they meet certain requirements. If the year given in the notice is within the publisher's years of occupation at the address from which the book was issued, it is accepted. Any exceptions to this general practice are explained in the notes under the main entries of the books concerned. The supplied date in the imprint is preceded by the abbreviation "cop." and both are placed in square brackets. An example is Phebe F. McKeen's *Theodora* (No. 1626). This undated novel is to be found with two different imprints but with the same copyright date of 1875. The book was published by the New York firm of Anson D. F. Randolph & Company at 770 Broadway and again at 900 Broadway. According to the directories, Randolph was at 770 Broadway from 1865 to 1875. From a notice in *Publishers' Weekly* it is learned that Randolph moved to 900 Broadway very early in 1876. So it is reasonably safe to consider novels issued at 770 Broadway to be within the date limits of this bibliography and to omit everything with the 900 Broadway address.

There are a few items with copyright dates much earlier than the possible publication dates of the copies recorded. For examples see numbers 335 and 340. Perhaps there are earlier separately printed editions more closely related to these copyright dates, but they will require further search.

Pagination Formal pagination is not given; usually only the last numbered page of text is noted, to afford an idea of the length of the contents. Deviations from this rule are explained in a note under the entry concerned. When the text is printed in double columns it is so noted, because the actual contents are greater than the last page number would indicate. The size of the books is omitted. To designate a novel printed on machine-made paper as octavo or duodecimo based on what evidence is available has little significance. And to state that a page is seven inches tall when such a measurement was usually derived from the examination of only one copy may be misleading.

Illustrations The abbreviation "illus." is used to designate all types of illustrations within the book: plates, portraits, textual illustrations, and frontispieces, provided the latter are not alone. If a book contains only a frontispiece it is noted by the abbreviation "front." Vignettes are not indicated or included in the abbreviation "illus."

Notes The notes are for the most part self-explanatory. Books containing two or more stories have one of the three following notes: "Contents," which lists all the stories in the book; "Also contains," which lists all stories following the first (the first being used as the title of the book); "Contains," which lists only those stories that fall within the scope of this work.

Annotations A note suggesting the topic of the novel or one of the subjects treated in it is occasionally added. Under some entries the note refers to the locale and date or period when the title furnished no clew.

Cross References Cross references, with the exception of titles, appear in the main body of the bibliography. Only the main entries are numbered. When there are two or more stories in one publication, those listed in the notes are analyzed, provided the authors' names are given. No attempt has been made to identify the anonymous stories.

TITLE INDEX

The title index lists the titles of all the main and analytical entries, including the change of titles recorded in the notes under the original titles.

March 25, 1957   Lyle H. Wright

ACKNOWLEDGMENTS

THERE now remains the pleasant task of acknowledging the assistance I have received in the compilation of this work. Without the generous help of the libraries included in the census and the answers to scores of questions addressed to innumerable other libraries and individuals, this list could not have attained any degree of completeness. It represents the joint efforts of librarians, collectors, bibliographers, and antiquarian booksellers.

I am grateful to the Trustees of the Huntington Library for making possible the publication of this book and to the Director John E. Pomfret and the Librarian Leslie E. Bliss for enabling me to work in several of the libraries included in the census. Miss Mary Isabel Fry, reference librarian, has contributed much to this project, including a preliminary survey of the holdings of some of the libraries concerned. I am indebted to Miss Eleanor Towles of the Publications Department for her careful editing of the manuscript and galleys and to her assistant, Mrs. Nancy English. Miss Gwen Staniforth of the Reference Department has also been of great assistance.

If I am obligated to any one person more than another, it is to Clarence Saunders Brigham of the American Antiquarian Society. His indefatigable help and keen interest in the work have played no small part in its completion. And to all the staff members of the Society's library, I am indebted in one way or another.

It is with pleasure that I acknowledge the invaluable aid of the following who were responsible for having my preliminary list checked, who answered a multitude of questions, or who rendered personal assistance when I visited their libraries:

Francis James Dallett, Jr., of the Athenaeum of Philadelphia.

Walter Muir Whitehill, of the Library of the Boston Athenaeum, and Marjorie Lyle Crandall, formerly of the Library.

Richard G. Hensley and Harriet Swift, of the Boston Public Library.

David A. Jonah, John R. Turner Ettlinger, and Marion E. Brown, of the Brown University Library.

ACKNOWLEDGMENTS

Roland Baughman and W. L. Williamson, of the Columbia University Libraries, Butler Division.

William A. Jackson, Robert H. Haynes, and Miss Audrey Hosford, of Harvard University Library.

Frederick R. Goff and J. M. Edelstein, of the Library of Congress.

Edwin Wolf, 2nd, of the Library Company of Philadelphia.

Stanley Pargellis and Frederick A. H. Hall, of the Newberry Library.

R. W. G. Vail and James J. Heslin, of the New York Historical Society Library, and Oscar Wegelin, formerly of the Library.

Lewis M. Stark and Mrs. Maud D. Cole, of the New York Public Library.

Robert Rosenthal, of the University of Chicago Library.

Miss Blanche Moen, of the University of Minnesota Library.

Miss Neda M. Westlake, of the University of Pennsylvania Library.

John Cook Wyllie, of the Alderman Library, University of Virginia. Mr. Wyllie also supplied the information about certain copies in C. Waller Barrett's library, "UVB" in the census, which Mr. Barrett has announced will go to the University of Virginia.

Donald G. Wing and Donald Gallup, of Yale University Library.

To Jacob Blanck I am particularly indebted, not only for his generosity in bibliographical matters, but also in a more personal way. And my thanks are due Edward R. Morrill and Frank Willson. Roger Butterfield and Thomas M. McDade generously permitted me to examine many items from their collections, and they supplied much useful information. I also wish to thank Edwin H. Carpenter, Jr., Richard B. Harwell, John S. Van E. Kohn, and Alexander D. Wainwright. Additional libraries and individuals are acknowledged in the text.

My wife Marjorie deserves my heartfelt thanks for her help on this book and for so patiently bearing with me during my more trying moments.

L. H. W.

KEY TO AUTHORS AND TITLES
OF BOOKS REFERRED TO IN THE NOTES

ALLIBONE
Allibone, S. A. *A Critical Dictionary of English Literature and British and American Authors*. Philadelphia, 1908.

AMER. CAT. 1876
The American Catalogue . . . Author and Title Entries of Books in Print . . . July 1, 1876. Compiled by Lynds E. Jones. New York, 1880.

APPLETON
Appleton's Cyclopaedia of American Biography. New York, 1887-1901.

BM
British Museum. *Catalogue of Printed Books*. London, 1881-1905, and the *General Catalogue of Printed Books*. London, 1931-1954.

CUSHING
Cushing, W. *Anonyms*. London, 1890.

KELLY 1861-1866, and 1866-1871
Kelly, J. *The American Catalogue of Books*. New York, 1866-1871.

PW
The Publishers' Weekly. New York, 1872-1875.

ROORBACH 1820-1852, 1852-1855, 1855-1858, and 1858-1861
Roorbach, O. A. *Bibliotheca Americana*. New York, 1852-1861.

SABIN
Sabin, J. *Bibliotheca Americana*. New York, 1868-1936.

WAGNER-CAMP
Wagner, H. R. *The Plains and the Rockies . . . Rev. by C. L. Camp*. Columbus, Ohio, 1953.

WRIGHT (1774-1850)
Wright, L. H. *American Fiction 1774-1850*. San Marino, Calif., 1948.

ABBREVIATIONS USED FOR LIBRARIES
APPEARING IN THE CENSUS

AAS
American Antiquarian Society, Worcester, Massachusetts

AP
Athenaeum of Philadelphia, Philadelphia, Pennsylvania

BA
Boston Athenaeum, Boston, Massachusetts

BP
Boston Public Library, Boston, Massachusetts

BU
Brown University Library, Providence, Rhode Island

CU
Columbia University Library, New York, N. Y.

H
Harvard University Library, Cambridge, Massachusetts

HEH
Henry E. Huntington Library and Art Gallery, San Marino, California

LC
Library of Congress, Washington, D.C.

LCP
Library Company of Philadelphia, Philadelphia, Pennsylvania

N
Newberry Library, Chicago, Illinois

NYH
New York Historical Society Library, New York, N. Y.

NYP
New York Public Library, New York, N. Y.

UC
University of Chicago Library, Chicago, Illinois

UM
University of Minnesota Library, Minneapolis, Minnesota

ABBREVIATIONS

UP
University of Pennsylvania Library, Philadelphia, Pennsylvania

UV
University of Virginia Library, Charlottesville, Virginia

UVB
C. Waller Barrett Collection for the University of Virginia

Y
Yale University Library, New Haven, Connecticut

BIBLIOGRAPHY

American Fiction

1851-1875

1   [ABBOT, ANNE WALES] *ed.* Autumn Leaves. Original Pieces in Prose and Verse ... Cambridge: John Bartlett, 1853. 200 p.

                    AAS, BA, BP, BU, CU, H, HEH, LC, N, NYP, Y

    Contains: Christmas Revived—A Tale: Found in the Repositories of the Abbots of the Middle Ages—From the Papers of Reginald Ratcliffe, Esq.

ABBOTT, AUSTIN, *jt. au.* *See* Benauly, *pseud.*, Nos. 257-258.

ABBOTT, BENJAMIN VAUGHAN, *jt. au.* *See* Benauly, *pseud.*, Nos. 257-258.

2   ABBOTT, MRS. ISABELLA (KENDRICK). Leah Mordecai: A Novel ... New York: Baker, Pratt & Company, 142 & 144 Grand Street [cop. 1875]. 238 p.   AAS

    Hebrew society in Charleston, S. C.

3   [ABBOTT, L. A.] Seven Wives and Seven Prisons; or, Experiences in the Life of a Matrimonial Monomaniac ... New York: published for the author, 1870. 205 p., illus.   AAS, H, HEH, LC, UP

    The trials of a bigamist.

4   ABBOTT, LYMAN. Laicus; or, The Experiences of a Layman in a Country Parish ... New York: Dodd & Mead, 1872. 358 p.

                    AAS, BA, BP, CU, HEH, LC, LCP, Y

    PW, Feb. 7, 1874, p. 146, indicates this was republished in 1873 with title "A Layman's Story."

    Laid in "Wheathedge," New York.

    ———— *jt. au.* *See* Benauly, *pseud.*, Nos. 257-258.

5   ABRAMS, ALEXANDER ST. CLAIR. The Trials of the Soldier's Wife: A Tale of the Second American Revolution ... Atlanta, Georgia: Intelligencer Steam Power Press, 1864. 188 p., 1 l.

                    HEH, NYH

ACKERMAN, MISS R. H. The Farmer's Daughters; or, Moving into Town. *In* S. Cobb, Orlando Chester (1852), No. 580.

6 ACONITE, TOBIAS, *pseud.* A Narrative of Startling Interest!! Edward Barnett, a Neglected Child of South Carolina, Who Rose to Be a Peer of Great Britain . . . By Tobias Aconite [pseud.], the Mayor of Hole Cum Corner. St. Louis, Philadelphia, Boston, and New York: H. H. Randall, 50 Ann Street [cop. 1855]. 50 p., illus.   LC
LC copy deposited for copyright Feb. 1, 1856.

7 THE ACTRESS IN HIGH LIFE: An Episode in Winter Quarters . . . New York: Derby & Jackson, 1860. 416 p.   BP, BU, HEH, N
The British in the Peninsular War.

ADAMS, ANNE P. Christine. *In* J. Griffiths, *ed.*, Autographs for Freedom [2d ser.] (1854), No. 1034.

8 [————] Otta Held and Other Stories, in Prose and Verse. By a Preacher. New York: Carlton & Porter, 1856. 124 p., illus.
Information from LC card for copy withdrawn from circulation.

9 [ADAMS, CHARLES.] The Adventures of My Cousin Smooth. By Timothy Templeton [pseud.], of Tewksbury. New York and Auburn: Miller, Orton & Mulligan. London: W. T. Tweedie and David Bryce, 1856. 236 p.   AAS, CU, H, HEH, LC, NYP, UC, Y
Humorous criticism of the administration of President Pierce.

10 ADAMS, FRANCIS COLBURN. Justice in the By-Ways: A Tale of Life . . . New York: Livermore & Rudd. London: David Bryce, 1856. 438 p.   AAS, BP, CU, H, HEH, LC, NYH, UC, UP, Y
Of antislavery interest; South Carolina.

11 [————] The Life and Adventures of Maj. Roger Sherman Potter; Together with an Accurate . . . Account of His Great Achievements in Politics, Diplomacy and War . . . By Pheleg Van Trusedale [pseud.]. New York: Stanford & Delisser, 1858. 522 p., illus.
AAS, BP, BU, CU, H, HEH, LC, LCP, N, NYH, NYP, UC, UM, UP, UV, Y

12 ———— Manuel Pereira; or, The Sovereign Rule of South Carolina. With Views of Southern Laws, Life, and Hospitality . . . Washington, D. C.: Buell & Blanchard, 1853. 302 p.
AAS, BA, BP, BU, CU, H, HEH, LC, LCP, N, NYH, NYP, UC, UP, UV, Y
Of antislavery interest.

13 [————] Our World; or, The Slaveholder's Daughter . . . New York and Auburn: Miller, Orton & Mulligan, 1855. 597 p., illus.   AAS, BP, CU, H, HEH, LC, N, NYH, NYP, UC, UM, UP, Y
Of antislavery interest; South Carolina.

14 ———— An Outcast; or, Virtue and Faith . . . New York: M. Doolady, 1861. 436 p.   BP, Y
Charleston, S. C., and New York underworlds in 1850.

15 ———— Siege of Washington, D. C. Written Expressly for Little People . . . New York: Dick & Fitzgerald [cop. 1867]. 130 p., illus.
    AAS, BA, BP, BU, H, HEH, LC, LCP, N, NYH, NYP, UC, UP, UV, Y
A satire on the generals of the North and the South.

16 ———— The Von Toodleburgs; or, The History of a Very Distinguished Family . . . Philadelphia: Claxton, Remsen & Haffelfinger, 1868. 290 p., illus.
    AAS, BP, CU, H, HEH, LC, LCP, NYH, NYP, UC, UM, UP, Y
Of whaling interest; Nyack, N.Y.

17 [ADAMS, MRS. H. A.] Dawn. Boston: Adams & Company. London: Trübner & Co., 1868. 404 p.
    AAS, BP, LC, LCP, NYP, UC, Y
Dawn, the heroine, dedicates herself to helping humanity.

18 ADAMS, MRS. HARRIET A. Allegories of Life . . . Boston: Lee & Shepard. New York: Lee, Shepard & Dillingham, 1872.   93 p.
    BP, LC

19 ADAMS, JOHN STOWELL. Town and Country; or, Life at Home and Abroad, without and within Us . . . Boston: J. Buffum, 1855. 368, [1] p., illus.   AAS, CU, H, HEH, NYH, UP, Y
Contains: Saved by Kindness—The Hope of the Fallen—The Wine-Dealer's Clerk—The Warrior's Bride—The Widow's Story—Autobiography of an Automaton—Better than Gold—Speculation and Its Consequence—Rich and Poor—Not Made for an Editor—The Jug Afloat—Little Nelly—The Disinherited.
Also published as: Half-Hour Stories of Choice Reading for Home and Travel. Boston: G. W. Cottrell, 1858.   LC

20 [ADAMS, JOHN TURVILL.] The Knight of the Golden Melice: A Historical Romance . . . New York: Derby & Jackson. Cincinnati: W. H. Derby [sic] & Co., 1857. 473 p.
    AAS, BA, BU, CU, HEH, LC, LCP, N, NYP, UC, UV, Y
Also published as: The White Chief among the Red Men; or, Knight of the Golden Melice. New York: Derby & Jackson, 1859.   CU, NYP
Early colonial Massachusetts.

21 [————] The Lost Hunter: A Tale of Early Times . . . New York: Derby & Jackson. Cincinnati: H. W. Derby, 1856. 462 p.   AAS, BA, CU, HEH, LC, NYP, UP, Y
Early 19th-century Connecticut.

ADAMS, MOSES, *pseud.* See Bagby, George William

22 [ADAMS, NEHEMIAH.] Bertha and Her Baptism . . . Boston: S. K. Whipple and Company, 1857. 297 p.   BA, BP, BU, LC, UV

23 [————] Catharine . . . Boston: J. E. Tilton and Company. London: Knight and Son, 1859. 192 p.   BP, BU, H, LC, UV
Meditations on death.

24 [————] The Sable Cloud: A Southern Tale, with Northern Comments . . . Boston: Ticknor and Fields, 1861. 275 p.
AAS, AP, BA, BP, BU, CU, H, HEH, LC, LCP, N, NYH, NYP, UC, UM, UP, UV, Y

25 [ADAMS, WILLIAM TAYLOR.] Hatchie, the Guardian Slave; or, The Heiress of Bellevue. A Tale of the Mississippi and the South-West. By Warren T. Ashton [pseud.] . . . Boston: B. B. Mussey and Company; and R. B. Fitts and Company, 1853. 313 p., illus.   AAS, BP, CU, N, NYH, UM, UV, Y

26 [————] In Doors and Out; or, Views from the Chimney Corner. By Oliver Optic [pseud.]. Boston: Brown, Bazin and Company [cop. 1854]. 330 p., illus.   AAS, H, HEH, UM
Engr. title page imprint: Boston: Brown, Bazin & Co. [n.d.].
AAS and H copies of the above contain advts. at end, dated "Dorchester, Sept. 12, 1855."
N copy with engr. title page dated 1855.
CU copy with title and engr. title pages dated 1855.
Also issued with imprint: Boston: Higgins and Bradley, 20 Washington Street [1855].   AP, H, NYP
Engr. title page imprint: Boston: Brown, Bazin & Co., 1855.
Also issued with imprint: Boston: Higgins and Bradley, 20 Washington Street [1855].   AAS, BP, BU, UP, Y
Engr. title page imprint: Boston: Higgins and Bradley, 1855.
Also published as: *Marrying a Beggar; or, The Angel in Disguise, and Other Tales.* Boston: Wentworth, Hewes & Co., 1859.   HEH, N, Y

27 ———— The Way of the World: A Novel. By William T. Adams (Oliver Optic). Boston: Lee and Shepard, 1867. 464 p.   AAS, BP, BU, CU, H, LCP, NYP, UC, UM

28 ADDISON, ALVIN. Eveline Mandeville . . . Cincinnati: U. P.
James, 167 Walnut Street [*ca.* 1856-1871]. 100 p. Printed in
double cols. AAS, BU, HEH, UC, UM, UP, Y
Copyright notice dated 1837 which is probably a printer's error.

ADDUMS, MOZIS, *pseud. See* Bagby, George William

ADELER, MAX, *pseud. See* Clark, Charles Heber

29 THE ADOPTED DAUGHTER; or, The Trials of Sabra. A Tale of Real
Life. Edition—Five Thousand Copies. Ogdensburgh [N.Y.]:
Hitchcock, Tillotson & Stilwell, printers, 1858. 199 p.
Upstate New York. BA, HEH, N, NYP, UP, Y

AFTON, EFFIE, *pseud. See* Monmouth, Mrs. Sarah Elizabeth
(Harper)

30 ALCOTT, LOUISA MAY. Hospital Sketches . . . Boston: James
Redpath, 1863. 102 p.
AAS, BA, BP, BU, CU, H, HEH, LC, LCP, N, NYH, NYP, UM, UP, UVB, Y

31 ———— Hospital Sketches and Camp and Fireside Stories . . .
Boston: Roberts Brothers, 1869. 379 p., illus.
AAS, BP, CU, HEH, NYP, UP, UVB, Y
Contents: Hospital Sketches—The King of Clubs and the Queen of Hearts
—Mrs. Podger's Teapot—My Contraband—Love and Loyalty—A Modern
Cinderella—The Blue and the Gray—A Hospital Christmas—An Hour.

32 ———— Moods . . . Boston: Loring, 1865. 297 p.
AAS, BP, CU, N, UC, UP, UVB, Y
Copyright notice dated 1864, printed on a slip of paper, found pasted on
verso of title page in some copies. The 1st ed. has the date 1865 on the title
page; the 2d ed. is so marked; and the 3d ed. is without date on title.

33 ———— On Picket Duty, and Other Tales . . . Boston: James
Redpath, 221 Washington Street. New York: H. Dexter,
Hamilton & Co. [cop. 1864]. 96 p.
AAS, CU, H, HEH, LC, NYH, NYP, UVB, Y
Also contains: The King of Clubs and the Queen of Hearts—The Cross on
the Old Church Tower—The Death of John.
On front cover: "Redpath's Books for the Camp Fires."

34 ———— Work: A Story of Experience . . . Boston: Roberts
Brothers, 1873. 443 p., illus.
AAS, BP, BU, CU, H, HEH, LC, LCP, N, NYP, UM, UP, UVB, Y

35 ALDRICH, THOMAS BAILEY. Daisy's Necklace: And What Came of It. (A Literary Episode.) . . . New York: Derby & Jackson. Cincinnati: H. W. Derby & Co., 1857. 225 p., 1 l.

AAS, BA, BP, BU, CU, H, HEH, LC, N, NYP, UC, UM, UP, UVB, Y

Laid in New York City.

36 ———— Marjorie Daw, and Other People . . . Boston: James R. Osgood and Company, 1873. 272 p.

AAS, BP, CU, H, HEH, LC, LCP, N, NYP, UC, UP, UVB, Y

Also contains: A Rivermouth Romance—Quite So—A Young Desperado—Miss Mehetabel's Son—A Struggle for Life—The Friend of My Youth—Mademoiselle Olympe Zabriski—Père Antoine's Date-Palm.

At head of title: "Thomas Bailey Aldrich."

37 ———— Out of His Head: A Romance . . . New York: Carleton, 1862. 226 p.

AAS, AP, BA, BP, BU, CU, H, HEH, LC, LCP, N, NYP, UC, UM, UP, Y

Also contains: Paul Lynde's Sketch Book: Pere Antoine's Date Palm, a Legend of New Orleans—A Word for the Town, a City Idyl—Miss Hepzibah's Lover, a Seaside Sketch—The Lady with the Balmoral, the Impressible Man's Story—The Cup and the Lip, a Christmas Story.

"Thackaray" for "Thackeray" on title page of 1st ed.

38 ———— Père Antoine's Date-Palm . . . Cambridge: Welch, Bigelow & Company, printers to the University, 1866. 20 p.

Twenty copies printed. H, NYP, UVB, Y

This tale is included in Nos. 36 and 37.

39 ———— Prudence Palfrey: A Novel. Boston: James R. Osgood and Company, 1874. 311 p., front.

AAS, BP, BU, CU, H, HEH, LC, LCP, N, NYP, UC, UM, UP, UVB, Y

At head of title: "Thomas Bailey Aldrich."

New England life.

40 ALECK AND PETE; or, 'The Hand of the Diligent Maketh Rich.' Saint Louis: S. W. Book and Publishing Co., 1870. 16 p. LC

41 ALETH, *pseud.* Ernestin; or, The Heart's Longing. By Aleth [pseud.] . . . New York: Stanford & Delisser, 1858. 532 p.

Laid in England. HEH, NYP

ALETHITHERAS, *pseud. See* Osborn, Laughton

42 [ALEXANDER, CHARLES WESLEY.] Angel Agnes; or, The Heroine of the Yellow Fever Plague in Shreveport . . . [N. p.] 1873. Illus.

Copy noted in Edward Morrill & Son, Cat. 18, item 19.

National Union Cat. contains a card for a copy with imprint: Philadelphia: Old Franklin Publishing House [cop. 1873], 30 p., which has been withdrawn from circulation.

43 [————] The Angel of the Battle-Field: A Tale of the Rebellion. By Wesley Bradshaw [pseud.]. New York: American News Company, 1865. 96 p. NYH

44 [————] Brigham Young's Daughter: A Most Thrilling Narrative of Her Escape from Utah with Her Intended Husband . . . Philadelphia: C. W. Alexander, No. 224 South Third Street, cop. 1870. 78 p., 1 l., illus. NYP, Y

45 [————] Carrie Clancy, the Heroine of the Atlantic. A Full Account of the Services Which This Noble Young Lady, Who Is a Poor Fisherman's Daughter, Rendered on the Occasion of the Wreck of the Atlantic on the Nova Scotian Coast . . . Philadelphia: Old Franklin Publishing House, 224 South Third Street, cop. 1873. 78 p., 1 l., illus. HEH

46 [————] General Sherman's Indian Spy: A Singularly Thrilling Narrative of Wenonah . . . Scouting from Atlanta through Georgia and South Carolina. By Wesley Bradshaw [pseud.] . . . Philadelphia: C. W. Alexander, 123 South Third Street, cop. 1865. 64 p., illus. NYP

47 [————] Maud of the Mississippi. A Companion to Pauline of the Potomac. By Wesley Bradshaw [pseud.] . . . Philadelphia: C. W. Alexander & Co., 123 South Third Street [1864]. 100 p., illus. (Paging irregular.) HEH, LC, NYP

Copyright notice dated 1863, but printed letter facing title page dated "Jan. 15, 1864." LC copy deposited for copyright Mar. 19, 1864.

48 [————] Pauline of the Potomac; or, General McClellan's Spy . . . Philadelphia: Barclay & Co., No. 56 North Sixth Street [cop. 1862]. 100 p., illus. (Paging irregular.)

AAS, LC, UM, UVB

LC copy deposited for copyright Oct. 20, 1862.

Barclay published an edition in German in 1863.

9

49 [————] The Picket Slayer: The Most Thrilling Story of the War . . . By Wesley Bradshaw [pseud.]. Philadelphia: Alexander & Co., 123 South Third Street, cop. 1863. 100 p., illus. (Paging irregular.) AAS

50 [————] Poor Lizzie Lee, Another Victim of the Notorious Madame La Farge. The Full History of How a Beautiful New York Heiress Was Induced to Elope with Her Father's Coachman . . . Deserted by the Brutal Husband, and Taken with Child to the Almshouse . . . Edited by Wesley Bradshaw [pseud.]. Philadelphia: Old Franklin Publishing House, cop. 1872. 30 p., illus. AAS, CU, NYP

51 [————] Washington's Vision . . . Philadelphia: C. W. Alexander & Co., 123 South Third St. [cop. 1864]. Cover title, 11-26 p., illus. AAS
Also contains: The South Carolina Seven—Still Knitting Stockings.

52 ALEXANDER, J. BELL. Malice: A Tale of Real Life in the South . . . Mobile: Strickland & Benjamin, 1852. 91 p., illus.
Title listed in Thos. M. Owen, "A Bibliography of Alabama," in Amer. Hist. Assn., *Annual Report . . . for . . . 1897* (Washington, 1898), p. 794.

53 ALGER, HORATIO. Bertha's Christmas Vision: An Autumn Sheaf . . . Boston: Brown, Bazin, and Company, 1856. 248 p., front. BU, CU, H, HEH, NYP, UM, UVB
Contains: Little Floy; or, How a Miser Was Reclaimed—Miss Henderson's Thanksgiving Day—Bertha's Christmas Vision—Wide-Awake—The Royal Carpenter of Amsterdam—The Veiled Mirror—The Prize Painting—Lost and Found—The Christmas Gift—Gottfried the Scholar—Peter Plunkett's Adventure.

———— Miss Henderson's Thanksgiving Day. *In* M. M. Ballou, The Sea-Witch [1855?], No. 207.

54 [————] Timothy Crump's Ward; or, The New Years Loan, and What Came of It. Boston: Loring [1866]. 188 p.
A copy is in the possession of Frank Gruber, Hollywood, California.
Also published as: *Timothy Crump's Ward: A Story of American Life.* Boston: Loring, 1866. Issued in "Loring's Railway Companions" series.
NYP
This was later rewritten and published under the title *Jack's Ward; or, The Boy Guardian*, Boston: Loring [cop. 1875], as a boys' book.

———— The Two Acre Lot. *In* S. Cobb, The Maniac's Secret [185-?], No. 576.

55 ALICE GRANGER: A Tale of the West. By a Lady. Cincinnati: I. Hart & Co., 1852. 98 p. UVB

ALLEN, AXIE, *pseud.* Emma Moore. *In* M. G. Clarke, *comp.*, Sunshine and Shadows (1865), No. 541.

ALLEN, MRS. JOSIAH, *pseud. See* Holley, Marietta

56 ALLEN, MARTHA. Day-Dreams . . . Philadelphia: Lippincott, Grambo & Co., 1852. 154 p. LC, NYP, UP, Y

ALMY, E. Convent Bride. *In* S. Cobb, The Iron Cross [185-?], No. 568.

57 AMES, MRS. ELEANOR MARIA (EASTERBROOK). Up Broadway, and Its Sequel. A Life Story. By Eleanor Kirk (Nellie Ames). New York: Carleton. London: S. Low, Son & Co., 1870. 271 p.
AAS, BP, CU, H, HEH, LC, NYP, UP, Y

58 AMES, MRS. MARY (CLEMMER). Eirene; or, A Woman's Right . . . New York: G. P. Putnam & Sons, 1871. 219 p. Printed in double cols. AAS, CU, H, LC, NYH, UC, UM, UP, Y
Civil War period; Harper's Ferry.

59 ———— His Two Wives . . . New York: Hurd and Houghton. Cambridge: the Riverside Press, 1875. 585 p.
AAS, BA, H, LC, LCP, UM
Washington, D.C.; early life.

60 [————] Victoire: A Novel . . . New York: Carleton, 1864. 392 p. AAS, H, HEH, LCP
The contemporary scene "overburdened" with spiritual emotion.

AMES, NELLIE. *See* Ames, Mrs. Eleanor Maria (Easterbrook)

61 THE AMOROUS INTRIGUES and Adventures of Aaron Burr. New York: published for the proprietors [ca. 1861]. 100 p. HEH
A scurrilous story.

62 AMOURS OF AN AMERICAN ADVENTURER in the New World and the Old. New York, 1865. 2 vols.
Title listed in H. C. Ashbee, *Catena Librorum Tacendorum* (London, 1885), p. 163.

63 ANDERSON, FLORENCE. Zenaida . . . Philadelphia: J. B. Lippincott & Co., 1858. 374 p. BP, LC, LCP, NYP, UC, UP, Y

ANGELA, *pseud.* Lights and Shadows, by Angela of Glen Cottage. *In* A. Cary, The Adopted Daughter (1859), No. 466.

64 ANNALS OF THE EMPIRE CITY, from Its Colonial Days to the Present. By a New Yorker. Tale I: The Quadroon; or, New-York under the English . . . New York: John F. Trow, printer, 1852. 238 p.　　　　　　　　　　　　　AAS, LC
The Negro plot of 1741.

65 APPELL, THERON B. Belshazzar; or, The Fall of Babylon. A Tale of the Orient . . . New Haven: Tuttle, Morehouse & Taylor, printers, 1861. 22 p.　　　　　　　　　　　　　　　　Y

66 ———— The Knight of Castille: A Spanish Tale . . . New Haven: printed by Tuttle, Morehouse & Taylor, 1862. Cover title, 12 p.　　　　　　　　　　　　　　　　　　　　Y

APPLETON, ELIZABETH HAVEN. A Half-Life and Half a Life. *In* Atlantic Tales (1866), No. 155.

67 THE ARCH FIEND; or, The Life, Confession, and Execution of Green H. Long . . . Who Was a Member of That Celebrated Gang, Known as the "Banditti of the West" . . . [New York] published by A. R. Orton, 1851. 31, [1] p., illus.　　　NYH

68 [ARCHER, GEORGE W.] More than She Could Bear: A Story of the Gachupin War in Texas, A.D. 1812-13. By Hesper Bendbow [pseud.] . . . Philadelphia: Claxton, Remsen & Haffelfinger, 1872. 439 p.　　　　　　　BP, HEH, LC, LCP, Y

69 ARCHIBALD CAMERON; or, Heart's Trial . . . New York: Charles Scribner, 1852. 352 p.　　　　　　　　　　　　　　LC

70 ARGYLE, ANNA. The Cecilias; or, The Force of Circumstances . . . New York: the American News Company, 1866. 177 p. Printed in double cols.　　　　　　　AAS, H, LC, LCP, NYP, Y

71 ———— The General's Daughter: A Romance . of History. Being a Sequel to "The Cecilias" . . . New York: the American News Company, 1869. 171 p., front. Printed in double cols.　　　　　　　　　　　　　　　　　　　H, LCP

72 ———— Money and Marriage: A Modern Story . . . New York: S. & A. Hoyt, 1862. 275 p.　　　　　　　HEH, NYP

73 ———— Olive Lacey: A Tale of the Irish Rebellion of 1798 . . .
Philadelphia: J. B. Lippincott & Co., 1874. 365 p.   BP, H, LC

74 ARGYLE, ARCHIE, *pseud.?* Cupid's Album . . . New York: M.
Doolady. St. Louis: Mat. B. Cullen, 1866. 332 p.
AAS, BU, CU, H, HEH, LC, LCP, N, NYP, Y
Overland to California and return by steamer via the Isthmus.

75 ARMSTRONG, HENRY S. Trifles for the Holidays. Philadelphia:
J. B. Lippincott & Co., 1868. 120 p.
Copy noted in BM.

76 [ARMSTRONG, WILLIAM H.] Red-Tape and Pigeon-Hole Generals as Seen from the Ranks during a Campaign in the Army
of the Potomac. By a Citizen-Soldier . . . New York: Carleton, 1864. 318 p.   AAS, CU, HEH, LC, LCP, N, NYP
HEH has author's ALS in which he states he wrote the story and that it was
instigated by the action of a superior in regard to a trifling clothing order.

77 [ARNOLD, ALEXANDER STREETER.] The Benson Family: A Story
for Old and Young . . . Central Falls, R. I.: E. L. Freeman,
1869. 196 p.   AAS, BU, LC

78 ARNOLD, AUGUSTUS C. L. The Signet of King Solomon; or, The
Templar's Daughter . . . To Which Is Added a Memoir of
Elizabeth Aldworth, the Female Freemason . . . New York:
Macoy & Sickels. Atlanta, Ga.: McPherson & Co., 1860.
307 p., illus.   AAS, LC
Also published as: *The Signet of King Solomon; or, The Freemason's
Daughter. New ed., enlarged.* New York: Masonic Publishing and Manu-
facturing Co., 1866. 288 p., illus.   BP, CU, NYP

ARNOLD, GEORGE. Why Thomas Was Discharged. *In* Atlantic
Tales (1866), No. 155.

ARP, BILL, *pseud. See* Smith, Charles Henry

79 ARREST, CONFESSION AND SUICIDE of Almira Cathcart, Who . . .
Was Arrested Last Week in Cincinnati. And, After Writing
Her Confession . . . Poisoned Herself . . . Philadelphia: C. W.
Alexander, 224 South Third Street, cop. 1869. 62 p., illus.
AAS, H, LC

13

80 ARRINGTON, ALFRED W. The Rangers and Regulators of the Tanaha; or, Life among the Lawless. A Tale of the Republic of Texas . . . New York: Robert M. DeWitt (Late DeWitt & Davenport), 160 & 162 Nassau Street [cop. 1856]. 397 p., illus.

AAS, BU, CU, H, HEH, LC, LCP, N, NYP, UM, UV, Y

LC copy deposited for copyright Feb. 14, 1857.

81 THE ARROW OF GOLD; or, The Shell Gatherer. A Story That Unfolds Its Own Mysteries and Moral. By the Author of "Secrets of the Cells." New York: Samuel French, 121 Nassau Street [185-?]. Cover title, 100 p. Printed in double cols.

AAS

Also contains: The Phantom Friar, by A. J. H. Duganne—Katy's Husband, by Emily Page—The Robber Baron, by Philip Lee, Jr.

82 ARTHUR, TIMOTHY SHAY. After a Shadow, and Other Stories . . . New York: Sheldon & Company, 1869. 248 p., illus.   UP

Also contains: In the Way of Temptation—Andy Lovell—A Mystery Explained—What Can I Do—On Guard—A Visit with the Doctor—Hadn't Time for Trouble—A Good Name—Little Lizzie—Alice and the Pigeon—Dressed for a Party—Coffee vs. Brandy—Amy's Question—An Angel in Disguise—Which Was Most the Lady?—Other People's Eyes.

83 ———— After the Storm . . . Philadelphia: John E. Potter and Company, 617 Sansom Street [cop. 1868]. 303 p.   AAS

84 ———— The Allen House; or, Twenty Years Ago and Now . . . Philadelphia: John E. Potter and Company, 617 Sansom Street [cop. 1860]. 307 p.   BP, NYP

85 ———— The Angel and the Demon: A Tale of Modern Spiritualism . . . Philadelphia: J. W. Bradley, 1858. 311 p.

AAS, BU, CU, LC, UM, UP

86 ———— The Angel of the Household . . . Philadelphia: J. W. Bradley. Auburn, N. Y.: H. A. Yates. New Haven: M. Bradley, 1854. 211 p., front.   CU, UC, UP, Y

Also issued with imprint: Boston: L. P. Crown & Co. Philadelphia: J. W. Bradley, 1854.   AAS, H

Also published as: *The Angel of the Household, and Other Tales*. Philadelphia: G. G. Evans, 1858. 211, 213 p.   AAS

The "Other Tales" comprise his *Home Mission* (1853), No. 100.

87 ———— Before and after the Election; or, The Political Experiences of Mr. Patrick Murphy . . . Philadelphia: J. W. Bradley, 1853. 46 p.

Copy noted in BM.

14

88 ———— Cast Adrift . . . Philadelphia: J. M. Stoddart & Co.
New York: Wm. Gibson, Jr. Boston: Geo. Maclean, 1873.
364 p., illus. AAS, BU, CU, LC, UP
Also issued with imprint: Cincinnati: Queen City Pub. Co., 1873. NYP

89 [————] Confessions of a Housekeeper. By Mrs. John Smith
[pseud.]. Philadelphia: Lippincott, Grambo & Co., 1852.
213 p., illus. LC
See also his *Trials and Confessions of an American Housekeeper* (1854),
No. 135.

———— The Cup of Cold Water. *In* The Mother Rewarded
(1851), No. 1758.

90 ———— Danger; or, Wounded in the House of a Friend . . .
Philadelphia: J. M. Stoddart & Co. Chicago: Western Publishing House. Boston: Geo. M. Smith & Co. [cop. 1875]. 334
p., illus. AAS, BU, CU, LC, NYP, UM, Y
A temperance novel.

———— The Eleventh Commandment. *In* J. V. Watson,
Tales and Takings (1857), No. 2663.

91 ———— Finger Posts on the Way of Life . . . Philadelphia:
J. W. Bradley, 1853. 214 p., front. BU, CU, UP, UVB
Contents: Shadows from a Clouded Brow—Gentle Hand—Will It Pay?—
The Lay Preacher—How to Destroy a Good Business—The Two Invalids—
Marrying Well—Blessing of a Good Deed—Paying the Doctor—The Little
Bound-Boy—Euthanasy—Three Scenes in the Life of a Worldling—Match-
Making—The Return; or, Who Is It?
Also issued with imprints: Boston: L. P. Crown & Co. Philadelphia: J. W.
Bradley, 1853. AAS, HEH
And, Philadelphia: J. W. Bradley. New Haven, Conn.: M. Bradley, 1853.
HEH

92 ———— Friends and Neighbours; or, Two Ways of Living in
the World. Edited by T. S. Arthur. Philadelphia: H. C. Peck
& Theo. Bliss, 1856. 300 p., front. AAS, BP, BU, LC, N, UM, UP

93 ———— The Good Time Coming . . . Philadelphia: J. W.
Bradley, 1855. 308 p., front.
AAS, BP, BU, CU, HEH, LC, UM, UP, Y
Also issued with imprints: Boston: L. P. Crown. Philadelphia: J. W.
Bradley, 1855. AAS, CU, N
And, Philadelphia: J. B. Lippincott & Co.; J. W. Bradley, 1855. NYP

94 ———— Growler's Income Tax . . . [New York: Francis & Loutrel, printers, 1864?]. Caption title, 4 p.

AAS, BA, BP, BU, H, HEH, LC, N, NYP, UM, UP

At head of title: "Loyal Publication Society. 863 Broadway. No. 57." Second copy variant, without printers' names at bottom of p. 4.   HEH, LC

Growler is convinced taxes are necessary.

95 ———— The Hand but Not the Heart; or, The Life-Trials of Jessie Loring . . . New York: Derby & Jackson, 1858. 317 p.

AAS, BU, CU, H, HEH, LC, LCP, N, NYP, UM, UP, Y

On unhappy marriages.

96 ———— Heart-Histories and Life-Pictures . . . New York: Charles Scribner, 1853. 350 p., front.   BU, CU, LC

Contents: The Book of Memory—The Brilliant and the Common-Place—Jenny Lawson—Shadows—The Thankless Office—Going to the Springs—The Wife—Not Great but Happy—The Married Sisters—Good-Hearted People—Slow and Sure—The School Girl—Unredeemed Pledges—Don't Mention It—The Heiress.

97 ———— Hidden Wings, and Other Stories . . . New York: Sheldon & Company, 1864. 245 p., illus.   H, NYP

Also contains: The Rich Man's Benefactor—More Nice than Wise—The Envied Lot—The Two Legacies—Catching a Sunbeam—Didn't Like His Wife—The Discipline of Misfortune—Work and Worry—Tell Your Wife—Uncle Phil's Remedy.

98 ———— Home-Heroes, Saints, and Martyrs . . . Philadelphia: J. B. Lippincott & Co., 1865. 296 p., front.

CU, LC, LCP, NYP, Y

Contents: Saint Barbara—Going Home—Sad Eyes—Guilty, or Not Guilty—The Father's Honor—Wounded—Little Martyrs—The Little Maid of All Work—Was It Murder or Suicide?—The Nursery Maid—My Father.

99 ———— Home Lights and Shadows . . . New York: Charles Scribner, 1853. 376 p., front.   CU

Contents: Rights and Wrongs—The Humbled Pharisee—Romance and Reality—Both to Blame—It's None of My Business—The Mother's Promise—The Two Husbands—Visiting as Neighbors—Not at Home—The Fatal Error—Following the Fashions—A Dollar on the Conscience—Aunt Mary's Suggestion—Helping the Poor—Common People—Making a Sensation—Something for a Cold—The Portrait—Very Poor.

Engr. title in CU's copy dated 1854.

100 ———— The Home Mission . . . Boston: L. P. Crown & Co. Philadelphia: J. W. Bradley, 1853. 213 p., front.

AAS, BP, BU, CU, H, HEH, N, NYP, UP, UVB, Y

16

Contents: A Vision of Consolation—The Step-Mother—Power of Kindness —Bear and Forbear—The Social Serpent—The Young Mother—The Gentle Warning—Kate's Experiment—My Fortune's Made—The Good Match— The Brother's Temptation—The Home of Taste—The Two Sisters—The Evening Prayer—A Peevish Day, and Its Consequences—Sisters—Brothers —Home—A Gleam of Sunshine on the Path of a Money-Lender—Engaged at Sixteen—The Daughter—Passing Away—The Love Secret.

Republished in 1858 in his *The Angel of the Household, and Other Tales*; see No. 86.

101 ———— Home Scenes and Home Influence . . . Philadelphia: Lippincott, Grambo & Co., 1852. 216 p. AAS, UP, Y

Contents: Taking Comfort—Children: A Family Scene—Losing One's Temper—Trouble with Servants—Haven't the Change—Old Maids' Children—The Mother and Boy—The Christmas Party—Is She a Lady?—Going into Mourning—If That Were My Child—I Will!—A Mother's Influence— The Power of Patience—An Old Man's Recollections.

———— The Humbled Pharisee. *In* B. P. Poore, The Mameluke (1852), No. 1928.

102 ———— The Iron Rule; or, Tyranny in the Household . . . Philadelphia: T. B. Peterson, No. 102 Chestnut Street [cop. 1853]. 93 p. AAS, BA, LC, UM, Y

103 ———— Leaves from the Book of Human Life . . . Boston: L. P. Crown & Co. Philadelphia: J. W. Bradley, 1855. 328 p., illus. AAS, CU, UP

A collection of temperance tales.

104 ———— Lessons in Life for All Who Will Read Them . . . Philadelphia: Lippincott, Grambo & Co., 1851. 215 p.
AAS, BP, CU, HEH, LC, NYP, UP

Contents: The Right of Way—Coals of Fire—A New Pleasure—The Daughter-in-Law—Smith and Jones; or, The Town Lot—He Must Have Meant Me—For the Fun of It—Forgive and Forget—Paying the Minister— Had I Been Consulted—The Mistakes of a "Rising Family"—The Means of Enjoyment.

105 ———— Light on Shadowed Paths . . . New York: Carleton, 1864. 355 p. AAS, AP, CU, H, HEH, LCP, NYP

106 ———— The Lights and Shadows of Real Life . . . Philadelphia: J. W. Bradley, 1851. 507 p., illus. AP, CU, HEH

This is Wright (1774-1850), No. 87, with eight new stories: The Eleventh Commandment—The Iron Will—A Cure for Low Spirits—Three Hundred a Year—I'll See about It—The Fiery Trial—The Sisters—The Maiden's Error.

107 ———— Lizzy Glenn; or, The Trials of a Seamstress . . . Philadelphia: T. B. Peterson and Brothers, 306 Chestnut Street [cop. 1859]. 253 p., front. AAS, CU, HEH, LC, LCP, NYP, UP, Y

108 ———— The Lost Bride; or, The Astrologer's Prophecy Fulfilled . . . Philadelphia: T. B. Peterson & Brothers, 306 Chestnut Street [cop. 1866]. 117 p. CU, NYP

109 ———— Married Life: Its Shadows and Sunshine . . . Philadelphia: Lippincott, Grambo & Co., 1852. 214 p. AAS, UP
Contents: Three Ways of Managing a Husband—Ruling a Wife—The Invalid Wife—The First and Last Quarrel—Guess Who It Is—Marrying a Tailor—The Maiden's Choice—The Fortune-Hunter—Is Marriage a Lottery?—The Unloved One.

110 ———— The Mother's Rule; or, The Right Way and the Wrong Way. Edited by T. S. Arthur. Philadelphia: H. C. Peck & Theo. Bliss, 1856. 300 p., front.
BU, CU, HEH, LC, UP, UVB, Y
Also issued with imprints: Chicago, Ill.: Keen & Lee, 1856. N
And, Rochester: E. Darrow & Brother, 1856. AAS
And, St. Louis: Edwards & Bushnell, 1856. AAS

———— The New Pleasure. *In* J. V. Watson, Tales and Takings (1857), No. 2663.

111 ———— Not Anything for Peace, and Other Stories . . . New York: Sheldon & Co., 1869. 240 p., illus.
Information from LC card for copy withdrawn from circulation.

112 ———— Nothing but Money: A Novel . . . New York: Carleton, 1865. 352 p. AAS, CU, H, HEH, LCP, UP, Y
Ambitious men versus happy men.

113 ———— Off-Hand Sketches, a Little Dashed with Humour . . . Philadelphia: Lippincott, Grambo & Co., 1851. 216 p.
AAS, BU, CU, Y
Contents: The Circuit-Preacher—The Protest—Retrenchment; or, What a Man Saved by Stopping His Newspaper—Hunting Up a Testimonial—Trying to Be a Gentleman—Taking a Prescription—The Yankee and the Dutchman; or, I'll Give or Take—A Tipsy Parson—Much Ado about Nothing; or, The Reason Why Mrs. Todd Didn't Speak to Mrs. Jones—Almost a Tragedy—That John Mason—A New Way to Collect an Old Debt—A Shocking Bad Memory—Driving a Hard Bargain—Out of the Frying-Pan into the Fire; or, The Love of a House—Marrying a Count—Job's Comforters; or, The Lady with Nerves—The Code of Honour—Treating a Case Actively.

114 ———— The Old Astrologer . . . Philadelphia: T. B. Peterson [1853?].
Title listed in Roorbach 1852-1855.

115 ———— The Old Man's Bride . . . New York: Charles Scribner, 1853. 347 p., front.   CU, H, LC, Y

116 ———— Orange Blossoms, Fresh and Faded . . . Philadelphia: J. M. Stoddart & Co. New York: Wm. Gibson, Jr. Boston: Geo. Maclean, 1871. 415 p., illus.   AAS, BU, CU, H, LC, NYP, UP
Contents: Little Foxes—Strength and Weakness—Love Not Constrained—Growing Cold—Little Things—In Danger—Ten Years after Marriage—A Hint to Husbands—A Young Wife's Sorrow—Looking for Wrinkles—A Nervous Wife—Only a Husband—The First Shadow—Not Appreciated—Smiles for Home—The Foiled Tempter—Drifting Away—Can You Afford It?—The Merest Trifle—Marrying a Beauty—John Armor's Scare—Nobody but John—Love, a Giver—Five Years Afterward—What Will the World Say?—When It Was Over.

117 ———— Our Homes: Their Cares and Duties, Joys and Sorrows. Edited by T. S. Arthur. Philadelphia: H. C. Peck & Theo. Bliss, 1856. 300 p., front.   BP, CU, LC, UP
Contains: Three New Years' Eves—Thanksgiving—An Evening at Home—A Thimble-Full of Romance—Mrs. Winterford and Her Servants—The Spare Bed-Room—Cousin Hettie and Her Mother-in-Law—The First Baby—Farmers' Sons.
Also issued with imprints: Chicago: Keen & Lee, 1856.   N
And, Rochester: E. Darrow & Brother, 1856.   Y

118 ———— Our Neighbors in the Corner House: A Novel . . . New York: Carleton. London: John Camden Hotten, 1866. 291 p.   AAS, HEH, LCP, NYP
Approaches a mystery story.

119 ———— Out in the World: A Novel . . . New York: Carleton, 1864. 312 p.   AAS, BU, CU, HEH, LCP, NYH, NYP, UM, UP, Y
Laid in New York City.

120 ———— The Peacemaker, and Other Stories . . . New York: Sheldon & Company, 1869. 239 p., illus.   AAS, CU, Y
Contents: A Cripple for Life—God Help the Poor—As You Have Opportunity—Compensation—He Lost His Reward—Grandpa and His Darling—Unforgotten Wrong—As We Forgive Our Debtors—Giving to the Poor—His Own Enemy—Only Words—What Did He Leave—The Motherless Boy—Oil on the Waters of Passion—An Indignation Visit.

121 ———— Seed-Time and Harvest; or, Whatsoever a Man Soweth, That Shall He Also Reap . . . Philadelphia: Lippincott, Grambo & Co., 1851. 216 p. BU, CU, UM

Contents: Action and Reaction—A Life Lesson—Unfading Flowers—Three Scenes in the Life of a Consumptive—The Overpaid Check—The Two Acts —The Lottery Ticket—The Mother and Sons—Better to Act the Gentleman—Principle and Interest—Is It Safe? Is It Honest?—Harmless Glass of Wine.

122 ———— The Seen and the Unseen . . . Philadelphia: J. B. Lippincott & Co., 1869. 205 p., illus.

Information from LC card for copy withdrawn from circulation.

———— Something Wrong; or, The Why and the Wherefore. In A. D. Milne, Uncle Sam's Farm Fence (1854), No. 1714.

123 [————] The Son of My Friend. Philadelphia: T. S. Arthur & Son, Nos. 809 and 811 Chestnut St. [1867]. Cover title, 16 p.

At head of title: "New Temperance Tales . . . No. 1." NYP

124 ———— Sowing the Wind, and Other Stories . . . New York: Sheldon & Company, 1865. 236 p., illus. UP, Y

Also contains: Growing Beautiful—Unforgotten Words—The Store Girl—The Broken Merchant—Not Thought Of—Long Afterwards—Somebody.

125 ———— Sparing to Spend; or, The Loftons and Pinkertons . . . New York: Charles Scribner, 1853. 358 p., front.

AAS, BU, LC, NYP, UC, UM, UP, UVB, Y

126 ———— Steps towards Heaven; or, Religion in Common Life. A Series of Lay Sermons for Converts in the Great Awakening . . . New York: Derby & Jackson, 1858. 403 p.

AAS, BP, BU, H, NYP, UC

127 ———— Stories for Parents . . . Philadelphia: Lippincott, Grambo & Co., 1851. 215 p. AAS, CU

Contents: The Temptation; or, Who Is to Blame—Obedience in Children—The Prodigal's Return—The Happy New Year—Origin and Destiny—What's in a Name—Seeing about It—The Iron Will—Haven't Time—Power of Kindness—Playing Mother.

128 ———— Stories for Young Housekeepers . . . Philadelphia: Lippincott, Grambo & Co., 1851. 212 p. LC, UP

Contents: Where the Money Goes—A Bad Habit Cured—Spoiling a Good Dinner—Opening an Account—Mr. and Mrs. Sunderland's Experiences—Doing as Other People—What Will People Say?—It's Only a Dollar—Hiring a Servant.

129 —————— Sunshine at Home, and Other Stories . . . New York: Sheldon & Company, 1864. 249 p., illus.   BU, CU, HEH, NYP, Y
Also contains: Thought for the Morrow—The Clerk's Marriage—Not Happy, and Why—Darkest before Day—My Whistling Neighbor—Honey vs. Vinegar—Poor Cousin Eunice—The Great Man—A Talk about Marriage—Words Fitly Spoken—Golden Days—The Company We Keep—Digging Up Seeds—The Shadow We Cast—A Little More Sunshine.

130 —————— The Tavern-Keeper's Victims; or, Six Nights with the Washingtonians . . . Philadelphia: Leary, Getz & Co., 1860. 301 p.   AAS, BU, LC
This is Wright (1774-1850), No. 154, with five new stories: The Reclaimed —The Man with the Poker—The Drunkard's Bible—After To-Day; or, Treating Resolution—Signing the Pledge.

131 —————— Ten Nights in a Bar-Room and What I Saw There . . . Philadelphia: Lippincott, Grambo & Co.; J. W. Bradley, 1854. 240 p., front.   CU, H, UM, UP, UV
Also issued with imprints: Philadelphia: J. W. Bradley, 1854.   AAS, HEH, LC, NYP, UVB, Y
And, Boston: L. P. Crown. Philadelphia: J. W. Bradley, 1854.   BP, BU, N, UVB

132 [——————] Three Years in a Man-Trap . . . Philadelphia: J. M. Stoddart & Co., 1872. 364 p., illus.
AAS, CU, LC, LCP, N, NYP, UC, UP, UV, Y

133 —————— Tom Blinn's Temperance Society, and Other Tales . . . New York: National Temperance Society and Publication House, 1870. 316 p., front.   LC
Also contains: The Unsteady Hand—One Fearful Night—The Son of My Friend—What One Man May Do—What Might Have Been—Not Myself —One Glass of Wine—Two Lives Wrecked—After Many Days—In League with Satan.

134 —————— Trial and Triumph; or, Firmness in the Household . . . Philadelphia: T. B. Peterson, No. 102 Chestnut Street [cop. 1855]. 107 p.   Printed in double cols.   HEH, UM
Also contains: The Gift of Beauty—The Young Music Teacher—The Unhappy Wife.

135 [——————] Trials and Confessions of an American Housekeeper. Philadelphia: Lippincott, Grambo & Co., 1854. 312 p., illus.
BP, CU, N, UC
"Under the title *Confessions of a Housekeeper*, a portion of the matter in this volume has already appeared"—Introd. Cf. No. 89.
Also published as: *Ups and Downs; or, Trials of a Housekeeper*. Philadelphia: J. B. Lippincott & Co., 1857.   AAS
And, *Trials and Confessions of a Housekeeper*. Philadelphia: G. G. Evans, 1859.   UM

136 ———— Trials of a Needlewoman . . . Philadelphia: T. B. Peterson, 102 Chestnut Street.
Title listed in Roorbach 1852-1855.

137 ———— The Tried and the Tempted . . . Philadelphia: Lippincott, Grambo & Co., 1852.   212 p.   AAS
The 1851 ed. not found.

138 ———— The True Path, and How to Walk Therein.   Edited by T. S. Arthur.   Philadelphia: H. C. Peck & Theo. Bliss, 1856. 300 p., front.   BP, BU, CU
Contains: Poverina—Filial Love Rewarded—The Adopted Child—Little Things the Index of Character—The Search for Happiness—Fruits of Sorrow—The Immortal Fountain—The Genii of the Gold Mines—Ada's Life Romance—The Step-Daughter—Blessed Are the Merciful—Tale-Telling—The Legend of Brother Alfus—The Friends; or, Luxuries Lost and Happiness Won—The Merchant's Son—Catharine Bloomer; or, New Aims in Life.
Also issued with imprints: Chicago: Keen and Lee, 1856.   CHICAGO HIST. SOC.
And, Cincinnati: H. W. Derby & Co., 1856.   AAS

139 ———— Twenty-Years Ago, and Now . . . Philadelphia: J. W. Bradley, 1860.   307 p.   LC, NYP
Also issued with imprint: Philadelphia: G. G. Evans, 1860.   AAS, H, Y

———— The Two Maidens. *In* The Smuggler's Daughter [1858?], No. 2280.

140 ———— The Two Wives; or, Lost and Won . . . Philadelphia: Lippincott, Grambo & Co., 1851.   184 p.   UM, UV, Y

141 ———— The Way to Prosper; or, In Union There Is Strength, and Other Tales . . . Philadelphia: J. W. Bradley, 1851.   203 p., illus.   AAS, CU, HEH, N, UC, UP, Y
Also contains: Where There's a Will There's a Way—Don't Be Discouraged.

142 ———— The Ways of Providence; or, "He Doeth All Things Well" . . . Philadelphia: Lippincott, Grambo & Co., 1852. 215 p.   CU, UV
Contents: The Bargain with Heaven—The Kind of Providence—Rich and Poor—Passing through the Fire—The Strange Providence—Mistook His Calling—Bad Luck—All for the Best—Both Sides of the Picture—A Strange Story—Mr. Barlow's Country-Seat—Don't Be Discouraged—The Merchant's Dream.

143 ———— The Wedding Guest: A Friend of the Bride and Bridegroom. Edited by T. S. Arthur. Philadelphia: H. C. Peck & Theo. Bliss, 1856. 300 p., front. H, HEH, LC

Also issued with imprint: Chicago: Keen & Lee, 1856. N

A collection of stories for the edification of newlyweds.

144 ———— What Came Afterwards: A Novel. Being a Sequel to "Nothing but Money" . . . New York: Carleton, 1865. 324 p.

AAS, CU, LCP, UM, UP

145 ———— What Can Woman Do? . . . Boston: L. P. Crown & Co. Philadelphia: J. W. Bradley, 1855. 326 p., front. UP

Copyright notice dated 1856; imprint date possibly a printer's error.

Also issued with imprints: Boston and Chicago: L. P. Crown & Co. Toronto: C. W. Bostwick & Barnard, 1856. AAS, HEH

And, Philadelphia: Evans and Co., 1856. UM

And, Philadelphia: J. W. Bradley. Auburn, N. Y.: H. A. Yates. New Haven: M. Bradley, 1856. Y

146 ———— The Withered Heart . . . Boston: L. P. Crown & Co. Philadelphia: J. W. Bradley, 1857. 318 p., front.

AAS, CU, LC, N, Y

Also issued with imprint: Philadelphia: J. W. Bradley, 1857. BU, LC, Y

147 ———— Woman to the Rescue: A Story of the New Crusade . . . Philadelphia: J. M. Stoddart & Co. Cincinnati: Queen City Publishing Co. Chicago: J. S. Goodman. New York: Douglass & Myers. Boston: Geo. M. Smith & Co. San Francisco: A. L. Bancroft & Co. [cop. 1874]. 226 p., front.

AAS, BP, BU, CU, H, HEH, N, NYP, UM, UP, Y

148 ———— Woman's Trials; or, Tales and Sketches from the Life around Us . . . Philadelphia: Lippincott, Grambo & Co., 1851. 216 p. AAS, LCP, NYP

Contents: A Lesson of Patience—I Didn't Think of That—Taking Boarders—Plain Sewing; or, How to Encourage the Poor—Jessie Hampton—The New Year's Gift—Aunt Mary's Preserving Kettle—Home at Last—Going Home.

149 ———— Words for the Wise . . . Philadelphia: Lippincott, Grambo & Co., 1851. 215 p. AAS, CU

Contents: The Poor Debtor—The Sunday Christian—I Knew How It Would Be—Jacob Jones; or, The Man Who Couldn't Get Along in the World—Starting a Newspaper. An Experience of Mr. Jones—The Way of Transgressors—Just Going to Do It—Making Haste to Be Rich—Let Her Pout It Out—A Fine, Generous Fellow—Taking It for Granted—Love and Law.

150 ——— Words of Cheer for the Tempted, the Toiling, and the Sorrowing. Edited by T. S. Arthur. Philadelphia: H. C. Peck & Theo. Bliss, 1856. 300 p., illus. BP

Contains: Aunt Mary—How to Be Happy—Arthur Leland—The Scarlet Poppy—Thistle-Down—The Neglected One—Ours, Loved, and "Gone Before"—The Grandfather's Advice—The Darkened Pathway—Have Patience.

Also issued with imprint: Chicago: Keen & Lee, 1856. UC

151 ASHETON, FRANCIS. A Modern Cressida, by Francis Asheton; and On the Church Steps, by Sarah [sic] C. Hallowell. Philadelphia: J. B. Lippincott & Co., 1875. 94 p., front. Printed in double cols. BA, BU, LC, LCP

"On the Church Steps," pp. 57-94.

152 ASHLAND, ARIA. The Rebel Scout: A Romance of the Revolution . . . New York: Stringer & Townsend, 222 Broadway [*ca.* 1852-55]. 109 p. AAS, BU, UP

The Cincinnati: U. P. James, No. 167 Walnut Street [n.d.], is a later ed.

ASHTON, WARREN T., *pseud.* *See* Adams, William Taylor

153 ASPENWOLD. New York: Livermore & Rudd, 1856. 408 p., front. AAS, BP

Laid in Kentucky and Washington, D.C.

154 AT ANCHOR: A Story of Our Civil War. By an American. New York: D. Appleton and Company, 1865. 311 p.
AAS, BP, CU, HEH, LC, N, NYH, NYP, UC, Y

Laid in Massachusetts, South Carolina, and Richmond.

ATHERN, ANNA, *pseud.* *See* Pike, Mrs. Frances West (Atherton)

155 ATLANTIC TALES: A Collection of Stories from the Atlantic Monthly. Boston: Ticknor and Fields, 1866. 479 p.
AAS, BP, HEH, LC, LCP, NYP, UC, UP, Y

Contents: My Double, and How He Undid Me, by E. E. Hale—The Diamond Lens, by F. J. O'Brien—Life in the Iron-Mills, by Miss R. B. Harding—The Pursuit of Knowledge under Difficulties, by Gail Hamilton—A Raft That No Man Made, by R. T. S. Lowell—Why Thomas Was Discharged, by G. Arnold—Victor and Jacqueline, by Caroline Chesebro'—Elkanah Brewster's Temptation, by C. Nordhoff—The Queen of the Red Chessmen, by L. P. Hale—Miss Lucinda, by Rose Terry—The Denslow Palace, by J. D. Whelpley—Friend Eli's Daughter, by B. Taylor—A Half-Life and Half a Life, by Miss E. H. Appleton—The Man without a Country, by E. E. Hale.

Also published as: *Modern Classics, Containing The Man without a Country* . . . Philadelphia: Porter & Coates, 822 Chestnut Street [n.d.].
BA
Copyright notice retains the Ticknor and Fields name and date 1865.

156 AUSTIN, MRS. JANE (GOODWIN). Cipher: A Romance . . . New York: Sheldon & Company, 1869. 175 p., illus.

AAS, BP, H, HEH, LC, LCP, N, UM, UVB, Y

For reference to Louisa May Alcott collaboration see Jacob Blanck, *Bibliog. of Amer. Lit.* (New Haven, 1955), No. 160.
Civil War period, but not concerned with it.

157 [————] Dora Darling, the Daughter of the Regiment. Boston: J. E. Tilton and Company, 1865. 370 p., illus.

AAS, HEH, LC, N, NYH, UM, UVB, Y

A young girl's adventures in a field hospital.

———— Harneyhow's Hummock. *In* Rougegorge (1870), No. 2130.

———— Nor Dead, nor Living. *In* Short Stories, 2d ser. (1869), No. 2211.

158 ———— Outpost . . . Boston: J. E. Tilton and Company, 1867. 411 p.   AAS, BP, CU, HEH, LC, NYP, UVB, Y

Concerns same characters as in her *Dora Darling*; story ends in Iowa.

159 ———— The Shadow of Moloch Mountain . . . New York: Sheldon & Company, 1870. 142 p., illus. Printed in double cols.   AAS, BA, BP, CU, H, HEH, LC, LCP, N, NYP, UM, UVB, Y

160 THE AUTOBIOGRAPHY of a Married Woman. No Girlhood. New York: S. A. Rollo & Co., 1859. 334 p.   AAS, LC, NYP

161 [AVERY, JANE GREENOUGH.] The Old Distillery; or, Hope Archer. By A. J. G., Author of "Tried and True." Boston: Henry Hoyt, 1865. 445 p., illus.   AAS, HEH, NYP

A temperance tale.

162 AVERY, M. A. The Rebel General's Loyal Bride. A True Picture of Scenes in the Late Civil War . . . Springfield, Mass.: W. J. Holland and Company, 1873. 417 p., illus.

AAS, BP, CU, HEH, LC, NYH, NYP

163 AVERY, SAMUEL PUTNAM. The Harp of a Thousand Strings; or, Laughter for a Lifetime . . . By Spavery . . . The Whole Engraved by S. P. Avery. New York: Dick & Fitzgerald, No. 18 Ann Street [cop. 1858]. 368 p., illus.

AAS, BU, CU, H, HEH, LC, LCP, N, NYP, UM, UP, UV, Y

164 ———— Mrs. Partington's Carpet-Bag of Fun . . . New York: Garrett & Co., 1854. 300 p., illus.

AAS, CU, LC, N, NYH, NYP, UM, UP, Y

AZILE, *pseud.* *See* Birdsall, Eliza R. M.

B., *Prof.* *See* Mansfield, Lewis William

165 B., J. Wolfsden: An Authentic Account of Things There and Thereunto Pertaining as They Are and Have Been. By J. B. . . . Boston: Phillips, Sampson and Company, 1856. 504 p.
This has been attributed to J. Barnes.   AAS, BP, BU, CU, HEH, N, UC
A plantation owner in Carolina is nearly enslaved.

166 [B., M.] Philip English's Two Cups. "1692." New York: Anson D. F. Randolph & Co., 1869. 109 p.

AAS, BA, BP, CU, H, HEH, LC, NYP, UP

Dedication signed "M. B." The "Introductory" gives author's maiden name as "Margaret Elton."
Salem witchcraft.

167 B., M. A. A. Clouded in Mystery: A Novel. By M. A. A. B. Philadelphia: Henry N. McKinney & Co., 1874. 393 p., front.

AAS, H

B., M. E. *See* Bennett, Mrs. Mary E.

168 B., N. Carrie Lee's Talisman: A Tale. By N. B. Philadelphia: T. K. Collins, Jr., 1854. 15 p.   HEH
A little tale to sell *Godey's Lady's Book.*

B., R. L., *pseud.* *See* Doutney, Mrs. Harriet G. (Storer)

B., W. T. *See* Barnitz, William Tell

169 BABCOCK, RETTA B. Clemence, the Schoolmistress of Waveland . . . Cleveland: Leader Printing Company, 1870. 277 p.   UV

170 —— Graham Lodge; or, Laura Clifford's Life Romance . . . Chicago: Rounds & James, book and job printers, 1868. 162 p.

HEH

171 BABCOCK, RUFUS. The Emigrant's Mother: A True Story of the Last Fifty Years, for the Old and the Young . . . With a Prefatory Authentication by Rufus Babcock, D.D. New York: Sheldon & Company, 1871. 144 p., illus. LC

172 [BABCOCK, SARAH A.] The Itinerant Side; or, Pictures of Life in the Itinerancy. New York: Carlton & Porter, 1857. 268 p., illus. AAS, CU, UV

173 BADEAU, ADAM. The Vagabond . . . New York: Rudd & Carleton, 1859. 368 p.

AAS, BP, BU, CU, H, HEH, LC, LCP, NYH, NYP, UC, UP, UV, Y

Contemporary scenes and prominent people.

BADEN, MRS. FRANCES (HENSHAW), jt. au. See Southworth, Mrs. E. D. E. N., Nos. 2291, 2298, and 2324.

174 BAER, MRS. BENJAMIN F. Irene; or, Beach-Broken Billows . . . New York: Authors' Publishing Company, 1875. 175 p.

BP, HEH, LC

175 [BAER, WARREN.] Carmine; or, The Trader at the Fort. Galveston: Advocate Publishing Company, 1872. Cover title, 140 p.

LC

On the Texas frontier.

176 —— Champagne Charlie! or, The "Sports" of New-York. Exhibiting in Lively Colors All the Ins and Outs, and Ups and Downs of Every Class of Fast Gothamites . . . New York: Robert M. DeWitt, No. 13 Frankfort Street, cop. 1868. 144 p. Printed in double cols. AAS, CU, H, LC, NYH, NYP, Y

177 —— The Sentinel at the Pass: A Novel . . . Galveston: printed at the "News" steam job office, 1873. 98 p. LC
Apache Pass, Arizona.

178 BAFFLED SCHEMES: A Novel. Boston: Loring, 1867. 159 p. Printed in double cols. LC

179 [BAGBY, GEORGE WILLIAM.] The Letters of Mozis Addums [pseud.] to Billy Ivvins. Richmond: West & Johnston, 1862. 87 p. BA

180 [————] Mozis Addums' New Letters. Lettur Wun. Richmond: MacFarlane & Fergusson, printers, 1860. 16 p.   HEH

181 [————] What I Did with My Fifty Millions. By Moses Adams [pseud.] . . . Philadelphia: J. B. Lippincott & Co., 1874. 128 p.   BA, BP, CU, H, HEH, LC, LCP, N, NYP, UM, UVB
At head of title: "For Virginians Only."

182 BAILEY, JAMES MONTGOMERY. Life in Danbury: Being a Brief but Comprehensive Record of the Doings of a Remarkable People . . . Boston: Shepard and Gill, 1873. 303 p., illus.
AAS, BA, BP, BU, CU, H, HEH, LC, LCP, N, NYH, NYP, UC, UM, UP, Y

183 BAILEY, MRS. MARGARET JEWETT (SMITH). The Grains; or, Passages in the Life of Ruth Rover, with Occasional Pictures of Oregon, Natural and Moral . . . To Be Published in Monthly Numbers Till Completed . . . Portland, Oregon: Carter & Austin, printers, 1854. 2 pts. (189, [1] p., 1 l.)   Y

184 THE BAKED HEAD, and Other Tales. Now First Collected, and Forming the Second Volume of "Putnam's Story Library." New York: G. P. Putnam & Co., 1856. 309 p.
AAS, BP, H, HEH, LC, LCP, NYP, Y
Also contains: The Wolf in Sheep's Clothing—Elkanah Smithers, Jun.—Infatuation—An Ordeal—A Royal Whim—A Story of Sweden—Major O'Shaughnessy's Adventure on the Duke's Moor—A Cock-Fight in Havana—Angelica Staggers—The Fall of the Janissaries—Leaves from the Diary of a Law Clerk—The Golden Guillotine—Edward Drysdale—The Story of the Unfinished Picture.
At head of title: "Putnam's Library of Choice Stories."

185 [BAKER, MRS. DELPHINE PARIS.] Solon; or, The Rebellion of '61. A Domestic and Political Tragedy. By Delphine [pseud.] . . . Chicago, Ill.: S. P. Rounds, 1862. 74 p.
AAS, BP, BU, H, HEH, LCP, UP

186 [BAKER, MRS. HARRIETTE NEWELL (WOODS).] Art and Artlessness. By Mrs. Madeline Leslie [pseud.]. Boston: Lee & Shepard, 1864. 256 p., illus.
Announced as "recently published" in *Amer. Lit. Gaz.*, II (Dec. 1, 1863), 96. LC and UC have Boston: Lee & Shepard. New York: Lee, Shepard & Dillingham, 1875.

187 [————] Behind the Curtain; or, Leelinau . . . Boston: Andrew F. Graves, No. 20 Cornhill [cop. 1869]. 335 p., illus.

Life in Savannah, Ga., and among the Pawnees.   AAS, BP

188 [————] The Breach of Trust; or, Professors and Possessors of Piety . . . Boston: Andrew F. Graves, 1869. 330 p.   BU

Announced as "recently published" in *Amer. Lit. Gaz.*, XIII (Oct. 15, 1869), 388.

189 [————] Cora and the Doctor; or, Revelations of a Physician's Wife. Boston: John P. Jewett & Co. Cleveland, Ohio: Jewett, Proctor & Worthington. New York: Sheldon, Lamport & Blakeman. London: Trübner & Co., 1855. 407 p.

New York City in the 1830's.   AAS, HEH, NYH, NYP

190 [————] The First and the Second Marriages; or, The Courtesies of Wedded Life. By Mrs. Madeline Leslie [pseud.]. Boston: C. Stone & Company, 1856. 428 p.

                       BA, BU, HEH, NYP, UC, UP

Also issued with imprint: Boston: Shepard, Clark & Co. New York: W. P. Fetridge & Co. Philadelphia: R. Cowperthwait & Co. Cleveland, Ohio: Jewett, Proctor & Worthington, 1856.   AAS, CU, H, NYH

191 [————] The Household Angel in Disguise. By Mrs. Madeline Leslie [pseud.] . . . Boston: Graves & Young, 1863. 440 p.

Copyrighted by Shepard, Clark & Co., 1856.   LCP, NYP

192 [————] Juliette; or, Now and Forever. By Mrs. Madeline Leslie [pseud.]. Boston: Lee and Shepard, 1869. 416 p.

                    AAS, BU, H, HEH, LC, LCP

193 [————] Old Moll and Little Agnes; or, The Rich Poor and the Poor Rich. By Madeline Leslie [pseud.] . . . Boston: Shepard, Clark and Company, 1857. 190 p., illus.

                    AAS, CU, UM

194 [————] The Two Homes; or, Earning and Spending. By Mrs. Madeline Leslie [pseud.]. Boston: Andrew F. Graves, 1862. 236 p., illus.   BP, BU

BAKER, JOSEPH C. Sweetbriar Cottage. *In* J. H. Robinson, The Lone Star (1852), No. 2071.

195 [BAKER, WILLIAM MUMFORD.] Inside: A Chronicle of Secession. By George F. Harrington [pseud.] . . . New York: Harper & Brothers, 1866. 223 p., illus. Printed in double cols.
AAS, BA, BP, BU, CU, H, HEH, LC, LCP, N, NYH, NYP, UC, UM, UVB, Y
Southern society during the Civil War.

196 ———— Mose Evans: A Simple Statement of the Singular Facts of His Case . . . New York: Hurd and Houghton. Cambridge: the Riverside Press, 1874. 317 p.
AAS, BA, BP, BU, CU, H, HEH, LC, LCP, N, NYP, UM, UV
Charleston in the late sixties.

197 ———— The New Timothy . . . New York: Harper & Brothers, 1870. 344 p.
AAS, BP, BU, CU, H, HEH, LC, LCP, N, NYP, UC, UP, Y
Life in the Southwest.

198 [BALDWIN, ISAAC.] The Wonderful Adventures and Horrible Disclosures of a Louisville Policeman. Written by Himself. Cincinnati: H. M. Rulison, 1852. 32 p., illus. NYP, UC

199 BALDWIN, JOSEPH GLOVER. The Flush Times of Alabama and Mississippi: A Series of Sketches . . . New York: D. Appleton and Company. London, 1853. 330 p., illus.
AAS, BP, H, HEH, LC, LCP, NYH, NYP, UC, UM, UVB, Y

200 [BALDWIN, OLIVER P.] *comp.* Southern and South-Western Sketches: Fun, Sentiment and Adventure. Edited by a Gentleman of Richmond. Richmond: J. W. Randolph, 121 Main St. [1855?]. 190 p., 1 l. HEH, LC, NYP
Contents: Rev. Peter Cartwright, the Methodist Presiding Elder—Uncle Bill—Drawing a Chalk Line; or, Reserving the Right of Passage—A Scene in Florida—How Mick Shouter Came Very Near "Walloping" Arch Coony, a Yazoo Sketch—Rousing a Hoosier, Scene at a Steamboat Dinner —Speculation in Whiskers; or, Shaving in a Broker's Office, by Sol Smith —The Volunteer Counsel, a Tale of John Taylor—A Hoosier Wedding, by Jacob Jenkins, Jr.—A Saw Log Blind; or, Poker Out West, by Frank Webber—A Trip to Texas, by Franklin Fox—The Hanimal Show, by Johnson Jones Hooper—Mrs. John Smith, Jr., of Arkansas, Whom It Was Hard to Make Scold—A Negro Beer Dance in Old Virginny—The Miniature: A Lynching Scene in California—A Narrow Escape—Sally Magus, the Woman Wot Knows How to Manage the Men—The Kentuckian in Havana—Fanny Moore, the Female Hunter of the West—Mr. Samson's House—A Clean Back Out—The Virginia Regiment—Incidents on Board a Steamboat—The Duel in the Dark, a True Incident in the Annals of Vicksburg—Backing Out a Stranger; or, The Tennessee Jockies Badly Sold—A Chip from a Sailor's Log—The Heroine of Wheeling—The Fatal Joke— "Dodging the Gambler;" or, The Man Who Bought the Ticket—Yankees Abroad; or, The Vermont Schoolmaster.

BALLOU, GIDDINGS H. La Tarantula. *In* M. M. Ballou, The Sea-Witch [1855?], No. 207.

201 BALLOU, JOHN. The Lady of the West; or, The Gold Seekers . . . Cincinnati: printed for the author by Moore, Wilstach, Keys and Overend, 1855. 544 p., illus.

AAS, HEH, LC, NYH, NYP, UM, Y

Overland to California and the injustice of law at the mines.

202 [BALLOU, MATURIN MURRAY.] The Circassian Slave; or, The Sultan's Favorite. A Story of Constantinople and the Caucasus. By Lieutenant Murray [pseud.]. Boston: F. Gleason, 1851. 67, [1] p. Printed in double cols. CU, Y

203 [————] The Duke's Prize: A Story of Art and Heart in Florence. By Lieutenant Murray [pseud.]. New York: Samuel French, 121 Nassau Street [185-?]. 100 p. Printed in double cols. Y

Also contains: The Prima Donna, by M. V. St. Leon—A Tale of a Crusader, by Charles E. Waite.

204 [————] The Gipsey Daughter; or, The Fortunes of a Spanish Cavalier. By Lieutenant Murray [pseud.] . . . Boston: F. Gleason, 1851. 100 p. Printed in double cols. AAS

205 [————] The Heart's Secret; or, The Fortunes of a Soldier. A Story of Love and the Low Latitudes. By Lieutenant Murray [pseud.]. Boston: F. Gleason's Publishing Hall, 1852. 100 p., illus. Printed in double cols. Y

Laid in Cuba.

206 [————] The Outlaw; or, The Female Bandit. A Story of the Robbers of the Apennines. By Lieutenant Murray [pseud.]. [New York, 187-?] Caption title, 63 p., illus. Printed in double cols. BP

This may be an extract.

207 [————] The Sea-Witch; or, The African Quadroon. A Story of the Slave Coast. By Lieutenant Murray [pseud.]. New York: Samuel French, 121 Nassau Street [1855?]. 100 p. Printed in double cols. Y

Also contains: La Tarantula, by Giddings H. Ballou—The Goldsmith of Paris, by H. W. Loring—Miss Henderson's Thanksgiving Day, by Horatio Alger, Jr.—The Fireman, by Miss M. C. Montaigne.

208 [————] The Turkish Spies Ali Abubeker Kaled and Zenobia Marrita Mustapha; or, The Mohammedan Prophet of 1854. A True History of the Russo-Turkish War. By Lieutenant Murray [pseud.] . . . Baltimore, Philadelphia, New York, and Buffalo: A. R. Orton, 1855. 267 p., illus.

AAS, BU, CU, H, LC, NYP, UM, Y

Also contains: The Circassian Slave–The Life and Confessions of Don Hernandez Romez de Arago–The Twin Brothers–The Two Sisters–The Robbers–The Adventures of a Medical Student–Madame Le Hocq.

209 BANVARD, JOSEPH. Priscilla; or, Trials for the Truth. An Historic Tale of the Puritans and the Baptists . . . Boston: Heath and Graves, 1854. 405 p., illus.

Colonial Rhode Island. AAS, BU, CU, H, HEH, LC, NYH, NYP, UM, Y

210 [BARBER, JOSEPH.] War Letters of a Disbanded Volunteer, Embracing His Experiences as Honest Old Abe's Bosom Friend and Unofficial Adviser . . . New York: Frederic A. Brady, 1864. 312 p., front.

AAS, BA, BP, BU, CU, H, HEH, LC, LCP, N, NYH, NYP, UC, UM, Y

Humorous satire.

211 [BARCLAY, GEORGE LIPPARD.] Little Cuba; or, Circumstantial Evidence. Being a True Story of Love, War, and Startling Adventures. The Massacre of the Young Students! Shooting the Men Found on the American Ship "Virginius" . . . Philadelphia: Barclay & Co., No. 21 North Seventh Street [cop. 1873]. 94 p., illus. BU, LC

212 BARKER, BENJAMIN. The Bandit of the Ocean; or, The Female Privateer. A Romance of the Sea . . . New York: Robert M. DeWitt, No. 13 Frankfort Street [186-?]. 115, [1] p. LC, Y

213 BARLOW, DAVID HATCH. The Howards: A Tale Founded on Facts . . . Philadelphia: Getz & Buck, 1851. 45 p. AAS, H, LC
Laid in New York City.

214 BARNARD, CHARLES. Camilla: A Tale of a Violin. Being the Artist Life of Camilla Urso . . . Boston: Loring, cor. Washington and Bromfield Streets [cop. 1874]. 141 p.

AAS, H, HEH, N, NYP, UP

215 [————] Farming by Inches; or, "With Brains, Sir" . . .
Boston: Loring, 319 Washington Street [cop. 1869]. 123 p.
AAS, BP, LC, LCP, NYP
Republished in his *Gardening for Money* [cop. 1869], No. 216.
In a humorous vein.

216 ———— Gardening for Money. How It Was Done in
Flowers, Strawberries, Vegetables . . . Boston: Loring, cor.
Bromfield and Washington Streets [cop. 1869]. 345 p. BP, LC
This contains his *My Ten-Rod Farm*, No. 218; *Farming by Inches*, No.
215; and *The Strawberry Garden*, No. 220.

217 ———— Money and Music: An Art Story. Being the Sequel
to "The Soprano" . . . [Colophon] Boston: Henry L. Shepard
& Co., 1874. 208 p. BA, N, NYP

218 [————] My Ten-Rod Farm; or, How I Became a Florist.
By Mrs. Maria Gilman [pseud.]. Boston: Loring, 1869.
119 p. BP, H, HEH, LC, LCP, NYP
Republished in his *Gardening for Money* [cop. 1869], No. 216.

219 [————] The Soprano: A Musical Story. By Jane Kingsford
[pseud.]. Boston: Loring, 319 Washington Street [cop. 1869].
179 p. AAS, BA, BP, BU, CU, H, HEH, LC, NYP, UC, UP, Y

220 ———— The Strawberry Garden. How It Was Planted . . . A
Very Practical Story . . . Boston: Loring, 205 Washington
Street [cop. 1871]. 104 p. AAS, BP, LC
First published [?] in his *Gardening for Money* [cop. 1869], No. 216.

221 BARNES, EUPHEMIA. Ellen Durand . . . Cincinnati: Moore,
Wilstach, Keys and Co., 1855. 228 p. AAS, LC, NYP, Y
Baltimore in the 1830's.

222 BARNES, JOSIAH. The Old Inn; or, The Travellers' Entertain-
ment . . . New York: J. C. Derby. Boston: Phillips, Sampson
& Co. Cincinnati: H. W. Derby, 1855. 360 p.
AAS, AP, BP, HEH, LC, NYP, UM, UP, Y
Also published as: *Green Mountain Travellers' Entertainment*. New
York: J. C. Derby. Boston: Phillips, Sampson & Co. Cincinnati: H. W.
Derby, 1856. AAS, CU, LCP, NYH
This title *also issued with imprint*: New York: Derby & Jackson. Cin-
cinnati: H. W. Derby, 1856. AAS
Also published as: *Wonderful Adventures by Land and Sea, of the Seven
Queer Travellers Who Met at an Inn*. Philadelphia: John E. Potter and
Company, 617 Sansom Street [cop. 1865]. UNIV. OF ILLINOIS LIBRARY

223 [BARNITZ, WILLIAM TELL.] The Recluse of the Conewaga; or, The Little Valley of the Blue Spring. A Legend of Adams County. By W. T. B. . . . Carlisle: E. Cornman, printer, 1853. 86 p.   HEH, LC, Y

224 BARRELL, GEORGE, JR. Bubbles of Fiction . . . New York: DeWitt & Davenport, 1852. 300 p.   AAS, BU, LC, NYP, UC, Y

   Contains: Javan—The Frost Imps—Zeno and Xara—The Bending Branch—Zell—My Last Waltz—The Violinist of Toledo—The Elixir of Life—The Statue of Marble—Eugene.

BARRETT, WALTER, *pseud*. *See* Scoville, Joseph Alfred

225 BARRINGTON, CHARLES F. Emily; or, The Orphan Sisters. A Tale of Mystery, Crime, and Terror . . . New York: Samuel French, 151 Nassau [cop. 1853]. 100 p. Printed in double cols.   HEH

226 [———] Nancy Waterman; or, Woman's Faith Triumphant. A Story of New York City. New York: Samuel French, 151 Nassau Street [cop. 1853]. Cover title, 100 p., illus.   CU, LC

BARRINGTON, F. CLINTON, *pseud*. *See* Piper, A. G.

227 [BARROW, MRS. FRANCES ELIZABETH (MEASE).] The Wife's Stratagem: A Story for Fireside and Wayside. New York: D. Appleton and Company. London, 1862. 336 p., illus.   HEH, NYP

228 BARTLETT, MRS. C. A. Lillie Ray; or, Every Cloud Has a Silver Lining. A Tale of Real Life . . . Hartford: press of the Case, Lockwood & Brainard Co., 1874. 268 p., front.

   Also contains: Eva, the Prairie Flower.   AAS, H, HEH, LC, UC
   Civil War period.

229 [BARTLETT, NAPIER.] Clarimonde: A Tale of New Orleans Life, and of the Present War. By a Member of the N. O. Washington Artillery. Richmond: M. A. Malsby, 1863. 79 p.   BA, HEH, LC, NYH, UVB

230 ——— Stories of the Crescent City . . . New Orleans: Steel & Company's time job print, 1869. Cover title, 100 p. Printed in double cols.   AAS

231 [BARTOL, MARY.] Honor May. Boston: Ticknor and Fields, 1866. 404 p.   AAS, BP, BU, CU, H, HEH, LC, NYP, UP, Y
Concerns music.

232 BARTON, K. Io: A Tale of the Olden Fane . . . New York: D. Appleton & Company, 1851. 251 p.
    AAS, BP, BU, H, HEH, LC, UC, UP, Y
A tale of Ephesus prior to the Christian era.

233 BASCOM, *Major* DICK, *pseud.* The Carpet-Bagger in Tennessee. By Major Dick Bascom [pseud.]. [Clarksville, Tenn.: J. Jay Buck, cop. 1869.] 208 p. Printed in double cols.   NYH
Imprint from cover. Pages 203-208 advts.

234 [BATES, LIZZIE.] Downward and Upward . . . Philadelphia: Claxton, Remsen & Haffelfinger, 1871. 245 p.   CU, N

235 [————] The Gabled House; or, Self-Sacrifice . . . Philadelphia: Claxton, Remsen & Haffelfinger, 1869. 214 p.
    BP, NYP, Y

236 ———— Had You Been in His Place . . . New York: Robert Carter and Brothers, 1873. 422 p.   AAS

237 ———— How It Was Paid . . . Philadelphia: Alfred Martien, 1871. 352 p., illus.   BP

238 ———— The Seymours . . . New York: National Temperance Society, 1871. 231 p.
Information from LC card for copy withdrawn from circulation.

BATKINS, JEFFERSON SCATTERING, *pseud.* *See* Jones, Joseph Stevens

239 [BEAL, NATHAN STONE REED.] Diamond Leaves from the Lives of the Dimond Family. By an Old, Old Bachelor. Macedon, N. Y.: published by the author, 1872. 384 p.   BP, LC
Contents: Dimond Introductory—First, Apples and Chestnuts; Next, Water; Then Love—The Manly Art of Self Defense—What Jules and I Did with the Wolves up on the Maquoketa—Eureka Dare—Boyd Dimond —Something Found by DeWitt among the Peninsular Pines—Lucy—The Value of an Old Negress Eighty-Seven Years Old at the Close of the Rebellion—Charley Bennett's Escape.
HEH has a copy identical to above but with a leaf inserted between pp. [iv] and [v], headed "A Statement."

240 [BEASLEY, FREDERICK WILLIAMSON.] Papers from Overlook-House. Philadelphia: J. B. Lippincott & Co., 1866. 238 p.

BP, BU, LC, NYP

241 THE BEAUTIFUL JEWESS, Rachel Mendoza. Her Lamentable Connection with the Dark and Eventful Career of Charles Bernard Otherwise Called "Prince Charles" . . . Revealing the Secrets of the Life of Queen Isabella. Philadelphia: E. E. Barclay, 1853. 39 p., illus. LC
Prefatory note signed "B. T."

242 THE BEAUTY OF WOMAN'S FAITH: A Tale of Southern Life . . . New York: Derby & Jackson, 1857. 310 p., front. BU, CU
Laid in Louisiana.

243 BECKWITH, MRS. J. R. House behind the Poplars: A Novel. New York: Hilton & Co., 1870.
Title listed in Kelly 1866-1871.

244 [————] The Winthrops: A Novel. New York: Carleton, 1864. 319 p. AAS, BP, CU, HEH, LCP, NYP, UC, UP, Y
From upstate New York to the West via Cuba and the South.

245 BEEBE, CARRIE D. Violets . . . Middletown, N. Y.: "Banner of Liberty" publishing house, 1873. 384 p. AAS, LC, NYP
Contemporary life and customs.

246 [BEEBE, CHARLES WASHINGTON.] Edmund Dawn; or, Ever Forgive. By Ravenswood [pseud.]. New York: G. W. Carleton & Co. London: S. Low, Son & Co., 1873. 301 p. HEH, LC
Laid in New York City.

247 [BEECHER, MRS. EUNICE WHITE (BULLARD).] From Dawn to Daylight; or, The Simple Story of a Western Home. By a Minister's Wife. New York: Derby & Jackson, 1859. 339 p.

AAS, BA, BP, CU, H, HEH, LC, LCP, N, NYP, UM, UP, UV, Y
Laid in Indiana.

248 BEECHER, HENRY WARD. Norwood; or, Village Life in New England . . . New York: Charles Scribner & Company, 1868. 549 p.

AAS, BA, BP, CU, H, HEH, LC, LCP, N, NYH, NYP, UC, UM, UP, UV, Y
At head of title: "From the New York Ledger."
Story covers the years 1840 to 1865.

249 BEHIND THE CURTAIN: A Tale of Elville . . . Danville, N. Y.: J. R. Trembly. New York: G. P. Putnam & Co., 1853. 442 p.
Life in a small town.   AAS, H, LC, NYP, Y

250 BELISLE, DAVID W. The American Family Robinson; or, The Adventures of a Family Lost in the Great Desert of the West . . . Philadelphia: Willis P. Hazard, 1854. 360 p., illus.
AAS, BU, HEH, LC, NYH, NYP, Y

251 BELISLE, ORVILLA S. The Arch Bishop; or, Romanism in the United States . . . Philadelphia: Wm. White Smith, 1855. 408 p., illus.   LCP
LCP copy "Second Thousand."
Anti-Catholic.

252 [————] The Prophets; or, Mormonism Unveiled . . . Philadelphia: Wm. White Smith. London: Trübner & Co., 1855. 412 p., illus.   AAS, BU, H, HEH, N, NYP, Y
Anti-Mormon.

253 BELL, ALFREDA EVA. Boadicea, the Mormon Wife. Life-Scenes in Utah . . . Baltimore, Philadelphia, New York, & Buffalo: Arthur R. Orton [cop. 1855]. 97 p., illus.   N, Y

254 ———— The Rebel Cousins; or, Life and Love in Secessia. The Autobiography of the Beautiful Bertha Stephens, the Accomplished Niece of the Hon. Alexander Hamilton Stephens, Vice-President of the Southern Confederacy . . . Written by Herself, and Prepared for Publication by Her Friend, Alfreda Eva Bell . . . Philadelphia: Barclay & Co., 1864. 48 p., illus.
At head of title: "New Era in American History."   BP, HEH
The story is not based on fact.

255 [BELLAMY, MRS. ELIZABETH WHITFIELD (CROOM).] Four-Oaks: A Novel. By Kamba Thorpe [pseud.]. New York: Geo. W. Carleton & Co. London: S. Low & Co., 1867. 420 p.
An ante bellum novel.   BP, CU, H, LCP

256 BELMONT, CARA. The City Side; or, Passages from a Pastor's Portfolio . . . Boston: Phillips, Sampson and Company. New York: J. C. Derby, 1854. 297 p., front.   AAS, BP, HEH
Presents the happier side of ministerial life.

BEN, *Uncle, pseud.* *See* White, Mrs. Rhoda Elizabeth (Waterman)

257 BENAULY, *pseud.* Cone Cut Corners: The Experiences of a Conservative Family in Fanatical Times; Involving Some Account of a Connecticut Village, the People Who Lived in It, and Those Who Came There from the City. By Benauly [pseud.]. New York: Mason Brothers, 23 Park Row [cop. 1855]. 456 p., illus. AAS, BP, BU, CU, H, HEH, LC, LCP, N, NYH, NYP, UP, Y
A joint temperance production of the Abbott brothers, Austin, Benjamin, and Lyman.

258 ———— Matthew Caraby: A Narrative of His Adventures during the Autumn of 1848, among Friends and Strangers in Country and in Town. By Benaulay [pseud.]. New York: Mason Brothers. Cincinnati: Rickey, Mallory & Co., 1859. 475 p. AAS, LCP, NYP
A joint production of the Abbott brothers, Austin, Benjamin, and Lyman.

BENDBOW, HESPER, *pseud.* *See* Archer, George W.

259 BENEDICT, FRANK LEE. John Worthington's Name: A Novel . . . New York: Harper & Brothers, 1874. 197 p. Printed in double cols. AAS, CU, H, HEH, LC, LCP, NYP, Y
Society in New York City.

260 ———— Miss Dorothy's Charge: A Novel . . . New York: Harper & Brothers, 1873. 195 p. Printed in double cols. AAS, BA, CU, H, LCP

261 [————] Miss Van Kortland: A Novel . . . New York: Harper & Brothers, 1870. 180 p. Printed in double cols. AAS, H, HEH, LC, LCP, NYP, UP
From coal mining region of Pennsylvania to New York.

262 ———— Mr. Vaughan's Heir: A Novel . . . New York: Harper & Brothers, 1875. 199 p. Printed in double cols. AAS, H, LC, LCP, NYP
A woman's rights woman; New York City and California.

263 [————] My Daughter Elinor: A Novel. New York: Harper & Brothers, 1869. 257 p. Printed in double cols. CU, H, HEH, LC, LCP, NYP
Politics in Washington, D.C.

———— The Price of a Dream. *In* Rougegorge (1870), No. 2130.

264 ———— St. Simon's Niece: A Novel . . . New York: Harper & Brothers, 1875. 189 p. Printed in double cols.

Includes a swindle in a Nevada silver mine. AAS, H, HEH, LC, LCP, NYP

265 BENJAMIN, SAMUEL GREENE WHEELER. The Choice of Paris: A Romance of the Troad . . . New York: Hurd and Houghton. Cambridge: Riverside Press, 1870. 342 p.

AAS, BA, BP, CU, H, LC, UP, Y

266 BENNETT, EMERSON. Alfred Moreland; or, The Legacy . . . Cincinnati: [H. M. Rulison] 1855. 1 p. l., 65-112 p. H, UC

The story is complete, but the pagination indicates that it is from a larger and unidentified work.

A 14-page extract, including title page, appended, of the Canadian A. M. Hart's *Life in the Far West*. Cincinnati: H. B. Pearson. This was first printed at St. Louis, 1853.

267 ———— The Artist's Bride; or, The Pawnbroker's Heir . . . New York: Garrett, Dick & Fitzgerald, No. 18 Ann Street [cop. 1856]. 414 p. LC, NYP

LC copy deposited for copyright April 27, 1857.

Also published as: *Villeta Linden; or, The Artist's Bride*. Philadelphia: Claxton, Remsen & Haffelfinger, 1874. LC

268 ———— The Bandit Queen: A Tale of Italy . . . [New York: Street & Smith, 1869.] Cover title, 16 p. Printed in double cols. AAS

Chapters 1-4 only, issued to promote the serial that began in the publishers' *New York Weekly*, Sept. 16, 1869.

269 ———— The Border Rover . . . Philadelphia: T. B. Peterson, No. 102 Chestnut Street [cop. 1857]. 33-524 p., front.

AAS, BU, CU, HEH, N, NYP, UM, Y

Pages 33-34 advts., p.[35] title page. Dedication dated "February 28, 1857." In and around Bent's Fort.

270 ———— The Bride of the Wilderness . . . Philadelphia: T. B. Peterson, No. 102 Chestnut Street [cop. 1854]. 325 p.

LC, NYP, Y

271 ———— Clara Moreland; or, Adventures in the Far South-West . . . Philadelphia: T. B. Peterson, No. 98 Chestnut [sic] Street [cop. 1853]. 334 p., illus.

AAS, BU, CU, H, HEH, LC, N, NYP, UC, UM

LC copy deposited for copyright Mar. 24, 1853.

39

272 ———— Ellen Norbury; or, The Adventures of an Orphan . . . Philadelphia: T. B. Peterson, No. 102 Chestnut Street [cop. 1855]. 309 p.   AAS, BU, HEH, LC, Y
Laid in Philadelphia.

273 ———— The Fair Rebel: A Tale of Colonial Times . . . Cincinnati: H. M. Rulison, 1853. 98 p. Printed in double cols.
Bacon's rebellion.   HEH, LC

274 ———— The Female Spy; or, Treason in the Camp. A Story of the Revolution . . . Cincinnati: Lorenzo Stratton, 131 Main Street [cop. 1851]. 112 p. Printed in double cols.   LC

275 ———— The Heiress of Bellefonte . . . Philadelphia: T. B. Peterson, No. 102 Chestnut Street [cop. 1855]. 157 p. Printed in double cols.   AAS, LC, NYP, UM
Also contains: Walde-Warren, pp. 57-157, with copyright notice at the bottom of p. 57 dated 1852 (see No. 286).
LC copy deposited for copyright Feb. 26, 1855.

276 ———— Intriguing for a Princess. An Adventure with Mexican Banditti . . . Philadelphia: J. W. Bradley, 1859. 96 p.   LC
At head of title: "Bradley's Railroad Library."

277 ———— The League of the Miami. A New and Stereotyped Edition, Enlarged, Revised, and Corrected by the Author . . . Cincinnati: Lorenzo Stratton, 1851. 116 p. Printed in double cols.   UVB
First separately published ed.; it had previously appeared in a newspaper in an "abbreviated form" according to the preface which is dated "Dec. 1850." Cincinnati Public Library also has a copy. Wright (1774-1850), No. 299 is in error; that ed. is a reprint of the above.

278 ———— The Orphan's Trials; or, Alone in a Great City . . . Philadelphia: T. B. Peterson & Brothers, 306 Chestnut Street [cop. 1874]. 302 p.   AAS, LC, NYP, Y

279 ———— The Outlaw's Daughter; or, Adventures in the South . . . Philadelphia: Claxton, Remsen & Haffelfinger, 1874. 343 p., front.   LC, LCP, UM
AAS has chapters 1-3 only: caption title, [Philadelphia, 1871], 8 p.; issued to promote the serial that began in *Saturday Night*, Feb. 11, 1871.

280 ——— The Phantom of the Forest: A Tale of the Dark and Bloody Ground . . . Author's Revised Edition. Philadelphia: John E. Potter and Company, 1868. 503 p. AAS, NYP, UM

No earlier ed. found in book form. Copyright notice dated 1867, the same as in the 1873 or later Philadelphia, Claxton, Remsen & Haffelfinger ed. which omits "author's revised edition" on the title page.

281 ——— The Pioneer's Daughter: A Tale of Indian Captivity . . . Philadelphia: T. B. Peterson, No. 98 Chesnut [sic] Street [cop. 1851]. 96 p. N, NYP, UC, UP, Y

NYP also has a Philadelphia: T. B. Peterson, No. 102 Chestnut Street [cop. 1851; actually *ca.* 1854], 145 p. ed. This contains Bennett's "Unknown Countess," pp. 97-145 (see Nos. 283-284).

282 ——— Rosalie Du Pont; or, Treason in the Camp. A Sequel to The Female Spy . . . Cincinnati: Lorenzo Stratton, 131 Main Street [cop. 1851]. 109 p. Printed in double cols.

AAS, LC, UM, UP, Y

283 ——— The Unknown Countess . . . Cincinnati: Lorenzo Stratton, 1851. 110 p. Printed in double cols. Y

Also contains: The Outlaws of New York; or, The Mysterious Marksman, pp. [49]-110.

In Roger Butterfield's private collection (New York) is an unidentified separate printing of *The Outlaws of New York; or, The Mysterious Marksman*, which collates: caption title, 108 p. This may have been published by U. P. James, of Cincinnati, *ca.* 1855. The Cincinnati Public Library, according to Yeatman Anderson III, curator, has in two states of covers and title pages, *The Mysterious Marksman; or, The Outlaws of New York* . . . Cincinnati: U. P. James [n.d.]. 64 p. Printed in double cols. Which of these two titles is the first separate printing of the tale has not been determined.

284 ——— The Unknown Countess; or, Crime and Its Results . . . Cincinnati: U. P. James [*ca.* 1854]. 96 p. Printed in double cols. UP, Y

Also contains (pp. 49-96): Blanche de Beaulieu—A Masked Ball—James I and James II.

Also issued with imprint: Louisville (Ky.): C. Hagen & Co. [185-?]. N

285 ——— Viola; or, Adventures in the Far South-West . . . A Companion to the "Prairie Flower." Philadelphia: T. B. Peterson, No. 98 Chesnut [sic] Street [cop. 1852]. 100 p. Printed in double cols. AAS, CU, HEH, UP, Y

AAS also has the 226-page ed. issued by T. B. Peterson, No. 102 Chestnut Street, *ca.* 1854.

286 ———— Walde-Warren: A Tale of Circumstantial Evidence . . . A Companion to the "Prairie Flower." Philadelphia: T. B. Peterson, No. 98 Chesnut [sic] Street [cop. 1852]. 107 p. Printed in double cols. LCP, NYP, UC

Reprinted in his *Heiress of Bellefonte* [cop. 1855], No. 275.

287 ———— Wild Scenes on the Frontiers; or, Heroes of the West . . . Philadelphia: Hamelin & Co., 1859. 421 p., illus.

AAS, CU, H, LC, N, NYP, UVB, Y

Contents: The Mingo Chief—The Kentucky Hero—The Maid of Fort Henry—Wrecked on the Lake—A Leap for Life—A Desperate Encounter —Love Triumphant—Mad Ann—The Daring Scouts—The Gamblers Out-witted—A Fight on the Prairie—An Arkansas Duel—The Poisoned Bride—Attacked by Indians—The Trapper's Story—A Miraculous Escape—A Mother's Courage—A Daring Exploit—Rocky Mountain Perils—The Dead Alive—Fight with a Bear—The Haunted House—Bill Luken's Run—The Faithful Negro—The Guerrilla Queen—The Last Stake—Adventure of a Colporteur—A Night with the Wolves—Colonel Bowie of Arkansas—The Backwoodsman's First Love—A Wolf in Sheep's Clothing—On the Scout.

Pages 409-411 misnumbered 419-421.

Also published as: *Forest and Prairie; or, Life on the Frontier.* Philadel-phia: J. W. Bradley, 1860. AAS, H, HEH, NYP, UC, UV, Y

288 BENNETT, MRS. MARTHA HAINES (BUTT). Antifanaticism: A Tale of the South. By Miss Martha Haines Butt. Philadelphia: Lippincott, Grambo and Co., 1853. 268 p.

In defense of slavery. AAS, BP, LC, LCP, N, NYH, NYP, UV

289 ———— Leisure Moments . . . New York: E. D. Long & Co., 1859.

Title listed in J. G. Johnson, *Southern Fiction* (Charlottesville, 1909), p. 11.

290 [BENNETT, MRS. MARY E.] Poems and Tales. By Mary Campbell, Mary Mel, etc., Noms de Plume of M. E. B. New York: T. W. Strong; Angell, Engel & Hewitt, printers, 1851. 160 p.

CU, HEH, LC, NYP, UC, UP

Contains: The Departure; or, One of the Caxtons—Rupert Ellsworth—The Artist's Dream; or, Love at First Sight—The History of Peter the Plasterer, and the Bachelor of Niagara.

291 BERKLEY, CORA. The Beauforts: A Story of the Alleghanies . . . Philadelphia: Peter F. Cunningham, 1866. 170 p. LC

292 ———— The Hamiltons; or, Sunshine in Storm . . . New York: Edward Dunigan & Brother; James R. Kirker, 1856. 216 p. LC, NYH

A pro-Catholic novel.

293 BERRIEDALE, *pseud.* Unforgiven: A Novel. By Berriedale [pseud.]. New York: G. S. Wilcox, 1869. 425 p. BP
Also issued with imprint: New York: T. W. Brown & Co., 1869. AAS, HEH, LC
Laid in New York and Europe.

294 [BERRY, MRS. MARTHA EUGENIA.] Bella; or, The Cradle of Liberty. A Story of Insane Asylums. By Mrs. Eugenia St. John [pseud.]. Boston: N. D. Berry, 1874. 351 p.
Primarily a writer for girls. AAS, BP, CU, H, HEH, LC, LCP, N, UP, Y

295 BICKFORD, MRS. J. T. Scandal . . . Boston: Shepard, Clark and Brown, 1857. 394 p. AAS, CU, HEH, N, NYP, UC, UP, UV, Y
On the evils of gossip.

296 BICKLEY, CHARLES POWELL. Garnelle; or, The Rover's Oath of Blood. An Exciting Tale of the Ocean and the Land . . . New York: Garrett & Co., 1853. 111 p. Printed in double cols. LC
Also contains: The Six Stages of Punishment; or, The Victim of a Vitiated Society, by Edwin F. Roberts—The Lapland Rat; or, The Loss of the Royal George.

297 BICKLEY, GEORGE W. L. Adalaska; or, The Strange and Mysterious Family of the Cave of Genreva . . . Cincinnati: H. M. Rulison, 1853. 106 p., illus. LC
Laid in Tazewell County, Va., about 1841.

298 [BIERCE, AMBROSE.] The Fiend's Delight. By Dod Grile [pseud.]. New York: A. L. Luyster, 1873. 197 p., 1 l.
This is preceded by the London ed. CU, HEH, LC, N, NYP, UVB, Y

299 BIGELOW, HARRIET HAMLINE. The Curse Entailed . . . Boston: Wentworth and Company. Cleveland, Ohio: Isaac I. Bigelow, 1857. 545 p., front.
AAS, BP, CU, HEH, LC, N, NYH, NYP, UC, UM, UP, Y
An antislavery novel.

BILLINGS, JOSH, *pseud.* *See* Shaw, Henry Wheeler

300 BINDER, WILLIAM EARLE. Madelon Hawley; or, The Jesuit and His Victim. A Revelation of Romanism . . . New York: H. Dayton, 1857. 277 p., illus. H, HEH, Y

301 ———— Viola; or, The Triumphs of Love and Faith. A Tale of Plots and Counterplots . . . New York: Evans and Company, 1858. 261 p., illus.   AAS, BU, Y

Also issued with imprint: New York: H. Dayton, 1858.   NYP
Anti-Catholic; Philadelphia.

302 [BIRDSALL, ELIZA R. M.]   Dora Raymond; or, Truth Triumphant. By Azile [pseud.] . . . Binghamton: printed at the Daily Republican book and job office, 1863.   32 p.   LC, NYP

303 THE BIRTHDAY GIFTS: A Story for Wives. New York: Sutton, Bowne & Co., 1867.   14 p.   LC

304 THE BLACK CROOK: A Most Wonderful History. Now Being Performed with Immense Success in All the Principal Theatres throughout the United States. Philadelphia: Barclay & Co., 602 Arch Street [cop. 1866].   148 p., illus.   Printed in double cols.   AAS, HEH, LC, Y

Charles M. Barras was the author of the drama "The Black Crook," but no evidence has been found that he wrote this prose version.

305 BLACKSON, LORENZO DOW. The Rise and Progress of the Kingdoms of Light and Darkness; or, The Reigns of Kings Alpha and Abadon . . . Philadelphia: J. Nicholas, printer, 1867. 288 p.   BU, LCP, NYH, NYP, Y

306 BLACKWELL, MRS. ANTOINETTE LOUISA (BROWN). The Island Neighbors: A Novel of American Life . . . New York: Harper & Brothers, 1871.   140 p., illus.   Printed in double cols.

Laid in Martha's Vineyard.   AAS, BP, BU, H, LC, LCP, NYP, Y

307 BLAKE, MRS. LILLIE (DEVEREUX) UMSTED. Fettered for Life; or, Lord and Master. A Story of Today . . . New York: Sheldon & Company, 1874.   379 p.   LC, NYP
Expounds woman's rights.

308 ———— Rockford; or, Sunshine and Storm . . . New York: Carleton, 1863.   308 p.
    AAS, AP, BP, CU, HEH, LC, LCP, NYH, NYP, UC, UP, Y
Laid in New York City.

309 ———— Southwold: A Novel . . . New York: Rudd & Carleton, 1859.   257 p.   AAS, BU, HEH, NYP, UP, Y

310 BLANCHE DEARWOOD: A Tale of Modern Life. New York: Bunce & Brother, 1855.   407 p.   AAS, CU, HEH

311 BLANCHE SEYMOUR: A Novel. By the Author of "Erma's Engagement" . . . Philadelphia: J. B. Lippincott & Co., 1873. 212 p. Printed in double cols. NYP

312 BLAND, WILLIAM. The Awful Doom of the Traitor; or, The Terrible Fate of the Deluded and Guilty. Being a Full Disclosure of the Character . . . of General Lopez, Who Decoyed a Multitude of Our . . . Citizens to an Awful and Untimely Grave in the Island of Cuba . . . Cincinnati: H. M. Rulison, 1852. 32 p., illus. N

313 [BLAUVELT, MRS. ISAAC REMSEN.] The Yoke and Burden. New York: United States Publishing Company, 1869. 401 p.
Laid in New York.   AAS, CU, HEH, LC, NYP, UP, Y

314 [BLOOMFIELD-MOORE, MRS. CLARA SOPHIA (JESSUP).] Tight Times; or, The Diamond Cross, and Other Tales. By Clara Moreton [pseud.] . . . Philadelphia: Willis P. Hazard, 1855. 431, [1] p. UP
Also contains: The Beckertons: A Tale for Christmas—Aunt Esther's Dowry—Elsie Gray; or, The Minister's Daughter—Lines—The Estranged Hearts: A Tale of Married Life—The Happy Thanksgiving, a New England Tale—Emma Dudley's Secret—The Father's Choice, a Story of New England Life—The Mother-in-Law; or, The Marriage Portion—Constance Lester; or, Love vs. Gratitude.

BLOUNT, MARGARET, *pseud*. *See* Francis, Mary O.

315 [BLOX, JOHN E.] Justo Ucundono, Prince of Japan. By Philalethes [pseud.]. Baltimore: John Murphy & Co. London: Charles Dolman, 1854. 343 p. BA, LC, N, NYP

316 BLUNT, MRS. ELLEN (KEY). Bread to My Children . . . Philadelphia: J. B. Lippincott & Co., 1856. 124 p.
Colonial America.   AAS, BU, HEH, LC, NYH, NYP, Y

317 [————] The +mas Star for the Poor . . . Washington: G. S. Gideon, printer, 1856. 37 p. LC

318 BOAZ, BEN, *pseud*. The Winged Chariot: An Allegory. By Ben Boaz [pseud.] . . . Cincinnati: A. B. Volney, 1858. 300 p., illus. LC, N
Also contains: The Way the World Goes—The Wheel of Fortune; or, The Ups and Downs of Life—Autobiography of Ben Boaz—The Fallen Angel—Light from Heaven; or, The Great Revival of 1858.

319 [BOGART, WILLIAM HENRY.] Quentin Durward, the Loser and the Winner ... Albany: Joel Munsell, 1869. 69 p.   BP, LC
A "proposed continuation of [Scott's] Quentin Durward," written jointly with his daughter.

BOGGS, ROBERT. Ricardo Il Falcone. *In* Short Stories, 2d ser. (1869), No. 2211.

320 BOLTON, MRS. SARAH (KNOWLES). The Present Problem ... New York: G. P. Putnam's Sons, 1874. 167 p.
A temperance tale.   BP, CU, LC, NYP, UC

321 BOUNDERBY, OLIVER, *pseud.?* The Law Student; or, The Struggles of a Heart ... New York: Samuel French, 121 Nassau Street [185-?]. 100 p. Printed in double cols.   BU
Also contains: The Little Errand Boy, by Mrs. Caroline Orne—Triumph of Love and Duty, by Mrs. E. Wellmont—The Lost Child; or, A Home in the West, by Mrs. Caroline Orne—The Forget-Me-Not, by Miss Anne T. Wilbur.
"From The Flag of Our Union."

322 [BOUTON, JOHN BELL.] Round the Block: An American Novel ... New York: D. Appleton and Company. London, 1864. 468 p., illus.
AAS, AP, BP, CU, HEH, LC, LCP, N, NYP, UC, UP, UVB, Y
Laid in New York City.

323 [BOWEN, MRS. SUE (PETIGRU) KING.] Busy Moments of an Idle Woman ... New York: D. Appleton & Co. London, 1854. 285 p.   AAS, BP, BU, H, LC, LCP, N, UC, UV
Contents: Edith—An Every-Day Life—The Widow—Old Maidism versus Marriage—An Episode in the Life of a Woman of Fashion.

324 [————] Gerald Gray's Wife ... [Augusta, Ga.] published by Stockton & Co. Southern Field and Fireside office, 1864. Cover title, 86 p.   BA
Society in Charleston, S. C.

325 [————] Lily: A Novel ... New York: Harper & Brothers, 1855. 330 p.   AAS, BP, BU, H, LC, N, NYP, UC, UV
Southern society life.

326 [————] Sylvia's World, [and] Crimes Which the Law Does Not Reach ... New York: Derby & Jackson, 1859. 384 p.
BU, CU, LC, LCP, N, NYP, UC
Also contains: The Heart History of a Heartless Woman.

327 BOWLINE, CHARLEY. The Iron Tomb; or, The Mock Count of
New York. A Local Tale . . . Boston: printed and published
by Geo. H. Williams at the office of "The Uncle Sam," No. 52
Washington Street [cop. 1852]. 100 p., illus.   AAS, LC
Also contains: Mina; or, The Lover's Mistake, by Miss A. Ingraham.

328 BOWMAN, JACOB L. You and Me; or, Sketches for Both of Us . . .
By Hans Patrick Le Connor (Jacob L. Bowman). St. Louis,
Mo.: George Knapp & Co., printers, 1867. 288 p., front.
Humorous sketches, essays, and poetry.   AAS, BU, LC, N, NYP, UM

329 [BOYCE, JOHN.] Mary Lee; or, The Yankee in Ireland. By Paul
Peppergrass [pseud.] . . . Baltimore: Kelly, Hedian & Piet.
Boston: P. Donahoe, 1860. 391 p.   AAS, UC, UP, Y

330 [————] The Spaewife; or, The Queen's Secret. A Story of
the Reign of Elizabeth. By Paul Peppergrass, Esq. [pseud.]
. . . Baltimore: John Murphy & Co. London: Charles Dolman, 1853. 2 vols. (742 p.), illus.   LC, UM, UP, UVB, Y

331 BOYESEN, HJALMAR HJORTH. Gunnar: A Tale of Norse Life . . .
Boston: James R. Osgood and Company, 1874. 292 p.
          AAS, BA, CU, HEH, LC, LCP, N, NYP, UC, UVB, Y

332 ———— A Norseman's Pilgrimage . . . New York: Sheldon
& Company, 1875. 301 p.   AAS, BA, BP, BU, CU, LC, LCP, NYP, Y

BRACE, JACK, *pseud.* *See* Jones, Justin

333 BRACE, JOHN PIERCE. The Fawn of the Pale Faces; or, Two
Centuries Ago . . . New York: D. Appleton & Company, 1853.
288 p.   AAS, BP, BU, CU, H, HEH, LC, N, NYH, NYP, UC, UM, UP, Y
Laid in Hartford, 1651.

BRADBURY, MARY L. *See* Savage, Mrs. Mary L. (Bradbury)

334 BRADBURY, OSGOOD. Agnes the Beautiful; or, The Gamblers'
Conspiracy. A Vivid Picture of the Secret Transactions of
New York Life . . . Boston: George H. Williams, cop. 1853.
100 p. Printed in double cols.   AAS
Copyright notice at head of title.

335 ———— Alice Barber; or, The Adventures of a Young Woman . . . New York: Samuel French [185-?]. 100 p. Printed in double cols. HEH

Copyright notice at head of title dated 1853, and in the name of George H. Williams. Addresses of publishers in the cover imprint of HEH copy indicate it was published in the late 1850's.

336 ———— The Banker's Victim; or, The Betrayed Seamstress . . . New York: Robert M. DeWitt, 160 & 162 Nassau Street [cop. 1857]. 100 p. Printed in double cols. NYP

337 ———— The Beautiful Half Breed; or, The Border Rovers. A Tale of 1812 . . . New York: Robert M. DeWitt, 13 Frankfort Street [cop. 1867]. 100 p. Printed in double cols. AAS, NYP

338 [————] Ellen Grant; or, Fashionable Life in New York . . . New York: Dick & Fitzgerald, No. 18 Ann Street [185-?]. 118 p. Printed in double cols. NYP, UP

339 ———— Ellen, the Pride of Broadway. New York: F. A. Brady [1865]. 103 p.

Copy noted in BM.

340 ———— The Fair Quakeress; or, The Perjured Lawyer . . . New York: Robert M. DeWitt, 13 Frankfort Street [186-?]. 99 p. Printed in double cols. NYP

Copyright notice dated 1857.

341 ———— Female Depravity; or, The House of Death . . . New York: Robert M. DeWitt, 13 Frankfort Street [186-?]. 100 p. Printed in double cols. NYP

Copyright notice dated 1857.

342 ———— The Flower of the Forest; or, The Discarded Daughter . . . New York: Robert M. DeWitt, 160 & 162 Nassau Street [cop. 1857]. 99 p. Printed in double cols. NYP

343 [————] The Gambler's League; or, The Trials of a Country Maid . . . New York: Robert M. DeWitt, 160 & 162 Nassau Street [cop. 1857]. 99 p. Printed in double cols. AAS, NYP

344 [————] The Haunted Castle; or, The Abducted Niece . . . New York: Robert M. DeWitt, 13 Frankfort Street [186-?]. 99 p. Printed in double cols. NYP

Copyright notice dated 1857.

345 ———— Jane Clark; or, Scenes in Metropolitan Life. A Tale Descriptive of New York Scenes . . . Boston: Geo. H. Williams, No. 52 Washington Street, cop. 1855. 100 p. Printed in double cols.   HEH

Copyright notice at head of title.

346 [————] Louise Martin, the Village Maiden; or, The Dangers of City Life. A Story of City Scenes and Thrilling Adventures . . . Boston: George H. Williams, No. 52 Washington Street, cop. 1853. 100 p. Printed in double cols.   H

Also contains: Woman's Love.

Copyright notice at head of title.

347 [————] The Modern Othello; or, The Guilty Wife. A Thrilling Romance of New York Fashionable Life . . . New York: Robert M. DeWitt, 13 Frankfort Street [186-?]. 84 p. Printed in double cols.   NYP

Copyright notice dated 1855, and in the name of Stringer & Townsend.

348 [————] The Mutineer; or, Heaven's Vengeance . . . New York: Robert M. DeWitt, 13 Frankfort Street [186-?]. 99 p. Printed in double cols.   NYP

Copyright notice dated 1857.

349 ———— The Mysterious Foundling; or, The Gamester's Fate . . . New York: Robert M. DeWitt, 160 & 162 Nassau Street [cop. 1857]. 99 p. Printed in double cols.   NYP

350 ———— The Old Distiller: A Tale of Truth . . . New York: Brognard & Co., 1851. 46 p., illus. Printed in double cols.   NYP

351 ———— The Rival Lovers; or, The Midnight Murder . . . New York: Robert M. DeWitt, 160 & 162 Nassau Street [cop. 1857]. 99 p. Printed in double cols.   NYP

352 ———— Therese; or, The Iroquois Maiden. A Tale of New York City and of Forest Life . . . Boston: George H. Williams, 52 Washington Street [cop. 1852]. 100 p. Printed in double cols.   BP, NYP, UM, Y

BRADFORD, MRS. ANNIE (CHAMBERS). *See* Ketchum, Mrs. Annie (Chambers) Bradford

353 [BRADFORD, MRS. SARAH ELIZABETH (HOPKINS).] Lewie; or, The Bended Twig. By Cousin Cicely [pseud.] . . . Auburn: Alden, Beardsley & Co. Rochester: Wanzer, Beardsley & Co., 1853. 344 p., front. AAS, BP, HEH, UP
Demonstrates results of lack of parental discipline.

354 ———— The Linton Family; or, The Fashion of This World ... New York: Pudney & Russell, 1860. 320 p.
CU, LC, NYP, Y

355 [————] Ups and Downs; or, Silver Lake Sketches. By Cousin Cicely [pseud.] . . . Auburn: Alden, Beardsley & Co. New York: James C. Derby, 1854. 341 p., illus. H
Contents: Miss Tod, M.D.; or, A Disease of the Heart—Uncle Caleb's Adopted Daughter—The Vermont Cousin—Ups and Downs—The Lonely Mourner—The Old Red School House—A Lesson of Contentment—The Husband of a Widow—Discriminating Charity—Lizzie Ellison's Story— The Heir of Glen Howard—Poor Nina, the Fugitive—What Makes the Difference—The Old Scotch Couple—The Burning of York Minster.

356 BRADLEY, JAMES A. Clayton Berry; or, New Year's Calls. A Temperance Story . . . New York: McDonald Bros., 1871. 39 p. NYP

BRADSHAW, WESLEY, pseud. See Alexander, Charles Wesley

357 BRADY, JAMES TOPHAM. A Christmas Dream . . . New York: printed by C. A. Alvord, 1860. 35 p., illus.
AAS, CU, HEH, LC, NYH, NYP

358 ———— ———— New York: D. Appleton & Co. London, 1860. 41 p., illus. BU, H, HEH
New material added to this ed.

BRAGANZA, pseud. See Bragg, Henry A.

359 [BRAGG, HENRY A.] Tekel; or, Cora Glencoe. A Novel ... By Braganza [pseud.]. Philadelphia: J. B. Lippincott & Co., 1870. 463 p. BP, LC, LCP, UM, UV
A Texan in New York and Maryland about 1850.

360 BRANDON, CURRIS. David Woodburn, the Mountain Missionary ... Boston: Henry Hoyt, No. 9 Cornhill [cop. 1865]. 310 p., illus. HEH
On the Wisconsin frontier.

BRENT, HENRY JOHNSON. The Iron Man. *In* The Knickerbocker Gallery (1855), No. 1492.

361 BREWSTER, ANNE MARIA HAMPTON. Compensation; or, Always a Future . . . Philadelphia: J. B. Lippincott & Co., 1860. 297 p.   AAS, BP, CU, H, HEH, LCP, NYP, UP, Y
On musical composers.

362 ———— St. Martin's Summer . . . Boston: Ticknor and Fields, 1866. 442 p.   AAS, AP, BA, BP, CU, H, HEH, LCP, NYP, UC, UP, Y
Laid in Italy.

———— Vox Humana. *In* Short Stories (1869), No. 2210.

BRICKTOP, *pseud. See* Small, George G.

363 BRIDGES, JAMES. The Collier's Tale: A True History . . . New York: Robert Carter & Brothers, 1853. 69 p., front.
New York State Library copy.

364 BRIERWOOD, FRANK, *pseud.?* Mabel Clifton: A Novel . . . Philadelphia: Claxton, Remsen & Haffelfinger, 1869. 304 p.
The downfall of an heiress.   AAS, LC, NYP

BRIGGS, CHARLES FREDERICK. A Literary Martyrdom. *In* The Knickerbocker Gallery (1855), No. 1492.

365 BRIGHT, MRS. AMANDA METCALF. The Three Bernices; or, Ansermo of the Crag . . . Philadelphia: Claxton, Remsen & Haffelfinger, 1869. 380 p.   CU, LC

366 [BRINTON, MRS. BULAH.] Man Is Love: An American Story. By One Who Knows . . . Philadelphia: J. B. Lippincott & Co., 1873. 471 p.   AAS, HEH, UC
Life on the border during the Civil War.

BRISBANE, WILLIAM HENRY. Narrative of Albert and Mary. *In* J. Griffiths, *ed.,* Autographs for Freedom [2d ser.] (1854), No. 1034.

367 BRISÉE . . . Philadelphia: J. B. Lippincott & Co., 1862. 255 p.
Washington society.   AAS, AP, CU, H, HEH, LC, N, NYP

368 BRISTED, CHARLES ASTOR. The Upper Ten Thousand: Sketches of
American Society . . . New York: Stringer & Townsend, 1852.
274 p., illus.

AAS, BA, BP, BU, CU, H, LC, LCP, N, NYH, NYP, UM, UP, UV, Y
New York City society.

369 BRITTAN, HARRIETTE G. Shoshie, the Hindoo Zenana Teacher
. . . New York: Thomas Whittaker, No. 2 Bible House [cop.
1873]. 222 p., illus.   LC, LCP

BROADLUCK, CEPHAS, *pseud.* *See* Gazlay, Allen W.

BROCK, SALLIE A. *See* Putnam, Mrs. Sallie A. (Brock)

BRODÉ, GERTRUDE. At Eve. *In* Stories and Sketches (1867),
No. 2386.

370 BROKEN COLUMNS . . . New York: Sheldon and Company, 1863.
558 p., 1 l.   AAS, AP, BA, CU, H, HEH, NYP, UP, Y
Laid in England.

371 BROOK FARM: The Amusing and Memorable of American Country
Life. New York: Robert Carter & Brothers, 1860. 208 p.,
front.   AAS, BP, LCP
Laid in New York.

BROOKE, WESLEY, *pseud.* *See* Lunt, George

371a [BROOKS, ALICE.] Day Dreams. Baltimore: Turnbull Brothers,
1874. 226 p.   AAS, H, HEH
Contents: Poor Phil—Marion—C. G.; or, The Tale of a Trunk—Compensation—Roger Ascott's Story—The Story of a Dream.
HEH author's presentation copy.

372 BROTHER MASON, the Circuit Rider; or, Ten Years a Methodist
Preacher . . . Cincinnati: H. M. Rulison. Philadelphia:
Quaker City Publishing House, 1855. 310 p., front.   LC, LCP

373 BROTHERHEAD, ALFRED PAXTON. Himself His Worst Enemy; or,
Philip Duke of Wharton's Career . . . Philadelphia: J. B.
Lippincott & Co., 1871. 374 p.   AAS, BP, LC, NYP
Early 18th-century London.

374 BROUGHAM, JOHN. A Basket of Chips . . . New York: Bunce & Brother, 1855. 408 p., illus.

AAS, BA, BP, BU, CU, HEH, LC, N, NYP, UC, UM, UP, UVB, Y

Contains: Some Passages in the Life of a Dog—Love and Loyalty, an Episode in English History—O'Dearmid's Ride—The Fairies' Warning—Kit Cobb, the Cabman, a Story of London Life—Fatality, a Condensed Novel—Ned Geraghty's Luck—The Eagle and Her Talons, an Eastern Apologue—Evenings at Our Club—Romance and Reality—Jasper Leech, the Man Who Never Had Enough—Nightmares—The Bunsby Papers.

375 ———— The Bunsby Papers (Second Series). Irish Echoes . . . New York: Derby & Jackson. Cincinnati: H. W. Derby & Co., 1856. 298 p., front. AAS, CU, H, HEH, LC, NYP, UC, UM, Y

Contents: Dan Duff's Wish, and What Came of It—The Blarney Stone—The Gospel Charm—The Test of Blood—The Morning Dream—The Fortune-Teller—The Fairy Circle—O'Bryan's Luck—The Tipperary Venus. Also published as: *Humorous Stories.* New York: Derby & Jackson, 1857. AAS

376 ———— The Light of Home: A Christmas Story . . . New York: American News Company, 1868. 96 p. UP, Y

———— *ed.* See Lotos Leaves (1875), No. 1588.

377 [BROWN, DAVID.] The Planter; or, Thirteen Years in the South. By a Northern Man . . . Philadelphia: H. Hooker, 1853. 275 p. BP, BU, CU, H, HEH, LC, LCP, NYH, NYP, UP

Arguments condoning slavery interspersed with tales.

378 [BROWN, EMMA ELIZABETH.] From Night to Light. By B. E. E. [pseud.]. Boston: D. Lothrop & Co. Dover, N. H.: G. T. Day & Co. [cop. 1872]. 290 p., illus. CU, LC

Laid in the Far East.

379 [BROWN, JAMES E.] Mose Skinner's [pseud.] Bridal Tour, and Other Sketches. Boston: New England News Company, No. 41 Court Street [cop. 1871]. Cover title, 21 p. AAS, LC, NYP

Also contains: A Popular Summer Resort—Mose Skinner as a Drummer—Woman's Rights, an Essay by Mrs. Skinner.

380 [————] Mose Skinner's Great World's Jubilee and Hum-strum Convulsion . . . Boston: printed by Warren Richardson, 1872. 21 p., illus. AAS, BP, BU, H, HEH, LC, NYP

Cover title: "Mose Skinner's Grand World's Jubilee . . ."

381 [————] Mose Skinner's Silver Wedding; to Which Is Added a Brief Biography of Mr. Skinner. Boston: printed by Warren Richardson, 112 Washington Street [cop. 1873]. 21 p.

AAS, H, HEH, LC

Cover title: "Mose Skinner's Silver Wedding and a Town at Auction."

382 [————] Our Great Peace Festival and Pow-Wow; to Be Held in Boston, June, 1869 . . . Boston: printed by Warren Richardson, 1869. 21 p.

AAS, BA, BP, BU, CU, H, HEH, LC, N, NYP

Cover title: "Mose Skinner's Grand Peace Jubilee and Jewsharp Oratorio."

383 [————] Recollections of a Lazy Life. By Mose Skinner [pseud.] . . . Boston: printed by Warren Richardson, 1869. 23 p. AAS, H, LC

384 [BROWN, NATHAN.] Œe Histori ov Magnus Maha'rba and de Blak Dragun. Bai Kristofur Kadmus [pseud.] . . . Nu-York: printed for de Filolojikal Gemána, 1866. 122 p.

AAS, BP, BU, CU, H, HEH, LC, NYP, UC, Y

AAS 2d copy: "Hurst, stereotyper; F. Somers, printer," verso of title page.
Allegorical history of the Civil War, in phonetic spelling.

385 [————] The History of Magnus Maharba and the Black Dragon. By Kristofur Kadmus [pseud.] . . . New York: printed for the proprietor, 1867. 105 p.

AAS, BA, BP, BU, HEH, LC, NYP

This is No. 384 in conventional spelling, but without index.

386 [————] ZYX and His Fairy; or, The Soul in Search of Peace. New York: Brown and Duer, 1867. 72 p. AAS, CU, LC, Y
An allegory.

BROWN, THURLOW WEED. Dodge's Ascent of Mount Washington. In Dodge's Sketches [1853], No. 1751.

387 ———— Minnie Hermon; or, The Night and Its Morning. A Tale for the Times . . . Auburn and Buffalo: Miller, Orton & Mulligan, 1854. 472 p., illus.

A temperance novel. AAS, BP, BU, CU, H, HEH, LC, NYP, UC, Y

388 ———— Minnie Hermon, the Rumseller's Daughter; or, Woman in the Temperance Reform. A Tale for the Times . . . New York and Boston: Henry S. Goodspeed & Co.; Thompson & Co., Woodstock, N. B.; Geo. Lawrence, London, Ont.; Ohio

Publishing Co., Ashland, O.; Goodspeed's Empire Publishing House, Chicago, Ill. [cop. 1874]. 542 p., illus.   AAS, CU, H, HEH
An introduction and two new chapters added to this ed.
Announced as "just published" in PW, V (June 13, 1874), 550.

389 ——— Why I Am a Temperance Man: A Series of Letters to a Friend. Together with Tales and Sketches from Real Life, and Hearth-Stone Reveries . . . Auburn: Derby and Miller. Buffalo: Derby, Orton and Mulligan. Cincinnati: Henry W. Derby, 1853. 384 p., illus.   AAS, LC

——— [*See also*] Cornyn, John K. Dick Wilson . . . With an Introduction by Thurlow W. Brown (1853), No. 640.

390 BROWN, WILLIAM WELLS. Clotelle: A Tale of the Southern States . . . Boston: James Redpath. New York: H. Dexter, Hamilton & Co. [cop. 1864]. 104 p., illus.   H, LC, LCP, NYP
On cover: "Redpath's Books for the Camp Fire."
An antislavery novel, first published in London, 1853, as *Clotelle; or, The President's Daughter* which is listed in M. Whiteman, *A Century of Fiction by American Negroes, 1853-1952* (Philadelphia, 1955), p. 12.

391 ——— Clotelle; or, The Colored Heroine. A Tale of the Southern States . . . Boston: Lee & Shepard, 1867. 114 p., illus.   BU, CU, NYH, NYP
There are a few alterations in this ed.

392 [BROWNE, CHARLES FARRAR.] Artemus Ward [pseud.], His Book . . . New York: Carleton, 1862. 262, [2] p., illus.
  AAS, AP, BP, BU, H, HEH, LC, LCP, N, NYP, UC, UVB, Y

393 [———] Artemus Ward, His Travels. Part I—Miscellaneous. Part II—Among the Mormons . . . New York: Carleton. London: S. Low, Son & Co., 1865. 231 p., illus.
  AAS, AP, BP, BU, CU, H, HEH, LC, LCP, N, NYP, UC, UM, UVB, Y

394 [———] Artemus Ward in London, and Other Papers . . . New York: G. W. Carleton & Co. London: S. Low, Son & Co., 1867. 229 p., illus.
  AAS, BP, BU, CU, H, HEH, LC, N, NYP, UC, UM, UP, UVB, Y

395 [———] Artemus Ward's Panorama. (As Exhibited at the Egyptian Hall, London.) Edited by His Executors, T. W. Robertson & E. P. Hingston . . . New York: G. W. Carleton. London: J. C. Hotten, 1869. 213 p., illus.
  AAS, BP, BU, CU, H, HEH, LC, N, NYP, UC, UM, UVB, Y

396 [————] Sandwiches, by Artemus Ward [pseud.]. New York: Carleton [cop. 1870]. Cover title, 31 p., illus. Printed in double cols.   NYH, NYP

397 BROWNE, JOHN ROSS. Adventures in the Apache Country. A Tour through Arizona and Sonora, with Notes on the Silver Regions of Nevada . . . New York: Harper & Brothers, 1869. 535 p., illus.

AAS, BA, BP, BU, CU, H, HEH, LC, LCP, N, NYH, NYP, UM, Y

The humorous illustrations are in keeping with the text.

398 ———— An American Family in Germany . . . New York: Harper & Brothers, 1866. 381 p., illus.

BU, CU, H, HEH, LC, LCP, N, NYP, Y

399 ———— Crusoe's Island. A Ramble in the Footsteps of Alexander Selkirk. With Sketches of Adventure in California and Washoe . . . New York: Harper & Brothers, 1864. 436 p., illus.   BP, CU, H, HEH, LC, LCP, N, NYH, NYP, Y

400 ———— The Land of Thor . . . New York: Harper & Brothers, 1867. 542 p., illus.

BA, BP, BU, CU, H, HEH, LC, LCP, N, NYP, UM, Y

401 ———— Yusef; or, The Journey of the Frangi. A Crusade in the East . . . New York: Harper & Brothers, 1853. 421 p., illus.   BU, CU, H, HEH, LC, LCP, N, NYP, UP, Y

402 [BROWNE, MRS. MATTIE (GRIFFITH).] Autobiography of a Female Slave. New York: Redfield, 1857. 401 p.

AAS, BP, CU, H, HEH, NYP, UM

HEH has author's ALS, dated May 21, 1904, in which she states that only a few copies were struck off "and then the book died a natural death without accomplishing its object. . . . The Story has one commendable virtue, every and each incident is a recited and well known fact."

403 BROWNING, MESHACH. Forty-Four Years of the Life of a Hunter: Being Reminiscences of Meshach Browning, a Maryland Hunter. Roughly Written Down by Himself. Revised and Illustrated by E. Stabler. Philadelphia: J. B. Lippincott & Co., 1859. 400 p., illus.   BP, H, HEH, Y

BROWNJOHN, BELLAMY, *pseud.* *See* Dunham, Robert Carr

404 BROWNSON, ORESTES AUGUSTUS. The Spirit-Rapper: An Autobiography . . . Boston: Little, Brown and Company. London: Charles Dolman, 1854. 402 p.
BA, BP, H, LC, NYP, UC, UM, UP

———— *ed. See* Clarke, Mrs. DeWitt. Lizzie Maitland (1857),
No. 538.

405 [BROWNSON, SARAH NICOLENA.] Marian Elwood; or, How Girls
Live. By One of Themselves. New York: E. Dunigan &
Brother; James B. Kirker, 1859. 360 p. LC
Of Catholic interest.

406 BRUCE, MRS. E. M. A Thousand a Year . . . Boston: Lee &
Shepard, 1866. 263 p. AAS, BP, LC, LCP, NYP, UM
The story of a clergyman and his family.

BUCKINGHAM, E. The Man-Owner. *In* J. Griffiths, *ed.*, Autographs for Freedom (1853), No. 1033.

407 BUCKINGHAM, EMMA MAY. A Self-Made Woman; or, Mary
Idyl's Trials and Triumphs . . . New York: S. R. Wells, 1873.
343 p. LC, NYP

408 BUCKINGHAM, HENRY A. Harry Burnham, the Young Continental; or, Memoirs of an American Officer during the
Campaigns of the Revolution, and Sometime a Member of
Washington's Staff . . . New York: Burgess & Garrett. Baltimore: Burgess, Taylor & Co., 1851. 256 p. Printed in double
cols. UC, UP

409 BUCKLEY, MRS. MARIA L. Amanda Willson; or, The Vicissitudes
of Life . . . New York: printed by Urner & Co., 1856. 40 p.,
front. AAS, BU, LC
Also contains: A Sketch of the Working Classes of New York; or, The
Sufferings of the Sewing Girls.

410 ———— Edith Moreton; or, Temperance versus Intemperance
. . . Philadelphia: published for the author, 1852. 48 p.
H, LC, NYP

BUDDINGTON, ZADEL BARNES. *See* Gustafson, Mrs. Zadel (Barnes)
Buddington

411 BULFINCH, STEPHEN GREENLEAF. Honor; or, The Slave-Dealer's
Daughter . . . Boston: William V. Spencer, 1864. 238 p.
Antislavery. AAS, H, HEH, N, NYP, UC, UM, UP, Y

412 [BULLARD, MRS. ANNE TUTTLE JONES.] Love Affairs in Our Village Twenty Years Ago. By Mrs. Caustic [pseud.]. St. Louis: printed and published at Intelligencer Buildings, 1852. 79, [1] p. Printed in double cols. LC

413 [————] Matrimony; or, Love Affairs in Our Village Twenty Years Ago. By Mrs. Caustic [pseud.]. Second Edition. New York: M. W. Dodd, 1853. 316 p. LC, NYP

This is her *Love Affairs* with a new title and preface.

414 BULLARD, MRS. LAURA J. (CURTIS). Christine; or, Woman's Trials and Triumphs. By Laura J. Curtis . . . New York: DeWitt & Davenport, 160 & 162 Nassau Street [cop. 1856]. 384 p.

Expounds woman's rights. AAS, HEH, UP

415 [————] Now-a-Days! New York: T. L. Magagnos & Co., 1854. 309 p., front. AAS, BP, CU, H, HEH, UC, UP, UV, Y

Also issued with imprint: New York: T. L. Magagnos & Co. Bangor, Me.: David Bugbee, 1854. This is listed as the 1st ed. by J. Williamson, *A Bibliography of the State of Maine* (Portland, 1896), No. 1725.

416 BUNCE, OLIVER BELL. A Bachelor's Story . . . New York: Rudd & Carleton, 1859. 247 p. AAS, BP, HEH, LCP, UM, UP, Y

417 [————] Bensley: A Story of To-Day . . . New York: James G. Gregory, 1863. 221 p. BU, H, LC, NYP

418 [————] Life before Him: A Novel . . . New York: W. A. Townsend & Company, 1860. 401 p.

AAS, AP, H, LC, NYP, UP, Y

BUNKER, TIMOTHY, *pseud.* *See* Clift, William

419 BUNKLEY, JOSEPHINE M., *pseud.?* The Testimony of an Escaped Novice from the Sisterhood of St. Joseph, Emmettsburg, Maryland . . . New York: Harper & Brothers, 1855. 338 p., illus.

BU, H, HEH, LC, N, NYH, UM, Y

At head of title: "Miss Bunkley's Book."

It is stated in the preface that an unauthorized anon. ed. was printed before the author could recover her ms. AAS has a copy entitled: *The Escaped Nun; or, Disclosures of Convent Life; and The Confessions of a Sister of Charity.* New York: DeWitt & Davenport [cop. 1855]. 344 p. Anti-Catholic.

BUNTLINE, NED, *pseud.* *See* Judson, Edward Zane Carroll

420 BURCKETT, FLORENCE. Wildmoor: A Novel . . . Philadelphia: J. B. Lippincott & Co., 1875. 464 p.   AAS, H, LC, NYP
Laid in England.

421 BURDETT, CHARLES. Dora Barton, the Banker's Ward: A Tale of Real Life in New York . . . New York: S. A. Rollo, 1860. 355 p.   AAS, HEH, NYP, Y

———— The Drunkard's Daughter. *In* C. B. Porter, *ed.*, The Silver Cup (1852), No. 1931.

422 ———— Margaret Moncrieffe, the First Love of Aaron Burr: A Romance of the Revolution . . . New York: Derby & Jackson, 1860. 437 p., front.
AAS, AP, BA, BP, BU, CU, H, HEH, LC, LCP, N, NYH, NYP, UM, UP, UVB, Y
Also published as: *The Beautiful Spy. An Exciting Story of Army and High Life in New York in 1776.* Philadelphia: J. E. Potter [cop. 1865].
CU, NYP, UVB

423 ———— The Second Marriage; or, A Daughter's Trials. A Domestic Tale of New York . . . New York: Charles Scribner, 1856. 238 p.   H, LC, NYP, UVB

424 ———— Three Per Cent a Month; or, The Perils of Fast Living . . . New York: Derby & Jackson. Cincinnati: H. W. Derby & Co., 1856. 395 p.   AAS, H, HEH, LC, N, NYP, UVB, Y
Also published as: *The Perils of Fast Living. A Warning to Young Men.* New York: Derby & Jackson, 1857.   AAS

BURDICK, AUSTIN C., *pseud.* *See* Cobb, Sylvanus

425 BURK, JAMES H., *ed.* First Quarrels and First Discords in Married Life. To Which Is Added: A Matrimonial Peace-Offering . . . Cincinnati: Applegate & Company, 1860. 291 p., front.   LC

BURKE, THOMAS A. Doing a Sheriff. [And] A Losing Game of Poker. *In* [the following entry].

426 ———— *ed.* Polly Peablossom's Wedding, and Other Tales. By the Hon. J. B. Lamar, Hon. R. M. Charlton . . . Edited by T. A. Burke . . . Philadelphia: A. Hart, 1851. 195 p., illus.
BA, BP, LC, N, UC
Contents: Polly Peablossom's Wedding [by John B. Lamar]—The Unclad Horseman [by Wm. T. Thompson]—The Thimble Game [by T. W. Lane]

59

—War's Yure Hoss? [by a Missourian]—A Losing Game of Poker [by T. A. Burke]—Mike Hooter's Bar Story [by a Missourian]—Electricity as a Temperance Agent [by Wm. C. Richards]—M'Cracken's Experience [by a Hoosier]—Bingo [by R. M. Charlton]—How Sally Hooter Got Snake-Bit [by a Missourian]—The "Experience" of the Blacksmith of the Mountain Pass [by John B. Lamar]—"Pertaters and Ternups" [by a South Carolinian]—The Coon-Hunt; or, A Fency Country [by Major Jos. Jones]—"Doing" a Sheriff [by T. A. Burke]—A Case of Supposition—The Amateur Ticket-Vender at the Varieties—The Telegraph in St. Louis—Smoking a Grizzly [by John S. Robb]—Ethan Spike's First and Last Visit to Portland —An Arkansas Original—A Fearful Tale of the Mississippi [by Falconbridge]—A Frightful Adventure in Mississippi [by "The Turkey Runner"] —Practical Jokes and Bad Liquor—Mississippi Legislature: The Way to Get a Vote—How Mike Hooter Came Very Near "Wolloping" Arch Cooney—The First Piano in Northern Illinois—A Modest Irishman—The Way Old Bill Went Off—A Sleep-Walking Incident—The Last Bloody Duel Fought in Ohio—Anecdotes of Western Travel—A Running Fight upon the Rackensac.

427 BURNHAM, GEORGE PICKERING. The Belle of the Orient; or, The Hindoo Merchant's Legacy. A Story of the East and West . . . New York: Samuel French, 121 Nassau Street; William V. Spencer, 128 Washington Street, Boston . . . C. P. Kimball, Long Wharf, San Francisco [185-?]. 100 p. Printed in double cols. HEH

428 ———— The History of the Hen Fever: A Humorous Record . . . Boston: James French and Company. New York: J. C. Derby. Philadelphia: T. B. Peterson [cop. 1855]. 326 p., illus. AAS, BA, BP, BU, CU, HEH, LC, LCP, N, NYH, NYP, UM, Y

429 ———— A Hundred Thousand Dollars in Gold. How to Make It. A Practical Narrative, Suggesting How to Use, and Not Abuse It . . . Springfield, Mass.: W. J. Holland, 1875. 407 p., illus. AAS, HEH, LC

430 ———— Nell Noell, the Light-Keeper's Treasure . . . New York: Samuel French, 121 Nassau Street [185-?]. 100 p. H

431 [————] The Rag-Picker; or, Bound and Free . . . New York: Mason Brothers, 1855. 431 p.
A temperance tale; Boston. AAS, BA, BU, H, HEH, NYH, UC, Y

432 BURNS, WILLIAM. Female Life in New York City . . . Philadelphia: T. B. Peterson and Brothers, 306 Chestnut Street [1875?]. 95 p., illus. Printed in double cols. UM, UV, Y
Roorbach 1852-1855 lists Life in New York, New York: Bunce and Brother.

433 [BURTON, MRS. HENRY S.] Who Would Have Thought It? A Novel . . . Philadelphia: J. B. Lippincott & Co., 1872. 438 p.

Civil War in background.   AAS, HEH, LC, LCP, NYP

434 [BURTS, ROBERT.] The Sea-King: A Nautical Romance. By the Author of the "Scourge of the Ocean." Edited and Completed by the Editor of "Valerie" . . . Philadelphia: A. Hart, 1851. 203 p.   HEH, LC, UC

435 [BURWELL, WILLIAM MACCREARY.] White Acre vs. Black Acre. A Case at Law, Reported by J. G., Esq. [pseud.], a Retired Barrister, of Lincolnshire, England. Richmond, Va.: J. W. Randolph, 1856. 251 p.   BP, H, HEH, LC, N, NYH, NYP, Y
A proslavery allegory.

436 BUSHNELL, WILLIAM H. Ah-Meek, the Beaver; or, The Copper-Hunters of Lake Superior. New York: American News Co. [1867]. 104 p.
Copy noted in BM.

437 ——— The Pearl of Panama; or, The Spaniard's Vengeance . . . Boston: Elliott, Thomes & Talbot, 63 Congress [cop. 1867]. 100 p.
University of Illinois Library copy.

438 ——— Prairie Fire! A Tale of Early Illinois . . . Chicago: Walter B. Sloan, publisher; Robert Fergus, printer, 1855. 96 p.
Illinois State Historical Society copy.

BUTLER, MRS. CAROLINE H. Amy. *In* Household Narratives (1854), No. 1278.

439 ——— Life in Varied Phases: Illustrated in a Series of Sketches . . . Boston: Phillips, Sampson and Company, 1851. 288 p.
       AAS, BP, Y
Contents: Nelly, the Rag-Gatherer—The Perplexed Student—Gaity—The Poet Lí—Little Winnie—The Widow and the Deformed—The Countess—The Curtain Lifted—The Maid of Che-Kyang.

——— The Perplexed Student. *In* Household Narratives (1854), No. 1278.

BUTT, MARTHA HAINES. *See* Bennett, Mrs. Martha Haines (Butt)

440 [BYRN, MARCUS LAFAYETTE.] The Life and Adventures of an Arkansaw Doctor. By David Rattlehead, M.D. [pseud.] . . . Philadelphia: Lippincott, Grambo and Co., 1851. 170 p., illus.
LC

441 [————] The Rambles of Fudge Fumble; or, The Love Scrapes of a Lifetime . . . New York: Frederic A. Brady, 1860. 232 p., illus. LC
Also published as: *The Adventures of Fudge Fumble . . . By David Rattlehead* [pseud.]. Philadelphia: T. B. Peterson & Brothers [cop. 1865]. NYP

442 [————] Rattlehead's Chronicles; or, A Little Experience with Old Maids and Young Maids, Old Bachelors, Fools, and Drunkards; Quack Doctors, Men of Science, and the World at Large. By David Rattlehead [pseud.]. Philadelphia: Lippincott, Grambo & Co. New York: Long & Brother; Stringer & Townsend. Boston: Redding & Co.; Fettridge & Co. Baltimore: Burgess, Taylor & Co., 1852. 175 p., illus. LC

443 [————] Rattlehead's Travels; or, The Recollections of a Backwoodsman, That Has Travelled Many Thousand Miles on the Highway of Human Destiny . . . By David Rattlehead, M.D. [pseud.] . . . Philadelphia: Lippincott, Grambo & Co. New York: Long & Brother; Stringer & Townsend. Boston: Redding & Co.; Fettridge & Co. Baltimore: Burgess, Taylor & Co., 1852. 175 p., illus. LC

C., M. A. *See* Cruse, Mary Anne

444 CABELL, MRS. JULIA (MAYO). An Odd Volume of Facts and Fictions, in Prose and Verse . . . Richmond: Nash and Woodhouse. J. W. Culley, printer, 1852. 275 p.
BU, HEH, NYH, UM
Contains: The Dead Bride; or, "The Fountain of Trevi." A Tale Founded on Fact—Wo and Weal; or, The Transitions of Life—Ilia, the High Priestess.

445 [CAFFREY, ANDREW.] The Adventures of a Lodger . . . Boston: printed for the author, 1868. 16 p. LC

446 [CALDCLEUGH, WILLIAM GEORGE.] Eastern Tales. By the Author of The Branch and Other Poems. Philadelphia: James Challen & Son, 1863. 280 p. AP, CU, LCP, UV

447 CALDOR, M. T. Oakenshaw; or, The Test of Heirs . . . Boston: F. Gleason, 1864. 80 p., illus.
Title listed in Allibone and announced as "recently published" in *Amer. Lit. Gaz.*, II (Feb. 1, 1864), 248.

448 [CALDWELL, JOHN H.] The Mysterious Messenger. Founded on Fact. By a Member of the Georgia Conference. Nashville, Tenn.: published for the author by J. B. M'Ferrin, Ag't., 1860. Cover title, 22 p. BA
A temperance tale.

449 ——— The Thurstons of the Old Palmetto State; or, Varieties of Southern Life. Illustrated in the Fortunes of a Distinguished Family of South Carolina . . . New York: Joseph Russell, 1861. 406 p. CU, LC, N, NYP, UC, UM, Y

450 [CAMBRIDGE, WILLIAM G.] Glenwood; or, The Parish Boy. Boston: Shepard, Clark and Co., 1855. 429 p., front.
AAS, BU, CU, H, HEH, N, UC
Village life and gossip.

451 ——— Henri; or, The Web and Woof of Life . . . Boston: Abel Tompkins and B. B. Mussey & Co., 1853. 432 p.
AAS, BP, H, HEH, NYP, UM, Y
Also published as: *Lelia Stewart; or, The Heart Unveiled.* Boston: Higgins, Bradley and Dayton, 1857. AAS, CU, HEH, N, Y

452 ——— The Mechanic's Bride; or, The Autobiography of Elwood Gorden . . . Boston: Shepard, Clark and Brown, 1857. 302 p. AAS, CU, HEH
Also issued with imprint: Boston: Bradley, Dayton & Co., 1857. UM

453 [CAMERON, REB.] Salted with Fire. By H. M. Le Grange [pseud.] . . . New York: E. J. Hale & Son, 1872. 177 p. LC

454 CAMPBELL, JANE C. The Money-Maker, and Other Tales . . . New York: J. C. Derby. Boston: Phillips, Sampson & Co. Cincinnati: H. W. Derby, 1854. 353 p.
AAS, CU, HEH, LC, NYP, UM
Also contains: Christine—Catharine Clayton—Paul Talbot—Robert Dunning—Blanche Acheson—Farmer's Daughter—The Seamstress—The First Step—A Wife's Love—Lazy Philanthropy.
Also published as: *American Evening Entertainments; or, Tales of City and Country Life.* New York: J. C. Derby [etc., etc.], 1856. AAS, BU, UV, Y

455 [CAMPBELL, MRS. JULIET HAMERSLEY (LEWIS).] Eros and Anteros; or, The Bachelor's Ward. By Judith Canute [pseud.]. New York: Rudd & Carleton, 1857. 360 p.

AAS, CU, HEH, LC, LCP, NYP, Y

Also published as: *The Old Love and the New.* New York: Rudd & Carleton, 1858. AAS, H

CAMPBELL, MARY, *pseud. See* Bennett, Mrs. Mary E.

456 [CANNON, CHARLES JAMES.] Bickerton; or, The Immigrant's Daughter ... New York: P. O'Shea, 1855. 191 p. CU, LC

457 [————] Ravellings from the Web of Life. By Grandfather Greenway [pseud.] ... New York, Boston, Montreal: D. & J. Sadlier & Co., 1855. 364 p. Y

458 [————] Tighe Lyfford: A Novel ... New York: James Miller, 1859. 270 p. AAS, LC, Y

459 CANNON, SUSAN. Maidee, the Alchemist; or, Turning All to Gold ... New York: M. Doolady, 1871. 249 p. AAS, CU, LC, Y

460 CANTY, SAMUEL. The Chip Boy of the Dry Dock: A Local Moral Story ... New York: printed and published for the author, 1855. 112 p., illus. CU, LC

Also published as: *George Seton; or, The Chip Boy of the Dry Dock. A Tale of New York Life.* New York: Garrett & Co., 18 Ann Street [cop. 1855]. AAS

CANUTE, JUDITH, *pseud. See* Campbell, Mrs. Juliet Hamersley (Lewis)

461 CAPRON, CARRIE. Helen Lincoln: A Tale ... New York: Harper & Brothers, 1856. 308 p.

AAS, CU, H, HEH, LC, N, NYP, UC, UM, UP, Y

Of shipping interest; New York.

CAPSADELL, LOU, *pseud. See* Hammond, Mrs. Henrietta (Hardy)

462 CAPTAIN LE DIABLE, *pseud.* Historical Sketch of the Third Annual Conquest of Florida. Captain Le Diable ... Port Royal, S. C., 1864. 19 p. H, HEH, LC

Humorous satire.

CARBOY, JOHN, *pseud. See* Harrington, John A.

463 THE CAREER OF JOHN MORTAL, a Man Who Enjoyed This Life. Baltimore: John F. Weishampel, Jr. Richmond, Va.: T. J. Starke. New York: Sheldon, Blakeman & Co. Harrisburg, Pa.: John Winebenner [cop. 1859]. 66 p., illus.   LC
Of the man who lost his soul.

CAREY, ALICE. *See* Cary, Alice

CAREY, M. F.   Adela Lincoln: A Tale of the Wine Cup.   *In* M. V. F. Victor, Fashionable Dissipation (1854), No. 2585.

CARLETON, *Cousin* MAY, *pseud. See* Fleming, Mrs. May Agnes (Early)

464 CARPENTER, WILLIAM HENRY.   The Regicide's Daughter: A Tale of Two Worlds . . .   Philadelphia: Lippincott, Grambo & Co., 1851.   213 p.   AAS

465 CARTER, JOHN HENTON.   The Log of Commodore Rollingpin: His Adventures Afloat and Ashore . . .   New York: G. W. Carleton & Co.   London: S. Low, Son & Co., 1874.   258 p., illus.
AAS, BP, BU, CU, HEH, LC, LCP, NYP, UC, UM, UP, Y

466 CARY, ALICE.   The Adopted Daughter . . . And Other Tales. Philadelphia: J. B. Smith & Co., 1859.   368 p.
AAS, CU, HEH, NYP

Contains: Three Scenes in the South, by C. B. Parsons—Mary Neilly, by Mrs. Jennie Dowling De Witt—The Last of Torconnier's Band, by Mrs. C. W. Denison—A Country Recollection; or, The Reformed Inebriate, by Mrs. E. F. Ellet—The Dying Husband, by Will. Willowill—Little Peleg, the Drunkard's Son, by William T. Coggeshall—Comfort, by Mrs. C. M. Kirkland—Rose May, the New School-Mistress, by F. H. Stauffer—My Early Friend, by Francis C. Woodworth—The Auction; or, The Wedding-Coat. A Tale of Truth—Wine Occasionally, Evelyn, by Mrs. E. J. Eames—Unequal Yoking: A Warning to Young Women, by Leroy M. Lee—The Basket-Maker. Dedicated to the Aristocracy—Lights and Shadows, by Angela of Glen Cottage—Idella Pemberton, by Rev. Philip P. Neely—The Two Clerks, by C. D. Colesworthy—A Tale of the Destroyer, by J. W. Field—The History of a Neighborhood, by Hon. Neal Dow.
Also issued with imprint: New York: Evans and Co., 1859.   UM

467 ———   The Bishop's Son . . .   New York: G. W. Carleton & Co.   London: S. Low, Son & Co., 1867.   416 p.
Laid in Ohio.   AAS, BU, CU, H, HEH, LC, N, NYP, UC, Y

468 ———— Clovernook; or, Recollections of Our Neighborhood in the West . . . New York: Redfield, 1852. 342 p., front.

AAS, BA, BU, CU, H, HEH, LC, LCP, N, NYH, NYP, UM, UV, Y

Sketches of life in Ohio.

469 ———————— Second Series. New York: Redfield, 1853. 364 p. AAS, HEH, LC, LCP, NYP, UM, UP, Y

470 ———— From Year to Year: A Token of Remembrance. Edited by Alice and Phoebe Cary. New York: Geo. A. Leavitt [1869?]. 312 p., illus. Y

471 ———— Hagar: A Story of To-Day . . . New York: Redfield, 1852. 300 p. AAS, BP, BU, CU, HEH, LCP, N, NYH, NYP, UC, Y

The story of an unwed mother.

472 ———— Married, Not Mated; or, How They Lived at Woodside and Throckmorton Hall . . . New York: Derby & Jackson. Cincinnati: H. W. Derby, 1856. 425 p.

AAS, BP, BU, CU, HEH, LC, N, NYP, UC, UM, UP, UVB, Y

———— My Grandmother That Might Have Been. *In* Rougegorge (1870), No. 2130.

473 ———— Pictures of Country Life . . . New York: Derby & Jackson, 1859. 359 p.

AAS, BP, BU, CU, HEH, LCP, N, NYH, NYP, UP, Y

Contents: Lem Lyon—Passages from the Married Life of Eleanor Holmes —The Outcast—Hasty Words and Their Apology—Sarah Morris—The House with Two Front Doors—Uncle John's Story—Making the Children Something—The Apple Cutting—Eliza Anderson—Mrs. Walden's Confidant—The Country Cousin—An Old Maid's Story.

CARY, PHOEBE, *jt. ed. See* Cary, Alice. From Year to Year [1869?], No. 470.

474 CASSEDAY, DAVIS B. The Hortons; or, American Life at Home . . . Philadelphia: James S. Claxton; D. Appleton & Co., New York; Lee & Sheppard [sic], Boston; R. W. Carroll & Co., Cincinnati; S. C. Griggs & Co., Chicago; Trübner & Co., London, 1866. 362 p. AAS, BP, CU, HEH, LC, Y

475 CASSIDY, PATRICK SARSFIELD. Glenveigh; or, The Victims of Vengeance. A Tale of Irish Peasant Life in the Present . . . Boston: Patrick Donahoe, 1870. 204 p. BP

CASTLETON, D. R., *pseud.* *See* Derby, Caroline Rosina

476 CATHERWOOD, MRS. MARY (HARTWELL). A Woman in Armor. By Mary Hartwell. New York: G. W. Carleton & Co. London: S. Low, Son & Co., 1875. 196 p., illus.
AAS, LC, N, NYP, UC, UVB
Also contains: Old Gargoyle—The Man Who "Hadn't Time."

CATIUS, JR., *pseud.* *See* Torrey, Elizabeth R.

CAUSTIC, MRS., *pseud.* *See* Bullard, Mrs. Anne Tuttle Jones

CAXTON, LAURA, *pseud.* *See* Comins, Elizabeth Barker

477 [CAZNEAU, MRS. WILLIAM LESLIE.] Eagle Pass; or, Life on the Border. By Cora Montgomery [pseud.] . . . New York: George P. Putnam & Co., 1852. 188 p.
AAS, AP, BA, BP, CU, H, HEH, LC, LCP, N, NYH, NYP, UC, UM, UVB, Y
A verisimilar story of Texas.

478 THE CHAINED WIFE; or, The Frightful Sufferings of Mary Lesley, a Beautiful Young American Girl, Who Foolishly Married the Notorious Lord Gorgon Who Lately Committed Suicide . . . Philadelphia: Old Franklin Publishing House [cop. 1874]. 62 p., illus.
AAS

479 CHALLEN, JAMES. Frank Elliott; or, Wells in the Desert . . . Philadelphia: James Challen & Son; Lindsay & Blakiston, 1859. 347 p.
BP, NYP, Y
Pages 349-352 advts.
Of religious interest; New Orleans.

480 CHAMBERLAIN, CHARLES, JR. Put to the Test . . . New York: Henry L. Hinton, 1874. 362 p.
LC
Laid in Alsace during Napoleon's time.

481 ———— The Servant-Girl of the Period the Greatest Plague of Life. What Mr. and Mrs. Honeydew Learned of Housekeeping . . . New York: J. S. Redfield, 1873. 215 p.
AAS, HEH, LC, LCP, UC, Y
The Honeydews preferred apartment living to housekeeping.

482 [CHAMBERLAIN, J. E.] Cotton Stealing: A Novel. Chicago: John R. Walsh & Co., 1866. 487 p.
AAS, BP, BU, CU, H, LC, N, NYH, NYP
Laid in Memphis and lower Mississippi Valley, 1861-1865.

483 CHAMBERLAIN, NATHAN HENRY. The Autobiography of a New England Farm-House . . . New York: Carleton, 1865. 365 p.
AAS, BA, BP, BU, CU, H, HEH, LC, NYH, NYP, UM, UV, Y

484 CHAMBERLAIN, PARTHENE BALLARD. Barbara St. John . . . Philadelphia: J. C. Garrigues & Co., 1869. 383 p., illus.
Information from LC card for copy withdrawn from circulation.

CHANDLER, ELLEN LOUISE. *See* Moulton, Mrs. Louise (Chandler)

485 CHANDLER, JOSEPH RIPLEY. The Beverly Family; or, Home Influence of Religion . . . Philadelphia: Peter F. Cunningham & Son, 1875. 166 p.   LC
Laid in Virginia about 1800.

486 CHANTER, WASHINGTON. The Nautch Girl! A Romance of the Indian Ocean . . . Philadelphia, Pa. and Dayton, O.: Oliver Crook & Co. [cop. 1868]. Caption title, 12 pts. (144 p.) Printed in double cols.   AAS (pts.1-8), BP, HEH
Story interspersed with advts. for Dr. Crook's wine tar.

487 CHAPIN, GARDNER B. Tales of the St. Lawrence . . . Rouse's Point: John Lovell & Sons, Lake Shore Press, 1873. 382 p., illus.   AAS, HEH, N, NYP, UC
Contents: Isadore—Maleeta, the River Waif—A Country Lost for a Love— The Triple Mistake—Given to the Wolves—The Church Bell of Caughnawaga—A Memory of a Masquerade—The Tale of Chateau Bigot—The Hidden Treasure of Isle Royal—The Battle of Wind Mill Point—William Johnson—Saved by an Earthquake—The Fatal Wager—The Captive of Crane's Island—Down the Rapids—The Isle of Massacre—Catching a Smuggler—The Phantom of Isle Perce—Little Mary of Villa Maria—The Hunter Lodge Movement of 1838.

488 CHAPIN, MRS. SALLIE F. (MOORE). Fitz-Hugh St. Clair, the South Carolina Rebel Boy; or, It Is No Crime to Be Born a Gentleman . . . Philadelphia: Claxton, Remsen & Haffelfinger. Charleston, S. C.: John M. Greer & Son, 1872. 252 p., illus.
An anti-North novel.   AAS, BP, CU, H, HEH, LCP, N, NYH, NYP, UV, Y

489 [CHAPLIN, MRS. JANE (DUNBAR).] The Convent and the Manse. By Hyla [pseud.] . . . Boston: John P. Jewett & Company. Cleveland, Ohio: Proctor & Worthington. London: Low & Co., 1853. 242 p.   CU, LC

490 ———— Out of the Wilderness . . . Boston: Henry A. Young & Co., 1870. 330 p.   AAS, BP, BU, CU, H, HEH, LC, NYH, NYP
Plantation problems during the Civil War and the events in the lives of a slave family following the war.

491 CHAPMAN, HELEN E. Paul Brewster and Son; or, The Story of Mary Carter . . . New York: National Temperance Society, 1875. 238 p., front.
Information from LC card for copy withdrawn from circulation.

492 CHARLEY HUNTER; or, The Forger's Fate . . . New York: Dick & Fitzgerald, No. 18 Ann Street [187-?]. 73 p., illus. Printed in double cols.   NYP

CHARLTON, R. M. Bingo. *In* T. A. Burke, *ed.*, Polly Peablossom's Wedding (1851), No. 426.

493 CHASE, LUCIEN BONAPARTE. English Serfdom and American Slavery; or, Ourselves as Others See Us . . . New York: H. Long & Brother, 43 Ann Street [cop. 1854]. 259 p.
    AAS, BP, CU, H, HEH, LC, N, NYP, UC, UP, Y

494 [CHEEVER, GEORGE BARRELL.] A Reel in a Bottle, for Jack in the Doldrums. Being the Adventures of Two of the King's Seamen in a Voyage to the Celestial Country. Edited from the Manuscripts of an Old Salt. By Rev. Henry T. Cheever . . . New York: Charles Scribner, 1852. 355 p.
    AAS, H, HEH, N, NYP, UC, UP

495 CHEEVER, HENRY P. The Rival Brothers; or, The Corsair and Privateer. A Tale of the Last War . . . New York: Samuel French, 151 Nassau [*ca.* 1852]. 100 p. Printed in double cols.
    AAS
Title story is Wright (1774-1850), No. 509, with new material added.
Contains: An Italian Duel, by Francis A. Durivage—The Mother's Lesson, by Austin C. Burdick—The Friend of the Family, by Francis A. Durivage —Going an Errand; or, Playing Deadhead, by George S. Raymond—Alice Tracey, by Emma T. Wilson—Mistaken Economy, by Sylvanus Cobb.

CHEEVER, HENRY THEODORE, *ed. See* Cheever, George Barrell. A Reel in a Bottle (1852), No. 494.

496 CHELLIS, MARY DWINELL. At Lion's Mouth . . . New York: National Temperance Society, 1872. 412 p., illus.   LC

497 ———— Aunt Dinah's Pledge . . . New York: National Temperance Society, 1869. 318 p., front. LC

498 ———— Bill Drock's Investment . . . Boston: Henry A. Young & Co., No. 24 Cornhill [cop. 1869]. 337 p., illus. BP, BU, LC
At head of title: "The Standard Series of Temperance Tales."

499 ———— Deacon Sims' Prayers . . . Boston: Henry A. Young & Co., No. 24 Cornhill [cop. 1868]. 393 p., front. UC

500 ———— Father Merrill . . . Boston: I. P. Warren [cop. 1872]. 410 p., illus. LC

501 ———— The Hermit of Holcombe . . . Boston: Henry A. Young & Co. [cop. 1871]. 336 p., illus. AAS, BP, BU, LC, NYP

502 ———— Mark Dunning's Enemy . . . Boston: Henry A. Young & Co. [cop. 1870]. 363 p., illus. BP, LC, NYP
At head of title: "The Standard Series of Temperance Tales."

503 ———— Molly's Bible . . . Boston: H. A. Young & Co. [cop. 1869]. 404 p., illus. LC

504 ———— The Old Doctor's Son . . . Boston: Henry A. Young & Co. [cop. 1870]. 354 p., illus. AAS, BU, HEH, LC
At head of title: "The Standard Series of Temperance Tales."

505 ———— Old Times . . . New York: National Temperance Society, 1873. 351 p., front. LC

506 ———— Out of the Fire . . . New York: National Temperance Society, 1869. 420 p., illus. LC

507 ———— The Temperance Doctor . . . New York: National Temperance Society, 1868. 370 p., front. AAS, LC

508 ———— Wealth and Wine . . . New York: National Temperance Society, 1874. 337 p., front. CU, LC

509 CHER, HENRY W. B., *pseud.* Gnaw-Wood; or, New England Life in a Village . . . Boston: A. K. Loring, 1868. Cover title, 22 p.
A parody on Beecher's *Norwood.* BA, CU, HEH, LC, LCP, NYH, UC, Y

510 CHESEBRO, CAROLINE. The Children of Light: A Theme for the Time . . . New York: Redfield, 1853. 374 p.
AAS, BP, CU, H, LC

511 ———— Dream-Land by Daylight: A Panorama of Romance . . . New York: Redfield, 1851. 428 p., front.
AAS, BP, CU, NYH, UC, UP, Y

512 ———— The Foe in the Household . . . Boston: James R. Osgood and Company, 1871. 114 p. Printed in double cols.
A study of a religious sect. AAS, H, HEH, LC, LCP, NYP

513 [————] Getting Along: A Book of Illustrations . . . New York: James C. Derby. Boston: Phillips, Sampson & Co. Cincinnati: H. W. Derby, 1855. 2 vols. (307, 325 p.) BP, LC
Also published as: *Susan, the Fisherman's Daughter; or, Getting Along.* New York: J. C. Derby [etc., etc.], 1855. AAS, HEH

514 ———— Isa: A Pilgrimage . . . New York: Redfield, 1852. 320 p.
AAS, BP, CU, H, LC, NYP

515 ———— Peter Carradine; or, The Martindale Pastoral . . . New York: Sheldon & Company. Boston: Gould & Lincoln, 1863. 399 p.
AAS, AP, BA, BP, CU, H, HEH, LC, LCP, N, NYP, UC, UP, Y
Of religious interest; Advent movement and Millerites.

516 ———— Philly and Kit; or, Life and Raiment . . . New York: Redfield, 1856. 342 p. AAS, BP, H, HEH, LC, NYP, UP, Y

———— The Prince at Land's End. *In* Gifts of Genius [cop. 1859], No. 1000.

———— The Record of Dorcas Bently. *In* Short Stories, 2d ser. (1869), No. 2211.

———— Victor and Jacqueline. *In* Atlantic Tales (1866), No. 155.

517 ———— Victoria; or, The World Overcome . . . New York: Derby and Jackson. Cincinnati: H. W. Derby & Co., 1856. 465 p. AAS, BP, CU, H, HEH, LC, NYH, NYP, UP
A tale of 1650; witchcraft.

518 CHILD, MRS. LYDIA MARIA (FRANCIS). Autumnal Leaves: Tales and Sketches in Prose and Rhyme . . . New York: C. S. Francis & Co. Boston, 1857. 365 p.

> AAS, BA, BP, BU, CU, H, HEH, LC, N, NYP, UC, UM, UP, Y
>
> *Contains:* The Eglantine, a Simple Love Story—The Juryman—The Emigrant Boy—Home and Politics. Founded on an Incident That Occurred in New York, during the Excitement Attending the Election of President Polk—The Catholic and the Quaker—The Rival Mechanicians—Utouch and Touchu—The Brother and Sister—The Man That Killed His Neighbours—Jan and Zaida. Founded on Circumstances Which Actually Occurred at Grésik, Island of Java, in 1854—The Ancient Clairvoyant—The Kansas Emigrants.

519 ———— A Romance of the Republic . . . Boston: Ticknor and Fields, 1867. 442 p.

> AAS, BA, BP, BU, CU, H, HEH, LC, LCP, N, NYP, UM, UP, Y
>
> A belated abolitionist novel.

———— *ed.* See Jacobs, Mrs. Harriet (Brent). Incidents in the Life of a Slave Girl (1861), No. 1333.

520 CHINQUOPIN, *pseud.* George Denny; or, Sketches of Life in the Far West. By "Chinquopin" [pseud.]. San Francisco: P. P. Hull & Co., 1856. 80 p., illus. Printed in double cols. HEH

> Gambling in St. Louis, and mining in California.

521 CHOAT, J. F. George Welding; or, Crime and Its Consequences . . . Cincinnati: H. M. Rulison, Queen City Publishing House, 141 Main Street [1859]. Cover title, 32 p., illus. HEH, LC

> LC copy deposited for copyright June 13, 1859.
> Laid in New York City.

522 CHOLULA; or, The Young Mexican. Philadelphia: J. P. Skelly & Co., 1869. 233 p., illus.

> Information from LC card for copy withdrawn from circulation.

523 DELETE

524 [CHURCH, MRS. ELLA RODMAN (MACILVAINE).] The Catanese; or, The Real and the Ideal. By Ella Rodman [pseud.] . . . New York: Bunnell & Price, 1853. 172 p. NYP, UP

525 [————] Flights of Fancy. By Ella Rodman [pseud.]. New York: John S. Taylor, 1853. 325 p. NYP

> *Contents:* First Impressions—Mr. Elmly's Pearl—The Widower; or, Leaves from an Old Maid's Journal—Amiability, with Variations—Taking Tea

Sociably—How to Get Rid of an Unwelcome Visitor—An Author's Vicissitudes—One of My Disappointments—The Higginbothams—The Wife's Revenge—Minna Clavers: A Sequel to "The Wife's Revenge"—The Wigwam in the Forest—A Leaf from the Portfolio of a Match-Maker.

526 [CHURCH, PHARCELLUS.] Mapleton; or, More Work for the Maine Law . . . Boston: Jenks, Hickling and Swan, 1853. 432 p.   AAS, BP, CU, H, HEH, LC, N, UM
A temperance novel.

CHURTON, HENRY, *pseud.* *See* Tourgée, Albion Winegar

CICELY, *Cousin, pseud. See* Bradford, Mrs. Sarah Elizabeth (Hopkins)

527 CLACK, MRS. LOUISE. Our Refugee Household . . . New York: Blelock & Co., 1866. 226 p.
                    AAS, BP, CU, H, HEH, LC, LCP, NYP, UV, Y
Louisiana during the Civil War.

528 CLARE, MRS. A. A Night at Isley's Grange: An Interesting Novelette . . . Cincinnati: the author; G. B. Bentley & Co., printers, 1859. 24 p.
Information from LC card for copy withdrawn from circulation.

CLARE, ADA, *pseud. See* McElhinney, Mrs. Jane

529 CLARE, MARIE J. The Trial . . . Albany: E. H. Pease & Co.; P. L. Gilbert, 1851. 70 p.   BP, NYP, Y
The trial of life.

530 CLAREMONT; or, The Undivided Household. Philadelphia: Parry and McMillan, 1857. 206 p.   LC

531 CLARK, ALEXANDER. The Old Log School House: Furnitured with Incidents of School Life, Notes of Travel . . . and Miscellaneous Sketches . . . Philadelphia: Leary, Getz & Co., 1861. 288 p., illus.   AAS, BP, BU, LC, NYH, NYP

532 [CLARK, CHARLES HEBER.] Out of the Hurly-Burly; or, Life in an Odd Corner. By Max Adeler [pseud.] . . . Philadelphia: "To-Day" Publishing Co., 1874. 398 p., illus.   H
Also issued with imprints: Philadelphia: "To-Day" Publishing Company, New York, Boston, and Chicago, 1874.   AAS, LC, UP
And, Philadelphia: "To-Day" Publishing Company, New York, Boston, and Chicago. San Francisco: F. Dewing & Co., 1874.   N, UVB
And, Philadelphia: George Maclean & Co. New York, Boston, Cincinnati, and Chicago. N. D. Thompson & Co., St. Louis, Mo., 1874.   AAS, CU, H, HEH, LCP, NYP, UC, UM, Y

73

533 CLARK, GEORGE EDWARD. Seven Years of a Sailor's Life . . .
Boston: Adams & Company, 25 Bromfield Street [cop. 1867].
358 p., illus.   AAS, BP, CU, LC, NYH, NYP
Includes Civil War period.

534 CLARK, S. W. From the Sublime to the Ridiculous . . . Chicago,
Ill., 1875. 101 p.   LC
Humor.

535 ———— Happy Home, Woman's Rights, and Divorce. By
S. W. Clark, Minneapolis, Minn. . . . Chicago, Ill., 1875. 45 p.,
illus.   LC
Laid in Wyoming territory.

536 [CLARK, THOMAS MARCH.] John Whopper the Newsboy . . .
Boston: Roberts Brothers, 1871. 128 p., illus.
A fantasy.   AAS, BA, BP, BU, CU, HEH, LCP, NYH, NYP, Y

537 [CLARK, WILLIAM ADOLPHUS.] Agnes Farriday; or, The Harlot's
Friend . . . New York: Frederic A. Brady [cop. 1869]. 301
p., front.   AAS, BP, LC
Laid in Boston.

538 CLARKE, MRS. DEWITT. Lizzie Maitland. Edited by O. A.
Brownson. New York: E. Dunigan & Brother, 1857. 340 p.
Information from LC card for copy withdrawn from circulation.

539 [CLARKE, E. G. H.] Lovers and Thinkers: A Novel. By Hewes
Gordon [pseud.] . . . New York: Carleton, 1865. 287 p.
Laid in New York City and Boston.   AAS, LC, LCP, NYP

540 CLARKE, MRS. HENRY STEELE. "Their Children" . . . Boston:
D. Lothrop & Co. Dover, N. H.: G. T. Day & Co. [cop. 1875].
414 p., illus.   LC

541 CLARKE, MRS. MARY G., comp. Sunshine and Shadows along the
Pathway of Life . . . Chicago: Clarke & Co., 1865. 400 p.,
illus.   HEH, UC
Contains: Frank Maynard; or, Aunt Mary's Way of Treating Passionate
Boys—Fashion, by Mrs. Thomas P. Smith—Love's Yearning, by Mrs. M. A.
Denison—A Day without Prayer, by L. B. M.—Emma Moore, by "Axie
Allen"—Daily Duties; or, Work for the Willing—The Stepmother; or,
How Mrs. Leighton "Did Manage Those Two Unruly Boys."

542 [CLAY, MRS. JOSEPHINE RUSSELL.] What Will the World Say?
A Novel of Every-Day Life. And Only a Woman. By Ojos
Morenos [pseud.]. Philadelphia: J. B. Lippincott & Co., 1873.
232 p.   CU
"Only a Woman," pp. 179-232.

CLEIGHMORE, *Capt., pseud. See* Judson, Edward Zane Carroll,
No. 1439.

543 [CLEMENS, JEREMIAH.] Bernard Lile: An Historical Romance,
Embracing the Periods of the Texas Revolution and the Mex-
ican War. Philadelphia: J. B. Lippincott & Co., 1856. 287 p.
AAS, CU, H, HEH, LC, UC, UM, UV
Another issue gives the author's name on title page. AAS, HEH, LC, N,
NYP, Y

544 ———— Mustang Gray: A Romance . . . Philadelphia: J. B.
Lippincott & Co., 1858. 296 p.   LC, LCP, NYP, UC, UM, Y
Exploits of Mabry Gray during the Texas revolution.

545 ———— The Rivals: A Tale of the Times of Aaron Burr and
Alexander Hamilton . . . Philadelphia: J. B. Lippincott & Co.,
1860. 286 p.
AAS, BP, BU, CU, H, HEH, LC, LCP, N, NYH, NYP, UC, UM, UP, UV, Y

546 ———— Tobias Wilson: A Tale of the Great Rebellion . . .
Philadelphia: J. B. Lippincott & Co., 1865. 328 p.
AAS, BA, CU, HEH, LC, LCP, NYH, NYP, UC, Y
Laid in northern Alabama.

547 [CLEMENS, SAMUEL LANGHORNE.] A Book for an Hour, Con-
taining Choice Reading and Character Sketches. A Curious
Dream, and Other Sketches. Revised and Selected for This
Work by the Author Mark Twain [pseud.] . . . New York:
published at 65 Liberty Street, 1873. 63, [1] p., illus.
H, HEH, LC, UVB, Y
For Clemens' contributions to this, and for contents of following work,
see Merle Johnson, *A Bibliography of the Work of Mark Twain* (New
York, 1910).

548 [————] The Celebrated Jumping Frog of Calaveras County,
and Other Sketches. By Mark Twain. Edited by John Paul
[pseud.]. New York: C. H. Webb, 1867. 198 p.
AAS, BP, CU, HEH, LC, N, NYP, UVB, Y
The title story—a condensed version—made its first appearance in book
form in *Beadle's Dime Book of Fun*, No. 3, April 21, 1866.

549 ——— The Gilded Age: A Tale of To-Day. By Mark Twain
... and Charles Dudley Warner ... Hartford: American Publishing Company, 1873. 574, [2] p., illus.

AAS, BP, CU, H, HEH, LC, LCP, N, NYP, UC, UM, UP, UVB, Y

The libraries credited with this title may not have the copy listed herein;
but, instead, one or more of the variant imprints dated either 1873 or 1874.
For discussion of variants see Frank C. Willson, "The Gilded Age," BSA,
Papers, XXXVII (1943), 141-156; and Denis Woodfield, "The 'Fake' Title-
Page of 'The Gilded Age:' A Solution," BSA, *Papers*, L (1956), 292-296.

550 ——— The Innocents Abroad; or, The New Pilgrim's
Progress. Being Some Account of the Steamship Quaker City's
Pleasure Excursion to Europe and the Holy Land ... Hartford, Conn.: American Publishing Company, 1869. 651 p.,
illus.

AAS, AP, BP, BU, CU, H, HEH, LC, LCP, N, NYP, UC, UM, UVB, Y

The libraries credited with this title may have one or more of the various
issues of the first edition. The first issue is identified by the lack of page
numbers in the table of "Contents" and the omission of "Conclusion" in
the last line of p. xviii; no illus. on p. 129, and chapter number "LXI"
printed "XLI."

551 [———] Mark Twain's (Burlesque) Autobiography and First
Romance. New York: Sheldon & Company, 677 Broadway
[cop. 1871]. 47 p., illus.

AAS, BA, BU, CU, H, HEH, LCP, N, NYH, NYP, UC, UM, UP, UVB, Y

The libraries credited with this title may have one or both issues of the first
edition. The first issue is identified by the centered copyright notice on
verso of title page and "Electrotyped by Smith & McDougal" at the
bottom of the page.

552 [———] Mark Twain's Sketches. Authorised Edition ...
New York: American News Company [1874]. 32 p.

AAS, BP, CU, H, HEH, N, NYH, NYP, UP, UVB, Y

At head of title: "Number One."
Blank back cover indicates the earliest state.

553 [———] Mark Twain's Sketches, New and Old. Now First
Published in Complete Form ... Hartford, Conn., and Chicago, Ill.: American Publishing Company, 1875. 320 p., illus.

AAS, BA, BP, BU, CU, H, HEH, LC, N, NYP, UC, UP, UVB, Y

The libraries credited with this title may have one or both issues of the
first edition. The first issue is identified by the duplication of the footnote
of p. 119 on p. 120; and "From Hospital Days" on p. 299, which is omitted
in the second issue.

554 ———— Roughing It . . . Hartford, Conn.: American Publishing Company; F. G. Gilman & Co., Chicago, Ill.; W. E. Bliss, Toledo, Ohio; Nettleton & Co., Cincinnati, Ohio; D. Ashmead, Philadelphia, Penn.; George M. Smith & Co., Boston, Mass.; A. Roman & Company, San Francisco, Cal., 1872. 591 p., illus.

AAS, BA, BP, BU, CU, H, HEH, LC, N, NYP, UC, UM, UP, UVB, Y

HEH has a canvasser's copy dated 1871, which contains plates and sample pages from various chapters.

555 CLEVELAND, CECILIA PAULINE. The Story of a Summer; or, Journal Leaves from Chappaqua . . . New York: G. W. Carleton & Co. London: S. Low, Son & Co., 1874. 274 p., illus.

AAS, BP, H, HEH, LC, LCP, NYH, NYP

CLEWLINE, CHARLEY, *pseud. See* Raymond, George S.

556 CLIFFORD, FRANK S. A Romance of Perfume Lands; or, The Search for Capt. Jacob Cole. With Interesting Facts about Perfumes and Articles Used in the Toilet . . . Boston: published by Clifford, perfumer, 1875. 295 p., illus.

AAS, BU, CU, H, HEH, LC, NYP, UM, Y

557 [CLIFT, WILLIAM.] The Tim Bunker Papers; or, Yankee Farming. By Timothy Bunker [pseud.] . . . New York: Orange Judd and Company, 245 Broadway [cop. 1868]. 314 p., illus.

AAS, BP, BU, CU, H, HEH, LC, LCP, NYP, UC, UP

558 CLINE, A. J. Henry Courtland; or, What a Farmer Can Do . . . Philadelphia: J. B. Lippincott & Co., 1870. 398 p. AAS, LC, LCP
Laid in New York.

CLINKER, GEOFFREY, *Esq., pseud. See* Sands, Alexander Hamilton

559 CLINTON, PARK. Glanmore: A Romance of the Revolution . . . New York: Stearns and Company, 25 Ann Street [cop. 1853]. 102 p. LC, UP, Y
Cover title reads: "Glanmore, the Bandit of Saratoga Lake."

560 COBB, CYRUS. The Veteran of the Grand Army: A Novel. By the Brothers Cobb. In Eight Parts. Boston: Cyrus and Darius Cobb, 1870. 384 p., front. AAS, BP, H, HEH, LC, NYH, NYP, UC
The parts originally issued in paper covers.
Darius Cobb, jt. au.

COBB, DARIUS, *jt. au. See* Cobb, Cyrus. The Veteran of the Grand Army (1870), No. 560.

561 COBB, JOSEPH BECKHAM. Mississippi Scenes; or, Sketches of Southern and Western Life and Adventure, Humorous, Satirical, and Descriptive, Including The Legend of Black Creek . . . Philadelphia: A. Hart, 1851. 250 p.

BA, BP, H, LC, LCP, N, NYH, NYP, UC, UM, UP, Y

"The Innkeeper's Wife: A Story of the Revolution," pp. 232-250.

562 COBB, SOPHIA DICKINSON. Hillsboro' Farms . . . Boston: Lee and Shepard, 1869. 423 p. AAS, BU, H, HEH, NYP

Laid in New England.

563 [COBB, SYLVANUS.] Alice the Fisher Girl; or, The Old Man of the Wreck. A Story of Old England. By Austin C. Burdick [pseud.]. New York: Samuel French, 121 Nassau Street [185-?]. 100 p. Printed in double cols. NYP

Contains: The Love and the Money Match, by Mrs. E. Wellmont.

564 —————— The Bravo's Secret; or, The Spy of the "Ten." A Venetian Tale. Founded on Incidents Which Occurred during the Latter Part of the Reign of Francesco Dandolo, Doge of Venice . . . Boston: F. Gleason, 1851. 99, [1]p., illus. Printed in double cols. LC, Y

Also contains: The Washerwoman's Windfall, by Falconbridge.

[——————] The Captain's Passage, by Austin C. Burdick [pseud.]. *In* C. G. Rosenberg, The Roman Soprano [185-?], No. 2128.

565 —————— The Child of the Bay; or, The Old Sailor's Protégé. A Tale of England, India, and the Ocean . . . Boston: F. Gleason, 1852. 100 p. Printed in double cols. CU, LC

—————— The Crossed Dollar. *In* B. P. Poore, The Mameluke (1852), No. 1928.

566 —————— The Earl's Ward; or, The Old Chapel and Its Mysteries. A Romance of the Land and Ocean . . . Boston: F. Gleason's Publishing Hall, 1852. 100 p., illus. Printed in double cols. AAS, NYP

567 —————— Fernando; or, The Moor of Castile. A Romance of Old Spain . . . Boston: F. Gleason's Publishing Hall, 1853. 100 p., illus. Printed in double cols. H, LC, UC, UM, Y

568 ——— The Iron Cross; or, The Countess of Errol. A Tale of High and Low Life. New York: Samuel French, 121 Nassau Street [185-?]. 84 p.

Also contains: Convent Bride, by E. Almy—A Winter in the Sierra Nevadas, by Frederick Stanhope.

No copy found; the T. B. Peterson & Brothers' reprint listed in the Amer. Cat. 1876.

569 ——— Isidore de Montigny; or, The Smuggler of St. Malo. A Story of Sea and Shore . . . New York: Samuel French, 121 Nassau Street [185-?]. 100 p. Printed in double cols.

HEH, UC

Also contains: The Lady Edith, by Francis P. Pepperell—Louise and Bertrand, by Mrs. Caroline A. Soule.

570 [———] Ivan the Serf; or, The Russian and Circassian. A Tale of Russia, Turkey, and Circassia. By Austin C. Burdick [pseud.]. New York: Samuel French, 121 Nassau Street [185-?]. 100 p. Printed in double cols. AAS, HEH

Also contains: Bianca; or, The Monk's Plot, by Dr. J. H. Robinson.

571 ——— The Juggler of Nankin; or, The Grandee's Plot. A Story of the Celestial Empire . . . New York: Samuel French, 121 Nassau Street [185-?]. 100 p. Printed in double cols.

Also contains: The Gipsy's Prediction, by M. V. St. Leon. H, UM, Y

572 [———] The King and Cobbler: A Romance of Ancient Persia. By Austin C. Burdick [pseud.]. New York: Samuel French, 121 Nassau Street [185-?]. 100 p. Printed in double cols. AAS

Also contains: The Governess, by T. A. Kimball—Reminiscences of California, by Frederick Stanhope—Broken Ear-Ring, by Mrs. Caroline Orne.

573 ——— The King's Talisman; or, The Young Lion of Mount Hor. An Eastern Romance . . . Boston: Frederick Gleason, 1851. 100 p. Printed in double cols. UM

574 ——— The Knight of Leon; or, The Monarch's Last Bride. A Tale of Moorish Granada . . . Boston: F. Gleason's Publishing Hall, 1853. 100 p. Printed in double cols. AAS

Also contains: The Orphan Boy's Prayer; or, The Perjured Witnesses, by S. Cobb.

575 ———— The Lost Heir; or, The Duke and the Lazzarone. A Tale of Naples and Its Environs . . . Boston: F. Gleason's Publishing Hall, 1853. 100 p. Printed in double cols. AAS, Y

576 ———— The Maniac's Secret; or, The Privateer of Massachusetts Bay. A Story of the Revolution . . . New York: Samuel French, 121 Nassau Street [185-?]. 84 p. Printed in double cols. AAS, CU

Also contains: The Two Acre Lot, by Horatio Alger, Jr.–The Unconquerable Conquered, by Maria M. Moore.

577 ———— Marco; or, The Female Smuggler. A Tale of Strange Incidents Afloat and Ashore . . . Boston, 1857. 100 p., illus. BU

———— Mistaken Economy. *In* H. P. Cheever, The Rival Brothers [*ca.* 1852], No. 495.

[————] The Mother's Lesson, by Austin C. Burdick [pseud.]. *In* H. P. Cheever, The Rival Brothers [ca. 1852], No. 495.

[————] The Mutineers. From the Papers of a London Detective Police Officer. By Austin C. Burdick [pseud.]. *In* S. Cobb, The Royal Yacht [185-?], No. 583.

578 [————] The Ocean Martyr; or, The Hunter Spy of Virginia. By Austin C. Burdick [pseud.]. New York: Samuel French, corner Spruce & Nassau . . . C. P. Kimball, Long Wharf, San Francisco [n. d.]. Cover title, 100 p. Printed in double cols. H

Also contains: A Country Residence, by Mrs. M. E. Robinson.

579 ———— Olivia Trevett; or, The Patriot Cruiser. A Story of the American Revolution . . . New York: Samuel French, 151 Nassau Street [185-?]. 100 p. Printed in double cols. AAS, NYP

580 ———— Orlando Chester; or, The Adventures of a Young Hunter. A Story of Old Virginia's Early Days . . . Boston: F. Gleason's Publishing Hall, 1852. 100 p., illus. Printed in double cols. UV

Also contains: The Farmer's Daughters; or, Moving into Town, by Miss R. H. Ackerman.

———— The Orphan Boy's Prayer; or, The Perjured Witnesses. *In* S. Cobb, The Knight of Leon (1853), No. 574.

581 ———— Paul Laroon; or, The Scourge of the Antiles. A Story of Ship and Shore ... New York: Samuel French, 121 Nassau Street [185-?]. 100 p. Printed in double cols.   H, UC, Y
Also contains: The Twin Daguerreotypes, by Edwin G. Mervin.

582 ———— The Phantom; or, The Wrecking Smuggler of the Ken ... Boston: National Publishing Company, 1851. 92 p. Printed in double cols.   UC

583 ———— The Royal Yacht; or, Logan the Warlock. A Story of the Revolution ... New York: Samuel French, 151 Nassau [185-?]. 100 p. Printed in double cols.   BP, NYP, Y
Also contains: The Tyrolese Lovers, by H. H. Heath—The Mutineers. From the Papers of a London Detective Police Officer, by Austin C. Burdick.

584 [————] The Sea Lion; or, The Privateer of the Penobscot. A Story of Ocean Life and the Heart's Love. By Austin C. Burdick [pseud.]. New York: Samuel French, 151 Nassau Street, 1853. 100 p., illus. Printed in double cols.   BP, LC, NYP

585 [————] The Storm Children; or, The Light-Keeper of the Channel. A Story of Adventure upon the Sea and the Shore. By Austin C. Burdick [pseud.]. Boston: F. Gleason's Publishing Hall, 1853. 100 p., illus. Printed in double cols.
Princeton University Library copy.

———— The Unfinished Will. *In* J. H. Robinson, The White Rover (1852), No. 2087.

———— The Unmeant Rebuke. *In* J. V. Watson, Tales and Takings (1857), No. 2663.

586 ———— The Wandering Guerrilla; or, The Infant Bride of Truxillo. A Story of the Troublous Times of Mexico ... New York: Samuel French, 121 Nassau Street [185-?]. 100 p. Printed in double cols.   NYP
Also contains: The Prima Donna; or, The Pearl Necklace, by Mrs. M. E. Robinson.

587 COCHRAN, WESLEY. The Emigrants, an Allegory; or, Christians vs. the World . . . Auburn, N. Y.: William J. Moses, 1854. 191 p.   UC
Copyrighted by publisher in 1854.
Also issued with imprint: New York: printed for the author, 200 Mulberry Street [cop. by author, 1854].   NYP

588 COFFIN, CHARLES CARLETON. Caleb Krinkle: A Story of American Life . . . Boston: Lee and Shepard. New York: Lee, Shepard, and Dillingham, 1875. 500 p.
Laid in "Millbrook," New England.   AAS, BA, CU, H, HEH, LC, UP, UV, Y

589 [COFFIN, ROBERT BARRY.] Cakes and Ale at Woodbine; from Twelfth Night to New Year's Day. By Barry Gray [pseud.] . . . New York: Hurd and Houghton, 1868. 229 p.
AAS, BP, BU, H, HEH, LC, LCP, NYP, UM, Y

590 [————] Castles in the Air, and Other Phantasies. By Barry Gray [pseud.] . . . New York: Hurd and Houghton, 1871. 352 p.   AAS, BU, CU, H, LC, LCP, NYH, UP, Y
Also contains: Broken Sheaves and Bitter Almonds—Wild Oats and Apple-Blossoms—Around the Mahogany—Musidora and My Southern Maid—Model Young Ladies.

591 [————] Matrimonial Infelicities, with an Occasional Felicity, by Way of Contrast. By an Irritable Man. To Which Are Added, as Being Pertinent to the Subject, My Neighbors, and Down in the Valley. By Barry Gray [pseud.]. New York: Hurd and Houghton. Boston: E. P. Dutton and Company, 1865. 269 p.   AAS, BP, H, HEH, LC, LCP, N, NYP, UM, UP, Y

592 [————] My Married Life at Hillside. By Barry Gray [pseud.]. New York: Hurd and Houghton. Boston: E. P. Dutton and Company, 1865. 290 p., illus.
AAS, BA, BP, BU, H, HEH, LC, LCP, NYP, UC, Y

593 [————] Out of Town: A Rural Episode. By Barry Gray [pseud.] . . . New York: Hurd and Houghton, 1866. 311 p., illus.   AAS, BU, H, LC, LCP, N, NYP, UM, Y

594 COGGESHALL, WILLIAM TURNER. Easy Warren and His Contemporaries: Sketched for Home Circles . . . New York: Redfield, 1854. 332 p.   AAS, BP, CU, LC, LCP, NYP
A collection of short stories.

595 ———— Frontier Life and Character in the South and West
. . . Columbus: Follett, Foster and Company, 1860. 313 p.
UV

Contents: The Everglade Heroes—Fleet Foot—Hunter Girty; or, The
Half-Breed Colony of Illinois—Golden Bird of Menomonee—The
Counterfeiters of the Cuyahoga, a Buckeye Romance—The Bright Eye
of the Settlement.
Also published as: *Stories of Frontier Adventure in the South and West.*
Columbus: Follett, Foster and Company, 1861.   CU

———— Little Peleg, the Drunkard's Son. *In* A. Cary, The
Adopted Daughter (1859), No. 466.

596 ———— Oakshaw; or, The Victims of Avarice. A Tale of
Intrigue . . . Cincinnati: U. P. James, 1855.   126 p.
Laid in rural Ohio.   AAS, BU, LC, NYP, UM, UVB

597 COLEMAN, WILLIAM MACON. The Wandering Jew in America:
A Novel . . . Washington, D. C.: J. G. Hester [cop. 1875].
57 p.   BP, LC, NYH

COLESWORTHY, C. D. The Two Clerks. *In* A. Cary, The
Adopted Daughter (1859), No. 466.

598 COLESWORTHY, DANIEL CLEMENT. The Old Bureau, and Other
Tales . . . Boston: Antique Book Store, 1861.   408 p.
AAS, CU, H, HEH, LC, N, NYP, UP, UVB, Y

599 COLLEY, JAMES, *ed.* The Thrilling Adventures of Alice Dunbar,
the Celebrated Horse Thief and Female Jack Sheppard . . .
Edited by James Colley, Detective. Philadelphia: Barclay &
Co. [cop. 1869].   62 p., illus.
A copy is in the possession of Roger Butterfield, New York.

600 COLLINS, MRS. ANGELINA MARIA (LORRAINE). Mrs. Ben Darby;
or, The Weal and Woe of Social Life . . . Cincinnati: Moore,
Anderson, Wilstach & Keys, 1853.   367 p.   AAS, BP, HEH
A temperance novel.

601 [COLLINS, J. L.] Queen Krinaleen's Plagues; or, How a Simple
People Were Destroyed. A Discourse in the Twenty-Second
Century, by "Jonquil" [pseud.] . . . New York: American
News Company, 1874.   151 p.   LC, NYH, NYP
A satire on American women.

602 [————] Was She Engaged? By "Jonquil" [pseud.]. Philadelphia: J. B. Lippincott & Co., 1871. 339 p.   BP, CU, LC, LCP

603 COLLIS, LAURISTON. The Mystery of Holly Tavern: A Story of Nine Travellers . . . Philadelphia: J. B. Lippincott & Co., 1873. 183 p.   UM
Laid in Virginia in the 1840's.

604 COLUMBIA, THE BEAUTIFUL BLONDE; or, Life in the Fifth Avenue, New York. Philadelphia: T. B. Peterson [185-?].
Title listed in Roorbach 1855-1858.

605 [COMINS, ELIZABETH BARKER.] The Hartwell Farm. By Laura Caxton [pseud.] . . . Boston: Loring, corner of Bromfield and Washington Sts. [cop. 1871]. 200 p., illus.
AAS, CU, H, LC, NYP, UC, Y

606 [COMSTOCK, WILLIAM.] Betsey Jane Ward <Better-Half to Artemus>. Hur Book of Goaks with a Full Akkownt of the Coartship and Maridge to A4said Artemus, and Mister Ward's Cutting-Up with the Mormon Fare Secks . . . New York: James O'Kane, No. 126 Nassau St. [cop. 1866]. 312 p., illus.
AAS, BP, CU, H, HEH, LC, LCP, N, NYP, UC, UP, UVB

———— The Village Slander. In J. V. Watson, Tales and Takings (1857), No. 2663.

CONINGSBY, CHRISTOPHER, pseud. See Harris, Samuel Smith

607 CONNELLY, EMMA MARY. Under the Surface . . . Philadelphia: J. B. Lippincott & Co., 1873. 332 p.   BP, LC, UC

608 THE CONSPIRACY OF COL. AARON BURR: A Historical Romance. Complete in One Volume. New York: G. W. Simmons, 1854. 311 p.   H, NYP

609 [COOK, MRS. MARY LOUISE (REDD).] Ante Bellum: Southern Life as It Was. By Mary Lennox [pseud.]. Philadelphia: J. B. Lippincott & Co., 1868. 322 p.
AAS, CU, H, HEH, LC, LCP, N, NYP, UM, UP, UVB, Y

610 COOK, Capt. WILLIAM, pseud. A History of the Great Narraticon Exploring Expedition of 1866. By Capt. Cook [pseud.] . . . Swedesboro, N. J.: published by the expedition, 1867. 18 p., illus.   LC, LCP

611 COOKE, JOHN ESTEN. Doctor Vandyke: A Novel . . . New York: D. Appleton and Company, 1872. 142 p., illus. Printed in double cols. AAS, BP, CU, H, LC, LCP, NYP, UC, UP, UVB, Y
Laid in Williamsburg, Va., about 1772.

612 ———— Ellie; or, The Human Comedy . . . Richmond: A. Morris, 1855. 576 p., illus.
Laid in Richmond. AAS, BP, CU, H, HEH, LC, N, UC, UM, UP, UVB, Y

613 ———— Fairfax; or, The Master of Greenway Court. A Chronicle of the Valley of the Shenandoah . . . New York: G. W. Carleton & Co. London: S. Low, Son & Co., 1868. 405 p.
  AAS, BP, BU, H, LC, LCP, N, NYP, UM, UP, UVB, Y
Laid in Virginia, 1748-1751.

614 ———— Hammer and Rapier . . . New York: Carleton. London: S. Low, Son & Co., 1870. 307 p.
  AAS, BP, BU, CU, H, HEH, LC, N, NYH, NYP, UM, UP, UVB, Y
Virginia in the Civil War.

615 ———— The Heir of Gaymount: A Novel . . . New York: Van Evrie, Horton & Co., No. 162 Nassau Street [cop. 1870]. 91 p. Printed in double cols. LC, NYP, UVB
At head of cover title: "Old Guard Library, No. 1."
Postwar Virginia.

616 ———— Henry St. John, Gentleman, of "Flower of Hundreds," in the County of Prince George, Virginia. A Tale of 1774-'75 . . . New York: Harper & Brothers, 1859. 503 p.
  AAS, AP, BP, BU, CU, H, HEH, LC, LCP, NYP, UC, UM, UP, UVB, Y
Sequel to *The Virginia Comedians*.

617 ———— Her Majesty, the Queen: A Novel . . . Philadelphia: J. B. Lippincott & Co., 1873. 330 p.
  AAS, BU, LC, LCP, UC, UM, UP, UVB, Y
France during the reign of Charles I.

618 ———— Hilt to Hilt; or, Days and Nights on the Banks of the Shenandoah in the Autumn of 1864. From the Mss. of Colonel Surry of Eagle's Nest . . . New York: G. W. Carleton. London: S. Low, Son & Co., 1869. 270 p.
  AAS, BP, HEH, LCP, N, NYH, NYP, UC, UM, UVB, Y

619 ———— Justin Harley: A Romance of Old Virginia . . . Philadelphia, New York, Boston, and Chicago: To-Day Printing and Publishing Company, 1874. 301 p., illus. UM, UVB

620 ———— The Last of the Foresters; or, Humors on the Border. A Story of the Old Virginia Frontier ... New York: Derby & Jackson. Cincinnati: H. W. Derby & Co., 1856. 419 p.

AAS, BP, BU, H, HEH, LC, N, NYH, NYP, UC, UM, UP, UVB, Y

621 [————] Leather Stocking and Silk; or, Hunter John Myers and His Times. A Story of the Valley of Virginia. New York: Harper & Brothers, 1854. 408 p.

AAS, BP, BU, CU, H, HEH, LC, LCP, N, NYH, NYP, UC, UM, UP, UVB, Y

622 ———— Mohun; or, The Last Days of Lee and His Paladins. Final Memoirs of a Staff Officer Serving in Virginia. From the Mss. of Colonel Surry, of Eagle's Nest ... New York: F. J. Huntington and Co., 1869. 509 p., illus.

BP, CU, HEH, LCP, N, NYH, NYP, UC, UM, UP, UVB

Sequel to *Surry of Eagle's-Nest.*

———— Out at Elbows: The Story of St. George Cleave. *In* Gifts of Genius [cop. 1859], No. 1000.

623 ———— Out of the Foam: A Novel ... New York: Carleton. London: S. Low, Son & Co., 1871. 340 p.

AAS, H, HEH, LC, LCP, N, NYP, UC, UM, UP, UVB

Anglo-French war, late 18th century.

624 ———— Pretty Mrs. Gaston, and Other Stories . . . New York: Orange Judd Company, 245 Broadway [cop. 1874]. 288 p., illus.

AAS, BA, BU, CU, H, HEH, LC, LCP, N, NYH, NYP, UC, UM, UP, UVB, Y

Also contains: Annie at the Corner—The Wedding at Duluth.

625 ———— Surry of Eagle's-Nest; or, The Memoirs of a Staff-Officer Serving in Virginia. Edited from the Mss. of Colonel Surry ... New York: Bunce and Huntington, 1866. 484 p., illus. AAS, BA, BP, CU, H, LC, LCP, N, NYP, UC, UM, UP, UVB, Y

Sequel: *Mohun.*

626 [————] The Virginia Comedians; or, Old Days in the Old Dominion. Edited from the Mss. of C. Effingham, Esq. [pseud.] ... New York: D. Appleton and Company. London, 1854. 2 vols. (332, 282 p.)

AAS, BP, BU, CU, H, HEH, LC, N, NYH, NYP, UC, UM, UP, Y

Sequel: *Henry St. John.*

627 ———— Wearing of the Gray: Being Personal Portraits, Scenes and Adventures of the War ... New York: E. B. Treat & Co. Baltimore, Md.: J. S. Morrow. New Orleans, La.: J. H. Hummel ... San Francisco, Cal.: H. H. Bancroft & Co., 1867. 601 p., illus.

AAS, BA, BP, BU, CU, H, HEH, LC, LCP, N, NYH, NYP, UM, Y

A few of the sketches are embellished.

628 [————] The Youth of Jefferson; or, A Chronicle of College Scrapes at Williamsburg, in Virginia, A.D. 1764 ... New York: Redfield, 1854. 249 p.

AAS, BA, BP, BU, CU, H, HEH, LC, N, NYH, NYP, UC, UM, UP, Y

COOKE, MRS. ROSE (TERRY). Miss Lucinda, by Rose Terry. In Atlantic Tales (1866), No. 155.

———— The Mormon's Wife, by Rose Terry. In J. T. Fields, ed., Good Company (1866), No. 900.

629 [COOLIDGE, SARAH E.] Ambition [by] Kate Willis [pseud.] ... Boston: James French and Company, 1856. 318 p.

AAS, HEH, UC

Laid in Hamilton and Albany, N. Y.

COOPER, FRANK, pseud. See Simms, William Gilmore

630 COOPER, S. M. Life in the Forest; or, The Trials and Sufferings of a Pioneer ... Philadelphia: Perry and Erety, 1854. 155 p., front.

AAS, LC

Colonial times.

631 COPCUTT, FRANCIS. Leaves from a Bachelor's Book of Life ... New York: S. A. Rollo, 1860. 250 p. AAS, HEH, LC, N, NYP, Y

Contents: The Raven—Seeking Dinner under Difficulties—Charlotte May—The Admiralty Papers—A Day in the Dead-Letter Office—Fire! Fire!—Edith.

632 [COPPINGER, JOHN B.] The Renegade: A Tale of Real Life. New York: Sherman & Co., 1855. 235 p.

AAS, BU, H, HEH, LC, NYP, UC, UP, UVB, Y

The Canadian (Ontario) wilderness.

633 CORBIN, MRS. CAROLINE ELIZABETH (FAIRFIELD). His Marriage Vow ... Boston: Lee and Shepard. New York: Lee, Shepard and Dillingham, 1874. 328 p. AAS, CU, HEH, LC, LCP, NYP

On the relation of the sexes.

634 ———— Our Bible-Class, and the Good That Came of It . . . New York: Derby & Jackson, 1860. 352 p.   BP, LC

Also published as: *Uncle Timothy; or, Our Bible Class.* Chicago: Clarke and Company, 1868. BP

635 ———— A Woman's Secret . . . Chicago: Central Publishing House, 1867. 440 p.   AAS, H, LCP, N, NYP

Also published as: *Rebecca; or, A Woman's Secret . . . New and Revised Edition.* Chicago: Clarke and Company, 1867. AAS, HEH

636 CORNELIO; or, The False Vocation. New York: P. O'Shea, 1863. 39 p.   AAS

With this was issued: *Valentine.* New York: P. O'Shea, 1863. 23 p.

637 CORNELIUS, MRS. MARY ANN (MANN). Little Wolf: A Tale of the Western Frontier . . . Cincinnati: Journal and Messenger, No. 178 Elm Street [cop. 1872]. 458 p.   AAS, HEH

Laid in Minnesota.

638 CORNWALLIS, KINAHAN. Adrift with a Vengeance: A Tale of Love and Adventure . . . New York: Carleton. London: S. Low, Son & Co., 1870. 319 p.

   AAS, H, HEH, LC, NYH, NYP, UP, Y

639 ———— Pilgrims of Fashion: A Novel . . . New York: Harper & Brothers, 1862. 337 p.   AAS, BP, H, LC, LCP, NYP, Y

640 CORNYN, JOHN K. Dick Wilson, the Rumseller's Victim; or, Humanity Pleading for the "Maine Law." A Temperance Story —Founded on Fact . . . With an Introduction, by Thurlow W. Brown. Auburn: Derby & Miller. Buffalo: Derby, Orton & Mulligan, 1853. 384 p., front.   AAS, CU, HEH, N

COSMOPOLITAN, A., *pseud.* *See* Pullen, Charles Henry

641 COTTAGE PIETY EXEMPLIFIED. By the Author of "Union to Christ," "Love of God," etc. Philadelphia: J. B. Lippincott & Co., 1869. 316 p.   LC

642 [COULSON, GEORGE JAMES ATKINSON.] Harwood: A Novel . . . New York: E. J. Hale & Son, 1875. 206 p., illus.

   AAS, BA, BP, CU, H, LC, LCP, NYP, Y

A journal of the Harwood family in the 1830's.

643 [————] The Lacy Diamonds: A Novel . . . New York: E. J. Hale & Son, 1875. 284 p.   AAS, BA, H, LC, LCP, NYP, UV

644 [————] The Odd Trump: A Novel. New York: E. J.
Hale & Son, 1875. 326 p.   AAS, BA, H, LC, LCP, NYP, UV
Old cathedral town of Gloucester.

645 COURTNEY, MRS. E. L.   Twice Tried; or, The Three Influences
... Philadelphia: Claxton, Remsen & Haffelfinger, 1870.   148
p., illus.
Information from LC card for copy withdrawn from circulation.

COUSIN CICELY, pseud. See Bradford, Mrs. Sarah Elizabeth
(Hopkins)

646 COWDIN, MRS. V. G.   Ellen; or, The Fanatic's Daughter . . .
Mobile: S. H. Goetzel & Company, 1860.   202 p.
Laid in Louisiana.   HEH, LC, NYP

647 [COWING, FANNY.]   Harvestings: Sketches in Prose and Verse.
By Sybil Hastings [pseud.] ... Boston: W. P. Fetridge & Co.
New York: J. C. Derby, 1855.   329 p.
AAS, BP, BU, CU, H, HEH, LC, LCP, NYP, Y
Contains: The Outcast and the Heiress—Florence Vassal; or, Reminis-
cences of My Youth—The Prima Donna; or, Mists of the Spirit—Heath
Hall; or, A Package of Letters—The Signet-Ring; or, Francoise de Foix—
The Homestead—The Crayon—Annie Rutledge; or, Reminiscences of a
Piano—Threads Drawn from Life: An Autobiography.
Information about author supplied by BU.

648 Cox, M. H.   Emily Mayland; or, The Faithful Governess . . .
Philadelphia: printed by Jas. B. Rodgers, 1864.   288 p.   LC

COZZENS, FREDERICK SWARTWOUT. Captain Belgrave. In The
Knickerbocker Gallery (1855), No. 1492.

649 [————] Father Tom and the Pope; or, A Night in the Vatican
... New York: Moorhead, Simpson & Bond, 1868.   63, [3] p.
AAS

650 [————] Prismatics, by Richard Haywarde [pseud.] . . .
New York: D. Appleton & Company. London, 1853.   235 p.,
illus.   AAS, BP, BU, CU, H, HEH, LC, LCP, N, NYH, NYP, UC, UVB, Y

651 ———— The Sayings of Dr. Bushwhacker, and Other Learned
Men ... New York: A. Simpson & Co., 1867.   213 p.
AAS, BA, BP, BU, CU, H, HEH, LC, LCP, N, NYH, NYP, UC, UM,
UP, UVB, Y

652 ———— The Sparrowgrass Papers; or, Living in the Country ... New York: Derby & Jackson. Cincinnati: H. W. Derby, 1856. 328 p., front.
AAS, BP, BU, CU, H, HEH, LC, LCP, N, NYP, UC, UP, UVB, Y

CRAFTS, WILLIAM AUGUSTUS, *jt. au.* *See* Tilton, Warren. Trifleton Papers (1856), No. 2516.

653 CRAIG, BENJAMIN FRANKLIN. The Border Ruffian; or, Kansas and Missouri. An Historical Western Story of the Present Time, with Interesting Conversations between Jeff and Abe on the Subject of Slavery ... Cincinnati: published for the author, 1863. 234 p.   LC

CRANE, ANNE MONCURE. *See* Seemüller, Mrs. Anne Moncure (Crane)

654 [CRAVEN, BRAXTON.] Mary Barker, by Charlie Vernon [pseud.]. Second Edition. Raleigh, N. C.: Branson & Farrar, 1865. 72 p.   AAS, BA, LC, N, NYH, NYP
Text ends on p. 69, p. 70 blank, advts. on pp. [71]-72.
Cover title: "Mary Barker, a Thrilling Narrative of Early Life in North Carolina."

CRAYON, PORTE, *pseud.* *See* Strother, David Hunter

655 CREAMER, HANNAH GARDNER. Delia's Doctors; or, A Glance behind the Scenes ... New York: Fowlers and Wells, 1852. 262 p.   AAS, H, LC, NYP, Y
Delia was a hypochondriac.

656 CREOLE WIFE; or, Love and Mystery. New York: F. Brady, 1856.
Title listed in Roorbach 1855-1858.

657 CRESWELL, MRS. JULIA (PLEASANTS). Callamura, by Julia Pleasants. Philadelphia: Claxton, Remsen & Haffelfinger, 1868. 454 p.   LC, LCP
An allegorical novel of life in the South.

CREYTON, PAUL, *pseud.* *See* Trowbridge, John Townsend

658 CRIDGE, ANNIE DENTON. Man's Rights; or, How Would You Like It? Comprising Dreams ... Boston: William Denton, 1870. 48 p.   BP, LC
Women take over men's work and men become housekeepers.

659 [CRIPPEN, WILLIAM G.] Green Peas, Picked from the Patch of Invisible Green, Esq. [pseud.] . . . Cincinnati: Moore, Wilstach, Keys & Overend. New York: Livermore & Rudd [cop. 1856]. 311 p.   AAS, LC, NYH, UM

660 CRISWELL, ROBERT. "Uncle Tom's Cabin" Contrasted with Buckingham Hall, the Planter's Home; or, A Fair View of Both Sides of the Slavery Question . . . New York: printed and published by D. Fanshaw, 1852. 152 p., illus.
    AAS, CU, H, HEH, LC, N, NYH, NYP, UC, UM, UP, Y

661 CROFTON, FRANCIS BLAKE. The Bewildered Querists and Other Nonsense . . . New York: G. P. Putnam's Sons, 1875. 127 p.
Humorous satire.   AAS, BP, BU, H, HEH, LC, NYP, Y

CROSBY, FRANCES J. See Van Alstyne, Mrs. Frances Jane (Crosby)

662 CROSBY, GEORGE S. The Mystery; or, Platonic Love . . . Philadelphia: J. B. Lippincott & Co., 1875. 564 p., illus.   BP, LC

663 CROSS, MRS. JANE TANDY (CHINN) HARDIN. Azile . . . Nashville, Tenn.: published for the author by A. H. Redford, 1868. 251 p.   LC, N
From Germany to the South and the beginning of the Civil War.

664 ———— Duncan Adair; or, Captured in Escaping. A Story of One of Morgan's Men . . . Macon, Ga.: Burke, Boykin & Company, 1864. 51 p.   BA, HEH, LC, NYH, UC

665 CROUCH, JULIA. Three Successful Girls . . . New York: Hurd and Houghton. Cambridge: Riverside Press, 1871. 382 p.
Laid in New York City.   AAS, BA, H, HEH, LCP, NYP, Y

CROWFIELD, CHRISTOPHER, pseud. See Stowe, Mrs. Harriet Elizabeth (Beecher)

666 CROZIER, ROBERT HASKINS. The Bloody Junto; or, The Escape of John Wilkes Booth. A Story Containing Many Interesting Particulars in Regard to the Trial and Execution of Mrs. Surratt and Other So-Called Conspirators . . . Little Rock, Ark.: Woodruff & Blocher, printers, 1869. 146 p. Printed in double cols.   HEH, LC

667 ———— The Confederate Spy: A Story of the War of 1861 . . . Gallatin, Tenn.: R. B. Harmon, 1866. 406 p.   H, LC

668 [CRUSE, MARY ANNE.] Cameron Hall: A Story of the Civil War. By M. A. C. . . . Philadelphia: J. B. Lippincott & Co., 1867. 543 p.   AAS, BU, CU, H, HEH, LC, LCP, NYH, UV
Laid in Alabama.

669 [CUDLIP, MRS. ANNIE HALL (THOMAS).] Lady Lorme's Stratagem, and Other Tales. New York: the American News Company, 121 Nassau Street [ca. 1865]. 102 p., illus. Printed in double cols.   HEH
This American reprint of an English novel contains three American tales: Clara, by John R. Williams, M.D.—Shot on Sight, by Frank Wood—Wreck of the Sylph, by an Ex-Member of Congress.

670 [CUMMINS, MARIA SUSANNA.] El Fureidîs . . . Boston: Ticknor and Fields, 1860. 379 p.
AAS, AP, BA, BP, BU, CU, H, HEH, LC, LCP, N, NYP, UC, UM, UP, UVB, Y
Laid in Palestine and Syria.

671 [————] Haunted Hearts . . . Boston: J. E. Tilton and Company, 1864. 554 p.
AAS, BA, BP, BU, CU, H, HEH, LCP, N, NYP, UC, UM, UP, UVB, Y
Story covers a half century from 1812; New Jersey.

672 [————] The Lamplighter. Boston: John P. Jewett & Company. Cleveland, Ohio: Jewett, Proctor and Worthington, 1854. 523 p.
AAS, AP, BA, BP, BU, CU, H, HEH, LCP, N, NYP, UVB, Y
Heroine experiences grim vicissitudes of life.

673 [————] Mabel Vaughan . . . Boston: John P. Jewett and Company. Cleveland, Ohio: Henry P. B. Jewett. London: Sampson Low, Son & Co., 1857. 508 p.
AAS, AP, BA, BP, BU, CU, H, HEH, LCP, N, NYH, UC, UM, UP, Y

674 CURRIER, MRS. SOPHRONIA. Alice Tracy; or, Faint Yet Pursuing. A Sketch from Real Life . . . Boston: E. P. Dutton and Company, 1868. 299 p.   AAS, CU, LC, NYP
Laid in Illinois.

675 ———— By the Sea . . . New York: E. P. Dutton and Company, 1871. 362 p.   AAS, BP, H, HEH, NYP, Y
On the Atlantic coast.

676 [CURTIS, GEORGE WILLIAM.] The Potiphar Papers . . . New York: G. P. Putnam and Company, 1853. 251 p., illus.
AAS, BP, BU, CU, H, HEH, LC, LCP, N, UC, UP, UVB, Y

677 ———— Prue and I . . . New York: Dix, Edwards & Co., 1856. 214 p.

AAS, BA, BP, BU, CU, H, HEH, LC, N, NYP, UC, UM, UP, UVB, Y

———— The Shrouded Portrait. *In* The Knickerbocker Gallery (1855), No. 1492.

———— A Story of Venice. *In* Gifts of Genius [cop. 1859], No. 1000.

678 ———— Trumps: A Novel . . . New York: Harper & Brothers, 1861. 502 p., illus.

AAS, BA, BP, BU, CU, H, HEH, LC, LCP, N, NYP, UC, UM, UVB, Y

New York City and Washington, D.C., in the 1830's.

CURTIS, LAURA J. *See* Bullard, Mrs. Laura J. (Curtis)

679 CUSTARD, MRS. ETHELINDA. The Discipline of Storms: A Tale of the Old World and the New . . . New York: H. Dayton. Indianapolis, Indiana: Dayton & Asher, 1859. 264 p.   HEH

Also published as: *Hester Warwick; or, The Triumph of Faith. A Tale of the Old World and the New.* New York: H. Dayton, 1860.   AAS

Of religious interest.

680 CUTLER, HELEN R. Jottings from Life; or, Passages from the Diary of an Itinerant's Wife . . . Cincinnati: Poe & Hitchcock; R. P. Thompson, printer, 1864. 282 p.   LC, Y

681 CUTLER, MRS. LIZZIE (PETIT). Household Mysteries: A Romance of Southern Life . . . New York: D. Appleton and Company, 1856. 300 p.   AAS, BP, BU, CU, H, LCP, N, NYP, UV

682 [————] Light and Darkness; or, The Shadow of Fate. A Story of Fashionable Life . . . New York: D. Appleton and Company, 1855. 319 p.   AAS, BU, CU, LC

683 CUTTER, LOUISE J. Cypress Leaves . . . With a Biography, by Mary W. Janvrin . . . Boston: J. M. Usher, 1856. 336 p., front.   AAS, BU, HEH

Contains: Little Effie; or, The Step-Mother's Lesson—Aunt Edith's Story; or, The History of a Heart—The Little Dancing Girl—Allie Rivers, the Young American Danseuse—The Masked Stranger—The Actress; or, Three Leaves from Life—The Castle and the Cottage—The Ball-Room Beauty—The Wife's Stratagem.

CYMON, *pseud. See* Somerby, Frederic Thomas

D., W. *See* Duane, William

684 DANA, JOHN JAY. Humpy Dumpy; or, The Corner Grocery . . .
New York: National Temperance Society, 1874. 314 p., front.
AAS, NYP

685 [DARDEN, JOHN P.] The Secret of Success; or, Family Affairs.
A Memoir . . . By a Mississippian. Cincinnati: Walter Scott,
1853. 364 p. AAS, CU, LC, LCP, NYP

DARGAN, CLARA VICTORIA. Riverland: A Charming Story of
Southern Life. *In* The Southern Field and Fireside Novelette
[1863], No. 2287.

686 DARK SHADES OF CITY LIFE. A Sequel to "River Pirates." New
York: H. Long & Brother [185-?].
Title listed in Roorbach 1852-1855.

DAVENPORT, *Capt.* HENRY E., *pseud.?* Rovings on Land and Sea
(1857). *See* The Yankee Enterprise; or, The Two Millionaires,
No. 2828.

687 DAVIES, THEODORE. Losing to Win: A Novel . . . New York:
Sheldon & Company, 1874. 407 p. H, HEH, LC, LCP, NYP
New York City society.

688 DAVIS, ANDREW JACKSON. Tale of a Physician; or, The Seeds and
Fruits of Crime. In Three Parts. Complete in One Volume . . .
Boston: William White & Company, 1869. 325 p.
AAS, BP, HEH, LC, NYP, UC, UM, UP, Y

689 DAVIS, ELIZA B. Edith; or, The Light of Home . . . Boston:
Crosby, Nichols and Company, 1856. 282 p.
AAS, H, LC, NYP, UC

DAVIS, LEMUEL CLARKE. Dick Lyle's Fee. *In* Rougegorge (1870),
No. 2130.

690 ———— A Stranded Ship: A Story of Sea and Shore . . .
New York: G. P. Putnam & Son, 1869. 175 p.
AAS, CU, H, HEH, LCP, NYP, UM, Y

———— A Wreck upon the Shore. *In* Short Stories (1869),
No. 2210.

691 [DAVIS, LUCIUS DANIEL.] Life in the Itinerancy, in Its Relations to the Circuit and Station, and to the Minister's Home and Family . . . New York and Auburn: Miller, Orton & Mulligan, 1856. 335 p.   AAS, HEH, LC, LCP, UM

692 ———— Life in the Laity; or, The History of a Station . . . New York: published for the author by Carlton & Porter, 1858. 200 p.   LC

693 DAVIS, MINNIE S. The Harvest of Love: A Story for the Home Circle . . . Boston: A. Tompkins, 1859. 256 p.   UP
Also published as: *Clinton Forrest; or, The Power of Kindness. A Story for the Home Circle.* Boston: Tompkins & Company, 1863.   HEH
Laid in "Oakville," New England.

694 ———— Marion Lester; or, The Mother's Mistake . . . Boston: A. Tompkins, 1856. 256 p.   AAS, BU, H, HEH, UC, UP, Y
Also published as: *Marion Lester: A Story of School Life.* Boston: A. Tompkins [cop. 1863].   UM

695 [DAVIS, PETER SEIBERT.] The Young Parson . . . Philadelphia: Smith, English & Co., 1863. 384 p.   AP, CU, H, N, NYP, UM, Y

696 DAVIS, MRS. REBECCA (HARDING). Dallas Galbraith . . . Philadelphia: J. B. Lippincott and Co., 1868. 242 p. Printed in double cols.
AAS, BA, BP, CU, H, HEH, LCP, N, NYP, UC, UM, UP, UVB, Y

697 ———— John Andross . . . New York: Orange Judd Company, 245 Broadway [cop. 1874]. 324 p., illus.
AAS, BA, CU, H, HEH, LC, LCP, N, NYP, UC, UM, UVB, Y

698 ———— Kitty's Choice: A Story of Berrytown . . . Philadelphia: J. B. Lippincott & Co., 1874. 74 p. Printed in double cols.   LCP, NYP, UVB
Also contains: Leonard Heath's Fortune—Balacchi Brothers.

———— Life in the Iron-Mills. *In* Atlantic Tales (1866), No. 155.

699 [————] Margaret Howth: A Story of To-Day . . . Boston: Ticknor and Fields, 1862. 266 p.
AAS, AP, BA, BP, BU, H, LC, N, NYH, NYP, UC, UM, UP, UVB, Y
Laid in a New England milling town.

———— The Pearl of Great Price. *In* Short Stories, 2d ser. (1869), No. 2211.

700 ———— Waiting for the Verdict . . . New York: Sheldon & Company, 1868. 361 p., illus.

AAS, BA, BP, CU, H, HEH, LC, LCP, N, NYP, UC, UM, UP, UVB, Y

Treats of the Negro problem.

DAVISON, HARRIET A. Count Von Lundstein. *In* A. J. H. Duganne, The Prince Corsair [185-?], No. 797.

701 DAY, CHARLES HENRY. Kate Vaugh; or, Spiders, Webs and Flies. A Life Tale . . . New Haven: C. H. Day, 1861. 72 p.   Y

At head of title: "Stories for Everybody, No. 1."

Y copy "seventh thousand."

702 THE DAY AFTER TO-MORROW. Boston: Henry Hoyt, No. 9 Cornhill [cop. 1871]. 397 p., front.   AAS

Deals with forgery.

703 DELETE.

704 [DAYTON, AMOS COOPER.] Theodosia Ernest; or, The Heroine of Faith. Nashville, Tenn.: Graves, Marks & Rutland. New York: Sheldon, Blakeman & Co., 1857. 2 vols. (399, 491 p.), illus.   BU, HEH, LC, LCP, UV(V.2), Y

Title page of vol. 2 reads: *Theodosia Ernest. Volume II; or, Ten Days' Travel in Search of the Church.* Nashville, Tenn.: South-Western Baptist Publishing House; Graves, Marks & Rutland. New York: Sheldon, Blakeman & Co., 1857.

Fictionalized treatment of the Baptist and Pedobaptist controversy.

705 [DE COSTA, BENJAMIN FRANKLIN.] Rector of Roxburgh: A Story of Our Own Times. By William Hickling [pseud.]. New York: E. P. Dutton & Company, 1873. 272 p.   H, NYH, Y

A small New England town.

706 [DEEN, MRS. E. W.] The Fixed Stars; or, The Goddess of Truth and Justice. New York: James Miller, 1865. 634 p.

AAS, LC, NYP, Y

707 DE FOREST, JOHN WILLIAM. Honest John Vane: A Story . . . New Haven, Conn.: Richmond & Patten, 1875. 259 p.

AAS, BA, BP, CU, H, LC, NYP, UM, UVB, Y

Political satire; Grant's administration.

———— The Hungry Heart. *In* Not Pretty, but Precious (1872), No. 1804.

708 ———— Kate Beaumont . . . Boston: James R. Osgood and Company, 1872. 165 p., illus. Printed in double cols.

AAS, BA, BU, CU, H, LC, LCP, N, NYP, UC, UM, UP, UVB, Y

At head of cover title: "Osgood's Library of Novels, Number 5."
Feuding in South Carolina.

709 ———— Miss Ravenel's Conversion from Secession to Loyalty ... New York: Harper & Brothers, 1867. 521 p.

AAS, BP, BU, CU, H, HEH, LC, LCP, NYH, NYP, UM, UP, UVB, Y

A realistic novel of the Civil War and its aftermath.

710 ———— Overland: A Novel . . . New York: Sheldon and Company, 677 Broadway, and 214 & 216 Mercer St. [cop. 1871]. 209 p., front.

AAS, CU, H, HEH, LC, LCP, N, NYP, UM, UP, UVB, Y

From Santa Fe to California.

711 ———— Playing the Mischief: A Novel . . . New York: Harper & Brothers, 1875. 185 p. Printed in double cols.

AAS, BA, CU, LC, LCP, NYP, UVB, Y

Corruption in Washington during Grant's administration.

712 ———— Seacliff; or, The Mystery of the Westervelts . . . Boston: Phillips, Sampson and Company, 1859. 466 p.

Long Island Sound.   AAS, H, LC, LCP, NYP, UM, UVB, Y

713 ———— The Wetherel Affair . . . New York: Sheldon and Company, 1873. 222 p.

A murder mystery.   AAS, BA, BP, HEH, LC, LCP, NYP, UM, UVB, Y

714 DELAPLAIN, SOPHIA, *pseud.* A Thrilling and Exciting Account of the Sufferings and Horrible Tortures Inflicted on Mortimer Bowers and Miss Sophia Delaplain, by the Spanish Authorities for a Supposed Participation with General Lopez in the Invasion of Cuba . . . Charleston, S. C.: E. E. Barclay; M. B. Crosson & Co., 1851. 31, [1] p., illus.   LC, N, NYP

DE LAZIE, ULRIC, *pseud. See* Griffin, Edmund D.

715 DE LEON, EDWIN. Askaros Kassis, the Copt: A Romance of Modern Egypt . . . Philadelphia: J. B. Lippincott & Co., 1870. 462 p.   BP, BU, H, LC, LCP, NYP, Y

716   DE LEON, THOMAS COOPER. Cross Purposes: A Christmas Experience in Seven Stages . . . Philadelphia: J. B. Lippincott & Co., 1871.   117 p., front.   AAS, BP, BU, LC

717   [DE LESDERNIER, MRS. EMILY PIERPONT.] Berenice: A Novel. Boston: Phillips, Sampson & Company, 1856.   332 p.
                                 AAS, BP, BU, CU, HEH, LC, LCP, N, NYP

718   ———— Fannie St. John: A Romantic Incident of the American Revolution . . . New York: Hurd and Houghton. Cambridge: the Riverside Press, 1874.   63 p.
                                 AAS, BA, BP, CU, H, HEH, LC, LCP, NYH, NYP, Y

719   ———— Headland Home; or, A Soul's Pilgrimage . . . New York: James Miller, 1868.   346 p.   AAS, HEH, LCP, NYP
      May be autobiographical.

720   ———— Hortense, the Last of a Noble Name: A Romance of Real Life . . . New York: Wentworth Maxwell & Co., 1867. 362 p.   AAS, H, HEH, NYP, UV, Y
      On the south Atlantic seaboard prior to the war.

      DELPHINE, pseud.   See Baker, Mrs. Delphine Paris

721   DENISON, MRS. MARY (ANDREWS). The Days and Ways of the Cocked Hats; or, The Dawn of the Revolution . . . New York: S. A. Rollo, 1860.   383 p., front.
                                 AAS, BP, CU, H, HEH, LC, NYP, UC, UP, Y

722   ———— Gracie Amber . . . New York: Sheldon, Blakeman & Co.   Chicago: S. C. Griggs & Co., 1857.   450 p.   NYP

723   ———— Home Pictures . . . New York: Harper & Brothers, 1853.   417 p.   AAS, BU, LC, NYH, NYP, Y

      ———— The Last of Torconnier's Band. In A. Cary, The Adopted Daughter (1859), No. 466.

724   ———— Led to the Light. A Sequel to Opposite the Jail . . . Philadelphia: J. S. Claxton, 1867.   352 p., illus.   CU, LC, NYP

725   ———— Lieutenant Messinger . . . Boston: Henry Hoyt, No. 9 Cornhill [cop. 1863].   119 p.   AAS, NYH

726 —————— The Lover's Trials; or, The Days before the Revolu-
tion . . . Philadelphia: T. B. Peterson & Brothers, 306 Chestnut
Street [cop. 1865]. 383 p.   HEH, NYP, UP
Andros rebellion in 1689.

—————— Love's Yearning. *In* M. G. Clarke, *comp.*, Sunshine
and Shadows (1865), No. 541.

727 —————— The Master . . . Boston: Walker, Wise and Company, 1862. 270 p.   AAS, BP, H, LC, LCP, NYP, UP, Y
Also published as: *The Music-Master.* Boston: Walker, Wise and Company, 1863.   NYP

728 —————— The Mill Agent . . . Boston: Graves and Young.
New York: Sheldon & Co. Cincinnati: Geo. S. Blanchard,
1864. 352 p.   AAS, BP, CU, NYP, Y
A temperance novel.

729 —————— Nobody's Child, and Other Stories . . . Philadelphia:
J. B. Lippincott & Co., 1857. 384 p., illus.   HEH
Copyright notice dated 1854.
Contains a few short tales.

730 —————— Old Hepsy . . . New York: A. B. Burdick, 1858.
459 p., illus.   AAS, BP, H, LC, NYH
Antislavery; Maryland.

731 [——————] Opposite the Jail . . . Boston: Henry Hoyt, 1859.
333 p., front.   AAS, BU, H

732 [——————] Out of Prison . . . Boston: Graves and Young.
New York: Sheldon and Company. Cincinnati: Geo. S. Blanchard, 1864. 358 p.   AAS, H, LC, NYP

733 —————— Victor Norman, Rector . . . Philadelphia: J. B. Lippincott & Co., 1873. 262 p.   AAS, LC, LCP

734 —————— What Not . . . Philadelphia: Lippincott, Grambo &
Co., 1855. 384 p., illus.   AAS, BA, BU, H, LC, UC
Also published as: *Orange Leaves.* Philadelphia: J. B. Lippincott & Co.
[1856].   Y

735 DE NORMAND, HUGH. The Brigand Captive; or, Gipsy Queen
. . . Auburn: Alden, Beardsley & Co. New York: J. C.
Derby, 1855. 354 p., front.   Y

736 ———— Julienne, the Daughter of the Hamlet . . . Auburn: Alden, Beardsley & Co. Rochester: Wanzer, Beardsley & Co., 1854. 354 p., front.   AAS, BP, CU, HEH, UC, UP, Y

737 DENSLOW, VAN BUREN. Owned and Disowned; or, The Chattel Child. A Tale of Southern Life . . . New York: H. Dayton, 1857. 302 p.   AAS, CU
New Orleans about 1814.

DE PONTE, MRS. S. A Night of Terror. *In* Thirteen Good Stories [1873?], No. 2457.

738 [DERBY, CAROLINE ROSINA.] Salem: A Tale of the Seventeenth Century. By D. R. Castleton [pseud.]. New York: Harper & Brothers, 1874. 336 p.
                    AAS, BP, BU, CU, H, HEH, LC, NYP, UC, UP, Y
On the persecution of witches.

739 [DERBY, GEORGE HORATIO.] Phoenixiana; or, Sketches and Burlesques. By John Phoenix [pseud.] . . . New York: D. Appleton and Company, 1856. 274 p., illus.
                    AAS, BP, BU, CU, H, HEH, LC, LCP, N, NYP, UM, UP, UVB, Y

740 ———— The Squibob Papers . . . New York: Carleton, 1865. 247 p., illus.
                    AAS, BA, BP, BU, CU, H, HEH, LC, N, NYH, NYP, UC, UM, UP, UVB, Y

741 THE DERIENNI; or, Land Pirates of the Isthmus. Being a True and Graphic History of Robberies . . . by Those Cool-Blooded Miscreants, Who Have Infested for Years the Great Highway to California . . . New Orleans, Charleston, Baltimore, and Philadelphia: A. R. Orton, 1853. 1 p. l., [15]-44 p., illus.
                    HEH, LC, NYP

742 DESLONDE, MRS. MARIA DARRINGTON. The Miller of Silcott Mill: A Novel . . . New York: G. W. Carleton & Co. London: Low & Co., 1875. 383 p.
Information from LC card for copy withdrawn from circulation.

743 DESMOS, *pseud.* Old Toney and His Master; or, The Abolitionist and the Land-Pirate. Founded on Fact. A Tale of 1824-1827. By Desmos [pseud.]. Nashville, Tenn.: Southwestern Publishing House, 1861. 393 p., front.   NYH, UC

744 DETTER, THOMAS. Nelli Brown; or, The Jealous Wife, with Other Sketches ... San Francisco: Cuddy & Hughes, printers, 1871. 160 p.   Y
Negro life in Nevada and Idaho.

745 DEVEREUX, GEORGE HUMPHREY. Sam Shirk: A Tale of the Woods of Maine ... New York: Hurd and Houghton, 1871. 391 p.   AAS, BA, BP, CU, HEH, LC, NYP, UC, Y

746 DEW OF EDEN: A Romance of the Harem. By "The Baronet's Son" ... New York: Ed. Harris & Co., 1865. Cover title, 22, [2] p.   LC
A "romance" to sell the Dew of Eden which is a potion to induce sleep.

747 DE WITT, MRS. JENNIE DOWLING. Kate Weston; or, To Will and to Do ... New York: DeWitt & Davenport, 160 & 162 Nassau Street [cop. 1855]. 456 p., illus.
AAS, BP, BU, CU, H, HEH, NYP, UC, UP

———— Mary Neilly. In A. Cary, The Adopted Daughter (1859), No. 466.

748 DEXTER, HENRY MARTYN. Street Thoughts ... Boston: Crosby, Nichols, and Company, 1859. 216 p., illus.
AAS, BA, BP, BU, CU, H, HEH, LC, NYH, NYP, UM, Y
Character sketches of Bostonians.

DHU, HELEN, pseud. See Lester, Mrs. Ellen (Brown)

749 DIAZ, MRS. ABBY (MORTON). Lucy Maria ... Boston: James R. Osgood and Company, 1874. 396 p., illus.
AAS, BP, CU, H, LC, LCP

750 ———— The Schoolmaster's Trunk Containing Papers on Home-Life in Tweenit . . . Boston: James R. Osgood and Company, 1874. 118 p., illus.   AAS, BA, BP, CU, H, HEH, UC

751 DICKINSON, ANNA ELIZABETH. What Answer? . . . Boston: Ticknor and Fields, 1868. 301 p.
AAS, BP, CU, H, HEH, LC, LCP, NYP, UC, UP, UVB, Y
Miscegenation during the Civil War.

752 DIMITRY, CHARLES PATTON. The House in Balfour-Street: A Novel ... New York: George S. Wilcox, 1868. 377 p.
Near London.   AAS, CU, LC, LCP

753 DIMMICK, FRANCIS MARION. Anna Clayton; or, The Enquirer after Truth . . . Philadelphia: Lindsay & Blakiston, 1859. 427 p.   BP, LC, UC, UV, Y
Pedobaptist doctrine.

754 DISOSWAY, ELLA TAYLOR. South Meadows: A Tale of Long Ago . . . Philadelphia: Porter and Coates, 822 Chestnut Street [cop. 1874]. 280 p.   AAS, BP, HEH, LC, LCP, N, NYP
Cotton Mather figures prominently in this story of Salem witchcraft.

755 DITSON, GEORGE LEIGHTON. Crimora; or, Love's Cross . . . Boston: George Leighton Ditson, 1852. 408 p.   BP, LC

756 ———— The Federati of Italy: A Romance of Caucasian Captivity . . . Boston: William White and Company, 1871. 319 p.   CU, LC

757 DIVOLL, WILLARD. The Fatal Stroke; or, The Philosophy of Intemperance . . . New York: Baker & Godwin, printers, 1869. 62 p.   LC, NYP, Y

758 DIXON, EDWARD H. Scenes in the Practice of a New York Surgeon . . . New York: DeWitt & Davenport, 160 & 162 Nassau Street [cop. 1855]. 407 p., illus.
AAS, BP, CU, H, HEH, LC, LCP, N, NYH, NYP, UC, UM, UP, Y
Sketches to dispel unpleasant reactions to doctors and medicines.

759 DOCWRA, EDWIN HILL. The Devil's Race Course: A Legend of Baltimore . . . Baltimore: Henry Taylor, 1854. 31 p.
BA, LC, LCP, UP

[DODGE, MARY ABIGAIL.] The Pursuit of Knowledge under Difficulties, by Gail Hamilton [pseud.]. In Atlantic Tales (1866), No. 155.

DODGE'S SKETCHES. [Boston, 1853.] 32 p., illus.
Issued with R. Morris, The Faithful Slave (1853), No. 1751.
The sketches relate to Ossian Euclid Dodge.

760 DOE, CHARLES HENRY. Buffets . . . Boston: James R. Osgood and Company, 1875. 143 p. Printed in double cols.
AAS, BA, BP, CU, H, HEH, LC, LCP, NYP
Business and social life during the Civil War.

DOESTICKS, JR., pseud. See Halsey, Harlan Page

DOESTICKS, Q. K. PHILANDER, P. B., *pseud. See* Thomson, Mortimer Neal

761 DOLLIE, *pseud.* Our Own Heroes: A Thrilling Narrative. By "Dollie" and "Mollie." Volume I. Atlanta, Ga.: office of "The Soldier's Friend," 1863. 128 p.   HEH
No more published.

DOMINIE, *pseud. See* Hamilton, John A.

762 [DONALDSON, JAMES LOWRY.] Sergeant Atkins: A Tale of Adventure. Founded on Fact. By an Officer of the United States Army . . . Philadelphia: J. B. Lippincott & Co., 1871. 317 p., illus.   AAS, BP, H, HEH, LC, LCP, N, NYP
The Seminole War, 1835-1842.

763 DOOWROF, *pseud.* The Young Empress and the Reclaimed Deserter: A Tale of the Vicissitudes of Human Life . . . Baltimore: printed by James Lucas & Son, 1857. 37 p.   Y
The American Revolution.

764 DORA GRAFTON; or, Every Cloud Has a Silver Lining. Boston: James French and Company, 1856. 406 p., front.   AAS, BU, UC

765 DORA, THE HEROINE OF THE CUMBERLAND; or, The American Amazon. A Startling but Authentic Narrative of Innumerable and Dangerous Feats Performed by This Daring Heroine, the Idol of the Loyal Armies. Philadelphia: Barclay & Co., No. 602 Arch Street [cop. 1864]. 116 p., illus.   NYP
Pagination irregular.

766 DORR, MRS. JULIA CAROLINE (RIPLEY). Expiation . . . Philadelphia: J. B. Lippincott & Co., 1873. 323 p.   AAS, BU, H

767 [————] Farmingdale, by Caroline Thomas [pseud.] . . . New York: D. Appleton & Co. London, 1854. 392 p.   BU, H, UP
Life in the Green Mountains.

768 ———— Lanmere . . . New York: Mason Brothers, 1856. 447 p.   AAS, CU, H, HEH, NYP, UP
A New England village.

769 ———— Sibyl Huntington: A Novel . . . New York: G. W. Carleton. London: S. Low, Son & Co., 1869. 359 p.   AAS, CU, HEH, NYP, UM, Y
Lake Champlain country.

DORR, LOUISE SNOW. The Mannerings. *In* Short Stories, 2d ser. (1869), No. 2211.

770 DORSEY, MRS. ANNA HANSON (MCKENNEY). Coaina, the Rose of the Algonquins . . . New York: P. O'Shea, 1867. 145 p.

CU, N, NYP, UM

771 ———— Conscience; or, The Trials of May Brooke. An American Catholic Tale . . . New York: Edward Dunigan & Brother (James B. Kirker), 1856. 2 vols. (, 183 p.) H(V.2)

772 ———— The Flemmings; or, Truth Triumphant . . . New York: P. O'Shea, 1870. 444 p. LC
At head of title: "The Notre Dame Series of Catholic Novels."

773 ———— Nora Brady's Vow, and Mona the Vestal . . . Philadelphia: J. B. Lippincott & Co., 1869. 324 p.
Laid in Ireland. AAS, CU, H, LC, NYP

774 ———— The Old Gray Rosary . . . New York: P. O'Shea, 37 Barclay Street [after 1873]. 147 p. AAS
At head of title: "The Notre Dame Series of Catholic Novels."
Kelly 1866-1871 notes an 1870 ed. which, when found, should give the publisher's address as 27 Barclay Street.

775 ———— Woodreve Manor; or, Six Months in Town. A Tale of American Life, to Suit the Merits and the Follies of the Times . . . Philadelphia: A. Hart, 1852. 334 p. AP, H, LC, NYP

DORSEY, D. B. Love and Ghosts. *In* Short Stories (1869), No. 2210.

———— Love on the Ohio. *In* Short Stories (1869), No. 2210.

776 [DORSEY, MRS. SARAH ANNE (ELLIS).] Agnes Graham: A Novel. By Filia [pseud.] . . . Philadelphia: Claxton, Remsen and Haffelfinger. New Orleans: J. A. Gresham, 1869. 121 p. Printed in double cols. UP
Of slavery interest; New Orleans.

777 [————] Athalie; or, A Southern Villeggiatura. "A Winters Tale." By "Filia" [pseud.] . . . Philadelphia: Claxton, Remsen and Haffelfinger. New Orleans: J. A. Gresham, 1872. 109 p. Printed in double cols. LC, NYH, NYP

778 [————]   Lucia Dare: A Novel. By Filia [pseud.] . . . New York: M. Doolady, 1867. 138 p. Printed in double cols.

Through the Civil War period.   AAS, BP, LC, LCP, NYP, UP

779 DOTEN, ELIZABETH. Hesper, the Home-Spirit: A Simple Story of Household Labor and Love . . . Boston: Abel Tompkins; Brown, Taggard & Chase, 1859. 251 p.

AAS, BP, BU, CU, HEH, Y

780 ————   My Affinity, and Other Stories . . . Boston: William White and Company. New York: the American News Company, 1870. 338 p.   AAS, CU, HEH, LC, NYP

Also contains: Madam Bonnifleur and Her Roses—Women and Wisdom—The Faith of Hasupha—The Bachelor's Defeat—The Great Carbuncle—Marrying for Money—The Prophet and the Pilgrims—Mr. Silverbury's Experience—Geraldine—Dr. Purdie's Patient—The Sunshine of Love—The Elfin Spring.

781 THE DOUBLE SUICIDE. The True History of the Lives of the Twin Sisters, Sarah and Maria Williams. Containing an Account of Maria's Love, Mock Marriage, Suffering and Degradation; Together with Sarah's Love and Suffering . . . New York: G. C. Holbrook, 1855. 62 p.   LC

Also issued with imprint: New York: H. H. Randall, No. 50 Ann Street [cop. 1855]. 64 p., illus. LC

782 DOUGLAS, AMANDA MINNIE. Claudia . . . Boston: Lee and Shepard, 1868. 381 p.   H, HEH, NYP

783 ————   Home Nook; or, The Crown of Duty . . . Boston: Lee and Shepard. New York: Lee, Shepard and Dillingham, 1874. 384 p.   AAS, BA, HEH, LC, UM

Laid on the Hudson.

784 ————   In Trust; or, Dr. Bertrand's Household . . . Boston: Lee and Shepard, 1866. 383 p.

In the vicinity of the Passaic.   AAS, CU, HEH, LCP, NYP, UC, UP, Y

785 ————   Lucia: Her Problem . . . New York: Sheldon & Company, 1872. 315 p.   AAS, CU, H, LC, NYP, UV

786 ————   Stephen Dane . . . Boston: Lee and Shepard, 1867. 253 p.   AAS, CU, H, HEH, LC, N, NYP, UM, UV, Y

In the Pennsylvania mining districts.

787 ———— Sydnie Adriance; or, Trying the World . . . Boston: Lee and Shepard, 1869. 355 p.   BA, H, LC, NYP, UM, Y

788 ———— There's No Place like Home . . . Boston: William F. Gill and Company, 1875. 380 p., illus.   AAS, CU, HEH, NYP

789 ———— With Fate against Him . . . New York: Sheldon & Company, 1870. 370 p.   AAS, BU, H, LC, NYP

DOUGLASS, FREDERICK. The Heroic Slave. *In* J. Griffiths, *ed.*, Autographs for Freedom (1853), No. 1033.

790 [DOUTNEY, MRS. HARRIET G. (STORER).] An Autobiography, Being Passages from a Life Now Progressing in the City of Boston . . . By R. L. B. [pseud.]. [Cambridge, Mass.] sold by subscription only, 1871. 240 p.   BP, CU, H, LC, N
Also published as: *Marrying a Moustache; or, An Autobiography.* [Cambridge, Mass.] published by subscription only, 1872.   AAS, UM
Also published as: *I Told You So; or, An Autobiography.* [Cambridge, Mass.] published by subscription only, 1873.   AAS, H, Y

DOW, NEAL. The History of a Neighborhood: A True Tale. *In* A. Cary, The Adopted Daughter (1859), No. 466.

791 DOWNING, MRS. FRANCES (MURDAUGH). Nameless: A Novel . . . Raleigh, N. C.: Wm. B. Smith & Co., 1865. 232 p.   AAS, LCP
Laid in England.

DOWNING, *Major* JACK, *pseud. See* Smith, Seba

792 DRAKE, RICHARD, *pseud.?* Revelations of a Slave Smuggler: Being the Autobiography of Capt. Rich'd Drake, an African Trader for Fifty Years—from 1807 to 1857 . . . With a Preface by His Executor, Rev. Henry Byrd West . . . New York: Robert M. DeWitt, 13 Frankfort Street [cop. 1860]. 100 p., illus.
H, HEH, LC, NYH, NYP

DRILLE, HEARTON, U.S.A., *pseud. See* Grey, Jeannie H.

793 DRURY, P. SHELDEN, *ed.* The Startling and Thrilling Narrative of the Dark and Terrible Deeds of Henry Madison, and His Associate and Accomplice Miss Ellen Stevens, Who Was Executed by the Vigilance Committee of San Francisco, on the 20th September Last . . . Cincinnati: Barclay & Co., 234 Main Street [cop. 1857]. 36 p., illus.   HEH, Y

794 [Duane, William.] Ligan: A Collection of Tales and Essays. "By W. D." Ninety-Nine Copies Printed. Philadelphia: Merrihew & Thompson, printers, 1857. 76 p.

AAS, HEH, LC, LCP, NYH, NYP, UC, Y

Contents: The African Fancy Ball—Erostratus—Verbal Criticisms—Passages from the Papers of the Late George Lepner—Extracts from the Diary of a Whig—Readings on Shenstone—The Military Excursion—Our Given Names—Chips and Shavings.

The "No." of each copy printed at head of title.

Dubh, Scian, *pseud. See* Scian Dubh, *pseud.*

795 Duffy, Owen. Walter Warren; or, The Adventurer of the Northern Wilds . . . New York: Stringer & Townsend, 222 Broadway [cop. 1854]. 105 p. Printed in double cols. LC

796 Duganne, Augustine Joseph Hickey. Bianca; or, The Star of the Valley. A Romance of the Alps . . . New York: Samuel French, 121 Nassau Street [185-?]. 100 p. Printed in double cols. AAS, CU

———— The Phantom Friar. *In* The Arrow of Gold [185-?], No. 81.

797 ———— The Prince Corsair; or, The Three Brothers of Guzan. A Tale of the Indian Ocean . . . New York: Samuel French, 121 Nassau Street [185-?]. 100 p. Printed in double cols. CU

Also contains: Blanchette Roso, by H. N. Hathaway—The Chevalier Tremlet, by Charles E. Waite—Count Von Lundstein, by Harriet A. Davison—The Concert, by Miss Anne T. Wilbur.

798 ———— The Ring of Destiny; or, The Astrologer's Plot. A Tale of Ancient Days . . . Boston: F. Gleason, 1863. 52 p., illus.

Announced as "recently published" in *Amer. Lit. Gaz.*, II (Nov. 2, 1863), 17.

It has not been determined whether this is a reprint with a new title, of an earlier ed., inasmuch as a copy has not been located.

799 [————] The Tenant-House; or, Embers from Poverty's Hearthstone . . . New York: Robert M. DeWitt, 160 & 162 Nassau Street [cop. 1857]. 490 p., front.

Laid in New York City.   AAS, BP, CU, H, HEH, NYP, UC

800 Dumond, Mrs. Annie (Hamilton) Nelles. Ravenia; or, The Outcast Redeemed. By Annie Nelles . . . Topeka, Kansas: Commonwealth Printing Company press, 1872. 251 p., front.

Tribulations of a deserted wife.   AAS, HEH, LC

801 DUMONT, MRS. JULIA LOUISA (CAREY). Life Sketches from Common Paths: A Series of American Tales ... New York: D. Appleton and Company, 1856. 286 p.

AAS, BP, H, HEH, LC, N, NYP, Y

Contents: Introductory Sketches—The First Temperance Pledge—The Brothers—Estrangement—The Soldier's Son—The Young Physician—The Debt—The Pauper—The Family History—The Rejected Manuscript—Aunt Hetty—Ashton Grey.

802 [DUNHAM, ROBERT CARR.] The Grecian Bend. What It Is ... New York: the Grecian Bend Publishing Company, 1868. Cover title, 22 p., illus. AAS, BP, H, NYH

Caption title: "A Severe Family Affliction. By Bellamy Brownjohn [pseud.]."

A humorous satire on bustles.

803 [———] No Throughfare. By C———s D———s, Bellamy Brownjohn [pseud.], and Domby. Second Edition. Revised, Corrected, and Enlarged upon by Brownjohn. Boston: Loring, 1868. Cover title, 15 p. Printed in double cols.

Humorous satire. BA, BP, HEH

804 DUNIWAY, MRS. ABIGAIL (SCOTT). Captain Gray's Company; or, Crossing the Plains and Living in Oregon ... Portland, Oregon: printed and published by S. J. McCormick, 1859. 342 p.

In the form of a journal. BP, CU, HEH, LC, NYP, UVB, Y

805 DUPUY, ELIZA ANN. The Adventures of a Gentleman in Search of Miss Smith ... Cincinnati: Edwards & Goshorn, 131 Main Street [cop. 1852]. 90 p.

Duke University Library copy.

806 ——— All for Love; or, The Outlaw's Bride ... Philadelphia: T. B. Peterson & Brothers, 306 Chestnut Street [cop. 1873]. 415 p. HEH, LC, UP

807 ——— Annie Selden; or, The Concealed Treasure ... Cincinnati: H. M. Rulison. New York: A. Ranney, 1854. 109 p., illus. Printed in double cols. Y

808 ——— Ashleigh: A Tale of the Olden Time ... Cincinnati: H. B. Pearson, 1854. 112 p. Printed in double cols. H, LC

809 ———— The Cancelled Will ... Philadelphia: T. B. Peterson & Brothers, 306 Chestnut Street [cop. 1872]. 493 p.

Sequel: *Who Shall Be Victor?*   AAS, CU, H, HEH, LC, NYP, UP, Y

810 ———— The Clandestine Marriage ... Philadelphia: T. B. Peterson & Brothers, 306 Chestnut Street [cop. 1875]. 454 p.

Sequel: *The Discarded Wife.*   CU, LC, UC

811 ———— The Country Neighborhood . . . New York: Harper & Brothers, 1855. 109, [1] p. Printed in double cols.

Plantation society near Natchez, Miss.   AAS, CU, H, LC, NYP, UVB

812 ———— The Dethroned Heiress . . . Philadelphia: T. B. Peterson & Brothers, 306 Chestnut Street [cop. 1873]. 471 p.

Sequel: *The Hidden Sin.*   BP, LC

813 ———— The Discarded Wife; or, Will She Succeed ... Philadelphia: T. B. Peterson & Brothers, 306 Chestnut Street [cop. 1875]. 595 p.   LC, UC
Sequel to *The Clandestine Marriage.*

814 ———— Emma Walton; or, Trials and Triumph . . . Cincinnati: J. A. & U. P. James, 1854. 179 p. Printed in double cols.
LC

815 ———— Florence; or, The Fatal Vow ... Cincinnati: Lorenzo Stratton, 131 Main Street [cop. 1852]. 120 p.
Princeton University Library copy.

816 ———— The Gipsy's Warning ... Philadelphia: T. B. Peterson & Brothers, 306 Chestnut Street [cop. 1873]. 450 p.
AAS, H, LC

817 ———— The Hidden Sin. A Sequel to "The Dethroned Heiress" . . . Philadelphia: T. B. Peterson & Brothers, 306 Chestnut Street [cop. 1874]. 357 p.   LC, UC
Not to be confused with the American reprint of Frances Browne's *Hidden Sin*, New York, 1866.

818 [————] How He Did It ... Philadelphia: T. B. Peterson & Brothers, 306 Chestnut Street [cop. 1871]. 456 p.   AAS
Also published as: *Was He Guilty? By Miss Eliza A. Dupuy*. Philadelphia: T. B. Peterson & Brothers, 306 Chestnut Street [cop. 1873]. Information from LC card for copy withdrawn from circulation.

819 [————] The Huguenot Exiles; or, The Times of Louis XIV.
A Historical Novel . . . New York: Harper & Brothers, 1856.
453 p.   AAS, BP, BU, H, HEH, LC, NYP, UC, UM, UP
Anti-Catholic.

820 ———— Michael Rudolph. "The Bravest of the Brave" . . .
Philadelphia: T. B. Peterson & Brothers, 306 Chestnut Street
[cop. 1870]. 481 p.   AAS, CU, H, UP
Napoleonic era.

821 ———— The Mysterious Guest . . . Philadelphia: T. B. Peterson & Brothers, 306 Chestnut Street [cop. 1873]. 406 p.   UP

822 [————] The Mysterious Marriage: A True Romance of
New York Life . . . Philadelphia: T. B. Peterson and Brothers,
306 Chestnut Street [cop. 1858]. 111 p., illus. Printed in
double cols.   Y
Roorbach 1855-1858 lists Rudd & Carleton, New York, as publishers.

823 ———— A New Way to Win a Fortune . . . Philadelphia:
T. B. Peterson & Brothers, 306 Chestnut Street [cop. 1875].
512 p.   AAS, LC, NYP, UVB

824 ———— The Planter's Daughter: A Tale of Louisiana . . .
New York: W. P. Fetridge & Company, 1857. 416 p.
        AAS, CU, HEH, N, NYP, UM, UP, Y

825 ———— The Separation. The Divorce. And the Coquette's
Punishment . . . Cincinnati: J. A. & U. P. James, 1851. 122 p.
Printed in double cols.   AAS, HEH, UP

826 ———— Who Shall Be Victor? A Sequel to "The Cancelled
Will" . . . Philadelphia: T. B. Peterson & Brothers, 306 Chestnut Street [cop. 1872]. 364 p.   AAS, H, HEH, NYP, Y

827 ———— Why Did He Marry Her . . . Philadelphia: T. B.
Peterson & Brothers, 306 Chestnut Street [cop. 1870]. 392 p.
        AAS, H

DURIVAGE, FRANCIS ALEXANDER. The Friend of the Family. *In*
H. P. Cheever, The Rival Brothers [*ca.* 1852], No. 495.

———— An Italian Duel. *In* H. P. Cheever, The Rival
Brothers [*ca.* 1852], No. 495.

828 ———— Life Scenes, Sketched in Light and Shadow from the World around Us . . . Boston: Benjamin B. Mussey and Company, 1853. 408 p., illus.   AAS, CU, H, LC, N, UC, UVB, Y
Also issued with imprint: Boston: Sanborn, Carter, Bazin and Co., 1853.
UM

829 ———— The Three Brides. Love in a Cottage, and Other Tales . . . Boston: Sanborn, Carter & Bazin, 1856. 408 p.
AAS, BP, H, LC, UC, UP, UVB
Contents: The Goldsmith's Daughter—Philetus Potts—The Gondolier—The Surrender of Cornwallis—The Three Brides—California Speculation—The French Guardsman—Personal Satisfaction—The Castle on the Rhine—Love in a Cottage—The Career of an Artist—Souvenirs of a Retired Oysterman in Ill Health—The New Year's Stockings—The Obliging Young Man—Eulalie Lasalle—The Old City Pump—The Two Portraits—Uncle Obed—The Casket of Jewels—Acting Charades—The Green Chamber—He Wasn't a Horse Jockey—Funeral Shadows—The Late Elias Muggs—The Soldier's Wife—A Kiss on Demand—The Rifle Shot—The Water Cure—The Cossack—Married for Money—The Emigrant Ship—The Last of the Stage Coaches—The Sexton of St. Hubert's—Jack Withers—The Silver Hammer—The Christ Church Chimes—The Polish Slave—Obeying Orders—The Deacon's Horse—The Contrabandista—The Stage-Struck Gentleman—The Diamond Star—The Game of Chance—The Soldier's Son—Taking Charge of a Lady—The New Year's Bells—The Old Year and the New.

830 DUTCHER, GEORGE M. Disenthralled: A Story of My Life . . . Hartford, Conn.: Columbian Book Company, 1872. 276 p., illus.   BP, H, LC, NYH
Temperance fiction.

E., B. E., *pseud. See* Brown, Emma Elizabeth

EAMES, MRS. E. J. Wine Occasionally, Evelyn. *In* A. Cary, The Adopted Daughter (1859), No. 466.

EARLIE, M. A. *See* Fleming, Mrs. May Agnes (Early)

831 EASTMAN, MRS. MARY (HENDERSON). Aunt Phillis's Cabin; or, Southern Life as It Is . . . Philadelphia: Lippincott, Grambo & Co., 1852. 280 p., illus.
AAS, BP, BU, CU, H, HEH, LC, LCP, N, NYH, NYP, UC, UM, UP, UV, Y
Proslavery.

832 ———— Fashionable Life . . . Philadelphia: J. B. Lippincott and Co., 1856. 394 p.   BP, LC, NYP, Y
Laid in New York City.

833 EASTMAN, P. O. The Young Captive Prince: A Tale of Allegory and Fact . . . Sandusky, Ohio: Register steam printing establishment, 1870. 60 p. BU, LC

834 EDGAR, MARY C. Father Drummond and His Orphans; or, The Children of Mary . . . Philadelphia: H. & C. McGrath, 1854. 178 p. LC
Roorbach 1820-1852 dates 1851.

835 EDGEVILLE, EDWARD. Castine . . . Raleigh: Wm. B. Smith & Co., 1865. 32 p. BA, BP, CU, H, HEH, LC, N, NYH, UVB, Y
Virginia, 1862-1865.

836 EDITH; OR, THE QUAKER'S DAUGHTER. A Tale of Puritan Times. By One of Her Descendants. New York: Mason Brothers, 1856. 407 p. BP, CU, H, HEH, LC, UC, UM, UP, Y
Laid in Boston.

837 EDWARDS, CHARLES R. A Story of Niagara. To Which Are Appended Reminiscences of a Custom House Officer . . . Buffalo: Breed, Lent & Co., 1870. 335 p.
AAS, CU, HEH, LC, NYH, NYP, UM

838 EDWARDS, HENRY. Annie: A Story of New York Life . . . New York: Manhattan Publishing Company [n.d.]. Cover title, 108 p. Printed in double cols. BU

839 ———— The Belle of Central Park: A Story of New York Life . . . New York: Advance Publishing Company [n.d.]. 100 p. Printed in double cols. NYH

840 ———— The Poor of New York . . . From the Play of "The Poor of New York" . . . New York: Hilton & Co., 1865. 96 [i.e., 46] p., illus. Printed in double cols. LC, NYH
Pages 38-46 misnumbered 88-96.
LC copy issued with E. Z. C. Judson, *Netta Bride* [cop. 1864].

EFFINGHAM, C., *Esq.*, *pseud.* *See* Cooke, John Esten

841 EGGLESTON, EDWARD. The Circuit Rider: A Tale of the Heroic Age . . . New York: J. B. Ford & Company, 1874. 332 p., illus. AAS, BU, CU, H, HEH, LC, LCP, N, NYP, UC, UM, UVB, Y
First state without word "Illustrated" on title page.

842 ———— The End of the World: A Love Story . . . New York: Orange Judd and Company, 245 Broadway [cop. 1872]. 299 p., illus.

       AAS, BA, BP, BU, H, HEH, LC, LCP, N, NYP, UM, UP, UVB, Y

Millerites in Indiana.

843 ———— The Hoosier School-Master: A Novel . . . New York: Orange Judd and Company, 245 Broadway [cop. 1871]. 226 p., illus.

       AAS, AP, BU, H, HEH, LC, LCP, N, NYP, UC, UP, UVB, Y

First state, p. 71, l. 3 reads "was out" instead of "is out"; and "(tinted)" appears after several plate titles in list of illus.

844 ———— The Mystery of Metropolisville . . . New York: Orange Judd and Company, 245 Broadway [cop. 1873]. 320 p., illus.

       AAS, BA, BU, CU, H, HEH, LC, LCP, N, NYP, UC, UM, UP, UVB, Y

Laid in Minnesota.

845 EGGLESTON, GEORGE CARY. A Man of Honor . . . New York: Orange Judd Company, 245 Broadway [cop. 1873]. 222 p., illus.   AAS, BU, CU, H, HEH, LC, LCP, N, NYP, UC, UM, UP, UVB, Y

Tidewater, Va.

846 ELDER, WILLIAM. The Enchanted Beauty, and Other Tales, Essays, and Sketches . . . New York: J. C. Derby. Boston: Phillips, Sampson & Son. Cincinnati: H. W. Derby, 1855. 406 p.   AAS, CU, H, LC, LCP, NYP, Y

847 ———— Periscopics; or, Current Subjects Extemporaneously Treated . . . New York: J. C. Derby. Boston: Phillips, Sampson & Co. Cincinnati: H. W. Derby, 1854. 408 p.

       AAS, BP, H, HEH, LCP, N, NYH, NYP, UC, UP, Y

ELDERKIN, JOHN, *jt. ed.* *See* Lotos Leaves (1875), No. 1588.

ELDRIDGE, ABBY. *See* Thomas, Mrs. Abby (Eldridge)

848 ELEMJAY, LOUISE, *pseud.?* Censoria Lictoria; or, What I Think of You. From the Notes and Minutes of Miss Betsey Trotwood's Official Tour . . . New York: John F. Trow, printer, 1855. 84 p.   LC

849 ———— Censoria Lictoria of Facts and Folks, from the Notes and Minutes of Miss Betsey Trotwood's Official Tour under the Frank Pierce Dynasty . . . Third Edition. Revised and Enlarged. New York: John F. Trow, printer, 1858. 162 p.
BP

Inserted between pages 6 and 7 are unnumbered pages of "Notices." With this was issued her *Rising Young Men* (1858).

NYH has a second issue of this ed. dated 1859, which collates 161, [2] p. With this was issued *Rising Young Men* (1859).

850 ———— ———— Eighth Edition. Revised and Enlarged. New York: John F. Trow, printer, 1859. 179 p. LC

With this was issued *Rising Young Men*, 4th ed. (1859).

It has not been determined whether textual changes were made in the eds. not listed.

851 ———— Rising Young Men, and Other Tales . . . New York: John F. Trow, printer, 1858. 208 p. BP, H

Contains: Our Experience—Rising Young Men—Trial of a Flirt—Church Brokers in the New Jerusalem.

Poem at end signed, "L. L. M. J." Pages 201-208, "Notices of the Work." Issued with her *Censoria Lictoria.*

NYH copy dated 1859.

852 ELIZABETH MASTERS, the Doubly Affianced: Being the Life of a Southern Belle; or, The Terrible Consequences of Being Betrothed to Two Lovers at Once. Philadelphia: Barclay & Co., 1859. 39 p., illus. AAS, LCP

AAS second copy without date on title page, a variant cover title, and differences in the illustrations.

853 ELLA CAMERON; or, The Maid, Wife, & Widow of a Day. An Extraordinary Revelation . . . of High Life in Washington, and Its Connection with the City of New York, at the Time of the Plotting of the Great Southern Rebellion. By an Ex-Member of Congress. Philadelphia: Barclay & Co., 1861. 42 p., illus.
UM, Y

854 ELLEN MAYNARD; or, The Death Wail of the Hawkshawes. A Story of Real Life and True Love. New York: F. A. Brady (Successor to H. Long & Bro.), 24 Ann Street [186-?]. 108 p. Printed in double cols. NYP

ELLET, MRS. ELIZABETH FRIES (LUMMIS). A Country Recollection; or, The Reformed Inebriate. *In* A. Cary, The Adopted Daughter (1859), No. 466.

855 ——— Love in a Maze; or, The Debutante's Disenchantment ... New York: Beadle and Adams [cop. 1865]. 96 p.   UM

At head of cover title: "Cheap Edition of Popular Authors."

856 ——— Nouvellettes of the Musicians ... New York: Cornish, Lamport & Co. St. Louis: McCartney & Lamport [cop. 1851]. 353 p., illus.   H, LCP, NYP, Y

Contents: Handel—Tartini—Haydn—Friedemann Bach—Sebastian Bach—The Old Musician—Mozart—The Artist's Lesson—Gluck in Paris—Beethoven—The Mission of Genius—Palestrina—Three Leaves from the Diary of a Traveller—The Young Tragedian—Francis Liszt—Tamburini—Bellini—Love versus Taste.

The first 13 stories were reissued as a gift book entitled: *The Philopoena: A Gift for All Seasons*. New York: Leavitt & Allen, No. 379 Broadway [185-?]. 260 p., illus.   H, LC

857 ——— Watching Spirits ... New York: Charles Scribner, 1851. 182 p., illus.

University of Illinois Library copy.

858 [ELLIOT, SAMUEL HAYES.] Dreams and Realities in the Life of a Pastor and Teacher ... New York: J. C. Derby. Boston: Phillips, Sampson & Co. Cincinnati: H. W. Derby, 1856. 439 p.   AAS, BP, LC, Y

Also published as: *Lights and Shadows of a Pastor's Life. By S. H. Elliott* [sic]. New York: Derby & Jackson; H. W. Derby & Company, Cincinnati, 1857.   NYP, Y

859 [———] New England's Chattels; or, Life in the Northern Poor-House ... New York: H. Dayton, 1858. 484 p., illus.
BP, CU, H, LC, NYH, UP, Y

Also issued with imprint: New York: H. Dayton. Indianapolis, Ind.: Dayton & Asher, 1858.   NYP

Also published as: *A Look at Home; or, Life in the Poor-House of New England ... By S. H. Elliot ... New and Rev. Ed.* New York: H. Dexter & Company. New Haven, Conn.: S. H. Elliot, 1860.   AAS, BU, NYP

860 [———] The Parish-Side. By the Author of Some Other Books, and Clerk of the Parish of Edgefield ... New York: Mason Brothers, 1854. 258 p., illus.
AAS, BP, CU, HEH, LC, N, NYP, UC, Y

Life in a small New England parish.

861 [ELLIOTT, CHARLES WYLLYS.] Wind and Whirlwind: A Novel. By Mr. Thom. White [pseud.]. New York: G. P. Putnam & Son, 1868. 307 p.   AAS, HEH, LC, NYP, UP

Laid in New York City.

862 ELLSWORTH, MRS. MARY WOLCOTT (JANVRIN). Peace; or, The Stolen Will. An American Novel. By Mary W. Janvrin . . . Boston: James French and Company. Galesburg, Ill.: Hastings and French, 1857. 407 p. AAS, H, HEH, NYP, Y

863 [————] Smith's Saloon; or, The Grays and the Grants. By Mrs. L. L. Worth [pseud.]. New York: Warren and Wyman, 13 Bible House [cop. 1871]. 299 p., illus. Y
  Also issued with imprint: New York: Broughton and Wyman [cop. 1871].
  NYP

———— Who Shall Separate Us? *In* Short Stories, 2d ser. (1869), No. 2211.

———— [*See also*] Cutter, Louise J. Cypress Leaves . . . With a Biography, by Mary W. Janvrin (1856), No. 683.

864 [ELLSWORTH, OLIVER.] A Single Gentleman. By Timothy Thistle [pseud.] . . . Boston: Oliver Ellsworth, 1867. 182 p., illus. AAS, BP, CU, H, HEH, LC, N, UC, Y

EMBURY, MRS. EMMA CATHERINE (MANLEY). The Lover's [sic]; or, The Double Error. *In* Household Narratives (1854), No. 1278.
This is entitled "The Lover's Appeal," in the 1858 reissue.

865 [EMERSON, NANNETTE SNOW.] The History of Dungeon Rock. Completed Sept. 17, 1856. By Enesee [pseud.]. Boston: Bela Marsh, 14 Bromfield St. [cop. 1856]. 75 p. AAS, BA, CU, H, Y
A pirate story.

866 EMERY, MISS E. B. Queens . . . Boston: Estes & Lauriat, 143 Washington Street [cop. 1872]. 349 p. AAS, BP, HEH, LC
Of religious interest.

867 EMERY, SARAH ANNA. Three Generations . . . Boston: Lee & Shepard. New York: Lee, Shepard and Dillingham, 1872. 244 p., illus. Printed in double cols.
At the turn of the 19th century. AAS, BA, BP, CU, H, HEH, LC, LCP, NYP

868 EMMA BARTLETT; or, Prejudice and Fanaticism. By an American Lady. Cincinnati: Moore, Wilstach, Keys & Overend, 1856. 502 p. HEH, NYH, UC, UM
Opposed to abolitionists and the Know-Nothing Party.

869 EMMA PARKER; or, Scenes in the Homes of the City Poor . . .
New York: Anson D. F. Randolph & Co., No. 770 Broadway
[cop. 1871]. 408 p. HEH
The tenements of New York City.

ENESEE, *pseud*. *See* Emerson, Nannette Snow

870 ENGLISH, THOMAS DUNN. Ambrose Fecit; or, The Peer and the
Printer. A Novel . . . New York: Hilton and Company, 1867.
135 p. Printed in double cols. AAS, BA, BP, NYP, UM, UVB, Y

871 ERNEST: A TRUE STORY. New York: A. D. F. Randolph, 1862.
177 p.
Information from LC card for copy withdrawn from circulation.

872 ESPERANZA: MY JOURNEY THITHER and What I Found There . . .
Cincinnati: Valentine Nicholson, 1860. 332 p. H, HEH, LC
An utopian novel advocating free love.

873 ESTELLE GRANT; or, The Lost Wife . . . New York: Garrett &
Co. [cop. 1855]. 350 p. CU, LC, UP
LC copy deposited for copyright Nov. 7, 1855.

874 ESTVAN, MATHILDE. Harry Delaware; or, An American in
Germany . . . New York: G. P. Putnam & Sons, 1872. 142 p.
Printed in double cols. HEH, LC, LCP, NYP
Life at a German spa.

875 EUGENE, MAURICE, *ed*. The Oak Shade; or, Records of a Village
Literary Association . . . Philadelphia: Willis P. Hazzard, 1855.
214 p. AAS, LC
Contents: Hans Dundermann, the Dutch Miser—The Wisdom of Preserv-
ing Moderation in Our Wishes—The Sick Mother—The Excellencies of
Lying—The Alchemist; or, The Magic Funnel—The Beauty of a Well-
Cultivated Heart—The Dream of a Loafer.

EVANS, AUGUSTA JANE. *See* Wilson, Mrs. Augusta Jane (Evans)

876 EVANS, WARREN FELT. The Happy Islands; or, Paradise Restored
. . . Boston: H. V. Degen & Son, 1860. 334 p. AAS
On the salvation of the soul.

EVELYN, W. MAUD. The Young Priest. *In* Short Stories, 2d ser.
(1869), No. 2211.

877 THE EVENTFUL LIVES of Helen and Charlotte Lenoxa, the Twin Sisters of Philadelphia ... The Former of Whom Was Hung at Knoxville, Tennessee, August 20th, 1852, for the Double Murder of Captain Gerald Vernon, and His Young Wife ... Memphis, Richmond, Baltimore and Philadelphia: A. R. Orton, 1853. 41 p., illus. NYP

F., M. A. *See* Fisher, Mary Ann

F., M. V. *See* Victor, Mrs. Metta Victoria (Fuller)

F., P. W. *See* Farmer, Mrs. P. W.

878 FABENS, JOSEPH WARREN. The Camel Hunt: A Narrative of Personal Adventure . . . Boston and Cambridge: James Munroe and Company, 1851. 219 p. AAS, LC, LCP, UC, UP, Y
Sequel: *A Story of Life.*
The camels are captured in Africa and landed in Panama.

879 [————] In the Tropics. By a Settler in Santo Domingo. With an Introductory Notice by Richard B. Kimball ... New York: Carleton, 1863. 306 p. BP, CU, H, LC, LCP, N, NYH, UC, Y
Also published as: *Life in Santo Domingo. By a Settler.* New York: G. W. Carleton & Co. London: Bentley & Son., 1873. BA, BP, LCP, NYP, UV

880 [————] The Prince of Kashna: A West Indian Story. By the Author of "In the Tropics." With an Editorial Introduction by Richard B. Kimball ... New York: Carleton, 1866. 450 p.
AAS, BP, CU, H, HEH, LC, LCP, NYP, UC, Y

881 ———— A Story of Life on the Isthmus . . . New York: George P. Putnam & Co., 1853. 215 p.
AAS, AP, BP, BU, CU, H, HEH, LC, N, NYH, NYP, UC, UP, Y
Sequel to *The Camel Hunt.*

FABRE, ALBERT. Golden Dreams. *In* Short Stories, 2d ser. (1869), No. 2211.

882 THE FACTORY GIRL. By a Friend. Providence: Knowles, Anthony & Co., printers, 1854. 78 p. AAS, BU, HEH
An anonymously rewritten version of Sarah Savage's *Factory Girl* (1814). Wright (1774-1850), No. 2308.

FADETTE, *pseud.* *See* Reeves, Marion Calhoun Legaré

FAIRFIELD, CAROLINE E. *See* Corbin, Mrs. Caroline Elizabeth (Fairfield)

FAIRFIELD, GENEVIEVE GENEVRA. The Vice President's Daughter. *In* G. F. Vingut, Irene (1853), No. 2595.

————— The Wife of Two Husbands. *In* G. F. Vingut, Irene (1853), No. 2595.

FALCONBRIDGE, *pseud.* *See* Kelly, Jonathan Falconbridge

883 FALCONER, WILLIAM. Bloom and Brier; or, As I Saw It, Long Ago. A Southern Romance . . . Philadelphia: Claxton, Remsen & Haffelfinger. Montgomery, Ala.: Joel White, 1870. 416 p.
AAS, H, HEH, LC, LCP, UM

884 FALKNER, WILLIAM C. The Spanish Heroine: A Tale of War and Love . . . Scenes Laid in Mexico. Cincinnati: I. Hart & Co., 1851. 136 p. LC
Also published as: *The Spanish Heroine: A Tale of Cuban Patriotism.* Cincinnati: H. B. Pearson, No. 17 East Fourth Street [185-?]. LC, Y

885 THE FALL OF FORT SUMTER; or, Love and War in 1860-61. "By the Private Secretary to —————, etc." New York: Frederic A. Brady, No. 22 Ann Street [cop. 1867]. 167 p., illus. Printed in double cols. AAS, BP, BU, H, HEH, LC, N, NYH, NYP
At head of cover title: "A Humorous Story."
Depicts Washington politics at the end of Buchanan's term.

FARMAN, ELLA. *See* Pratt, Mrs. Ella (Farman)

886 [FARMER, MRS. P. W.] Louisa Williams; or, The Orphan Bound-Girl. A Tale of the Queen City. Founded on Facts. By P. W. F. Cincinnati: printed for the author at the office of the "Cincinnatus," 1859. 112 p. LC

887 FARNHAM, MRS. ELIZA WOODSON (BURHANS). The Ideal Attained: Being the Story of Two Steadfast Souls, and How They Won Their Happiness and Lost It Not . . . New York: C. M. Plumb & Co., 1865. 510 p. AAS, BP, H, LC, LCP, NYP
Social life in San Francisco.

888 ———— My Early Days . . . New York: Thatcher & Hutchinson, 1859. 425 p. AAS

Also published as: *Eliza Woodson; or, The Early Days of One of the World's Workers. A Story of American Life.* New York: A. J. Davis & Co., 1864. AAS, BP, BU, CU, H, HEH, LC, NYP, UC, UM, UP, Y

FARQUHARSON, MARTHA, *pseud. See* Finley, Martha

FARREN, MRS., *attrib. au. See* Varnham, Mrs. R. G.

889 FARRENC, EDMUND. Carlotina and the Sanfedesti; or, A Night with the Jesuits at Rome . . . New York: John S. Taylor, 1853. 432 p. AAS, BU, HEH, LC, NYP, UP, Y
Anti-Catholic.

890 THE FATAL SECRET; or, Crime and Retribution! Facts Most Singular and Fearful . . . New York: A. F. Joy. Philadelphia: E. E. Barclay, 1852. 36 p., illus. LC

891 FAWCETT, EDGAR. Purple and Fine Linen: A Novel . . . New York: G. W. Carleton & Co. London: S. Low, Son & Co., 1873. 483 p. AAS, BP, BU, CU, H, HEH, LC, LCP, N, NYP, UC, UM, Y
New York City society.

892 FAY, ALICE. Lily Bell; or, The Lost Child . . . Boston: James French and Company, 1857. 343 p. AAS, BU, HEH
Laid in New York City and Boston.

893 FEARFUL ADVENTURES IN PENNSYLVANIA'S WILDS; or, The Startling Narrative of Adelaide Lane . . . Philadelphia: Barclay & Co. [cop. 1857]. 35 p., illus. LC, NYP

894 THE FEMALE SKEPTIC; or, Faith Triumphant . . . New York: Robert M. DeWitt, 160 & 162 Nassau Street [cop. 1859]. 449 p. AAS, H, NYP

895 THE FEMALE VOLUNTEER; or, The Life, and Wonderful Adventures of Miss Eliza Allen, a Young Lady of Eastport, Maine . . . [N. p., cop. 1851.] 68 p., illus. AAS, H, HEH, LC
Eliza fought in the Mexican War, and mined gold in California.

FERN, FANNY, *pseud. See* Parton, Mrs. Sara Payson (Willis)

896 FIELD, MRS. ADA M. Altha; or, Shells from the Strand . . . Boston: James French and Company, 1856. 300 p.
Refers to the California mines. BP, BU, H, NYP, Y

FIELD, J. W. A Tale of the Destroyer. *In* A. Cary, The Adopted Daughter (1859), No. 466.

897 FIELD, KATE. Planchette's Diary ... New York: J. S. Redfield, 1868. 95 p. AAS, BP, H, HEH, LC, LCP, NYH, NYP
On spiritualism.

898 FIELD, MARGARET. Bertha Percy; or, L'Espérance . . . New York: D. Appleton and Company, 1860. 567 p.
AAS, AP, H, HEH, LCP, NYP

———— Not Pretty, but Precious. *In* Not Pretty, but Precious (1872), No. 1804.

FIELD, MAUNSELL BRADHURST, *jt. au.* *See* James, G. P. R. Adrian; or, The Clouds of the Mind (1852), No. 1334.

899 [FIELDS, MRS. ANNIE (ADAMS).] Asphodel . . . Boston: Ticknor and Fields, 1866. 224 p. AAS, BA, BP, H, HEH, LC, NYP, Y
A tragic love story in the genteel manner.

900 [FIELDS, JAMES THOMAS] *ed.* Good Company for Every Day in the Year . . . Boston: Ticknor and Fields, 1866. 326 p., illus.
AAS, BP, H, HEH, LC, NYP, Y
Contains: The Mormon's Wife, by Rose Terry—Little Pansie, a Fragment, by Nathaniel Hawthorne.

FILIA, *pseud.* *See* Dorsey, Mrs. Sarah Anne (Ellis)

901 [FINLEY, MARTHA.] Casella; or, The Children of the Valleys. By Martha Farquharson [pseud.] ... Philadelphia: J. B. Lippincott & Co., 1869. 389 p. AAS, LC, LCP, Y
Laid in Italy, mid-17th century; anti-Catholic.

902 [————] Lilian; or, Did She Do Right? By Martha Farquharson [pseud.] ... Philadelphia: William B. Evans & Co., 740 Sansom Street [*ca.* 1873]. 104 p., front. Printed in double cols. AAS, LC
Also published as: *Did She Do Right?* Philadelphia: S. T. Souder [cop. 1875]. AAS, NYP
Laid in the Midwest.

903 ———— Wanted—A Pedigree . . . Philadelphia: William B. Evans & Co., No. 740 Sansom Street [cop. 1871]. 528 p., front.
LC, LCP, NYP

904 [FISHER, MARY ANN.] A Spinster's Story. By M. A. F. ... New York: Carleton, 1866. 399 p.   AAS, BP, LC, LCP, NYP, Y

905 FITCH, ANNA M. Bound Down; or, Life and Its Possibilities ... Philadelphia: J. B. Lippincott & Co., 1870. 338 p.
Laid in San Francisco in the 1850's.   AAS, BP, HEH, NYP, UVB, Y

FITTS, JAMES FRANKLIN. Myra's Mirror. *In* Rougegorge (1870), No. 2130.

FITZGERALD, RITER. The Shadow of Fate. *In* Rougegorge (1870), No. 2130.

906 THE FIVE FIENDS; or, The Bender Hotel Horror in Kansas ... Philadelphia: Old Franklin Publishing House, cop. 1874. 60, [1] p., illus.
Title listed in R. F. Adams, *Six-Guns & Saddle Leather* (Norman, Okla., 1954), No. 96.

907 FLAGG, WILLIAM JOSEPH. A Good Investment: A Story of the Upper Ohio ... New York: Harper & Brothers, 1872. 116 p., illus. Printed in double cols.
    AAS, BA, BP, H, HEH, LC, LCP, N, NYP

908 [FLANDERS, MRS. G. M.] The Ebony Idol ... New York: D. Appleton & Company, 1860. 283 p., illus.
    AAS, AP, BP, BU, CU, H, HEH, LC, LCP, N, NYH, NYP, UC, UM, UP, UVB, Y
Satire on an abolitionist organization.

909 FLEMING, MRS. MAY AGNES (EARLY). The Dark Secret ... New York: the Federal Book Company [cop. 1875]. 361, 22 p.
Contains: Poor and Proud, by Marion Harland, 22 p. at end.
Information from National Union Cat. for copy withdrawn from circulation.

910 [————] Erminie; or, The Gipsy's Vow. A Tale of Love and Vengeance. By Cousin May Carleton [pseud.]. New York: F. A. Brady, 24 Ann Street [cop. 1862]. 158 p., illus. Printed in double cols.   HEH, UC
Laid in London and "Judestown," Maryland.

911 ———— Eulalie; or, The Wife's Tragedy. By Miss M. A. Earlie ... New York: Frederic A. Brady, No. 22 Ann Street [cop. 1866]. 119 p., illus. Printed in double cols.   AAS, BP, HEH, NYP
Machinations and blackmail.

912 —————— Guy Earlscourt's Wife: A Novel . . . New York: G. W. Carleton & Co. London: S. Low, Son & Co., 1873. 438 p. HEH, LCP, UV

913 —————— A Mad Marriage: A Novel . . . New York: G. W. Carleton & Co. London: S. Low, Son & Co., 1875. 459 p.
Laid in London and Quebec. H, HEH, LC, LCP, NYP

914 [—————] La Masque; or, The Midnight Queen. A Tale of Illusion, Delusion, and Mystery. By Cousin May Carleton [pseud.]. New York: F. A. Brady, 1863. 108 p., illus.
Announced as "recently published" in *Amer. Pub. Cir.*, I (Aug. 1, 1863), 281.

915 —————— Nathalie Marsh; or, Redmon's Heiress. By Miss M. A. Earlie. New York: F. A. Brady, 1867. 231 p.
Announced as "recently published" in *Amer. Lit. Gaz.*, X (Nov. 1, 1867), 16.

916 —————— Norine's Revenge, and Sir Noel's Heir . . . New York: G. W. Carleton & Co. London: S. Low, Son & Co., 1875. 402 p. AAS, LCP, NYP
Also contains: A Dark Conspiracy—For Better for Worse.

917 [—————] Silver Star; or, The Mystery of Fontelle Hall. A Tale of New Jersey in the Olden Time. By Cousin May Carleton [pseud.]. New York: Frederic A. Brady, No. 24 Ann Street [cop. 1861]. 142 p., illus. Printed in double cols.
NYP, UC

918 [—————] Sybil Campbell; or, The Queen of the Isle. A Tale. By Cousin May Carleton [pseud.]. New York: F. A. Brady [1863]. 151 p.
Copy noted in BM.
Later published as Beadle's "New 25 Cent Novels," No. 1, [1869]. BP, HEH, NYP, UC

919 —————— A Terrible Secret: A Novel . . . New York: G. W. Carleton & Co. London: S. Low, Son & Co., 1874. 410 p.
Laid in England. AAS, HEH, LCP, NYP

920 [—————] Victoria; or, The Heiress of Castle Cliffe. By Cousin May Carleton [pseud.]. New York: Frederic A. Brady, 24 Ann Street [cop. 1862]. 124 p., illus. Printed in double cols.
AAS

921 ———— A Wonderful Woman: A Novel . . . New York: G. W. Carleton & Co. London: S. Low, Son & Co., 1873. 544 p.   H, HEH, NYP
Laid in England.

922 [FLETCHER, MISS A.] Ballyshan Castle: A Tale Founded on Fact. By Sheelah [pseud.] . . . New York: N. Tibbals, 1857. 355 p., illus.   LC
Also published as: *The Mother's Request; or, Ballyshan Castle.* New York: N. Tibbals, 1866.   AAS, CU

923 FLETCHER, MIRIAM. The Methodist; or, Incidents and Characters from Life in the Baltimore Conference . . . With an Introduction by W. P. Strickland, D.D. . . . New York: Derby & Jackson, 1859. 2 vols. (384, 360 p.)
                         AAS, BP, H, LC, LCP, N, NYH, NYP, Y

924 FLORENCE ERWIN'S THREE HOMES: A Tale of North and South. Boston: Crosby and Nichols, 1862. 327 p., front.
The Southerner frees her slaves.   AAS, BP, CU, HEH, Y

925 FLOYD, MARY FAITH. The Nereid . . . Macon, Georgia: J. W. Burke & Company, 1871. 102 p. Printed in double cols.   LC
An ante bellum tale.

926 FOLIO, FRED, *pseud.* Lucy Boston; or, Woman's Rights and Spiritualism, Illustrating the Follies and Delusions of the Nineteenth Century. By Fred Folio [pseud.] . . . Auburn and Rochester: Alden and Beardsley. New York: J. C. Derby, 1855. 406 p., illus.   CU, HEH, LC, N, NYH, UC, UM, UP
Also issued with imprint: Boston: Shepard, Clark & Co. Auburn and Rochester: Alden and Beardsley, 1855.   AAS, H
At head of title: "A Book for the Times."

927 FORD, E. L. Madelaine Darth . . . Chicago: Western News Company, 1867. Cover title, 71 p.   LC
Laid in Wisconsin.

928 FORD, MRS. SALLIE (ROCHESTER). Evangel Wiseman; or, The Mother's Question . . . St. Louis: Barns & Beynon, 1874. 507 p.   AAS, LC, Y
On infant baptism.

929 ———— Grace Truman; or, Love and Principle . . . New York: Sheldon, Blakeman & Co. Boston: Gould & Lincoln. Chicago: S. C. Griggs & Co., 1857. 499 p., front.
Religious controversy; pro-Baptist. AAS, BU, H, LC, N, NYP, UC, UM, Y

930 ———— Mary Bunyan, the Dreamer's Blind Daughter: A Tale of Religious Persecution . . . New York: Sheldon & Company. Boston: Gould & Lincoln, 1860. 488 p., illus.
AAS, BP, BU, H, LC, NYH, NYP, UC, Y
At the time of John Bunyan; England.

931 ———— Raids and Romance of Morgan and His Men . . . Mobile: S. H. Goetzel & Co., 1863. 319 p.
Copy noted in BM.

932 ———— ———— 2d ed. Mobile: S. H. Goetzel, 1864. 332 p.
BA, BP, H, HEH, NYH, NYP, UP, UVB, Y
Also issued with imprint: New York: Charles B. Richardson, 1864. 417 p., front. BP, LC, LCP, N, NYH, NYP, UM, UV

933 THE FORSAKEN DAUGHTER . . . Philadelphia: T. B. Peterson & Brothers, 306 Chestnut Street [cop. 1865]. 461 p. AAS
On spine: "Compn to Linda."

934 FORT, G. We Four Villagers: A Tale of Domestic Life in Pennsylvania . . . Philadelphia: J. S. McCalla, printer, 1861. 339 p.
AAS, LC, UP

935 FOSDICK, WILLIAM WHITEMAN. Malmiztic the Toltec and the Cavaliers of the Cross . . . Cincinnati: Wm. H. Moore & D. Anderson, 1851. 356 p.
AAS, BP, H, LC, LCP, N, NYH, NYP, UC, UM

936 FOSTER, GEORGE G. Fifteen Minutes around New York . . . New York: DeWitt & Davenport, 160 & 162 Nassau Street [cop. 1854]. 111 p. CU, H, LC, NYP, UP

937 ———— New York Naked . . . New York: DeWitt and Davenport, 160 & 162 Nassau Street [185-?]. 168 p.
BP, LC, NYH, NYP, UP, Y
At head of cover title: "G. G. Foster's Last & Best Local Work."

938 THE "FOURTH," 1854. Log of the Smoothing Iron. New York: W. H. Tinson, printer, No. 24 Beckman Street [1854]. 20 p.
AAS, NYP
Humorous log of a "voyage up North River shore of New York city."

Fox, FRANKLIN. A Trip to Texas. *In* O. P. Baldwin, *comp.*, Southern and South-Western Sketches [1855?], No. 200.

FOXTON, E., *pseud*. *See* Palfrey, Sara Hammond

939 FRAME, ELIZABETH. The Twilight of Faith . . . Boston: H. D. Brown & Co., 1873. 128 p.   AAS, H

940 FRANCES, MARGARET. Rose Carleton's Reward . . . Cincinnati: Bosworth, Chase & Hall, 1871. 283 p., illus.
Information from LC card for copy withdrawn from circulation.

941 [FRANCIS, MARY O.] Clifford and the Actress; or, The Reigning Favorite. By Margaret Blount [pseud.]. Philadelphia: Peterson [187-?].
Title listed in Amer. Cat. 1876.
Mr. Albert Johannsen was kind enough to supply new information he had found which led to the correction of the name "Mary O'Francis" as it appears in his *The House of Beadle and Adams* (Norman, Okla., [1950]), to Mary O. Francis. This was confirmed by Messrs. Lewis M. Stark and Edwin Carpenter, of the New York Public Library.

942 [———] A Dangerous Woman: A Study from Life. By Margaret Blount [pseud.]. New York: Frederic A. Brady, 24 Ann Street [186-?]. 69 p., illus. Printed in double cols.   AAS
Announced as "recently published" in *Amer. Lit. Gaz.*, II (Feb. 15, 1864), 280. Copyright notice dated 1858.

943 [———] The Downe Reserve; or, The Mystery at Wishing Well. By Margaret Blount [pseud.]. New York: F. A. Brady, 1864. 117 p., illus.
Announced as "recently published" in *Amer. Lit. Gaz.*, III (Sept. 1, 1864), 258.

944 [———] Hallow-Ash Hall: A Story of a Haunted House. By Margaret Blount [pseud.] New York: F. A. Brady, 1864. 80 p., illus.
Announced as "recently published" in *Amer. Lit. Gaz.*, III (Sept. 1, 1864), 258.

945 [———] Kitty Atherton; or, A Broken Life. By Margaret Blount [pseud.]. New York: Frederic A. Brady, 24 Ann Street [1863]. 64 p., illus. Printed in double cols.   NYP

946 [————] The Orphan of Charnley. By Margaret Blount [pseud.]. New York: F. A. Brady, 1864. 80 p.
Announced as "recently published" in *Amer. Lit. Gaz.*, III (July 15, 1864), 178. Copy noted in BM.

947 [FRANCIS, SAMUEL WARD.] The Autobiography of a Latin Reader. By Samuel Syntax, Esq. [pseud.]. New York: Anson D. F. Randolph, 1859. 50 p.   BP, BU, H, LC, NYH, NYP, Y
Information about authorship supplied by NYH.

948 ———— A Christmas Story . . . New York: G. H. Mathews, 1867. Cover title, 16 p.   LC, NYP
Caption title: "Man in His Element; or, A New Way to Keep House."

949 [————] Inside Out: A Curious Book. By a Singular Man . . . New York: Miller, Mathews & Glasback, 1862. 364 p.
AAS, H, LC, NYP, UM, UP, Y

950 [————] Life and Death: A Novel. By Your Humble Servant. New York: Carleton. London: S. Low & Co., 1871. 264 p.
Laid in New York City.   AAS, CU, LC, LCP, NYH, NYP

951 FRANKLIN, JOSEPHINE. Rachel: A Romance . . . Boston: Thayer & Eldridge, 1860. 300 p.   AAS, BU, HEH, LC
A schoolteacher's experiences in New Jersey.

FRAZAER, MARY, *pseud. See* Hayden, Mrs. Sarah Marshall

952 FREDAIR, ANNA. Minor Place . . . New York: E. J. Hale & Sons, 1869. 281 p.   CU, LC
Laid in Georgia.

953 FREELANCE, RADICAL, *Esq., pseud.* The Philosophers of Foufouville. By Radical Freelance, Esq. [pseud.] . . . New York: G. W. Carleton. London: S. Low, Son & Co., 1868. 297 p.
A satire upon utopian groups.   AAS, CU, H, HEH, LCP, NYP

954 FREEMAN, MRS. THERESA J. Silver Lake; or, The Belle of Bayou Luie. A Tale of the South . . . Saint Louis: P. M. Pinckard, 1867. 344 p.   AAS, LC
Ante bellum.

955 [FRENCH, MRS. LUCY VIRGINIA (SMITH).] Kernwood; or, After Many Days. A Historical Romance, Founded on the Events of the Late War, from the Manuscript of a Confederate Spy. By L'Inconnue [pseud.]. Louisville, Ky.: published for the author, 1867. 390 p. BP, UC

956 ———— My Roses: The Romance of a June Day . . . Philadelphia: Claxton, Remsen & Haffelfinger, 1872. 278 p.

New Orleans in the 1850's. AAS, BP, CU, LC, Y

957 FRIEND, JULIA M. The Chester Family; or, The Curse of the Drunkard's Appetite . . . Boston: William White and Company; New York agents, the American News Company, 1869. 224 p., front. AAS, BU, CU, HEH, LC, Y
A temperance tale, written in a series of letters.

958 THE FRONTIERSMEN: A Narrative of 1783 . . . New York: Stringer & Townsend, 222 Broadway [cop. 1854]. 166 p.
HEH, LC
Author may be Harvey Hubbard (1821-1862), of Norwich, N.Y.
Laid in western New York.

959 FROST, MRS. JENNETT BLAKESLEE. The Gem of the Mines: A Thrilling Narrative of California Life . . . Hartford, Conn.: published by the authoress, 1866. 276 p. H, HEH, LC, NYP
Based on fact, but "most of the names are assumed."

960 FROST, JOHN. Border Wars of the West, Comprising the Frontier Wars of Pennsylvania, Virginia, Kentucky, Ohio, Indiana, Illinois, Tennessee and Wisconsin . . . Auburn: Derby & Miller. Buffalo: Derby, Orton and Mulligan. Cincinnati: Henry W. Derby, 1853. 608 p., illus. H, LC, LCP, NYP

FROST, SARAH E. A. See Shields, Mrs. Sarah Annie (Frost)

961 FROTHINGHAM, CHARLES W. The Convent's Doom: A Tale of Charlestown in 1834. Also, The Haunted Convent . . . Fifth Edition. Boston: Graves & Weston, 1854. 32 p. Printed in double cols. AAS, LC, N, NYP

962 ———— Six Hours in a Convent; or, The Stolen Nuns! A Tale of Charlestown in 1834 . . . Boston: Graves & Weston, 1855. 44 p. N
This is not his *Convent's Doom*.

963 [FROTHINGHAM, WASHINGTON.] Zoe; or, The Martel Papers. A
Manuscript of the Conciergerie . . . New York: Sheldon & Co.,
1865. 468 p., illus. AAS, CU, H, HEH, LC, N, NYP
Also published as: *Martel Papers; or, Life-Scenes in the Reign of Terror.*
2d Ed. New York, 1867.
Listed in *Catalogue of the Astor Library* (Cambridge, 1887), p. 1364.

964 FULLER, EDWIN WILEY. Sea-Gift: A Novel . . . New York:
E. J. Hale & Son, 1873. 408 p. BU, LC
Southern life prior to and during the Civil War.

965 FULLER, JANE GAY. Bending Willow: A Tale of Missionary Life
in the Northwest . . . Saint Paul: D. D. Merrill & Co. [cop.
1871]. 305 p., illus.
Information from NYP card for copy withdrawn from circulation.

966 ———— The Brownings: A Tale of the Great Rebellion . . .
New York: M. W. Dodd, 1867. 310 p., illus.
AAS, BP, BU, H, N, NYP
Also contains: Lucy Lee; or, All Things for Christ, pp. [122]-310.

967 ———— The Grahams: A Story of the Florida War . . . New
York: M. W. Dodd, 1864.
Title listed in Kelly 1861-1866.

968 FULLER, LYDIA. Mistaken; or, The Seeming and the Real . . .
Philadelphia: J. B. Lippincott & Co., 1870. 286 p.
AAS, BP, LC, LCP, UM

FULLER, METTA VICTORIA. *See* Victor, Mrs. Metta Victoria
(Fuller)

969 FULTON, CHANDOS. A Brown Stone Front: A Story of New
York and Saratoga . . . New York: Henry L. Hinton, 1873.
147 p. AAS, CU, H, NYH, NYP
At head of title: "The Puck Novels."

970 FURBER, GEORGE C. Ike McCandliss, and Other Stories; or,
Incidents in the Life of a Soldier . . . Cincinnati: U. P. James,
No. 167 Walnut Street [cop. 1852]. 96 p., illus. Printed in
double cols. CU, HEH, N, Y

G., A. J. *See* Avery, Jane G.

G., H. B. *See* Talcott, Mrs. Hannah Elizabeth (Bradbury) Goodwin

G., J., *Esq., pseud. See* Burwell, William MacCreary

971 GAGE, MRS. FRANCES DANA (BARKER). Elsie Magoon; or, The Old Still-House in the Hollow. A Tale of the Past . . . Philadelphia: J. B. Lippincott & Co., 1867. 324 p., front.

A temperance tale; Ohio.   AAS, H, HEH, NYP

972 ———— Gertie's Sacrifice; or, Glimpses at Two Lives . . . New York: National Temperance Society, 1869. 189 p., front.

Information from LC card for copy withdrawn from circulation.

973 ———— Steps Upward . . . Utica, N. Y.: Temperance Patriot office, 1870. 360 p.   BP, NYP

GALPIN, MRS. The Two Ghosts of New London Turnpike. *In* Stories and Sketches (1867), No. 2386.

974 GARANGULA, THE ONGUA-HONWA CHIEF: A Tale of Indian Life among the Mohawks and Onondagas, Two Hundred Years Ago. By a Citizen of Milwaukee. Milwaukee: Strickland & Co., 1857. 160 p.   H, N, UVB

GARDETTE, EMILE B. The Crevasse. *In* Household Narratives (1854), No. 1278.

975 [GARDINER, FREDERICK.] The Island of Life: An Allegory. By a Clergyman . . . Boston and Cambridge: James Munroe & Company, 1851. 89 p., illus.   BP, LC

976 [GARDNER, ————.] The Life and Death of Sam, in Virginia. By a Virginian . . . Richmond: published for the author. A. Morris, 1856. 308 p.   AAS, BP, BU, H, HEH, LC, NYH, NYP, Y

Post-mortem of the "Know-Nothing" campaign in Virginia.

977 GARDNER, CELIA EMMELINE. Rich Medway's Two Loves . . . New York: G. W. Carleton & Co., 1875. 463 p.

Information from LC card for copy withdrawn from circulation.

978 ———— Tested; or, Hope's Fruition. A Story of Woman's Constancy... New York: G. W. Carleton & Co., 1874. 430 p.
Information from LC card for copy withdrawn from circulation.

979 GARDNER, MRS. H. C. Extracts from the Diary of a Country Pastor . . . Cincinnati: Poe & Hitchcock. E. P. Thompson, printer, 1864. 240 p. LC

980 ———— Fault-Finding, and Madeline Hascall's Letters . . . Cincinnati: Hitchcock & Walden, 1869. 249 p.
Information from LC card for copy withdrawn from circulation.

981 ———— Glimpses of Our Lake Region in 1863, and Other Papers... New York: Nelson & Phillips. Cincinnati: Hitchcock & Walden [cop. 1874]. 420 p. AAS, LC
Also contains: Natural History—"Provoking One Another to Love and Good Works"—"A Patch on the Knee and Gloves on"—Miss Phillissa's Letters—Sympathy—The Reverend Didymus Ego, M.D.

982 ———— Mehetabel: A Story of the Revolution . . . New York: Nelson & Phillips, 1875. 372 p.
Information from LC card for copy withdrawn from circulation.

983 ———— The Power of Kindness . . . New York: Carlton & Porter, 1865. 247 p., illus.
Information from LC card for copy withdrawn from circulation.

984 ———— Rosedale: A Story of Self-Denial . . . Cincinnati: Poe & Hitchcock, 1863. 410 p. AAS, H, LC, NYH, UP

985 GAY, MRS. M. M. Gleanings from Real Life... Buffalo: C. E. Felton, printer, 1858. 291 p. LC

986 GAY, MARY ANN HARRIS. The Pastor's Story, and Other Pieces; or, Prose and Poetry . . . 6th ed. Nashville, Tenn.: published for the author, 1860. 266 p. BU
This may be a revised ed. of the following entry.

987 [————] Prose and Poetry. By a Georgia Lady. First Edition. Nashville: published for the author, 1858. 196 p.
Contains: The Pastor's Story, pp. 35-77.
Atlanta Public Library copy.

988 GAYARRÉ, CHARLES ÉTIENNE ARTHUR. Fernando de Lemos.
Truth and Fiction: A Novel ... New York: G. W. Carleton &
Co. London: S. Low, Son & Co., 1872. 486 p.

AAS, BP, CU, H, HEH, LC, LCP, NYH, UC, UVB, Y

989 ———— The School for Politics: A Dramatic Novel ... New
York: D. Appleton and Co., 1854. 158 p.

BP, BU, CU, H, LC, LCP, NYH, NYP, UC, UM, UP, Y

Political degradation in Baton Rouge.

990 GAYLER, CHARLES. Out of the Streets: A Story of New York
Life ... New York: Robert M. DeWitt, No. 13 Frankfort
Street [cop. 1869]. 360 p.   AAS, LC, NYP, UC

LC copy deposited for copyright July 9, 1869.

991 [GAZLAY, ALLEN W.] Races of Mankind; with Travels in Grub-
land. By Cephas Broadluck [pseud.]. Cincinnati: Longley
Brothers, 168½ Vine St.; U. P. James, 167 Walnut St. [cop.
1856]. 310 p., illus.   H, LC, NYP

LC copy deposited for copyright Sept. 8, 1856.

Anti-utopian novel.

992 GENERAL SHERIDAN'S SQUAW SPY, and Mrs. Clara Blynn's Captivity
among the Wild Indians of the Prairies: A Thrilling Narrative
of the Daring Exploits and Hair-Breadth Escapes of Viroqua
... Philadelphia, Pa.: the Cooperative Publishing House, cop.
1869. 1 p. l., [17]-78 p., illus.   Y

An ed. in German also issued in 1869; both eds. copyrighted by C. W.
Alexander.

Relates to Sheridan's Washita campaign.

993 GERALD O'REILLY; or, The Triumph of Principle. And Eva
O'Brien. Two Tales. Baltimore: J. Murphy & Co., 1857.

Title listed in Roorbach 1855-1858.

994 [GERARD, JAMES WATSON.] Full and True Report after the
Manner of the Abbé Rabelais, of the Suit Recently Promoted
in the Superlative Court of Gother ... New York: Wm. C.
Bryant & Co., printers, 1853. 16 p.   AAS

995 GERARD CARLTON: A Novel. By the Author of "Twice Married."
New York: the American News Company, 1866. 205 p.
Printed in double cols.   LCP

Laid in England.

996 GERRY, MRS. MARTHA FOSTER (CLOUGH). The Man of the Golden Mask: A Romance of Olden Times . . . Boston: F. Gleason, 1864. 50 p., illus.
Announced as "recently published" in *Amer. Lit. Gaz.*, II (Feb. 1, 1864), 249.

997 GERSONI, HENRY. Sketches of Jewish Life and History . . . New York: Hebrew Orphan Asylum printing establishment, 1873. 224 p.   BA, LC, NYP
Contents: Characteristic Sketches: The Singer's Revenge—Appendix: Mutual Death Insurance Co.—Metamorphose of a Lithuanian Boy: Part First, as Told by Himself; Part Second, as Gathered from Reliable Sources —Rabbi Elchanan, a Legend of Mayence—Historical Sketches: The Fall of Bethar and the Martyrs—The Converted Nobleman.

998 GERTRUDE LESLIE; or, The Queen's Vengeance. New York: Stearns & Co., 1852.
Title listed in Roorbach 1820-1852.

999 GERTRUDE MORGAN; or, Life and Adventures among the Indians of the Far West. Philadelphia: Barclay & Co., 602 Arch Street [cop. 1866]. 40 p., 1 l., illus.   HEH, LC, NYP

GIFTIE, *pseud.* The Knight of the Ringlet. *In* C. B. Porter, *ed.* The Silver Cup (1852), No. 1931.

1000 GIFTS OF GENIUS: A Miscellany of Prose and Poetry. By American Authors. New York: printed for C. A. Davenport [cop. 1859]. 264 p.
            BP, BU, CU, H, HEH, LC, N, NYH, NYP, UC, UP, Y
Contains: Out at Elbows: The Story of St. George Cleave, by John Esten Cooke—The Prince at Land's End, by Caroline Chesebro—A Story of Venice, by George William Curtis.
Written for the benefit of Miss Davenport who was blind. "To the Public" signed and dated, "W. C. Bryant, New York, June, 1859." The "Introductory" signed "S[amuel] O[sgood]."

GILDERSLEEVE, MRS. C. H. *See* Longstreet, Mrs. Rachel Abigail (Buchanan) Gildersleeve

GILES, DAPHNE SMITH. *See* Jenkins, Mrs. Daphne Smith (Giles)

GILES, ELLA AUGUSTA. *See* Ruddy, Mrs. Ella Augusta (Giles)

1001 GILL, JULIA. Legends of New England . . . New York: Carlton & Porter [cop. 1864]. 171 p., illus.
American University Library copy.

GILMAN, MRS. MARIA, *pseud.* *See* Barnard, Charles

1002 [GILMORE, JAMES ROBERTS.] Among the Guerillas. By Edmund Kirke [pseud.] . . . New York: Carleton, 1866. 286 p.
AAS, BP, CU, H, HEH, LC, LCP, N, NYH, NYP, UC, UM, UV, Y
The Civil War; Virginia, 1864.

1003 [————] Among the Pines; or, South in Secession-Time. By Edmund Kirke [pseud.]. New York: J. R. Gilmore, Charles T. Evans, 1862. 310 p.
BA, BP, BU, CU, H, LC, LCP, NYH, UC, UM, Y
Also issued with imprint: New York: G. P. Putnam, 1862.   N

1004 [————] Down in Tennessee, and Back by Way of Richmond. By Edmund Kirke [pseud.] . . . New York: Carleton, 1864. 282 p.
AAS, BA, BP, BU, CU, H, HEH, LC, LCP, NYH, NYP, UC, UM, UVB, Y
A highly embellished personal narrative.

1005 [————] My Southern Friends. "All of Which I Saw, and Part of Which I Was." By Edmund Kirke [pseud.] . . . New York: Carleton, 1863. 308 p.
AAS, BA, BP, BU, CU, H, HEH, LC, LCP, N, NYH, NYP, UC, UVB, Y
Also issued with imprint: New York: the Tribune Association, 1863.
AAS, HEH, LC, UM
Antislavery; North Carolina.

1006 [————] On the Border. By Edmund Kirke [pseud.] . . . Boston: Lee and Shepard, 1867. 333 p.
AAS, BA, BP, CU, H, HEH, LC, LCP, N, NYP, UC, UM, UVB, Y
Col. Garfield's campaign in eastern Kentucky.

1007 GLADDING, MRS. E. N. Leaves from an Invalid's Journal, and Poems . . . Providence: George H. Whitney, 1858. 235 p.
AAS, BP, BU, H, HEH, LC, NYH, NYP, Y
Contains: Minnie: A Temperance Tale—Alice; or, The Victim of Revenge—A Dialogue on Peace.

1008 GLEN, KNELLER. Isabel Carollton: A Personal Retrospect . . . Boston: Phillips, Sampson and Company. New York: J. C. Derby, 1854. 340 p.   AAS, BP

GLENN, JESSIE, *pseud.* *See* Schenck, Mrs. J. V.

GLENWOOD, IDA, *pseud.* *See* Gorton, Mrs. Cynthia M. R.

1009 GLOSSNAP, FRANCIS. The Victim of the Mysterious Mark; or, The Magic Mirror. A Tale for the Times . . . New York: published at No. 11 Park Row. Baker, Godwin & Co., printers, 1851. 22 p.   NYH

GLOVER, CAROLINE HOWARD (GILMAN). *See* Jervey, Mrs. Caroline Howard (Gilman) Glover

1010 GODMAN, STUART ADAIR. The Ocean-Born: A Tale of the Southern Seas . . . New York: Bunce & Brother, 134 Nassau Street [cop. 1852]. 100 p., illus.   H, NYP

1011 GODWIN, PARKE. Vala: A Mythological Tale . . . New York: George P. Putnam, 1851. 46, [4] p., illus.
                    AAS, BP, BU, CU, H, HEH, LC, N, NYP, UM, Y
The Vala of this tale is Jenny Lind.

GOLDSMITH, CHRISTABEL, *pseud. See* Smith, Fannie N.

1012 GOOD STORIES . . . Boston: Ticknor and Fields, 1867-68. 4 pts. in 3 vols., illus.
          BA(1,3-4), BP, BU(3), H(1-2), LC, LCP, NYP(1-3)
Contains: pt. 1, Peter Goldthwaite's Treasure, by N. Hawthorne—Love and Skates, by T. Winthrop; pt. 3, The Christmas Banquet, by N. Hawthorne—Three of a Trade; or, Red Little Kriss Kringle, by F. J. O'Brien; pt. 4, From Hand to Mouth, by F. J. O'Brien.

1013 GOODWIN, EDWARD. Lily White: A Romance . . . Philadelphia: J. B. Lippincott & Co., 1858. 315 p.   AAS

GOODWIN, MRS. H. B. *See* Talcott, Mrs. Hannah Elizabeth (Bradbury) Goodwin

1013a [GORDON, CLARENCE.] Christmas at Under-Tor: An American Christmas Story. New York: Mohun, Ebbs & Hough, 1864. 47 p.   H, HEH

GORDON, HEWES, *pseud. See* Clarke, E. G. H.

1014 [GORTON, MRS. CYNTHIA M. R.] The Fatal Secret. By Ida Glenwood [pseud.], "the Blind Bard of Michigan" . . . Philadelphia: John E. Potter and Company, 617 Sansom Street [cop. 1873]. 415 p., front.   AAS, BU, CU, HEH, NYP, UM
Laid in New York City and England.

1015 GOULD, EDWARD SHERMAN. John Doe and Richard Roe; or, Episodes of Life in New York... New York: Carleton, 1862. 312 p.   AAS, AP, BP, CU, H, HEH, LC, LCP, NYH, NYP, UV, Y

GOULD, JOHN W. Cruise of a Guineaman. *In* Swell Life at Sea (1854), No. 2414.

1016 GRAINGER, ARTHUR M. Golden Feather; or, The Buccaneer of King's Bridge. A Warlike Romance of the Rivers and the Bay of New York. Being a Tale of Love and Glory of the War of 1812-'15 ... New York: Frederic A. Brady, No. 24 Ann Street [1863]. 90 p., illus. Printed in double cols.   LC
LC copy deposited for copyright April 9, 1863. First published in the *New York Mercury* beginning July 7, 1860, the year of the copyright date in the book.

1017 ——— Guy Ravenel; or, How Will It End? A Tale of New York Twenty Years Ago ... New York: Frederic A. Brady, 1864. 86 p., illus.
Announced as "recently published" in *Amer. Lit. Gaz.*, IV (Nov. 15, 1864), 42.

GRANDFATHER GREENWAY, *pseud. See* Cannon, Charles James

GRANICE, ROWENA. *See* Steele, Mrs. Rowena (Granice)

GRAY, ALICE, *pseud. See* Mathews, Julia A.

GRAY, BARRY, *pseud. See* Coffin, Robert Barry

GRAY, ROBERTSON, *pseud. See* Raymond, Rossiter Worthington

GRAYSON, ELDRED, *pseud. See* Hare, Robert

1018 THE GREAT "TRUNK MYSTERY" of New York City. Murder of the Beautiful Miss Alice A. Bowlsby, of Patterson, N. J. Philadelphia, Pa.: Barclay & Co., 21 North Seventh Street [cop. 1871]. 102 p., illus.   BA, LC, LCP, NYP

1019 GREELEY, ROBERT F. The Partisan's Oath; or, The Trooper's Revenge. A Tale of the Revolution ... New York: Bunce & Brother, 134 Nassau Street [185-?]. 96 p.   HEH, LC
Also contains: Edgar Edgerton, a Tale of the Revolution.

1020 ———— Violet, the Child of the City: A Story of New York Life . . . New York: Bunce & Brother, 1854. 336 p.

AAS, CU, H, N

GREEN, INVISIBLE, *pseud. See* Crippen, William G.

1021 GREENE, JOSEPH H., JR. Athaliah: A Novel . . . New York: Carleton. London: S. Low, Son & Co., 1869. 378 p.

HEH, LC, LCP, NYP

At the time of King David.

1022 GREENE, TALBOT. American Nights' Entertainments, Compiled from Pencilings of a United States Senator, Entitled: A Winter in the Federal City . . . Jonesborough, Tenn.: Wm. A. Sparks & Co., book and job printers, 1860. 266 p.

AAS, BP, BU, LC, N, NYH, NYP, UP

GREENHORN, *pseud. See* Thompson, George

1023 [GREENOUGH, HENRY.] Apelles and His Contemporaries: A Novel . . . Boston: T. O. H. P. Burnham, 1860. 342 p.

AAS, BP, CU, H, HEH, N, NYP, UP, Y

1024 [————] Ernest Carroll; or, Artist-Life in Italy. A Novel . . . Boston: Ticknor and Fields, 1858. 344 p.

AAS, BA, BP, H, LC, LCP, NYP, Y

Covers of LC and NYP copies dated 1859.

1025 GREENOUGH, MRS. SARAH DANA (LORING). Arabesques: Monarè; Domitia; Apollyona; Ombra . . . Boston: Roberts Brothers, 1872. 213 p., illus.   AAS, BA, BP, CU, H, HEH, LC, NYP, UP

1026 ———— In Extremis: A Novelette . . . Boston: Roberts Brothers, 1872. 202 p.   BP, BU, H, HEH, LC, NYP, UP

1027 [————] Lilian. Boston: Ticknor and Fields, 1863. 312 p.

AAS, AP, BP, CU, H, HEH, LC, N, NYP, UC, UP

From Indian country to Rome, Italy.

1028 ———— Treason at Home: A Novel . . . Philadelphia: T. B. Peterson & Brothers, 306 Chestnut Street [187-?]. 400 p.

BP, H

Appleton's Cyclop. of Amer. Biog. lists this as being published in London, 1865, in 3 vols.

GREENWAY, *Grandfather, pseud.* *See* Cannon, Charles James

GREENWOOD, GRACE, *pseud.* *See* Lippincott, Mrs. Sara Jane (Clarke)

1029 GREEY, EDWARD. The Queen's Sailors: A Nautical Novel. By Edward Greey . . . (Sungtie) . . . New York: E. Greey and Co., 1870. 3 vols. (314, 283, 335 p.), front.   LC

Also published in one volume as: *Blue Jackets; or, The Adventures of J. Thompson, A.B. among "the Heathen Chinese."* Boston: J. E. Tilton & Co., 1871. 236 p., front.   AAS, BP, BU, CU, HEH, LCP, NYP, UM

GREGORY, JAMES, *attrib. au.* *See* Throop, George Higby

1030 [GREY, JEANNIE H.] Tactics; or, Cupid in Shoulder-Straps. A West Point Love Story. By Hearton Drille, U.S.A. [pseud.] . . . New York: Carleton, 1863. 250 p.

AAS, CU, H, LC, LCP, Y

1031 GRIEST, ELLWOOD. John and Mary; or, The Fugitive Slaves. A Tale of South-Eastern Pennsylvania . . . Lancaster, Pa.: Inquirer Printing and Publishing Company, 1873. 226 p.

BP, H, LC, NYH, NYP, Y

1032 [GRIFFIN, EDMUND D.] Dreams within Dreams; a Plagiarism of the Seventeenth Century. Being like Most Visions of the Night, a Medley of Old Things and New. By Ulric De Lazie [pseud.] . . . New York: P. O'Shea, 1864. 534 p.   LC

GRIFFITH, MATTIE. *See* Browne, Mrs. Mattie (Griffith)

1033 [GRIFFITHS, JULIA] *ed.* Autographs for Freedom. Boston: John P. Jewett and Company. Cleveland, Ohio: Jewett, Proctor, and Worthington. London: Low and Company, 1853. 263 p., illus.

AAS, BA, BP, CU, H, LC, N, NYH, NYP, UC, UM, Y

Contains: Momma Charlotte, by Mrs. C. M. Kirkland—Passages in the Life of a Slave Woman, by Annie Parker—The Man-Owner, by Rev. E. Buckingham—The Two Altars; or, Two Pictures in One, by Harriet Beecher Stowe—The Heroic Slave, by Frederick Douglass.

1034 ——————————— [2d ser.] Auburn: Alden, Beardsley & Co. Rochester: Wanzer, Beardsley & Co., 1854. 309 p., illus.

AAS, BP, BU, CU, H, HEH, LC, N, NYH, NYP, Y

Contains: Narrative of Albert and Mary, by William Henry Brisbane—Christine, by Anne P. Adams.

GRILE, DOD, *pseud. See* Bierce, Ambrose

GRINGO, HARRY, *pseud. See* Wise, Henry Augustus

1035 GRISWOLD, MRS. FRANCES IRENE (BURGE) SMITH. Asleep. By F. Burge Smith . . . Brooklyn, N. Y.: T. B. Ventres, 62 Court Street [cop. 1871]. 149 p.   H, LC, NYP
On death.

1036 ——— The Bishop and Nannette . . . New York: Thomas Whittaker, No. 2 Bible House [cop. 1873]. 329 p., illus.
CU, H, LC, UV

1037 ——— Elm Tree Tales . . . New York: Mason Brothers, 1856. 342 p.   AAS, H
Contents: Jennie Grigg, the Street-Sweeper—Nannie Bates, the Huckster's Daughter—Archibald Mackie, the Little Cripple.

1038 ——— Nina; or, Life's Caprices. A Story Founded upon Fact . . . New York: published for the Home of the Aged and Orphan of the Brooklyn Church Charity Foundation, by Daniel Dana, agent, 1861. 426, [1] p., front.
CU, LC, NYP, UP, Y

GRISWOLD, HATTIE TYNG. Down by the Sea. *In* Stories and Sketches (1867), No. 2386.

1039 [GRISWOLD, V. M.] Hugo Blanc, the Artist: A Tale of Practical and Ideal Life. By an Artist. New York: Hilton & Co. Philadelphia: J. B. Lippincott & Co. San Francisco: A. Roman & Co. St. Louis: J. F. Torrey & Co., 1867. 411 p.
BP, HEH, LC, NYP
Refers to New York City studios.

GUERNSEY, CLARA FLORIDA. The Cold Hand. *In* Not Pretty, but Precious (1872), No. 1804.

——— The Red Fox. *In* Not Pretty, but Precious (1872), No. 1804.

1040 GUERNSEY, LUCY ELLEN. Lady Betty's Governess; or, The Corbet Chronicles . . . New York: T. Whittaker, 1872. 369 p.   CU, LC, LCP, NYP

1041 ———— Lady Rosamond's Book, Being the Second Part of the Stanton-Corbet Chronicles . . . New York: Thomas Whittaker, 2 Bible House [cop. 1874]. 344 p.   BP, LCP, NYP
Anti-Catholic.

1042 ———— The Merman and the Figure-Head: A Christmas Story . . . Philadelphia: J. B. Lippincott & Co., 1871. 117 p., illus.   BP, CU, Y

1043 ———— Winifred; or, "After Many Days" . . . New York: Thomas Whittaker, No. 2 Bible House [cop. 1869]. 335 p.
At the time of James II and William and Mary.   AAS, BP, NYP, UV

1044 [GUILD, MRS. CAROLINE SNOWDEN (WHITMARSH).] The Sisters of Soleure: A Tale of the Sixteenth Century. By C. S. W. Concord [N. H.]: Edson C. Eastman, 1860. 272 p.   AAS, BP

GUILD, CURTIS. Dodge's Private Performance. *In* Dodge's Sketches [1853], No. 1751.

1045 "GUILTY OR NOT GUILTY:" The True Story of Manhattan Well. New York: Carleton. London: S. Low, Son & Co., 1870. 396 p.   AAS, CU, NYP
New York City at the turn of the 19th century.

1046 GUNN, THOMAS BUTLER. The Physiology of New York Boarding-Houses . . . New York: Mason Brothers, 1857. 300 p., illus.   AAS, BP, CU, H, HEH, LCP, NYH, NYP, UC

1047 GUSTAFSON, MRS. ZADEL (BARNES) BUDDINGTON. Can the Old Love? A Novel, by Zadel Barnes Buddington . . . Boston: James R. Osgood and Company, 1871. 198 p., illus. Printed in double cols.   AAS, BP, CU, HEH, LC, N

1048 GUTHRIE, MRS. M. J. The Silver Lining; or, Fair-Hope Prospect . . . Philadelphia, 1872. 203 p.   AAS, LC

H., MRS. E. A. W. *See* Hopkins, Mrs. Eliza Ann (Woodruff)

H., HD. *See* Hinton, Howard

H., H. L. *See* Hosmer, Hezekiah Lord

H.

H., L. C. *See* Hill, L. C.

H., M. J. *See* Haw, Mary Jane

H., M. R. *See* Higham, Mrs. Mary R.

1049   HACO, DION.   The Private Journal and Diary of John H. Surratt, the Conspirator. Edited and Arranged by Dion Haco, Esq. . . . New York: Frederic A. Brady, 22 Ann Street [cop. 1866].   104 p.   BU, H, HEH

HADERMANN, JEANNETTE R. *See* Walworth, Mrs. Jeannette Ritchie (Hadermann)

1050   HADSELL, O. D.   Heroine of Manassas; or, The Female Volunteer. A Romance in High Life. Kalamazoo, Mich.: the author, 1870.
Title listed in Kelly 1866-1871 and Allibone.

1051   HALE, EDWARD EVERETT.   Christmas Eve and Christmas Day: Ten Christmas Stories . . . Boston: Roberts Brothers, 1873. 4 p.l., 39, 39^1-39^{14}, [40]-294 p., front.
                                   AAS, BP, BU, CU, H, HEH, LC, LCP, Y
Contents: They Saw a Great Light–Christmas Waits in Boston–Alice's Christmas-Tree–Daily Bread–Stand and Wait–The Two Princes–The Story of Oello–Love Is the Whole–Christmas and Rome–The Survivor's Story–The Same Christmas in Old England and New.

1052   ———— His Level Best, and Other Stories . . . Boston: James R. Osgood and Company, 1873.   293 p.
                                   AAS, BA, BP, CU, H, HEH, LC, N, UVB, Y
Also contains: The Brick Moon–Water Talk–Mouse and Lion–The Modern Sindbad–A Tale of a Salamander–The Queen of California–Confidence.
Preface dated "November 30, 1872."

1053   ———— If, Yes, and Perhaps. Four Possibilities and Six Exaggerations, with Some Bits of Fact . . . Boston: Ticknor and Fields, 1868.   296 p.
                                   AAS, BA, BP, BU, CU, H, HEH, LC, LCP, N, NYP, UC, UM, UVB, Y
Contents: The Children of the Public–A Piece of Possible History–The South American Editor–The Old and the New, Face to Face–The Dot and Line Alphabet–The Last Voyage of the Resolute–My Double, and How He Undid Me–The Man without a Country–The Last of the Florida–The Skeleton in the Closet–Christmas Waits in Boston.

1054 ———— In His Name: A Christmas Story . . . Boston: published by the proprietors of Old and New, 1873. 87 p. Printed in double cols.

> AAS, BA, BP, BU, CU, H, HEH, LC, LCP, UP, UVB, Y
>
> At head of title: "Old and New Series; No. 2."
>
> *Also issued with imprint*: Boston: Roberts Brothers, 1873. AAS, NYP, Y
>
> Title page reset, and note at head of title omitted.

1055 ———— The Ingham Papers: Some Memorials of the Life of Capt. Frederic Ingham, U.S.N., Sometime Pastor of the First Sandemanian Church in Naguadavick, and Major-General by Brevet in the Patriot Service in Italy . . . Boston: Fields, Osgood & Co., 1869. 266 p.

> AAS, BA, BP, BU, CU, H, HEH, LC, LCP, N, NYP, UC, UM, UP, UVB, Y
>
> *Contents*: Memoir of Captain Frederic Ingham—The Good-Natured Pendulum—Paul Jones and Denis Duval—Round the World in a Hack—Friends' Meeting—Did He Take the Prince to Ride?—How Mr. Frye Would Have Preached It—The Rag-Man and the Rag-Woman—Dinner Speaking—Good Society—Daily Bread.

1056 [————] The Man without a Country. Boston: Ticknor and Fields, 1865. 23 p.

> AAS, BP, CU, H, HEH, LC, N, NYH, NYP, UVB, Y
>
> Also in *Atlantic Tales* (1866), No. 155.

————My Double, and How He Undid Me. *In* Atlantic Tales (1866), No. 155.

1057 ———— Our New Crusade: A Temperance Story . . . Boston: Roberts Brothers, 1875. 287 p.

> AAS, BA, BP, CU, H, LC, LCP, N, NYH, NYP, Y
>
> Also published as: *The Good Time Coming; or, Our New Crusade.* Boston: Roberts Brothers, 1875. Y

1058 ————, ed. Six of One by Half a Dozen of the Other: An Every Day Novel. By Harriet Beecher Stowe, Adeline D. T. Whitney, Lucretia P. Hale, Frederic W. Loring, Frederick B. Perkins, Edward E. Hale. Boston: Roberts Brothers, 1872. 245 p.   AAS, BP, BU, CU, H, HEH, LC, NYP, UC, UM, UVB, Y

1059 ———— Sybaris, and Other Homes . . . Boston: Fields, Osgood & Co., 1869. 206 p.

> AAS, BA, BU, CU, H, HEH, LC, NYH, NYP, UC, UM, UVB, Y
>
> *Contents*: My Visit to Sybaris—How They Lived at Naguadavick—How They Live in Vineland—How They Live in Boston, and How They Die There—Homes for Boston Laborers—Appendix.

1060 [————] Ten Times One Is Ten; the Possible Reformation. A Story in Nine Chapters. By Col. Frederic Ingham [pseud.]. Boston: Roberts Brothers, 1871. 148 p.
AAS, BA, BP, BU, CU, H, HEH, LC, N, NYP, UC, UP, UVB, Y

———— Two Princes. *In* Thirteen Good Stories [1873?], No. 2457.

1061 ———— Ups and Downs: An Every-Day Novel ... Boston: Roberts Brothers, 1873. 319 p.
AAS, BA, BP, CU, H, HEH, LC, LCP, NYP, UC, Y

1062 ———— Workingmen's Homes: Essays and Stories. By Edward E. Hale and Others, on the Homes of Men Who Work in Large Towns. Boston: James R. Osgood and Company, 1874. 182 p., front.   AAS, BA, BP, CU, LC, LCP, NYH, NYP, Y
Contains: How They Lived at Naguadavick, from Rev. Frederic Ingham's Papers—How They Live in Boston, and How They Die There.

HALE, LUCRETIA PEABODY. The Queen of the Red Chessmen. *In* Atlantic Tales (1866), No. 155.

1063 [————] Struggle for Life . . . Boston: Walker, Wise & Co., 1861. 311 p.   LC

———— jt. au. *See* Hale, Edward Everett, *ed.* Six of One (1872), No. 1058.

1064 HALE, MRS. SARAH JOSEPHA (BUELL). Liberia; or, Mr. Peyton's Experiments. Edited by Sarah J. Hale . . . New York: Harper & Brothers, 1853. 304 p.
AAS, BP, H, LC, LCP, N, NYP, UC, UVB, Y

1065 ———— Northwood; or, Life North and South, Showing the True Character of Both . . . New York: H. Long & Brother, 43 Ann Street [cop. 1852]. 408 p., illus.
AAS, BP, BU, CU, H, HEH, LC, LCP, N, NYH, NYP, UV
Originally published as *Northwood: A Tale of New England* (1827), Wright (1774-1850), No. 1083.
Antislavery material added to this ed.

1066 HALL, ABRAHAM OAKEY. The Congressman's Christmas Dream, and the Lobby Member's Happy New Year: A Holiday Sketch . . . New York: Scribner, Welford & Co. London, 1870-71. 64 p., illus.   BU, CU, H, LC, N, NYH, NYP, UC, UM, Y

1067 ———— Old Whitey's Christmas Trot: A Story for the Holidays ... New York: Harper & Brothers, 1857. 237 p., illus.

AAS, BU, CU, H, HEH, NYP, Y

1068 HALL, BAYNARD RUSH. Frank Freeman's Barber Shop: A Tale ... New York: Charles Scribner, 1852. 343 p., illus.

Proslavery.　　　　　AAS, CU, H, HEH, LC, N, NYP, UC, UP, UV, Y

1069 HALL, CHARLES WINSLOW. Twice Taken: An Historical Romance of the Maritime British Provinces ... Boston: Lee and Shepard, 1867. 242 p.

The siege of Louisburg.　　AAS, BP, BU, CU, H, HEH, LC, N, NYP, UP, Y

1070 [HALL, MRS. LOUISA JANE (PARK).] The Sheaves of Love: A Fireside Story. Boston: L. J. Pratt, 1861. 274 p.

Preface signed "Miss L. J. P."　　　　　AAS, HEH, NYP

1071 [HALLETT, MISS E. V.] Natalie; or, A Gem among the Sea-Weeds. By Ferna Vale [pseud.]. Andover: printed by W. F. Draper, 1858. 324 p.　　　AAS, BU, CU, LC, Y
Laid in Nantucket.

HALLOWELL, MRS. SARA CATHERINE (FRALEY). On the Church Steps. *In* F. Asheton, A Modern Cressida (1875), No. 151.

1072 [HALPINE, CHARLES GRAHAM.] Baked Meats of the Funeral: A Collection of Essays, Poems, Speeches, Histories, and Banquets. By Private Miles O'Reilly [pseud.] ... New York: Carleton, 1866. 378 p.

AAS, BA, BP, BU, CU, H, HEH, LC, LCP, N, NYH, NYP, UC, UP, Y

1073 [————] The Life and Adventures, Songs, Services, and Speeches of Private Miles O'Reilly. (47th Regiment, New York Volunteers.) ... With Comic Illustrations ... New York: Carleton, 1864. 237 p., illus.

AAS, BA, BP, BU, CU, H, HEH, LC, LCP, N, NYH, NYP, UC, UM, UP, UVB, Y

HEH has a 2d copy with textual variations pp. 219-223; the song "Our Lady of the Hospital," pp. 220-222, omitted.

1074 HALSEY, HARLAN PAGE. Annie Wallace; or, The Exile of Penang. A Tale ... New York: Miller & Holman, 1857. 304 p.
Information from LC card for copy withdrawn from circulation.

1075   [————] Dare Devil Pat; or, The Dashing Rider of the Plains. By Tony Pastor [pseud.] ... New York: Independent News Company [1872]. 88 p.
Information from LC card for copy withdrawn from circulation.

1076   [————] Something to Wear, and Some Other Things. By Doesticks, Junior [pseud.]. Brooklyn: Brockway, 1857. 67 p., illus.
Brooklyn College Library copy.

HAMILTON, ADAM, *pseud.*   *See* Leppere, Adam Hamilton

HAMILTON, GAIL, *pseud.*   *See* Dodge, Mary Abigail

1077   HAMILTON, JOHN A. Chris Spangler: A Tale of the War. By Dominie [pseud.]. Orangeburg, S. C.: Berry & Howell [186-?]. Cover title, 125 p. Printed in double cols.
University of Texas Library copy.

1078   HAMILTON, MRS. M. J. R. Cachet; or, The Secret Sorrow. A Novel ... New York: G. W. Carleton & Co., 1873. 351 p.
BP, LC

1079   [HAMMETT, SAMUEL ADAMS.] Piney Woods Tavern; or, Sam Slick in Texas ... Philadelphia: T. B. Peterson and Brothers, 306 Chestnut Street [cop. 1858]. 309 p., front.
AAS, BP, BU, CU, HEH, LC, LCP, N, NYP, UC, UM

1080   [————] A Stray Yankee in Texas. By Philip Paxton [pseud.]. New York: Redfield, 1853. 416 p., front.
AAS, AP, BP, BU, CU, H, LC, LCP, N, NYP, UC, Y

1081   [————] The Wonderful Adventures of Captain Priest: A Tale of But Few Incidents, and No Plot in Particular. With Other Legends ... New York: Redfield, 1855. 335 p., front.
AAS, BU, CU, H, HEH, LC, N, NYP, UC, UM, UP, UVB
Contents: Adventures of Captain Priest—Legends of City and Country—Midsummer Chapters.

1082   HAMMOND, MRS. ADELAIDE F. Josephine Eloise: A Novel ... Baltimore: published by the Baltimore News Company; John W. Woods, printer, 1872. 93 p. Printed in double cols. LC
Life in a New England village.

145

1083 [HAMMOND, MRS. HENRIETTA (HARDY).] Her Waiting Heart. By Lou Capsadell [pseud.] . . . New York: the Authors' Publishing Company, 1875. 192 p.   LC, NYP

1084 HAMMOND, SAMUEL H. Country Margins and Rambles of a Journalist. By S. H. Hammond . . . and L. W. Mansfield . . . New York: J. C. Derby. Boston: Phillips, Sampson & Co. Cincinnati: H. W. Derby, 1855. 356 p.
AAS, BA, BP, BU, CU, H, HEH, LC, LCP, UC, UM, UP, Y
Included because of the humorous style of the authors' letters.

1085 HAMMOND, WILLIAM ALEXANDER. Robert Severne, His Friends and His Enemies: A Novel . . . Philadelphia: J. B. Lippincott & Co., 1867. 369 p.   AAS, BP, CU, H, HEH, LC, NYP, UM, Y
The rare book business in New York City.

1086 HAMPDEN, ALLEN. Hartley Norman: A Tale of the Times . . . New York: Rudd & Carleton, 1859. 429 p.
AAS, BP, H, HEH, LCP, NYP
Laid in New York City and Central America.

HAMPTON, MOULTON, *pseud.?* The Mirror of the World (1856). *See* The Yankee Enterprise; or, The Two Millionaires, No. 2828.

1087 HANAFORD, MRS. PHEBE ANN (COFFIN). Lucretia, the Quakeress; or, Principle Triumphant . . . Boston: J. Buffum, 1853. 172 p.   UM
Antislavery.

1088 HANCOCK, SALLIE J. Etna Vandemir: A Romance of Kentucky and "The Great Uprising" . . . New York: Cutter, Tower & Co., 1863. 366 p.   AAS, BU, HEH, LC, N, NYH, NYP, UC

1089 ——— The Montanas; or, Under the Stars. A Romance . . . New York: Carleton, 1866. 320 p.
AAS, BP, CU, HEH, LC, LCP, UC
New England family life; Civil War background.

1090 HANKINS, *Colonel.* Dakota Land; or, The Beauty of St. Paul. An Original, Illustrated, Historic, and Romantic Work . . . To Which Is Added: "A Round of Pleasure," with Interesting Notes of Travel . . . Forming a Comprehensive Guide to the Great North-West . . . New York City: Hankins & Son, 1868. 460 p., illus.   BA, BU, NYH, NYP, UC, Y

1091 HANKINS, MARIE LOUISE. Reality; or, A History of Human Life
. . . New York and Philadelphia: Marie Louise Hankins &
Co., 1858. 98 p. LC, NYP, Y
Pages 89-98 advts. in NYP copy.

1092 ──────── Women of New York . . . New York: Marie Louise
Hankins & Co., 1861. 354 p., illus.
Pages [350]-354 advts. AAS, BP, CU, H, HEH, LC, N, NYP, UC, UM, Y

1093 HANNA, ABIGAIL STANLEY. Withered Leaves, from Memory's
Garland . . . Providence: A. Crawford Greene & Brother,
Printers to the State, 1857. 390 p.
AAS, BP, BU, HEH, NYH, NYP
Contains: The History of a Household—The Angel Cousin—The
Unhappy Marriage—Consumption—A Long Night in the Eighteenth
Century—Henriette Clinton; or, Reverses of Fortune.

HANNAY, JAMES. Fitz-Gubin; or, The Admiral's Pet. *In* Swell
Life at Sea (1854), No. 2414.

──────── Mr. Snigsby's Yacht. *In* Swell Life at Sea (1854),
No. 2414.

HANNIBAL, *Professor* JULIUS CAESAR, *pseud. See* Levison,
William H.

1094 [HANNIGAN, DENNIS.] The Orange Girl of Venice; or, The
Secret Council of Ten. By the Author of "The Swamp Steed"
. . . New York: Dick & Fitzgerald, No. 18 Ann Street
[185-?]. 89 p., illus. Printed in double cols. AAS, UM
This is Wright (1774-1850), No. 1125, with "Agnes," pp. 60-89, added.

1095 [────────] The Swamp Steed; or, The Days of Marion and
His Merry Men. A Romance of the American Revolution.
New York: DeWitt & Davenport, Tribune Building [cop.
1852]. 198 p. AAS, CU, HEH, NYH, NYP, UC, Y
Laid in South Carolina.

1096 HARBERT, MRS. ELIZABETH MORRISSON (BOYNTON). Out of Her
Sphere . . . Des Moines: Mills & Co., printers and publishers,
1871. 184 p. BU, HEH, LC, NYP
Woman's rights propaganda.

1097 HARDIMAN, H. M. The Free Flag of Cuba; or, The Martyrdom of Lopez. A Tale of the Liberating Expedition of 1851 . . . New York: DeWitt & Davenport, 1855. 206 p.   NYH

HARDMAN, FRANCIS, ed. See Sealsfield, Charles. Frontier Life (1853), No. 2172.

HARDWICK, MRS. J. P. See M'Keehan, Hattia. Liberty or Death, No. 1624n.

1098 HARE, MRS. R. Standish: A Story of Our Day . . . Boston: Loring, 1865. 185 p.   BP, LC
Boston, Minnesota, and the battlefields of Virginia.

1099 [HARE, ROBERT.] Overing; or, The Heir of Wycherly. A Historical Romance. By Eldred Grayson [pseud.] . . . New York: Cornish, Lamport & Co., 1852. 416 p.   BP, BU, NYP, UC
Laid in Rhode Island.

1100 HARLAN, MARY B. Ellen; or, The Chained Mother. And Pictures of Kentucky Slavery. Drawn from Real Life . . . Cincinnati: published for the author by Applegate & Co., 1853. 259 p., illus.   CU, LC, UM
Antislavery.

HARLAND, MARION, pseud. See Terhune, Mrs. Mary Virginia (Hawes)

1101 [HARRELLE, ALBERT J.] The Life and Private Confessions of an Ex-Convict, as Told by Himself . . . Indianapolis, Ind.: the Novelty Publishing Company, 1875. 64 p.   LC
At head of title: "A Thrilling Narration."

HARRINGTON, GEORGE F., pseud. See Baker, William Mumford

1102 HARRINGTON, J. Josephine; or, The Romish Poison. A Romance of the Present . . . New York: Burgess & Day, 100 Nassau Street [185-?]. Cover title, 103 p., illus. Printed in double cols.   LC

1103 [HARRINGTON, JOHN A.] Between the Crusts; or, "Ticket 1939." By John Carboy [pseud.] . . . New York: Collin & Small, 1875. 109 p., illus. Printed in double cols.   LC

————— Kicked into Good Luck. In Searching for the White Elephant [cop. 1872], No. 2173.

1104 HARRIS, GEORGE WASHINGTON. Sut Lovingood. Yarns Spun by a "Nat'ral Born Durn'd Fool:" Warped and Wove for Public Wear ... New York: Dick & Fitzgerald [cop. 1867]. 299 p., illus.   AAS, BP, CU, H, HEH, LC, LCP, N, NYP, UC, UM, UP, UV, Y

1105 HARRIS, MRS. HELENA J. Southern Sketches. Cecil Gray; or, The Soldier's Revenge. Rosa Sherwood; or, The Avenger. By Mrs. Helena J. Harris, Native of Alabama. New Orleans: Crescent Job Print., 1866. 20 p.
At the time of the Civil War.   AAS, HEH, LC, N, NYP, UC, UVB

1106 HARRIS, LOUISE S. Linden Hill; or, The Vanquished Life-Dream . . . St. Louis: Southwestern Book and Publishing Company, 1874. 455 p.   AAS, HEH, LC
Of religious interest.

1107 [HARRIS, MRS. MIRIAM (COLES).] Frank Warrington ... New York: Carleton, 1863. 478 p.
  AAS, BU, CU, HEH, LCP, NYP, UM, UP, UVB, Y
Civil War background.

1108 [————] A Perfect Adonis ... New York: G. W. Carleton & Co. London: S. Low, Son & Co., 1875. 380 p.
  AAS, BA, CU, H, HEH, LC, LCP, N, UP, Y
Contemporary life and manners.

1109 ———— Richard Vandermarck: A Novel. By Mrs. Sidney S. Harris ... New York: Charles Scribner & Company, 1871. 330 p.
  AAS, BA, BP, BU, CU, H, HEH, LC, LCP, N, NYP, UC, UVB, Y
The well to do in early New York.

1110 [————] Rutledge. New York: Derby & Jackson, 1860. 504 p.
  AAS, BU, CU, H, HEH, LC, N, NYH, NYP, UC, UM, UVB, Y
Conventional story of trials and tribulations.

1111 [————] St. Philip's . . . New York: Carleton, 1865. 340 p.   AAS, AP, CU, HEH, LC, LCP, N, NYP, UC, UP, UVB, Y

1112 [————] The Sutherlands ... New York: Carleton, 1862. 474 p.   AAS, BP, CU, HEH, LCP, N, NYP, UP, Y
Laid in England.

1113 [HARRIS, SAMUEL SMITH.] Sheltern: A Novel. By Christopher Coningsby [pseud.] . . . New York: Blelock & Co., 1868. 272 p.   AAS, BP, LC, LCP, N

HARRIS, MRS. SIDNEY S. *See* Harris, Mrs. Miriam (Coles)

1114 [HARRISON, WILLIAM POPE.] Theophilus Walton; or, The Majesty of Truth. A Reply to Theodosia Ernest. By a Member of the Alabama Conference . . . Nashville, Tenn.: published for the author by Stevenson & Owen, 1858.   408 p.
                                                                    HEH, LC, Y
Also issued with imprint: Nashville, Tenn.: Southern Methodist Publishing House, 1858.   HEH, UC, UM, Y
The Baptist and Pedobaptist controversy.

HART, GERALD, *pseud.*   *See* Irving, Thomas J.

1115 HARTE, BRET. Condensed Novels, and Other Papers. By F. Bret Harte. With Comic Illustrations by Frank Bellew. New York: G. W. Carleton & Company. London: S. Low, Son & Co., 1867.   307 p., illus.
                        AAS, BP, CU, H, HEH, LC, LCP, N, NYP, UC, UP, UVB, Y
Contents: Condensed Novels: Muck a Muck, an Indian Novel, after Cooper—Terence Deuville, by Ch-ls Lo-r—Selina Sedilia, by Miss B-dd-n and Mrs. H-y W-d—Ninety-Nine Guardsmen, by Al-x-ndr D-m-s—The Dweller of the Threshold, by Sir Ed-d L. B-lw-r—The Haunted Man, by Ch-l-s D-k-ns—Miss Mix, by Ch-l-tte Br-nte—Guy Heavystone, by Author of Sword and Gun—Mr. Midshipman Breezy, by Capt. M-ry-t—John Jenkins, by T. S. A-rth-r—No Title, by W-lk-e C-ll-ns—N N., A French Paragraphic Novel—Fantine, after the French of Victor Hugo—La Femme, after the French of M. Michelet—Mary McGillup, a Southern Novel. Civic Sketches: A Venerable Impostor—From a Balcony—Melons—Surprising Adventures of Mr. Chas. Summerton—Sidewalkings—A Boy's Dog—Charitable Reminiscences—Seeing the Steamer Off—Neighborhoods I Have Moved From—My Suburban Residence—A Vulgar Little Boy—Waiting for the Ship. Legends and Tales: The Legend of Monte del Diablo—Adventures of Padre Vincentio—The Legend of Devil's Point—The Devil and the Broker—The Ogress of Silver Land—Ruins of San Francisco—Night at Wingdam.
Full name, Francis Bret Harte.

1116 ———— ———— With Illustrations by S. Eytinge, Jr. Boston: James R. Osgood and Company, 1871.   212 p., illus.
                        AAS, BA, BP, CU, H, HEH, LC, N, NYP, UM, UP, UVB, Y
Reprints the above "condensed novels" only, with two added: Handsome Is as Handsome Does, by Ch-s R-de—Lothaw, by Mr. Benjamins.

1117 ———— The Luck of Roaring Camp, and Other Sketches . . . Boston: Fields, Osgood & Co., 1870. 239 p.

AAS, H, HEH, LCP, N, NYP, UP, UVB, Y

Also contains: Sketches: The Outcasts of Poker Flat—Miggles—Tennessee's Partner—The Idyl of Red Gulch—High-Water Mark—A Lonely Ride—The Man of No Account. Stories: Mliss—The Right Eye of the Commander—Notes by Flood and Field. Bohemian Papers: Mission Dolores—John Chinaman—From a Back Window—Boonder.

1118 ——————————— Boston: Fields, Osgood & Co., 1870. 256 p.

This ed. adds "Brown of Calaveras." AAS, CU, HEH, UP, UVB, Y

1119 ———— Mrs. Skaggs's Husbands, and Other Sketches . . . Boston: James R. Osgood and Company, 1873. 352 p.

AAS, BA, BP, CU, HEH, LC, LCP, N, NYP, UC, UP, UVB, Y

Also contains: How Santa Claus Came to Simpson's Bar—The Princess Bob and Her Friends—The Iliad of Sandy Bar—Mr. Thompson's Prodigal —The Romance of Madroño Hollow—The Poet of Sierra Flat—The Christmas Gift That Came to Rupert—A Venerable Impostor—From a Balcony—Melons—Surprising Adventures of Master Charles Summerton —Sidewalkings—A Boy's Dog—Charitable Reminiscences—"Seeing the Steamer Off"—Neighborhoods I Have Moved From—My Suburban Residence—On a Vulgar Little Boy—Waiting for the Ship—The Legend of Monte del Diablo—The Adventure of Padre Vicentio—The Legend of Devil's Point—The Devil and the Broker—The Ogress of Silver Land— The Ruins of San Francisco—A Night at Wingdam.

1120 ———— Mliss: An Idyl of Red Mountain. A Story of California in 1863 . . . New York: Robert M. DeWitt, No. 33 Rose Street [1873]. 148 p. Printed in double cols.

AAS, HEH, NYP, UVB, Y

There is another issue without Harte's name on the title page; for discussion of priority see "The Question of Bret Harte's Mliss," by Jacob Blanck, in PW, CXXX (Nov. 28, 1936), 2102-2105.

1121 ———— Tales of the Argonauts, and Other Sketches . . . Boston: James R. Osgood and Company, 1875. 283 p.

AAS, BA, BP, BU, CU, H, HEH, LC, LCP, N, NYP, UC, UM, UP, UVB, Y

Contents: The Rose of Tuolumne—A Passage in the Life of Mr. John Oakhurst—Wan Lee, the Pagan—How Old Man Plunkett Went Home— The Fool of Five Forks—Baby Sylvester—An Episode of Fiddletown—A Jersey Centenarian.

1122 HARTMANN, THEODORE. Charity Green; or, The Varieties of Love . . . New York: John W. Norton, 1859. 601 p.

AAS, CU, H, HEH, LC, NYP, UC, Y

From New England to Charleston via London.

HARTWELL, MARY. *See* Catherwood, Mrs. Mary (Hartwell)

1123 HASTINGS, ANNA. The Russell Family . . . New York: M. W. Dodd, 1861. 201 p. AAS
Preface dated Nov. 22, 1856 and copyright notice dated 1856; Roorbach 1855-1858 dates the book 1857.

HASTINGS, SYBIL, *pseud. See* Cowing, Fanny

1124 HATCH, ALICE J. Under the Cedars; or, What the Years Brought . . . Boston: Lee and Shepard. New York: Lee, Shepard and Dillingham, 1872. 264 p. AAS, BP, CU, H, HEH, LC, NYP
Laid in "Millbrook" in the 1850's.

HATHAWAY, HARRIET N. Blanchette Roso. *In* A. J. H. Duganne, The Prince Corsair [185-?], No. 797.

——— The Child's Tear; or, The Miser's Heart Unsealed. *In* G. C. Hill, Esmerelda (1852), No. 1208.

——— The Village Gossip; or, The New Minister. *In* A. G. Piper, The Young Fisherman (1851), No. 1912.

1125 HATHAWAY, WILLIAM E. Christopher Crooked: A Christmas Story . . . New York: G. P. Putnam & Sons, 1873. 96 p., illus. Y
A temperance tale.

1126 [———] My Grandfather's Old Coat: A Political Allegory. By Reisender [pseud.]. Cincinnati: Robert Clarke & Co., print., 1873. 15 p. LC, LCP

1127 THE HAUNTED SCHOOL-HOUSE at Newburyport, Mass. Boston: Loring, cor. Washington and Bromfield Streets [cop. 1873]. 21 p., illus. Printed in double cols.

AAS, BA, BP, CU, H, LC, LCP, N, Y

1128 ——— Boston: Loring, cor. Washington and Bromfield Streets [cop. 1873]. 24 p., illus. NYP
Pages [22]-24, "Continuation."

HAVEN, MRS. ALICE (BRADLEY). Charity Envieth Not. *In* J. V. Watson, Tales and Takings (1857), No. 2663.

1129 ———— The Coopers; or, Getting Under Way . . . New York: D. Appleton and Company, 1858. 336 p.

AAS, BP, BU, CU, H, HEH, LC, LCP, NYP, UM, UP, Y

A young married couple in upstate New York.

1130 ———— Home Stories . . . New York: D. Appleton and Company, 1869. 372 p. AAS, H, LC, LCP

Contents: Spring Winds—Carriage Friends—Miss Bremer's Visit to Cooper's Landing—"Only a Family Party"—The Furnished House—The Ordeal; or, The Spring and Midsummer of a Life—Single Lessons Five Dollars—Counsel: The Evil and the Good.

———— [See also] Whitcher, Mrs. Frances M. B. The Widow Bedott Papers. With an Introduction by Alice B. Neal (1856), No. 2697.

1131 [HAW, MARY JANE.] The Rivals: A Chickahominy Story. By Miss M. J. H., of Virginia . . . Richmond: Ayres & Wade, 1864. 61 p., illus. BA, HEH, LC, NYH, UVB

1132 HAWTHORNE, JULIAN. Bressant: A Novel . . . New York: D. Appleton and Company, 1873. 383 p.

AAS, BA, BP, H, HEH, LC, LCP, N, NYH, NYP, UC, UP, UVB, Y

1133 ———— Idolatry: A Romance . . . Boston: J. R. Osgood and Company, 1874. 372 p.

AAS, BA, BU, CU, H, HEH, LC, LCP, N, NYP, UP, UVB, Y

1134 HAWTHORNE, NATHANIEL. The Blithedale Romance . . . Boston: Ticknor, Reed and Fields, 1852. 288 p.

AAS, AP, BA, BP, BU, H, HEH, LC, N, NYH, NYP, UC, UM, UP, UVB, Y

———— The Christmas Banquet. In Good Stories (1867-68), No. 1012.

1135 ———— The House of Seven Gables: A Romance . . . Boston: Ticknor, Reed and Fields, 1851. 344 p.

AAS, BA, BP, BU, CU, H, HEH, LC, N, NYH, NYP, UC, UM, UP, UVB, Y

———— Little Pansie, a Fragment. In J. T. Fields, ed., Good Company (1866), No. 900.

1136 ——————— The Marble Faun; or, The Romance of Monte Beni
... Boston: Ticknor and Fields, 1860. 2 vols. (283, 284 p.)

AAS, AP, BA, BP, BU, H, HEH, LC, LCP, N, NYH, NYP,
UC, UM, UP, UVB, Y

I have seen three different make-ups of the 1st issue: 1) Title, preface,
table of contents; p. ix signed "1*;" advts. dated Feb. 2) Title, table of
contents, preface; p. vii signed "1*;" advts. (some differences), dated
Mar. 3) Title, preface, table of contents; no signature on p. vii or ix;
advts. dated Mar.

1137 ——————— ——————— Boston: Ticknor and Fields, 1860. 2 vols.
(283, 288 p.)   AAS, CU, HEH, LC, LCP, N, NYP, UM, UV, Y

Text on p. 284, Vol. II, reset, and a "Conclusion" dated "Leamington,
Mar. 14, 1860" added, pp. 284-88.

1138 ——————— Mosses from an Old Manse ... Carefully Revised by
the Author. Boston: Ticknor and Fields, 1854. 2 vols.
(286, 297 p.)   AAS, BA, BP, H, HEH, LC, N, NYP, UVB, Y

This is a new ed. of Wright (1774-1850), Nos. 1143-1145, with three
sketches added: Feathertop—Passages from a Relinquished Work—
Sketches from Memory.

——————— Peter Goldthwaite's Treasure. *In* Good Stories
(1867-68), No. 1012.

1139 ——————— Septimius Felton; or, The Elixir of Life ... Boston:
James R. Osgood and Company, 1872. 229 p.

AAS, AP, BA, BP, CU, H, HEH, LC, LCP, N, NYP, UM, UP, UVB, Y

1140 ——————— The Snow-Image, and Other Twice-Told Tales ...
Boston: Ticknor, Reed and Fields, 1852. 273 p.

AAS, BA, BP, BU, CU, H, HEH, LC, LCP, N, NYH, NYP,
UC, UM, UP, UVB, Y

For contents see W. H. Cathcart, *Bibliography of the Works of Nathaniel
Hawthorne* (Cleveland, 1905), pp. 39-41.

HAY, JOHN. The Blood Seedling. *In* Not Pretty, but Precious
(1872), No. 1804.

1141 HAYDEN, MRS. CAROLINE A. Carrie Emerson; or, Life at Clifton-
ville ... Boston: James French and Company, 1855. 360 p.

Vicious gossip in a small town.   AAS, BP, BU, CU, HEH, UP, UVB

1142 [HAYDEN, MRS. SARAH MARSHALL.] Early Engagements, and Florence (A Sequel). By Mary Frazaer [pseud.]. Cincinnati: Moore, Anderson, Wilstach & Keys, 1854. 281 p.

"Florence" appears on pp. 189-281. AAS, LC, NYP

Opposes early marriages; laid in the Southwest.

1143 HAYWARD, MARIA LOUISE. The Huntingdons; or, Glimpses of Inner Life . . . Boston: H. V. Degen & Son, 1863. 306 p.

AAS, HEH, Y

HAYWARDE, RICHARD, *pseud.* See Cozzens, Frederick Swartwout

1144 HAZARD, ANN. Emma Stanley; or, The Orphans . . . New York: Clark, Austin & Smith, 1852. 161 p. CU

The 1842 ed. listed in Wright (1774-1850), No. 1151, is a citation from T. M. Owen, "A Bibliography of Mississippi," in Amer. Hist. Assn., *Annual Report . . . for the Year 1899* (Washington, 1900), p. 725, which now appears to be in error.

HAZEL, HARRY, *pseud.* See Jones, Justin

1145 HAZEN, JACOB A. Five Years before the Mast; or, Life in the Forecastle Aboard of a Whaler and Man-of-War . . . Philadelphia: Willis P. Hazard, 1854. 444 p., illus.

Purportedly factual. AAS, H, LC, N, UP, Y

1146 HAZLETT, HELEN. The Cloud with a Golden Border . . . Philadelphia: T. Ellwood Zell, 1861. 412 p. AAS, LC, LCP, UP

1147 ———— Glennair; or, Life in Scotland . . . Philadelphia: Claxton, Remsen & Haffelfinger, 1869. 332 p. LC, LCP, UC

1148 ———— The Heights of Eidelberg . . . Philadelphia: William S. & Alfred Martien, 1859. 419 p. AAS, LCP

1149 HEADS AND HEARTS; or, My Brother the Colonel. A Novel . . . By the Author of "Cousin Cecil," "Miser's Daughter," &c. . . . New York: DeWitt & Davenport, Tribune Bldgs. [1852?]. 200 p. HEH

Emily Appleton wrote a *Miser's Daughter*, Wright (1774-1850), No. 38; but I cannot prove that she wrote *Heads and Hearts*.

1150 THE HEART OF MABEL WARE: A Romance. New York: J. C. Derby. Cincinnati: H. W. Derby, 1856. 411 p.

AAS, BU, CU, HEH, LC, UP, Y

Occasional unflattering remarks about Quakers.

1151 THE HEART OF THE WEST: An American Story. By an Illinoian. Time: 1860. Scene: On the Mississippi . . . Chicago: steam printing house of Hand & Hart, 1871. 229, iii p.

AAS, BP, CU, H, HEH, LC, N, NYH, NYP, UC, UM, UP

Preface dated: "Grand Prairie, Ill., July 21st, 1870."

HEATH, H. H. The Moorish Captives. In C. G. Rosenberg, The Roman Soprano [185-?], No. 2128.

———— The Tyrolese Lovers. In S. Cobb, The Royal Yacht [185-?], No. 583.

1152 [HEAVEN, MRS. LOUISE (PALMER).] Aldeane: A Novel. By Laura Preston [pseud.] . . . New York: A. Roman & Co. San Francisco, 1868. 403 p. AAS, BP, LC, LCP

1153 [————] In Bonds: A Novel. By Laura Preston [pseud.] . . . San Francisco: A. Roman & Company. New York, 1867. 247 p. Printed in double cols. HEH

Reprinted with imprint: New York: A. Roman & Company. San Francisco, 1867. 438 p. AAS, BU, LC, LCP, NYP

A brother and sister learn that they are of Negro descent.

1154 HELEN LEESON: A Peep at New-York Society . . . Philadelphia: Parry & McMillan, 1855. 367 p. AAS, AP, CU, H, NYP, Y

1155 HELEN MULGRAVE; or, Jesuit Executorship. New York: DeWitt & Davenport, 160 & 162 Nassau Street [185-?]. 312 p.

Anti-Catholic; laid in England. H, N, NYP

1156 HENTZ, MRS. CAROLINE LEE (WHITING). Courtship and Marriage; or, The Joys and Sorrows of American Life . . . Philadelphia: T. B. Peterson, No. 102 Chestnut Street [cop. 1856]. 522 p., front. BP, BU, LC, UC, Y

Contents: The Pet Beauty—The Fortunes of a Young Physician—The Two Sisters and the Two Uncles—The Mob Cap; or, My Grandmother's Trunk—The Pedler, the Sequel to the Mob Cap—The Beauty Transformed—The Drunkard's Daughter—Father Hilario, the Catholic—The Tempted—Aunty Mercy—The Village Pastor's Wife—Thanksgiving Day —The Stranger at the Banquet.

Also issued with paper covers in two vols. AAS (v.1)

1157 ———— Eoline; or, Magnolia Vale. A Novel . . . Philadelphia: A. Hart, 1852. 261 p.

Life in the South.   AAS, BU, CU, H, HEH, LCP, N, UC, UP

1158 ———— Ernest Linwood: A Novel . . . Boston: John P. Jewett and Company. Cleveland, Ohio: Jewett, Proctor and Worthington. New York: Sheldon, Lamport and Blakeman, 1856. 467 p.

               AAS, BA, BP, BU, CU, H, LCP, N, UC, UM, UP, UVB, Y

A tale of New York City.

1159 ———— Helen and Arthur; or, Miss Thusa's Spinning-Wheel. A Novel . . . Philadelphia: A. Hart, 1853. 238 p., front.

               AAS, BU, CU, H, N, NYP, UC, UVB

1160 ———— The Lost Daughter, and Other Stories of the Heart . . . Philadelphia: T. B. Peterson & Brothers, 306 Chestnut Street [cop. 1857]. 308 p., front.

               AAS, BU, CU, H, NYP, UC, UM, UP, Y

Contains: The Pea-Green Taffeta—The Purple Satin Dress—The Red Velvet Bodice—The Soldier's Bride—The Premature Declaration of Love —Aunt Patty's Scrap-Bag.

1161 ———— Marcus Warland; or, The Long Moss Spring. A Tale of the South . . . Philadelphia: A. Hart, 1852. 287 p.

Proslavery.   AP, BP, BU, CU, H, LC, LCP, UC

1162 ———— The Mob Cap, and Other Tales . . . Philadelphia: T. B. Peterson, No. 98 Chestnut Street [1852?]. 192 p., illus.
               CU

Contains: The Pedler, the Sequel to The Mob Cap—The Catholic—The Drunkard's Daughter—A Legend of the Silver Wave—Mary Hawthorne —The Premature Declaration—Thanksgiving Day.
See also No. 1166.

1163 ———— The Planter's Northern Bride: A Novel . . . Philadelphia: A. Hart, late Carey & Hart, 1854. 2 vols. (300, 281 p.), illus.   AAS, BU, CU, H, LCP, UV, Y
Copyrighted by A. Hart in 1854.
Also issued with imprint: Philadelphia: Parry & M'Millan, successors to A. Hart, 1854.   HEH, LC
The T. B. Peterson, No. 102 Chestnut St. [n.d.], ed. records the fictitious copyright notice: "In the Year 1851, by A. Hart."   UM
Proslavery.

1164 ———— Rena; or, The Snow Bird. A Nouvellette . . . Philadelphia: A. Hart, 1851. 273 p. AAS, AP, BU, CU, UC, UM

1165 ———— Robert Graham: A Novel . . . Philadelphia: Parry & McMillan, 1855. 256 p. AAS, CU, H, HEH, LC, LCP, UC, UP, Y
At head of title: "A Sequel to Linda", Wright (1774-1850), No. 1157.

1166 ———— Ugly Effie; or, The Neglected One and the Pet Beauty, and Other Tales . . . Philadelphia: T. B. Peterson, No. 98 Chestnut Street [1852?]. 195-374 p. NYP
Also contains: The Two Uncles—Neglecting a Fee—The Young Physician and His Fortunes—The Tempted—Aunt Mercy—The Village Pastor's Wife—The Stranger at the Banquet.
This is uniform with her *Mob Cap*, and the pagination is continuous to it; but I have not found the two together. The contents of both items were republished in her *Courtship and Marriage* [cop. 1856], No. 1156.

1167 ———— The Victim of Excitement; The Bosom Serpent, etc. . . . Philadelphia: A. Hart, 1853. 257 p.
AAS, BP, H, LC, UP, UVB, Y
Also contains: The Blind Girl's Story—The Parlour Serpent—The Shaker Girl—The Rainy Evening—Three Scenes in the Life of a Belle—The Fatal Cosmetic—The Abyssinian Neophyte—The Village Anthem—The Bosom Serpent—My Grandmother's Bracelet—The Mysterious Reticule—Love after Marriage.
Also published as: *Love after Marriage, and Other Stories of the Heart.* Philadelphia: T. B. Peterson, No. 102 Chestnut Street [cop. 1857].
HEH, N, UM, UVB

1168 ———— Wild Jack; or, The Stolen Child, and Other Stories. Including the Celebrated Magnolia Leaves . . . Philadelphia: A. Hart, 1853. 277 p. LC
Also contains: Bell and Rose—Percy; or, The Banished Son—The Little Broom Boy—Selim: An Oriental Tale—Howard, the Apprentice Boy—The Black Mask—A Tale of the Land of Flowers—Magnolia Leaves—A Trip to the Bay—Paradise of the Dead—The Sex of the Soul.
Also published as: *The Banished Son, and Other Stories of the Heart.* Philadelphia: T. B. Peterson, No. 102 Chestnut Street [cop. 1856].
AAS, LC, NYP, Y

1169 HERBERT, HENRY WILLIAM. The Cavaliers of England; or, The Times of the Revolutions of 1642 and 1688 . . . New York: Redfield, 1852. 428 p.
AAS, BP, CU, H, HEH, LC, N, NYP, UC, UM, UP, Y
Contents: The Brothers in Arms—The Rival Sisters—Jasper St. Aubyn—Vernon in the Vale.
Half-title: "Legends of Love and Chivalry."

1170 ———— The Chevaliers of France, from the Crusaders to the Marechals of Louis XIV . . . New York: Redfield, 1853.
399 p.   AAS, BP, CU, H, HEH, LC, NYP, UC, UM, UP, UVB, Y
Contents: Sir Hugues de Coucy—Eustache de St. Pierre—The Fortunes of the Maid of Arc—Hamilton of Bothwelhaugh—Ahsahgunushk Numamahtahseng.
Half-title: "Legends of Love and Chivalry."

1171 ———— The Knights of England, France and Scotland . . . New York: Redfield, 1852. 426 p.
AAS, BP, CU, H, HEH, LC, NYP, UC, UM, UP, Y
Contents: The Saxon's Oath—The Norman's Vengeance—The Faith of Woman—The Erring Arrow—The Saxon Prelate's Doom—The Fate of the Blanche Navire—The Saxon's Bridal—The Syrian Lady—The Templar's Trials—The Renegado—The False Ladye—The Vassal's Wife—True Love's Devotion—Passages in the Life of Mary Stuart—Elizabeth's Remorse—The Moorish Father.
Half-title: "Legends of Love and Chivalry."

1172 ———— Persons and Pictures from the Histories of France and England, from the Norman Conquest to the Fall of the Stuarts . . . New York: Riker, Thorne & Co., 1854. 440 p.
AAS, BP, CU, H, HEH, LC, NYP, UC, UM, UP, UVB, Y
Contents: Editha, the Swan-Necked—The Countess of Montfort—Philippa of Hainault—The Forest of Le Mans—The Maid of Orleans—The Lady Catherine Douglass—Margaret of Anjou—Henry VIII and His Wives—Anne Ascue—Jane Grey and Guilford Dudley—Elizabeth Tudor and Mary Stuart—Sir Walter Raleigh and His Wife—Cromwell and Charles I—Charlotte de La Tremouille—The King's Gratitude—The Lady Alice Lisle—Ditton-in-the-Dale.

1173 ———— The Quorndon Hounds; or, A Virginian at Melton Mowbray . . . Philadelphia: Getz, Buck & Co., 1852. 173 p., illus.   AAS, CU, LC, NYP, UP, UVB, Y

1174 ———— Wager of Battle: A Tale of Saxon Slavery in Sherwood Forest . . . New York: Mason Brothers, 1855. 336 p.
AAS, BA, BP, BU, CU, H, HEH, LC, NYH, NYP, UC, UM, UP, UVB, Y

1175 [HERBERT, MRS. SARAH ANN (FLANDERS).] Trust; or, A Peep at Eaton Parsonage . . . New York: Anson D. F. Randolph, 1866. 190 p., front.   AAS

1176 HERBERT TRACY; or, The Trials of Mercantile Life, and the Morality of Trade. By a "Counting-House Man." New York: John C. Riker, 1851. 180 p.   AAS, H, NYP, Y

1177 THE HERMIT OF THE CHESAPEAKE; or, Lessons of a Lifetime. Philadelphia: Barclay & Co., 610 Arch Street [cop. 1869]. 82 p., illus. Printed in double cols. AAS
Amer. Cat. 1876 enters under G. R. Price.

1178 HERNDON, MRS. MARY ELIZA (HICKS). Louise Elton; or, Things Seen and Heard. A Novel . . . Philadelphia: Lippincott, Grambo & Co., 1853. 407 p. AAS, LC, NYP, Y
A reply to *Uncle Tom's Cabin.*

1179 HERNE, PEREGRINE, *pseud.* Perils and Pleasures of a Hunter's Life; or, The Romance of Hunting. By Peregrine Herne [pseud.]. Boston: L. P. Crown. Philadelphia: J. W. Bradley, 1854. 336 p., illus. HEH, LC, Y
Also issued with imprint: Philadelphia: J. W. Bradley. New Haven, Auburn, 1854. See Wagner-Camp, 239a.

1180 HERRINGTON, W. D. The Captain's Bride: A Tale of the War. By W. D. Herrington, 3rd N. C. Cavalry, Author of "The Refugee's Niece," "The Deserter's Daughter," etc. . . . Raleigh: William B. Smith, 1864. 22 p. BA, NYH, Y

1181 ———— The Deserter's Daughter . . . Raleigh: Wm. B. Smith & Co., 1865. 27 p.
BA, BP, CU, H, HEH, LC, LCP, N, NYH, NYP, UC, UP, UVB, Y

1182 HERTFORD, JOSEPH. Personals; or, Perils of the Period . . . New York: printed for the author, 1870. 339, viii p., front.
Extramarital affairs. AAS, CU, H, HEH, LC, N, NYH, Y

1183 HERVEY, JAMES WALTER. The Scroll and Locket; or, The Maniac of the Mound. A Temperance Tale . . . Indianapolis: Indianapolis Journal Company, printers, 1858. 109 p.
Indiana University Library copy.

1184 HEYWOOD, JOSEPH CONVERSE. How Will It End? A Romance . . . Philadelphia: J. B. Lippincott & Co., 1872. 301 p.
At the end of the Civil War. AAS, BP, H, HEH, LC, NYP

1185 HIATT, JAMES M. The Test of Loyalty . . . Indianapolis: Merrill and Smith, 1864. 180 p. BU, CU, LC, UP, UVB
On desertion; early war period in Indiana and eastern Tennessee.

HICKLING, WILLIAM, *pseud.* *See* De Costa, Benjamin Franklin

HICKOX, CHAUNCEY. The Marquis. *In* Not Pretty, but Precious (1872), No. 1804.

1186 [HICKS, JENNIE E.] Sparkles from Saratoga. By Sophie Sparkle [pseud.] . . . New York: American News Co., 1873. 340 p., illus.   AAS, BP, CU, H, NYH, NYP

1187 HICKS, MRS. REBECCA. The Lady Killer . . . Philadelphia: Lippincott, Grambo and Co., 1851. 127 p.   LC, NYP
Laid in Virginia.

1188 —————— The Milliner and the Millionaire . . . Philadelphia: Lippincott, Grambo & Co., 1852. 167 p.
Laid in the South.   AAS, BU, HEH, LC, UM

1189 [HIGGINS, ALVIN S.] The Mishaps of Mr. Ezekiel Pelter . . . Chicago: S. C. Griggs and Company, 1875. 302 p., illus.
Humorous satire.   AAS, CU, H, HEH, LC, LCP, UC, Y

1190 [HIGGINS, THOMAS W.] The Crooked Elm; or, Life by the Way-Side . . . Boston: published for the author, by Whittemore, Niles, and Hall, 1857. 452 p., front.
Laid in New York City.   AAS, BP, BU, CU, HEH, Y

1191 HIGGINSON, THOMAS WENTWORTH. Malbone: An Oldport Romance . . . Boston: Fields, Osgood & Co., 1869. 244 p.
    AAS, BA, BP, CU, HEH, LC, N, Y

1192 [HIGHAM, MRS. MARY R.] Athol. By M. R. H. . . . New York: Pott, Young & Co., 1873. 423 p.   AAS, BP, BU, CU, HEH, LCP, Y
Civil War background.

1193 —————— Cloverly . . . New York: Anson D. F. Randolph & Company, 770 Broadway [cop. 1875]. 256 p.
    AAS, BP, H, LC, LCP, NYP
LCP has two variant copies: one with the author's name only on the title page; the other with the author's name, followed by a listing of her works.

HILBORN, MRS. CHARLOTTE. *See* Hilbourne, Mrs. Charlotte S.

1194 HILBOURNE, MRS. CHARLOTTE S. Alice Waters; or, The Sandown Victory. A Temperance Story, for Old and Young . . . Portland [Me.]: F. G. Rich, 1867. 22 p.   CU, LC

1195 ———— The Diamond Necklace; or, The Island Recluse. A Tale of Interesting Incidents and Adventures, Connected with the Life of a Young Nobleman, in Pursuit of His Birthplace and Parentage . . . Lowell, Mass., 1852. 31 p. Printed in double cols.   LC

1196 ———— Effie and I; or, Seven Years in a Cotton Mill. A Story of the Spindle City . . . Cambridge: printed by Allen and Farnham, 1863. 276 p.   AAS, BP, CU, H, HEH, N, NYP, Y
     Laid in Lowell, Mass.

1197 ———— Elmwood; or, The Children of the Manse . . . Lowell: S. N. Merrill, printer, 1857. 73 p.   Y

1198 [HILDRETH, RICHARD.] The White Slave; or, Memoirs of a Fugitive . . . Boston: Tappan and Whittemore, 1852. 408 p., illus.
             AAS, BA, BP, BU, CU, H, HEH, LC, LCP, N, NYH, NYP, UC, UP, Y
     This is Wright (1774-1850), Nos. 1185-1191, with the events brought up to date.
     Also issued with imprint: Boston: Tappan and Whittemore. Milwaukie, Wis.: Rood and Whittemore, 1852.   HEH

1199 HILL, MRS. AGNES (LEONARD) SCANLAND. Heights and Depths . . . Chicago: Henry A. Sumner; J. B. Lippincott & Co., Philadephia; Lee & Shepard, Boston, 1871. 271 p.
                                                           BP, LC, N, NYP

1200 [————] Myrtle Blossoms. By Molly Myrtle [pseud.] . . . Chicago, Ill.: published for the authoress by J. C. W. Bailey, 1863. 304 p.   BU, LC, N, NYH, Y

1201 ———— Vanquished: A Novel. By Agnes Leonard . . . New York: G. W. Carleton & Co. London: S. Low, Son & Co., 1867. 392 p.   AAS, HEH, LC, LCP

1202 HILL, ALONZO F. John Smith's Funny Adventures on a Crutch; or, The Remarkable Peregrinations of a One-Legged Soldier after the War . . . Philadelphia: John E. Potter and Company, 1869. 374 p., illus. BP, CU, HEH, LC, LCP, N, UC, UM, Y
AAS copy without date on title page.
From city to city, and to California via the Isthmus.

1203 ——— Our Boys. The Personal Experiences of a Soldier in the Army of the Potomac . . . Philadelphia: John E. Potter, 1864. 412 p., front. AAS, BP, CU, HEH, LC, LCP, N, NYH

1204 ——— The White Rocks; or, The Robbers' Den. A Tragedy of the Mountains . . . Philadelphia: John E. Potter, 1866. 390 p., front. LC

1205 [HILL, GEORGE CANNING.] Amy Lee; or, Without and Within . . . Boston: Brown, Bazin and Company, 1856. 376 p.
AAS, CU, Y

1206 [———] Cap Sheaf, a Fresh Bundle. By Lewis Myrtle [pseud.]. New York: Redfield, 1853. 313 p.
Country living in early New York. CU, H, LC, NYP, UP

1207 [———] Dovecote; or, The Heart of the Homestead . . . Boston: John P. Jewett and Company. Cleveland, Ohio: Jewett, Proctor and Worthington. London: Sampson Low, Son and Co., 1854. 361 p. AAS, CU, HEH, LC, N, UC, Y
Also published as: *Sweet Home; or, Life in the Country. Showing the Joys and Sorrows of Every-Day Home-Life in New England.* Boston: Albert Colby & Co., 1858. CU, NYP

1208 ——— Esmerelda, the Italian Peasant Girl: A Tale of Ravenna . . . Boston: Frederick Gleason, 1852. 100 p. Printed in double cols. AAS, UP
Also contains: The Child's Tear; or, The Miser's Heart Unsealed, by H. N. Hathaway.

1209 [———] Homespun; or, Five and Twenty Years Ago. By Thomas Lackland [pseud.] . . . New York: Hurd and Houghton, 1867. 346 p. AAS, BA, BP, LC, LCP, NYH, UC, UP

1210 [———] Our Parish; or, Annals of Pastor and People. Boston: L. P. Crown & Co. Philadelphia: J. W. Bradley, 1854. 452 p., front. AAS, BP, HEH, NYP, UP, Y
Also published as: *Our Parish; or, Pen Paintings of Village Life.* Boston: Crown & Co. Philadelphia: J. W. Bradley, 1857. AAS, HEH

———— Peggy Dawson: A Leaf from the Life of a Seamstress.
In A. G. Piper, The Young Fisherman (1853), No. 1913.

1211 [HILL, L. C.] Laure: The History of a Blighted Life. By
L. C. H. Philadelphia: Claxton, Remsen & Haffelfinger, 1869.
371 p.   AAS
Occupation of New Orleans by Union troops mentioned.

1212 HILLIARD, HENRY WASHINGTON. De Vane: A Story of Plebeians
and Patricians . . . New York: Blelock & Company, 1865.
2 vols. in 1. (552 p.)
      AAS, BA, CU, H, HEH, LC, LCP, N, NYP, UC, UV, Y
A defense of the Methodist church.

1213 HILLS, ALFRED C. MacPherson, the Great Confederate Philos-
opher and Southern Blower. A Record of His Philosophy,
His Career . . . and . . . Election to the Office of Governor of
Louisiana . . . New York: James Miller, 1864. 209 p.
      AAS, BA, BP, CU, H, LC, LCP, N, NYH, NYP, UM, Y
Humorous satire.

1214 HINCKLEY, MARY. The Camphene Lamp; or, Touch Not,
Taste Not, Handle Not . . . Lowell [Mass.]: James P. Walker,
1852. 62 p.   AAS, LC
A temperance tale.

1215 HINE, LUCIUS ALONZO. Currie Cummings; or, Love's Labor Not
Lost . . . Cincinnati: Longley & Brother, 1853. 96 p.
Printed in double cols.   H
At head of title: "All Is Fiction That Is Not Truth."

1216 [HINTON, HOWARD.] School Days at Mount Pleasant, Includ-
ing Sketches and Legends of the Neutral Ground. By Ralph
Morley [pseud.]. New York: H. L. Hinton, 1871. 327 p.,
illus.   NYP
Also published as: *My Comrades: Adventures in the Highlands and
Legends of the Neutral Ground. By Hd. H.* New York: Henry L.
Hinton & Co., 1874.   AAS, CU, H, HEH, LC, N, NYH, Y
A military school on the Hudson.

1217 HITS AND HINTS. Contents: How to Make Millionaires. The
Late Captain Fume. Canonical Amusements. Skipper
Sinker. Jonathan on the Road to Gentility. Mr. Blot Gored
by Bulls. Aunt Diadama. Luckless Wight. Hospitality.
Manners. Boston: John J. Dyer & Co., 1867. 70 p., illus.
      AAS, BP, H, NYP, UC

1218 HOFFMAN, MRS. MARY JANE. Agnes Hilton; or, Practical Views of Catholicity. A Tale of Trials and Triumphs . . . New York: P. O'Shea, 1864. 477 p. AAS, LC

1219 ———— Alice Murray: A Tale . . . New York: P. O'Shea, 37 Barclay Street [cop. 1869]. 490 p. HEH, LC

1220 ———— Felix Kent; or, The New Neighbors . . . New York: P. O'Shea, 1871. 430 p. AAS, NYP
Laid in central New York.

1221 ———— The Orphan Sisters; or, The Problem Solved . . . New York: D. & J. Sadlier & Co. Montreal, 1875. 352 p. LC

1222 HOLCOMBE, WILLIAM HENRY. In Both Worlds . . . Philadelphia: J. B. Lippincott & Co., 1870. 387 p. AAS, NYP, Y
Written as the autobiography of Lazarus of Bethany.

1223 HOLDING, C. B. Green Bluff: A Temperance Story. By Rev. C. B. Holding. Sold by Thomas Soper, for His Benefit. St. Louis, Mo.: J. W. McIntyre, 1874. 215 p. HEH
Preface dated "May, 1874," and signed "C. B. H."
HEH also has a reprint: Boston: Rand, Avery, and Company [n.d.], which records "by T. N. Soper" on title page and omits "C. B. H." at the end of preface.

1224 HOLGATE, JEROME BONAPARTE. Noachidae; or, Noah and His Descendants . . . Buffalo: Breed, Butler & Co., 1860. 354 p.
Fictional history of early nations. H, HEH, LC, NYP

1225 HOLLAND, C. Aspasia . . . Philadelphia: J. B. Lippincott & Co., 1869. 192 p. AAS, CU, LC, UC
Purported autobiography.

1226 HOLLAND, JOSIAH GILBERT. Arthur Bonnicastle: An American Novel . . . New York: Scribner, Armstrong & Co., 1873. 401 p., illus.
AAS, BA, BP, BU, CU, H, HEH, LC, LCP, N, NYP, UC, UP, UVB, Y
Life at Yale and temptations in New York City.

1227 ———— The Bay-Path: A Tale of New England Colonial Life . . . New York: G. P. Putnam & Co., 1857. 418 p.
AAS, BA, BP, CU, H, HEH, LC, LCP, N, NYP, UC, UVB, Y
Laid in the Connecticut Valley, 1638-1652.

1228 ———— Miss Gilbert's Career: An American Story ... New York: Charles Scribner. London: Sampson Low, Son & Co., 1860. 476 p.

AAS, BA, BU, CU, H, HEH, LC, LCP, N, NYP, UC, UVB, Y

Miss Gilbert wrote novels and then she married a minister.

1229 ———— Sevenoaks: A Story of To-Day . . . New York: Scribner, Armstrong & Co., 1875. 441 p., illus.

AAS, BA, CU, H, HEH, LC, LCP, N, NYP, UVB, Y

Laid in New York City.

1230 [HOLLEY, MARIETTA.] My Opinions and Betsey Bobbet's, Designed as a Beacon Light, to Guide Women to Life, Liberty, and the Pursuit of Happiness, but Which May Be Read by Members of the Sterner Sect, without Injury to Themselves or the Book. By Josiah Allen's Wife [pseud.] . . . Hartford, Conn.: American Publishing Company; W. E. Bliss & Co., Toledo, Ohio; F. G. Gilman & Co., Chicago, Ill.; Nettleton & Co., Cincinnati, Ohio, 1873. 432 p., illus.

AAS, BU, HEH, LC, LCP, NYP, UP, Y

1231 HOLLISTER, GIDEON HIRAM. Mount Hope; or, Philip, King of the Wampanoags. An Historical Romance . . . New York: Harper & Brothers, 1851. 280 p.

AAS, AP, BA, BP, BU, CU, H, HEH, LC, N, NYP, UC, UM, UP, UVB, Y

HOLM, SAXE, *pseud*. *See* Jackson, Mrs. Helen Maria (Fiske) Hunt

1232 HOLMES, ALICE A. Arcadian Leaves . . . New York: Pudney & Russell, printers, 1858. 122 p. AAS, BU, H, LC, UM, UP

Contains: Eva; or, The Basket of Wild Flowers—The Father's Curse; or, The Bride of the Wave.

1233 HOLMES, MRS. MARY JANE (HAWES). The Cameron Pride; or, Purified by Suffering. A Novel . . . New York: G. W. Carleton & Co. London: S. Low, Son & Co., 1867. 415 p.

AAS, CU, HEH, LC, UVB, Y

1234 ———— Cousin Maud, and Rosamond . . . New York: C. M. Saxton, Barker & Co., 1860. 374 p. H

Also contains: Rosamond; or, The Youthful Error—Diamonds—Bad Spelling—Maggie Lee—The Answered Prayer.

1235 ——— Darkness and Daylight: A Novel . . . New York: Carleton, 1864. 384 p.   AAS, CU, LCP, UC, UVB, Y

1236 ——— Dora Deane; or, The East India Uncle. And Maggie Miller; or, Old Hagar's Secret . . . New York: C. M. Saxton, 1859. 474 p.   AAS, UP

1237 ——— Edna Browning; or, The Leighton Homestead. A Novel . . . New York: G. W. Carleton & Co. London: S. Low, Son & Co., 1872. 423 p.
AAS, BU, CU, H, HEH, LC, LCP, N, NYP, UC, UM, Y
Upstate New York.

1238 ——— The English Orphans; or, A Home in the New World . . . New York: D. Appleton & Company. London, 1855. 331 p.   AAS, BA, HEH, NYP, UC

1239 ——— Ethelyn's Mistake; or, The Home in the West. A Novel . . . New York: G. W. Carleton. London: S. Low, Son & Co., 1869. 380 p.
AAS, BU, CU, H, HEH, LC, LCP, N, NYP, UC, UP, UVB, Y
Laid in "Olney," Iowa.

1240 ——— The Homestead on the Hillside, and Other Tales . . . New York and Auburn: Miller, Orton & Mulligan, 1856. 379 p.   AAS, LC
Also contains: Rice Corner—The Gilberts; or, Rice Corner Number Two—The Thanksgiving Party and Its Consequences—The Old Red House among the Mountains—Glen's Creek—The Gable-Roofed House at Snowdon.

1241 ——— Hugh Worthington . . . New York: Carleton, 1865. 370 p.   AAS, CU, HEH, LC, LCP, N, UM, UP, UV, Y
Concerns a pro-Union man from the Bluegrass country.

1242 ——— 'Lena Rivers . . . New York and Auburn: Miller, Orton & Mulligan, 1856. 416 p.   HEH, UM, UVB
Ante bellum Kentucky.

1243 ——— Marian Grey; or, The Heiress of Redstone Hall . . . New York: Carleton, 1863. 400 p.
Laid in Kentucky.   AAS, HEH, LC, LCP, N, NYP, UVB

1244 ———— Meadow-Brook . . . New York: Miller, Orton & Co., 1857. 380 p.   AAS, LC, NYP, UC, UP
A plantation in Georgia.

1245 ———— Millbank; or, Roger Irving's Ward. A Novel . . . New York: G. W. Carleton & Co. London: S. Low, Son & Co., 1871. 402 p.   AAS, H, HEH, LC, LCP, NYP, UC, UP, UVB, Y

1246 ———— Rose Mather: A Tale . . . New York: G. W. Carleton & Co. London: S. Low, Son & Co., 1868. 407 p.
A Civil War story.   AAS, CU, HEH, LC, LCP, UC, UP, Y

1247 ———— Tempest and Sunshine; or, Life in Kentucky . . . New York: D. Appleton & Company, 1854. 381 p.
AAS, H, UC, UVB, Y

1248 ———— West Lawn, and The Rector of St. Mark's . . . New York: G. W. Carleton & Co. London: S. Low, Son & Co., 1874. 413 p.   AAS, CU, H, HEH, LCP, N, NYP, UM, UP, UVB, Y

1249 HOLMES, OLIVER WENDELL. Elsie Venner: A Romance of Destiny . . . Boston: Ticknor and Fields, 1861. 2 vols. (288, 312 p.)
AAS, BA, BP, BU, CU, H, HEH, LC, LCP, N, NYH(V.1), NYP,
On prenatal influence.   UC, UM, UP, UVB, Y

1250 ———— The Guardian Angel . . . Boston: Ticknor and Fields, 1867. 420 p.
AAS, BA, BP, BU, CU, H, HEH, LCP, N, NYP, UC, UP, UVB, Y
The Civil War period.

1251 [HOLT, JOHN SAUNDERS.] Abraham Page, Esq.: A Novel . . . Philadelphia: J. B. Lippincott & Co., 1868. 354 p.
The South prior to the war.   AAS, BP, H, HEH, LC, LCP, N, UM, UVB

1252 [————] What I Know about Ben Eccles. By Abraham Page [pseud.]. Philadelphia: J. B. Lippincott & Co., 1869. 407 p.   AAS, BP, H, HEH, LC, LCP, N, NYP
Of religious interest.

1253 HOME IS HOME: A Domestic Tale. New York: D. Appleton and Company, 1851. 299 p.   H

1254　HOME ON A FURLOUGH: A Sketch of Real Life. Springfield, Mass.: W. J. Holland, 1864. 16 p.　　　　　AAS

1255　A HOME ON THE DEEP; or, The Mariner's Trials on the Dark Blue Sea. By a Son of the Ocean. Boston: Higgins, Bradley & Dayton, 1857. 483 p., illus.　　　　　BP, H, LC, N

1256　[HOMES, MRS. MARY SOPHIE (SHAW) ROGERS.] Carrie Harrington; or, Scenes in New Orleans. A Novel. By Millie Mayfield [pseud.] . . . New York: A. Atchison, 1857. 354 p.
　　　　　NYP

1257　[HOOPER, GEORGE W.] Down the River; or, Practical Lessons under the Code Duello. By an Amateur . . . New York: E. J. Hale & Son, 1874. 267, [1] p., illus.
　　　　　AAS, BP, CU, H, HEH, LC, LCP, N, NYP, UC
Fictional treatment of famous southern duels.

1258　HOOPER, HENRY. The Lost Model: A Romance . . . Philadelphia: J. B. Lippincott & Co., 1874. 386 p.　　　　　BP, LC

　　　　HOOPER, JOHNSON JONES. The Hanimal Show. In O. P. Baldwin, comp., Southern and South-Western Sketches [1855?], No. 200.

1259　———— The Widow Rugby's Husband. A Night at the Ugly Man's, and Other Tales of Alabama . . . Philadelphia: A. Hart, 1851. 169 p., illus.　　　　　BP, CU, UP, UVB
This is a reprint of Hooper's A Ride with Old Kit Kuncker (Tuscaloosa, 1849), according to W. Blair, Native American Humor (New York [1937]), p. 185.

　　　　HOOPER, MRS. LUCY HAMILTON (JONES). The Blue Cabinet. In Short Stories, 2d ser. (1869), No. 2211.

　　　　———— The Photographer's Story. In Short Stories, 2d ser. (1869), No. 2211.

　　　　———— Snow upon the Waters. In Rougegorge (1870), No. 2131.

　　　　———— Under False Colors. In Not Pretty, but Precious (1872), No. 1804.

1260 HOPE, CECIL. Seabury Castle . . . Philadelphia: J. B. Lippincott & Co., 1869. 96 p. LC, LCP, NYP, UM

1261 HOPE'S ANCHOR. New York: Everit Bros., printers, 1870. 34 p.
Laid in Rhode Island. LC, NYP

1262 HOPKINS, ALPHONSO ALVA. His Prison-Bars, and the Way of Escape . . . Rochester, N. Y.: Rural Home Publishing Co. New York: Hurd and Houghton [cop. 1874]. 256 p.
The Civil War and politics. LC, LCP

1263 [HOPKINS, MRS. ELIZA ANN (WOODRUFF).] Ella Lincoln; or, Western Prairie Life. An Autobiography. By Mrs. E. A. W. H. Boston: James French & Company, 1857. 359 p.
AAS, CU, H, LC, N
Also published as: Ella Lincoln; or, Early Haste and Late Repentance. An Autobiography. Boston: E. O. Libby and Company, 1858. HEH

1264 HOPKINS, SAMUEL. The Youth of the Old Dominion . . . Boston: John P. Jewett & Co. Cleveland, Ohio: Jewett, Proctor, and Worthington. New York: Sheldon, Blakeman & Co., 1856. 473 p.
AAS, BA, BP, CU, H, HEH, LC, N, NYH, NYP, UC, UM, Y
From Jamestown to Bacon's rebellion.

1265 [HORN, HENRY J.] ed. Strange Visitors: A Series of Original Papers, Embracing Philosophy . . . Fiction, Satire . . . Narrative . . . By the Spirits of Irving, Willis, Thackeray . . . and Others Now Dwelling in the Spirit World. Dictated through a Clairvoyant . . . New York: Carleton. London: S. Low, Son & Co., 1869. 249, [1] p. BP, BU, H, HEH, LC, LCP, NYP

1266 [HORNBLOWER, MRS. JANE ELIZABETH (ROSCOE).] "The Julia" . . . New York: Robert Carter & Brothers, 1859. 388 p.
A tale of the sea. BP, CU, LC, NYP

1267 [————] Nellie of Truro . . . New York: Robert Carter & Brothers, 1856. 432 p. BP, BU, CU, HEH, LC, Y
The domestic life of a wealthy family.

1268 [————] Vara; or, The Child of Adoption. New York: Robert Carter & Brothers, 1854. 316 p.
AAS, BP, CU, HEH, NYP, UP, Y

1269 HORRIBLE AND AWFUL DEVELOPMENTS, from the Confession of William Morrison, the Rocky Mountain Trapper; Giving a True and Faithful Account of His Murders and Depredations on the Plains . . . To Which Is Attached the Narrative of His Wife . . . Philadelphia: E. E. Barclay, 1852. 31 p., illus. Y

1270 HORTON, MRS. M. B. The Wife's Messengers . . . Philadelphia: J. B. Lippincott & Co., 1869. 323 p.
AAS, BP, H, HEH, LC, LCP, NYP

1271 HOSMER, HEZEKIAH LORD. Adela, the Octoroon . . . Columbus: Follett, Foster & Co., 1860. 400 p.
AAS, HEH, N, NYH, NYP, UP, Y
Antislavery.

1272 [————] The Octoroon. By H. L. H. New York: Follett, Foster & Co., 1863. 310 p. CU, HEH, NYP
This is a condensed version of his *Adela, the Octoroon* (1860).

1273 HOSMER, JAMES KENDALL. The Thinking Bayonet . . . Boston: Walker, Fuller and Company, 1865. 326 p.
AAS, BA, BP, BU, CU, H, HEH, LC, LCP, N, NYH, NYP, UM, UP, Y
A Civil War story.

1274 HOSMER, MRS. MARGARET (KERR). Blanche Gilroy: A Girl's Story . . . Philadelphia: J. B. Lippincott & Co., 1871. 330 p.
AAS, BP, CU, HEH, LCP, NYP

1275 ———— The Morrisons: A Story of Domestic Life . . . New York: John Bradburn, 1864. 382 p. BP, CU, LCP, NYP

1276 ———— The Subtle Spell: A Temperance Story . . . Philadelphia: Alfred Martien, 1873. 288 p., illus. AAS

1277 ———— Ten Years of a Lifetime . . . New York: M. Doolady, 1866. 422 p. AAS, BP, CU, H, HEH, LC, LCP, NYP

———— To Please Aunt Martha. *In* Short Stories (1869), No. 2210.

———— The Victims of Dreams. *In* Not Pretty, but Precious (1872), No. 1804.

1278 HOUSEHOLD NARRATIVES, for the Family Circle. Philadelphia: H. C. Peck & Theo. Bliss, 1854. 300 p., illus.   AAS, CU, UC
Contains: The Lover's [sic]; or, The Double Error, by Mrs. Emma C. Embury—The Perplexed Student: A Lesson for Bachelor Bookworms, by Mrs. C. H. Butler—Amy, by Mrs. Caroline H. Butler—The Crevasse; or, The Widow Morel, by E. B. Gardette, M.D.
Also published as: *Home Made Happy; or, Pictures of Every Day Life for the Family Circle*. Philadelphia: H. C. Peck & T. Bliss, 1858.   LC

1279 HOUSEKEEPER, M. R. My Husband's Crime . . . New York: Harper & Brothers, 1868. 115 p., illus. Printed in double cols.   AAS, BP, LC, LCP, NYP

HOUSTON, JAMES A., *ed. See* Jones, Buehring H. The Sunny Land (1868), No. 1366.

HOWARD, BLANCHE WILLIS. *See* Teuffel, Mrs. Blanche Willis (Howard) von

1280 [HOWARD, JOSEPH.] Corry O'Lanus [pseud.]: His Views and Experiences . . . New York: G. W. Carleton & Co. London: S. Low, Son & Co., 1867. 236 p., illus.
AAS, BP, CU, HEH, LCP, NYH, NYP

1281 HOWE, MARY A. The Merchant-Mechanic: A Tale of "New England Athens" . . . New York: John Bradburn, 1865. 453 p.   AAS, BP, CU, H, HEH, LCP, N, NYP

1282 ———— The Rival Volunteers; or, The Black Plume Rifles . . . New York: John Bradburn, 1864. 377 p.
AAS, BA, BU, CU, HEH, LC, N, NYH, NYP, UC, Y
False marriage and blackmail; Civil War background.

HOWE, SARAH M. Blue-Eyed Jessie. *In* A. G. Piper, The Young Fisherman (1851), No. 1912.

1283 ———— Eustatia; or, The Sybil's Prophecy. A Tale of England, France and Spain . . . Boston: F. Gleason's Publishing Hall, 1852. 100 p. Printed in double cols.   Y

1284 ———— The Soldier's Daughter; or, The Conspirators of La Vendee. A Romance of Napoleon's Times . . . New York: Garrett & Co., 18 Ann Street [cop. 1853]. 112 p. Printed in double cols.   UC, UP

1285 ———— The Woodman's Rifle, and the Forest Maiden . . . New York: Dick & Fitzgerald, No. 18 Ann Street [187-?]. 88 p. Printed in double cols.   AAS

1286 [HOWE, WILLIAM WIRT.] The Pasha Papers: Epistles of Mohammed Pasha [pseud.], Rear Admiral of the Turkish Navy, Written from New York to His Friend Abel Ben Hassen. Translated into Anglo-American from the Original Manuscripts . . . New York: Charles Scribner. London: Sampson Low, Son & Co., 1859. 312 p.

   AAS, BA, BP, BU, CU, HEH, LC, LCP, N, NYH, NYP, UM, UP, Y
   Satire on New York City society.

1287 HOWELLS, WILLIAM DEAN. A Chance Acquaintance . . . Boston: James R. Osgood and Company, 1873. 279 p.

   AAS, AP, BP, BU, CU, H, HEH, LC, LCP, N, NYP, UC, UM, UP, UVB, Y

1288 ———— A Foregone Conclusion . . . Boston: James R. Osgood and Company, 1875. 265 p.

   AAS, BA, BP, BU, CU, H, HEH, LC, LCP, N, NYP, UC, UM, UP, UVB, Y
   Laid in Italy.

1289 ———— Their Wedding Journey . . . Boston: James R. Osgood and Company, 1872. 287 p., illus.

   AAS, BA, BP, CU, H, HEH, LC, LCP, N, NYP, UP, UVB, Y

1290 HOWLAND, MRS. MARIE. Papa's Own Girl: A Novel . . . New York: John P. Jewett. Boston: Lee & Shepard, 1874. 547 p.

   AAS, BP, H, HEH, LC, NYP, Y

1291 HOYT, JEHIEL KEELER. The Romance of the Table, in Three Parts. I, Breakfast; II, Dinner; III, Tea . . . New Brunswick, N. J.: Times Publishing Co., 1872. 445 p.

   HEH, LC, NYH, NYP, UM, UP, UV

1292 [HUBBELL, MRS. MARTHA (STONE).] The Shady Side; or, Life in a Country Parsonage. By a Pastor's Wife . . . Boston: John P. Jewett and Company. Cleveland, Ohio: Jewett, Proctor & Worthington, 1853. 349 p.

   BP, BU, CU, H, LC, LCP, N, NYH, NYP, UC, UM, UP, UV
   Also issued with imprint: Boston: John P. Jewett and Company. Cleveland, Ohio: Jewett, Proctor & Worthington. London: Low and Company, 1853. AAS, UP

Hudson, Mrs. Mary (Clemmer) Ames. *See* Ames, Mrs. Mary (Clemmer)

1293 [Huet, M. M.]   Alexander Tardy, the Poisoner or Pirate Chief of St. Domingo. By Author of "Morgan, the Buccaneer; or, The History of the Freebooters of the Antilles;" "Silver and Pewter: A Tale of High and Low Life in New York;" "The Seven Brothers of Wyoming . . ." Philadelphia: T. B. Peterson and Brothers, 306 Chestnut Street [1866?].   107 p.   AAS

1294 ——— Davis, the Pirate; or, The True History of the Freebooters of the Pacific . . . New York: H. Long & Brother, No. 43 Ann Street [cop. 1853].   104 p.   LC

1295 ——— Eva May, the Foundling; or, The Secret Dungeon. A Romance of New York . . . New York: Garrett & Co., 1853.   105 p.   Printed in double cols.   LC

1296 [———]   Kit Clayton; or, The Hero of the Road. By the Author of "Morgan, the Buccaneer; or, The History of the Freebooters of the Antilles" . . . Philadelphia: T. B. Peterson & Brothers, 306 Chestnut Street [1867?].   110 p.   AAS, H

1297 ——— Morgan, the Buccaneer; or, The True History of the Freebooters of the Antilles . . . New York: H. Long & Brother, No. 43 Ann Street [cop. 1853].   112 p.   LC

1298 ——— Silver and Pewter: A Tale of High Life and Low Life in New York . . . New York: H. Long & Brother, 43 Ann Street. Cincinnati, O.: H. B. Pearson & Co., 17 East Fourth St. [cop. 1852].   106 p., illus.   Printed in double cols.
AAS, H, HEH, LC, N, Y

1299 Hughes, Margie S.   Annetta; or, The Story of a Life . . . Cincinnati: Hitchcock and Walden. New York: Nelson and Phillips, 1873.   282 p., illus.   AAS, LC

1300 [Hughes, Mrs. Reginald.]   Margaret: A Story of Life in a Prairie Home. By Lyndon [pseud.]. New York: Charles Scribner & Co., 1868.   360 p.
AAS, BU, CU, H, HEH, LC, LCP, NYP, UP, Y

1301 [————] Oxley. By Lyndon [pseud.] . . . New York: Scribner, Armstrong & Company, 1873. 441 p.

AAS, BP, H, HEH, LC, LCP, NYP

HULSE, GEORGIANA A. *See* McLeod, Mrs. Georgiana A. (Hulse)

1302 [HUME, JOHN FERGUSON.] Five Hundred Majority; or, The Days of Tammany. By Willys Niles [pseud.]. New York: G. P. Putnam & Sons, 1872. 200 p. Printed in double cols.

AAS, BU, CU, H, HEH, LC, LCP, N, NYH, NYP, UM, Y

1303 HUME, MRS. R. S. Woman's Wrongs: A History of Mary and Fidelia . . . Portland [Me.]: printed by B. Thurston and Company, 1872. 223 p. AAS, LC

1304 HUNGERFORD, JAMES. The Old Plantation, and What I Gathered There in an Autumn Month . . . New York: Harper & Brothers, 1859. 369 p.

AAS, BP, BU, CU, H, HEH, LC, LCP, N, NYH, NYP, UP, UV, Y

Eastern Maryland in the 1830's.

1305 HUNT, JEDEDIAH. An Adventure on a Frozen Lake: A Tale of the Canadian Rebellion of 1837-8 . . . Cincinnati: printed at the Ben Franklin Book and Job Office, 1853. 46 p. LC

Also contains: The Massacre at Owego: An Indian Tale.

1306 [HUNT, SARA KEABLES.] The Brook, and The Tide Turning. New York: National Temperance Society, 1875. 91, 129 p., front. NYP

Cushing indicates that an unidentified Bates was jt. au.

1307 [HUNTER, MRS. MARTHA FENTON.] The Clifford Family; or, A Tale of the Old Dominion. By One of Her Daughters . . . New York: Harper & Brothers, 1852. 430 p.

AAS, H, LC, N, NYP

1308 [HUNTINGTON, CORNELIA.] Sea-Spray, a Long Island Village. By Martha Wickham [pseud.]. New York: Derby & Jackson. Cincinnati: H. W. Derby & Co., 1857. 460, [1] p.

AAS, BP, BU, CU, HEH, LC, NYH, NYP, Y

1309 [HUNTINGTON, JEDEDIAH VINCENT.] Alban: A Tale of the New World . . . New York: George P. Putnam. London: Colburn & Co., 1851. 496 p.

Sequel: *The Forest.* AAS, BA, BP, BU, CU, HEH, LCP, NYP, UC, UP, Y

Following the War of 1812.

1310 [————] Blonde and Brunette; or, The Gothamite Arcady . . . New York: D. Appleton and Company, 1858. 316 p.

AAS, BA, CU, H, HEH, LCP, N, NYP, UM, Y

Also published as: *A Tale of Real Life; or, Blonde and Brunette.* New York: D. W. Evans & Co., 1860. AAS

1311 ———— The Forest . . . New York: Redfield, 1852. 384 p.

AAS, BA, BP, BU, CU, HEH, LC, LCP, NYH, NYP, UC, UM, UP, Y

Sequel to *Alban.*
Upstate New York.

1312 ———— Rosemary; or, Life and Death . . . New York, Boston, Montreal: D. & J. Sadlier & Co., 1860. 522 p., front.

AAS, CU, H, HEH, LC, LCP, NYP, UC

HYLA, *pseud.* See Chaplin, Mrs. Jane (Dunbar)

1313 I WAS LEAN, and I Became Stout . . . Boston: A. Williams & Co., 1868. 36 p. AAS

The "Appendix," pp. [27]-36, sets forth good health practices.
A tale which emphasizes the importance of diet.

IANTHE, *pseud.* See Mendenhall, Mrs. V. L.

1314 ILSLEY, CHARLES PARKER. Forest and Shore; or, Legends of the Pine-Tree State . . . Boston: John P. Jewett and Company. Cleveland: Jewett, Proctor and Worthington. New York: Sheldon, Blakeman and Company, 1856. 426 p.

AAS, BP, CU, H, NYH, NYP, UM, Y

Contents: The Wrecker's Daughter—The Scout—The Light-Keeper—The Settlers—The Liberty Pole—The Storm at Sea—The Canadian Captive.

Also published as: *The Wrecker's Daughter, and Other Tales.* Boston: Albert Colby and Company, 1860. AAS

INCONNU, *pseud.* See Marsh, Mrs. Jeannie S.

L'INCONNUE, *pseud.* *See* French, Mrs. Lucy Virginia (Smith)

INGHAM, *Col.* FREDERIC, *pseud.* *See* Hale, Edward Everett

INGRAHAM, MISS A. Mina; or, The Lover's Mistake. *In* C. Bowline, The Iron Tomb [cop. 1852], No. 327.

1315 INGRAHAM, JOSEPH HOLT. Mortimer; or, The Bankrupt's Heiress. A Home Romance . . . New York: Frederic A. Brady, No. 22 Ann Street [cop. 1865]. 87 p., illus. Printed in double cols. UP

1316 [————] Nobody's Son; or, The Life and Adventures of Percival Mayberry [pseud.]. Written by Himself . . . Philadelphia: A. Hart, 1851. 225 p. LC
Also published as: *The Life and Adventures of Percival Mayberry. An Autobiography.* Philadelphia: T. B. Peterson [cop. 1854]. BU, NYP, UM, UP, UVB

1317 ———— The Pillar of Fire; or, Israel in Bondage . . . New York: Pudney & Russell, 1859. 600 p., front.
AAS, CU, H, LCP, N, UC, UP, UV, Y
Also issued with imprints: New York: Pudney & Russell; Sheldon & Co., 1859. AAS, UVB
And, New York: Pudney & Russell; H. Dayton, 1859. BU, HEH, LC, NYP
And, Philadelphia: G. G. Evans, 1859. UM

1318 [————] The Pirate Chief; or, The Cutter of the Ocean . . . New York: Dick & Fitzgerald, No. 18 Ann Street [186-?]. 99 p. Printed in double cols. HEH

1319 ———— The Prince of the House of David; or, Three Years in the Holy City. Being a Series of the Letters of Adina . . . Edited by J. H. Ingraham . . . New York: Pudney & Russell, 1855. 456 p., front. BP, BU, LC, NYP, UVB, Y

1320 ———— The Sunny South; or, The Southerner at Home, Embracing Five Years' Experience of a Northern Governess in the Land of the Sugar and the Cotton. Edited by Professor J. H. Ingraham . . . Philadelphia: G. G. Evans, 1860. 526 p.
AAS, BA, BP, BU, CU, H, HEH, LC, LCP, N, NYH, NYP, UC, UM, UP, UV, Y
Written in the form of letters by "Kate Conynghan," a pseudonym used by Ingraham.

1321 ———— The Throne of David, from the Consecration of the Shepherd of Bethlehem, to the Rebellion of Prince Absalom . . . In a Series of Letters Addressed by an Assyrian Ambassador, Resident at the Court of Saul and David, to His Lord and King on the Throne of Nineveh . . . Philadelphia: G. G. Evans, 1860. 603 p., illus.

AAS, AP, BP, BU, CU, H, LC, NYP, UP, UVB, Y
Also issued with imprint: Philadelphia: G. G. Evans, 1860. New York: H. Dayton. HEH

1322 AN INTERESTING LOVE STORY Found in a Rebel Camp Ground. Written by a Southern Soldier, Drafted into the Rebel Army, Whose Sympathies Were with the North. New York, 1863. 12 p. LC

INVISIBLE SAM, *pseud. See* Vose, Reuben

1323 IRENE: A TALE OF SOUTHERN LIFE; and Hathaway Strange. Philadelphia: J. B. Lippincott & Co., 1871. 69 p., front. Printed in double cols. H, NYP, Y

1324 [IRION, ALFRED BRIGGS.] Boaz: His Tribulations. Nashville, Tenn.: Wheeler, Marshall & Bruce [cop. 1874]. 244 p. LC
A Louisiana farmer in 1866.

1325 [IRVING, JOHN TREAT.] Harry Harson; or, The Benevolent Bachelor . . . New York: Samuel Hueston, 1853. 364 p., illus. AAS, BU, CU, HEH, N, UV, Y

———— Zadoc Town: A Legend of Dosoris. *In* The Knickerbocker Gallery (1855), No. 1492.

———— [Author of the stories listed in note below.] *In* Tales of the Time [1861], No. 2426.
Obed Groot—Derrick Van Dam—The Van Gelders of Matinecock.

1326 [IRVING, THOMAS J.] In the Rapids: A Romance. By Gerald Hart [pseud.]. Philadelphia: J. B. Lippincott & Co., 1871. 319 p. AAS, LC, NYP, UVB

1327 IRVING, WASHINGTON. Wolfert's Roost, and Other Papers, Now First Collected . . . New York: G. P. Putnam & Co., 1855. 383 p., front.

AAS, BA, BP, BU, CU, H, HEH, LC, LCP, N, NYH, NYP,
UC, UM, UP, UV, Y

Also contains: The Birds of Spring—The Creole Village—Mountjoy—
The Bermudas—The Widow's Ordeal—The Knight of Malta—A Time of
Unexampled Prosperity—Sketches in Paris in 1825—A Contented Man—
Broek, or the Dutch Paradise—Guests from Gibbet-Island—The Early
Experiences of Ralph Ringwood—The Seminoles—The Count Van Horn
—Don Juan: A Spectral Research—Legend of the Engulphed Convent—
The Phantom Island—Recollections of the Alhambra.

1328 ISABEL MORTIMER; or, The Southerner's Revenge. An Autobi-
ography. Cincinnati: H. M. Rulison, 1858. 36 p., illus.
Printed in double cols. HEH, UVB
Copyright notice dated 1854.

1329 ISABELLA GRAY: A NOVEL. By a Lady ... Philadelphia: Charles
Desilver. Chicago: W. B. Keen, 1858. 252 p.
AAS, CU, H, HEH, LC, N, UP, Y
Laid in New York City and San Francisco.

1330 IVY FENNHAVEN; or, Womanhood in Christ. A Story of Processes
... Boston: D. Lothrop & Co. Dover, N. H.: G. T. Day &
Co. [cop. 1872]. 200 p. LC

IZAX, IKABOD, *pseud*. *See* Stebbins, George Stanford

1331 JACK CADE; or, The Bondsman's Struggle. A Tale of Feudal
Oppression. New York: DeWitt & Davenport, 160 & 162
Nassau Street [cop. 1853]. 100 p., illus. BU

1332 [JACKSON, MRS. HELEN MARIA (FISKE) HUNT.] Saxe Holm's
[pseud.] Stories. New York: Scribner, Armstrong & Com-
pany, 1874. 350 p.
AAS, BA, BU, CU, H, HEH, LCP, N, NYP, UP, UVB, Y
Contents: Draxy Miller's Dowry—The Elder's Wife—Whose Wife Was
She?—The One-Legged Dancers—How One Woman Kept Her Husband
—Esther Wynn's Love-Letters.

1333 [JACOBS, MRS. HARRIET (BRENT).] Incidents in the Life of a
Slave Girl. Written by Herself ... Edited by L. Maria Child.
Boston: published for the author, 1861. 306 p.
AAS, BP, H, HEH, LC

1334 JAMES, GEORGE PAYNE RAINSFORD. Adrian; or, The Clouds of
the Mind. A Romance. By G. P. R. James, Esq. and Maunsell B. Field, Esq. ... New York: D. Appleton & Company,
1852. 301 p. AAS, BP, BU, CU, H, HEH, LC, N, UC, UP, Y
Preface dated: "Stockbridge, Mass., Sept. 1, 1851."
Included because the joint author, M. B. Field, was an American.

1335 JAMES, HENRY. A Passionate Pilgrim, and Other Tales ... Boston: James R. Osgood and Company, 1875. 496 p.

AAS, BA, BP, BU, CU, H, HEH, LC, LCP, N, NYP, UC, UM, UP, UVB, Y

Also contains: The Last of the Valerii—Eugene Pickering—The Madonna of the Future—The Romance of Certain Old Clothes—Madame de Mauves.

1336 [JAMISON, MRS. CECILIA VIETS (DAKIN).] A Crown from the Spear ... Boston: James R. Osgood and Company, 1872. 172 p. Printed in double cols. BA, BP, H, HEH, LC, NYP

Laid in France.

1337 [————] Ropes of Sand, and Other Stories ... Boston: James R. Osgood and Company, 1873. 176 p. Printed in double cols. BA, BP, H, LC, LCP, NYP

Also contains: A Woman's Story—Mrs. Gordon's Confession—Every String Broken—A Domestic Tragedy—Mr. John.

1338 [————] Something to Do: A Novel. Boston: James R. Osgood and Company, 1871. 150 p. Printed in double cols. AAS, CU, H, HEH, LC, LCP, NYP, Y

About the theater, actresses, and small town gossip.

1339 [————] Woven of Many Threads ... Boston: James R. Osgood and Company, 1871. 128 p. Printed in double cols. AAS, BA, BP, CU, H, HEH, LCP, NYP

Laid in England and Italy about 1860.

JANVRIN, MARY W. *See* Ellsworth, Mrs. Mary Wolcott (Janvrin)

1340 JARVES, JAMES JACKSON. Kiana: A Tradition of Hawaii ... Boston and Cambridge: James Munroe and Company. London: S. Low, Son and Company, 1857. 277 p., illus. AAS, BA, BP, CU, H, HEH, LC, LCP, N, NYP, UC, UP, Y

1341 ———— Why and What Am I? The Confessions of an Inquirer. In Three Parts. Part 1, Heart-Experience; or, The Education of the Emotions ... Boston: Phillips, Sampson and Company. London: Sampson Low, Son & Co., 1857. 320 p. AAS, BA, BP, CU, H, LC, NYH, NYP, UM, UP, Y

1342 JAY, CHARLES W. My New Home in Northern Michigan, and Other Tales ... Trenton, N. J.: printed by W. S. & E. W. Sharp, 1874. 180 p. AAS, BA, BU, CU, H, HEH, LC, N, NYH, NYP, UM, UP, Y

Also contains: How the "Old Settler" Settled My Potato Bugs—The First Death in Our Little Sunday School—Darwinism Vindicated and Confirmed—A Tale of the Wars of Pontiac—My First Hunt in My New Home—My Maple—Another Interesting Interview with the "Old Settler" —The Deserted Cabin, a Tale of Northern Michigan—I Meet My First "Ingin"—The Spectre of the Hemlock Gorge—My Mother—The "Old Settler" Goes to Church in Full Dress—To My Little Sparrow—My Angel—To the Reader.

JAY, W. M. L., *pseud.* *See* Woodruff, Mrs. Julia Louisa Matilda (Curtiss)

1343 JEANIE MORISON; or, The Discipline of Life. By the Author of "The Pastor's Family." New York: R. Carter & Brothers, 1855. 348 p., illus.
Information from LC card for copy withdrawn from circulation.

1344 JEFFREY, MRS. ROSA (GRIFFITH) VERTNER JOHNSON. Woodburn: A Novel . . . New York: Sheldon & Company, 1864. 356 p.   AP, CU, HEH, LCP, NYP, UM
Ante bellum social life.

1345 JENKINS, MRS. DAPHNE SMITH (GILES). East and West . . . By Daphne S. Giles. New York: printed by R. Craighead, 1853. 246 p.   BU, LC, UC
A temperance novel.

1346 ———— Half-Past Ten . . . [Mount Holyoke?] published for the author, 1860. 381 p.   HEH

JENKINS, JACOB, JR. A Hoosier Wedding. *In* O. P. Baldwin, *comp.*, Southern and South-Western Sketches [1855?], No. 200.

1347 JENNY AMBROSE; or, Life in the Eastern States. A Charming Domestic Story. By the Author of "Lights and Shadows of Factory Life" . . . Philadelphia: T. B. Peterson & Brothers, 306 Chestnut Street [cop. 1866]. 116 p.   HEH, Y

1348 JERVEY, MRS. CAROLINE HOWARD (GILMAN) GLOVER. Helen Courtenay's Promise: A Romance . . . New York: Carleton, 1866. 390 p.   AAS, NYP
A tale of a man who lost his sight.

1349 ——— Vernon Grove; or, Hearts as They Are. A Novel. By Mrs. C. H. Glover. New York: Rudd & Carleton, 1859. 384 p. AAS, CU, HEH, NYP

1350 JEWETT, MRS. SUSAN W. From Fourteen to Fourscore . . . New York: Hurd and Houghton. Cambridge: Riverside Press, 1871. 416 p. BA, H, HEH, LC, LCP, NYP, Y

1351 [———] The Old Corner Cupboard; or, The Every-Day Life of Every-Day People . . . Cincinnati: Truman and Spofford, 1856. 304 p. AAS, BP, LC, N, NYP, UC, UVB, Y

1352 JOHN, the Outcast, pseud. The Homeless Heir; or, Life in Bedford Street. A Mystery of Philadelphia. By John, the Outcast [pseud.]. Philadelphia: J. H. C. Whiting, 1856. 39 p. LCP

1353 JOHN NORTON'S CONFLICT. A Story of Life in New York City. Buffalo: Express Printing Co., No. 4 E. Swan St. [between 1866 & 1867]. Cover title, 23 p. Printed in double cols. HEH

Date of publication established from information supplied by Mr. C. S. Brigham.

JOHNSON, EFFIE, pseud. See Richmond, Mrs. Euphemia Johnson (Guernsey)

1354 JOHNSON, VIRGINIA WALES. The Calderwood Secret: A Novel . . . New York: Harper & Brothers, 1875. 136 p. Printed in double cols. AAS, LC, LCP, NYP

Laid in New York City.

1355 [———] Duties and Difficulties; or, Mary Mathieson . . . Philadelphia: James S. Claxton, 1867. 270 p., front. CU

1356 [———] Joseph the Jew: The Story of an Old House . . . New York: Harper & Brothers, 1874. 131 p. Printed in double cols. AAS, BA, BP, H, HEH, LC, LCP, NYP

1357 ——— A Sack of Gold: A Novel . . . New York: Harper & Brothers, 1874. 121 p. Printed in double cols.

AAS cover imprint dated 1874, but title page dated 1875. AAS, BA, BP, LC

1358 ———— Travels of an American Owl: A Satire . . . Philadelphia: Claxton, Remsen & Haffelfinger, 1871. 179 p., illus.
AAS, BU, CU, HEH, LC, LCP, NYH, NYP, UC, UM, Y
A satire on current events.

1359 [————] What the World Made Them . . . New York: G. P. Putnam & Sons, 1871. 284 p.   H, HEH, LC, NYP

1360 JOHNSTON, MRS. MARIA ISABELLA (BARNETT). The Siege of Vicksburg . . . Boston: Pratt Brothers, 1869. 330 p.
CU, HEH, LC, N, NYH

1361 [JOHNSTON, RICHARD MALCOLM.] Dukesborough Tales. By Philemon Perch [pseud.]. Baltimore: Turnbull Brothers, 1871. 232 p.   AAS, BA, BU, HEH, LC, LCP, NYP, UVB, Y
Contents: The Goosepond School—Judge Mike's Court—How Mr. Bill Williams Took the Responsibility—The Pursuit of Mr. Adiel Slack—The Early Majority of Mr. Thomas Watts—The Organ-Grinder—Mr. Williamson Slippey and His Salt—Investigations Concerning Mr. Jonas Lively.

———— Five Chapters of a History: A Georgia Court Forty Years Ago. In The Southern Field and Fireside Novelette [1863], No. 2287.

1362 [————] Georgia Sketches, Containing: Mr. Israel Meadows and His School; Judge Mike and His Court; How Bill Williams Took the Responsibility; Miss Pea, Miss Spouter, and the Yankee; from the Recollections of an Old Man; by Philemon Perch [pseud.] . . . [Augusta, Ga.] Stockton & Co., 1864. Cover title, 114 p.   Y
These tales were later included in his Dukesborough Tales.

1363 [JOHNSTONE, MISS O. A.] Sophie de Brentz; or, the Sword of Truth. A Story of Italy and Switzerland . . . Boston: Henry Hoyt. Chicago: Wm. Tomlinson. Cincinnati: Geo. Crosby, 1859. 190 p., illus.   HEH
Anti-Catholic.

1364 [JOLLIFFE, JOHN.] Belle Scott; or, Liberty Overthrown! A Tale for the Crisis . . . Columbus: D. Anderson. Cincinnati: G. S. Blanchard, 1856. 426 p.   CU, H, LC, N, NYP

1365 [————] Chattanooga . . . Cincinnati: Wrightson & Company, printers, 1858. 400 p.

BU, CU, HEH, LC, NYH, NYP, UC, UP, Y

Also issued with imprint: Cincinnati: Anderson, Gates & Wright, 1858. LC, NYP

Antislavery; Indians and the Tennessee frontier.

1366 JONES, BUEHRING H. The Sunny Land; or, Prison Prose and Poetry, Containing the Productions of the Ablest Writers in the South . . . Edited, with Preface . . . and Stories, by J. A. Houston . . . Baltimore: Innes & Company, printers, 1868. 540 p., 1 l.   BA, BP, CU, HEH, LC, N, NYP, UM

The title story by Jones occupies the first 246 pages.

1367 [JONES, CORNELIA.] Heavenward Led; or, The Two Bequests. By Jane R. Sommers [pseud.] . . . Philadelphia: Porter & Coates, 822 Chestnut Street [1870]. 488 p.   HEH

HEH copy contains inserted erratum, printed on purple paper. This explains the discrepancy between the title and running headlines which read "Heavenward Bound; or, The Two Bequests." The copyright date is given as 1871; but the advts. at end are dated "September, 1870."

The Porter & Coates reissue with title *The Two Bequests; or, Heavenward Led* omits the address in the imprint and gives copyright date as 1870. Running headlines changed to "Heavenward Led; or, The Two Bequests."

1368 JONES, ERASMUS W. The Captive Youths of Judah . . . New York: J. C. Derby & Co., 1856. 465 p.   LC, NYP

A temperance tale.

JONES, GEORGE. Dick Libby. *In* Rougegorge (1870), No. 2130.

1369 JONES, JOHN BEAUCHAMP. Adventures of Col. Gracchus Vanderbomb, of Sloughcreek, in Pursuit of the Presidency; also the Exploits of Mr. Numerius Plutarch Kipps, His Private Secretary . . . Philadelphia: A. Hart, 1852. 202 p.

AAS, H, LC, NYH, NYP, UM, UP

1370 ————— Border War: A Tale of Disunion . . . New York: Rudd & Carleton, 1859. 502 p.

AAS, BA, CU, H, HEH, LC, LCP, N, NYH, NYP, UC, UM, UP, UVB, Y

Also published as: *Wild Southern Scenes: A Tale of Disunion and Border War.* Philadelphia: T. B. Peterson & Brothers [cop. 1859].   AAS, BU, H, LC, N, NYH, NYP, UM, UV

And: *Secession, Coercion and Civil War. The Story of 1861.* Philadelphia: T. B. Peterson & Brothers [cop. 1861].   HEH, LC, N, UV

1371 ———— The City Merchant; or, The Mysterious Failure . . .
Philadelphia: Lippincott, Grambo & Co., 1851. 235 p., illus.
AAS, BU, HEH, UM

1372 ———— Freaks of Fortune; or, The History and Adventures
of Ned Lorn . . . Philadelphia: T. B. Peterson, No. 102
Chestnut Street [cop. 1854]. 401 p., illus.
AAS, H, HEH, LC, NYP, UV, Y

1373 ———— Life and Adventures of a Country Merchant: A Narrative of His Exploits at Home, during His Travels, and in
the Cities . . . Philadelphia: Lippincott, Grambo & Co., 1854.
396 p., front. AAS, HEH, LC, LCP, N, NYH, NYP, UC, UP, Y

1374 ———— Love and Money . . . Philadelphia: T. B. Peterson &
Brothers, 306 Chestnut Street [cop. 1865]. 407 p. NYP

1375 ———— The Monarchist: An Historical Novel, Embracing
Real Characters and Romantic Adventures . . . Philadelphia:
A. Hart, 1853. 336 p. AAS, AP, BP, LC, UC, UM, UP, UVB
At the time of the American Revolution.

1376 ———— The Spanglers and Tingles; or, The Rival Belles. A
Tale, Unveiling Some of the Mysteries of Society and Politics
as They Exist at the Present Time in the United States . . .
Philadelphia: A. Hart, 1852. 270 p. LC, NYP
Also published as: *The Rival Belles; or, Life in Washington.* Philadelphia: T. B. Peterson and Brothers, 306 Chestnut Street [cop. 1864].
AAS, LCP

1377 ———— Wild Western Scenes—Second Series. The Warpath:
A Narrative of Adventures in the Wilderness . . . Philadelphia: J. B. Lippincott & Co., 1856. 335 p., illus.
CU, LC, LCP, N, NYH, NYP, UC, UM

1378 ———— Wild Western Scenes; or, The White Spirit of the
Wilderness. Being a Narrative of Adventures, Embracing the
Same Characters Portrayed in the Original "Wild Western
Scenes" . . . New Series. Richmond: M. A. Malsby, 1863.
123, [1] p. BA, BP, HEH, LC, N, NYH, UV, Y

1379 [————] The Winkles; or, The Merry Monomaniacs. An
American Picture with Portraits of the Natives . . . New
York: D. Appleton and Company. London, 1855. 424 p.
AAS, AP, BP, BU, CU, H, HEH, LC, LCP, N, NYH, NYP,
UC, UM, UP, UV, Y
AAS copy in original paper covers in 2 vols.

1380 JONES, JOHN HILTON. The Dominie's Son: A Novel . . . New York [G. P. Putnam's Sons], 1874. 264 p. AAS, HEH
Laid in New York.

1381 [JONES, JOHN RICHTER.] The Quaker Soldier; or, The British in Philadelphia. An Historical Novel . . . Philadelphia: T. B. Peterson and Brothers, 306 Chestnut Street [cop. 1858]. 569 p., front. AAS, CU, HEH, LC, LCP, N, NYP, UC, UM, Y
LC copy deposited for copyright May 5, 1858.

JONES, *Major* JOSEPH. The Coon-Hunt; or, A Fency Country. *In* T. A. Burke, *ed.*, Polly Peablossom's Wedding (1851), No. 426.

1382 [JONES, JOSEPH STEVENS.] Life of Jefferson S. Batkins, Member from Cranberry Centre . . . Boston: Loring, cor. Bromfield and Washington Streets [cop. 1871]. 496 p., illus.
AAS, BA, BP, BU, CU, H, HEH, LC, NYP, UC, UV, Y

1383 [JONES, JUSTIN.] The Brigand; or, The Mountain Chief . . . New York: H. Long & Brother, 43 Ann Street [cop. 1852]. 121 p., illus. AAS

1384 [————] The Doomed Ship; or, The Wreck of the Arctic Regions. By Harry Hazel [pseud.]. Philadelphia: T. B. Peterson & Brothers, 306 Chestnut Street [cop. 1864]. 96 p.
BA, UP

1385 [————] The Flying Artillerist; or, The Child of the Battle-Field. A Tale of Mexican Treachery. By Harry Hazel [pseud.] . . . New York: H. Long & Brother, 1853. 92 p., illus.
Information from LC card for copy withdrawn from circulation.
AAS & H have the T. B. Peterson & Brothers, Philadelphia, reprint.

1386 [————] The Flying Dutchman; or, The Wedding Guest of Amsterdam. A Mysterious Tale of the Sea. By Captain Merry, United States Navy [pseud.]. New York: H. Long & Brother, 43 Ann Street. Cincinnati: H. B. Pearson & Co., 17 East Fourth Street [185-?]. 118 p., illus. Y

1387 [————] The Flying Yankee; or, The Cruise of the Clippers. A Tale of Privateering in the War of 1812-'15. New York: H. Long & Brother, No. 121 Nassau Street [cop. 1853]. 100 p., illus. UC

1388 [————] Gallant Tom; or, The Perils of the Ocean. An Interesting Sea-Tale . . . New York: H. Long & Brother, 43 Ann Street [cop. 1852]. 111 p.   AAS, BA, HEH, LC, NYP

Not to be confused with *Gallant Tom* by the English author T. P. Prest.

1389 [————] The Gold Seekers; or, The Cruise of the Lively Sally. By Captain Merry, U.S.N. [pseud.] . . . New York: H. Long & Brother, 43 Ann Street [cop. 1853]. 103 p., illus. Printed in double cols.   NYP

1390 [————] Harry Helm; or, The Cruise of the Bloodhound. By Harry Hazel [pseud.] . . . Philadelphia: T. B. Peterson & Brothers, 306 Chestnut Street [186-?]. 100 p.   AAS

1391 [————] Harry Tempest; or, The Pirate's Protege. By Harry Hazel [pseud.] . . . Philadelphia: T. B. Peterson & Brothers, 306 Chestnut Street [1866?]. 103, [1] p., illus.   HEH, NYP

Also contains: The Rose of Matanzas; or, Diableto, the Gulf Pirate.

1392 [————] Jack Junk; or, The Tar for All Weathers . . . New York: H. Long & Brother [cop. 1853]. 112 p., illus.   UP

1393 [————] Jack Waid, the Cobbler of Gotham. By Harry Hazel [pseud.]. Philadelphia: A. Winch, 505 Chestnut Street [cop. 1856]. 97 p. Printed in double cols.   AAS

1394 [————] Jane Horton; or, The Wife's Martyrdom. By Jack Brace [pseud.]. New York: Frederic A. Brady [186-?]. 93, [1], 4-9 p.   NYP

Also contains: The Lady and the Artist—The Gold Piece—Boarding a Buccaneer—The Young Continental; or, The Ranger's Bride—Leone, the Corsair.

"The Virgin Wife" separately paged at end.

At head of title: "Tales of the Metropolis."

1395 [————] Marie; or, The Gambler of the Mississippi. By Jack Brace [pseud.]. New York, 1861.

Title listed in L. C. McVoy, *A Bibliography of Fiction by Louisianians* [Baton Rouge, 1935], p. 12.

1396 [————] Old Put; or, The Days of Seventy-Six. A Tale of the Revolution . . . New York: H. Long & Brother, 43 Ann Street. Cincinnati: H. B. Pearson & Co., 17 East Fourth St. [cop. 1852]. 104 p. Printed in double cols.   HEH, UC, UM

1397 [————] The Pirate's Son: A Sea Novel of Great Interest ... Philadelphia: T. B. Peterson and Brothers, 306 Chestnut St. [after 1858]. 98 p., illus. AAS
Copyright notice dated 1855.

1398 [————] Ralph Runnion; or, The Outlaw's Doom. A Romance of the Revolution ... New York: H. Long & Brother, 121 Nassau St. [cop. 1858]. 119 p. AAS

1399 [————] The Rebel Bride: A Revolutionary Romance, and Other Tales. By Jack Brace [pseud.]. New York: H. Long & Brother, 43 Ann Street [cop. 1853]. 105 p. NYP, Y
Also contains: The Cruise of the Wasp—Constance Beverly; or, Love and Loyalty—The Sea Chase—The Baffled Tory—The Escape.
AAS copy of the T. B. Peterson & Brothers reprint gives "By Harry Hazel" on the title page; and it is credited to him in various advts. of the same publishers.

1400 [————] Sweeny Todd; or, The Ruffian Barber. By Harry Hazel [pseud.]. Philadelphia: T. B. Peterson & Brothers [1865].
Title listed in Kelly 1861-1866.

1401 [————] The Three Pirates; or, The Virgin of the Islet. By Harry Hazel [pseud.] ... New York: H. Long & Brother, 1853. 112 p., illus.
Information from LC card for copy withdrawn from circulation.

1402 [————] Valdez, the Pirate; or, Scenes off Long Island. By Jack Brace [pseud.]. New York: H. Long & Brother, 43 Ann Street [cop. 1853]. 98 p. LC
AAS has a copy of the above publisher's reprint, *ca.* 1854, which gives the copyright date as 1846; they also have the later T. B. Peterson & Brothers reprint which gives "By Harry Hazel" on the title page.

1403 ———— Virginia Graham, the Spy of the Grand Army ... Boston: Loring, 319 Washington Street [cop. 1867]. 165 p. Printed in double cols. LC, LCP, NYP, Y

1404 [————] Yankee Jack; or, The Perils of a Privateersman. By Harry Hazel [pseud.]. New York: H. Long & Brother, 43 Ann Street [cop. 1852]. 127 p., illus. H

1405 [————] The Yankee Middy; or, The Two Frigates. A Romance of the Coast of Maine. By William Robinson [pseud.]. New York: H. Long & Brother, 43 Ann Street [cop. 1853]. 112 p., illus. AAS

JONES, *Dr.* PLEASANT, *pseud.* *See* Starnes, Ebenezer

JONQUIL, *pseud.* *See* Collins, J. L.

1406 JOSEPH, *pseud.* New-York Aristocracy; or, Gems of Japonica-dom. By Joseph [pseud.] . . . New York: Charles Norton. Philadelphia: W. P. Hazard. Boston: Fetridge & Co., 1851. 152 p., illus. BP, H, N, NYH, UC, Y

1407 JOYCE, ROBERT DWYER. Irish Fireside Tales . . . Boston: Patrick Donahoe, 1871. 376 p., front. BP

1408 ———— Legends of the Wars in Ireland . . . Boston: James Campbell, 1868. 352 p. BP, H, LCP, UC
Contents: A Batch of Legends—The Master of Lisfinry—The Fair Maid of Killarney—An Eye for an Eye—The Rose of Drimnagh—The House of Lisbloom—The White Knight's Present—The First and Last Lords of Fermoy—The Chase from the Hostel—The Whitethorn Tree—Rosaleen; or, The White Lady of Barna—The Bridal Ring—The Little Battle of Bottle Hill.

1409 JUDD, H. O. Look Within for Fact and Fiction, Consisting of Instructive Sketches, and Thrilling Narratives . . . Macon, Ga.: published for the author, 1864. 204 p. BA

1410 [JUDD, SYLVESTER.] Margaret: A Tale of the Real and the Ideal, Blight and Bloom; Including Sketches of a Place Not Before Described, Called Mons Christi . . . Revised Edition . . . Boston: Phillips, Sampson and Company, 1851. 2 vols. (321, 304 p.) AAS, BA, BU, H, HEH, LC, NYP(V.2), UM, UP, UV, Y
This is Wright (1774-1850), No. 1512, with many alterations in text, and with an "Author's Note" dated "May 12, 1851," added.

1411 [JUDSON, EDWARD ZANE CARROLL.] Agnes; or, The Beautiful Milliner. By Ned Buntline [pseud.] . . . New York: publishers and booksellers, Nassau Street [*ca.* 1874]. 100 p. Printed in double cols.
Oberlin College Library copy.

1412 [————] The Battle of Hate; or, Hearts Are Trump. By Ned Buntline [pseud.]. New York: Frederic A. Brady, No. 22 Ann Street [cop. 1865]. 79 p., illus. Printed in double cols. BU

1413 [————] The Beautiful Nun. By Ned Buntline [pseud.] . . . Philadelphia: T. B. Peterson & Brothers, 306 Chestnut Street [cop. 1866]. 183 p. Printed in double cols. AAS, UVB

1414 ———— Delete.

1415 [————] Charley Bray; or, The Fireman's Mission. The Story of a New York Fireman. New York [published for the trade, 1870?]. 78 p. UM

Jay Monaghan, *The Great Rascal* (Boston, 1952), p. 323, gives imprint: New York: Hilton & Co., 1865.

1416 ———— Child of the Sun: A Tale of Mexico. New York: Hilton & Co., 1865.

Monaghan, p. 323.

1417 ———— Clara St. John [Sequel to Mermet Ben]. New York: Hilton & Co., 1865.

Monaghan, p. 323.

1418 ———— Clarence Rhett; or, The Cruise of a Privateer. An American Sea Story . . . New York: Frederic A. Brady, No. 22 Ann Street [cop. 1866]. 78 p. Y

1419 [————] The Convict; or, The Conspirator's Victim. By Ned Buntline [pseud.] . . . New York: W. F. Burgess, 1851.

Monaghan, p. 323.

1420 [————] The Death-Mystery: A Crimson Tale of Life in New York. By Ned Buntline [pseud.]. New York: Frederic A. Brady [cop. 1861]. 88 p., illus.

Information from LC card for copy withdrawn from circulation.

1421 [————] Elfrida, the Red Rover's Daughter: A New Mystery of New York. By Ned Buntline [pseud.]. New York: Frederic A. Brady, No. 24 Ann Street [cop. 1863]. 103 p., illus. Printed in double cols. AAS, CU

1422 [————] Ella Adams; or, The Demon of Fire. A Tale of the Charleston Conflagration. By Ned Buntline [pseud.]. New York: Frederic A. Brady, 24 Ann Street [cop. 1862]. 84 p., illus. Printed in double cols. LC

1423 [————] English Tom; or, The Smuggler's Secret. A Tale of Ship and Shore. By Ned Buntline [pseud.]. New York: Frederic A. Brady, 24 Ann Street [186-?]. 82 p., illus. Printed in double cols. Y

Copyright notice dated 1858.

1424 [————] Fanny, the Belle of Central Park . . . New York: Hilton & Co., 1866.

Monaghan, p. 324.

1425 [————] The Grossbeak Mansion: A Mystery of New York. By Ned Buntline [pseud.]. New York: Frederic A. Brady, 24 Ann Street [cop. 1862]. 90 p., illus. Printed in double cols.   AAS, HEH

1426 [————] Hilliare Henderson; or, The Secret Revealed. An Antecedent to "The Death Mystery." By Ned Buntline [pseud.]. New York: Frederic A. Brady, No. 24 Ann Street [1865]. 88 p., illus. Printed in double cols.   CU, LC

LC copy deposited for copyright April 9, 1865. Probably first published in the *New York Mercury* in 1861, the year of the copyright date in the book.

1427 [————] The Jesuit's Daughter: A Novel for Americans to Read. By Ned Buntline [pseud.]. New York, 1854.

Copy noted in Edward Morrill & Son, Cat. 32, item 320.

1428 ———— The Jew's Daughter: A Tale of City Life. New York: Garrett & Co. [185-?].

Title listed in Roorbach 1855-1858. Monaghan notes a Dick & Fitzgerald [n.d.] ed., with title *Miriam; or, The Jew's Daughter*.

1429 ———— The Lady Thief. New York: Hilton & Co., 1866.

Monaghan, p. 325.

1430 [————] The Last of the Buccaneers: A Yarn of the Eighteenth Century. By Ned Buntline [pseud.] . . . New York: Garrett & Co., 18 Ann Street [1856?]. 97 p., illus. Printed in double cols.   H

Contents: The Pirate of the Gulf—Lalla Zara, the Flower of the Desert— The Grecian Wife, a Tale of the Archipelago—Bianca's Bridal Eve, a Tale of Venice—The Buccaneer's Daughter, a Tale of the Southern Seas— The Treason of Gomez Arias, a Tale of Man's Perfidy—Zuleika, Queen of the Harem, a Brief Story of the East—Wanesa, the Wabinga Queen, a Legend of the Forest—Chased by a Bear—Fatal Curiosity; or, The Abstracted Letter—The Last of the Buccaneers.

Dedication to Garrett & Co. dated "May 17th, 1856."

1431 ———— Lenore; or, The Highwayman's Bride. New York: Hilton & Co., 1866.

Monaghan, p. 326.

1432 [————] Life in the Saddle; or, The Cavalry Scout. By Ned
Buntline [pseud.] . . . New York: Frederic A. Brady, No. 22
Ann Street [cop. 1864]. 81 p., illus. Printed in double cols.
Lehigh University Library copy.

1433 [————] Luona Prescott; or, The Curse Fulfilled. A Tale of
the American Revolution. By Ned Buntline [pseud.]. New
York: Frederic A. Brady, No. 24 Ann Street [186-?]. 64 p.,
illus. Printed in double cols.   AAS, CU, HEH
Copyright notice dated 1858.

1434 ———— Magdalena, the Outcast; or, The Millionaire's Daugh-
ter. A Story of Life in the Empire City . . . New York:
Hilton & Co., 128 Nassau Street [cop. 1866]. 96 p. Printed
in double cols.   LC
On cover: "Ned Buntline's Own Series."
LC copy deposited for copyright May 19, 1866.

1435 [————] The Man-o'-War's-Man's Grudge: A Romance of
the Revolution. By Ned Buntline [pseud.]. New York:
Frederic A. Brady, No. 24 Ann Street [186-?]. 95 p., illus.
Printed in double cols.   AAS
CU has Brady reprint published at 22 Ann St., with copyright notice dated
1859. Brady moved to this address from No. 24 Ann St. late in 1864.

1436 [————] Mermet Ben; or, The Astrologer King. Sequel to
Rose Seymour . . . New York: Hilton & Co., 1865. 96 p.,
front. Printed in double cols.   LC
On cover: "Ned Buntline's Own Series."

1437 [————] Morgan; or, The Knight of the Black Flag. A
Strange Story of By-Gone Times. By Ned Buntline [pseud.].
New York: Frederic A. Brady, 24 Ann Street [cop. 1860].
118 p., illus. Printed in double cols.   AAS, LC

1438 [————] The Mysteries and Miseries of New Orleans. By
Ned Buntline [pseud.] . . . New York: Akarman and
Ormsby, 102 Nassau Street [cop. 1851]. 104 p. Printed in
double cols.   AAS, HEH
At head of cover title: "Ned Buntline's Last Novel."
Cover title imprint: New York, Thomas Ormsby (late Akarman &
Ormsby).

1439 [————] Netta Bride; or, The King of the Vultures. By Capt. Cleighmore [pseud.] ... New York: published for the trade [cop. 1864]. 48 p. Printed in double cols.   LC

With this was issued: *The Poor of New York, by Henry Edwards* (New York, 1865).

LC cover title: "Ned Buntline's Own Series, No. 5. Netta Bride, and The Poor of New York."

1440 [————] Our Mess; or, The Pirate-Hunters of the Gulf. A Tale of Naval Heroism and Wild Adventure in the Tropics. By Ned Buntline [pseud.]. New York: Frederic A. Brady, No. 24 Ann Street [186-?]. 71 p., illus. Printed in double cols.   AAS, HEH

Copyright notice dated 1859.

1441 [————] The Parricides; or, The Doom of the Assassins, the Authors of a Nation's Loss. By Ned Buntline [pseud.]. New York: Hilton & Co., 1865. 94 p., front. Printed in double cols.   BU, HEH, LC, LCP

1442 [————] The Rattlesnake; or, The Rebel Privateer. A Tale of the Present Time. By Ned Buntline [pseud.]. New York: Frederic A. Brady, 24 Ann Street [1865]. 79 p., illus. Printed in double cols.   LC, NYP

LC copy deposited for copyright Oct. 29, 1865. First published in the *New York Mercury* in 1862, the year of the copyright date in the book.

1443 [————] Red Ralph; or, The Daughter of Night. A Novel. From Ned Buntline's Own Series. New York: published for the trade [n.d.]. Cover title, 96 p. Printed in double cols.   NYH

At head of cover title: "Price 25 Cents."

Monaghan, p. 329, notes a Hilton & Co. 1865 ed. which may be the first.

1444 [————] Rosa, the Indian Captive: A Story of the Last War with England . . . New York: Hilton & Company, 128 Nassau Street [1867?]. 94 p. Printed in double cols.

Princeton University Library copy.

1445 [————] Rose Seymour; or, The Ballet Girls' Revenge. A Tale of the New York Drama. New York: Hilton & Co., 1865. 96 p., illus. Printed in double cols.   LC

On cover: "Ned Buntline's Own Series."

1446 [————] Sadia: A Heroine of the Rebellion. By Ned Buntline [pseud.]. New York: Frederic A. Brady, No. 22 Ann
Street [cop. 1864]. 92 p., illus. Printed in double cols. UC

1447 [————] Saul Sabberday; or, The Idiot Spy. A Tale of the
Men and Deeds of '76. By Ned Buntline [pseud.]. New
York: Frederic A. Brady, No. 24 Ann Street [186-?]. 95 p.,
illus. Printed in double cols. AAS, HEH
Copyright notice dated 1858.

1448 [————] Sea Waif; or, The Terror of the Coast. A Tale of
Privateering in 1776. By Ned Buntline [pseud.]. New York:
Frederic A. Brady, No. 24 Ann Street [186-?]. 128 p., illus.
Printed in double cols. AAS
Copyright notice dated 1859.
UP has Brady reprint published at 22 Ann St., with copyright notice
dated 1858.

1449 [————] The Shell Hunter; or, An Ocean Love-Chase. A
Romance of Land and Sea. By Ned Buntline [pseud.]. New
York: Frederic A. Brady, 24 Ann Street [1863]. 78 p., illus.
Printed in double cols. H, LC, UP
LC copy deposited for copyright April 9, 1863. Copyright notice in book
dated 1858.

1450 [————] Stella Delorme; or, The Comanche's Dream. A
Wild and Fanciful Story of Savage Chivalry. By Ned Bunt-
line [pseud.]. New York: Frederic A. Brady, No. 24 Ann
Street [cop. 1860]. 71 p., illus. Printed in double cols.
AAS, HEH, LC, NYP, UM

1451 [————] Thayendanegea, the Scourge; or, The War-Eagle
of the Mohawks. A Tale of Mystery, Ruth, and Wrong. By
Ned Buntline [pseud.]. New York: Frederic A. Brady, No.
24 Ann Street [186-?]. 77 p., illus. Printed in double cols.
Copyright notice dated 1858. UC, UM
AAS has Brady reprint published at 22 Ann St., with copyright notice
dated 1859.

1452 [————] The Wheel of Misfortune; or, The Victims of
Lottery and Policy Dealers. A Yarn from the Web of New
York Life. By Ned Buntline [pseud.]. New York: Garrett &
Co. [cop. 1853]. 100 p.
Information from LC card for copy removed from circulation.

1453 [————] The White Cruiser; or, The Fate of the Unheard-Of. A Tale of Land and Sea, of Crime and Mystery. By Ned Buntline [pseud.]. New York: Garrett & Co., 1853. 103 p. Printed in double cols. BA

Listed in Roorbach 1852-1855, under title "Cruise of the White Squall; or, Fate of the Unheard Of."

1454 [————] The White Wizard; or, The Great Prophet of the Seminoles. A Tale of Strange Mystery in the South and North. By Ned Buntline [pseud.]. New York: Frederic A. Brady, No. 24 Ann Street [186-?]. 104 p., illus. Printed in double cols. HEH, UP

Copyright notice dated 1858.

1455 JULIA TREMAINE; or, The Father's Wish and Husband's Duty. A Tale for All Time. By ****. Philadelphia: Whilt and Yost, 1855. 354 p. CU, NYP

Laid in England.

K., A. H., *pseud.* *See* Warner, Eliza A.

KADMUS, KRISTOFUR, *pseud.* *See* Brown, Nathan

1456 KATE KILBORN; or, Sowing and Reaping. By the Author of "Jeanie Morrison"... New York: Robert Carter & Brothers, 1856. 284 p., illus. AAS, Y

1457 KATE MARSTONE; or, Happy Hearts Make Happy Homes. A Fireside Story . . . New York: Carleton, 1866. 303 p.

AAS, CU, H, HEH, LC, LCP, NYP, UP, Y

Laid in "Clairsville," New Hampshire.

1458 KATE STANTON: A Page from Real Life . . . Boston: James French and Company, 1855. 332 p. AAS, N

KATINKA, *pseud.* *See* Yale, Mrs. Catherine (Brooks)

1459 KEELER, RALPH OLMSTEAD. Gloverson and His Silent Partners . . . Boston: Lee and Shepard, 1869. 372 p.

Mines and stocks; San Francisco. AAS, CU, H, HEH, LC, LCP, UM, Y

1460 [KEENER, JOHN CHRISTIAN.] Post-Oak Circuit. By a Member of the Red River Conference ... Edited by Thos. O. Summers, D.D. Nashville, Tenn.: published for the author, by E. Stevenson & F. A. Owen, 1857. 275 p.   AAS HEH, N
On the problems of raising money.

KELLEY, JONATHAN F. *See* Kelly, Jonathan Falconbridge

1461 KELLOGG, SARAH WINTER. The Livelies, and Other Short Stories ... Philadelphia: J. B. Lippincott & Co., 1875. 90 p., front. Printed in double cols.   AAS, BA, BP, LC, LCP
Also contains: Deshler & Deshler—When I Was a Boarder—Her Chance —Mrs. Twitchell's Inventions.

1462 [KELLY, JOHN L.] Fact and Fiction: Disappointed Love. A Story, Drawn from Incidents in the Lives of Miss Clara C. Cochran and Miss Catharine B. Cotton, Who Committed Suicide, by Drowning in the Canal at Manchester, N. H., August 14, 1853. Manchester, N. H.: from the Daily and Weekly Mirror steam printing works, 1853. 32 p. Printed in double cols.   AAS, BP, BU, HEH, LC, UVB
Cover imprint: "Manchester: printed at the Daily and Weekly Mirror printing establishment, 1853."
For the same story by another writer see No. 2480.

[KELLY, JONATHAN FALCONBRIDGE.] A Fearful Tale of the Mississippi, by Falconbridge [pseud.]. *In* T. A. Burke, *ed.*, Polly Peablossom's Wedding (1851), No. 426.

1463 ———— The Humors of Falconbridge [pseud.]: A Collection of Humorous and Every Day Scenes ... Philadelphia: T. B. Peterson, No. 102 Chestnut Street [cop. 1856]. 436 p.
   AAS, BU, CU, H, HEH, LC, N, NYP, UC, UM
A tour through the Southern states in 1839.

1464 [————] Marie Lessaire; or, The Ballet-Girl's Love. By Falconbridge [pseud.] ... New York: William Skelly, No. 280 Greenwich Street [cop. 1854]. 108 p.   UM
NYP has New York: F. A. Brady, 1858, with copyright notice dated 1854.

[————] The Washerwoman's Windfall, by Falconbridge [pseud.]. *In* S. Cobb, The Bravo's Secret (1851), No. 564.

————— [Under his pseudonym "Falconbridge," he wrote the stories listed in note below.] *In* Dodge's Sketches [1853], No. 1751.

The Thin Abolitionist and the Caged Madman—Marrying 'Em Over Again; or, A Joker Forestalled—Magnetism Triumphant; or, The Way Dodge "Done" the Old Maids—Doing the Artist; or, The Ups and Downs of a Genius—Dodge's Elopment; or, The Captain Outwitted—Dodging a Crowd: A Scene in a Chinese Junk.

1465 KELSO, ISAAC. Danger in the Dark: A Tale of Intrigue and Priestcraft . . . Cincinnati: published for the author by Moore, Anderson, Wilstach & Keys, 1854. 300 p., front.

Anti-Catholic. UC

1466 ————— Light, More Light; or, Danger in the Dark . . . Cincinnati: Epenetus Hampson; Longley Brothers, printers, 1855. 300 p., front. LC, N

This is a different story from his *Danger in the Dark*, No. 1465. Anti-Catholic.

1467 ————— The Stars and Bars; or, The Reign of Terror in Missouri . . . Boston: A. Williams & Co., 1863. 324 p.

AAS, BA, BP, CU, H, HEH, N, NYH, NYP

Covers the first two years of the Civil War.

1468 KELVIN, KIT, *pseud.* Kit Kelvin's Kernels . . . New York: Rollo, 1860. 270 p., illus. AAS, CU, H, HEH, LC, N, NYP, UC

Humor.

1469 KENNERLY, AUGUSTIN. The Heiresses of Fotheringay: A Tale Founded on Fact . . . Saint Louis: E. K. Woodward, 1856. 487 p. AAS, HEH, LC, NYP

KEREVEN, KATE P. Doctor Aar. *In* Short Stories, 2d ser. (1869), No. 2211.

————— Loyal en Tout. *In* Short Stories (1869), No. 2210.

KERR, ORPHEUS C., *pseud.* *See* Newell, Robert Henry

1470 KETCHUM, MRS. ANNIE (CHAMBERS) BRADFORD. Nelly Bracken: A Tale of Forty Years Ago. By Annie Chambers Bradford. Philadelphia: Lippincott, Grambo & Co., 1855. 377 p.

Laid in Kentucky. AAS, AP, H, HEH, LC, UC

1471 [KEYES, F.] Evan Dale . . . Boston: A. Williams & Co., 1864.
387 p.   AAS, CU, HEH, LC, N, NYP, UC, Y
Life in a New England seacoast town.

1472 KIMBALL, RICHARD BURLEIGH. Henry Powers (Banker); How
He Achieved a Fortune, and Married. A Novel . . . New
York: G. W. Carleton & Co. Leipsic: Tauchnitz, 1868.
335 p.   AAS, CU, H, HEH, LCP, N, NYP, UP, Y
Laid in New York City.

1473 ———— Romance of Student Life Abroad . . . New York:
G. P. Putnam & Co., 1853. 261 p.   AP, BA, BP, H, LCP, UM, Y
Also published as: *Students Abroad*. New York: G. P. Putnam, 1862.   Y

———— The Sun-Dial of Isella. *In* The Knickerbocker
Gallery (1855), No. 1492.

1474 ———— To-Day: A Romance . . . New York: Carleton.
Leipsic: Tauchnitz, 1870. 480 p.   AAS, HEH, LC, LCP, NYP, Y
Laid in New York City.

1475 ———— Undercurrents of Wall-Street: A Romance of Business . . . New York: G. P. Putnam, 1862. 428 p.
AAS, AP, BA, BP, BU, CU, H, HEH, LCP, N, NYP, UC, UM, UP, UV, Y

1476 ———— Was He Successful? A Novel . . . New York:
Carleton. Leipsic: Tauchnitz, 1864. 407 p., front.
About a New York millionaire.   AAS, CU, H, HEH, LCP, UP, Y

———— [*See also*] Fabens, Joseph Warren. In the Tropics
. . . With an Introductory Notice by Richard B. Kimball
(1863), No. 879.

———— [*See also*] Fabens, Joseph Warren. The Prince of
Kashna . . . With an Editorial Introduction by Richard B.
Kimball (1866), No. 880.

KIMBALL, T. A. The Governess. *In* S. Cobb, The King and
Cobbler [185-?], No. 572.

1477 KING, EDWARD SMITH. Kentucky's Love; or, Roughing It
around Paris . . . Boston: Lee and Shepard. New York:
Lee, Shepard and Dillingham, 1873. 287 p.
At the time of the Franco-Prussian war.   AAS, BA, BP, H, HEH, LCP

King, Mrs. Sue (Petigru). *See* Bowen, Mrs. Sue (Petigru) King

1478 Kingsbury, John H. Kingsbury Sketches: A Truthful and Succinct Account of the Doings and Misdoings of the Inhabitants of Pine Grove; Their Private Trials and Public Tribulations . . . New York: G. W. Carleton & Co., 1875. 296 p., illus. AAS, CU, H, HEH, LCP, NYH, NYP, UC, UP, Y

Kingsford, Jane, *pseud. See* Barnard, Charles

1479 Kinzie, Mrs. Juliette Augusta (Magill). Mark Logan, the Bourgeois . . . Two Volumes in One . . . Philadelphia: J. B. Lippincott & Co., 1871. 678 p. HEH
On the Wisconsin frontier.

1480 [———] Walter Ogilby: A Novel . . . Philadelphia: J. B. Lippincott & Co., 1869. 2 vols. in 1. (619 p.)
LC, LCP, NYP, UC, Y

1481 ——— Wau-Bun, the "Early Day" in the North-West . . . New York: Derby & Jackson. Cincinnati: H. W. Derby & Co., 1856. 498 p., illus.
AAS, BP, HEH, LC, LCP, N, NYP, UC, UM, Y
Written in the form of an autobiography. Several of the characters are carried over to her *Mark Logan.*

1482 [Kip, Leonard.] AEnone: A Tale of Slave Life in Rome. New York: John Bradburn, 1866. 308 p.
AAS, H, HEH, LC, LCP, NYP, UM, Y

——— Alas, Poor Ghost. *In* Short Stories (1869), No. 2210.

1483 ——— The Dead Marquise: A Romance . . . New York: G. P. Putnam's Sons, 1873. 356 p. BP, H, LC, NYP, Y
Also published as: *The Story of the Dead Marquise.* New York: G. P. Putnam's Sons, 1873. AAS

1484 ——— Hannibal's Man . . . Albany: the Argus Company, printers, 1873. 46 p. LC
At head of title: "The Argus Christmas Story."

1485 ——— In Three Heads: The Argus Christmas Story . . . Albany: the Argus Company, printers, 1874. 70 p. N
Laid in Albany in 1758.

1486 [————] The Volcano Diggings: A Tale of California Law. By a Member of the Bar ... New York: J. S. Redfield, 1851. 131 p. HEH, LC, NYP

1487 KIRK, CHARLES D. Wooing and Warring in the Wilderness ... New York: Derby & Jackson. Louisville, Ky.: F. A. Crump, 1860. 288 p. AAS, BP, H, HEH, LC, N, NYH, NYP, UC, Y
At head of title: "A Story of Canetuckey."

KIRKE, EDMUND, *pseud*. *See* Gilmore, James Roberts

1488 KIRKLAND, MRS. CAROLINE MATILDA (STANSBURY). Autumn Hours, and Fireside Reading ... New York: Charles Scribner, 1854. 311 p., illus. AAS, BP, CU, NYP, UC, Y
Contains: Search after Pleasure—The Island Story—What Must Be Must —The Hermit's Story.

1489 ———— A Book for the Home Circle; or, Familiar Thoughts on Various Topics, Literary, Moral and Social ... New York: Charles Scribner, 1853. 312 p., illus.
BU, CU, H, HEH, LC, N, NYP, UP, Y
Contains: Mrs. Pell's Pilgrimage—Sense, Common and Uncommon— Sinecures; or, A Country Minister's Day—Faith and Fortune: A Romance of Central America—Recollections of Rural Life in the West—Is Patience a Virtue?

———— Comfort. *In* A. Cary, The Adopted Daughter (1859), No. 466.

1490 ———— The Evening Book; or, Fireside Talk on Morals and Manners, with Sketches of Western Life ... New York: Charles Scribner, 1852. 312 p., illus.
AAS, CU, H, LCP, NYH, NYP, UM, UP

———— Momma Charlotte. *In* J. Griffiths, *ed.*, Autographs for Freedom (1853), No. 1033.

1491 KIRKPATRICK, MRS. JANE (BAYARD). The Light of Other Days: Sketches of the Past and Other Selections from the Writings of the Late Mrs. Jane Kirkpatrick. New Brunswick, N. J.: press of J. Terhune, 1856. 89 p. CU, H, LC, NYH, NYP

1492 THE KNICKERBOCKER GALLERY: A Testimonial to the Editor [Louis G. Clark] of the Knickerbocker Magazine from Its Contributors ... New York: Samuel Hueston, 1855. 505 p., illus.

AAS, BA, BP, BU, CU, HEH, LC, LCP, N, NYH, NYP, UC, UM, UP, Y

Contains: The Bride of the Ice-King, by Donald G. Mitchell—Gentle Dove: An Indian Legend, by F. W. Shelton—On Lake Pepin, by Epes Sargent—Anteros: A Life with One Passion, by Donald MacLeod—Captain Belgrave, by Frederic S. Cozzens—A Dutch Belle, by P. Hamilton Myers—The Iron Man, by Henry J. Brent—Marie Lefrette: A Story of Kaskaskia, by J. L. M'Connel—The Shrouded Portrait, by George W. Curtis—The Loves of Mary Jones, by J. M. Legaré—The Sun-Dial of Isella, by Richard B. Kimball—A Literary Martyrdom, by C. F. Briggs—Zadoc Town: A Legend of Dosoris, by J. T. Irving.
Editorial preparation by John W. Francis, George P. Morris, Rufus W. Griswold, Richard B. Kimball, and Frederick W. Shelton.

1493 [KNIGHT, MRS. S. G.] Man's Wrongs; or, Woman's Foibles. By Kate Manton [pseud.]. Boston: Crosby & Damrell, 1870. 272 p.   AAS, BP, HEH, LC, LCP

Also published as: *Minnie Maverick; or, Man's Wrongs and Woman's Foibles. By S. G. K.* New York: Broughton & Wyman, 1870.   AAS

1494 KNORR, JAMES. The Two Roads; or, The Right and the Wrong ... Philadelphia: Lippincott, Grambo & Co., 1854. 372 p.

AAS, BU, LC, NYP

Of temperance interest.

1495 THE KNOW NOTHING? Boston: John P. Jewett & Company. Cleveland, Ohio: Jewett, Proctor & Worthington. New York: Sheldon, Lamport & Blakeman, 1855. 347 p.

AAS, BP, BU, CU, H, HEH, LC, N, NYH, UC, UM, UVB, Y

A political novel.

1496 KNOX, MRS. ADELINE (TRAFTON). An American Girl Abroad. By Adeline Trafton ... Boston: Lee and Shepard. New York: Lee, Shepard and Dillingham, 1872. 245 p., illus.

AAS, BA, BP, BU, CU, H, HEH, LC, LCP, NYP, UC, UP

A guide book in narrative form with some dialogue.

1497 ———— Katherine Earle. By Miss Adeline Trafton ... Boston: Lee and Shepard. New York: Lee, Shepard and Dillingham, 1874. 325 p., illus.

AAS, BA, HEH, LC, LCP, NYP, UC

L.

L., E. L.   *See* Lasselle, Mrs. E. L.

L., J. W.   *See* Lawson, Mrs. J. W.

1498   LABREE, LAWRENCE.   Rebels and Tories; or, The Blood of the
       Mohawk! A Tale of the American Revolution . . . New
       York: DeWitt & Davenport [cop. 1851]. 202 p.
                                   BU, CU, H, HEH, LC, NYH, UC, Y
       LC copy deposited for copyright April 10, 1851.

       LACKLAND, THOMAS, *pseud.*   *See* Hill, George Canning

1499   THE LADY LIEUTENANT: A Wonderful, Startling and Thrilling
       Narrative of the Adventures of Miss Madeline Moore, Who,
       in Order to Be Near Her Lover, Joined the Army . . . and
       Fought in Western Virginia under the Renowned General
       McClellan and Afterwards at the Great Battle of Bull's Run
       . . . Philadelphia: Barclay & Co., 1862.   40 p., illus.
                                        AAS, H, LC, NYP, Y

1500   LAING, MRS. CAROLINE HYDE (BUTLER).   The Old Farm House
       . . . Philadelphia: C. H. Davis, 1855.   461 p., illus.
                                              CU, H, NYP

       LAMAR, JOHN B.   The "Experience" of the Blacksmith of the
       Mountain Pass.   *In* T. A. Burke, *ed.*, Polly Peablossom's Wed-
       ding (1851), No. 426.

       ———— Polly Peablossom's Wedding. *In* T. A. Burke, *ed.*,
       Polly Peablossom's Wedding (1851), No. 426.

1501   LAMB, MRS. MARTHA JOANNA READE (NASH).   Spicy: A Novel
       . . . New York: D. Appleton and Company, 1873.   178 p.,
       illus.   Printed in double cols.
                                   AAS, CU, HEH, LC, LCP, N, NYH, NYP, Y
       Laid in Chicago and New York City.

1502   LAMSON, CHARLES HUTCHINS.   The Exiles, and Other Tales . . .
       Bangor: E. F. Duren, 1856.   156 p.   AAS, BU, HEH, Y
       Title story in verse; also contains two prose tales: The White Lily—Fred
       Howard.

       LANDER, META, *pseud.*   *See* Lawrence, Mrs. Margaret Oliver
       (Woods)

1503 LANDIS, SIMON MOHLER. An Entirely New Feature of a Thrilling Novel! Entitled, The Social War of the Year 1900; or, The Conspirators and Lovers . . . Philadelphia, Pa.: Landis Publishing Society, 1872. 416 p.   AAS, HEH, LC, N, NYP, Y
Text ends on p. 401, pp. 403-416 advts.

1504 LANDON, MELVILLE DE LANCEY. Eli Perkins (at Large): His Sayings and Doings . . . New York: J. B. Ford & Company, 1875. 248 p., illus.
    AAS, BP, BU, CU, H, HEH, LCP, N, NYP, UC, UM, UP, Y

1505 [————] Saratoga in 1901. By Eli Perkins [pseud.]. Fun, Love, Society, & Satire . . . New York: Sheldon & Company, 1872. 249, [1] p., illus.
    AAS, BP, BU, CU, H, HEH, LC, LCP, N, NYH, NYP, UC, UM, UP

LANE, T. W. The Thimble Game. In T. A. Burke, ed., Polly Peablossom's Wedding (1851), No. 426.

LANGDON, MARY, pseud. See Pike, Mrs. Mary Hayden (Green)

1506 LANIER, CLIFFORD ANDERSON. Thorn-Fruit: A Novel . . . New York: Blelock & Co., 1867. 116 p. Printed in double cols.
The Confederate army, 1864-1865.   HEH, NYP

1507 LANIER, SIDNEY. Tiger-Lilies: A Novel . . . New York: Hurd and Houghton, 1867. 252 p.
    AAS, CU, HEH, LC, LCP, N, NYP, UC, UP, UV, Y
Southern life before and during the war.

1508 [LASSELLE, MRS. E. L.] Magdalen, the Enchantress. Founded on Fact. By E. L. L. Philadelphia: J. B. Lippincott & Co., 1858. 302 p.   LC

1509 LASSELLE, MRS. NANCY POLK. Annie Grayson; or, Life in Washington . . . Washington: H. Lasselle, 1853. 345 p.
    AAS, CU, H, LC
Also issued with imprint: New York: Bunce & Brother, 1853.   AAS, N, Y
Also published as: *The Belle of Washington: A True Story of the Affections*. Philadelphia: T. B. Peterson and Brothers, 306 Chestnut Street [cop. 1858].   H, HEH, UC

1510 ———— Hope Marshall; or, Government and Its Offices . . . Washington: H. Lasselle, 1859. 396 p.   CU, HEH, N, NYP, Y
Also published as: *High Life in Washington: A True Picture from Life, of Real Persons & Characters*. Philadelphia: T. B. Peterson & Brothers, 306 Chestnut Street [cop. 1865].   BP, HEH, N

1511 LATIMER, MRS. MARY ELIZABETH (WORMELEY). Amabel: A Family History . . . New York: George P. Putnam & Co., 1853. 466 p.   AAS, CU, HEH, LC, NYP

1512 ———— Our Cousin Veronica; or, Scenes and Adventures over the Blue Ridge . . . New York: Bunce & Brother, 1855. 437 p.   AAS, BU, H, HEH, LC, N, NYP, UP, UV

1513 LAUGHLIN, GEORGE. Ashmore; or, The Reclaimed Husband, and Other Tales . . . Boston: printed for Mrs. Laughlin by John Wilson and Son, 1858. 48 p.   AAS, BA, BU, H, NYP
Also contains: The Student's Last Offering—Writing for Bread.

1514 [LAWRENCE, MRS. MARGARET OLIVER (WOODS).] Esperance. By Meta Lander [pseud.] . . . New York: Sheldon and Company, 1865. 336 p.   BU, LC, LCP, NYP, UC

1515 [————] Marion Graham; or, "Higher Than Happiness." By Meta Lander [pseud.] . . . Boston: Crosby, Nichols, Lee and Company, 1861. 506 p.   AAS, LC, NYP

1516 [LAWSON, MRS. J. W.] Brockley Moor: A Novel. By J. W. L. New York: D. Appleton and Company, 1874. 307 p.
Laid in England.   BP, LC, LCP, NYP

1517 LEANDRO; OR, THE SIGN OF THE CROSS. A Catholic Tale. Philadelphia: Peter F. Cunningham, 1870. 318 p.   LC
At head of title: " 'Messenger' Series."

1518 LEAVES FROM THE DIARY of a Celebrated Burglar and Pickpocket . . . New York: George W. Matsell & Co., proprietors of the National Police Gazette, 1865. 174 p., illus.   LC
At bottom of p. 174: "End of First Series." No more found.

1519 [LEAVITT, JOHN M'DOWELL.] The American Cardinal: A Novel. New York: Dodd & Mead, 1871. 315 p.
   AAS, BP, CU, H, HEH, LC, NYP, UM, Y
The Civil War and then to Rome; anti-Catholic.

1520 LE CATO, NATHANIEL JAMES WALTER. Mahalinda; or, The Two Cousins . . . Locust Mount, Va.: printed for the author by John A. Gray, New York, 1858. 271 p.

Laid in Virginia; 1751. HEH, LC, LCP, NYP, UV

1521 LEE, DAY KELLOGG. The Master Builder; or, Life at a Trade . . . New York: Redfield, 1852. 322 p.

Of labor interest. AAS, BP, BU, CU, H, HEH, N, NYP, UP, Y

1522 ———— Merrimack; or, Life at the Loom. A Tale . . . New York: Redfield, 1854. 353 p.

AAS, BP, BU, CU, H, HEH, LC, LCP, N, NYH, Y

Mill towns of Massachusetts.

1523 ———— Summerfield; or, Life on a Farm . . . Auburn: Derby and Miller, 1852. 246 p. BP, CU, LC, N, NYP, Y

Finger Lakes region, New York.

1524 LEE, MRS. ELIZA (BUCKMINSTER). Florence, the Parish Orphan, and A Sketch of the Village in the Last Century . . . Boston: Ticknor and Fields, 1852. 176 p. AAS, BP, CU, H, LC, UP, Y

Also issued with imprint: Boston: Ticknor, Reed and Fields, 1852.
NYP

1525 ———— Parthenia; or, The Last Days of Paganism . . . Boston: Ticknor and Fields, 1858. 420 p.

AAS, BA, BP, BU, CU, H, LC, LCP, UC, UP, UVB, Y

1526 LEE, FRANCES. False Shame . . . New York: Carlton & Porter [cop. 1866]. 215 p., illus.

Information from LC card for copy withdrawn from circulation.

1527 ———— Laying the Keel . . . New York: Carlton & Lanahan [cop. 1872]. 178 p., illus.

Information from LC card for copy withdrawn from circulation.

1528 [LEE, J. WILKE.] Seven Stories of the River Counties. By Dirck St. Remy [pseud.] . . . Saratoga Springs: A. S. Baker & Co., 1868. 163 p. HEH, NYP

Contents: The Magian's Daughter—Polipel's Island—Last of a Generation —St. Anthony's Nose—Mystery of Danskammer—Almost Married— Warden of Mahopac.

Caption title: "Tales of the Hudson."

1529 [————] Stories of the Hudson River Counties. By Dirck St. Remy [pseud.] . . . New York: for the author; G. P. Putnam and Sons [cop. 1871]. 174 p.   H, HEH

> Contents: Polipel's Island—Last of a Generation—The Mystery of Danskammer—A Waif of the War [poem]—Almost Married—Warden of Mahopac—St. Antony's Nose—Gold Underground—The Magian's Daughter.
> Caption title: "Stories of the Hudson."
> His *Seven Stories* republished with additions.

LEE, LEROY MADISON. Unequal Yoking: A Warning to Young Women. *In* A. Cary, The Adopted Daughter (1859), No. 466.

1530 LEE, MARGARET. Dr. Wilmer's Love; or, A Question of Conscience. A Novel . . . New York: D. Appleton and Company, 1868. 416 p.   AAS, BP, HEH, LC, NYP

> A few chapters devoted to the Civil War and Libby Prison.

LEE, MINNIE MARY, *pseud. See* Wood, Mrs. Julia Amanda (Sargent)

LEE, PHILIP, JR. The Robber Baron. *In* The Arrow of Gold [185-?], No. 81.

LEGARÉ, JAMES MATHEWES. The Loves of Mary Jones. *In* The Knickerbocker Gallery (1855), No. 1492.

LE GRANGE, H. M., *pseud. See* Cameron, Reb

LEIGH, MRS. EDWARD. *See* Leigh, Mrs. Ella

1531 LEIGH, MRS. ELLA. Confessions of a Flirt: "An Ower True Tale." By Mrs. Edward Leigh . . . Milledgeville, Ga.: Boughton, Nisbet, Barnes & Moore, 1865. 72 p.   LC, UVB

> Preface signed: "Ella Leigh."
> LC copy lacks all after p. 16.

1532 LELAND, ANNA. Home . . . New York: J. C. Derby. Boston: Phillips, Sampson & Co. Cincinnati: H. W. Derby, 1856. 352 p.   AAS, BP, HEH, LC, NYP, UC, UP

> Also published as: *Joys and Sorrows of Home: An Autobiography.* New York: Derby & Jackson, 1857.   BU

1533 LELAND, HENRY PERRY. Americans in Rome . . . New York: Charles T. Evans, 1863. 311 p.

AAS, BA, BP, BU, CU, H, LCP, NYP, UC, UM, Y

1534 ———— The Grey-Bay Mare, and Other Humorous American Sketches . . . Philadelphia: J. B. Lippincott & Co., 1856. 314 p., illus. AAS, BU, H, LCP, NYH, UP

———— The Little Black Slipper. *In* Tales of the Time [1861], No. 2426.

LENNOX, MARY, *pseud. See* Cook, Mrs. Mary Louise (Redd)

LEONARD, AGNES. *See* Hill, Mrs. Agnes (Leonard) Scanland

1535 LEONHARDT, JOSEPHUS, *pseud.* The Confessions of a Minister: Being Leaves from the Diary of the Rev. Josephus Leonhardt [pseud.] . . . Philadelphia: H. Peterson & Co., 1874. 136 p.
HEH, LC, UC

1536 LEONHART, RUDOLPH. Dolores: A Tale of Maine and Italy . . . Pittsburgh, Pa.: Ernst Luft, job printer and book binder, 1870. 432 p. AAS, LC

1537 ———— Through Blood and Iron: A Story of the French-German War . . . Pittsburgh, Pa.: Ernst Luft & Co., 1871. 325 p., illus. LC, NYP

1537a ———— The Wild Rose of the Beaver . . . Tidioute [Pa.]: G. A. Needle & Company, 1873. 111 p. HEH
An Indian tale; western Pennsylvania, 1782.

1538 [LEPPERE, ADAM HAMILTON.] The Rainbow Creed: A Story of the Times . . . Boston: William F. Gill & Co., 1875. 271 p.
AAS, CU, H, HEH, NYP, Y
Of religious interest.

1539 LESLIE, ELIZA. The Dennings and Their Beaux, and Alina Derlay . . . Philadelphia: A. Hart, 1851. 111 p. BP, LC
Also contains: Eliza Farnham—Nothing Morally Wrong.

1540 ———— The Maid of Canal Street, and The Bloxhams . . . Philadelphia: A. Hart, 1851. 115 p. AAS, LC, UVB
Also contains: Barclay Compton; or, The Sailor's Return.

LESLIE, MADELINE, *pseud. See* Baker, Mrs. Harriette Newell (Woods)

1541 [LESTER, MRS. ELLEN (BROWN).] Stanhope Burleigh. The
       Jesuits in Our Homes: A Novel. By Helen Dhu [pseud.].
       New York: Stringer & Townsend, 1855. 406 p., front.

    AAS, BP, CU, H, HEH, LC, N, NYH, NYP, UC, UM, Y

HEH presentation copy with inscription: "Presented to Dr. Bassett by the
Author, Mrs. C. Edwards Lester."
Has been previously attributed to Charles Edwards Lester, and to Helen
Black.
Anti-Catholic.

1542 LETTERS OF MAJOR JACK DOWNING, of the Downingville Militia.
       "The Constitution Is a Dimmycratic Machine . . ." New
       York: Bromley & Co.; J. F. Feeks, 1864. 254 p., illus.

Not by Charles A. Davis; cf. Sabin 84179.   AAS, H, HEH, NYP
Ridicules Lincoln's Civil War policies.

1543 [LEVISON, WILLIAM H.] Black Diamonds; or, Humor, Satire,
       and Sentiment, Treated Scientifically. By Professor Julius
       Caesar Hannibal [pseud.]. In a Series of Burlesque Lectures,
       Darkly Colored . . . New York: A. Ranney. Chicago:
       Rufus Blanchard. Cincinnati: H. M. Rulison, 1855. 364 p.,
       illus.   AAS, H, HEH, LC, NYP

1544 [———] Professor Julius Caesar Hannibal's Scientific Dis-
       courses... New York: Stringer and Townsend, 1852. 128 p.
            AAS, BA, NYP

1545 [LEWIS, CHARLES BERTRAND.] "Quad's Odds" by "M. Quad
       [pseud.], the Detroit Free Press Man:" Anecdote, Humor and
       Pathos ... Detroit: R. D. S. Tyler & Co., 1875. 480 p., illus.
            AAS, BU, CU, LC, N, NYP, UM

1546 [LEWIS, MRS. ESTELLE ANNA (ROBINSON).] Minna Monte. By
       Stella [pseud.]. Philadelphia: J. B. Lippincott & Co., 1872.
       224 p.   BP, LCP

LEWIS, JULIUS WARREN. See Piper, A. G.

1547 THE LIFE AND ADVENTURES OF EBO JUBE; in Connexion with,
       and as More Fully Illustrated by, What Befel His Master,
       Charley Brief, at Various Times, and in Different Parts of the
       World. Part I. New York: Adriance, Sherman & Co., 1852.
       69 p., illus.   LC
       No more published.

1548 THE LIFE AND ADVENTURES OF MISS EMMA HOWARD, a Model of Female Virtue . . . New York: George C. Holbrook, 1853. 38 p.   H

1549 LIFE AND ALONE. Boston: Lee and Shepard, 1870. 407 p.   AAS, CU, H, LC, NYP, Y
Laid in Middleton, England.

1550 THE LIFE OF ANSON BUNKER, "the Bloody Hand," the Perpetrator of No Less Than Fifteen Cold-Blooded Murders, amongst Which Were the Great Nathan Murder of New York City . . . Philadelphia: Barclay & Co., 21 North Seventh Street [cop. 1875]. 95 p., illus.   LC, NYP

1551 THE LIFE OF GENERAL M. D. STANLEY, an American Militia General, the Celebrated Roué, Swindler, Pickpocket, and Murderer, Who Was Executed at Vienna, Austria, September 17, 1853 . . . Baltimore, Philadelphia, Cincinnati, and St. Louis: A. R. Orton, 1855. 49, [1] p., illus.   LC

1552 THE LIFE OF JOAQUIN MURIETA, the Brigand Chief of California: Being a Complete History of His Life, from the Age of Sixteen to the Time of His Capture and Death at the Hands of Capt. Harry Love, in the Year 1853. San Francisco: published at office of the "California Police Gazette," 1859. 71 p., illus. Printed in double cols.
Listed by R. F. Adams, Six-Guns and Saddle Leather (Norman, Okla. [1954]), No. 710, who notes that it is a plagiarism of J. R. Ridge's Life (1854), No. 2039.
Reissued with imprint on front paper cover: San Francisco: Butler & Co., publishers of the "California Police Gazette," 1861. At head of cover title: "Second Edition." HEH has a photostat of the copy formerly in possession of Francis Farquhar.

1553 LINDEN, CLARENCE. Our General . . . Philadelphia: Barclay & Co., No. 21 North Seventh Street [cop. 1872]. 1 p.l., 19-20, iv, 21-201 p., illus.   BP, LC, UV
Union armies in the West.

1554 LINDEN, LIELE. Chestnut Wood: A Tale . . . New York: D. Appleton and Company. London, 1854. 2 vols. (359, 360 p.)   AAS, BP, BU, H(V.1), NYP

LINKINWATER, TIM, pseud. See Waldo, James Curtis

1555 LINWOOD, WITH OTHER STORIES. New York: Oliver S. Felt, 1865. 183 p. AAS, BP, CU

Contents: Linwood; or, The Christmas Gift—The Spirit of the Fountain —Ernest's Choice; or, The Fireside Fairy—Ida Leslie—The Mother's Dream—The Crucible—Florence Lambert.

1556 LIPPARD, GEORGE. The Midnight Queen; or, Leaves from New-York Life ... New York: Garrett & Co., 18 Ann Street [cop. 1853]. 110 p. Printed in double cols. LC, NYH

Also contains: The Life of a Man of the World—Margaret Dunbar.

For information concerning Lippard's works, particularly in reference to the different titles under which the same work was published, see Roger Butterfield, "George Lippard and His Secret Brotherhood," *Penn. Mag. of Hist. & Biog.*, LXXIX (1955), 285-309.

1557 ———— New York: Its Upper Ten and Lower Million ... Cincinnati: H. M. Rulison, 1853. 284 p. Printed in double cols. AAS, BU, CU, H, LC, N, NYP, UM, UP

1558 [LIPPINCOTT, MRS. SARA JANE (CLARKE).] A Forest Tragedy, and Other Tales. By Grace Greenwood [pseud.] ... Boston: Ticknor and Fields, 1856. 343 p.

AAS, BP, BU, CU, H, HEH, LC, LCP, NYH, NYP, UM, UV

Also contains: The Minister's Choice—St. Pierre, the Soldier—Alice's Tryst—The Child-Seer.

1559 [————] Greenwood Leaves: A Collection of Sketches and Letters. By Grace Greenwood [pseud.]. Second Series. Boston: Ticknor, Reed and Fields, 1852. 382 p., front.

AAS, BU, CU, HEH, LCP, NYH, NYP, UP, Y

Contains: Philip Hamilton and His Mother—The Two Thompsons—The Step-Mother—The Irish Patriots of '48—A Mere Act of Humanity—Effie Mather—Apollonia Jagiello—The Volunteer—The Poetry of Whittier—The Darkened Casement—Dora's Children—A Few Words about Actors and Plays—The Story of a Violet—Selections from Letters—A Good Story Spoiled in the Telling—Preachers and Politics: A Contrast.

1560 [LITTLE, MRS. SOPHIA LOUISE (ROBBINS).] The Reveille; or, Music at Dawn ... Providence: printed by Benjamin T. Albro, 1854. 3 pts. (140 p.) AAS(pt.2), BU, LC(pt.1)

Author's name supplied by BU.

A temperance tale.

1561 ———— Thrice through the Furnace: A Tale of the Times of the Iron Hoof ... Pawtucket, R. I.: A. W. Pearce, printer, 1852. 190 p. AAS, BP, BU, CU, HEH, N, NYH, NYP, UP, Y

Antislavery.

LIVELY, BOB, *pseud.* Mysterious Rappings Explained; or, An Artful Dodge. *In* Dodge's Sketches [1853], No. 1751.

1562 LIVERMORE, MRS. ELIZABETH D. Zoë; or, The Quadroon's Triumph. A Tale for the Times . . . Cincinnati: Truman and Spofford, 1855. 2 vols. (327, 306 p.), illus.
Antislavery. AAS, BP, BU, CU, H, HEH, LC, N, NYH, NYP, UM, UP

1563 LIVERMORE, KATE. Mary Lee . . . New York: D. Appleton & Co., 1860. 161 p., illus. Y

1564 LIVERMORE, MRS. MARY ASHTON (RICE). Pen Pictures; or, Sketches from Domestic Life . . . Chicago: S. C. Griggs & Co., 1862. 216 p. AAS, BP, HEH
Contains: The Life-Long Sacrifice—The Sale of the Homestead—The Sewing Society—Lost and Found—The Race with the Mill-Stream—The Mission of Sorrow—The First Quarrel.

1565 LIZZIE LEE's DAUGHTER; or, A Rich Father's Remorse . . . Truly a Most Romantic Incident of Real Life in Fifth Avenue, New York City. [New York, 18—?] 62 p., illus. NYP

1566 [LOCKE, DAVID ROSS.] Divers Views, Opinions, and Prophecies of Yoors Trooly Petroleum V. Nasby [pseud.] . . . Cincinnati: R. W. Carroll & Co.; Jos. L. Topham & Co., general agents, 1866. 424 p., illus.
AAS, BA, BU, HEH, LC, N, NYH, NYP, UC, UM, UP, Y
At head of title: "Nasby."

1567 ———— Eastern Fruit on Western Dishes. The Morals of Abou Ben Adhem. Edited by D. R. Locke . . . Boston: Lee and Shepard. New York: Lee, Shepard and Dillingham, 1875. 231 p. AAS, BA, BP, CU, H, HEH, LC, LCP, N, NYP, UC, Y
Satire on society and politics.

1568 [————] Ekkoes from Kentucky. By Petroleum V. Nasby [pseud.] . . . Bein a Perfect Record uv the Ups, Downs, and Experiences uv the Dimocrisy, doorin the Eventful Year 1867, ez Seen by a Naturalized Kentuckian . . . Boston: Lee and Shepard, 1868. 324 p., illus.
AAS, BP, BU, H, HEH, LC, N, NYH, NYP, UC, UM, UVB, Y

1569 ———— Nasby on Inflation: A New Comic Book by Petroleum V. Nasby (D. R. Locke), Mark Twain's Only Rival . . . Philadelphia: Barclay & Co., No. 21 North Seventh Street [cop. 1875]. 78 p., illus. AAS

At head of title: "Deep-Seated Mirth Holds a Place in Every Line."

1570 [————] The Nasby Papers: Letters and Sermons Containing the Views on the Topics of the Day, of Petroleum V. Nasby [pseud.] . . . Indianapolis, Ind.: C. O. Perrine & Co., 1864. 64 p.

AAS, BA, BP, BU, CU, H, HEH, LC, LCP, NYP, UC, UM, UP, Y

AAS has 2d copy with imprint on front cover: "T. R. Dawley, New York."

1571 [————] The Struggles (Social, Financial and Political) of Petroleum V. Nasby [pseud.] . . . With an Introduction by Hon. Charles Sumner . . . Boston: I. N. Richardson and Company, 1872. 720 p., illus.

Pages 721-727 are advts. AAS, BP, BU, H, HEH, LC, NYH, NYP, UC

Also published as: *The Moral History of America's Life-Struggle.* Boston, Mass.: I. N. Richardson and Company. St. Louis, Mo.: Etna Publishing Co. [cop. 1874]. BP, CU, H, HEH, LC, N

1572 [————] "Swingin round the Cirkle." By Petroleum V. Nasby [pseud.] . . . His Ideas of Men, Politics, and Things, as Set Forth in His Letters to the Public Press during the Year 1866 . . . Boston: Lee and Shepard, 1867. 299 p., illus.

AAS, BA, BP, BU, CU, H, HEH, LC, LCP, N, NYH, NYP, UC, UM, UP, UVB, Y

1573 LOFLAND, JOHN. The Poetical and Prose Writings of Dr. John Lofland, the Milford Bard . . . Collected and Arranged by J. N. M'Jilton, A.M. Baltimore: John Murphy & Co. Wilmington: J. T. Heald, 1853. 587 p., front.

BU, CU, H, LC, NYH, NYP, UM, UV, Y

Contains: The Wizard of Valley Forge; or, The Revenge of the Mysterious Man—Ono-Keo-Co; or, The Bandit of the Brandywine—The Dream of Love—The Broken Heart; or, Virtue Triumphant in Death—The Quaker Merchant; or, The Generous Man Rewarded—The Courtship versus the Rum Jug—The Duel; or, The Dream of Love—Love a la Mode; or, The Boatman's Daughter—Helen MacTrever: A Tale of the Battle of Brandywine—The Muzzled Dog—The Humming-Bird's Nest—Manitoo, the Indian Beauty of the Brandywine and Wild Harry, of Wilmington. The 1846 ed. with the above title contains no fiction.

LOGAN, *pseud.* *See* Thorpe, Thomas Bangs

1574 LOGAN, OLIVE. Chateau Frissac; or, Home Scenes in France . . . New York: D. Appleton and Company, 1865. 329 p.
First published, London, 1862.   AAS, BP, BU, CU, H, LCP, NYP, UC, Y
Olive Logan was first married to Henry A. De Lille, then to William Wirt Sikes, and finally to James O'Neill.

1575 ———— The Good Mr. Bagglethorpe . . . New York: the American News Company, 1869. 27 p. Printed in double cols.   AAS, H, LC, LCP
At head of title: "Olive Logan's New Story."

1576 ———— Olive Logan's Christmas Story: Somebody's Stocking . . . New York: the American News Company [cop. 1867]. 16 p. Printed in double cols.   H, LC

1577 ———— Olive Logan's New Christmas Story: John Morris's Money . . . New York: the American News Company, 1867. 55 p. Printed in double cols.   LC, Y

1578 ———— They Met by Chance: A Society Novel . . . New York: Adams, Victor & Co., 98 William Street [cop. 1873]. 320 p.   AAS, CU, H, HEH, LC, LCP, NYP, UC, Y

1579 [LOMAX, E. VICTORIA.] Mary Austin; or, The New Home. By Byrd Lyttle [pseud.]. Philadelphia: A. Martien, 1870.
Title listed in Kelly 1866-1871.

1580 LONG, R. H. Harry Todd, the Deserter; or, The Soldier's Wife. With Scenes of the Present Rebellion . . . New York: American News Company, 1864. 58 p., illus. Printed in double cols.   LC, NYH

1581 [LONGSTREET, AUGUSTUS BALDWIN.] Master William Mitten; or, A Youth of Brilliant Talents, Who Was Ruined by Bad Luck . . . Macon, Ga.: Burke, Boykin & Company, 1864. 239 p.   BA, HEH, LC, NYH, UV, Y

1582 LONGSTREET, MRS. RACHEL ABIGAIL (BUCHANAN) GILDERSLEEVE. Remy St. Remy; or, The Boy in Blue. By Mrs. C. H. Gildersleeve . . . New York: James O'Kane, 1865. 352 p.
AAS, HEH, LCP, Y

LORD, J. L. The Romance of a Western Trip. *In* Stories and Sketches (1867), No. 2386.

1583 LORIMER, GEORGE CLAUDE. Under the Evergreens; or, A Night
with St. Nicholas . . . Boston: Shepard and Gill, 1874. 234
p., illus.   BP

LORING, FREDERIC WADSWORTH. The Improvisatore and the
Heeler. *In* Thirteen Good Stories [1873?], No. 2457.

———— Rebecca's Ma. *In* Thirteen Good Stories [1873?],
No. 2457.

1584 ———— Two College Friends . . . Boston: Loring, corner
Bromfield & Washington Sts. [cop. 1871]. 161 p.
The Union army in Virginia.   AAS, BA, BP, BU, H, LC, LCP, NYP, Y

———— *jt. au. See* Hale, Edward Everett, *ed.* Six of One
(1872), No. 1058.

LORING, H. W. The Goldsmith of Paris. *In* M. M. Ballou, The
Sea-Witch [1855?], No. 207.

1585 LORRAINE, *pseud.* Why She Refused Him. By Lorraine
[pseud.]. Philadelphia: J. B. Lippincott & Co., 1873. 330 p.
Information from LC card for copy withdrawn from circulation.

1586 LOTH, MORITZ. "The Forgiving Kiss;" or, Our Destiny. A
Novel . . . New York: George W. Carleton & Co. London:
S. Low, Son & Co., 1874. 364 p.   LC

1587 ———— Our Prospects: A Tale of Real Life . . . Cincinnati:
Robert Clarke & Co., printers, 1870. 377 p.
                                       AAS, BU, LC, NYP, UM

LOTHROP, AMY, *pseud. See* Warner, Anna Bartlett

1588 LOTOS LEAVES: Original Stories, Essays and Poems. By White-
law Reid, Wilkie Collins, Mark Twain, John Hay, John
Brougham . . . Edited by John Brougham and John Elderkin
. . . Boston: William F. Gill and Company, 1875. 411 p.,
illus.   AAS, BU, CU, H, HEH, LC, NYP, UC, UM, UP, Y
Verso of title page: "Welch Bigelow Co., University Press, Cambridge,
Mass."
Also published as: *Lotos Leaves: Original Stories, Poems, and Essays. By
the Great Writers of America and England.* Boston: William F. Gill and
Company, 1875.   NYP, Y
Verso of title page: "Press of Rockwell & Churchill, 39 Arch St.,
Boston."

1589 LOUD, JEREMY. Gabriel Vane, His Fortune and His Friends . . . New York: Derby & Jackson. Cincinnati: H. W. Derby & Co., 1856. 423 p.   AAS, BP, H, HEH, LC
Also published as: *The Orphan Boy; or, Lights and Shadows of Northern Life.* New York: Derby & Jackson, 1857. 423 p., front.   AAS, CU

LOVERING, MRS. E. C. The Isle of Crows. *In* J. H. Robinson, Rosalthe (1853), No. 2081.

1590 LOWELL, ROBERT TRAILL SPENCE. Antony Brade . . . Boston: Roberts Brothers, 1874. 415, [1] p.
AAS, BA, BP, BU, CU, H, HEH, LC, LCP, UP, UVB, Y
One chapter devoted to the Rosicrucians.

1591 [————] The New Priest in Conception Bay . . . Boston: Phillips, Sampson and Company, 1858. 2 vols. (309, 339 p.)
AAS, BA, BU, CU, H, HEH, LC, LCP, N, NYP, UC, UM, UV, Y
Laid in Newfoundland.

———— A Raft That No Man Made. *In* Atlantic Tales (1866), No. 155.

1592 [LUDLOW, FITZ HUGH.] The Hasheesh Eater: Being Passages from the Life of a Pythagorean . . . New York: Harper & Brothers, 1857. 371 p.
AAS, BA, CU, H, HEH, LC, LCP, N, NYH, NYP, UC, UM, UP, UVB, Y

1593 ———— Little Brother, and Other Genre-Pictures . . . Boston: Lee and Shepard, 1867. 293 p.
AAS, BP, CU, H, HEH, LC, N, NYP, UC, UM, UVB, Y
Also contains: Fleeing to Tarshish—Little Briggs and I—A Brace of Boys.

———— The Proper Use of Grandfathers. *In* Stories and Sketches (1867), No. 2386.

———— The Taxidermist. *In* Tales of the Time [1861], No. 2426.

1594 LUNARIUS: A VISITOR FROM THE MOON. New York: National Temperance Society, 1869. 72 p.   AAS, LC, NYP

1595 [LUNT, GEORGE.] Eastford; or, Household Sketches. By Wesley Brooke [pseud.] . . . Boston: Crocker & Brewster, 1855. 328 p.   AAS, BA, BP, CU, LC, NYP, UM, UP, UVB, Y
New England life and characters.

LYNDON, *pseud.* *See* Hughes, Mrs. Reginald

1596 LYNN, CORA. Durham Village: A Temperance Tale . . . Boston: John P. Jewett & Company. Cleveland, Ohio: Jewett, Proctor & Worthington, 1854. 174 p. AAS, BP, HEH, NYP, UM

LYTTLE, BYRD, *pseud.* *See* Lomax, E. Victoria

M., C. L. *See* McIlvain, Mrs. Charlotte L.

1597 M., E. H. Mariamne; or, The Queen's Fate. A Tale of the Days of Herod . . . New York: Pudney & Russell, and Dayton & Burdick, 1856. 275 p., illus. AAS, HEH, NYH

M., J. A. *See* Maitland, James A.

M., L. B. A Day without Prayer. *In* M. G. Clarke, *comp.*, Sunshine and Shadows (1865), No. 541.

1598 M., L. M. Olie; or, The Old West Room. The Weary at Work and the Weary at Rest . . . New York: Mason Brothers, 1855. 525 p. BP

M., M. L. *See* Meaney, Mary L.

1599 M., N. Hester Somerset: A Novel. Philadelphia: A. Hart, 1853.
Title listed in Roorbach 1852-1855.

1600 M., S. H. Miranda Elliot; or, The Voice of the Spirit . . . Philadelphia: Lippincott, Grambo & Co., 1855. 308 p.
Sarah H. Maxwell may be the author. AAS, BP, HEH, LC, NYP

1601 McAFEE, MRS. NELLY NICHOL (MARSHALL). As by Fire . . . Harrodsburg: published by the author, 1868. 323 p. LCP
Appleton lists the following three titles: "Eleanor Morton; or, Life in Dixie, New York, 1865; Sodom Apples, New York, 1866; Wearing the Cross, Cincinnati, 1868."

1602 [————] Gleanings from Fireside Fancies. By "Sans Souci" [pseud.]. Chicago: J. C. W. Bailey, 1866. 396 p., front.
BU, UC

1603 [MCALPINE, EMILY ELIZA JOURS.] Doings in Maryland; or, Matilda Douglas . . . Philadelphia: J. B. Lippincott & Co., 1871. 316 p.   AAS, CU, HEH, LC, LCP, N, NYP, UV, Y
A fictitious biography of Washington Allston.

1604 MCCABE, JAMES DABNEY. The Aid-de-Camp: A Romance of the War . . . Richmond: W. A. J. Smith, 1863. 113 p.
CU, H, HEH, LC, NYH, UP, UV, Y

1605 MCCONNEL, JOHN LUDLUM. The Glenns: A Family History . . . New York: Charles Scribner, 1851. 280 p.
Western manners and scenery.   AAS, LC, N, UC, UP, Y

———— Marie Lefrette: A Story of Kaskaskia. In The Knickerbocker Gallery (1855), No. 1492.

1606 ———— Western Characters; or, Types of Border Life in the Western States . . . New York: Redfield, 1853. 378 p., illus.
AAS, BA, BP, CU, H, HEH, N, NYH, NYP, Y

MCCOOMB, FLORENCE, pseud. See Meline, Mary Miller

1607 [MCCORMICK, M. R.] The Duke's Chase; or, The Diamond Ring vs. the Gold Ring. By Forest Warbler [pseud.]. Cincinnati: Robert Clarke & Co., printers, 1871. 271 p.   LC
At bottom of p. 271: "End of Vol. 1." No more published.

1608 [MCCORRY, PETER.] Irish Widow's Son; or, The Pikeman of '98. By C. O'Leary [pseud.]. Boston: P. Donahoe, 1869.
Title listed in S. J. Brown, Ireland in Fiction (Dublin, 1919), No. 1342, and in Kelly 1866-1871.

1609 [————] The Lost Rosary; or, Our Irish Girls, Their Trials, Temptations, and Triumphs. By Con O'Leary [pseud.]. Boston: P. Donahoe, 1870. 230 p.   BP, LC

1610 ———— Mount Benedict; or, The Violated Tomb. A Tale of Charlestown the Convent, by Peter McCorry, Author of "The Irish Widow's Son," "The Lost Rosary; or, Our Irish Girls," "The Lighthouse of the Lagan," etc., etc. Boston: Patrick Donahoe, 1871. 239 p., illus.   N

1611 [MCDONNELL, WILLIAM.] Exeter Hall: A Theological Romance . . . New York: the American News Company, 1869. 186 p. Printed in double cols.   AAS, BP, CU, H, LC, NYP

1612 ———— Heathens of the Heath: A Romance . . . New York: D. M. Bennett, 1874. 498 p. CU, NYP, UC
Laid in England.

1613 [McDougall, Mrs. Frances Harriet (Whipple) Greene).] Shahmah in Pursuit of Freedom; or, The Branded Hand. Translated from the Original Showiah, and Edited by an American Citizen. New York: Thatcher & Hutchinson, 1858. 599 p., front. AAS, BP, BU, HEH, LC, N, NYP
On slavery.

1614 McElgun, John. Annie Reilly; or, The Fortunes of an Irish Girl in New York. A Tale Founded on Fact . . . New York: J. A. McGee, 1873. 245 p., front. H, LC, Y

1615 [McElhinney, Mrs. Jane.] Only a Woman's Heart. By Ada Clare [pseud.] . . . New York: M. Doolady, 1866. 336 p.
AAS, HEH, LC

1616 M'Gaw, James F. Philip Seymour; or, Pioneer Life in Richland County, Ohio. Founded on Facts . . . Mansfield: R. Brinkerhoff, 1858. 295 p., illus. AAS, H, N, NYH
Indian campaigns.

1617 MacGregor, Annie Lyndsay. John Ward's Governess: A Novel . . . Philadelphia: J. B. Lippincott & Co., 1868. 303 p.
CU, H, HEH, LCP, NYP

1618 ———— The Professor's Wife; or, It Might Have Been . . . Philadelphia: J. B. Lippincott & Co., 1870. 305 p.
Laid in New London, Conn. BP, HEH, LC, LCP, NYP

1619 [McIlvain, Mrs. Charlotte L.] Ebon and Gold: A Novel. By C. L. M. . . . New York: G. W. Carleton & Co. London: S. Low, Son & Co., 1874. 335 p. AAS, LC
Begins and ends in the South.

1620 McIntosh, Maria Jane. Evenings at Donaldson Manor; or, The Christmas Guest . . . New York: D. Appleton & Company. Philadelphia: Geo. S. Appleton, 1851. 286 p., illus.
AAS, BP, CU, H, HEH, LC, LCP, N, NYH, UC, UP, UV, Y

1621 ———— The Lofty and the Lowly; or, Good in All and None
All-Good . . . New York: D. Appleton & Company, 1853.
2 vols. (299, 323 p.)
Southern life.   AAS, AP, CU, H, HEH, LC, LCP, NYP, UC, UV, Y

1622 ———— Two Pictures; or, What We Think of Ourselves, and
What the World Thinks of Us . . . New York: D. Appleton
and Company. London, 1863. 476 p.
                                   AAS, AP, H, HEH, LC, LCP, NYH, NYP, UC, Y
Southern life, ante bellum.

1623 ———— Violet; or, The Cross and the Crown . . . Boston:
John P. Jewett and Company. Cleveland, Ohio: Henry P. B.
Jewett. New York: Sheldon, Blakeman & Company, 1856.
448 p.   AAS, BP, BU, CU, H, HEH, LCP, NYP, UC, Y

McJILTON, JOHN NELSON, ed. See Lofland, John. The Poetical
and Prose Writings . . . Collected and Arranged by J. N.
M'Jilton (1853), No. 1573.

McKAY, J. T. Ranlock Branch. In Short Stories (1869), No.
2210.

1624 M'KEEHAN, HATTIA. Liberty or Death; or, Heaven's Infraction
of the Fugitive Slave Law . . . Cincinnati: published for and
by the author, 1858. 104 p.   N
Also published as: Liberty or Death; or, The Mother's Sacrifice. By
Hattia M'Keehan. Indianapolis: published for and by the author, 1859.
NYH
Also published as: Liberty or Death; or, The Mother's Sacrifice. By
Mrs. J. P. Hardwick. Harrisburg: printed for the author, 1862.   LC

1625 ———— The Life and Trials of a Hoosier Girl . . . New
York: printed for the authoress, 1863. 31 p.   H
Preface dated: "Dec. 22nd, 1859."

1626 McKEEN, PHEBE FULLER. Theodora: A Home Story . . . New
York: Anson D. F. Randolph & Company, 770 Broadway [cop.
1875]. 480 p.   H, HEH, LC, LCP, NYP, Y
Laid in New York; Civil War background.

1627 McKEEVER, HARRIET BURN. Edith's Ministry . . . Philadelphia:
Lindsay & Blakiston, 1860. 431 p.   AAS, UP
Many of her stories were for teenage readers.

1628 ———— The House on the Heights . . . Philadelphia: H. N. McKinney & Co. [cop. 1873]. 373 p.   AAS, BP, LCP, NYP

1629 ———— Maude and Miriam; or, The Fair Crusader . . . Philadelphia: Claxton, Remsen & Haffelfinger, 1871. 337 p.
The Crusades, 1189-1192.   AAS, BP, H, HEH, LC, LCP, NYP

1630 ———— Silver Threads . . . Philadelphia: Claxton, Remsen & Haffelfinger, 1868. 376 p., front.   AAS, CU, LC, UP

1631 ———— Twice Crowned: A Story of the Days of Queen Mary . . . Philadelphia: Claxton, Remsen & Haffelfinger, 1873. 360 p.   AAS, BP, H, LC, NYP
Persecution of the Protestants.

1632 ———— Westbrook Parsonage . . . Philadelphia: Claxton, Remsen & Haffelfinger, 1870. 359 p., front.
   AAS, LC, LCP, NYP

1633 ———— Woodcliff . . . Philadelphia: Lindsay & Blakiston, 1865. 464 p.   AAS, BU, CU, HEH, LC, UP, Y

1634 MacKenzie, Mrs. Adelheid (Zwissler). Aureola; or, The Black Sheep. A Story of German Social Life. By Mrs. Adelheid Shelton-MacKenzie . . . Philadelphia: Claxton, Remsen & Haffelfinger, 1871. 263 p.   BP, HEH, LC

1635 ———— Married against Reason . . . Boston: Loring, 319 Washington Street [cop. 1869]. 97 p.   LC, LCP, NYP

1636 MacKenzie, Robert Shelton. Bits of Blarney . . . New York: Redfield, No. 34 Beekman Street [1855]. 426 p.   H, LC, Y
Contents: Legends—Irish Stories—Eccentric Characters—Irish Publicists. Dedication dated "Aug. 20, 1855."

1637 ———— Tressilian and His Friends . . . Philadelphia: J. B. Lippincott & Co., 1859. 372 p.
   AAS, BP, CU, H, HEH, LC, LCP, NYP, UC, UP, Y
Short stories and sketches.

1638 McKnight, Charles. Old Fort Duquesne; or, Captain Jack, the Scout. An Historical Novel, with Copious Notes . . . Pittsburgh: Peoples Monthly Publishing Co., 1873. 501 p., illus.   AAS, BA, CU, HEH, LC, LCP, N, NYP
Also published as: Captain Jack, the Scout; or, The Indian Wars about Old Fort Duquesne. Philadelphia: Porter & Coates [cop. 1873].
AAS, LCP, N

1639 [McLain, Mary Webster.] Lifting the Veil . . . New York: Charles Scribner & Co., 1870. 200 p.

On bereavement.   AAS, BP, BU, H, LC, LCP, NYP

MacLeod, Donald. *See* MacLeod, Xavier Donald

1640 McLeod, Mrs. Georgiana A. (Hulse). Mine and Thine; or, The Step Mother's Reward. New York: Derby & Jackson, 1857.

Title listed in J. G. Johnson, *Southern Fiction* (Charlottesville, 1909), p. 40.

1641 ———— Sea Drifts . . . New York: Robert Carter and Brothers, 1864. 264 p., illus.

Peabody Library copy.

1642 ———— Sunbeams and Shadows, and Buds and Blossoms; or, Leaves from Aunt Minnie's Portfolio . . . New York: D. Appleton & Co., 1851. 262 p.   H, LC, LCP

MacLeod, Xavier Donald. Anteros: A Life with One Passion. *In* The Knickerbocker Gallery (1855), No. 1492.

1643 ———— The Bloodstone . . . New York: Charles Scribner, 1853. 215 p.   BP, BU, CU, LC, LCP, NYP, Y
Laid in Germany.

1644 [————] Legends of Holy Mary. Cincinnati: John P. Walsh [n.d.]. 71 p.

Preface signed "X. D. ML."
Cincinnati Public Library copy.

1645 ———— Our Lady of Litanies . . . Cincinnati: printed and published by John P. Walsh, 1861. 225, 11 p.   BU, LC
Eleven pages at end, music.

1646 ———— Pynnshurst: His Wanderings and Ways of Thinking . . . New York: Charles Scribner, 1852. 431 p.

      AAS, BA, BP, BU, CU, HEH, LC, LCP, NYP, Y

1647 McMechan, I. V. V. Time; or, The Incidents of a Life . . . Clay [N. Y.?]: P. Childs & Co., book and job printers, 1851. 40 p. Printed in double cols.   UP

1648 McSHERRY, JAMES. Willitoft; or, The Days of James the First
. . . Baltimore: John Murphy & Co. Pittsburgh: George
Quigley, 1851. 293, [1] p.   BP

1649 MAFFITT, JOHN NEWLAND. Nautilus; or, Cruising under Canvas
. . . New York, Cincinnatti [sic], Chicago, and St. Louis:
United States Publishing Company. San Francisco: A. L.
Bancroft & Co., 1871. 352 p.   CU, HEH, LC, LCP

1650 MAGA STORIES. New York: G. P. Putnam & Son, 1867. 325 p.
                              AAS, BA, BP, HEH, LC, LCP, NYP
Contents: Found and Lost—My Three Conversations with Miss Chester
—Mrs. MacSimum's Bill—The Feast of the Cranberries—Tolliwotte's
Ghost—Professor Phantillo—The Mormon's Wife—The Rich Merchant
of Cairo—The Legend of Goodman Poverty—The Double Veil—My
Husband's Mother—The Old Woman Who Dried Up and Blew Away
—The Ambassador in Spite of Himself—Elegant Tom Dillar—A Toss-up
for a Husband—Uncle Bernard's Story—How I Came to Be Married.
Also published as: Found and Lost, and Other Maga Stories. New York:
G. P. Putnam & Son, 1868.   AAS, LCP
At head of title: "Putnam's Railway Classics."

1651 MAGGIE AND HER LOVERS. Providence: Knowles, Anthony and
Company, 1866. 48 p.   AAS, BU, CU, HEH

1652 MAGILL, MARY TUCKER. The Holcombes: A Story of Virginia
Home-Life . . . Philadelphia: J. B. Lippincott & Co., 1871.
290 p.   AAS, BP, CU, HEH, LC, LCP, N, NYP, UV, Y
Ante bellum.

1653 ——— Women; or, Chronicles of the Late War . . . Baltimore: Turnbull Brothers, 1871. 393 p.
                    AAS, BA, BP, CU, H, HEH, LC, LCP, N, NYP, UV, Y
From the Southern viewpoint.

1654 [MAITLAND, JAMES A.] The Cabin Boy's Story: A Semi-
Nautical Romance. Founded on Fact . . . New York: Gar-
rett & Co., 18 Ann Street [cop. 1854]. 438 p., front.
On the African slave trade.   AAS, CU, HEH, N, UC

1655 ——— The Cousins; or, The Captain's Ward . . . New
York: Evans & Co., 1858. 384 p.   AAS, UC
Also published as: The Three Cousins. Philadelphia: T. B. Peterson &
Brothers, 306 Chestnut St. [cop. 1860].   AAS, LC

1656 —————— The Diary of an Old Doctor: Being Sketches of the Most Interesting Reminiscences of an Old Physician . . . Philadelphia: T. B. Peterson & Brothers, 306 Chestnut Street [cop. 1858]. 400 p., illus.   AAS
This is his *The Old Doctor* with a new "Author's Preface" which states that this is a revised ed.

1657 [—————] The Lawyer's Story; or, The Orphan's Wrongs. By a Member of the New-York Bar. New York: H. Long & Brother [cop. 1853]. 374 p., illus.   AAS, BU, UP, Y
Also issued with imprint: New York: H. Long & Brother, 43 Ann Street. Cincinnati: H. B. Pearson & Co., 17 East Fourth St. [cop. 1853].
CU, HEH, N

1658 [—————] The Old Doctor; or, Stray Leaves from My Journal. Being . . . Reminiscences of a Retired Physician. New York: H. Long & Brother, 43 Ann St., 1853. 384 p., illus.   AAS
Revised ed. published under title: *The Diary of an Old Doctor* [cop. 1858].

1659 —————— The Old Patroon; or, The Great Van Broek Property . . . Philadelphia: T. B. Peterson & Brothers, 306 Chestnut Street [1866?]. 392 p.   AAS, NYP

1660 [—————] The Pirate Doctor; or, The Extraordinary Career of a New-York Physician. By a Naval Officer. New York: Garrett & Co., No. 18 Ann Street [185-?]. 126 p. Printed in double cols.   LC

1661 —————— Sartaroe: A Tale of Norway . . . Philadelphia: T. B. Peterson & Brothers, No. 306 Chestnut Street [cop. 1858]. 448 p.   AAS, BU, CU, HEH, LCP, NYP, UC, Y

1662 [—————] The Wanderer: A Tale of Life's Vicissitudes . . . New York: E. D. Long, 121 Nassau Street [cop. 1856]. 377 p.   AAS, BU, CU, HEH, N, NYP, UC, UV, Y

1663 [—————] The Watchman. By J. A. M. . . . New York: H. Long & Brother, 121 Nassau Street [cop. 1855]. 400 p.
AAS, BU, CU, H, HEH, LC, NYH, NYP, UC, UP, UV, Y

1664 MANDEVILLE, AUGUSTUS H., *pseud.?* A Faithful and Authentic Narrative of the Abduction, Captivity, Sufferings, and Heart-Rending Misfortunes of Payneta Mandeville, Wife of Augustus H. Mandeville, of Baltimore, Maryland, Who Was Abducted by the Spanish Bandits of New Grenada . . . Richmond, Va.: M. L. Barclay [cop. 1854]. 35 p., illus.

AAS, HEH, NYP

Mandeville's name not in Baltimore directories, 1850-1860.
AAS copy without copyright notice.

1665 [MANIGAULT, GABRIEL.] St. Cecilia: A Modern Tale from Real Life. Part First: Adversity . . . Philadelphia: J. B. Lippincott & Co., 1871. 372 p. LC, NYP

MANNERS, MRS., *pseud. See* Richards, Mrs. Cornelia Holroyd (Bradley)

1666 [MANSFIELD, LEWIS WILLIAM.] Up-Country Letters. Edited by Prof. B———, National Observatory . . . New York: D. Appleton and Company. London, 1852. 331 p., front.

AAS, BA, BP, BU, CU, H, HEH, LC, LCP, N, NYH, NYP

Letters signed "Z. P." [i.e., Zachary Pundison], a pseudonym used by Mansfield, according to Cushing.

———— *jt. au. See* Hammond, S. H. Country Margins (1855), No. 1084.

MANTON, KATE, *pseud. See* Knight, Mrs. S. G.

MARCH, *Major, pseud. See* Willcox, Orlando Bolivar

MARCH, WALTER, *pseud. See* Willcox, Orlando Bolivar

1667 MARGARET; OR, PREJUDICE AT HOME, and Its Victims. An Autobiography. New York: Stringer & Townsend, 1854. 362 p.

BP, H, NYP, UV, Y

Laid in England.

1668 MARIAN ELLIS; or, Unfading Flowers. By a Clergyman's Wife. New York: Routledge, 1873.
Title listed in Amer. Cat. 1876.

1669 MARLBY VILLA. By the Authoress, Rome, Georgia. Atlanta, Georgia: William Kay, 1858. Cover title, 96 p. UC

1670 MARRS, HENRY W. The Refugees of the Revolution; or, The Cow Boys of Plumstead. A Thrilling History of Local Events in Bucks County . . . Doylestown, Pa.: Beans & Kuster, 1860. 55 p. Printed in double cols.   NYH
At head of title: "Interesting Local History."

1671 [MARSH, MRS. JEANNIE S.] Cathara Clyde: A Novel. By Inconnu [pseud.]. New York: Charles Scribner, 1860. 377 p.   AAS, BP, CU, HEH, LC

1672 MARSH, MRS. JENNY. Toiling and Hoping: The Story of a Little Hunchback . . . New York: Derby & Jackson, 1856. 398 p.   CU, LC, NYP
Kelly 1861-1866 lists *The Deformed*. Philadelphia: Petersons, 1864, which may be the above novel with a new title.

1673 MARTELL, MARTHA, *pseud.?* Second Love. By Martha Martell. New York: G. P. Putnam, 1851. 356 p.   LC
Roorbach 1820-1852 indicates that Martha Martell was Mrs. Tuthill; but I have been unable to verify the attribution.

1674 [MARTIN, MRS. CLARA BARNES.] The Story of Muff. A Contribution to the Fair of the Second Parish, for the Payson Memorial Church. Portland [Me.]: Short and Loring, 1868. 27 p.   AAS, BA
CU 1877 ed. gives author's name on title page.
About the Portland fire, July 4, 1866.

MARTINGALE, HAWSER, *pseud.* *See* Sleeper, John Sherburne

1675 THE MARTYR OF THE CATACOMBS: A Tale of Ancient Rome . . . New York: Hunt & Eston. Cincinnati: Cranston & Curts [187-?]. 202 p., illus.   Y
Kelly 1861-1866 records a copy with imprint: New York: Carlton & Porter, 1865.

MARVEL, IK., *pseud.* *See* Mitchell, Donald Grant

1676 THE MASKED LADY OF THE WHITE HOUSE; or, The Ku-Klux-Klan. A Most Startling Exposure of the Doings of This Extensive Secret Band, Whose Mysterious Lodges Exist in Every City and County in the Land . . . Philadelphia: C. W. Alexander, cop. 1868. 62 p., illus.   H, LC

1677 MASON, CHARLES WELSH. Rape of the Gamp: A Novel . . . New York: Harper & Brothers, 1875. 152 p., illus. Printed in double cols.   AAS, BA, LC, LCP, NYP

1678 MASSETT, STEPHEN C. "Drifting About;" or, What "Jeems Pipes of Pipesville" Saw-and-Did. An Autobiography . . . New York: Carleton, 1863. 371 p., illus.
AAS, BP, BU, CU, H, HEH, LC, LCP, N, NYH, NYP, UC, UM, UP, Y

1679 THE MASSINGERS; or, The Evils of Mixed Marriages. Baltimore: Walker, Wise & Co., 1862.
Title listed in Kelly 1861-1866.

1680 THE MATCH GIRL; or, Life Scenes as They Are . . . Philadelphia: Wm. White Smith, 1855. 418 p., illus.   AAS, H, N, Y

1681 [MATHEWS, ALBERT.] Walter Ashwood: A Love Story. By Paul Siogvolk [pseud.] . . . New York: Rudd & Carleton, 1860. 296 p.   AAS, CU, H, HEH, LC, LCP, NYP, Y

1682 MATHEWS, JOANNA HOOE. Guy Hamilton: A Story of Our Civil War . . . New York: American News Company, 119 & 121 Nassau Street [cop. 1866]. 96 p.   LC, LCP
Also issued with original paper covers dated 1866.

1683 [MATHEWS, JULIA A.] Lily Huson; or, Early Struggles 'Midst Continual Hope. A Tale of Humble Life. Jotted Down from the Pages of Lily's Diary. By Alice Gray [pseud.]. New York: H. Long and Brother, 121 Nassau Street [cop. 1855]. 384 p.   AAS, CU, HEH, NYP, UP
Also contains: Clara Neville, and Other Tales—The Veiled Picture—My Father's Head Farming-Man; or, Peter Mulroon's Adventures in New York—The Red Cloak; or, The Murder at the Roadside Inn. A Tale of New York in Olden Times—The Recognition and the Recompense—Tom Richard's Adventure with the Malay Pirates—The Ruined House—Save Me from My Friends, a Tale of English Life.

1684 MATURIN, EDWARD. Bianca: A Tale of Erin and Italy . . . New York: Harper & Brothers, 1852. 395 p.
AAS, BU, CU, H, HEH, LC, LCP, NYP, UP, UV, Y

MAURICE, JACQUES, *pseud. See* Morris, James W.

1685 MAXWELL, MARIA. Ernest Grey; or, The Sins of Society. A Story of New York Life . . . New York: T. W. Strong, 1855. 335 p., illus.   AAS, BP, CU, H, HEH, LC, N, NYP, UP, Y
On prison reform.

MAYBERRY, PERCIVAL, *pseud.* See Ingraham, Joseph Holt

1686 MAYER, NATHAN. Differences: A Novel . . . Cincinnati, Ohio: Bloch & Co., 1867.   462 p.   NYP, Y
Civil War background.

1687 ———— The Fatal Secret; or, Plots and Counterplots. A Novel of the Sixteenth Century. Founded on Facts . . . Cincinnati: printed at the office of "The Israelite," and "Deborah," 1858.   176 p.   Printed in double cols.
Dropsie College Library copy.

1688 MAYFIELD, CORA, *pseud.?* Elmwood; or, Helen and Emma . . . Boston and Cambridge: James Munroe and Company, 1856. 350 p.   AAS, BP, H, LC

MAYFIELD, MILLIE, *pseud.* See Homes, Mrs. Mary Sophie (Shaw) Rogers

MAYNARD, MARY. Sketches from the Backwoods. *In* A. Morton, The Ducal Coronet [185-?], No. 1757.

1689 MAYO, WILLIAM STARBUCK. Never Again . . . New York: G. P. Putnam & Sons, 1873.   714 p., illus.
     AAS, BA, BU, CU, H, HEH, LC, LCP, N, NYP, UC, UM, UP, UV, Y
Society life.

1690 ———— Romance Dust from the Historic Placer . . . New York: Geo. P. Putnam. London: Richard Bentley, 1851. 284 p.
     AAS, BP, BU, CU, H, HEH, LC, LCP, N, NYH, NYP, UC, UM, UP, UV, Y
Contains: Don Sebastian, from the Chronicles of Portugal—The Captain's Story—A Legend of the Cape de Verdes—A Real Pirate—The Astonishing Adventure of James Botello—Dragut, the Corsair—The Pious Constancy of Inez de Mencia Mont-Roy.
Pages [277]-284 advts.
Also published as: *Flood and Field; or, Tales of Battles on Sea and Land.* Philadelphia: Willis P. Hazard, 1855.   AAS, BU, CU, H, N, NYH, Y

1691 [MEANEY, MARY L.] The Confessors of Connaught; or, The Tenants of a Lord Bishop. A Tale of Our Times. By M. L. M. . . . Philadelphia: Peter F. Cunningham, 1865. 319 p.   LC

1692 [————] Grace Morton; or, The Inheritance. A Catholic Tale. By M. L. M. . . . Philadelphia: Peter F. Cunningham, 1864. 324 p.   AAS, LC
Laid in Pennsylvania.

1693 [MEEKER, NATHAN COOK.] Life and Adventures of Captain Jacob D. Armstrong . . . New York: DeWitt and Davenport, 1852. 72 p.   BP, LC, UC, UP
Depicts a social utopia.

1694 ———— Life in the West; or, Stories of the Mississippi Valley . . . New York: Samuel R. Wells, 1868. 360 p.
AAS, BP, CU, H, HEH, LC, LCP, N, NYH, NYP, UC, UM, Y

MEL, MARY, *pseud.* See Bennett, Mrs. Mary E.

1695 MELINE, MARY MILLER. Charteris: A Romance . . . Philadelphia: J. B. Lippincott & Co., 1874. 260 p.   BP, LC
Laid in England.

1696 ———— In Six Months; or, The Two Friends . . . Baltimore: Kelly, Piet and Company, 1874. 299 p.   BP, LC

1697 [————] The Montarges Legacy: A Tale. By Florence McCoomb [pseud.] . . . Philadelphia: Peter F. Cunningham, 1869. 294 p.   CU, LC, LCP
A Catholic tale.

1698 MELVILLE, CHARLES K. The Forest Witch; or, The Terror of the Odjibwes . . . Providence, R. I.: General Intelligence and Publishing Co., 68 Arcade [cop. 1874]. Cover title, 20 p. Printed in double cols.   LC
At head of title: "Indian Tales, No. 1."

1699 MELVILLE, HERMAN. The Confidence-Man: His Masquerade . . . New York: Dix, Edwards & Co., 1857. 394 p.
AAS, BP, H, HEH, LC, LCP, N, NYH, NYP, UC, UM, UP, UVB, Y

1700 ——— Israel Potter: His Fifty Years of Exile . . . New York: G. P. Putnam & Co., 1855. 276 p.

AAS, AP, BA, BP, BU, CU, H, HEH, LC, LCP, N, NYP, UC, UM, UP, UVB, Y

Also published as: *The Refugee*. Philadelphia: T. B. Peterson & Brothers [cop. 1865]. 286 p. (Repaged.) H, NYP

1701 ——— Moby-Dick; or, The Whale . . . New York: Harper & Brothers. London: Richard Bentley, 1851. 634 p., 1 l.

AAS, AP, BP, H, HEH, LC, LCP, N, NYP, UC, UP, UVB, Y

1702 ——— The Piazza Tales . . . New York: Dix & Edwards. London: Sampson Low, Son & Co., 1856. 431 p.

AAS, BA, BP, CU, H, HEH, LC, LCP, N, NYP, UC, UM, UP, UVB, Y

Contents: The Piazza—Bartleby—Benito Cereno—The Lightning-Rod Man—The Encantadas; or, Enchanted Islands—The Bell-Tower.

1703 ——— Pierre; or, The Ambiguities . . . New York: Harper & Brothers, 1852. 495 p.

AAS, BA, BP, BU, H, HEH, LC, LCP, N, NYH, NYP, UC, UM, UP, UVB, Y

1704 [MENDENHALL, MRS. V. L.] The Greek Slave: A Story. By Ianthe [pseud.]. San Francisco: A. Roman and Company. New York, 1867. 151 p. AAS, BU, H

Inscription on the flyleaf in H copy: "Rev. Richard F. Putnam. With the kindest wishes of the writer. Mrs. V. L. Mendenhall. San Francisco, Cal. July 12th, 1867."

MERCHANT, MATTHEW, *pseud*. *See* Wood, W. S.

MERRY, *Captain, United States Navy, pseud*. *See* Jones, Justin

MERVIN, EDWIN G. The Twin Daguerreotypes. *In* S. Cobb, Paul Laroon [185-?], No. 581.

1705 MIGNONETTE, MINNIE. The Armless Sleeve . . . New York: Manhattan Publishing Company, 1870. Cover title, 15 p. LC

A Civil War episode.

1706 MILES, GEORGE HENRY. The Governess; or, The Effects of Good Example. An Original Tale . . . Baltimore: Hedian & O'Brien, 1851. 256 p. Y

A Catholic tale.

1707 ———— Loretto; or, The Choice. A Story, Written for the Old and for the Young. In Four Parts . . . First Stereotype Edition, Revised and Enlarged by the Author. Baltimore: Hedian & O'Brien, 1851. 324 p.   Y
Probably 1st ed. in book form.

1708 ———— The Truce of God: A Tale of the Eleventh Century . . . Baltimore: J. Murphy & Co. New York: Catholic Publication Society, 1871. 384 p.   AAS, LC

MILES, HENRY ADOLPHUS. The Companion of Paradise. *In* Thirteen Good Stories [1873?], No. 2457.

1709 [MILLER, MRS. ANNA CUMMINGS (JOHNSON).] The Myrtle Wreath; or, Stray Leaves Recalled. By Minnie Myrtle [pseud.]. New York: Charles Scribner, 1854. 380 p., front.
    BP, BU, CU, HEH, LC, NYP
Her pseudonym "Minnie Myrtle" so spelled on engraved title and binding.

1710 MILLER, JOAQUIN. Unwritten History: Life amongst the Modocs . . . Hartford, Conn.: American Publishing Company, 1874. 445 p., illus.
    AAS, BP, CU, H, HEH, LCP, N, NYH, NYP, UC, UVB, Y
First published in London, 1873, under title: *Life amongst the Modocs.*

1711 MILLER, STEPHEN FRANKS. Wilkins Wylder; or, The Successful Man . . . Philadelphia: J. B. Lippincott & Co., 1860. 420 p.
    AAS, H, LC, NYP
Also contains: Mind and Matter: A Story of Domestic Life.

1712 MILLER, WILLIAM. A Thrilling Narrative of the Life, Adventures and Terrible Crimes of James Bagwell, Who . . . Made a Full Confession of His Dark and Terrible Crimes to the Rev. W. Miller, His Spiritual Advisor . . . Published by the Rev. William Miller. [Cincinnati: H. M. Rulison, cop. 1851.] 42 p., illus.   HEH, LC

1713 MILLS, J. C. Manvers; or, The Child of Crime. A Romance. New York: Akarman & Ormsby, 1851.
Title listed in Roorbach 1820-1852.

1714 MILNE, A. D. Uncle Sam's Farm Fence . . . New York: C. Shepard & Co., 1854. 282 p., illus.
    AAS, BP, CU, H, HEH, LC, N, NYH, NYP, UC, UM, UP, Y

Also contains: Something Wrong; or, The Why and the Wherefore, by T. S. Arthur.
A temperance tale.

MINOR, R. D. Old Sadler's Resurrection. *In* Not Pretty, but Precious (1872), No. 1804.

1715 MINSTER, ANNIE MARIA, *pseud.* Glenelvan; or, The Morning Draweth Nigh . . . New York: A. B. Burdick, 1861. 384 p.
On the banks of the Hudson. AAS, BU, HEH, NYP

1716 MISS ANNIE COLESON'S OWN NARRATIVE of Her Captivity among the Sioux Indians. An Interesting and Remarkable Account of the Terrible Sufferings and Providential Escape of This Beautiful Young Lady. Written by Herself. Philadelphia: Barclay & Co., No. 21 North Seventh Street [cop. 1875]. 94 p., illus. AAS, HEH
Also contains: My Revenge, a Beautiful Story—The Ordeal of Battle—The Student's Story.
This is No. 1717 with new material added.

1717 MISS COLESON'S NARRATIVE of Her Captivity among the Sioux Indians . . . a Victim of the Late Indian Outrages in Minnesota. Philadelphia: Barclay & Co., 1864. 70 p., illus. HEH, NYH

1718 MISS JANE CLARK, the Buried Alive; or, The Confessions of a Suicide. Cincinnati: H. M. Rulison, 34 East Third St. [cop. 1852]. 32 p., illus. LC
LC copy deposited for copyright June 25, 1852.

1719 MR. WINKFIELD: A Novel. New York: American News Company, 1866. 160 p. Printed in double cols. LC
Laid in New York City.

MITCHELL, DONALD GRANT. The Bride of the Ice-King. *In* The Knickerbocker Gallery (1855), No. 1492.

1720 [————] Doctor Johns: Being a Narrative of Certain Events in the Life of an Orthodox Minister of Connecticut . . . New York: Charles Scribner and Company, 1866. 2 vols. (300, 295 p.)
AAS, BA, BU, CU, H, HEH, LC, LCP, N, NYP, UC, UM, UP, UVB, Y
Covers the period from 1812 to 1848.

1721 [————] Dream Life: A Fable of the Seasons. By Ik. Marvel [pseud.] . . . New York: Charles Scribner, 1851. 286 p., front.

AAS, BA, BP, BU, CU, H, HEH, LC, LCP, N, NYH, NYP, UC, UVB, Y

Y has seven copies which have been identified as different issues, by Donald Gallup, curator of the Yale collection of American literature.

1722 [————] Fudge Doings: Being Tony Fudge's Record of the Same. In Forty Chapters. By Ik. Marvel [pseud.] . . . New York: Charles Scribner, 1855. 2 vols. (235, 257 p.), fronts.

AAS, AP, BA, BP, BU, CU, H, HEH, LC, LCP, N, NYH, NYP, UC, UM, Y

Commentary on the times.

1723 [————] Seven Stories, with Basement and Attic . . . New York: Charles Scribner, 1864. 314 p.

AAS, BP, BU, CU, H, HEH, LC, LCP, N, NYH, NYP, UC, UP, UVB, Y

1724 [MITCHELL, JOHN.] Rachel Kell. By the Author of "My Mother" . . . New York: M. W. Dodd, 1853. 312 p.

AAS, BP, CU, LC, UC, UP, Y

1725 MITCHELL, WALTER. Bryan Maurice; or, The Seeker . . . Philadelphia: J. B. Lippincott & Co., 1867. 288 p.

AAS, LC, LCP, UC, UV

MIZZEN, MAT, *pseud. See* Williams, Henry Llewellyn

Also spelled "Matt Mizzen" and "Mat Mizen."

1726 THE MODERN NIOBE; or, Leoni Loudon. A Tale of Suffering Loyalty in the Heart of Rebeldom . . . Philadelphia: Barclay & Co., 1864. 70 p., illus. LC

1727 THE MODERN STORY-TELLER; or, The Best Stories of the Best Authors, Now First Collected. New York: G. P. Putnam & Co., 1856. 324 p. BP, BU, CU, H, HEH, LC, LCP, NYP

Contents: The Unlucky Present—The Sultan's Bear—The Ghost-Raiser —The Pierced Skull—Cornet Winthrop's Story—Opposite Neighbors—A Night Adventure—The Two Isabels—Popping the Question—Captain Withers' Engagement—The Twin Sisters—The Judge Who Always Anticipated—The Satisfaction of a Gentleman—The Counter-Stroke— The Betrothal—Love Passages in the Life of Perron the Breton—Match-Making—The Tapis Vert of Versailles—The White Lace Bonnet—The First and Last Dinner—The Cock-Fight—Our Major's Story.

At head of title: "Putnam's Story Library."

1728 MODÊT, HELEN. Light . . . New York: D. Appleton and Company. London, 1863. 339 p.
Society life.   AAS, BP, H, HEH, LC, LCP, NYP, Y

MOFFETT, EMMA L. *See* Wynne, Mrs. Emma L. (Moffett)

MOLLIE, *pseud. See* Dollie, *pseud.*

1729 MONK, *pseud.* Going and Son: A Novel. By "Monk" [pseud.]. New York: published for the author, by the American News Company, 1869. 167 p. Printed in double cols.   AAS, H, LC
Laid in New York City.

1730 [MONMOUTH, MRS. SARAH ELIZABETH (HARPER).] Eventide: A Series of Tales and Poems. By Effie Afton [pseud.] . . . Boston: Fetridge and Company, 1854. 431 p.
           AAS, BP, BU, CU, HEH, NYH, UP, Y
Contains: Wimbledon; or, The Hermit of the Cedars—Scraggiewood: A Tale of American Life—Alice Orville; or, Life in the South and West.

1731 MONTAGUE; or, The Rejected Suitor. New York: E. D. Long, 1856.
Title listed in Roorbach 1855-1858.

MONTAIGNE, MISS M. C. The Fireman. *In* M. M. Ballou, The Sea-Witch [1855?], No. 207.

1732 [MONTAN, DOUGLAS C.] Redstick; or, Scenes in the South. By B. R. Montesano, Esq. [pseud.], of Louisiana . . . Cincinnati: U. P. James, 1856. 90 p.   H, HEH, LC
Social life in Baton Rouge.

MONTESANO, B. R., *Esq., pseud. See* Montan, Douglas C.

MONTGOMERY, CORA, *pseud. See* Cazneau, Mrs. William Leslie

1733 THE MONTGOMERYS: A Tale Drawn from Real Life. Buffalo: Wanzer, McKim & Co., 1856.
HEH and N have title leaf and 48 pages of text used as advt. in E. W. Reynolds, *Tangletown Letters* (1856).

MOORE, ANNIE. Waveline, for Children. *In* Thirteen Good Stories [1873?], No. 2457.

MOORE, MRS. CLARA SOPHIA (JESSUP). *See* Bloomfield-Moore, Mrs. Clara Sophia (Jessup)

1734 MOORE, EMILY H. A Lost Life: A Novel . . . New York: G. W. Carleton & Co. London: S. Low, Son & Co., 1871. 300 p.   AAS, BP, HEH, LC, NYP
The doctor's wife tells the story in the first person.

1735 [MOORE, MRS. H. J.] Anna Clayton; or, The Mother's Trial. A Tale of Real Life . . . Boston: James French and Company. New York: J. C. Derby, 1855. 352 p.   NYP, UC, UP
Laid in New England.

1736 [————] The Golden Legacy: A Story of Life's Phases. By a Lady . . . New York: D. Appleton and Company, 1857. 382 p.   AAS, HEH, LC, NYP, UC

1737 ———— Wild Nell, the White Mountain Girl . . . New York: Sheldon & Company. Philadelphia: J. B. Lippincott & Company. Boston: Brown & Taggard, 1860. 293 p., illus.
AAS, BA, BP, CU, LC, UP, Y

1738 [MOORE, M. A.] Dinah. New York: Charles Scribner, 1861. 466 p.   AAS, AP, BP, H, HEH, LCP, NYP

MOORE, MARIA M. The Unconquerable Conquered. In S. Cobb, The Maniac's Secret [185-?], No. 576.

1739 Moos, HERMAN M. Carrie Harrington. Sequel to "Hannah." Cincinnati: Bloch & Co. [187-?].
Title listed in Amer. Cat. 1876.

1740 ———— Hannah; or, A Glimpse of Paradise. A Tale in Four Parts . . . Cincinnati: Literary Eclectic Publishing House [cop. 1868]. 351 p., illus. Printed in double cols.   LC
Of Hebrew interest.

MORENOS, OJOS, pseud. See Clay, Mrs. Josephine Russell

MORETON, CLARA, pseud. See Bloomfield-Moore, Mrs. Clara Sophia (Jessup)

1741 MORFORD, HENRY. The Coward: A Novel of Society and the Field in 1863 . . . Philadelphia: T. B. Peterson & Brothers, 306 Chestnut Street [cop. 1864]. 520 p.
AAS, CU, H, HEH, LC, LCP, N, NYH, NYP, UC, UM, UP, UVB, Y

1742 ———— The Days of Shoddy: A Novel of the Great Rebellion in 1861 ... Philadelphia: T. B. Peterson & Brothers, 306 Chestnut Street [cop. 1863]. 478 p., front.

AAS, BP, BU, CU, H, HEH, LC, LCP, N, NYH, NYP, UM, UP, UVB, Y

Dedication dated "Dec. 1st, 1863."

1743 [————] John Jasper's Secret. A Sequel to Charles Dickens' Unfinished Novel "The Mystery of Edwin Drood" ... Philadelphia: T. B. Peterson & Brothers, 306 Chestnut Street [cop. 1871]. 408 p., illus.

AAS, BA, BP, H, HEH, LCP, NYP, UM, Y

1744 ———— Shoulder-Straps: A Novel of New York and the Army, 1862 ... Philadelphia: T. B. Peterson & Brothers, 306 Chestnut Street [cop. 1863]. 482 p., front.

AAS, AP, BP, CU, H, HEH, LC, LCP, N, NYH, NYP, UC, UM, UP, UVB, Y

1745 ———— Sprees and Splashes; or, Droll Recollections of Town and Country. A Book for Railroad Rides and Odd Half-Hours . . . New York: Carleton, 1863. 240 p., front.

AAS, BP, BU, CU, H, HEH, LC, LCP, N, NYP, UC, UM, UP, UVB, Y

1746 ———— Turned from the Door: A Christmas Story for 1869-70 ... New York: the American News Company, 1869. 80 p.   LC, NYP

At head of cover title: "The Governor's Christmas Story."

1747 ———— Utterly Wrecked: A Novel of American Coast Life . . . New York: the American News Company, 119 & 121 Nassau Street [cop. 1866]. 182 p. Printed in double cols.

AAS, LC, LCP, UM

1748 MORGAN, CHARLES P. The Phantom Cruiser; or, The Pilot of the Gulf ... Boston: F. Gleason, 1864. 50 p., illus.

Announced as "recently published" in *Amer. Lit. Gaz.*, II (Feb. 1, 1864), 249.

1749 MORGAN, NATHAN DENISON. George Cardwell; or, A Month in a Country Parish ... New York: Dana and Company, 1856. 62 p.   AAS, CU, H, HEH, LC, NYP, UP, Y

"Appendix," pp. [55]-62, sells the idea of the need for life insurance.

MORLEY, RALPH, *pseud. See* Hinton, Howard

1750 [MORRIS, JAMES W.] K. N. Pepper, and Other Condiments Put Up for General Use. By Jacques Maurice [pseud.] . . . New York: Rudd & Carleton, 1859. 258 p.

AAS, BP, BU, CU, H, HEH, LC, LCP, NYH, UC, UM, UP, UV, Y

At head of title: "Vive la Bagatelle!"

MORRIS, JOHN, *pseud.* *See* O'Connor, John

1751 MORRIS, ROBERT. The Faithful Slave . . . Boston: office of Dodge's Literary Museum, 1853. Cover title, 48 p., illus. Printed in double cols. LC

At head of title: "A $500 Story."

With this was issued: *Dodge's Sketches* [1853], which contains: The Thin Abolitionist and the Caged Madman, by Falconbridge—Marrying 'Em Over Again; or, A Joker Forestalled, by Falconbridge—Magnetism Triumphant; or, The Way Dodge "Done" the Old Maids, by Falconbridge—Doing the Artist; or, The Ups and Downs of a Genius, by Falconbridge—Dodge's Ascent of Mount Washington, by Thurlow W. Brown—Dodge's Private Performance, by Curtis Guild—The Way Dodge Started Himself, by Charles Sheppard—Dodge's Elopment; or, The Captain Outwitted, by Falconbridge—Mysterious Rappings Explained; or, An Artful Dodge, by Bob Lively—Dodging a Crowd: A Scene in a Chinese Junk, by Falconbridge.

1752 ———— Life in the Triangle; or, Freemasonry at the Present Time . . . Louisville: printed by J. F. Brennan & Co., 1854. 284 p. HEH, LC

1753 ———— The Lights and Shadows of Freemasonry: Consisting of Masonic Tales, Songs, and Sketches . . . Louisville, Ky.: J. F. Brennan, for the author, 1852. 384 p. NYP

1754 ————————— Louisville, Ky.: J. F. Brennan, for the author, 1852. 390, ii p. BP, HEH, LC, NYH, UC

This ed. extends the last story and adds an index.

1755 ———— Tales of Masonic Life . . . Louisville, Ky.: Morris & Monsarrat, 1860. 352 p. AAS, LC, UC

1756 MORTIMER, CHARLOTTE B. Marrying by Lot: A Tale of the Primitive Moravians . . . New York: G. P. Putnam & Son, 1868. 405 p. AAS, CU, HEH, LC, LCP, NYH, NYP, UP

Laid in Pennsylvania at the time of the American Revolution.

1757 MORTON, ARTHUR. The Ducal Coronet; or, The Heir and the Usurper. A Romance of Italy in the 16th Century ... New York: Samuel French, 121 Nassau Street [185-?]. 71, 12 p.

"Sketches from the Backwoods," by Mary Maynard, 12 p. at end. AAS

MOSE, *Buckskin, pseud.* *See* Perrie, George W.

1758 THE MOTHER REWARDED and the Son Reclaimed: A Temperance Narrative ... Portland [Me.]: William Hyde & Son, 1851. 36 p. LC

Also contains: The Cup of Cold Water, by T. S. Arthur.
Cover title: "The Son Reclaimed and Mother Rewarded."

MOULTON, MRS. LOUISE (CHANDLER). Dr. Huger's Intentions. *In* Stories and Sketches (1867), No. 2386.

1759 [————] Juno Clifford: A Tale. By a Lady. New York: D. Appleton and Company, 1856. 408 p., front.

AAS, BP, NYP, UV, Y

1760 ———— My Third Book: A Collection of Tales ... New York: Harper & Brothers, 1859. 434 p.

AAS, BP, BU, CU, HEH, LC, N, NYP

Contents: The Pride of Moses Grant—How One Woman Came to Marry —The Tenant of the Old Brown House—Uncle Roger's Story and Mine —The Mist over the Valley—Joseph Thorne, His Calling—Olive Winchester Wight—My Inheritance—Number 101—Leona: A Blind Man's Story—The Mountain Road—The Story of a Man of Business—The Cottage on the Hill—Joanna, the Actress—The Record of a Troubled Life— Four Letters from Helen Hamilton—The Phantom Face: A Story for Christmas.

1761 ———— Some Women's Hearts ... Boston: Roberts Brothers, 1874. 364 p. AAS, BA, BP, LC, NYP

Contents: Fleeing from Fate—Brains—Twelve Years of My Life—Little Gibraltar—Household Gods—The Judge's Wife—A Letter, and What Came of It—Out of Nazareth.

1762 ———— This, That, and the Other ... Boston: Phillips, Sampson and Company. New York: James C. Derby, 1854. 412 p., illus. AAS, BU, CU, HEH, N, NYH, UVB

Contains: The Orphan's Task—Heaven's Chancery—Poor Maud—Christiana; or, The Christmas Gift—Kate Lynn's Bridal—The First Quarrel— Silence Adams: An Old Man's Story—Sweet Ellen Adair—Valerie—The Bishop's Bride—A Husking-Party at Ryefield—My Aunt Patience—The Scotch Pastor's Bride—Agnes Lee: An Autobiography—The Secret Marriage—Aline—Bessie Green.

1763 MOUNTFORD, WILLIAM. Thorpe, a Quiet English Town, and Human Life Therein . . . Boston: Ticknor, Reed and Fields, 1852. 390 p.

AAS, AP, BA, BP, BU, H, HEH, LC, LCP, N, NYP, UC, UP

MOWATT, MRS. ANNA CORA (OGDEN). *See* Ritchie, Mrs. Anna Cora (Ogden) Mowatt

1764 MURDOCH, DAVID. The Dutch Dominie of the Catskills; or, The Times of the "Bloody Brandt" . . . New York: Derby & Jackson, 1861. 471 p.

AAS, BP, CU, H, HEH, LC, LCP, N, NYH, NYP, UC, UM, UP, Y

Also published as: *The Royalist's Daughter and the Rebels*. Philadelphia: J. E. Potter [cop. 1865]. AAS, NYH, NYP, Y

1765 MURPHY, MRS. ROSALIE (MILLER). Destiny; or, Life as It Is . . . New York: M. Doolady, 1867. 336 p.

AAS, BP, CU, HEH, LC, NYP, Y

MURRAY, *Lieutenant, pseud. See* Ballou, Maturin Murray

1766 MURRAY, WILLIAM HENRY HARRISON. Adventures in the Wilderness; or, Camp-Life in the Adirondacks . . . Boston: Fields, Osgood & Co., 1869. 236 p., illus.

AAS, BA, BU, CU, H, HEH, LCP, NYP, UC, Y

1767 —————— Deacons . . . Boston: Henry L. Shepard and Company, 1875. 82 p., illus.

AAS, BA, BP, H, HEH, LC, NYH, NYP, UM

1768 THE MUSEUM OF PERILOUS ADVENTURES and Daring Exploits: Being a Record of Thrilling Narratives, Heroic Achievements . . . Found in History . . . New York: G. & F. Bill, 1858. 504 p., illus. NYH

1769 MY CONFESSION: The Story of a Woman's Life, and Other Tales . . . New York: J. C. Derby. Boston: Phillips, Sampson & Co. Cincinnati: H. W. Derby, 1855. 306 p. AAS

Contents: My Confession—Sybil Rivers—Lorraine Gordon, a Biography —A Fragment of Autobiography—Zoe Bell's Birthday—An Old Man's Story—The Swallows in Mr. Pip's Chimney—The Story of Hagar.

1770 MY LOST HOME, and Other Tales. New York: Frederic A. Brady.

Title listed in Roorbach 1858-1861.

1771 [MYERS, PETER HAMILTON.] Bell Brandon, and The Withered Fig Tree. A Prize Novel . . . Philadelphia: T. B. Peterson, No. 98 Chestnut Street [cop. 1851]. 114 p.   UP
Laid in New York City; 1810.

———— A Dutch Belle. *In* The Knickerbocker Gallery (1855), No. 1492.

1772 ———— The Emigrant Squire . . . Philadelphia: T. B. Peterson, No. 98 Chestnut Street [cop. 1853]. 109 p.   Printed in double cols.   AAS, CU, LC, N, Y
Caption title: "The Emigrant Squire; or, The Dillons of Dillonborough."

1773 ———— The Miser's Heir; or, The Young Millionaire . . . Philadelphia: T. B. Peterson, No. 102 Chestnut Street [cop. 1854]. 222 p.
AAS, BP, BU, CU, HEH, LC, N, NYP, UC, UM, UP, Y
Also contains: Ellen Welles; or, The Siege of Fort Stanwix.
Laid in New York City.

1774 ———— The Prisoner of the Border: A Tale of 1838 . . . New York: Derby & Jackson, 1857. 378 p., illus.
AAS, BU, CU, H, HEH, NYP, UC, UM, UP, UV, Y
Also published as: *Thrilling Adventures of the Prisoner of the Border.*
New York: Derby & Jackson, 1860.   NYP

MYRTLE, LEWIS, *pseud. See* Hill, George Canning

MYRTLE, MINNIE, *pseud. See* Miller, Mrs. Anna Cummings (Johnson)

MYRTLE, MOLLY, *pseud. See* Hill, Mrs. Agnes (Leonard) Scanland

1775 MYSELF: A Romance of New England Life. Philadelphia: J. B. Lippincott & Co., 1872. 488 p.   AAS, H, HEH, LCP
This may be by Enoch Emery.

1776 THE MYSTERIES AND MISERIES OF SAN FRANCISCO. By a Californian . . . New York: Garrett & Co., No. 18 Ann Street [cop. 1853]. 208 p. Printed in double cols.   LC
HEH has the New York: Dick & Fitzgerald, 18 Ann St., reprint.

1777 MYSTERIES OF CRIME as Shown in Remarkable Capitol Trials. By a Member of the Massachusetts Bar . . . Boston: Samuel Walker and Company, 1870. 431 p., illus.   BA, NYH

1778 THE MYSTERIES OF ST. LOUIS; or, The Jesuits on the Prairie de Noyers. A Western Tale in Four Parts. St. Louis, 1852. 357 (i.e., 359) p., illus.
Wagner-Camp, No. 208a, locates a copy in possession of Thomas W. Streeter, Morristown, N. J.

NASBY, PETROLEUM V., *pseud.* *See* Locke, David Ross

NAUMAN, MARY DUMMETT. *See* Robinson, Mrs. Mary Dummett (Nauman)

NEAL, ALICE B. *See* Haven, Mrs. Alice (Bradley)

1779 NEAL, JOHN. True Womanhood: A Tale . . . Boston: Ticknor and Fields, 1859. 487 p.
AAS, BP, BU, CU, H, HEH, LC, LCP, N, NYP, UM, UP, UVB, Y
Laid in New York City.

1780 NEALE, FLORENCE. Thine and Mine; or, The Stepmother's Reward. New York: Derby & Jackson, 1857.
Title listed in Roorbach 1855-1858.

NEELY, PHILIP P. Idella Pemberton. *In* A. Cary, The Adopted Daughter (1859), No. 466.

1781 NEIGHBORLY LOVE, and Margaret Lawrence. Boston: D. Lothrop Company, Franklin and Hawley Streets [*ca.* 1870]. 184 p., front. UM
"Margaret Lawrence," pp. [111]-184.

NELLES, ANNIE. *See* Dumond, Mrs. Annie (Hamilton) Nelles

1782 [NELSON, AUGUSTA R.] The Prize Essay, and The Mitherless Bairn, Originally Published in the Missouri Republican. By Roswytha [pseud.]. St. Louis: Geo. Knapp & Co., printers, 1857. Cover title, 104 p. Printed in double cols. LC

1783 NEPENTHE: A NOVEL. By the Author of "Olie" . . . New York: Carleton, 1864. 323 p. BP, H, HEH, LCP
Civil War background.

1784 NEVILLE, LAURENCE. Edith Allen; or, Sketches of Life in Virginia . . . Richmond: J. W. Randolph, 1855. 311 p. UV, Y
Proslavery.

1785 [NEWELL, ROBERT HENRY.] Avery Glibun; or, Between Two Fires. A Romance. By Orpheus C. Kerr [pseud.]. New York: G. W. Carleton & Co. London: S. Low, Son & Co., 1867. 2 vols. in 1. (301 p.) Printed in double cols.

AAS, BP, CU, H, HEH, LC, N, NYP, UC, UM, UP, UV, Y

Satire upon New York City life and politics.

1786 [————] The Cloven Foot: Being an Adaptation of the English Novel "The Mystery of Edwin Drood" (by Charles Dickens), to American Scenes, Characters, Customs, and Nomenclature. By Orpheus C. Kerr [pseud.]. New York: Carleton. London: S. Low, Son & Co., 1870. 279 p.

AAS, BP, CU, H, HEH, LC, LCP, N, NYP, UC, UM, UP, Y

1787 [————] The Orpheus C. Kerr Papers. New York, 1862-65. 3 vols. (382, 367, 300 p.), illus.

AAS, BA(1-2), BP, BU, CU, H(1), HEH, LC, N(1-2), NYH, NYP, UC, UM, UP(1,3), UV, Y

1st ser. published by Blakeman & Mason, 1862.
2d ser. published by Carleton, 1863.
3d ser. published by Carleton, 1865.
Written in a series of letters from Washington, D.C.

1788 [————] Smoked Glass. By Orpheus C. Kerr [pseud.] . . . New York: G. W. Carleton. London: S. Low, Son & Co., 1868. 277 p., illus.

AAS, BP, BU, CU, H, HEH, LC, LCP, N, NYH, NYP, UC, UM, UP, UV, Y

Humorous satire upon impeachment of President Johnson.

1789 ———— The Walking Doll; or, The Asters and Disasters of Society . . . New York: Francis B. Felt & Company, 1872. 391 p.

AAS, BP, CU, H, HEH, LC, LCP, N, NYH, NYP, UC, UM, UP, UV, Y

1790 [NEWHALL, JAMES ROBINSON.] Liñ; or, Jewels of the Third Plantation . . . By Obadiah Oldpath [pseud.]. Lynn [Mass.]: Thomas Herbert & James M. Munroe, 1862. 400 p.

AAS, BA, BP, H, HEH, LC, NYH, UC, Y

1791 NICHOLS, GEORGE WARD. The Sanctuary: A Story of the Civil War . . . New York: Harper & Brothers, 1866. 286 p., illus.

Union army in Georgia. AAS, CU, H, HEH, LC, LCP, N, NYP, UC, UV, Y

1792 [NICHOLS, MRS. MARY SARGEANT (NEAL) GOVE.] Mary Lyndon; or, Revelations of a Life. An Autobiography. New York: Stringer and Townsend, 1855. 388 p.

BU, CU, HEH, LC, LCP, NYP, UM, UP, Y

1793 NICHOLS, THOMAS LOW. Father Larkin's Mission in Jonesville: A Tale of the Times . . . Baltimore: Kelly, Hedian & Piet, 1860. 64 p.
Feehan Memorial Library copy, St. Mary of the Lake Seminary.

1794 NICHOLSON, JOSEPH JOHN. The Blemmertons; or, Dottings by the Wayside . . . New York: Dana and Company. London: Sampson Low, Son and Company, 1856. 423 p.   BP, BU, LC

1795 [NICKERSON, SUSAN D.] Bread-Winners, by a Lady of Boston. Boston: Nichols and Hall, 1871. 295 p.   AAS, HEH, LC, NYP
On working women.

1796 THE NIGHT WATCH; or, Social Life in the South. By Somebody . . . Cincinnati: Moore, Wilstach, Keys & Co., 1856. 525 p.
Copyrighted by C. O. Hoffman.   AAS, N

NILES, WILLYS, *pseud.*   *See* Hume, John Ferguson

1797 NOLAN, ALICE. The Byrnes of Glengoulah: A True Tale . . . New York: P. O'Shea, 1870. 362 p.   LC
Copyright notice dated 1869.
NYP copy without date on title page.

1798 NORDHOFF, CHARLES. Cape Cod and All along Shore: Stories . . . New York: Harper & Brothers, 1868. 235 p.
AAS, BA, BP, H, HEH, LC, LCP, N, NYH, NYP, UM, UVB, Y
Contents: Captain Tom: A Resurrection—What Is Best?—A Struggle for Life—Elkanah Brewster's Temptation—One Pair of Blue Eyes—Mehetabel Rogers's Cranberry Swamp—Maud Elbert's Love Match.

——— Elkanah Brewster's Temptation. *In* Atlantic Tales (1866), No. 155.

1799 NORTHUP, SOLOMON, *pseud.* Twelve Years a Slave: Narrative of Solomon Northup, a Citizen of New-York, Kidnapped in Washington City in 1841, and Rescued in 1853, from a Cotton Plantation near the Red River, in Louisiana. Auburn: Derby and Miller. Buffalo: Derby, Orton and Mulligan. London: Sampson Low, Son & Company, 1853. 336 p., illus.
Preface signed: "David Wilson."   BU, LCP, N, Y

1800 NORTON, JOHN NICHOLAS. The Boy Who Was Trained Up to Be a Clergyman . . . Philadelphia: H. Hooker, 1854. 152 p.

NYP, UC, Y

1801 ———————— 2d ed. Philadelphia: H. Hooker, 1854. 201 p.

NYP

Seven new chapters added to this ed.

1802 ——— Full Proof of the Ministry. A Sequel to The Boy Who Was Trained Up to Be a Clergyman . . . New York: Redfield, 1855. 245 p.

BP, H, LC, NYP

1803 ——— Rockford Parish; or, The Fortunes of Mr. Mason's Successors . . . New York: Dana & Company. London: Sampson Low, Son and Company, 1856. 216 p.

Laid in Kentucky.

BU, H, LC, NYP

1804 NOT PRETTY, BUT PRECIOUS, and Other Short Stories . . . Philadelphia: J. B. Lippincott & Co., 1872. 144 p., illus. Printed in double cols.

BA, H, Y

Contents: Not Pretty, but Precious, by Margaret Field—The Victims of Dreams, by Margaret Hosmer—The Cold Hand, by Clara F. Guernsey—The Blood Seedling, by John Hay—The Marquis, by Chauncey Hickox—Under False Colors, by Lucy Hamilton Hooper—The Hungry Heart, by J. W. De Forest—"How Mother Did It," by J. R. Hadermann—The Red Fox, by Clara F. Guernsey—Louie, by Harriet Prescott Spofford—Old Sadler's Resurrection, by R. D. Minor.

1805 NOTES OF HOSPITAL LIFE, from November, 1861 to August, 1863 . . . Philadelphia: J. B. Lippincott & Co., 1864. 210 p.

Apparently written by a woman.

AAS, BP, BU, H, HEH, N, NYP, UP, Y

1806 NOWELL, SARAH ALLEN. The Shadow on the Pillow, and Other Stories . . . Boston: A. Tompkins, 1860. 404 p.

AAS, BA, BU, CU, HEH, N, UC, UP, Y

Also contains: Carlotta's Awakening—The Knights of Saint John—Catherine Petroff—The Regalia of Scotland—The Idol of the Tyrolese—The Garrison of Cape Ann—The Spirit Bride—The Blue Chamber—The Maid of Bregenz—The Tower of Torre Mozza—Robert Harmon's Spirit—Casa della Sirena—Maud; or, The Bridal of Malahide—The Coronach—The Scar of the White Cross—The Wreck of the Pirate Ship—The Scarf of Prince Charles—Hope Clifton, the Quaker—The Insurrection—Twenty Years in the Tower of London—The Pass of Plumes—The Widow's Curse—A Legend of Nantucket—The Prisoner of State—The Old Block House—A Legend of Meiland—The Infanta of Spain—The Fate of a Queen—The Victim of the Grand Duke Constantine.

1807 NYE, E. C.   Life, Trial, and Conviction of Zella de Chalue; also The Life, Confession, and Startling Disclosures of the Notorious Clarence O. Alderman . . . [Burlington, Iowa: Osborn & Acres steam book and job printers, 1873.]   104 p.   LC
Cover title: "The False Marriage; or, The Broken Pledge."

O., C. A.   *See* Ogden, Mrs. C. A.

1808 O'BRIEN, DILLON.   The Dalys of Dalystown . . .   Saint Paul: Pioneer Printing Co., 1866.   518 p.   AAS, LC, NYH, UM
An Irish schoolteacher in Wisconsin.

1809 ———— Dead Broke: A Western Tale . . .   Saint Paul: Pioneer Company print., 1873.   193 p.   LC, UM
Laid in Michigan Territory.

O'BRIEN, FITZ-JAMES.   Bob O'Link.   *In* Tales of the Time [1861], No. 2426.

———— The Diamond Lens.   *In* Atlantic Tales (1866), No. 155.

———— From Hand to Mouth.   *In* Good Stories (1867-68), No. 1012.

———— Three of a Trade; or, Red Little Kriss Kringle.   *In* Good Stories (1867-68), No. 1012.

1810 THE OCEAN QUEEN; or, The Seaman's Bride.   By the Author of "The Pale Lily," etc.   New York: Dick & Fitzgerald, No. 18 Ann Street [185-?].   82 p.   Printed in double cols.   NYP
Also contains: The Marquis de Letoriere; or, The Art of Pleasing—A Brace of Law Students; or, The Dangers of Rowdyism.

OCKSIDE, KNIGHT RUSS, *M.D.*, *pseud.*   *See* Underhill, Edward Fitch

1811 O'CONNOR, FLORENCE J.   The Heroine of the Confederacy; or, Truth and Justice . . .   New Orleans: A. Eyrich, successor to Blelock & Co., 1869.   408 p.   BP, CU
First published in London [1864].

1812 [O'CONNOR, JOHN.] Wanderings of a Vagabond: An Autobiography. Edited by John Morris [pseud.] . . . New York: published by the author [cop. 1873]. 492 p.
BA, BU, CU, H, HEH, LC, LCP, N, NYH, NYP, UM, Y
On gambling and gamblers.

1813 O'CONNOR, WILLIAM DOUGLAS. The Ghost . . . New York: G. P. Putnam & Son. London: Sampson Low & Co., 1867. 93 p., front.
AAS, BP, BU, H, HEH, LC, LCP, N, NYP, UP, UVB, Y
Also published as: Netty Renton; or, The Ghost. New York: G. P. Putnam's Sons, 1869. AAS, H, Y
Beacon Hill, Boston.

1814 [————] Harrington: A Story of True Love . . . Boston: Thayer & Eldridge, 1860. 558 p.
Antislavery. AAS, BA, BP, BU, H, HEH, LC, LCP, N, NYP, UP, UVB, Y

OELAND, PETER JOSEPH. Myra Bruce; or, True Love Running Roughly. In The Southern Field and Fireside Novelette [1863], No. 2287.

O'FRANCIS, MARY. See Francis, Mary O.

1815 [OGDEN, MRS. C. A.] Into the Light; or, The Jewess. By C. A. O. . . . Boston: Loring, 1868. 322 p. AAS, BA, H, LC

1816 [OGDEN, ROBERT N.] Who Did It? A Novel. Philadelphia: Claxton, Remsen and Haffelfinger. New Orleans: J. A. Gresham, 1870. 87 p. Printed in double cols. LC
Laid in Louisiana.

O'LANUS, CORRY, pseud. See Howard, Joseph

1817 [OLCOTT, MRS. HARRIET A. (HINSDALE).] Isora's Child . . . New York: J. C. Derby. Boston: Phillips, Sampson & Co. Cincinnati: H. W. Derby, 1855. 504 p. AAS

1818 ———— The Torchlight; or, Through the Wood . . . New York: Derby & Jackson. Cincinnati: H. W. Derby & Co., 1856. 447 p. AAS, BP, CU, H, HEH, NYP, UP, Y

1819 OLD HAUN, THE PAWNBROKER; or, The Orphan's Legacy. A Tale of New York Founded on Facts. New York: Rudd & Carleton, 1857. 463 p., front. AAS, CU, H, HEH

1820 THE OLD PINE FARM; or, The Southern Side. Comprising Loose Sketches from the Experience of a Southern Country Minister, S. C. Nashville: Southwestern Publishing House, 1859. 202 p., illus. NYH

OLDPATH, OBADIAH, *pseud. See* Newhall, James Robinson

O'LEARY, C., *pseud. See* McCorry, Peter

1821 THE OLIVE-BRANCH; or, White Oak Farm . . . Philadelphia: J. B. Lippincott & Co., 1857. 329 p.
Proslavery. AAS, H, LC, N, NYH, UC, UM, UP

1822 ONE LINK IN THE CHAIN of Apostolic Succession; or, The Crimes of Alexander Borgia . . . Boston: E. W. Hinks & Co., 1854. 171 p., front. AAS, BU, HEH, LC, NYP
Anti-Catholic.

OPTIC, OLIVER, *pseud. See* Adams, William Taylor

O'REILLY, *Private* MILES, *pseud. See* Halpine, Charles Graham

ORNE, MRS. CAROLINE (CHAPLIN). Broken Ear-Ring. *In* S. Cobb, The King and Cobbler [185-?], No. 572.

1823 ———— Lionel Ainsworth; or, The Young Partisan's Doom. A Story of the American Revolution . . . New York: Samuel French, 151 Nassau, corner of Spruce Street [185-?]. 100 p. Printed in double cols. H

———— The Little Errand Boy. *In* O. Bounderby, *pseud.?,* The Law Student [185-?], No. 321.

———— The Lost Child; or, A Home in the West. *In* O. Bounderby, *pseud.?,* The Law Student [185-?], No. 321.

———— The Walbridge Family. *In* B. P. Poore, The Mameluke (1852), No. 1928.

1824 ORTON, JASON ROCKWOOD. Camp Fires of the Red Men; or, A Hundred Years Ago . . . New York: J. C. Derby. Boston: Phillips, Sampson & Co. Cincinnati: H. W. Derby, 1855. 401 p., illus. AAS, BP, CU, HEH, LC, N, NYH, NYP, Y
Laid in New York.

1825   [OSBORN, LAUGHTON.]   Travels by Sea and Land of Alethitheras [pseud.]. New York: Moorhead, Sampson & Bond, 1868. 381 p.   CU, H, LCP, NYP
A satire.

1826   [————]   ———— New York: James Miller, 1868. 390 p.
This ed. adds a "key" to the satire.   AAS, UM, Y

1827   [OSBORNE, ELISE.]   Life and Its Aims, in Two Parts. Part First —Ideal Life. Part Second—Actual Life. Philadelphia: Lippincott, Grambo & Co., 1854. 362 p.   AP, BP, LC, NYP
Also published as: *Life's Lottery; or, Life and Its Aims*. Philadelphia: Claxton, Remsen & Haffelfinger, 1869.   LC

OTIS, BELLE, *pseud.*   *See* Woods, Caroline H.

1828   OTIS, MRS. ELIZA HENDERSON (BOARDMAN).   The Barclays of Boston . . . Boston: Ticknor, Reed and Fields, 1854. 419 p.
AAS, AP, BU, CU, H, HEH, LC, LCP, N, NYP, UC, UP, UV, Y

1829   OUR "FIRST FAMILIES:" A Novel of Philadelphia Good Society. By a Descendant of the "Pens." . . . Philadelphia: Whilt & Yost, 1855. 408 p.
AAS, AP, BP, BU, CU, HEH, LC, LCP, NYH, NYP, UC, UM, UVB, Y
BP credits this to a J. G. Koster.
Pages 405-408 advts.

1830   [OUTWEST, OLIVER] *pseud.*   Adventures of Lena Rouden, a "Southern Letter Carrier," or Rebel Spy: A Story of the Late War. Chicago: Horton & Leonard, book and job printers, 1872. 69 p.   HEH
Signed at end: "Oliver Outwest."
Laid in Tennessee.

1831   OWEN, FARLEIGH.   Aden Power; or, The Cost of a Scheme . . . Boston: T. O. H. P. Burnham, 1862. 155 p. Printed in double cols.   AP, BP, H, NYP

1832   OWEN, GEORGE WASHINGTON.   The Leech Club; or, The Mysteries of the Catskills . . . Boston: Lee & Shepard. New York: Lee, Shepard & Dillingham, 1874. 298 p.
AAS, CU, H, HEH, LC, NYH, NYP, UM
Political and moral machinations.

1833 OWEN, ROBERT DALE. Beyond the Breakers: A Story of the
Present Day . . . Philadelphia: J. B. Lippincott & Co., 1870.
274 p., illus. Printed in double cols.
AAS, BU, CU, H, HEH, LC, LCP, N, NYP, UP, UV, Y
At head of title: "Village Life in the West."

OWSTON, FRANCES W. The Brothers Leinhardt. *In* Prize
Papers (1865), No. 1968.

P., H. F. *See* Parker, Mrs. Helen Eliza (Fitch)

1834 P., M. C. Miriam Rivers, the Lady Soldier; or, General Grant's
Spy . . . Philadelphia: Barclay & Co., 1865. 2 p. l., 39-116
(i.e., 114) p., illus. HEH, LC, NYP
Pages 51-52 omitted in numbering.

P., Z., *pseud.* *See* Mansfield, Lewis William

PAGE, ABRAHAM, *pseud.* *See* Holt, John Saunders

PAGE, EMILY. Katy's Husband. *In* The Arrow of Gold
[185-?], No. 81.

1835 PAGE, JOHN W. Uncle Robin in His Cabin in Virginia, and Tom
without One in Boston . . . Richmond, Va.: J. W. Randolph,
1853. 299 p., illus. BP, HEH, LC, N, NYH, UM, UV, Y
Proslavery.

1836 PAINE, SUSANNA. Roses and Thorns; or, Recollections of an
Artist. A Tale of Truth, for the Grave and the Gay . . .
Providence: B. T. Albro, printer, 1854. 204 p.
AAS, BU, CU, H, HEH, LC, NYH, UC, UP
Purportedly an autobiography.

1837 ———— Wait and See . . . Boston: printed by John Wilson
and Son, 1860. 400 p. AAS, BP, BU, CU, HEH, LC, N
Laid in and around Boston.

1838 [PALFREY, SARA HAMMOND.] Agnes Wentworth. By E. Foxton [pseud.] . . . Philadelphia: J. B. Lippincott & Co., 1869.
316 p. BA, H, LC, LCP, NYP
Boston and New York City society.

1839 [————] Herman; or, Young Knighthood. By E. Foxton [pseud.] . . . Boston: Lee and Shepard, 1866. 2 vols. (416, 391 p.)

AAS, BA, BP, CU, H, HEH, LC, LCP, NYP, UP, UV, Y(V.1)

State of the country prior to the war.

1840 PARADOX, PETER, *pseud.?* The Paradox Papers: A Medley of Original Humorous Articles, Including a Re-Print of the Old Dutch Legislative Sour Drout Message . . . [Albany: J. Munsell, printer.] 1873. 48 p. AAS, BP

PARKER, ANNIE. Passages in the Life of a Slave Woman. *In* J. Griffiths, *ed.*, Autographs for Freedom (1853), No. 1033.

1841 [PARKER, MRS. HELEN ELIZA (FITCH).] Constance Aylmar: A Story of the Seventeenth Century. By H. F. P. New York: Charles Scribner & Company, 1869. 347 p.

BP, LCP, NYP, UM, UP

Laid in New Amsterdam.

1842 ———— Sunrise and Sunset: A True Tale . . . Auburn: Derby and Miller. Buffalo: Derby, Orton and Mulligan. Cincinnati: Henry W. Derby, 1854. 220 p. LC

Home life; Ireland and eastern New York.

1843 PARKER, MRS. JANE (MARSH). Barley Wood; or, Building on the Rock . . . New York: Daniel Dana, Jr., 1860. 320 p.

LC, NYP

Of Episcopal interest.

1844 PARKMAN, FRANCIS. Vassall Morton: A Novel . . . Boston: Phillips, Sampson and Company, 1856. 414 p.

AAS, BA, BP, BU, CU, H, HEH, LC, LCP, N, NYP, UC, UM, UP, UV, Y

An American, imprisoned in Austria, charged with inciting revolution.

PARSONS, CHARLES BOOTH. Three Scenes in the South. *In* A. Cary, The Adopted Daughter (1859), No. 466.

1845 [PARTON, MRS. SARA PAYSON (WILLIS).] Fern Leaves from Fanny's Port-Folio . . . Auburn: Derby and Miller. Buffalo: Derby, Orton and Mulligan. Cincinnati: Henry W. Derby, 1853. 400 p., illus.

AAS, AP, BA, BU, CU, H, N, NYH, NYP, UC, UM, UP, UVB, Y

UVB two copies: one with and one without stereotyper's name on verso of title page.

1846 [————] ———— 2d ser. Auburn and Buffalo: Miller, Orton & Mulligan. London: Sampson Low, Son & Co., 1854. 400 p., illus. AAS, AP, BU, CU, H, N, NYH, NYP, UC, UM

1847 [————] Fresh Leaves. By Fanny Fern [pseud.]. New York: Mason Brothers, 1857. 336 p.
CU, H, HEH, LC, N, NYH, NYP, UC, UM, UP, UVB, Y

1848 [————] Rose Clark. By Fanny Fern [pseud.]. New York: Mason Brothers, 1856. 417 p.
AAS, BU, CU, H, HEH, LC, N, NYP, UC, UM, UP, UVB, Y

1849 [————] Ruth Hall: A Domestic Tale of the Present Time. By Fanny Fern [pseud.]. New York: Mason Brothers, 1855. 400 p. AAS, AP, BA, BP, BU, CU, H, HEH, LC, LCP, N, NYH, NYP, UC, UM, UP, UVB, Y

PASHA, MOHAMMED, *pseud.* *See* Howe, William Wirt

PASTOR, TONY, *pseud.* *See* Halsey, Harlan Page

1850 [PATTERSON, MRS. JANE (LIPPITT).] Victory ... Boston: R. A. Ballou, 1866. 304 p. AAS
At head of title: "Prize Series."
The Civil War.

PAUL, JOHN, *pseud.* *See* Webb, Charles Henry

PAXTON, PHILIP, *pseud.* *See* Hammett, Samuel Adams

1851 PAYNE, MRS. E. S. N. Election Times; or, Social and Domestic Influence ... Cincinnati: American Reform Tract and Book Society, 1860. 251 p. AAS, CU, UC
Western politics.

1852 [PAYSON, GEORGE.] Golden Dreams and Leaden Realities. By Ralph Raven [pseud.]. With an Introductory Chapter, by Francis Fogie, Sen., Esq. New York: G. P. Putnam & Co., 1853. 344 p. AAS, BP, H, HEH, LCP, N, NYH, NYP, UC
Around the Horn to the California mines in 1849.

1853 [————] The New Age of Gold; or, The Life and Adventures of Robert Dexter Romaine [pseud.]. Written by Himself . . . Boston: Phillips, Sampson and Company, 1856. 403 p. AAS, BP, BU, H, HEH, LC, N, NYH, NYP, UC, UM, Y

1854 ———— Totemwell . . . New York: Riker, Thorne & Co., 1854. 519 p.   AAS, BP, H, LC, N, NYH, NYP, UC, Y

New England village life.

PEABODY, MRS. MARK, *pseud. See* Victor, Mrs. Metta Victoria (Fuller)

1855 PEACOCKE, JAMES S. The Creole Orphans; or, Lights and Shadows of Southern Life. A Tale of Louisiana . . . New York: Derby & Jackson. Cincinnati: H. W. Derby, 1856. 365 p.   AAS, BP, BU, HEH, LC, N, NYP, UP

Also published as: *The Orphan Girls: A Tale of Southern Life.* Philadelphia: G. G. Evans, 1859.   N, Y

1856 [PEARSON, MRS. EMILY (CLEMENS).] Cousin Franck's Household; or, Scenes in the Old Dominion. By Pocahontas [pseud.]. Boston: Upham, Ford and Olmstead, 1853. 259 p., illus.   AAS, BP, BU, CU, H, HEH, NYH, UC, UM, UP

Also published as: *Ruth's Sacrifice; or, Life on the Rappahannock.* Boston: Charles H. Pearson; Graves and Young, 1863.   AAS, BP, NYP, UVB, Y

Antislavery.

1857 ———— Gutenberg, and the Art of Printing . . . Boston: Noyes, Holmes and Company, 1871. 292 p., illus.

A fictitious biography.   AAS, BP, CU, H, HEH, NYP, UC, UM, Y

1858 ———— Our Parish: A Temperance Tale. New York: National Temperance Society, 1868.

Title listed in Kelly 1866-1871.

1859 [————] The Poor White; or, The Rebel Conscript . . . Boston: Graves and Young. New York: Sheldon and Company. Cincinnati: Geo. S. Blanchard, 1864. 320 p., illus.   AAS, CU, HEH, UC

1860 PEARSON, HELEN C. Roy's Search; or, Lost in the Cars . . . New York: National Temperance Society, 1870. 364 p., front.

Information from LC card for copy withdrawn from circulation.

1861 [PECK, ELLEN.] Ecce Femina. New York: Schuyler & Gracie, 1874. 46 p.   LC

1862 [————] Ecce Femina; or, The Woman Zoe. By Cuyler
Pine [pseud.]. New York: G. W. Carleton & Co. London:
S. Low, Son & Co., 1875. 133 p.   AAS, CU, LC, LCP, NYP, UP
This is a different story from No. 1861.

1863 [————] Mary Brandegee: An Autobiography. Edited by
Cuyler Pine [pseud.]. New York: Carleton, 1865. 389 p.
AAS, BP, CU, HEH, LCP, NYP, UP, UV, Y

1864 [————] Renshawe: A Novel . . . Edited by Cuyler Pine
[pseud.]. New York: G. W. Carleton & Co. London: S.
Low, Son & Co., 1867. 384 p.   AAS, BP, HEH, LC, NYP
The early phases of the Civil War.

1865 PECK, GEORGE WILBUR. Adventures of One Terence McGrant,
a Brevet Irish Cousin of President Ulisses S. Grant . . . New
York: James H. Lambert, 1871. 261 p., illus.
AAS, BP, BU, H, HEH, LC, N, NYH, NYP, UM, UVB

1866 PECK, WILLIAM HENRY. The Confederate Flag on the Ocean:
A Tale of the Cruises of the Sumter and Alabama . . . New
York: Van Evrie, Horton & Co., 1868. 96 p.   LC

1867 ———— The Conspirators of New Orleans; or, The Night of
the Battle . . . Greenville, Ga.: Peck & Wells [cop. 1863].
132 p.
Emory University Library copy.

1868 ———— The M'Donalds; or, The Ashes of Southern Homes.
A Tale of Sherman's March . . . New York: Metropolitan
Record Office, 1867. 192 p.
AAS, BP, CU, H, HEH, LC, LCP, N, NYH, NYP, UC, UM, UP, UV, Y

PENCILLER, HARRY, pseud. See Wetmore, Henry Carmer

1869 PENN, A. SYLVAN, pseud. My Three Neighbors in the Queen
City. By A. Sylvan Penn [pseud.]. Cincinnati: Hibbon &
Webster, 1858. 250 p.   CU

1870 THE PENNIMANS; or, The Triumph of Genius . . . Boston:
Gardner A. Fuller [cop. 1862]. 296 p., front.
Beacon Hill, Boston, in the 1850's.   AAS, H, HEH, NYP, Y

PEPPERELL, FRANCIS P. The Lady Edith. *In* S. Cobb, Isidore de Montigny [185-?], No. 569.

PEPPERGRASS, PAUL, *Esq., pseud. See* Boyce, John

1871 PERCE, ELBERT. Gulliver Joi: His Three Voyages. Being an Account of His Marvelous Adventures in Kailoo, Hydrogenia and Ejario . . . New York: Charles Scribner, 1851. 272 p., illus. AAS, BP, LC, UC, UM

1872 ———— The Last of His Name . . . New York: Riker, Thorne & Co., 1854. 369 p. AAS, BP, LC, UC
Laid in Sweden.

PERCH, PHILEMON, *pseud. See* Johnston, Richard Malcolm

PERKINS, ELI, *pseud. See* Landon, Melville de Lancey

PERKINS, FREDERIC BEECHER. Devil-Puzzlers. *In* Thirteen Good Stories [1873?], No. 2457.

1873 ———— Scrope; or, The Lost Library. A Novel of New York and Hartford . . . Boston: Roberts Brothers, 1874. 278 p. Printed in double cols.
AAS, BA, BP, CU, H, HEH, LC, LCP, N, NYP, UM, UP, Y
Of antiquarian books, book auctions, and subscription books.

———— *jt. au. See* Hale, Edward Everett, *ed.* Six of One (1872), No. 1058.

1874 [PERKINS, MRS. SUE (CHESTNUTWOOD).] Honor Bright: A Romance. By Author of "Malbrook." New York: Carleton. London: S. Low, Son & Co., 1870. 312 p. NYP, UV

1875 [————] Malbrook: A Novel. New York: G. W. Carleton & Co. London: S. Low, Son & Co., 1868. 353 p.
Dedication signed: "Ruth Woodland," [pseud.]. AAS, HEH, LCP, NYP

1876 [PERRIE, GEORGE W.] Buckskin Mose [pseud.]; or, Life from the Lakes to the Pacific, as Actor, Circus-Rider, Detective, Ranger, Gold-Digger, Indian Scout, and Guide. Written by Himself . . . Edited, and with Illustrations, by C. G. Rosenberg. New York: Henry L. Hinton, 1873. 285 p., illus.
AAS, BP, BU, H, HEH, LC, NYP, Y

1877 PERRYMAN, E. G. Our New Minister: A Story. New York: T. Whittaker, 1875. 157 p.

Information from LC card for copy withdrawn from circulation.

1878 [PETERSON, CHARLES JACOBS.] The Cabin and Parlor; or, Slaves and Masters. By J. Thornton Randolph [pseud.] . . . Philadelphia: T. B. Peterson, No. 98 Chesnut [sic] Street [cop. 1852]. 324 p., illus.

AAS, BP, CU, H, HEH, LC, LCP, N, NYH, NYP, UC, UM, UV, Y

Also published as: *Courtenay Hall; or, The Hospitality and Life in a Planter's Family. A True Tale of Virginia Life. By James T. Randolph [pseud.].* Philadelphia: T. B. Peterson & Brothers, 306 Chestnut Street [185-?]. Virginia State Library copy.

1879 ———— Kate Aylesford: A Story of the Refugees . . . Philadelphia: T. B. Peterson, 102 Chestnut Street. Boston: Phillips, Sampson & Co. New York: J. C. Derby [cop. 1855]. 356 p.

AAS, H, LC, LCP, NYP, UM

Also published as: *Heiress of Sweetwater: A Love Story. By J. Thornton Randolph [pseud.].* Philadelphia: T. B. Peterson & Brothers [cop. 1873]. Announced as "just published" in PW, IV (July 26, 1873), 113.
Laid in Pine Barrens, N. J., during the Revolution.

1880 ———— The Old Stone Mansion . . . Philadelphia: T. B. Peterson and Brothers, 306 Chestnut Street [cop. 1859]. 367 p., front. AAS, BP, BU, H, HEH, LC, NYH, Y

Laid in and around Philadelphia.

1881 PETERSON, HENRY. Pemberton; or, One Hundred Years Ago . . . Philadelphia: J. B. Lippincott & Co., 1873. 393 p., illus.

On the American Revolution. AAS, H, LC, LCP, N, UP

PETIT, LIZZIE. *See* Cutler, Mrs. Lizzie (Petit)

1882 PHELPS, MRS. ALMIRA (HART) LINCOLN. Ida Norman; or, Trials and Their Uses . . . Two Volumes in One. New York: Sheldon, Lamport & Blakeman, 1854. 2 vols. in 1 (432 p.), illus. AAS, HEH, LC, NYP, UC, UM

Vol. I is a reprint of Wright (1774-1850), No. 2041; Vol. II is new material.

1883 [PHELPS, MRS. ELIZABETH (STUART).] The Angel over the Right Shoulder; or, The Beginning of a New Year . . . Andover: Warren F. Draper. Boston: J. P. Jewett and Co., 1852. 29 p., front. AAS, BP, CU, H, NYP

1884 [————] The Last Leaf from Sunny Side. By H. Trusta [pseud.] . . . With a Memorial of the Author, by Austin Phelps. Boston: Phillips, Sampson & Co., 1853. 342 p., front.

AAS, BA, BU, H, LCP, UP, Y

Contents: Memorial—The Puritan Family—The Cloudy Morning—The Country Cousins—The Night after Christmas.

1885 [————] A Peep at "Number Five;" or, A Chapter in the Life of a City Pastor. By H. Trusta [pseud.] . . . Boston: Phillips, Sampson and Company, 1852. 296 p., front.

AAS, BP, BU, CU, H, HEH, LC, NYP, UP, Y

1886 [————] The Sunny Side; or, The Country Minister's Wife. By H. Trusta [pseud.]. Boston: John P. Jewett and Co. Andover: Warren F. Draper, 1851. 135 p.

AAS, BA, BP, BU, CU

Later revised and enlarged by the author, and published by the American Sunday School Union.

1887 [————] The Tell-Tale; or, Home Secrets Told by Old Travellers. By H. Trusta [pseud.] . . . Boston: Phillips, Sampson and Company, 1853. 262 p., illus.

AAS, BP, BU, CU, H, HEH, LC, LCP, NYP, UP, Y

Contents: What Sent One Husband to California—The First Cross Word —The Old Leather Portfolio; or, A House-Cleaning—The May-Queens— The Husband of a Blue—The Wife of a Student—Old Witch Moll, and Her Brown Pitcher—The Glorious Fourth in Boston—First Trials of a Young Physician.

PHELPS, ELIZABETH STUART, *the younger*. *See* Ward, Mrs. Elizabeth Stuart (Phelps)

PHILALETHES, *pseud*. *See* Blox, John E.

1888 [PHILLEO, CALVIN WHEELER.] Twice Married: A Story of Connecticut Life . . . New York: Dix & Edwards. London: Sampson Low & Son, 1855. 264 p.

AAS, BP, BU, CU, H, HEH, N, NYH, NYP, UC, UM, Y

BP copy inscribed: "Eliz. P. Philleo from the author C. W. Philleo."

1889 PHILLIPS, GEORGE SEARLE. The Gypsies of the Danes' Dike: A Story of Hedge-Side Life in England in the Year 1855 . . . Boston: Ticknor and Fields, 1864. 416 p.

AAS, BA, BP, H, HEH, LC, LCP, NYP, Y

1890 PHILLIPS, WALDORF HENRY. The World to Blame: A Novel
. . . Philadelphia: Claxton, Remsen & Haffelfinger, 1874.
190 p   AAS, LC, NYP

1891 PHILLIPS, WILLIAM BARNET. The Diamond Cross: A Tale of
American Society . . . New York: Hilton & Company.
Philadelphia: J. B. Lippincott & Co. St. Louis: J. F. Torrey
& Co. [cop. 1866]. 353 p.   BP, LC, Y
Also published as: *Wooed and Won; or, The True Value of Woman.*
New York: W. E. Hilton, 1871.   AAS, NYP

PHOENIX, JOHN, *pseud.* See Derby, George Horatio

1892 [PIATT, MRS. LOUISE (KIRBY).] Bell Smith Abroad . . . New
York: J. C. Derby. Boston: Phillips, Sampson & Co. Cin-
cinnati: H. W. Derby, 1855. 326 p., illus.
                      AAS, BP, BU, CU, H, HEH, LC, LCP, NYP, UC, UM, UP, Y
Humorous letters.

1893 PICKARD, MRS. KATE E. R. The Kidnapped and the Ransomed:
Being the Personal Recollections of Peter Still and His Wife
"Vina," after Forty Years of Slavery . . . Syracuse: William T.
Hamilton. New York and Auburn: Miller, Orton and
Mulligan, 1856. 409 p., illus.
                      AAS, CU, H, HEH, LCP, N, NYH, NYP, UC, UM, UP, Y

1894 [PICTON, THOMAS.] The Alpine Guide; or, The Veteran of
Marengo. An Historical Tale of the Napoleonic Empire. By
Paul Preston [pseud.] . . . New York: E. D. Long, 26 Ann
St. [186-?]. 104 p.   AAS

1895 [————] The Bootmaker of the Fifth Avenue: A Story of
the Petroliomania in New-York City. By Paul Preston
[pseud.] . . . New York: Hilton & Co. [cop. 1866]. 93 p.
Printed in double cols.   LC
LC copy deposited for copyright July 30, 1866.
Erroneously credited to E. Z. C. Judson in J. Monaghan, *The Great
Rascal* (1952), p. 322.

1896 [————] The Princess of Viarna; or, The Spanish Inquisi-
tion in the Reign of the Emperor Charles the Fifth. New
York: Pudney & Russell, 1857. 359 p., illus.   BU, H

1897 PIERSON, MRS. B. A. Lillian; or, The Battle of Life . . . Cincinnati: E. Morgan & Sons, print., 1865. 366 p.

Laid in Italy. AAS, HEH, N, NYP

1898 PIERSON, MRS. EMILY CATHARINE. Jamie Parker, the Fugitive . . . Hartford: Brockett, Fuller and Co., 1851. 192 p.

CU, N, NYH, NYP, Y

1899 [PIKE, MRS. FRANCES WEST (ATHERTON).] Every Day . . . Boston: Noyes, Holmes and Company, 1871. 282 p.

AAS, CU, H, LC

1900 [————] Here and Hereafter; or, The Two Altars. By Anna Athern [pseud.] . . . Boston: Crosby, Nichols and Company. London: Sampson Low, Son & Co., 1858. 376 p.

Laid in New York City. AAS, BP, LC, UC

1901 [————] Katherine Morris: An Autobiography . . . Boston: Walker, Wise and Company, 1860. 353 p. AAS, BU, H, LC

1902 [————] Step by Step; or, Delia Arlington. A Fireside Story. By Anna Athern [pseud.] . . . Boston and Cambridge: James Munroe and Company, 1857. 448 p.

AAS, BP, CU, H, HEH, LC, Y

1903 [PIKE, MRS. MARY HAYDEN (GREEN).] Agnes: A Novel . . . Boston: Phillips, Sampson & Company, 1858. 509, [1] p.

AAS, HEH, LC, LCP, UC, UM, Y

Quakers, Indians, and the American Revolution.

1904 [————] Caste: A Story of Republican Equality. By Sydney A. Story, Jr. [pseud.]. Boston: Phillips, Sampson and Company. New York: J. C. Derby, 1856. 540 p.

Antislavery. AAS, CU, H, HEH, N, NYH, UC, UM, Y

1905 [————] Ida May: A Story of Things Actual and Possible. By Mary Langdon [pseud.] . . . Boston: Phillips, Sampson and Company. New York: J. C. Derby, 1854. 478 p.

AAS, AP, BP, CU, H, HEH, N, NYH, NYP, UC, UV, Y

Antislavery; South Carolina.

PINE, CUYLER, *pseud. See* Peck, Ellen

1906 PINKERTON, ALLAN. Claude Melnotte as a Detective, and Other Stories ... Chicago: W. B. Keen, Cooke & Co., 1875. 282 p., illus.   AAS, BA, H, HEH, LC, LCP, N, NYP, UM, UVB

Also contains: L'Envoi—The Two Sisters; or, The Avenger—The Frenchman and the Bills of Exchange.

1907 ———— The Detective and the Somnambulist. The Murderer and the Fortune Teller ... Chicago: W. B. Keen, Cooke & Co., 1875. 241 p., illus.   AAS, CU, HEH, LC, LCP, N, NYP

1908 ———— The Expressman and the Detective ... Chicago: W. B. Keen, Cooke & Co., 1874. 278 p., illus.

AAS, BA, H, HEH, LC, LCP, N, NYH, UVB

1909 [PIPER, A. G.] The Arrest: A Tale of the Revolution. Founded on Fact. By F. Clinton Barrington [pseud.]. Little Falls, N. Y.: printed at the office of the Herkimer Journal, 1852. 32 p.   HEH

The tale is interspersed with advts.

The case for Piper as author of this title and the following titles, as recorded by A. Johannsen, *The House of Beadle and Adams* (Norman, Okla., 1950), II, 226, is stronger than the former attribution to Julius Warren Lewis.

1910 [————] Conrado de Beltran; or, The Buccaneer of the Gulf. A Romantic Story of the Sea and Shore. By F. Clinton Barrington [pseud.]. Boston: Frederick Gleason, 1851. 100 p. Printed in double cols.   HEH, LC, UVB

BP has a copy of this story with title: "Captain Belt; or, The Buccaneer of the Gulf. A Romantic Story of the Sea and Shore." N.p., n.d. 72 p., illus. Printed in double cols. It appears to be an extract.

1911 [————] The Young Fisherman; or, The Cruiser of the English Channel. A Story of the Olden Times. By F. Clinton Barrington [pseud.]. Boston: F. Gleason, 1851. 84 p. Printed in double cols.   UVB

1912 [————] ———— Boston: F. Gleason, 1851. 100 p. Printed in double cols.   AAS

Also contains: Iva; or, The Twin Brothers, by Dr. J. H. Robinson—The Village Gossip; or, The New Minister, by Harriet N. Hathaway—Blue-Eyed Jessie, by Miss Sarah M. Howe.

1913 [————] ———— Boston: F. Gleason's Publishing Hall, 1853. 100 p. Printed in double cols.   LC, NYP, Y

Also contains: Peggy Dawson: A Leaf from the Life of a Seamstress, by G. C. Hill—Iva; or, The Twin Brothers, by Dr. J. H. Robinson.

1914 EL PIRATA. [N.p., n.d.] Caption title, 56 p. Printed in double cols.   AAS, Y
Laid in New Orleans; ante bellum.

1915 PITRAT, JOHN CLAUDIUS. Paul and Julia; or, The Political Mysteries, Hypocrisy, and Cruelty of the Leaders of the Church of Rome . . . Boston: Edward W. Hinks and Company, 1855. 319 p., illus.   AAS, BU, CU, HEH, LC, N, NYP, Y
Laid in Italy and Greece.

1916 PLATNER, MRS. LOIS L. Cecilia Grey; or, The Vicissitudes of Fortune . . . New York: Derby & Jackson, 1859. 392 p., illus.   AAS
At head of title: "The Clermont Family."

1917 PLATT, S. H. The Martyrs and the Fugitive; or, A Narrative of the Captivity, Sufferings and Death of an African Family, and the Slavery and Escape of Their Son . . . New York: printed by Daniel Fanshaw, 1859. 95 p.   BP, CU, N, NYH, NYP, UM, Y

1918 THE PLEASANT AND GRAVE HISTORY of the First Adventures of That Good-Intentioned Gentleman, the Renowned Bartholomew Peregru. By a Member of the Philadelphia Bar . . . Philadelphia: Whilt & Yost, 1856. 331 p.   LC

PLEASANTS, JULIA. See Creswell, Mrs. Julia (Pleasants)

POCAHONTAS, pseud. See Pearson, Mrs. Emily (Clemens)

1919 POMEROY, MARCUS MILLS. Brick-Dust: A Remedy for the Blues, and a Something for People to Talk About . . . New York: G. W. Carleton & Co. London: S. Low, Son & Co., 1871. 255 p., illus.   H, HEH, LC, LCP, NYP, UM

1920 ———— Gold-Dust: For the Beautifying of Lives and Homes . . . New York: G. W. Carleton & Co. London: S. Low, Son & Co., 1871. 275 p., illus.
AAS, CU, H, HEH, LC, LCP, NYP, UC, UM, UP

1921 ———— Nonsense; or, Hits and Criticisms on the Follies of the Day . . . New York: G. W. Carleton & Co. London: S. Low, Son & Co., 1868. 274 p., illus.
AAS, BU, CU, H, HEH, LC, LCP, N, NYP, UC, UV, Y
Another ed. with same imprint ends on p. 275; type reset.   BP, NYP

1922 ———— Our Saturday Nights . . . New York: Carleton. London: S. Low, Son & Co., 1870. 272 p., illus.

AAS, BP, H, HEH, LC, LCP, NYP, UC, UM, Y

1923 ———— Sense; or, Saturday-Night Musings and Thoughtful Papers . . . New York: G. W. Carleton & Co. London: S. Low, Son & Co., 1868. 273 p., illus.

AAS, BP, H, HEH, LC, LCP, NYH, NYP, UV

POOL, MARIA LOUISE. Made Whole. *In* Short Stories (1869), No. 2210.

1924 A POOR FELLOW. By the Author of "Which, the Right, or Left?" . . . New York: Dick & Fitzgerald, 1858. 480 p.

A New York millionaire. AAS, LC, NYP, UP, Y

1925 POOR MARY POMEROY! The Jersey City Music Teacher. Also, a Full and Authentic Account of the Trial of Rev. John S. Glendenning before the Authorities of Prospect Avenue Church. Startling Details and Curious Statements. What a Lady Saw One Night. Philadelphia: Old Franklin Publishing House, No. 224 South Third Street, cop. 1874. 86 p., illus.

AAS, H, NYP

1926 POORE, BENJAMIN PERLEY. Aurora; or, The Sharpshooters' Scout. A Romance of the Revolution . . . New York: Samuel French, 121 Nassau Street [185-?]. 100 p. Printed in double cols. HEH

Also contains: Harry Percy Howard, by M. V. St. Leon.

1927 ———— Claude, the Artist; or, Rivalries of Art and Heart . . . New York: Samuel French, 121 Nassau Street [185-?].

Advertised in G. P. Burnham, *The Belle of the Orient* [185-?].

1928 ———— The Mameluke; or, The Sign of the Mystic Tie. A Tale of the Camp and Court of Bonaparte . . . Boston: F. Gleason's Publishing Hall, 1852. 100 p. Printed in double cols. AAS, HEH, LC, NYP, UP, Y

Also contains: The Story of a Genius, by Rev. H. H. Weld—The Crossed Dollar, by S. Cobb—The Humbled Pharisee, by T. S. Arthur—The Walbridge Family, by Mrs. C. Orne.

1929 ———— The Russian Guardsman: A Tale of the Seas and Shores of the East . . . New York: Samuel French, 151 Nassau [1852?]. 100 p. Printed in double cols. UC

Pages 94-100 advt. for an English tale.

1930 ———— The West Point Cadet; or, The Turns of Fortune's Wheel. Boston [1863].

Title listed in BM.

1931 PORTER, MISS C. B., *ed.* The Silver Cup of Sparkling Drops from Many Fountains for the Friends of Temperance . . . Buffalo: Derby and Co., 1852. 312 p.

AAS, BP, HEH, NYP, UM, Y

Contains: The Silver Cup, by M. G. Sleeper—Seed Time and Harvest, by Lucius M. Sargent [Wright (1774-1850), No. 2300]—There Is Hope for the Fallen—Emma Alton, by Mrs. C. H. Butler [Wright (1774-1850), No. 996n]—The Drunkard's Daughter, by Charles Burdett—The Knight of the Ringlet, by Giftie—The Dissipated Husband—The Widowed Bride—The Poor Girl and the Angels.

1932 PORTER, LINN BOYD. Caring for No Man: A Novel . . . Boston: William F. Gill & Company, 1875. 173 p. Printed in double cols.

BP, LC, NYP

Laid in New York City.

1933 [PORTER, MRS. LYDIA ANN (EMERSON).] Captain John; or, Loss Is Sometimes Gain. Boston: Henry Hoyt, 1870. 354 p., illus.

AAS, BU, CU

1934 ———— Glencoe Parsonage . . . Boston: D. Lothrop & Co. Dover, N. H.: G. T. Day & Co., 1870. 256 p., illus.   LC

1935 ———— The Lost Will . . . Boston: Henry Hoyt, No. 9 Cornhill [cop. 1860]. 294 p., illus.   AAS, CU, HEH

Laid in Vermont.

1936 ———— Married for Both Worlds . . . Boston: Lee and Shepard. New York: Lee, Shepard and Dillingham, 1871. 281 p.

AAS, CU, H, LC, NYP, UC

1937 ———— My Hero; or, Contrasted Lives . . . Boston: D. Lothrop & Co. Dover, N. H.: G. T. Day & Co., 1872. 332 p., illus.   LC

1938 PORTER, ROSE. Foundations; or, Castles in the Air . . . New York: Anson D. F. Randolph & Co., 770 Broadway [cop. 1871]. 194 p.

AAS, BP, H, HEH, LC, LCP, UM, Y

1939 ———— Summer Drift-Wood for the Winter Fire . . . New York: Anson D. F. Randolph & Co., 1870. 175 p.

Page 174 blank, p. 175 contains a poem.   CU, H, LC, LCP, UM, Y

1940 ——— Uplands and Lowlands; or, Three Chapters in a Life . . . New York: Anson D. F. Randolph & Company, 770 Broadway [cop. 1872]. 303 p.   BP, H, HEH, LC, LCP, NYP, UM

1941 ——— The Winter Fire. A Sequel to "Summer Drift-Wood" . . . New York: Anson D. F. Randolph & Company, 770 Broadway [cop. 1874]. 231 p.

                                   AAS, CU, H, HEH, LC, LCP, NYP, UM, Y

1942 ——— The Years That Are Told . . . New York: Anson D. F. Randolph & Company, 770 Broadway [cop. 1875]. 233, [1] p.   BP, HEH, LC, LCP, NYP, UM, Y

1943 [POTTER, ELIZA.] A Hairdresser's Experience in High Life. Cincinnati: published for the author, 1859. 294 p.

From New York to southern plantations.   AAS, LC, LCP, N, NYH, NYP

1944 POTWIN, MRS. H. K. Ruby Duke . . . Boston: Lee and Shepard. New York: Lee, Shepard and Dillingham, 1872. 421 p.

                                   AAS, BP, H, LC

1945 [POWELL, THOMAS.] Chit-Chat of Humor, Wit, and Anecdote . . . Edited by Pierce Pungent [pseud.]. New York: Stringer & Townsend, 1857. 398 p., illus.

                                  AAS, H, LC, LCP, UP, UVB

1946 PRATT, MRS. ELLA (FARMAN). A White Hand: A Story of Noblesse Oblige. By Ella Farman . . . Boston: D. Lothrop & Co. Dover, N. H.: G. T. Day & Co., 1875. 251 p., front.

                                  AAS, HEH, LC, NYP, Y

1947 PRATT, FRANCES HAMMOND. La Belle Zoa; or, The Insurrection of Hayti . . . Albany: McGoun and Kewin, 1854. 96 p.   N

Also issued with imprint: Albany: Weed, Parsons and Co., 1854.   NYP

1948 PRATT, L. J. The Blind Girl's Offering; or, Stray Thoughts in Poetry and Prose . . . Swanton, Vermont: P. P. R. Ripley, printer, 1853. 142 p.   AAS, BU

1949 ——— The Unfortunate Mountain Girl: A Collection of Miscellanies in Prose and Verse . . . Middlebury [Vt.]: printed at the Register book and job office, 1854. 176 p.

Page 175 blank, p. 176 "Index."   AAS, BU, CU, H, HEH, UM

1950 PRENTISS, MRS. ELIZABETH (PAYSON). Aunt Jane's Hero . . . New York: A. D. F. Randolph & Co., 770 Broadway [cop. 1871]. 292 p.

AAS, BA, BU, CU, H, HEH, LC, LCP, NYP, UC, UM, Y

1951 [————] Fred, and Maria, and Me . . . New York: Charles Scribner & Company, 1868. 71 p., illus.

In a humorous vein.   AAS, H, HEH, LCP, NYP

1952 [————] The Little Preacher . . . New York: Anson D. F. Randolph, 1867. 223 p., front.

Information from LC card for copy withdrawn from circulation.

1953 ———— Old Brown Pitcher. New York: National Temperance Society, 1868.

Title listed in G. L. Prentiss, *Life and Letters of Elizabeth Prentiss* (New York [1882]), p. 569.

1954 ———— Stepping Heavenward . . . New York: Anson D. F. Randolph & Co., 1870. 426 p.

AAS, BA, BU, H, LCP, N, NYP, UM, Y

1955 ———— Urbané and His Friends . . . New York: Anson D. F. Randolph & Company, 770 Broadway [cop. 1874]. 287 p.

AAS, BP, CU, HEH, LCP, NYP, Y

1956 PRESBURY, B. F. The Mustee; or, Love and Liberty . . . Boston: Shepard, Clark & Brown, 1859. 487 p.

Antislavery.   AAS, BP, BU, CU, H, HEH, NYH, NYP, UP, Y

PRESCOTT, HARRIET ELIZABETH. *See* Spofford, Mrs. Harriet Elizabeth (Prescott)

1957 PRESTON, HARRIET WATERS. Aspendale . . . Boston: Roberts Brothers, 1871. 219 p.

AAS, BA, BP, CU, H, HEH, LC, LCP, N, NYP, UM, Y

1958 ———— Love in the Nineteenth Century: A Fragment . . . Boston: Roberts Brothers, 1873. 153 p.

AAS, BA, BU, CU, H, HEH, LC, N, NYP, UC, Y

PRESTON, LAURA, *pseud. See* Heaven, Mrs. Louise (Palmer)

263

1959 [PRESTON, MRS. MARGARET (JUNKIN).] Silverwood: A Book of Memories . . . New York: Derby & Jackson. Cincinnati: H. W. Derby & Co., 1856. 405 p.   AAS, CU, HEH, LCP, N
Southern life.

PRESTON, PAUL, *pseud.* *See* Picton, Thomas

1960 PRICHARD, SARAH JOHNSON. Faye Mar of Storm-Cliff . . . New York: Wynkoop & Sherwood, 1868. 351 p.   AAS, H, LC, UV
Mother-in-law problems; Civil War in background.

1961 PRIME, WILLIAM COWPER. I Go A-Fishing . . . New York: Harper & Brothers, 1873. 365 p.
AAS, BA, BP, BU, H, LCP, NYP, UC, UP, Y

1962 [————] Later Years . . . New York: Harper & Brothers, 1854. 353 p.
AAS, BP, CU, H, HEH, LC, LCP, N, NYH, NYP, UC, UM, UP, Y
A series of sketches.

1963 [————] The Old House by the River . . . New York: Harper & Brothers, 1853. 318 p.
AAS, AP, BP, BU, CU, H, HEH, LC, N, NYH, NYP, UC, UM, UP, UV, Y
A series of sketches.

1964 [PRINCE, GEORGE.] Rambles in Chili, and Life among the Araucanian Indians in 1836. By "Will, the Rover" [pseud.]. Thomaston [Me.]: D. J. Starrett, 1851. 88 p. Printed in double cols.   AAS, N, NYP
Based upon an actual trip.

1965 PRINCE, PAUL. The Story of Fort Hill: Giving an Account of Many Interesting Adventures between the White and Indians, Previous to the Settlement of Auburn . . . Auburn: P. J. Becker, 1859. 50 p. Printed in double cols.   LC

1966 THE PRINCESS OF THE MOON: A Confederate Fairy Story. Written by a Lady of Warrenton, Va. Warrenton, Va., 1869. 72 p., front.   BA, HEH, LC, UC
Berates the North and forgives the South.

1967 PRITCHARD, PAUL. The Refugee; or, The Union Boys of '61. A Tale of the Rebellion . . . New York: T. W. Strong, No. 98 Nassau Street [cop. 1862]. 80 p.   Y

1968 PRIZE PAPERS, Written for the New York Observer: Essays, Poems, and Tales. New York: A. D. F. Randolph, 1865. 47 p.   BP, BU, H
Contains: The Brothers Leinhardt, by Miss Frances W. Owston, Pittsburg, Penn.

1969 PROSPERO, pseud. Caliban. A Sequel to "Ariel." By Prospero [pseud.] . . . New York: published for the proprietor, 1868. 32 p.   NYP, Y

1970 PUGH, MRS. ELIZA LOFTON (PHILLIPS). In a Crucible: A Novel . . . Philadelphia: Claxton, Remsen & Haffelfinger. New Orleans: J. A. Gresham, 1872. 389 p.   AAS, HEH, LC
Louisiana during the Civil War.

1971 ————— Not a Hero: A Novel . . . New York: Blelock & Co., 1867. 131 p. Printed in double cols.   LC
Laid in New Orleans; 1850-1862.

1972 [PULLEN, CHARLES HENRY.] Miss Columbia's Public School; or, Will It Blow Over? By A. Cosmopolitan [pseud.] . . . New York: Francis B. Felt & Co., 1871. 82 p., illus.
         AAS, BA, BP, CU, H, HEH, LC, LCP, N, NYP, UC, UM, UP, Y

PUNGENT, PIERCE, pseud. See Powell, Thomas

1973 PURITAN, JOB, pseud. Household Tales. By Job Puritan [pseud.] . . . Boston: James Munroe and Company, 1861. 367 p.   AAS, BP, HEH, LC
Contents: The Old Windmill—The Trial of Genius—The Profane Swearer—Love a Victor—Dora Norton—The Forest Bride—A Will and a Way—Married for a Dinner—Stella Lea—The Betrayed—The Skipper's Daughter—The Sabbath Breakers.

1974 [PUTNAM, MRS. ELLEN TRYPHOSA HARRINGTON.] The Bridle of Vanity. Boston: Donahoe, 1863.
Title listed in Kelly 1861-1866.

1975 [—————] Captain Molly: The Story of a Brave Woman. By Thrace Talmon [pseud.]. New York: Derby & Jackson, 1857. 349 p., illus.   AAS
Also published as: Heroine of the Revolution; or, Captain Molly, the Brave Woman. New York: Derby & Jackson, 1860.   H
And, The Hero Girl and How She Became a Captain in the Army. Philadelphia: John E. Potter and Company, 617 Sansom Street [cop. 1865].   H

1976 [————] Edith Hale: A Village Story. By Thrace Talmon [pseud.]. Boston: Phillips, Sampson & Company, 1856. 521 p. AAS, BU, H, HEH, UP, Y

1977 [————] The Red Bridge: A Temperance Story. By Thrace Talmon [pseud.]. New York: National Temperance Society, 1867. 321 p., illus. CU

1978 [————] Where Is the City? Boston: Roberts Brothers, 1868. 349 p. LC, LCP, N

1979 [PUTNAM, MRS. MARY TRAILL SPENCE (LOWELL).] Fifteen Days: An Extract from Edward Colvil's Journal ... Boston: Ticknor and Fields, 1866. 299, [1] p.
AAS, BA, BP, CU, H, HEH, LC, LCP, N, NYP, UP, Y
Laid in the South; "April 5-19, 1844."

1980 [————] Record of an Obscure Man ... Boston: Ticknor and Fields, 1861. 216 p.
AAS, AP, BA, BP, CU, H, HEH, LC, LCP, N, NYP, UC, UV, Y

1981 [————] ———— Boston: Ticknor and Fields, 1861. 228 p. Y
Pages [217]-228 "Notes."
Also issued with imprint: Cambridge: printed at the Riverside Press, 1861. 229 p. La. paper copy. "Notes" on pp. 217-229. HEH, UM
Story incidental to the discourse upon Negroes and slaves.

1982 PUTNAM, MRS. SALLIE A. (BROCK). Kenneth, My King: A Novel ... New York: G. W. Carleton & Co. London: S. Low, Son & Co., 1873. 417 p. AAS, HEH, LCP, NYH, NYP, UV
The ante bellum South.

QUAD, M., *pseud.* See Lewis, Charles Bertrand

1983 QUEST ... New York: Carleton, 1864. 312 p.
AAS, CU, H, HEH, LCP, NYP, UC, Y

1984 QUID, TERTIUM, *pseud.* One of the Family. By Tertium Quid [pseud.]. Portland: Bailey & Noyes, 1868. Cover title, 24 p.
A humorous tale of a dog. AAS

1985 QUIET THOUGHTS FOR QUIET HOURS . . . Boston: J. E. Tilton and Company, 1861. 268 p., illus. AP, H, UV
Contains a few didactic stories.

1986 [QUIGLEY, HUGH.] The Cross and the Shamrock; or, How to Defend the Faith. An Irish-American Catholic Tale of Real Life . . . Written by a Missionary Priest. Boston: Patrick Donahoe, Franklin Street [cop. 1853]. 264 p. AAS, NYP, UM

1987 ——— Profit and Loss: A Story of the Life of the Genteel Irish-American, Illustrative of Godless Education . . . New York: T. O'Kane, 1873. 458 p. BP, LC

1988 [———] The Prophet of the Ruined Abbey; or, A Glance of the Future of Ireland . . . New York: Edward Dunigan and Brother, 1855. 293 p. CU, HEH, LC

1989 [QUINCY, EDMUND.] Wensley: A Story without a Moral. Boston: Ticknor and Fields, 1854. 302 p.
AAS, BP, BU, CU, H, HEH, LC, N, NYP, UC, UM, UP, Y

R., F. W. *See* Rankin, Fannie W.

R., W. D. *See* Ritner, William D.

1990 [RAM, STOPFORD JAMES.] Greatness in Little Things; or, Way-Side Violets. By Ruth Vernon [pseud.] . . . New York: Dayton & Wentworth; A. Ranney. Cincinnati: H. M. Rulison, 1854. 322 p., front. LC, Y
Also published as: *The Bride of Love; or, The True Greatness of Female Heroism. By Ruth Vernon.* Philadelphia: D. Rulison, 1859. LC

1991 [———] Unseen Hand. By Ruth Vernon [pseud.]. Cincinnati: J. R. Hawley, 1863. 321 p., illus. H, LC, UC
Contents: Eustace Corrie; or, The Somnambulist—The Unknown Prisoner—Lilian; or, Sketches from Life—Live for Something; or, The Brother's Choice—The Railroad Inn; or, "The Lost One Found"—The Bank Notes; or, The Story of an Old Gown.

RANDOLPH, J. THORNTON, *pseud. See* Peterson, Charles Jacob

1992 [RANDOLPH, PASCHAL BEVERLY.] Dealings with the Dead: The Human Soul, Its Migrations and Its Transmigrations. Penned by the Rosicrucian... Utica, N. Y.: M. J. Randolph, 1861-62. 268 p.   H, LC, N, NYP, UM
Based, in part, on the life and experiences of the author.

1993 ———— The Rosicrucian's Story: The Wonderful Things That Happened to Mr. Thomas W., and His Wife. Embracing the Celebrated "Miranda Theory"... Utica: M. J. Randolph, 1863. 106 p.   LC
At head of title: "Dr. P. B. Randolph's Thrilling Tale."

1994 ———— The Wonderful Story of Ravalette. Also, Tom Clark and His Wife: Their Double Dreams and the Curious Things That Befell Them Therein; or, The Rosicrucian's Story... New York: Sinclair Tousey, 1863. 249, 146 p.
           AAS, HEH
The second story has its own title page and pagination; but the signatures are continuous.

1995 [RANKIN, FANNIE W.] True to Him Ever: A Novel. By F. W. R. New York: G. W. Carleton & Co. London: S. Low, Son & Co., 1874. 290 p.   AAS, LC, NYP, UV

1996 [RANSOM, A.] A Terrible History of Fraud and Crime. The Twin Brothers of Texas, Lives, Trial, Confession, and Execution, at Savannah, Georgia... Philadelphia: M. A. Milliette [cop. 1858]. 41 p., illus.   LC
At head of title: "Just Published."
Signed at end: "Rev. A. Ransom."

RATTLEHEAD, DAVID, *M.D., pseud. See* Byrn, Marcus Lafayette

RAVEN, RALPH, *pseud. See* Payson, George

RAVENSWOOD, *pseud. See* Beebe, Charles Washington

1997 [RAYMOND, GEORGE S.] The Empress of the Isles; or, The Lake Bravo. A Romance of the Canadian Struggle in 1837. By Charley Clewline [pseud.]. New York: Stringer & Townsend, 222 Broadway [1853?]. 127, [1] p.   BU, LC
First word, last line at end: "Isles." It reads "les" in the Cincinnati: U. P. James, No. 167 Walnut St. [n.d.], reprint.

———— Going an Errand; or, Playing Deadhead. *In* H. P. Cheever, The Rival Brothers [*ca.* 1852], No. 495.

1998 [————] Red Wing; or, The Weird Cruiser of Van Dieman's Land. By Charley Clewline [pseud.] . . . New York: Stringer & Townsend, 222 Broadway [cop. 1853]. 122 p.   LC
Y reprint without copyright notice, includes in title, "A Romance of Two Continents." A later undated ed. gives the author's name on the title page.

1999 [RAYMOND, ROSSITER WORTHINGTON.] Brave Hearts: An American Novel. By Robertson Gray [pseud.] . . . New York: J. B. Ford and Company, 1873. 284 p., illus.
AAS, BP, CU, H, HEH, LC, LCP, N, NYP, UM
Mining towns in California's Sierra Nevada mountains.

2000 READ, EMILY. Aytoun: A Romance . . . Philadelphia: J. B. Lippincott & Co., 1872. 79 p. Printed in double cols.
LCP, NYP

2001 READ, HARRIETTE FANNING. The Haunted Student: A Romance of the Fourteenth Century . . . Washington, D. C.: published by the author, 1860. 396 p.   BA, LC, NYP

2002 THE RECORDED WILL; or, Truth and Not Fiction, Remarkably Illustrating the Care of Divine Providence. By a Clergyman's Widow. Boston: Tappan & Whittemore; Jewett, Proctor & Worthington, Cleveland; A. Whittemore & Co., Milwaukie; J. R. Whittemore, Chillicothe, 1855. 234 p.   BP, H
BP credits this to a Mrs. E. Bigelow.

2003 [REED, ISAAC GEORGE.] Erring yet Noble: A Tale of and for Women . . . New York: John Bradburn, 1865. 569 p.
AAS, BP, LC, Y

2004 REED, PETER FISHE. Beyond the Snow: Being a History of Trim's Adventures in Nordlichtschein . . . Chicago: the Lakeside Press, 1873. 323, [3] p., illus.   AAS, HEH

2005 REEDER, LOUISE. Currer Lyle; or, The Stage in Romance and the Stage in Reality . . . New York: E. D. Long, 1856. 361 p.
BP, CU, LC

Also published as: *Currer Lyle: A History of My Life; or, The Stage in Romance and the Stage in Reality*. Philadelphia: T. B. Peterson, No. 102 Chestnut Street [cop. 1857].   AAS, H, HEH, UM
A semi-autobiographical novel.

2006 REES, JAMES. The Tinker Spy: A Romance of the Revolution
... Buffalo: A. Burke, 1855. 103 p.   AAS, H, NYP

2007 [REEVES, MARIAN CALHOUN LEGARÉ.] Ingemisco. By Fadette
[pseud.] ... New York: Blelock & Co., 1867. 341 p.
                                    AAS, LC, LCP, NYP, Y
Also issued with imprint: New York: Blelock & Co., 1867.   BU
Laid in Switzerland and Bavaria.

2008 [————] Randolph Honor ... New York: Richardson
and Company, 1868. 382 p.   LC
At the time of the Civil War.

2009 [————] Sea-Drift. By Fadette [pseud.]. Philadelphia:
Claxton, Remsen & Haffelfinger, 1869.
Title listed in I. Raymond, *Southland Writers* (Philadelphia, 1870),
II, 909.

2010 [————] Wearithorne; or, In the Light of To-Day. By
"Fadette" [pseud.] ... Philadelphia: J. B. Lippincott & Co.,
1872. 214 p.   AAS, BP, H, HEH, LC, LCP, NYP
Laid in Scotland.

REGESTER, SEELEY, *pseud*. *See* Victor, Mrs. Metta Victoria
(Fuller)

REID, CHRISTIAN, *pseud*. *See* Tiernan, Mrs. Frances Christine
(Fisher)

REISENDER, *pseud*. *See* Hathaway, William E.

2011 [REMBERT, W. R.] The Georgia Bequest: Manolia; or, The
Vale of Tallulah. By a Georgia Huntsman. Augusta:
McKinne & Hall, 1854. 192 p., illus.
Supposed author.   AAS, HEH, LC, NYH, NYP, UM, UP, UV, Y

2012 REMICK, MARTHA. Agnes Stanhope: A Tale of English Life ...
Boston: James M. Usher, 1862. 444 p.   BP, H, LC, NYP, UM

2013 ———— Millicent Halford: A Tale of the Dark Days of Kentucky in the Year 1861 ... Boston: A. Williams & Co., 1865.
424 p.   AAS, CU, HEH, LC, N, Y

2014 ———— Richard Ireton: A Legend of the Early Settlement of New England ... Boston: Loring [1875?]. 466 p.

AAS, BP, UM

2015 REMINGTON, E. F. The City of Sin and Its Capture by Immanuel's Army: An Allegory ... New York: Carlton & Porter, 206 Mulberry Street [cop. 1857]. 336 p.

Slocum Library copy, Ohio Wesleyan University.

2016 THE REV. J. W. LOGUEN, as a Slave and as a Freeman: A Narrative of Real Life. Syracuse, N. Y.: J. G. K. Truair & Co., stereotypers and printers, 1859. 444 p., front. HEH, NYP, Y

This biography of Jermain Wesley Loguen is partly fictitious.

2017 ———— Syracuse, N. Y.: J. G. K. Truair & Co., stereotypers and printers, 1859. 455 p., front. H, HEH, N

This issue adds an "Appendix" which contains a letter dated "March 28, 1860."

2018 REVERIES OF AN OLD MAID. New York: DeWitt & Davenport, 1852.

Title listed in Roorbach 1820-1852.

2019 [REYNOLDS, ELHANAN WINCHESTER.] Records of the Bubbleton Parish; or, Papers from the Experience of an American Minister ... Boston: A. Tompkins and B. B. Mussey & Co., 1854. 340 p., illus.

AAS, BP, BU, CU, H, HEH, LC, LCP, NYH, NYP, UP

2020 [————] The Tangletown Letters: Being the Reminiscences, Observations, and Opinions of Timotheus Trap [pseud.] ... Buffalo: Wanzer, McKim & Co., 1856. 300 p., illus.

AAS, BU, CU, H, HEH, LC, LCP, N, NYH, NYP, UM, UP, UV, Y

Title page and 48 p. of text of "The Montgomerys" (advt.) at end.

2021 REYNOLDS, JOSEPH. Peter Gott, the Cape Ann Fisherman ... Boston: John P. Jewett & Company. Cleveland, Ohio: Jewett, Proctor & Worthington. New York: Sheldon, Blakeman and Company, 1856. 280 p., front.

AAS, BP, BU, CU, H, LC, NYH, NYP

Also issued with imprints: Portland: Francis Blake. Boston: John P. Jewett & Co., 1856. HEH

And, Salem: D. B. Brooks & Brother. Boston: John P. Jewett & Co., 1856. AAS, H

2022 REYNOLDS, WILLIAM D. Miss Martha Brownlow; or, The Heroine of Tennessee . . . Philadelphia: Barclay & Co., 56 North Sixth St. [cop. 1863]. 1 p.l., 21-49, [1] p., illus.

BU, HEH, LC, LCP, N, NYP

Also published as: *The Rebel Fiend; or, The Scout of Secessia. A Stirring Historical Romance of the War in the West.* Philadelphia: Reichner & Company [n.d.].   AAS, LC

Mr. Brigham reported no Reichner in the Philadelphia directories, 1856-1872, that he searched.

2023 RICE, ROSELLA. Mabel; or, Heart Histories. A Tale of Truth . . . Second Edition . . . Columbus, Ohio: Follett, Foster and Company, 1859. 414 p.   BU

2024 RICHARDS, A., *ed.* Zilla Fitz James, the Female Bandit of the South-West; or, The Horrible, Mysterious and Awful Disclosures in the Life of the Creole Murderess, Zilla Fitz James, Paramour and Accomplice of Green H. Long . . . An Autobiographical Narrative, Edited by Rev. A. Richards. Little Rock, Ark.: A. R. Orton, 1852. 31 p., illus.

Information from card in Nat'l Union Cat.

2025 [RICHARDS, MRS. A. M.] Memories of a Grandmother. By a Lady of Massachusetts . . . Boston: Gould and Lincoln. New York: Sheldon, Lamport & Blakeman, 1854. 141 p.

AAS, BP, BU, H, HEH, LC, NYP, UM

2026 RICHARDS, C. FRENCH. John Guilderstring's Sin: A Novel . . . New York: Carleton, 1864. 244 p.

Civil War background.   AAS, BP, BU, H, HEH, LC, LCP, NYP, UVB, Y

2027 [RICHARDS, MRS. CORNELIA HOLROYD (BRADLEY).] Aspiration: An Autobiography of Girlhood. By Mrs. Manners [pseud.] . . . New York: Sheldon, Lamport and Blakeman, 1855. 334 p.   AAS, BP, CU, H, HEH

2028 RICHARDS, MRS. ELIZABETH BARNES. Elisiner; or, The Mysteries of an Old Stone Mansion. A Historical Story Founded upon Facts . . . Worcester: printed by Adams & Brown, 1864. 309 p., illus.   AAS, CU, HEH, NYP, Y

Copyright notice dated 1861.
Laid in New Hampshire.

2029 RICHARDS, MRS. MARIA (TOLMAN). Life in Israel; or, Portraitures of Hebrew Character ... New York: Sheldon, Blakeman and Company. Chicago: S. C. Griggs and Company, 1857. 389 p.   AAS, BP, H, HEH, LC, NYP

2030 RICHARDS, THOMAS ADDISON. The Romance of American Landscape ... New York: Leavitt and Allen [cop. 1854]. 310 p., illus.   CU, LC, UP, UV, Y

Also published as: *American Scenery*. New York: G. A. Leavitt [cop. 1854].   AAS, BP, LC, N, UM, Y

2031 ———— Tallulah and Jocassee; or, Romances of Southern Landscape, and Other Tales ... Charleston: Walker, Richards & Co., 1852. 255 p.
      AAS, BP, BU, CU, LC, N, NYP, UC, UM, UVB

Contents: Tallulah; or, The Trysting Rock—Jocassee; or, Il Capannetto—The Phrenologist; or, The Tactics of Dr. Cranium—The Travellers' Club; or, Lights and Shades of Locomotion—"Don't Be Bashful"—One Good Turn Deserves Another.
Also published as: *Summer Stories of the South*. Philadelphia: Lippincott, Grambo & Co., 1853.   AAS, H, HEH, NYP

RICHARDS, WILLIAM CAREY. Electricity as a Temperance Agent. *In* T. A. Burke, *ed.*, Polly Peablossom's Wedding (1851), No. 426.

2032 RICHMOND, MRS. EUPHEMIA JOHNSON (GUERNSEY). The Fatal Dower ... New York: the National Temperance Society, 1874. 219 p., front.   LC

2033 [————] The Harwoods; or, The Secret of Happiness. By Effie Johnson [pseud.]. New York: American Female Guardian Society, 1857. 83 p., front.   AAS

2034 RICHTER, PAUL. Lizzie West, the Printer's Daughter: A Tale of Filial Heroism ... Philadelphia: S. C. Lamb, 310 Chestnut Street [cop. 1859]. 106 p., illus.   LC
Pages 103-106 advts.
A temperance tale.

2035 ———— The Lottery Ticket; or, The Forlorn Hope. A Tale of the Present Times ... Philadelphia: Barclay & Co., 734 Market Street [cop. 1858]. 94 p., 1 l., illus.   LC, UP
NYP has copy with above address in cover imprint; but title page imprint is "No. 1 South Sixth Street," which makes it a later printing.

2036 RIDDLE, ALBERT GALLATIN. Alice Brand: A Romance of the Capital . . . New York: D. Appleton and Company, 1875. 384 p.   AAS, BU, CU, H, HEH, LC, LCP, N, NYP, Y
Also issued with imprint: Cleveland: Cobb, Andrews & Co., 1875.
AAS, UV

2037 [————] Bart Ridgeley: A Story of Northern Ohio. Boston: Nichols and Hall, 1873. 374 p.   AAS, CU, H, UC, UV, Y
Also issued with imprint: Boston: Nichols and Hall. Cleveland: Cobb, Andrews & Co., 1873.   HEH, LC, NYP

2038 ———— The Portrait: A Romance of the Cuyahoga Valley . . . Boston: Nichols & Hall. Cleveland: Cobb, Andrews & Co., 1874. 378 p.   CU, H, LC, UC, UP
Also issued with imprint: Cleveland: Cobb, Andrews & Co. Boston: Nichols & Hall, 1874.   AAS, HEH, NYP, UM, Y
A Mormon novel.

2039 [RIDGE, JOHN ROLLIN.] The Life and Adventures of Joaquín Murieta, the Celebrated California Bandit. By Yellow Bird [pseud.]. San Francisco: W. B. Cooke and Company, 1854. 91 p., illus.
For an anonymous plagiarism see No. 1552.
A copy is in the possession of Thomas W. Streeter, Morristown, N. J.

2040 ———— ———— 3d ed. San Francisco: Fred'k MacCrellish & Co., 1871. 81 p. Printed in double cols.   LC
Ridge revised this ed.

2041 ———— ———— 3d ed. Revised and Enlarged. San Francisco: Fred'k MacCrellish & Co. [1874]. 98 p. Printed in double cols.   H, HEH
This is No. 2040 with the "Career of Tiburcio Vasquez" added, pp. [83]-98. On cover: "The Lives of Joaquin Murieta and Tiburcio Vasquez. The California Highwaymen. San Francisco, 1874."

2042 RIGHTED AT LAST: A Novel . . . New York: D. Appleton and Company, 1872. 172 p., illus. Printed in double cols.
This has been attributed to Martha Russell.   AAS, CU, HEH, LCP, NYP

2043 RILEY, HENRY HIRAM. Puddleford and Its People . . . New York: Samuel Hueston, 1854. 269 p., illus.
AAS, BU, CU, H, HEH, LC, LCP, NYP, UC, UM, UP, UVB, Y

2044 ———— The Puddleford Papers; or, Humors of the West . . . New York: Derby & Jackson. Cincinnati: H. W. Derby & Co., 1857. 353 p., illus.

AAS, BU, CU, HEH, LC, NYP, UM, UP, Y

This adds five chapters to the 1854 ed., No. 2043.

2045 RITCHIE, MRS. ANNA CORA (OGDEN) MOWATT. The Clergyman's Wife, and Other Sketches . . . New York: G. W. Carleton & Co. London: S. Low, Son & Co., 1867. 384 p.

AAS, BA, BP, BU, CU, LC, LCP, NYP, Y

2046 ———— Fairy Fingers: A Novel . . . New York: Carleton, 1865. 460 p.   AAS, CU, HEH, LC, LCP, N, NYP, UC, UP, UVB, Y

French diplomats of Napoleon III, in Washington, D. C.

2047 ———— Mimic Life; or, Before and behind the Curtain. A Series of Narratives . . . Boston: Ticknor and Fields, 1856. 408 p., front.

AAS, BP, BU, CU, H, HEH, LC, LCP, N, NYH, NYP, UC, UM, UP, UVB, Y

Contents: Stella—The Prompter's Daughter—The Unknown Tragedian.

2048 ———— The Mute Singer: A Novel . . . New York: Carleton, 1866. 360 p.

AAS, BP, BU, CU, H, HEH, LC, LCP, NYP, UC, UP, Y

2049 ———— Twin Roses: A Narrative . . . Boston: Ticknor and Fields, 1857. 273 p.

On the theater.   AAS, BU, H, HEH, LC, N, NYH, NYP, UP, UVB, Y

2050 RITNER, WILLIAM D. The Great Original and Entrancing Romance: The Fireman's Bride; or, Beautiful Myria, the Mad Actress . . . Philadelphia: M. A. Milliette. New York, Baltimore, Buffalo, and Chicago, 1858. 86 p., illus.   LC

Also published as: *Myria, the Mad Actress; or, The Mysterious Murder.* Philadelphia: Barclay & Co. [cop. 1873]. 110 p., illus.   LC

2051 [————] Juan; or, The White Slave. A History of Wrongs, Trials, Sufferings and Daring. By W. D. R., Author of the "Nobleman's Daughter," "Juan, the Unknown," "Mysterious Robbery," "Julia Davis," "Ella Dale," "Amy Florence," "Lovely Quakeress." Philadelphia: J. H. C. Whiting, 1857. 98 p., illus.   LCP

Also published as: *Juan, the White Slave and the Rebel Planter's Daughter. A Stirring Story of Slavery, Secession, Suffering, and Revenge . . . By W. D. R., Author of "The Jeweler's Daughter," "The Fireman's Bride," "The Knights of the Golden Circle," etc.* Philadelphia: Barclay & Co., 1865. 97, [1] p., illus.   AAS, LC, UM, Y

2052 [————] The Rival's Revenge! or, The Lovely Quakeress, Catherine Middleton, the Skilful Gamester in Disguise! Her Singular Career with the Startling Developments in the Life of Don Senor Jacinto, "the Maniac Priest" . . . Philadelphia, Cincinnati, & Richmond, Va.: M. L. Barclay [cop. 1854]. 36 p., illus.   AAS, BU

2053 THE RIVER PIRATES: A Tale of New York. Taken from the Records of the New York Police Courts. New York: H. Long & Brother, 43 Ann Street [cop. 1853]. 92 p.   LC

2054 [RIVES, MRS. JUDITH PAGE (WALKER).] Home and the World . . . New York: D. Appleton and Company, 1857. 408 p.
AAS, BA, BP, CU, LCP, NYP, UC

2055 ROATH, DAVID L. The Five Love Adventures of Solomon Slug, and Other Sketches . . . New York: Bunce & Brother, 1852. 167 p.   H
Also contains: A Georgia Court—The Village Inn—The Man Whose Mother Didn't Know He Was Out—The Great Used Up—Ichabod Icicle —Blood.

ROBB, JOHN S. Smoking a Grizzly. *In* T. A. Burke, *ed.*, Polly Peablossom's Wedding (1851), No. 426.

2056 ROBERTS, EDWIN F. The Road to Ruin; or, The Dangers of the Town. A Career of Crime . . . Cincinnati: U. P. James, No. 167 Walnut Street [1855 or later]. 107 p. Printed in double cols.   HEH, UM, UP, Y
Also contains: The Road to Happiness in Six Steps—The Gamester's Progress.
Copyright notice dated 1854, in name of Stringer & Townsend.

———— The Six Stages of Punishment; or, The Victim of a Vitiated Society. *In* C. P. Bickley, Garnelle (1853), No. 296.

2057 ———— The Twin Brothers; or, The Victims of the Press-gang. A Romance of the Land and Sea . . . Cincinnati: U. P. James, No. 167 Walnut Street [185-?]. 96 p.   HEH

ROBERTS, LESTER A., *attrib. au. See* Griswold, V. M.

2058 [ROBERTS, MAGGIE.] Home Scenes during the Rebellion. By Eiggam Strebor [pseud.] . . . New York: John F. Trow & Son, 1875. 204 p., illus.   AAS, BP, H, HEH, LC, N
Laid in Washington, D. C., and New Orleans.

2059 [ROBERTS, SARAH.] My Step-Mother; or, The Power of Love. New York: D. Dana, Jr., 1857. 203 p.
Information from LC card for copy withdrawn from circulation.

2060 ROBERTSON, JOSEPH R. The Brinkley Female College Ghost Story . . . Based upon Facts . . . Memphis, Tenn.: R. C. Floyd & Co., printers, 1871. 36 p.   HEH, LC

2061 ROBINSON, BENJAMIN. Dolores: A Tale of Disappointment and Distress, Compiled, Arranged and Edited from the Journal, Letters and Other MSS of Roland Vernon, Esq. . . . New York: E. J. Hale & Sons, 1868. 180 p. Printed in double cols.
Laid in North Carolina.   H, N

2062 ROBINSON, FAYETTE. The Wizard of the Wave: A Romance . . . New York: Stringer & Townsend [cop. 1853]. 107 p.   BU

2063 ROBINSON, JOHN HOVEY. Alethe; or, The Child of the Cero . . . New York: F. A. Brady, 1867. 75 p.
Announced as "recently published" in *Amer. Lit. Gaz.*, IX (Aug. 15, 1867), 216.

2064 ———— Barnaby, the Sandhiller; or, The Planter's Ruse . . . New York: Frederic A. Brady, 22 Ann Street [186-?]. 89 p., illus. Printed in double cols.   H
Copyright notice dated 1862.

———— Bianca; or, The Monk's Plot. *In* S. Cobb, Ivan the Serf [185-?], No. 570.

2065 ———— Black Ralph, the Forest Fiend! or, Wanderers of the West. A Tale of Wood and Wild . . . Boston: National Publishing Company, 1851. 97 p., front.
Wagner-Camp 203a locates a copy in the Bancroft Library, University of California.

2066 ———— The Buckeye Ranger: A Tale of the Kansas Hunting Grounds! . . . New York: Frederic A. Brady, No. 24 Ann Street [186-?]. 79 p., illus. Printed in double cols.   Y

2067 ——— Catholina; or, The Niche in the Wall. A Tale of Louisiana . . . New York: Frederic A. Brady, No. 24 Ann Street [cop. 1861]. 101 p., illus. Printed in double cols. Y

2068 ——— Cepherine; or, The Secret Cabal . . . New York: Frederic A. Brady [cop. 1863]. 114 p., illus. LC

2069 ——— Good-for-Nothing Dick; or, A Hero of Humble Life. A Story of Our Own Times . . . New York: Frederic A. Brady, No. 24 Ann Street [1864]. 189 p., front. Printed in double cols. LC
LC copy deposited for copyright Mar. 15, 1864.

——— Iva; or, The Twin Brothers. *In* A. G. Piper, The Young Fisherman (1851 & 1853), Nos. 1912-1913.

2070 ——— The Life and Adventures of Wm. Harvard Stinchfield; or, the Wanderings of a Traveling Merchant. "An Owre True Tale" of the Gaming Table and Bowl . . . Portland, Me.: for the author, printed by Thurston & Co., 1851. 81 p. BP, H, LC, Y
Cover title: "The Yankee Pedlar or Traveling Merchant."
Also published as: *Wanderings of a Traveling Merchant.* Portland: Charles J. Clark, 1862. HEH

2071 ——— The Lone Star; or, The Texan Bravo. A Tale of the Southwest . . . Boston: F. Gleason's Publishing Hall, 1852. 100 p., illus. Printed in double cols. H, LC, N, NYP, UC
Also contains: Sweetbriar Cottage, by Joseph C. Baker.

2072 ——— The Maid of the Ranche; or, The Regulators and Moderators. A Story of Life on the Texan Border . . . New York: Frederic A. Brady, No. 24 Ann Street [186-?]. 100 p., illus. Y

2073 ——— Marion's Brigade; or, The Light Dragoons. A Tale of the Revolution . . . Boston: F. Gleason's Publishing Hall, 1852. 100 p., illus. Printed in double cols. AAS, BU, LC, UVB

2074 ——— Milrose; or, The Cotton-Planter's Daughter. A Tale of South Carolina . . . New York: Frederic A. Brady, 24 Ann Street [cop. 1862]. 110 p., illus. Printed in double cols.
Princeton University Library copy.

2075 ———— Mountain Max; or, Nick Whiffles on the Border. A Tale of the Bushwhackers in Missouri . . . New York: Frederic A. Brady, 24 Ann Street [cop. 1862]. 77 p., illus. Printed in double cols.   LC
LC copy deposited for copyright Aug. 8, 1863.

2076 ———— Nightshade; or, The Masked Robber of Hounslow Heath. A Romance of the Road . . . New York: Frederic A. Brady, 24 Ann Street [cop. 1861]. 100 p., illus. Printed in double cols.   AAS, LC

2077 ———— Noll Darker; or, The Ghost of Black Alley . . . New York: Frederic A. Brady, 1864.
Title listed in Kelly 1861-1866.

2078 ———— Pathaway; or, The Mountain Outlaws. A Tale of the Northern Hunting-Grounds . . . New York: Frederic A. Brady, 24 Ann Street [186-?]. 127 p., illus. Printed in double cols.   AAS
Laid in southern Alberta and northern Montana.

2079 ———— The Rebel Spy; or, The King's Volunteers. A Romance of the Siege of Boston . . . Boston: F. Gleason's Publishing Hall, 1852. 100 p., illus. Printed in double cols.   LC

2080 ———— Redpath; or, The Western Trail. A Story of Frontier Life and Adventure . . . New York: Samuel French, 121 Nassau Street [185-?]. 84 p. Printed in double cols.
Platte River country in Wyoming.   HEH, Y

2081 ———— Rosalthe; or, The Pioneers of Kentucky. A Tale of Western Life . . . Boston: F. Gleason's Publishing Hall, 1853. 100 p., illus. Printed in double cols.   NYP
Also contains: The Isle of Crows, by Mrs. E. C. Lovering.

2082 ———— The Round Pack: A Tale of the Forked Deer . . . New York: Frederic A. Brady, 22 Ann Street [186-?]. 72 p., illus. Printed in double cols.   AAS, HEH
Copyright notice dated 1862.

2083 ———— The Royal Greens; or, The Scout of the Susquehanna. A Tale of the Valley of Wyoming . . . New York: Samuel French, 121 Nassau Street [185-?]. 100 p. Printed in double cols.   BA, UM, Y

2084 ———— Scotto the Scout; or, The Union Rangers. A Tale of the Great Rebellion . . . New York: Frederic A. Brady, No. 24 Ann Street [cop. 1861]. 69 p., illus. Printed in double cols. Y

2085 ———— The Silver Bell; or, The Heir of Motcombe Manor. A Romance of Merry England . . . Boston: F. Gleason's Publishing Hall, 1853. 100 p., illus. Printed in double cols. AAS, UP

2086 ———— The Swordmaker of the Santee; or, Hirl the Hunchback . . . New York: Frederic A. Brady, No. 24 Ann Street [cop. 1861]. 95 p., illus. Printed in double cols. AAS, HEH
The American Revolution.

2087 ———— The White Rover; or, The Lovely Maid of Louisiana. A Romance of the Wild Forest . . . Boston: Frederick Gleason, 1852. 100 p. Printed in double cols. CU, NYP, Y
Also contains: The Unfinished Will, by Sylvanus Cobb.

2088 ———— Whitelaw; or, Nattie of the Lake Shore. A Tale of the Ten Mile Trace . . . New York: Frederic A. Brady, 24 Ann Street [cop. 1861]. 83 p., illus. Printed in double cols.
Lake Superior. N, Y

ROBINSON, MRS. M. E. A Country Residence. *In* S. Cobb, The Ocean Martyr [n.d.], No. 578.

———— The Prima Donna; or, The Pearl Necklace. *In* S. Cobb, The Wandering Guerrilla [185-?], No. 586.

2089 ROBINSON, MRS. MARTHA HARRISON. Helen Erskine . . . Philadelphia: J. B. Lippincott & Co., 1870. 255 p.
Laid in England. BP, HEH, LC, NYP, UV

2090 ROBINSON, MRS. MARY DUMMETT (NAUMAN). Clyde Wardleigh's Promise . . . Philadelphia: Claxton, Remsen & Haffelfinger, 1873. 300 p. BP, LC

2091 ———— Enchanted Princess . . . Philadelphia: Claxton, Remsen & Haffelfinger, 1871.
Title listed in Amer. Cat. 1876.

2092 ———— Sidney Elliott: A Novel . . . Philadelphia: Claxton, Remsen & Haffelfinger, 1869. 235 p. AAS, BP, HEH, LC

2093 ———— Twisted Threads . . . Philadelphia: Claxton, Remsen & Haffelfinger, 1870. 202 p. AAS, BP, LC

2094 ROBINSON, MRS. MARY STEPHENS. Glen Elm; or, Life in the West . . . Philadelphia: H. N. McKinney & Co., 1873. 59 p.
Announced as "ready, May 1" in PW, II (Apr. 5, 1873), 367.

2095 [ROBINSON, SOLON.] The Green-Mountain Girls: A Story of Vermont. By Blythe White, Jr. [pseud.] . . . New York: Derby & Jackson. Cincinnati: H. W. Derby, 1856. 406 p.
AAS, BP, BU, CU, HEH, UM, UP, Y

2096 [————] Home Comforts; or, Economy Illustrated by Familiar Scenes of Every-Day Life. By Lillie Savery [pseud.] . . . New York: Bunce & Brothers, 1855. 278 p.
Pages 277-278 advts. AAS, BP, H, LC, Y

2097 ———— Hot Corn: Life Scenes in New York Illustrated. Including the Story of Little Katy, Madalina, the Rag-Picker's Daughter, Wild Maggie, &c. . . . New York: DeWitt and Davenport, 1854. 408 p., illus.
AAS, BA, BU, CU, H, HEH, LC, N, NYH, NYP, UC, UM, UV, Y

2098 ———— How to Live: Saving and Wasting; or, Domestic Economy Illustrated by the Life of Two Families of Opposite Character, Habits, and Practices, in a Pleasant Tale of Real Life . . . New York: Fowler and Wells, 1860. 343 p.
BP, BU, LC, NYP
This is his *Home Comforts*, No. 2096, with an additional chapter. Miss Harriet Swift of BP determined this.

2099 ———— Me-Won-I-Toc: A Tale of Frontier Life and Indian Character . . . New York: New York News Company, 1867. 133 p. Printed in double cols.
AAS, BP, BU, H, HEH, LC, N, NYH, NYP, UM, UV, Y
Michigan and Illinois country.

2100 [ROBINSON, MRS. THERESE ALBERTINE LOUISE (VON JACOB).] The Exiles: A Tale. By Talvi [pseud.] . . . New York: G. P. Putnam & Co., 1853. 400 p. AAS, H, HEH, LCP, NYH, NYP, Y
Also published as: *Woodhill; or, The Ways of Providence*. New York: DeWitt & Davenport, 1856. BU, HEH, LCP, NYP
This ed. prints a new table of contents which changes the chapter headings, but the changes have not been made in the text. The running headlines have been changed.
The trials of a German couple in America.

2101 ———— Fifteen Years: A Picture from the Last Century ...
New York: D. Appleton & Company, 1871. 315 p.
AAS, BA, BP, CU, H, HEH, LCP, NYP

2102 [————] Life's Discipline: A Tale of the Annals of Hungary.
By Talvi [pseud.] ... New York: D. Appleton & Co. Phila-
delphia: Geo. S. Appleton, 1851. 171 p.
AAS, H, LC, LCP, NYP

ROBINSON, WILLIAM, *pseud*. *See* Jones, Justin

2103 ROCKWELL, MRS. M. E. Tom Miller; or, After Many Days ...
Philadelphia: J. C. Garrigues & Co., 1867. 351 p., illus.
Information from LC card for copy withdrawn from circulation.

RODMAN, ELLA, *pseud*. *See* Church, Mrs. Ella Rodman (Mac-
Ilvaine)

RODNEY, MRS. MARION CALHOUN LEGARÉ (REEVES). *See* Reeves,
Marion Calhoun Legaré

2104 ROE, AZEL STEVENS. The Cloud on the Heart: A Novel ...
New York: G. W. Carleton. London: S. Low, Son & Co.,
1869. 315 p. AAS, LCP, NYP

2105 ———— How Could He Help It? or, The Heart Triumphant
... New York: Derby & Jackson, 1860. 443 p.
Laid in New York City. AAS, CU, H, LC, NYP, UC

2106 ———— Like and Unlike ... New York: Carleton, 1862.
501 p. AAS, AP, BU, CU, NYP
Laid in New York City.

2107 ———— A Long Look Ahead; or, The First Stroke and the
Last ... New York: J. C. Derby. Boston: Phillips, Sampson
& Co. Cincinnati: H. W. Derby, 1855. 441 p.
BP, CU, NYP, UP

2108 ———— Looking Around: A Novel ... New York: Carleton, 1865. 312 p. AAS, CU, H, HEH, NYP, UM, Y
Laid in New York City.

2109 ———— Resolution; or, The Soul of Power ... New York:
G. W. Carleton & Co. London: S. Low, Son & Co., 1871.
348 p. AAS, CU, HEH, NYP

2110 ———— The Star and the Cloud; or, A Daughter's Love . . . New York: Derby & Jackson. Cincinnati: H. W. Derby & Co. London: Sampson Low, Son & Co., 1857. 410 p.
Laid in New Jersey.   AAS, CU, HEH, LCP, NYP, UP, Y

2111 ———— Time and Tide; or, Strive and Win . . . New York: D. Appleton & Company, 1852. 243 p.
New England farm and city life.   AAS, BP, CU, H, HEH, N, UP, Y

2112 ———— To Love and to Be Loved: A Story . . . New York: D. Appleton & Company. Philadelphia: Geo. S. Appleton, 1851. 190 p.   AAS, HEH, LC, NYP, Y
Laid in New York City.

2113 ———— True to the Last; or, Alone on a Wide Wide Sea . . . New York: Derby & Jackson, 1858. 384 p.
                    AAS, BU, CU, HEH, NYP, UP

2114 ———— Woman Our Angel: A Novel . . . New York: Carleton. London: S. Low, Son & Co., 1866. 312 p.
                    AAS, CU, H, HEH, NYP

2115 ROE, EDWARD PAYSON. Barriers Burned Away . . . New York: Dodd & Mead, 1872. 488 p.
                    AAS, BU, CU, H, HEH, LC, LCP, N, UP, UV, Y
At the time of the Chicago fire.

2116 ———— From Jest to Earnest . . . New York: Dodd & Mead [cop. 1875]. 548 p.   AAS, H, HEH, LC, LCP, UM, Y

2117 ———— Gentle Woman Roused: A Story of the Temperance Movement in the West . . . New York: National Temperance Society, 1874. Cover title, 24 p.   BP, NYP

2118 ———— Opening a Chestnut Burr . . . New York: Dodd & Mead, 762 Broadway [cop. 1874]. 561 p.
Laid in New York City.   AAS, H, HEH, LC, LCP, N, NYP, UP, UV, Y

2119 ———— What Can She Do? . . . New York: Dodd & Mead [cop. 1873]. 509 p.   AAS, BU, CU, H, HEH, LC, LCP, UM, UV, Y

2120 ROE, MRS. ELIZABETH A. Aunt Leanna; or, Early Scenes in Kentucky . . . Chicago: published for the author, 1855. 280 p., 1 l., illus.   HEH, N, NYH, NYP, UC, UM, Y
Antislavery.

2121 ROLAND TREVOR; or, The Pilot of Human Life. Being an Autobiography of the Author, Showing How to Make and Lose a Fortune, and Then to Make Another. Philadelphia: Lippincott, Grambo and Co., 1853. 415 p.   AAS, H, Y
LC enters under Trevor, Roland, as though this were authentic, which it may be.

ROMAINE, ROBERT DEXTER, *pseud.* See Payson, George

2122 THE ROMANCE OF AN IRISH GIRL; or, Life in Two Worlds. An Autobiography, with an Introduction by a Lady of New York. New York: Derby & Jackson, 1860. 408 p.   LCP
Introduction signed "F. F. B."

2123 ROOSEVELT, ROBERT BARNWELL. Five Acres Too Much: A Truthful Elucidation of the Attractions of the Country, and a Careful Consideration of the Question of Profit and Loss as Involved in Amateur Farming . . . New York: Harper & Brothers, 1869. 296 p., illus.
               AAS, BA, BP, H, HEH, LC, LCP, N, NYH, NYP, UC, UM, Y
Humorous satire.

2124 ―――― Progressive Petticoats; or, Dressed to Death. An Autobiography of a Married Man . . . New York: G. W. Carleton & Co. London: S. Low, Son & Co., 1874. 316 p.
Humorous satire.   AAS, CU, H, HEH, LC, LCP, NYP, Y

2125 ROPES, MRS. HANNAH ANDERSON. Cranston House: A Novel . . . Boston: Otis Clapp, 1859. 388 p., front.
                    AAS, BP, CU, H, HEH, NYP, Y

2126 ROSE, HENRIETTA. Nora Wilmot: A Tale of Temperance and Woman's Rights . . . Columbus [Ind.]: Osgood & Pearce, stereotypers and printers, 1858. 368 p., front.
                    HEH, NYH, UM

2127 ROSE MILTON: A ROMANCE . . . Philadelphia: Parry and McMillan, 1855. 275 p.   LC
Southern society; on the evils of dueling.

2128 ROSENBERG, CHARLES G.   The Roman Soprano; or, The Captain of the Swiss Guard . . . New York: Samuel French, 121 Nassau Street [185-?].   100 p.   Printed in double cols.

AAS, H, HEH, NYP

Also contains: The Moorish Captives, by H. H. Heath—The Captain's Passage, by Austin C. Burdick.

———— *ed. See* Perrie, George W. Buckskin Mose . . . Edited . . . by C. G. Rosenberg (1873), No. 1876.

ROSWYTHA, *pseud. See* Nelson, Augusta R.

2129 ROTH, EDWARD.   Christus Judex: A Traveller's Tale . . .   Philadelphia: Frederick Leypoldt, 1864.   78 p.

AAS, BP, CU, H, HEH, LC, LCP, NYP, UP

2130 ROUGEGORGE and Other Short Stories . . .   Forming the Third Series of "Short Stories for Spare Moments," Reprinted from Lippincott's Magazine.   Philadelphia: J. B. Lippincott & Co., 1870.   148 p., front.   Printed in double cols.   AAS, BP, LC

Contents: Rougegorge, by Harriet Prescott Spofford—Sam's Sermon, by S. Watkins Tuttle—The Shadow of Fate, by Riter Fitzgerald—The Prince's Surprise—My Grandmother That Might Have Been, by Alice Cary—Snow upon the Waters, by Lucy H. Hooper—That Man—Harney-how's Hummock, by Jane G. Austin—Myra's Mirror, by James Franklin Fitts—Dick Libby, by George Jones—Dick Lyle's Fee, by L. Clarke Davis—Peter Crisp's Spectacles, by Solomon Soberside—Only No Love, Trans. by Mrs. A. L. Wister—The Price of a Dream, by Frank Lee Benedict.

2131 RUBINA.   New York: James G. Gregory, 1864.   468 p.

A novel of life and manners.   BP, CU, H, HEH, LCP, NYP, Y

2132 RUDDY, MRS. ELLA AUGUSTA (GILES).   Bachelor Ben . . .   Madison, Wis.: Atwood & Culver.   Chicago: Jansen, McClurg & Company, 1875.   308 p.   AAS, BP, CU, LC, UM

Also issued with imprint: Chicago: Jansen, McClurg & Co. Madison: Atwood & Culver, 1875.   HEH

2133 RUFFIN, MRS. R. M.   Tales and Sketches for the Fireside; Which Is Most Respectfully Dedicated to Every Southern Home Circle . . .   Marion, Ala.: printed at the book and job office of Dennis Dykous, 1858.   173 p.

Title listed in R. C. Ellison, *A Check List of Alabama Imprints, 1807-1870* (University, Ala., 1946), No. 1092.

2134 [RULISON, H. M.] The Mock Marriage; or, The Libertine's
Victim. Being a Faithful Delineation of the Mysteries and
Miseries of the Queen City. Cincinnati: Barclay & Co.
[1855]. 102 p., illus.   NYH

2135 RUNKEL, WILLIAM M. Wontus; or, The Corps of Observation
. . . Philadelphia: J. B. Lippincott & Co., 1874. 363 p., illus.
The Civil War, 1861-1862 period.   AAS, BP, HEH, LC, LCP, UP

2136 RUNNING A TIME TABLE: A Brakeman's Story. Burlington,
Vt.: Henry & Johnson [cop. 1873]. 16 p.   AAS
At head of title: "A Thrilling Tale."

2137 [RUSH, MRS. CAROLINE E.] The Dew-Drop of the Sunny South:
A Story Written from Every Day Life . . . Philadelphia:
published for the authoress by Crissy & Markley, 1851. 213
p., illus.   HEH, NYH

2138 [———] The North and South; or, Slavery and Its Contrasts.
A Tale of Real Life . . . Philadelphia: published for the
author by Crissy & Markley, 1852. 350 p., illus.
            BU, CU, H, HEH, LC, N, NYH, NYP, UC, UM, UP, Y
In answer to "Uncle Tom."

2139 [———] Way-Marks in the Life of a Wanderer. The Incidents Taken from Real Life . . . Philadelphia: published for
the author by Crissy & Markley [1855?]. 310 p., front.
                      AAS, BP, CU, HEH, N, NYP, UM, UP

2140 [RUSSELL, CHARLES WELLS.] Roebuck: A Novel. New York:
M. Doolady, 1866. 329 p.
The Civil War, 1861-1862 period.   AAS, BP, HEH, LC, N, NYP, UV, Y

2141 RUSSELL, DAVID, *pseud.?* Autobiography of David Russell, a
Boston Boy and True American. An Account of His Travels,
Romantic Adventures and Hair Breadth Escapes by Sea and
Land . . . from the Age of Sixteen Years to Sixty-Seven . . .
Boston: printed for the author, 1857. 372 p., illus.
                              BA, BP, H, HEH, NYH

2142 RUSSELL, JOHN. Claudine Lavalle; or, The First Convict. The
Mormoness; or, The Trials of Mary Maverick . . . Alton
[Ill.]: Courier Steam Press print., 1853. 89 p.   Y

2143 RUSSELL, MARTHA. Leaves from the Tree Igdrasyl . . . Boston: John P. Jewett and Company. Cleveland, Ohio: Jewett, Proctor & Worthington. New York: Sheldon, Lamport & Blakeman, 1854. 348 p. AAS, CU, H, HEH, NYP, UC, UP, Y
Contents: The Diary—Love's Labor Not Lost—A Tale of the Colony Times—Uncle John's Visit—An Incident on the Sea-Shore—Death by the Way-Side—Little Bessie—Sketches of Our Village.
Also published as: Stories of New England Life; or, Leaves from the Tree Igdrasyl. Boston: John P. Jewett and Company. Cleveland, Ohio: Jewett, Proctor and Worthington. New York: Sheldon, Lamport and Blakeman, 1856. BP, CU, HEH, LC, NYP, UP

2144 ———— Sibyl; or, Out of the Shadow into the Sun . . . Boston and Chicago: L. P. Crown and Company. Philadelphia: J. W. Bradley. Toronto: C. W. Bostwick & Barnard, 1857. 368 p. AAS, HEH, Y
Also published as: Sybil Monroe, the Forger's Daughter; or, Out of the Shadow into the Sun. Boston: L. P. Crown and Company, 1859. LC
This title also issued with imprint: Philadelphia: G. G. Evans, 1859. NYP

2145 RUTH: A SONG IN THE DESERT . . . Boston: Gould and Lincoln, 1864. 64 p. AAS
On the loss of a soldier-husband.

2146 RUTH CHURCHILL; or, The True Protestant. A Tale for the Times. By a Lady of Virginia. New York: C. Shepard & Co., 1851. 224 p. BU

2147 S., E. O. Isolina; or, The Actor's Daughter . . . Philadelphia: J. B. Lippincott & Co., 1873. 479 p. AAS, H, LCP

2148 [SAGE, ROBERT F.] Charette: A Tale "of Lovers' Sorrows and Their Tangled Sin" . . . New York: G. W. Carleton & Co. London: Low & Co., 1875. 327 p. AAS, BP, H, HEH, LC

2149 ST. CLAIR, FRANK. Six Days in the Metropolis; or, Phases of Life in Town . . . Boston: Redding & Company, 1854. 96 p.
Laid in Boston. H, LC, NYP, UC, UM, Y

2150 ST. CLAR, ROBERT. The Metropolites; or, Know Thy Neighbor. A Novel . . . New York: American News Company, 121 Nassau Street [cop. 1864]. 575 p.
Laid in New York City. AAS, BU, CU, H, HEH, LC, LCP, NYP, Y

2151 ST. GEORGE DE LISLE; or, The Serpent's Sting. A Tale of Woman's Devotion & Self-Sacrifice . . . A True and Thrilling Narrative of Crime in High Life in the City of New York. Philadelphia: Barclay & Co., 734 Market Street [cop. 1858]. 34 p., 1 l., illus.   LC, NYH, Y

ST. JOHN, MRS. EUGENIA, *pseud.* *See* Berry, Mrs. Martha Eugenia

ST. LEON, M. V. The Gipsy's Prediction. *In* S. Cobb, The Juggler of Nankin [185-?], No. 571.

———— Harry Percy Howard. *In* B. P. Poore, Aurora [185-?], No. 1926.

———— The Prima Donna. *In* M. M. Ballou, The Duke's Prize [185-?], No. 203.

ST. REMY, DIRCK, *pseud.* *See* Lee, J. Wilke

SAM, *Invisible, pseud.* *See* Vose, Reuben

2152 [SANDS, ALEXANDER HAMILTON.] Some Passages in the Life of Geoffrey Clinker, Esq. [pseud.], Written by Himself. Richmond: MacFarlane & Fergusson, 1854. 34 p.   HEH
At head of title: "The Clinker Manuscripts."
Introduction and footnotes signed "I. W."
Laid in Virginia, 1773-1783.

SANS SOUCI, *pseud.* *See* McAfee, Mrs. Nelly Nichol (Marshall)

SARGENT, EPES. On Lake Pepin. *In* The Knickerbocker Gallery (1855), No. 1492.

2153 ———— Peculiar: A Tale of the Great Transition . . . New York: Carleton, 1864. 500 p.
AAS, AP, BA, BP, BU, CU, H, HEH, LC, LCP, N, NYH, NYP, UM, UV, Y
From slavery to freedom.

2154 SAUZADE, JOHN S. Garret Van Horn; or, The Beggar on Horseback . . . New York: Carleton, 1863. 376 p.
AAS, BP, CU, H, HEH, LC, NYH, NYP
Laid in New York and New Jersey about 1840.

2155 ———— Mark Gildersleeve: A Novel . . . New York: G. W. Carleton & Co. London: S. Low, Son & Co., 1873. 379 p.
"Belton" on the Passaic River.   AAS, BP, CU, H, HEH, LC, NYP, Y

2156 [SAVAGE, MRS. MARY L. (BRADBURY).] Miramichi. First Edition. Boston: Loring, 1865. 232 p.   AAS, CU, HEH, LC, NYP
Also published as: *Adèle Dubois: A Story of the Lovely Miramichi Valley in New Brunswick.* Boston: Loring [cop. 1865].   LC

SAVERY, LILLIE, *pseud. See* Robinson, Solon

2157 SAWYER, MOSES H. Lieutenant Colborn; or, The Disinherited ... Portland: published by the author. For sale by Bailey & Noyes, 1861. 349 p.   AAS, BU, UM
England at the end of the 18th century.

2158 SAYMORE, SARAH EMERY. Hearts Unveiled; or, "I Knew You Would Like Him" ... New York: D. Appleton & Company, 1852. 300 p.   AAS, HEH, LC, NYP, UP, Y

SCANLAND, AGNES LEONARD. *See* Hill, Mrs. Agnes (Leonard) Scanland

2159 [SCHENCK, MRS. J. V.] Cousin Paul. By Jessie Glenn [pseud.]. New York: G. W. Carleton & Co. London: S. Low, Son & Co., 1868. 332 p.   AAS, BP, LCP, NYP
Allibone gives her name as Mrs. J. W. Schenck.
Fashionable life in New York City.

2160 SCHILLER, EDWARD. Cherry Blossom; or, "Love Thy Neighbor as Thyself" ... New York: Robert M. DeWitt, 1860. 366 p.   CU

2161 [SCHMUCKER, SAMUEL MOSHEIM.] The Planter's Victim; or, Incidents of American Slavery ... Philadelphia: Wm. White Smith, 1855. 365 p., illus.
   AAS, CU, H, HEH, LC, N, NYH, UC, UP
Also published as: *The Yankee Slave Driver; or, The Black and White Rivals.* New York: H. Dayton. Indianapolis, Ind.: Asher & Co., 1859. H
Antislavery; Louisiana.

2162 SCHOOLCRAFT, MRS. MARY (HOWARD). The Black Gauntlet: A Tale of Plantation Life in South Carolina ... Philadelphia: J. B. Lippincott & Co., 1860. 569 p.
   AAS, BA, BU, CU, H, HEH, LC, N, NYP, UM, UV

2163 SCHUYLER, MONTGOMERY. The Pioneer Church; or, The Story of a New Parish in the West ... New York: Hurd and Houghton. Boston: E. P. Dutton and Company, 1867. 211 p., illus.   BA, BP, HEH, LC, LCP, N, NYP

2164 SCIAN DUBH, *pseud.* Ridgeway: An Historical Romance of the Fenian Invasion of Canada. By Scian Dubh [pseud.] . . . Buffalo: McCarroll & Co., 1868. 262 p.   BP, HEH, UM

2165 SCOTFORD, JOHN. The Judd Family; or, An Evening Visit and What Came of It. Being an Elucidation of Baptism—Ceremonial and Spiritual—or, Scriptural Baptism . . . Ann Arbor, Michigan: Dr. Chase's Steam Printing House, 1869. 304 p., 1 l.   BP, CU, HEH

2166 SCOTT, ROSA. Marian Wallace; or, Life's Changes. A Tale of Truth . . . New York: Derby & Jackson, 1858. 369 p.   LC

2167 SCOVILLE, JOSEPH ALFRED. Clarence Bolton: A New York Story, with City Society in All Its Phases . . . New York: Garrett & Co., 1852. 104 p., illus.   AAS, UC
Cover title: "The Adventures of Clarence Bolton; or, Life in New York."

2168 [————] Vigor: A Novel. By Walter Barrett [pseud.] . . . New York: Carleton, 1864. 428 p.
AAS, H, HEH, LC, LCP, N, NYH, NYP, UVB

2169 [SCRIBNER, ISAAC W.] Laconia; or, Legends of the White Mountains and Merry Meeting Bay. By an Old Mountaineer . . . Boston: B. B. Mussey and Company, 1854. 489 p.
AAS, BA, BP, HEH, N, NYP, Y
Also published as: *Rozella of Laconia; or, Legends of the White Mountains.* Boston: James French & Co., 1857.   AAS, BP, CU, UP

2170 SEA STORIES Now First Collected and Forming the Fifth Volume of "Putnam's Story Library." New York: G. P. Putnam, 1858. 276 p., front.   AAS, H
At head of title: "Putnam's Library of Choice Stories."

2171 SEALS, A. B. Rockford: A Romance . . . Atlanta, Georgia: Franklin Printing House; Wood, Hanleiter, Rice & Co., 1861. 275, [1] p.   BA, BP, HEH, LC

2172 [SEALSFIELD, CHARLES.] Frontier Life; or, Scenes and Adventures in the Southwest. By Francis [i.e., Frederick] Hardman [Ed. and Trans.]. Buffalo: Derby, Orton & Mulligan, 1853. 376 p., front.   NYP

Contents: Adventures in Louisiana—Adventures in Texas—Two Nights in Southern Mexico—A Sketch in the Tropics—A Tale of the Mexican War —The Texan Ranger's Best Shot.

Also issued with imprint: Buffalo: Derby, Orton and Mulligan. Auburn: Derby and Miller, 1853. BP, CU, Y

2173 SEARCHING FOR THE WHITE ELEPHANT IN NEW YORK: A Humorous Record of Many Adventures. New York: published at the office of "Wild Oats," 113 Fulton Street [cop. 1872]. 47, 47 p., illus. Printed in double cols. LC
Also contains: Kicked into Good Luck, by John Carboy (2d numbering).

2174 SEARS, EDMUND HAMILTON. Pictures of the Olden Time, as Shown in the Fortunes of a Family of the Pilgrims ... Boston: Crosby, Nichols and Company. Cincinnati: George S. Blanchard. London: Sampson Low, Son and Co., 1857. 342 p.
AAS, BA, BP, BU, CU, H, HEH, LC, LCP, N, NYH, NYP, UC, UP, Y
Contents: The Exile—The Adventurer—The Pilgrim.

2175 SEATON, WALTER. A Man in Search of a Wife; or, The Adventures of a Bachelor in New York ... New York: DeWitt & Davenport, 160 & 162 Nassau Street [cop. 1853]. 100 p., illus. BU, LC
LC copy deposited for copyright Apr. 15, 1853.

SEAWORTHY, *Capt.* Gregory, *pseud.* *See* Throop, George Higby

2176 SECRETS OF A YOUNG GIRL in Words and Pictures. New York: F. Kahlau, 60 New Chambers Street [n.d.]. 50 p. HEH
A tale of the London music halls.

2177 [SEDGWICK, CATHARINE MARIA.] Married or Single? ... New York: Harper & Brothers, 1857. 2 vols. (261, 284 p.)
AAS, BA, BP, BU, CU, H, HEH, LC, LCP, N, NYP, UC, UP, UVB, Y
Laid in New York City.

2178 ———— A New England Tale, and Miscellanies ... New York: George P. Putnam & Co., 1852. 388 p.
AAS, CU, H, LC, N, NYP, UM, UP, UVB
Also contains: A Berkshire Tradition—The White Scarf—Fanny McDermot.
Title story is Wright (1774-1850), No. 2356; additional material is new.

2179 [SEDGWICK, MRS. SUSAN ANNE LIVINGSTON (RIDLEY).] Walter Thornley; or, A Peep at the Past . . . New York: Harper & Brothers, 1859. 486 p.

AAS, BU, CU, H, HEH, LCP, NYP, UC, UP, Y

Laid in Massachusetts about 1780.

2180 [SEDLEY, HENRY.] Dangerfield's Rest; or, Before the Storm. A Novel of American Life and Manners. New York: Sheldon & Company, 1864. 392 p. AAS, H, HEH, LCP, NYP, UP, Y

2181 ———— Marian Rooke; or, The Quest for Fortune. A Tale of the Younger World . . . New York: Sheldon & Company, 1865. 475 p. AAS, BP, CU, HEH, LCP, N, NYP, Y

California, New York, etc., 1850's.

2182 THE SEDLEY FAMILY; or, The Effect of the Maine Liquor Law. Boston: T. O. Walker, 1853. 209 p., illus. AAS, CU, NYP

2183 [SEEMÜLLER, MRS. ANNE MONCURE (CRANE).] Emily Chester: A Novel . . . Boston: Ticknor and Fields, 1864. 367 p.

Laid in Baltimore. AAS, BA, BP, CU, H, HEH, LC, NYP, UC, UP, Y

2184 ———— Opportunity: A Novel . . . Boston: Ticknor and Fields, 1867. 336 p.

AAS, BA, BP, BU, H, HEH, LC, LCP, NYP, UP, UV, Y

Pre-Civil War Maryland.

2185 ———— Reginald Archer: A Novel . . . Boston: James R. Osgood & Company, 1871. 386 p.

AAS, BA, BP, CU, H, HEH, LC, LCP, NYP, UP, UV, Y

Also issued with imprint: Boston: James R. Osgood & Company, 1871. 147 p. Printed in double cols. NYP

2186 SELDON, WILLIAM N., *pseud.* The Extraordinary and All-Absorbing Journal of Wm. N. Seldon, One of a Party of Three Men Who Belonged to the Exploring Expedition of Sir John Franklin, and Who Left the Ship Terror, Frozen Up in Ice, in the Arctic Ocean, on the 10th Day of June, 1850 . . . Detroit, Mich.: E. E. Barclay; A. R. Orton & Co., 1851. 36 p., illus. CU, LC

2187 SELLES, MRS. S. E. Amy's Temptation; or, One Year with the Leonard Family. Cincinnati: Hitchcock & Walden, 1875. Announced as "just published" in PW, VIII (Aug. 21, 1875), 366.

2188 SENTER, A. E. The Diddler ... New York: M. Doolady, 1868.
96, 34, 21, 40 p., illus.   AAS, H, HEH, LC, NYP, UM, Y
Also contains: Hodge-Podge—Items from Joe Miller—Raising the Wind:
A Farce, by James Kenney.

2189 SETON, WILLIAM. Nat Gregory; or, The Old Maid's Secret. A
Novel . . . New York: Hilton & Company, 1867. 144 p.
Printed in double cols.   BP, CU, LC

2190 ———— The Pride of Lexington: A Tale of the American
Revolution ... New York: P. O'Shea, 45 Warren St. [1874].
365 p.   AAS, BU
Announced as "just published" in PW, V (Jan. 17, 1874), 46.

2191 ———— Romance of the Charter Oak: A Picture of Colonial
Times ... New York: P. O'Shea, 1871. 2 vols. (424, 350 p.)
Laid in Connecticut, late 17th century.   AAS, CU, NYH, NYP

SEVERANCE, MARK SIBLEY. Spoons in a Wherry. *In* Thirteen
Good Stories [1873?], No. 2457.

2192 SHADOW, BEN, *pseud.* Echoes of a Belle; or, A Voice from the
Past. By Ben Shadow [pseud.] ... New York: George P.
Putnam & Co., 1853. 196 p.
      AAS, BP, BU, HEH, LC, N, NYP, UM, UP, Y
Author may be a Mrs. Middleton, nee Irving.
Southern social life prior to and including the War of 1812.

SHANLY, CHARLES DAWSON. A Night in the Sewers. *In* Stories
and Sketches (1867), No. 2386.

2193 [SHARON, THOMAS.] Viola; or, Life in the Northwest. By a
Western Man. This Book Illustrates the Peculiar Habits and
Customs of the People . . . with Incidents of the Minnesota
Massacre ... Chicago: R. R. McCabe & Co., printers, 1874.
422 p., illus.   AAS, CU, H, HEH, LC, N, NYP, UM, UP, Y
Editor's preface signed "C. D. P." and dated "Menasha, Wis., June, 1874."

2194 [SHAW, HENRY WHEELER.] Everybody's Friend; or, Josh
Billing's [pseud.] Encyclopedia and Proverbial Philosophy of
Wit and Humor ... Hartford, Conn.: American Publishing
Company, 1874. 617 p., illus.
Humorous sketches.   AAS, BP, CU, HEH, LC, LCP, N, UC, UM

2195 [————] Josh Billings, Hiz Sayings . . . New York: Carleton, 1866. 232 p., illus.

AAS, BP, H, HEH, LC, LCP, N, NYP, UC, Y

2196 [————] Josh Billings on Ice, and Other Things . . . New York: G. W. Carleton & Co. London: J. C. Hotton, 1868. 263 p., illus. AAS, BP, HEH, LC, LCP, NYP, UC, UM, Y

SHEELAH, *pseud. See* Fletcher, Miss A.

2197 SHELTON, FREDERICK WILLIAM. Crystalline; or, The Heiress of Fall Down Castle. A Romance . . . New York: Charles Scribner, 1854. 202 p., illus.

AAS, BP, CU, H, HEH, LC, LCP, N, NYP, UC, UP, Y

Also contains: Clarence: A Domestic Story.

———— Gentle Dove: An Indian Legend. *In* The Knickerbocker Gallery (1855), No. 1492.

2198 ———— Peeps from a Belfry; or, The Parish Sketch Book . . . New York: Charles Scribner, 1855. 294 p.

AAS, BP, CU, H, NYP, UC, UV, Y

Contents: The Lost Tomb-Stone—Golden-Mouthed Taylor—A Burial among the Mountains—St. Peter's at Rosendale—The Square Pew—The Model Parish—The Child's Funeral—The Two Neighbors—The Heart of Adamant.

2199 ———— Peeps from a Belfry. By Rev. F. W. Shelton . . . New York: Dana and Company, 1856. 304 p. H, LC

Contents: [same as above and two new stories] The Seven Sleepers—Father Boyle.

2200 ———— The Rector of St. Bardolph's; or, Superannuated . . . New York: Charles Scribner, 1853. 344 p., front.

AAS, BP, BU, CU, H, HEH, LC, NYP, UP, UVB, Y

SHELTON-MACKENZIE, MRS. ADELHEID. *See* MacKenzie, Mrs. Adelheid (Zwissler)

2201 [SHEPHERD, DANIEL.] Saratoga: A Story of 1787. New York: W. P. Fetridge & Co. Boston: Williams & Co., 1856. 400 p.

AAS, BU, CU, HEH, LC, NYP, UC, UP, Y

SHEPPARD, CHARLES. The Way Dodge Started Himself. *In* Dodge's Sketches [1853], No. 1751.

SHEPPARD, MRS. EDWIN. *See* Sheppard, Mrs. Lydia H.

2202 SHEPPARD, FRANCIS HENRY. Love Afloat: A Story of the American Navy . . . New York: Sheldon & Company, 677 Broadway [cop. 1875]. 483 p.

Piracy in the West Indies, 1823.   AAS, BA, BU, HEH, LC, LCP, NYP, Y

2203 SHEPPARD, MRS. LYDIA H. "Judge Not;" or, Hester Powers' Girlhood . . . Boston: Loring, 1868. 224 p.   AAS, BP, LC, NYP
Laid in England.

2204 SHERTZER, ABRAM TREGO. Trials and Triumphs: A Novel . . . Baltimore: printing house of Sherwood & Co., 1875. 249 p.

Concerns an American surgeon in the Prussian war.   AAS, NYP, UV

2205 SHERWOOD, JOHN D. The Comic History of the United States from a Period Prior to the Discovery of America to Times Long Subsequent to the Present . . . Boston: Fields, Osgood & Co., 1870. 549 p., illus.

AAS, BP, BU, CU, H, HEH, LC, LCP, NYH, NYP, UC, UM, Y

2206 SHIELDS, MRS. SARAH ANNIE (FROST). A Coat of Many Colors . . . Albany: J. Munsell, 1862. 300 p.   AAS, BP, CU, H, HEH
Short stories.

2207 SHILLABER, BENJAMIN PENHALLOW. Knitting-Work: A Web of Many Textures, Wrought by Ruth Partington (B. P. Shillaber) . . . Boston: Brown, Taggard & Chase. New York: Sheldon & Company. Philadelphia: J. B. Lippincott & Co., 1859. 408 p., illus.

AAS, AP, BP, BU, CU, HEH, LC, LCP, N, NYH, NYP, UC, UM, UP, UVB, Y

Also published as: *Mrs. Partington's Knitting Work.* Philadelphia: John E. Potter, 1868.   AAS

2208 ———— Life and Sayings of Mrs. Partington and Others of the Family. Edited by B. P. Shillaber . . . New York: J. C. Derby. Boston: Phillips, Sampson and Company. Cincinnati: H. W. Derby, 1854. 384 p., illus.

AAS, BA, BP, BU, CU, H, HEH, LCP, N, NYP, UC, UM, UP, UVB, Y

Also issued with imprint: New York: J. C. Derby. Chicago: D. B. Cooke & Co., 1854.   NYH

2209 ——— Partingtonian Patchwork. Blifkins the Martyr: The Domestic Trials of a Model Husband. The Modern Syntax: Dr. Spooner's Experiences in Search of the Delectable . . . Boston: Lee and Shepard. New York: Lee, Shepard and Dillingham, 1873. 360 p., illus.

AAS, BA, BP, BU, CU, HEH, LC, LCP, NYP, UC, UM, UVB, Y

2210 SHORT STORIES FOR SPARE MOMENTS. Selected from Lippincott's Magazine. Philadelphia: J. B. Lippincott and Co., 1869. 146 p. Printed in double cols. AAS, LC

Contents: Alas, Poor Ghost, by Leonard Kip—Lady Haughton's Mistake, by Annie Thomas—To Please Aunt Martha, by Margaret Hosmer—Ranlock Branch, by J. T. McKay—The Forget-Me-Not, by Gustave zu Putlitz—A Wreck upon the Shore, by L. Clark Davis—The Strange Passengers, by Harriet Prescott Spofford—Love and Ghosts, by D. B. Dorsey—Loyal en Tout, by Kate P. Kereven—The Legend of Ball's Lake, by Rev. R. Wilson—Vox Humana, by Anne Brewster—Willie's Wife, by Rosamond Dale Owen—Made Whole, by Maria L. Pool—Love on the Ohio, by D. B. Dorsey.

2211 ——— 2d ser. Philadelphia: J. B. Lippincott and Co., 1869. 150 p. Printed in double cols. LC

Contents: The Record of Dorcas Bently, by Caroline Chesebro'—The Blue Cabinet, by Lucy Hamilton Hooper—Golden Dreams, by Albert Fabre—The Pearl of Great Price, by Rebecca Harding Davis—Nor Dead, nor Living, by Jane G. Austin—Doctor Aar, by Kate P. Kereven—The Mannerings, by Louise S. Dorr—Mahala's Drive, by F. R. Stockton—The Photographer's Story, by Lucy H. Hooper—Who Shall Separate Us, by Mary W. Janvrin—The Young Priest, by W. Maud Evelyn—Ricardo Il Falcone, by Robert Boggs.

2212 [SHREVE, THOMAS HOPKINS.] Drayton: A Story of American Life. New York: Harper & Brothers, 1851. 274 p.

AAS, HEH, LC, N, NYP, UC, UP, UV

2213 SHRIMPTON, CHARLES. The Black Phantom; or, Woman's Endurance. A Narrative Connected with the Early History of Canada and the American Revolution . . . New York: James Miller, 1867. 358 p. AAS, BP, H, HEH, Y

Also issued with imprint: New York: Crowen & Company, 1867. LC, NYP

Also published as: Lillian; or, Woman's Endurance. New York: N. Tibbals & Co., 1868. LCP

2214 [SHUBRICK, MRS. HARRIET CORDELIA (WETHERED).] Violet; or, The Times We Live in. Philadelphia: J. B. Lippincott & Co., 1858. 247 p. LC, NYP, UC, Y

Laid in Philadelphia.

2215 SHUMAN, ANDREW. The Loves of a Lawyer, His Quandary and How It Came Out . . . Chicago: W. B. Keen, Cooke & Co., 1875. 214 p. CU

2216 THE SIGNET OF HIRAM: A Tale of the First Temple. New York: Masonic Tidings Publishing House, 1874. Cover title, 74 p. LC

At head of title: "Ransom's Library of Cheap Masonic Publications."

2217 SIGOURNEY, MRS. LYDIA HOWARD (HUNTLEY). Lucy Howard's Journal . . . New York: Harper & Brothers, 1858. 343 p.

AAS, BA, BP, BU, CU, H, HEH, LC, LCP, N, NYH, NYP,
The journal begins in 1810.   UC, UM, UP, UV, Y

2218 SIKES, WILLIAM WIRT. A Book for the Winter-Evening Fireside . . . Watertown, N. Y.: Ingalls & Haddock, 1858. 96 p., illus. H, LC

2219 ———— One Poor Girl: The Story of Thousands . . . Philadelphia: J. B. Lippincott & Co., 1869. 255 p.

AAS, LC, LCP, NYP

———— The Rev. Mr. Tympan's Misfortune. *In* Tales of the Time [1861], No. 2426.

———— Under a Cloud. *In* Stories and Sketches (1867), No. 2386.

SIKES, MRS. WILLIAM WIRT. *See* Logan, Olive.

SILVERVALE, LUMINA, *pseud. See* Suddoth, Mrs. Harriet Almaria (Baker)

2220 [SIMMS, WILLIAM GILMORE.] As Good as a Comedy; or, The Tennesseean's Story. By an Editor . . . Philadelphia: A. Hart, 1852. 251 p.   H, HEH, LC, UVB, Y

2221 ———— The Cassique of Kiawah: A Colonial Romance . . . New York: Redfield, 1859. 600 p., front.

AAS, BA, CU, H, HEH, LCP, N, NYP, UP, UVB, Y

2222 ———— Charlemont; or, The Pride of the Village. A Tale of Kentucky . . . New York: Redfield, 1856. 447 p., front.

AAS, BA, BP, BU, CU, H, HEH, N, NYH, NYP, UC, UM, UP, UVB, Y

2223 ———— Eutaw. A Sequel to The Forayers; or, The Raid of the Dog-Days. A Tale of the Revolution . . . New York: Redfield, 1856. 582 p., front.

AAS, BA, BU, CU, H, HEH, LC, N, UC, UM, UP, UVB, Y

2224 ———— The Forayers; or, The Raid of the Dog-Days . . . New York: Redfield, 1855. 560 p., front.

AAS, BA, BU, H, HEH, LC, N, UM, UP, UVB, Y

Laid in South Carolina during the American Revolution.

2225 [————] The Golden Christmas: A Chronicle of St. John's, Berkeley. Compiled from the Notes of a Briefless Barrister . . . Charleston: Walker, Richards and Co., 1852. 168 p.

AAS, BP, H, HEH, LC, LCP, NYH, NYP, UP, UVB, Y

Social life on a Southern plantation.

2226 [————] Katharine Walton; or, The Rebel of Dorchester. An Historical Romance of the Revolution in Carolina . . . Philadelphia: A. Hart, 1851. 186 p. Printed in double cols.

AAS, H, LC, NYH, UP, UVB, Y

2227 [————] ———— New and Revised Edition. New York: Redfield, 1854. 474 p., front.

AAS, BP, BU, HEH, LCP, N, NYH, UP, UV, Y

Four-page dedication to the "Hon. Edward Frost, of South Carolina," dated "Woodland, April 1854," added.

2228 ———— Marie de Berniere: A Tale of the Crescent City . . . Philadelphia: Lippincott, Grambo and Co., 1853. 422 p.

AAS, AP, BU, H, HEH, LC, LCP, NYP, UM, UP, UVB, Y

Also contains: The Maroon: A Legend of the Caribbees—Maize in Milk: A Christmas Story of the South.

Also published as: *The Maroon: A Legend of the Caribbees, and Other Tales.* Philadelphia: Lippincott, Grambo & Co., 1855. AAS, H, HEH

The title story *Marie de Berniere* was published separately as: *The Ghost of My Husband: A Tale of the Crescent City.* New York: Chapman & Company, 116 Nassau Street [cop. 1866]. 114 p., front. AAS, H

2229 ———— Southward Ho! A Spell of Sunshine . . . New York: Redfield, 1854. 472 p.

AAS, BA, CU, H, HEH, LC, LCP, N, NYH, NYP, UC, UP, UVB, Y

2230 [————] The Sword and the Distaff; or, "Fair, Fat and Forty." A Story of the South at the Close of the Revolution . . . Second Edition. Charleston: Walker, Richards & Co., 1852. 591 p. BA, UVB

2231 [————] ———— Philadelphia: Lippincott, Grambo &
Co., 1853. 591 p.   CU, LC, N, NYP, UP, UV
Also published as: *Woodcraft; or, Hawks about the Dovecote . . . New
and Revised Edition.* New York: Redfield, 1854. 518 p.   BU, CU,
H, HEH, LC, NYP, UV, Y

2232 [————] Vasconselos: A Romance of the New World. By
Frank Cooper [pseud.] . . . New York: Redfield, 1853.
531 p.   AAS, BP, H, HEH, NYP, UP, UVB, Y
At the time of De Soto.

SIOGVOLK, PAUL, *pseud.* *See* Mathews, Albert

2233 SISTER AGNES; or, The Captive Nun. A Picture of Convent Life.
By a Clergyman's Widow . . . New York: Riker, Thorne &
Co., 1854. 412 p., illus.   AAS, NYH, UM

2234 THE SISTERS OF ORLEANS: A Tale of Race and Social Conflict.
New York: G. P. Putnam & Sons, 1871. 341 p.
AAS, BP, H, HEH, LC, NYH, Y

2235 SIX HUNDRED DOLLARS A YEAR. A Wife's Effort at Low Living,
under High Prices. Boston: Ticknor and Fields, 1867.
183 p.   AAS, H, HEH, LC
Depicts income taxes and the cost of living during the Civil War.

2236 SKETCH, WALTER. The Down-Trodden; or, Black Blood and
White . . . New York: Jonathan Miller, Jr., 1853. 89 p.
Printed in double cols.   AAS, LC, NYH, NYP, UC, UP
Also contains: The Maid of Honor.

SKINNER, MOSE, *pseud.* *See* Brown, James E.

2237 SKINNER, P. H. The Little Ragged Ten Thousand; or, Scenes of
Actual Life among the Lowly in New York . . . New York:
Charles Scribner, 1853. 118 p.   N

2238 ———— ———— New York: published for a committee,
1854. 122 p., front.   NYP
This ed. adds chapter 17.

SKITT, *pseud.* *See* Taliaferro, Harden E.

2239 SLAUGHTER, JAMES SUMMERFIELD. Madeline; or, Love, Treachery and Revenge. A Romance . . . Atlanta, Georgia: printed by C. R. Hanleiter, 1859. 193 p.

Copy noted in *Georgia 1800-1900. A Series of Selections from the Georgiana Library of a Private Collector* (Atlanta Public Library, 1954), ser. 3, item 63.

SLAUGHTER, WILLIAM BANK. Marrying Rich. *In* J. V. Watson, Tales and Takings (1857), No. 2663.

2240 [SLEEPER, JOHN SHERBURNE.] Jack in the Forecastle; or, Incidents in the Early Life of Hawser Martingale [pseud.] . . . Boston: Crosby, Nichols, Lee and Company, 1860. 452 p., illus.   AAS, BP, CU, H, UP

2241 [————] Mark Rowland: A Tale of the Sea. By Hawser Martingale [pseud.] . . . Boston: Loring, 1867. 206 p.
AAS, CU, H, HEH, LC, NYP, UC, UM, UP, Y

2242 [————] Salt Water Bubbles; or, Life on the Wave. By Hawser Martingale [pseud.] . . . Boston: Wm. J. Reynolds & Co., 1854. 408 p., illus.
AAS, BP, BU, CU, H, HEH, LC, NYH, NYP, UC, UM, Y

Also published as: *Ocean Adventures; or, Cabin and Forecastle Yarns. By Hawser Martingale.* Boston: G. W. Cottrell, 36 Cornhill [cop. 1854].
AP, Y

Also published as: *Wonderful Adventures on the Ocean: Being True Descriptions of Battles, Tempests . . . By Capt. Hawser Martingale.* Boston: G. W. Cottrell, No. 36 Cornhill [n.d.].   BP

SLEEPER, MRS. MARTHA G. (QUINCY). The Silver Cup. *In* C. B. Porter, *ed.*, The Silver Cup of Sparkling Drops (1852), No. 1931.

2243 [SLOCOM, MARY S. F.] Lucy Gelding: A Tale of Land and Sea, Showing the Evil Effects of Gambling as It Is Practiced upon the Atlantic Coast . . . By Willa West [pseud.]. Chicago: E. B. Myers, 1862. 285 p.   AAS, BP, HEH, LC

2244 [SMALL, GEORGE G.] Farming for Fun; or, Back-Yard Grangers. By Bricktop [pseud.]. New York: Collin & Small, 1874. 59 p., illus.   LC

2245 [————] Fred Douglass and His Mule: A Story of the War. By Bricktop [pseud.]. New York: Collin & Small, 1873. 95 p., illus.   LC, NYP

2246 [————] Joining the Grangers; or, Trying to Be a Patron of Husbandry. By Bricktop [pseud.]. New York: Collin & Small, 1873. 64 p., illus. BP, LC

2247 [————] The Knights of Pythias Shown Up. By Bricktop [pseud.]. New York: Collin & Small, 1873. 67 p., illus. LC, NYP

2248 [————] My Mother-in-Law. By Bricktop [pseud.] . . . New York: Collin & Small, 1875. 79 p., illus. LC

2249 [————] Parson Beecher and His Horse: A Humorous Adventure. By Bricktop [pseud.]. New York: Winchell & Small, 1871. 96 p., illus. AAS, LC, NYP, Y

2250 [————] The Trip of the Porgie; or, Tacking up the Hudson. The Sentiment and Humor of Events en Route. By Bricktop [pseud.]. New York: Collin & Small, 1874. 124 p., illus. LC, NYP

2251 SMART, CHARLES. Driven from the Path: A Novel. Edited by Dr. Charles Smart . . . New York: D. Appleton and Company, 1873. 467 p. AAS, HEH, LC, LCP, UC, Y
A young man's adventures from Scotland to California, and through the Civil War.

2252 [SMITH, CHARLES HATCH.] George Melville: An American Novel . . . New York: W. R. C. Clark & Co., 1858. 386 p., front. AAS, LC, N
Laid in New York City and state.

2253 [SMITH, CHARLES HENRY.] Bill Arp [pseud.], So Called. A Side Show of the Southern Side of the War . . . New York: Metropolitan Record Office, 1866. 204 p., illus.
AAS, BA, BU, CU, H, HEH, LCP, NYH, NYP, UC, UM, UP, UVB, Y

2254 [————] Bill Arp's Peace Papers . . . New York: G. W. Carleton & Co. London: S. Low, Son & Co., 1873. 271 p., illus. AAS, BP, BU, CU, H, HEH, LC, LCP, N, NYH, NYP, UM, Y
Humorous tales dealing with the Civil War and reconstruction.

2255 SMITH, DENIS E. Leaves from a Physician's Journal . . . New York: the New York Publishing Company, 1867. 336 p.
AAS, CU, LC

2256 SMITH, MRS. ELIZABETH OAKES (PRINCE). Bertha and Lily; or, The Parsonage of Beech Glen. A Romance . . . New York: J. C. Derby. Boston: Phillips, Sampson & Co. Cincinnati: H. W. Derby, 1854. 336 p., illus.

AAS, BP, CU, H, HEH, LC, N, NYP, UVB, Y

Of social reforms and woman's rights.

2257 [————] The Newsboy. New York: J. C. Derby. Boston: Phillips, Sampson & Co. Cincinnati: H. W. Derby, 1854. 527 p., front.

AAS, CU, HEH, LC, N, NYH, NYP, UC, UP, UVB, Y

Laid in the slums of New York City.

SMITH, F. BURGE. *See* Griswold, Mrs. Frances Irene (Burge) Smith

2258 [SMITH, FANNIE N.] Brazen Gates: A True History of the Blossoms Which Grew in the Garden at Cragenfels. Compiled by Christabel Goldsmith [pseud.]; and Preface by the Author of "Widow Goldsmith's Daughter" . . . New York: G. W. Carleton & Co. London: S. Low & Co., 1872. 248 p., illus.

AAS, BU, HEH, LC, LCP, NYP

Preface by Julie P. Smith.

2259 [————] Shiftless Folks: An Undiluted Love Story. By Christabel Goldsmith [pseud.] . . . New York: G. W. Carleton & Co. London: S. Low, Son & Co., 1875. 454 p.

AAS, BA, BP, BU, H, HEH, LC, LCP, Y

2260 [SMITH, FRANCIS SHUBAEL.] Eveleen Wilson; or, The Trials of an Orphan Girl. New York: H. Long & Brother. Cincinnati: H. B. Pearson & Co. [cop. 1853]. 108 p., illus. Printed in double cols.

LC

Also published as: *Pictorial Life and Adventures of Eveleen Wilson; or, The Trials of an Orphan Girl.* Philadelphia: T. B. Peterson & Brothers, 306 Chestnut Street [1864?]. AAS

2261 SMITH, J. N. The Way of the World; or, Honesty the Best Policy. A Tale of New England and New York . . . Dedham: printed by Cox & Hutchins, 1854. 221 p., front.

AAS, CU, HEH, NYP, UP, Y

SMITH, MRS. JOHN, *pseud. See* Arthur, Timothy Shay

2262 SMITH, JOHN HYATT. Gilead; or, The Vision of All Souls' Hospital. An Allegory . . . New York: Charles Scribner. Buffalo: Breed, Butler & Co., 1863. 360 p., front.

AAS, BP, BU, CU, LC

2263 ————— The Open Door; or, Light and Liberty . . . New York: Theodore E. Perkins, 1870. 216 p.   AAS, BU, LC, UC

2264 SMITH, JOSEPH EMERSON. Oakridge: An Old-Time Story . . . Boston: James R. Osgood and Company, 1875. 415 p.

AAS, BU, H, HEH, LC, NYP, UC

A New England village at the turn of the century.

2265 [SMITH, MRS. JULIE P.] Chris and Otho; the Pansies and Orange-Blossoms They Found in Roaring River and Rosenbloom. A Sequel to "Widow Goldsmith's Daughter" . . . New York: Carleton. London: S. Low, Son & Co., 1870. 528 p.   AAS, CU, H, NYP, Y

2266 ————— The Married Belle; or, Our Red Cottage at Merry Bank. A Novel . . . New York: G. W. Carleton & Co. London: S. Low, Son & Co., 1872. 359 p.

Social life in the country.   AAS, HEH, LC, LCP, NYP, Y

2267 ————— Ten Old Maids, and Five of Them Were Wise and Five of Them Were Foolish: A Novel . . . New York: G. W. Carleton & Co. London: S. Low, Son & Co., 1874. 406 p.

Farm and city life.   AAS, BA, H, HEH, LC, LCP, NYP

2268 ————— The Widow Goldsmith's Daughter . . . Hartford: Brown & Gross, 1870. 664 p.   AAS

Also issued with imprint: Hartford: S. W. Barrows, 1870.   H

2269 [—————] The Widower; also, A True Account of Some Brave Frolics at Craigenfels . . . New York: G. W. Carleton & Co. London: S. Low, Son & Co., 1871. 389 p.

AAS, BA, HEH, LC, NYP

————— [*See also*] Smith, Fannie N. Brazen Gates . . . Preface by the Author of "Widow Goldsmith's Daughter" (1872), No. 2258.

2270 SMITH, M. M. Kick Him Down Hill; or, Ups and Downs in Business . . . New York: United States Publishing Company, 1875. 312 p.   AAS, HEH, LC

The social and financial world with prominent people mentioned.

2271 [SMITH, NATHAN RYNO.] Legends of the South. By Somebody Who Desires to Be Considered Nobody. Baltimore: steam press of William K. Boyle, 1869. 70 p.   CU, LC, UV

Contains five tales of White Sulphur Springs and the Mammoth Caves.

2272 [————] ———— By Viator [pseud.]. Baltimore: steam press of William K. Boyle, 1869. 95 p.   AAS, CU, H

This ed. adds one tale, "Somnambula."

2273 [SMITH, SEBA.] My Thirty Years Out of the Senate. By Major Jack Downing [pseud.] . . . New York: Oaksmith & Company, 1859. 458 p., illus.

     AAS, BA, BP, BU, CU, H, HEH, LC, LCP, N, NYH, NYP, UC, UM, UP, UVB, Y

Reprints a number of his letters first published in the 1830's and includes his later letters.

2274 ———— 'Way Down East; or, Portraitures of Yankee Life . . . New York: J. C. Derby. Boston: Phillips, Sampson & Co. Cincinnati: H. W. Derby, 1854. 384 p., illus.

     AAS, AP, BP, BU, H, HEH, LC, LCP, NYP, UP, UVB

SMITH, SOLOMON FRANKLIN. Speculation in Whiskers; or, Shaving in a Broker's Office. *In* O. P. Baldwin, *comp.*, Southern and South-Western Sketches [1855?], No. 200.

2275 SMITH, STEPHE R. Romance and Humor of the Road: A Book for Railway Men and Travellers . . . Chicago: Horton & Leonard, railroad printers, 1871. 219 p., illus.

     BU, CU, LC, NYH, UC, UM

Contains: Engineer's Gossip—At Jack Short's—Way-Car Gossip—Telegraph Gossip—The Side-Track—Miscellaneous Railway Gossip—Colossus of Roads.

SMITH, MRS. THOMAS P. Fashion. *In* M. G. Clarke, *comp.*, Sunshine and Shadows (1865), No. 541.

2276 SMITH, TOM WASHINGTON. The Bridle on the Heart; or, Pictures from Life. By Tom Wash. Smith, Alias Harold. Philadelphia: J. Nicholas, printer, 1860. 116 p., front.

Pages [113]-116 advts.   LC, N, NYP

2277 SMITH, WILLIAM B. Slippers and Gown . . . Philadelphia: J. B. Lippincott & Co., 1873.
Advt. in PW, IV (Sept. 13, 1873), 284, as "a curious novel."

2278 SMITH, WILLIAM L. G. Life at the South; or, "Uncle Tom's Cabin" as It Is. Being Narratives, Scenes, and Incidents in the Real "Life of the Lowly" . . . Buffalo: Geo. H. Derby and Co., 1852. 519 p., illus.
AAS, BP, BU, CU, H, HEH, LCP, N, NYP, UC, UM, UP, Y
Also issued with imprints: Buffalo: Geo. H. Derby and Co. Cincinnati: H. W. Derby and Co. Chicago: D. B. Cooke and Co., 1852. HEH
And, Buffalo: Geo. H. Derby and Co. Cleveland: Tooker and Gatchel. Sandusky: C. L. Derby and Co. Chicago: D. B. Cooke and Co., 1852. NYH

2279 [SMITH, WILLIAM RUSSELL.] As It Is . . . Albany: Munsell & Rowland, 1860. 260 p., 1 l. AAS, H, HEH, LC, NYP, UP
Congressmen and gambling.

2280 THE SMUGGLER'S DAUGHTER, and Other Tales. Also: The Two Maidens, by T. S. Arthur. Cincinnati: U. P. James, 167 Walnut Street [1858?]. 98 p. Printed in double cols. HEH
Title story and "other tales" probably of foreign origin.

2281 [SMYTHE, JAMES M.] Ethel Somers; or, The Fate of the Union. By a Southerner. Augusta, Ga.: H. D. Norrell, 1857. 382 p.
On slavery and states' rights. AAS, LC, NYH

2282 SNOWBALL, *Deacon, pseud.* Comic Lectures on Every Thing in General and Nothing in Particular. By Deacon Snowball and Diedrich Lager-Blatter [pseuds.]. New York: Frederic A. Brady, 126 Nassau Street [185-?]. 216 p. CU, NYH, Y

SOBERSIDE, SOLOMON, *pseud.* Peter Crisp's Spectacles. *In* Rougegorge (1870), No. 2130.

2283 [SOMERBY, FREDERIC THOMAS.] Hits and Dashes; or, A Medley of Sketches and Scraps, Touching People and Things. By "Cymon" [pseud.] . . . Boston: Redding & Co., 1852. 152 p. AAS, BP, LC, N, NYP, UP, UVB, Y

SOMMERS, JANE R., *pseud. See* Jones, Cornelia

SOPER, THOMAS N. *See* Holding, C. B.

SOUCI, SANS, *pseud. See* McAfee, Mrs. Nelly Nichol (Marshall)

2284 SOULE, MRS. CAROLINE AUGUSTA (WHITE). Home Life; or, A Peep across the Threshold . . . Boston: A. Tompkins and B. B. Mussey & Co., 1855. 249 p., illus. HEH, NYP

Contents: The Haunted Hearthstone—The Patient Hope—The Only Daughter—The Mother's Temptation—"I Haven't the Change"—The Anonymous Letters—The Thanksgiving Presents—Pride and Pity—The Children and the Novel—The Slattern Cured—"Company Every Day"— The Broken Windows.

———— Louise and Bertrand. In S. Cobb, Isidore de Montigny [185-?], No. 569.

2285 ———— The Pet of the Settlement: A Story of Prairie-Land ... Boston: A. Tompkins, 1860. 256 p., front.

AAS, BP, N, NYP, UP, Y

Also published as: Little Alice; or, The Pet of the Settlement. Boston: Tompkins & Company, 1863. HEH

———— The Poor Washerwoman. In J. V. Watson, Tales and Takings (1857), No. 2663.

2286 ———— Wine or Water: A Tale of New England . . . Boston: Abel Tompkins; Brown & Taggard, 1862. 354 p.

AAS, HEH, NYP, UM

2287 THE SOUTHERN FIELD AND FIRESIDE NOVELETTE, No. 1, Containing: "Myra Bruce; or, True Love Running Roughly," with Illustrations. "Riverland:" A Charming Story of Southern Life. And "Five Chapters of a History: A Georgia Court, Forty Years Ago." Augusta, Ga.: James Gardner [1863]. 35, 41, 19 p., illus.

"Myra Bruce," by Peter Joseph Oeland; "Riverland," by Clara Victoria Dargan; and "Five Chapters," by Richard Malcolm Johnston. University of North Carolina Library copy.

2288 [SOUTHWOOD, MARION.] Tit for Tat: A Novel. By a Lady of New Orleans . . . New York: Garret & Company, 18 Ann Street. London: Clarke, Beeton & Company [cop. 1856]. 356 p. AAS, CU, HEH, LCP, N, NYH, NYP, UP

For discussion of authorship see G. L. Phillips, "Tit for Tat: A Novel of Social Criticism," in Mid-America, XXXIII (1951), 225-241.

2289 SOUTHWORTH, ELLA. Sarah de Vaughan: A Story of the Times of Aaron Burr. New York: Dean and Salter, 1858.

Title listed in R. L. Boyle, Mrs. E. D. E. N. Southworth, Novelist (Washington, D. C., 1939), p. 29.

2290 SOUTHWORTH, MRS. EMMA DOROTHY ELIZA (NEVITTE). All-worth Abbey . . . Philadelphia: T. B. Peterson & Brothers, 306 Chestnut Street [cop. 1865]. 421 p.   LC, NYP, UM
LC copy deposited for copyright Dec. 1, 1865.

2291 ———— The Artist's Love. By Mrs. Emma D. E. N. South-worth. And Stories by Her Sister, Mrs. Frances Henshaw Baden . . . Philadelphia: T. B. Peterson & Brothers, 306 Chestnut Street [cop. 1872]. 479 p.   AAS, CU, LC, NYP, UP, Y

2292 ———— A Beautiful Fiend; or, Through the Fire . . . Phila-delphia: T. B. Peterson & Brothers, 306 Chestnut Street [cop. 1873]. 452 p.   AAS, CU, HEH, UC, Y
Sequel: *Victor's Triumph.*

2293 ———— The Bridal Eve . . . Philadelphia: T. B. Peterson & Brothers, 306 Chestnut Street [cop. 1864]. 446 p.
AAS, NYP, UP, Y

2294 ———— The Bride of Llewellyn . . . Philadelphia: T. B. Peterson & Brothers, 306 Chestnut Street [cop. 1866]. 550 p.
LC copy deposited for copyright Dec. 14, 1866.   LC, UV

2295 ———— The Bride's Fate. A Sequel to "The Changed Brides" . . . Philadelphia: T. B. Peterson & Brothers, 306 Chestnut Street [cop. 1869]. 488 p.   AAS, H, NYP, UP, Y

2296 ———— The Broken Engagement; or, Speaking the Truth for a Day . . . Philadelphia: T. B. Peterson and Brothers, 306 Chestnut Street [cop. 1862]. 92 p.   H, LC, LCP, UC, UVB
LC copy deposited for copyright Jan. 23, 1862.

2297 ———— The Changed Brides . . . Philadelphia: T. B. Peter-son & Brothers, 306 Chestnut Street [cop. 1869]. 503 p.
Sequel: *The Bride's Fate.*   AAS, H, HEH, LC, NYP, UM, UP

2298 ———— The Christmas Guest: A Collection of Stories. By Mrs. Emma D. E. N. Southworth and Her Sister, Mrs. Frances Henshaw Baden . . . Philadelphia: T. B. Peterson & Brothers, 306 Chestnut Street [cop. 1870]. 338 p.   LC
LC copy deposited for copyright May 10, 1870.

2299 ———— The Coral Lady; or, The Bronzed Beauty of Paris . . . Philadelphia: C. W. Alexander, 224 South Third Street, cop. 1867. 78 p., illus.   LC
LC copy deposited for copyright Jan. 7, 1868.

2300 ———— Cruel as the Grave . . . Philadelphia: T. B. Peterson & Brothers, 306 Chestnut Street [cop. 1871]. 372 p.

Sequel: *Tried for Her Life.* AAS, H, HEH, LC, NYP, UP

2301 ———— The Curse of Clifton: A Tale of Expiation and Redemption . . . Philadelphia: A. Hart, 1853. 2 vols. (234, 248 p.) AAS, UP

Also published as: *Fallen Pride; or, The Mountain Girl's Love.* Philadelphia: T. B. Peterson & Brothers, 306 Chestnut Street [cop. 1867]. 467 p. AAS, H

2302 ———— The Discarded Daughter; or, The Children of the Isle. A Tale of the Chesapeake . . . Philadelphia: A. Hart, 1852. 2 vols. (224, 204 p.) AAS, HEH, NYP(V.1), UM

Also found 2 vols. in 1.

2303 ———— Fair Play; or, The Test of the Lone Isle . . . Philadelphia: T. B. Peterson & Brothers, 306 Chestnut Street [cop. 1868]. 670 p. AAS, CU, H, HEH, NYP, UM, UP, Y

Sequel: *How He Won Her.*

2304 ———— The Family Doom; or, The Sin of a Countess . . . Philadelphia: T. B. Peterson & Brothers, 306 Chestnut Street [cop. 1869]. 350 p. AAS, CU, UP, Y

Sequel: *The Maiden Widow.*

2305 ———— The Fatal Marriage . . . Philadelphia: T. B. Peterson & Brothers, 306 Chestnut Street [cop. 1863]. 487 p.

AP, HEH, NYP, UP

2306 ———— The Fortune Seeker . . . Philadelphia: T. B. Peterson & Brothers, 306 Chestnut Street [cop. 1866]. 498 p. LC, UP

LC copy deposited for copyright Mar. 14, 1866.

2307 ———— The Gipsy's Prophecy: A Tale of Real Life . . . Philadelphia: T. B. Peterson & Brothers, 306 Chestnut Street [cop. 1861]. 455 p. AAS, Y

2308 ———— The Haunted Homestead, and Other Nouvellettes. With an Autobiography of the Author . . . Philadelphia: T. B. Peterson and Brothers, 306 Chestnut Street [cop. 1860]. 292 p., front. AAS, H, HEH, NYP, UC, UP

Contents: Biographical Sketch of the Author—The Haunted Homestead—The Presentiment—The Spectre Revels—The Widow's Son.

2309 ———— Hickory Hall; or, The Outcast. A Romance of the Blue Ridge . . . Philadelphia: T. B. Peterson and Brothers [cop. 1861]. 136 p.

Information from LC card for copy withdrawn from circulation.

2310 ———— How He Won Her. A Sequel to "Fair Play" . . . Philadelphia: T. B. Peterson & Brothers, 306 Chestnut Street [cop. 1869]. 512 p.   AAS, CU, H, HEH, LC, NYP, UC, UM, Y

2311 ———— India: The Pearl of Pearl River . . . Philadelphia: T. B. Peterson, No. 102 Chestnut Street [cop. 1855]. 402 p., front.   HEH, LCP, UP

HEH copyright notice on verso of title page dated 1855, with dedication and preface dated "February 16th, 1856."

2312 ———— The Lady of the Isle: A Romance from Real Life . . . Philadelphia: T. B. Peterson and Brothers, 306 Chestnut Street [cop. 1859]. 598 p., front.

AAS, CU, HEH, LC, UC, UM, UP, UV, Y

2313 ———— The Lost Heir of Linlithgow . . . Philadelphia: T. B. Peterson & Brothers, 306 Chestnut Street [cop. 1872]. 570 p.

Sequel: *A Noble Lord.*   H, LC, UM, UP

2314 ———— The Lost Heiress . . . Philadelphia: T. B. Peterson, No. 102 Chestnut Street [cop. 1854]. 502 p., front.

AAS, BU, H, NYP, Y

2315 ———— Love's Labor Won . . . Philadelphia: T. B. Peterson & Brothers, 306 Chestnut Street [cop. 1862]. 383 p.

AAS, NYP, UP

2316 ———— The Maiden Widow. A Sequel to "The Family Doom" . . . Philadelphia: T. B. Peterson & Brothers, 306 Chestnut Street [cop. 1870]. 313 p.

AAS, CU, H, HEH, LC, NYP, UM, UP, Y

2317 ———— The Missing Bride; or, Miriam the Avenger . . . Philadelphia: T. B. Peterson, 102 Chestnut Street [cop. 1855]. 635 p., front.   UC

Also published as: *Miriam the Avenger; or, The Missing Bride.* Philadelphia: T. B. Peterson & Brothers [cop. 1874].   AAS

2318 ———— The Mother-in-Law; or, The Isle of Rays. A Tale
. . . New York: D. Appleton & Company, 1851. 187 p.
Printed in double cols.   HEH, NYP, UC, UP, Y

2319 ———— The Mystery of Dark Hollow . . . Philadelphia:
T. B. Peterson & Brothers, 306 Chestnut Street [cop. 1875].
366 p.   AAS, H, HEH, LC, NYP, UC

2320 ———— A Noble Lord. The Sequel to "The Lost Heir of
Linlithgow" . . . Philadelphia: T. B. Peterson & Brothers, 306
Chestnut Street [cop. 1872]. 428 p.   AAS, H, HEH, LC

2321 ———— Old Neighbourhoods and New Settlements; or,
Christmas Evening Legends . . . Philadelphia: A. Hart, 1853.
370 p., front.   AAS, HEH, LC, UC, UP, UVB, Y
Contents: The Better Way; or, The Wife's Victory—The Married
Shrew, a Sequel to "The Better Way"—The Thunderbolt to the Hearth
—Neighbours' Prescriptions—The Temptation—Across the Street: A
New Year's Story—The Irish Refugee—New Year in the Little Rough-
Cast House—Winny—The Fine Figure.
Also published as: The Wife's Victory and Other Nouvellettes. Phila-
delphia: T. B. Peterson, No. 102 Chestnut Street [cop. 1854].
AAS, CU, LC

2322 ———— The Prince of Darkness: A Romance of the Blue
Ridge . . . Philadelphia: T. B. Peterson & Brothers, 306
Chestnut Street [cop. 1869]. 370 p.
     AAS, CU, HEH, LC, NYP, UV
Also contains: The Broken Engagement—Winny—The Thunderbolt to
the Hearth.
According to R. L. Boyle, Mrs. E. D. E. N. Southworth, Novelist
(Washington, D. C., 1939), p. 74, the title story above is the same as
Hickory Hall.

2323 ———— Shannondale . . . New York: D. Appleton & Com-
pany. Philadelphia: George S. Appleton, 1851. 170 p.
Printed in double cols.   AAS, H, HEH, NYP, UC, UP, UVB, Y
Also published as: The Three Beauties. Philadelphia: T. B. Peterson &
Brothers [cop. 1858]. 523 p., front.   CU, N, NYP, UP, UV, Y

2324 ———— The Spectre Lover. By Mrs. Emma D. E. N. Southworth. And Other Stories by Her Sister Mrs. Frances Henshaw Baden . . . Philadelphia: T. B. Peterson & Brothers
[1875]. 416 p.
Information from LC card for copy withdrawn from circulation.

2325 ———— Tried for Her Life. A Sequel to "Cruel as the Grave" . . . Philadelphia: T. B. Peterson & Brothers, 306 Chestnut Street [cop. 1871]. 356 p.   AAS, CU, H, LC, NYP

2326 ———— Victor's Triumph. The Sequel to "A Beautiful Fiend" . . . Philadelphia: T. B. Peterson & Brothers, 306 Chestnut Street [cop. 1874]. 348 p.   AAS, NYP

2327 ———— Virginia and Magdalene; or, The Foster-Sisters. A Novel . . . Complete in One Volume. Philadelphia: A. Hart, 1852. 159 p. Printed in double cols.   AAS, BA, BU, Y
Also published as: *The Two Sisters.* Philadelphia: T. B. Peterson and Brothers, 306 Chestnut Street [cop. 1858]. 497 p., front.   AAS, CU, HEH

2328 ———— Vivia; or, The Secret of Power . . . Philadelphia: T. B. Peterson, No. 102 Chestnut Street [cop. 1857]. 540 p., front.   AAS, CU, H, HEH, UC, UM, UP, Y

2329 ———— The Widow's Son . . . Philadelphia: T. B. Peterson & Brothers, 306 Chestnut Street [cop. 1867]. 649 p.   CU, LCP

2330 SOUTHWORTH, MRS. S. A. Hester Strong's Life Work; or, The Mystery Solved . . . Boston: Lee and Shepard, 1870. 453 p.
AAS, H, HEH, LC, NYP, UM, Y

2331 ———— The Inebriate's Hut; or, The First Fruits of the Maine Law . . . Boston: Phillips, Sampson and Company, 1854. 240 p., illus.   AAS, CU, H, LC, UM
Also published as: *Alice Lee; or, The Maine Law Triumphant.* New York: Hall and Brother, 1855.   AAS, BU, HEH, LC, UP

2332 SPANGLER, HELEN KING. The Physician's Wife: A Novel . . . Philadelphia: J. B. Lippincott & Co., 1875. 305 p.
Laid in London.   AAS, H, HEH, LC

2333 DELETE.

SPARKLE, SOPHIE, *pseud.* *See* Hicks, Jennie E.

2334 SPARKS, *pseud.* Flora Montgomerie, the Factory Girl: A Tale of Lowell Factories. Being a Recital of the Adventures of a Libidinous Millionaire Whose Wealth Was Used as a Means of Triumphing over Virtue. By Sparks [pseud.]. New York: George Akarman, 1856. 99 p., front.
Title listed in H. C. Ashbee, *Catena Librorum Tacendorum* (London, 1885), p. 227.

SPAVERY, *pseud.* *See* Avery, Samuel Putnam

2335 [SPENCER, MRS. BELLA ZILFA.] Ora, the Lost Wife . . . Cincinnati: P. C. Browne, 1863. 384 p.   LC

2336 [————] Right and Wrong; or, She Told the Truth at Last. With Other Stories . . . Springfield, Mass.: W. J. Holland & Co., 1870. 384 p., front.   AAS, CU, Y
Also contains: Woman in the War—The Prisoner's Child—Presentiments —The Coquette's Faith.

2337 ———— Tried and True; or, Love and Loyalty. A Story of the Great Rebellion . . . Springfield, Mass.: W. J. Holland, 1866. 394 p., illus.
AAS, H, HEH, LC, LCP, N, NYH, NYP, UM, UP, Y

2338 SPOFFORD, MRS. HARRIET ELIZABETH (PRESCOTT). The Amber Gods and Other Stories . . . Boston: Ticknor and Fields, 1863. 432 p.
AAS, AP, BA, BP, BU, CU, H, HEH, LC, LCP, N, NYP, UM, UP, UV, Y
Also contains: In a Cellar—Knitting Sale-Socks—Circumstance—Desert Sands—Midsummer and May—The South Breaker.

2339 ———— Azarian: An Episode . . . Boston: Ticknor and Fields, 1864. 251 p.
AAS, BA, BP, BU, CU, H, HEH, LC, LCP, N, NYP, UC, UM, UP, Y

———— Louie. *In* Not Pretty, but Precious (1872), No. 1804.

2340 ———— New-England Legends . . . Boston: James R. Osgood and Company, 1871. 40 p., illus. Printed in double cols.
AAS, BA, BP, BU, CU, H, HEH, LC, LCP, N, NYH, NYP, UC, UM, UVB, Y
Contents: The True Account of Captain Kidd—Charlestown—Salem— Newburyport—Dover—Portsmouth.

———— Rougegorge. *In* Rougegorge and Other Short Stories (1870), No. 2130.

2341 [————] Sir Rohan's Ghost: A Romance. Boston: J. E. Tilton and Company, 1860. 352 p.
AAS, BA, BP, BU, CU, H, HEH, LC, LCP, NYP, UC, UM, UP, UVB, Y
Laid in England.

———— The Strange Passengers. *In* Short Stories (1869), No. 2210.

2342 ———— The Thief in the Night . . . Boston: Roberts Brothers, 1872. 217 p.
AAS, BA, BP, CU, H, HEH, LC, LCP, NYP, UC, UM, UP, Y

2343 SPRINGER, MRS. REBECCA (RUTER). Beechwood . . . Philadelphia: J. B. Lippincott & Co., 1873. 288 p. AAS, LC

2344 THE SPUYTENDUYVEL CHRONICLE. New York: Livermore & Rudd, 1856. 318 p. BP, H, LC, NYP, UP, Y
Life in New York City and a Saratoga season.

STABLER, EDWARD. *See* Browning, Meshach

2345 [STABLER, MRS. JENNIE LATHAM.] Left to Herself. By Jennie Woodville [pseud.]. Philadelphia: J. B. Lippincott & Co., 1872. 311 p. AAS, BP, LC, LCP, UC, UV
Also published as: *Edith's Mistake; or, Left to Herself.* Philadelphia: J. B. Lippincott & Co. [cop. 1874]. LC

STAHL, *pseud. See* Wharton, George M.

STANHOPE, FREDERICK. Reminiscences of California. *In* S. Cobb, The King and Cobbler [185-?], No. 572.

———— A Winter in the Sierra Nevadas. *In* S. Cobb, The Iron Cross [185-?], No. 568.

2346 STANLEY, HARVEY. Pilate and Herod: A Tale Illustrative of the Early History of the Church of England in the Province of Maryland . . . Philadelphia: H. Hooker, 1853. 2 vols. (284, 283 p.) H, HEH, LC, NYP, UM, UP, UV

2347 [STANTON, BENJAMIN F.] The Haps and Mishaps of the Three Jolly Students: A Veritable History . . . Manchester, N. H.: press of Gaywell, Webster & Gabbles, 1866. 12 p., illus. AAS

2348 STARBUCK, CALEB. Hampton Heights; or, The Spinster's Ward . . . New York: Mason Brothers, 1856. 504 p.
BU, CU, HEH, LC, UC

2349 [STARNES, EBENEZER.]   The Slaveholder Abroad; or, Billy Buck's
Visit with His Master, to England.   A Series of Letters from
Dr. Pleasant Jones [pseud.] to Major Joseph Jones, of Georgia
. . . Philadelphia: J. B. Lippincott & Co., 1860.   512 p., illus.
                                        BP, H, HEH, LC, N, NYP, UC, UP, Y
Has been wrongly attributed to William T. Thompson.

2350 THE STARTLING CONFESSIONS OF ELEANOR BURTON: A Thrilling
Tragedy from Real Life.   Exhibiting a Dark Page in the Man-
ners, Customs, and Crimes of the "Upper Ten" of New York
City . . . Philadelphia: E. E. Barclay, 1852.   34 p., illus.
                                        H, LC, NYP

2351 STARTLING DISCLOSURES! Mysteries Solved! or, The History of
Esther Livingstone and Dark Career of Henry Baldwin. This
Narrative . . . Pictures . . . the Scenes in Which They Were
Actors in the Mammoth Cave . . . Philadelphia: E. Elmer
Barclay, 1853.   50 p., illus.   HEH, LC

STAUFFER, FRANK H.   Rose May, the New School-Mistress.   In
A. Cary, The Adopted Daughter (1859), No. 466.

2352 [STEBBINS, GEORGE STANFORD.]   My Satchel and I; or, Literature
on Foot.   By Ikabod Izax [pseud.] . . .   Springfield, Mass.:
D. E. Fisk and Company [cop. 1873].   326 p., illus.
                                        AAS, BP, BU, CU, H, LC, NYP, UM, UP, Y

2353 STEELE, JAMES WILLIAM.   The Sons of the Border: Sketches of
the Life and People of the Far Frontier . . . Topeka, Kansas:
Commonwealth Printing Company, 1873.   260 p.
                                        AAS, CU, H, HEH, LC, N, NYH, NYP, Y
Also contains: Chuck—New Mexican Common Life—The Scout's Mis-
take—Copper-Distilled—Jack's   Divorce—A   Harvest-Day   with   the
Pueblos—Brown's Revenge—A Day with the Padres—Joe's Pocket—
Woman under Difficulties—The Reunion of the Ghosts—Coyotes—The
Priest of El Paso—La Senorita—Peg—Captain Jinks—Jornado del Muerto.

2353a STEELE, MRS. ROWENA (GRANICE).   Dell Dart; or, Within the
Meshes . . . Merced: printed at the San Joaquin Valley Argus
office, 1874.   69 p.
California State Library copy.

2353b ———— The Family Gem: Miscellaneous Stories. By Rowena Granice. Sacramento: printed at the old State Journal steam presses, 1858. 40 p.   HEH

Contains: The Two Wives: A Tale of Domestic Life in California—Rosalie Irving; or, Life Scenes in the City of New York—The Rag Party; or, The First and Last Love of Aunt Debbie—Blanche Blakely; or, the Curse of Beauty.

2353c ———— Leonnie St. James; or, The Suicide's Curse! A Novelette. Written by Rowena Granice Steele, Author of "The Family Gem," "Victims of Fate," "Camorie; or, The Kanaka Girl's Revenge," "The Early Doomed," "Lights and Shadows in the Life of the Widow Platt"... Auburn, Cal.: printed at the Union Advocate office, 1862. 62 p.   HEH

Also contains her sketch on "Lola Montez," pp. 61-62.

STELLA, pseud. See Lewis, Mrs. Estelle Anna (Robinson)

2354 STEPHENS, MRS. ANN SOPHIA (WINTERBOTHAM). Bellehood and Bondage... Philadelphia: T. B. Peterson & Brothers, 306 Chestnut Street [cop. 1873]. 458 p.   AAS, H, HEH, NYP, UM

2355 ———— Bertha's Engagement... Philadelphia: T. B. Peterson & Brothers, 306 Chestnut Street [cop. 1875]. 552 p.
HEH, LC, NYP

2356 ———— The Curse of Gold... Philadelphia: T. B. Peterson & Brothers, 306 Chestnut Street [cop. 1869]. 406 p.
AAS, CU, HEH, LC, NYP, UM, UP, Y

2357 ———— Doubly False . . . Philadelphia: T. B. Peterson & Brothers, 306 Chestnut Street [cop. 1868]. 556 p.
CU, NYP, UP, Y

2358 ———— Fashion and Famine . . . New York: Bunce & Brother, 1854. 426 p.
AAS, BP, BU, CU, H, HEH, LC, N, NYP, UC, UP, UVB, Y

2359 ———— The Gold Brick... Philadelphia: T. B. Peterson and Brothers, 306 Chestnut Street [cop. 1866]. 514 p.
AAS, CU, HEH, NYP, UM, UP, Y

2360 ———— The Heiress of Greenhurst: An Autobiography ... New York: Edward Stephens, 1857. 430 p.
AAS, CU, H, HEH, NYP, UP, UVB, Y

2361 ———— Lord Hope's Choice . . . Philadelphia: T. B. Peterson & Brothers, 306 Chestnut Street [cop. 1873]. 312 p.

Sequel: *The Old Countess.*   AAS, CU, H, HEH, LC, NYP, Y

2362 ———— Mabel's Mistake . . . Philadelphia: T. B. Peterson & Brothers, 306 Chestnut Street [cop. 1868]. 431 p.

AAS, CU, H, HEH, NYP, UM, UP, Y

2363 ———— Married in Haste . . . Philadelphia: T. B. Peterson & Brothers, 306 Chestnut Street [cop. 1870]. 383 p.

AAS, LC, NYP, Y

2364 ———— Mary Derwent . . . Philadelphia: T. B. Peterson and Brothers, 306 Chestnut Street [cop. 1858]. 408 p.

AAS, BA, BU, CU, H, HEH, LC, NYH, NYP, UC, UM, UP, UV, Y

2365 ———— A Noble Woman . . . Philadelphia: T. B. Peterson & Brothers, 306 Chestnut Street [cop. 1871]. 479 p.

CU, H, HEH, LC, NYP, UVB

2366 ———— The Old Countess; or, The Two Proposals . . . A Sequel to "Lord Hope's Choice." Philadelphia: T. B. Peterson & Brothers, 306 Chestnut Street [cop. 1873]. 301 p.

AAS, BU, CU, H, HEH, LC, NYP

2367 ———— The Old Homestead . . . New York: Bunce & Brother, 1855. 435 p.

AAS, BP, BU, CU, H, HEH, LC, N, NYH, NYP, UM, UP, UVB, Y

On the "evils" of political appointment.

2368 ———— Palaces and Prisons . . . Philadelphia: T. B. Peterson & Brothers, 306 Chestnut Street [cop. 1871]. 592 p.

AAS, H, LC, NYP, Y

2369 ———— Phemie Frost's Experiences . . . New York: G. W. Carleton & Co. London: S. Low, Son & Co., 1874. 408 p.

AAS, BP, BU, CU, H, HEH, LC, NYP, UC, UVB, Y

2370 ———— The Reigning Belle . . . Philadelphia: T. B. Peterson & Brothers, 306 Chestnut Street [cop. 1872]. 317 p.

AAS, CU, HEH, LC, NYP, UM, UP, Y

2371 ———— The Rejected Wife . . . Philadelphia: T. B. Peterson
& Brothers, 306 Chestnut Street [cop. 1863]. 436 p.

AAS, CU, H, HEH, LC, NYP, UP, Y

Of a secret marriage of Benedict Arnold.

2372 ———— Ruby Gray's Strategy . . . Philadelphia: T. B. Peterson & Brothers, 306 Chestnut Street [cop. 1869]. 393 p.

AAS, BU, CU, HEH, NYP, UM, UP, Y

2373 ———— Silent Struggles . . . Philadelphia: T. B. Peterson & Brothers, 306 Chestnut Street [cop. 1865]. 460 p.

AAS, BU, CU, H, HEH, LCP, NYP

2374 ———— The Soldier's Orphans . . . Philadelphia: T. B. Peterson and Brothers, 306 Chestnut Street [cop. 1866]. 330 p.

H, HEH, LC, NYP, UM

2375 ———— The Wife's Secret . . . Philadelphia: T. B. Peterson & Brothers, 306 Chestnut Street [cop. 1864]. 480 p.

H, LC, NYP, UM

2376 ———— Wives and Widows; or, The Broken Life . . . Philadelphia: T. B. Peterson & Brothers, 306 Chestnut Street [cop. 1869]. 409 p.

AAS, HEH, NYP, UM, UP, Y

2377 STEPHENS, MRS. HARRIET MARION (WARD). Hagar the Martyr; or, Passion and Reality. A Tale of the North and South . . . Boston: W. P. Fetridge & Co., 1855. 360 p., front.

AAS, BP, BU, CU, H, HEH, NYP, UC, UP, UV

2378 ———— Home Scenes and Home Sounds; or, The World from My Window . . . Boston: Fetridge and Company, 1854. 288 p., illus.

AAS, BP, BU, CU, H, HEH, LC, NYH, NYP, UC, UM, UP, UV, Y

Contains: The Maniac's Curse: A Legend of Wyoming—What Katy Did; or, Mr. Watkins's Wife—The Warning Dream—Liberty vs. Love; or, The Soldier's Triumph—Leoline, the Child of Shadows—Gracy Green—Agnes Doyle: A Christmas Story—The Maniac Lover; or, The Three Trials of Norah Shehaine—Retribution—My Aunt Fanny: A Country Sketch.

2379 THE STEP-SISTER: A NOVELETTE. By a Southern Gentleman. Richmond: Ayres & Wade, 1863. 260 p.

HEH, LCP, NYH

2380 [STEVENS, WILLIAM.] The Unjust Judge; or, The Evils of Intemperance on Judges, Lawyers, and Politicians. By a Member of the Ohio Bar ... Mansfield, O., 1854. 352 p.
Authorship established by Ernest J. Wessen.   HEH, LC, NYP, UM

2381 STIMSON, ALEXANDER LOVETT. Easy Nat; or, The Three Apprentices. A Tale of Life in New York and Boston ... New York: J. C. Derby. Boston: Phillips, Sampson & Co. Cincinnati: H. W. Derby, 1854. 465 p., illus.
AAS, BU, CU, H, N, NYP, UC, UM
Also published as: *New England Boys; or, The Three Apprentices.* New York: J. C. Derby, 1856.   HEH, LC

2382 [————] Waifwood: A Novel . . . Boston: Wm. V. Spencer, 1864. 472 p.   AAS, LC, LCP, N, NYP

STOCKTON, FRANCIS RICHARD. Mahala's Drive. *In* Short Stories, 2d ser. (1869), No. 2211.

2383 STODDARD, MRS. ELIZABETH DREW (BARSTOW). The Morgesons ... New York: Carleton, 1862. 259 p.
AAS, AP, HEH, LCP, N, UP, UVB, Y

2384 ———— Temple House: A Novel . . . New York: G. W. Carleton & Co. [cop. 1867]. 347 p.   AAS, BP, LCP, NYP

2385 ———— Two Men: A Novel . . . New York: Bunce and Huntington, 1865. 291 p.   AAS, CU, HEH, LCP, N, UC, UV, Y

2386 STORIES AND SKETCHES by Our Best Authors. Boston: Lee and Shepard, 1867. 307 p.
AAS, BP, BU, CU, HEH, LC, NYP, UM, UP, Y
Contents: The Skeleton at the Banquet, by Seeley Regester—Let Those Laugh Who Win, by Samuel W. Tuttle—The Proper Use of Grandfathers, by Fitz Hugh Ludlow—At Eve, by Gertrude Brodé—Broken Idols, by Richmond Wolcott—Dr. Huger's Intentions, by Louise Chandler Moulton—The Man Whose Life Was Saved—The Romance of a Western Trip, by J. L. Lord—The Two Ghosts of New London Turnpike, by Mrs. Galpin—Down by the Sea, by Hattie Tyng Griswold—Why Mrs. Radnor Fainted—Under a Cloud, by William Wirt Sikes—Coming from the Front, by Richmond Wolcott—A Night in the Sewers, by Chas. Dawson Shanly.

2387 STORIES FOR CHRISTMAS AND WINTER EVENINGS. Now First Collected, and Forming the Third Volume of "Putnam's Story Library." New York: G. P. Putnam & Co., 1857. 324 p.

BA, BP, HEH, NYP

Contents: The Christmas Bride–The Christmas-Eve Letter–Adventures of a New-Year's Eve–Christmas Changes–A Story of a New-Year's Eve–Mrs. Ranford's New-Year's Dinner–A Merry Christmas–Mrs. Peck's Pudding–How We Made Money Last Year–Miss Brightington's Polka Jacket–Christmas-Eve in a Sponging-House–Myself and Julia Arran.

At head of title: "Putnam's Library of Choice Stories."

2388 STORY, JAMES P. Choisy: A Novel . . . Boston: James R. Osgood and Company, 1872. 131 p. Printed in double cols.

AAS, BA, CU, H, HEH, LC, LCP, NYP, Y

Laid in New York City and Paris.

STORY, SYDNEY A., JR., *pseud*. *See* Pike, Mrs. Mary Hayden (Green)

2389 STOWE, MRS. HARRIET ELIZABETH (BEECHER). Agnes of Sorrento . . . Boston: Ticknor and Fields, 1862. 412 p.

AAS, H, HEH, LC, LCP, N, UP, UVB, Y

Laid in Italy at the time of Pope Alexander VI.

2390 [————] The Chimney-Corner. By Christopher Crowfield [pseud.] . . . Boston: Ticknor and Fields, 1868. 311 p.

AAS, BP, BU, CU, H, HEH, LC, LCP, N, NYP, UM, UP, UVB, Y

2391 ———— Dred: A Tale of the Great Dismal Swamp . . . Boston: Phillips, Sampson and Company, 1856. 2 vols. (329, 370 p.)   AAS, AP, BA, BP, BU, CU, H, HEH, LC, LCP, N, NYH, NYP, UC, UM, UP, UVB, Y

Also published as: *Nina Gordon: A Tale of the Great Dismal Swamp*. Boston: Ticknor and Fields, 1866. LC

2392 [————] House and Home Papers. By Christopher Crowfield [pseud.]. Boston: Ticknor and Fields, 1865. 333 p.

AAS, BP, BU, CU, H, HEH, LCP, N, NYP, UC, UVB, Y

2393 ———— The Minister's Wooing . . . New York: Derby and Jackson, 1859. 578 p.

AAS, AP, BU, CU, H, HEH, LC, LCP, N, NYP, UC, UM, UP, UVB, Y

Copies found with and without the three-line stereotype notice on verso of title page.

Also issued with imprint: New York: Derby and Jackson. Boston: Brown, Taggard and Chase, 1859. AAS, BP, LC

2394 ———— My Wife and I; or, Harry Henderson's History . . .
New York: J. B. Ford and Company, 1871.   474 p., illus.

AAS, BA, H, LC, LCP, N, UC, UVB, Y

2395 ———— Oldtown Fireside Stories . . .   Boston: James R.
Osgood & Company, 1872.   199 p., illus.

AAS, BA, CU, H, HEH, LCP, N, NYP, UC, UM, UP, Y

Contents: The Ghost in the Mill—The Sullivan Looking-Glass—The
Minister's Housekeeper—The Widow's Bandbox—Captain Kidd's Money
—"Mis' Elderkin's Pitcher"—The Ghost in the Cap'n Brown House—
Colonel Eph's Shoe-Buckles—The Bull-Fight—How to Fight the Devil.

2396 ———— Oldtown Folks . . .   Boston: Fields, Osgood & Co.,
1869.   608 p.   AAS, BA, BP, BU, CU, H, HEH, LC, LCP, N,

NYH, NYP, UC, UM, UP, UVB, Y

2397 ———— The Pearl of Orr's Island: A Story of the Coast of
Maine . . .   Boston: Ticknor and Fields, 1862.   437 p.

AAS, AP, H, HEH, LC, LCP, N, NYP, UVB, Y

2398 ———— Pink and White Tyranny: A Society Novel . . .   Boston: Roberts Brothers, 1871.   331 p., illus.

AAS, BA, BP, BU, CU, H, HEH, LC, LCP, N, NYP, UC, UM, UP, UVB, Y

2399 ———— The Two Altars; or, Two Pictures in One . . .   [Bos-
ton: John P. Jewett & Co., cop. 1852.]   Caption title, 12 p.

At head of title: "Liberty Tracts—No. 1."   AAS, BA, BU, NYH, UM, Y

LC copy deposited for copyright July 24, 1852.
Reissued by the American Anti-Slavery Society as Tract No. 13.
In J. Griffiths, *ed.*, *Autographs for Freedom* (1853), No. 1033.

2400 ———— Uncle Sam's Emancipation. Earthly Care a Heav-
enly Discipline, and Other Sketches . . .   With a Sketch of
Mrs. Stowe's Family.   Philadelphia: Willis P. Hazard, 1853.
124 p.

AAS, BA, BP, CU, H, HEH, LC, N, NYH, NYP, UC, UM, UP, UVB, Y

Also contains: A Scholar's Adventures in the Country—Children—The
Two Bibles—Christmas; or, The Good Fairy.
Table of contents calls for "Deacon Enos" on p. 125 which apparently
was not printed.

2401 ———— Uncle Tom's Cabin; or, Life among the Lowly . . . Boston: John P. Jewett & Company. Cleveland, Ohio: Jewett, Proctor & Worthington, 1852. 2 vols. (312, 322 p.), illus.

AAS, BA, BP, BU, CU, H, HEH, LC, LCP, N, NYH, NYP, UC, UM, UP, UVB, Y

The *Key to Uncle Tom's Cabin* was published in 1853.

2402 ———— We and Our Neighbors; or, The Records of an Unfashionable Street. (Sequel to "My Wife and I.") A Novel . . . New York: J. B. Ford & Company [cop. 1875]. 480 p., illus. AAS, AP, BA, BP, BU, H, HEH, LC, LCP, N, NYH, NYP, UC, UM, UP, UVB, Y

———— *jt. au. See* Hale, Edward Everett, *ed.* Six of One (1872), No. 1058.

STREBOR, EIGGAM, *pseud. See* Roberts, Maggie

2403 STREET, ALFRED BILLINGS. Woods and Waters; or, The Saranacs and Racket . . . New York: M. Doolady, 1860. 345 p., illus.

AAS, BP, BU, CU, H, HEH, LC, LCP, N, NYP, UC, UM, UVB

2404 STRICKLAND, WILLIAM PETER. The Astrologer of Chaldea; or, The Life of Faith . . . Cincinnati: Jacob Ernst, 1855. 268 p.

HEH, LC, NYP

———— [*See also*] Fletcher, M. The Methodist . . . With an Introduction by W. P. Strickland (1859), No. 923.

2405 [STROTHER, DAVID HUNTER.] Virginia Illustrated: Containing a Visit to the Virginian Canaan, and the Adventures of Porte Crayon [pseud.] and His Cousins . . . New York: Harper & Brothers, 1857. 300 p., illus. AAS, BP, H, HEH, LC, NYP, Y

2406 STROUT, MRS. C. W. D. Slippery Paths: A Temperance Story . . . Portland: Hoyt, Fogg and Breed, 1872. 71 p., front.

AAS, NYP

2407 [SUDDOTH, MRS. HARRIET ALMARIA (BAKER).] An Orphan of the Old Dominion: Her Trials and Travels. Embracing a History of Her Life, Taken Principally from Her Journals and Letters. By Lumina Silvervale [pseud.] . . . Philadelphia: J. B. Lippincott & Co., 1873. 390 p. BP, CU, LC, LCP, Y

SUMMERFIELD, CHARLES. The Texas Camp-Meeting. *In* J. V. Watson, Tales and Takings (1857), No. 2663.

2408 THE SUMMER-LAND: A Southern Story. By a Child of the Sun . . . New York: D. Appleton and Company, 1855. 264 p.   AAS, BP, H, HEH, LC, N, NYH, NYP, UC, UP, UVB, Y
Life on a plantation and in New Orleans.

SUMMERS, THOMAS OSMOND, *ed. See* Keener, John Christian. Post-Oak Circuit (1857), No. 1460.

2409 SUMMERTON, WINTER, *pseud.* Will He Find Her? A Romance of New York and New Orleans . . . New York: Derby and Jackson, 1860. 491 p.   AAS, CU, H, HEH, LC, LCP, NYP

2410 SUMNER, CHARLES ALLEN. 'Round the Horn: A Christmas Yarn . . . San Francisco: Bacon & Company [*ca.* 1865]. Cover title, 18 p.   HEH

2411 [SWAN, CHARLES RED.] Minny Lawson; or, The Outlaws League. A Romance of Gotham. New York: Garrett & Co., 18 Ann Street [185-?]. 109 p. Printed in double cols.
LC, NYP

2412 SWAYZE, JASON C. The Lime-Kiln Man; or, The Victim of Misfortune . . . New York: DeWitt & Davenport, 160 & 162 Nassau St. [cop. 1855]. 98 p.   LC, NYH

2413 SWEAT, MRS. MARGARET JANE (MUSSEY). Ethel's Love-Life: A Novel . . . New York: Rudd & Carleton, 1859. 232 p.
AAS, CU, H, HEH, NYP, UC, UM, UP, Y
Written in a series of letters which treat of Lesbianism.

2414 SWELL LIFE AT SEA; or, Fun, Frigates and Yachting. A Collection of Nautical Yarns . . . New York: Stringer & Townsend, 1854. 432 p.   AAS, BP, CU, H, HEH, LC, N, NYP, UP
Contents: Cruise of a Guineaman, by J. W. Gould—Fitz-Gubin; or, The Admiral's Pet, by J. Hannay—Homeward Bound—An Aquatic Expedition from Gibraltar to Barcelona—Mr. Snigsby's Yacht, by J. Hannay—The Death Shot: A Tale of the Coast Guard.
Also published as: *Thrilling Scenes on the Ocean; or, Swell Life at Sea.* New York: Derby & Jackson, 1860.   LC

2415 SWIFT, JOHN FRANKLIN. Robert Greathouse: An American Novel . . . New York: Carleton. London: S. Low, Son & Co., 1870. 573 p.   BP, H, HEH, LC, NYP
Life on the Comstock Lode.

SYNTAX, SAMUEL, *Esq., pseud.* *See* Francis, Samuel Ward

2416 THE TABLES TURNED: Being an Interesting Incident in the Life of Jack Small and His Companions. Richmond, Ind.: Central B. and T. Committee of Friends, 1865. 16 p.   NYP
A temperance tale.

2417 TALCOTT, MRS. HANNAH ELIZABETH (BRADBURY) GOODWIN. Dr. Howell's Family . . . Boston: Lee & Shepard, 1868. 361 p.
AAS, BU, LCP, UM

2418 [————] Madge; or, Night and Morning. By H. B. G. . . . New York: D. Appleton and Company. London, 1863. 407 p.   AAS, AP, CU, H, HEH, LCP, NYP, UM, Y
Of domestic service and factory life.

2419 [————] Roger Deane's Work. By H. B. G. . . . Boston: Graves and Young, 1863. 48 p.   AAS, BP, HEH, NYH
A farm boy becomes a surgeon during the war.

2420 [————] Sherbrooke. By H. B. G. . . . New York: D. Appleton and Company, 1866. 463 p.
AAS, BP, BU, CU, HEH, N

2421 ———— A Spray from Lucerne . . . Cambridge: printed at the Riverside Press, 1873. 36 p.   AAS, NYP

2422 TALES FOR WINTER NIGHTS: A Choice Collection of Interesting Adventures, Marvellous Stories . . . Philadelphia: Jas. B. Smith & Co., 1855. 288 p.   HEH
Running headline: "Marvellous Repository." See also No. 2424.
On leaves with signature marks is printed: "Vol. II."

2423 TALES OF EUROPEAN LIFE. Boston: Loring, 319 Washington Street [cop. 1870]. 126 p.   BA, BP, LC, NYH

2424 TALES OF ROMANCE: A Series of Entertaining Tales of Manners and Customs, Adventures . . . Philadelphia: Jas. B. Smith & Co., 1855. 288 p.   HEH

Running headline: "Marvellous Repository." See also No. 2422.

2425 TALES OF THE PICKET-GUARD; or, The Blue Devils Driven from Camp. A Collection of Stories Told by Three Rollicking Boys on Picket-Guard. Philadelphia: Barclay & Co., 1864. 84 p., front.   NYH

2426 TALES OF THE TIME. Fitz-Hugh Ludlow, John T. Irving . . . New York: H. Dexter & Co., and Ross & Tousey. Boston: A. Williams & Co., and J. J. Dyer & Co. [1861]. Cover title, 96 p.   UVB

Contains: The Taxidermist, by Fitz-Hugh Ludlow—The Rev. Mr. Tympan's Misfortune, by William Wirt Sikes—Obed Groot, by John T. Irving—Bob O'Link, by Fitz-James O'Brien—Derrick Van Dam, by John T. Irving—The Van Gelders of Matinecock, by John T. Irving—The Little Black Slipper, by Henry P. Leland.

At head of title: "Price Twenty-Five Cents."

2427 [TALIAFERRO, HARDEN E.] Fisher's River (North Carolina): Scenes and Characters. By "Skitt [pseud.], Who Was Raised Thar" . . . New York: Harper & Brothers, 1859. 269 p., illus.

AAS, BA, BP, H, HEH, LC, LCP, N, NYP, UC, UP, UVB, Y

TALMON, THRACE, *pseud.* *See* Putnam, Mrs. Ellen Tryphosa Harrington

TALVI, *pseud.* *See* Robinson, Mrs. Therese Albertine Louise (von Jacob)

2428 TARTAN, *pseud.* Philadelphia Malignants . . . By Tartan [pseud.]. Philadelphia: Weir & Co., 1863. 28 p.

A satire on Philadelphia politics in Biblical style.   HEH, LC, LCP

TATEM, M. H., *pseud.* *See* Hazlett, Helen

2429 TATOR, HENRY H. Brother Jonathan's Cottage; or, A Friend to the Fallen . . . New York: F. Hart, 1854. 235 p.

A temperance novel.   LC, NYP, UM

2430 TAYLOR, BAYARD. Beauty and the Beast, and Tales of Home . . . New York: G. P. Putnam & Sons, 1872. 340 p.

AAS, BA, CU, H, HEH, LC, LCP, N, NYP, UP, UVB, Y

Also contains: The Strange Friend—Jacob Flint's Journey—Can a Life Hide Itself?—Twin-Love—The Experiences of the A. C.—Friend Eli's Daughter—Miss Bartram's Trouble—Mrs. Strongitharm's Report.

————— Friend Eli's Daughter. *In* Atlantic Tales (1866), No. 155.

2431 ————— Hannah Thurston: A Story of American Life . . . New York: G. P. Putnam, 1863. 464 p.

AAS, BA, BP, H, HEH, LC, LCP, N, UC, UP, UVB, Y

2432 ————— John Godfrey's Fortunes, Related by Himself: A Story of American Life . . . New York: G. P. Putnam; Hurd and Houghton, 1864. 511 p. AAS, LC, LCP, N, NYP, Y

2433 ————— Joseph and His Friend: A Story of Pennsylvania . . . New York: G. P. Putnam & Sons. London: S. Low, Son & Marston, 1870. 361 p.

AAS, BA, CU, H, HEH, LC, LCP, N, NYP, UM, UP, UVB, Y

2434 ————— The Story of Kennett . . . New York: G. P. Putnam; Hurd and Houghton, 1866. 418 p.

AAS, AP, BA, BP, BU, H, HEH, LCP, N, NYP, UC, UP, UVB, Y

2435 TAYLOR, BENJAMIN FRANKLIN. The World on Wheels, and Other Sketches . . . Chicago: S. C. Griggs & Co., 1874. 258 p., illus. AAS, CU, H, LC, LCP, N, NYP, UC, UV, Y

2436 TAYLOR, JOSEPH. A Fast Life on the Modern Highway: Being a Glance into the Railroad World from a New Point of View . . . New York: Harper & Brothers, 1874. 220 p., illus.

BA, H, HEH, LC, LCP, NYP, UM, Y

TEMPLETON, TIMOTHY, *pseud. See* Adams, Charles

2437 TEN YEARS OF TORTURE; or, Sutten's Death-Bed Confession of How He Married Miss Martha Morton, an Accomplished Young Lady of Baltimore, with the Hellish Design of Torturing Her to Death . . . Philadelphia, Pa.: C. W. Alexander [cop. 1871]. 76 p., illus. BA, LC

2438 [TERHUNE, MRS. MARY VIRGINIA (HAWES).] Alone. By
Marion Harland [pseud.] . . . Richmond: A. Morris, 1854.
499 p.   H, UV
Life in the south.

2439 [————] At Last: A Novel. By Marion Harland [pseud.]
. . . New York: Carleton. London: S. Low, Son & Co., 1870.
360 p.   AAS, BU, CU, HEH, LC, LCP, UM, UV, Y

2440 [————] The Christmas Holly. By Marion Harland
[pseud.]. New York: Sheldon & Co., 1867. 86, [1] p., illus.
                         AAS, CU, H, HEH, LC, NYH, NYP, UC, UV, Y
Contents: Nettie's Prayer—A Christmas Talk with Mothers.

2441 [————] The Empty Heart; or, Husks. "For Better, for
Worse." By Marion Harland [pseud.]. New York: Carleton,
1871. 353 p.   LC, LCP, NYP, UC
The first story Empty Heart was published in 1863 as Husks; see No.
2446.
This is the first printing in book form of "For Better, for Worse," pp.
[245]-353.

2442 [————] From My Youth Up. By Marion Harland [pseud.]
. . . New York: G. W. Carleton & Co. London: S. Low, Son
& Co., 1874. 390 p.   AAS, CU, H, HEH, LC, LCP, NYP, UP, Y

2443 [————] Helen Gardner's Wedding-Day; or, Colonel Floyd's
Wards. A Battle Summer. By Marion Harland [pseud.].
New York: Carleton. London: S. Low, Son & Co., 1870.
382 p.   AAS, H, HEH, LC, LCP, NYP
The first story Helen Gardner's Wedding-Day was published as "Colonel
Floyd's Wards" in her Husks (1863), No. 2446.
This is the first printing in book form of "A Battle Summer," pp.
[285]-382.

2444 [————] The Hidden Path. By Marion Harland [pseud.]
. . . New York: J. C. Derby. Boston: Phillips, Sampson &
Co. Cincinnati: H. W. Derby, 1855. 434 p.
                              AAS, AP, BU, HEH, LCP, UP, UV

2445 [————] Husbands and Homes. By Marion Harland
[pseud.] . . . New York: Sheldon and Company. Boston:
Gould and Lincoln, 1865. 390 p.
                    AAS, BP, BU, CU, H, HEH, LCP, NYP, UP, UV, Y
Also contains: A Hasty Speech and What Came of It.

2446 [————] Husks. Colonel Floyd's Wards. By Marion Harland [pseud.] . . . New York: Sheldon & Company, 1863. 526 p.   AAS, AP, BU, CU, HEH, LC, LCP, N, NYP, UC, UM, UP, Y
Title story also published as: *The Empty Heart* (1871); see No. 2441. "Colonel Floyd's Wards" also published as: *Helen Gardner's Wedding-Day* (1870), No. 2443.

2447 [————] Jessamine: A Novel. By Marion Harland [pseud.] . . . New York: G. W. Carleton & Co. London: S. Low, Son & Co., 1873. 387 p.   AAS, BU, CU, HEH, LC, LCP, N, NYP, UM

2448 [————] Miriam. By Marion Harland [pseud.] . . . New York: Sheldon & Company. Boston: Gould & Lincoln, 1862. 549 p.   AAS, AP, BA, BU, H, LCP, UM, UP, UV, Y

2449 [————] Moss-Side. By Marion Harland [pseud.] . . . New York: Derby & Jackson, 1857. 450 p.
   AAS, BP, BU, CU, H, HEH, LCP, NYP, UC, UM, UP, UV, Y

2450 [————] Nemesis . . . By Marion Harland [pseud.] . . . New York: Derby & Jackson, 1860. 499 p.
   AAS, BP, BU, CU, H, HEH, LCP, N, NYP, UC, UM, UP, UV, Y

2451 [————] Phemie's Temptation: A Novel. By Marion Harland [pseud.] . . . New York: Carleton. London: S. Low, Son & Co., 1869. 396 p.
   AAS, CU, H, HEH, LC, LCP, NYP, UC, UM, UP
Also contains: Charybdis.

   [————] Poor and Proud, by Marion Harland [pseud.]. *In* M. A. E. Fleming, The Dark Secret [1875], No. 909.

2452 [————] Ruby's Husband. By Marion Harland [pseud.] . . . New York: Sheldon and Company, 1869. 392 p.
   AAS, CU, HEH, LC, LCP, NYP, UP, UV, Y

2453 [————] Sunnybank. By Marion Harland [pseud.] . . . New York: Sheldon and Company, 1866. 415 p.
   AAS, BA, CU, H, HEH, LC, LCP, N, NYP, UC, UM, UP, UV, Y

2454 [————] True as Steel: A Novel. By Marion Harland [pseud.] . . . New York: G. W. Carleton & Co. London: S. Low, Son & Co., 1872. 350 p.
   AAS, H, HEH, LC, LCP, NYP, UC, UM, UP, Y

TERRY, ROSE. *See* Cooke, Mrs. Rose (Terry)

2455 [TEUFFEL, MRS. BLANCHE WILLIS (HOWARD) VON.] One Summer . . . Boston: J. R. Osgood and Company, 1875. 254 p. AAS, CU, H, LC, LCP, NYP, UC, UP, UV, Y

2456 THANKFULLA, *pseud.* Travels of the De le Telle Family. Letters from Europe. By Thankfulla [pseud.]. Buffalo: the Courier Company, printers, 1869. 27 p., illus. NYP, Y
Satire.

2457 THIRTEEN GOOD STORIES FROM OLD AND NEW . . . Boston, Mass.: Old and New office, 143 Washington Street [1873?]. 94 p.
BA

Contents: Devil-Puzzlers, by Fred B. Perkins—The Improvisatore and the Heeler, by Fred W. Loring—Two Princes, by E. E. Hale—In the Wide World, by Theodor Federhorn, tr. from Swedish—Rebecca's Ma, by Fred Loring—What Happened to the Khan and the Poor Man's Son —The Companion of Paradise, by Henry A. Miles—A Tartar Fairy Tale— Spoons in a Wherry, by Mark Sibley Severance—Waveline, by Annie Moore—A Night of Terror, by Mrs. S. De Ponte.

THISTLE, TIMOTHY, *pseud. See* Ellsworth, Oliver

2458 THOMAS, MRS. ABBY (ELDRIDGE). Norman Brill's Life-Work . . . New York: National Temperance Society, 1875. 218 p., front. LC, NYP

THOMAS, CAROLINE, *pseud. See* Dorr, Mrs. Julia Caroline (Ripley)

2459 [THOMAS, FREDERICK WILLIAM.] An Autobiography of William Russell . . . Baltimore: Gobright, Thorne & Co., 1852. 119 p. Printed in double cols. LC, NYP
Laid in Baltimore.

2460 ———— John Randolph, of Roanoke, and Other Sketches of Character, Including William Wirt. Together with Tales of Real Life . . . Philadelphia: A. Hart, 1853. 375 p.
AAS, BA, BU, CU, H, HEH, LC, LCP, N, NYH, NYP, UC, Y
Also contains: Rev. Henry B. Bascom—A Visit to Simon Kenton, the Last of the Pioneers—Old Nat: A Fact—"Old Kentuck:" A True Story —A Frolic among the Lawyers—The Missionary's Convert—My Aunt Betsy—Mary M'Intyre Has Arrived—The Unsummoned Witness—Life in Washington—The Development of Mind and Character—A Chapter of Accidents—The Late Charles Hammond, of Cincinnati—Changes in Our Cities—Shobal Vail Clevenger, the Sculptor—Powell, the Artist— Death of Mr. Webster.

2461   THOMAS, J. N. The Man Whom Everybody Snubbed: A Story of Fact and Fancy . . . Providence: Tillinghast & Mason, 1869. 13 p. Printed in double cols.   AAS, BU

2462   [THOMAS, MARTHA McCANNON.] Life's Lesson: A Tale. New York: Harper & Brothers, 1854. 398 p.
      AAS, CU, H, HEH, LC, NYP, UC, UP

2463   THOMES, WILLIAM HENRY. The Bushrangers. A Yankee's Adventures during His Second Visit to Australia . . . Boston: Lee and Shepard, 1866. 480 p., illus.   NYP

2464   ———— The Gold Hunters' Adventures; or, Life in Australia . . . Boston: Lee & Shepard, 1864. 564 p., illus.
      AAS, H, HEH, Y

2465   ———— The Gold Hunters in Europe; or, The Dead Alive . . . Boston: Lee and Shepard, 1869. 384 p., illus.
At head of title: "The Gold Hunter's Library."   AAS, HEH, NYP

2466   ———— Life in the East Indies . . . Boston: Lee and Shepard. New York: Lee, Shepard and Dillingham, 1873. 354 p., illus.
At head of title: "The Ocean Life Series."   LC, NYP
Copies without date on title page of later issue.

2467   ———— Running the Blockade; or, U. S. Secret Service Adventures . . . Boston: Lee and Shepard. New York: Lee, Shepard and Dillingham, 1875. 474 p., illus.   HEH, LC, NYP

2468   ———— A Slaver's Adventures on Land and Sea . . . Boston: Lee and Shepard. New York: Lee, Shepard and Dillingham [cop. 1872]. 406 p., illus.   CU, LC, NYP
At head of title: "The Ocean Life Series."

2469   ———— The Whaleman's Adventures in the Sandwich Islands and California . . . Boston: Lee and Shepard. New York: Lee, Shepard and Dillingham, 1872. 444 p., illus.
At head of title: "The Ocean Life Series."   AAS, HEH, LC, N
Copies without date on title page of later issue.

2470   [THOMPSON, MRS. CLARA M.] The Chapel of St. Mary . . . Boston: J. E. Tilton and Company, 1861. 396 p.
      AAS, AP, BP, BU, CU, H, HEH, LC, LCP, NYP, UV, Y

2471 ———— Hawthorndean; or, Philip Benton's Family. A Story of Every Day Life . . . Philadelphia: Peter F. Cunningham, 1873. 426 p.   AAS, LC
Laid in Illinois in the 1840's.

2472 [————] The Rectory of Moreland; or, My Duty . . . Boston: J. E. Tilton and Company, 1860. 339 p.
AAS, BP, BU, CU, H, HEH, LC, LCP, NYP, UC, Y

2473 [THOMPSON, DANIEL PIERCE.] Centeola, and Other Tales . . . New York: Carleton, 1864. 312 p.
AAS, BA, BP, CU, H, HEH, LC, LCP, N, NYP, UM, UVB, Y
Contents: Centeola; or, The Maid of the Mounds—The Starving Settlers—The Unfathomable Mystery: A Tale of Circumstantial Evidence—The Rustic Financiers—The Counterfeiter.

2474 [————] The Doomed Chief; or, Two Hundred Years Ago . . . Philadelphia: J. W. Bradley, 1860. 473 p.
BU, CU, H, HEH, LC, N, NYP, UC, UM, UP, UVB, Y
Also issued with imprint: Philadelphia: G. G. Evans. Boston: G. G. Evans, 1860.   AAS, BP

2475 ———— Gaut Gurley; or, The Trappers of Umbagog. A Tale of Border Life . . . Boston: John P. Jewett and Company. Cleveland, Ohio: Henry P. B. Jewett, 1857. 360 p.
AAS, BP, BU, H, HEH, LC, LCP, N, UM, UP, UVB, Y

2476 [————] The Rangers; or, The Tory's Daughter. A Tale Illustrative of the Revolutionary History of Vermont and the Northern Campaign of 1777 . . . Boston: Benjamin B. Mussey and Company, 1851. 2 vols. in 1. (155, 174 p.)
AAS, BP, BU, CU, H, LC, NYP, UVB, Y

THOMPSON, GEORGE. ["One of the most prolific American writers of cheap, racy literature . . . He has escaped the attention of the biographers, and I would refer my readers for particulars of his career to his Autobiography," H. C. Ashbee, *Catena Librorum Tacendorum* (London, 1885), p. 219. The "Jack Harold Series," which includes some of the titles listed below, is a publisher's series, and as such, is outside the scope of this bibliography. Ashbee lists additional titles with no indication of place or date.]

2477 ———— Anna Mowbray; or, Tales of the Harem. New York: Henry R. J. Barkley [n.d.]. 100 p., front. Printed in double cols.

Ashbee, p. 219.

2478 ———— The Brazen Star; or, The Adventures of a New York M. P. A True Tale of the Times We Live In . . . New York: George W. Hill, 1853. 59 p. UP

2479 ———— The Bridal Chamber and Its Mysteries; or, Life at Our Fashionable Hotels. By George Thompson, Esq., Author of "Jack Harold," "His Own Autobiography," "Dashington," "Lady's Garter," "The Actress," and One Hundred Other Popular Tales. New York: published for the author, 1856. 82 p., illus.

Ashbee, p. 218.

2480 [————] Catharine and Clara; or, The Double Suicide. A True Tale of Disappointed Love . . . New York: George W. Hill, 1853. 46 p., illus. BP

Reprinted in his *Harry Glindon* (1854), No. 2484.

The New Hampshire State Library has a copy of the above ed. and a 2d copy, dated 1853, without the publisher's name in imprint.

2481 [————] The Criminal; or, The Adventures of Jack Harold. Being a Sequel to the Tale of "Jack Harold; or, The Criminal's Career." By Greenhorn [pseud.], Author of City Crimes, Venus in Boston, Gay Deceiver, Dissipation, Radcliff, Housebreaker . . . Boston: William Berry & Co., publishers, No. 19 State Street [1851].

Title page and 18 p. of text appended to his *Life and Exploits of "Bristol Bill"* (1851). HEH

Later included as No. 3 in the Frederic A. Brady, publisher [186-?], "Jack Harold Series." UP

AAS has a copy of *Jack Harold; or, The Criminal's Career*, "Jack Harold Series," No. 1.

2482 ———— The Delights of Love; or, The Lady Libertine. Being the Adventures of an Amorous Widow . . . New York: J. H. Farrell, 15 Ann Street [186-?]. 100 p.
Ashbee, p. 203.

2483 ———— The Gay Girls of New York; or, Life on Broadway. Being a Mirror of the Fashions, Follies and Crimes of a Great City. New York: George W. Hill, 1854. 118 p.

Advt. at end of his *Harry Glindon* (1854).

2484 ———— Harry Glindon; or, The Man of Many Crimes. A Startling Narrative of the Career of a Most Desperate Villain ... New York, 1854. 104 p., illus. NYP

Also contains: Catharine and Clara; or, The Double Suicide. A True Tale of Disappointed Love. This was first published in 1853; cf. No. 2480.

2485 ———— Kate Castleton, the Beautiful Milliner; or, The Wife and Widow of a Day. New York: George W. Hill, 1853.

Advt. in his *The Brazen Star* (1853).

2486 [————] The Ladies' Garter. By Greenhorn [pseud.] ... New York: Henry S. G. Smith & Co. [185-?]. 89 p., illus. Printed in double cols. HEH

Caption title: "The Lady's Garter; or, The Platonic Marriage."

2487 [————] Life and Exploits of "Bristol Bill," the Notorious Burglar: Being Compiled from His Own Confessions and the Records of Crime in England and America. Boston: Willis Little & Co., publishers, No. 19 State Street [1851]. 100 p., illus. Printed in double cols. HEH, NYH

Cover imprint: "William Berry & Co., publishers, No. 19 State Street, 1851."

2488 ———— The Locket: A Romance of New York ... New York: P. F. Harris, 1855. 89 p., illus. LC

2489 ———— The Mysteries of Bond Street; or, The Seraglios of Upper Tendom. New York: 1857. 84 p.

Ashbee, p. 219.

2490 [————] The Outlaw; or, The Felon's Fortunes. New York: W. Berry & Co., 1851.

Ed. listed in Roorbach 1820-1852.

Later included as No. 4 in the Frederic A. Brady, publisher [186-?], "Jack Harold Series." AAS, UP

2491 [————] Road to Ruin; or, The Felon's Fortune. New York: W. Berry & Co., 1851.

Ed. listed in Roorbach 1820-1852.

Later included as No. 5 in the Frederic A. Brady, publisher [186-?], "Jack Harold Series," with title: *The Road to Ruin; or, Felon's Doom.*
UP

2492 THOMPSON, MAURICE. Hoosier Mosaics . . . New York: E. J. Hale & Son, 1875. 196 p.

AAS, BP, BU, CU, H, HEH, LC, N, NYP, UVB, Y

Contents: Was She a Boy?—Trout's Luck—Big Medicine—The Venus of Balhinch—The Legend of Potato Creek—Stealing a Conductor—Hoiden —The Pedagogue—An Idyl of the Rod.

THOMPSON, WILLIAM TAPPAN. The Unclad Horseman. *In* T. A. Burke, *ed.*, Polly Peablossom's Wedding (1851), No. 426.

2493 [THOMSON, MORTIMER NEAL.] Doesticks, What He Says. By Q. K. Philander Doesticks, P.B. [pseud.]. New York: Edward Livermore, 1855. 330 p., illus.

AAS, AP, BP, BU, CU, H, HEH, LC, N, NYH, NYP, UC, UM, UVB, Y

Also published as: *Doesticks' Letters and What He Says*. Philadelphia: T. B. Peterson and Brothers, 306 Chestnut Street [after 1857]. AAS, BP, NYP, UP

Copyright notice dated 1855.

[————] *jt. au. See* Underhill, Edward Fitch. The History and Records of the Elephant Club (1856), No. 2572.

2494 THORNTON, JAMES DOUGLAS. Chorronessee, and Other Tales . . . Norfolk [Va.]: printed at the Journal office, 1868. 212 p.

BU, NYP

Also contains: Esther; or, Love and Gratitude—Songs of the Aeronauts —Miscellaneous Poems.

THORPE, KAMBA, *pseud. See* Bellamy, Mrs. Elizabeth Whitfield (Croom)

2495 THORPE, THOMAS BANGS. The Hive of "The Bee-Hunter:" A Repository of Sketches, Including Peculiar American Character, Scenery, and Rural Sports . . . New York: D. Appleton and Company. London, 1854. 312 p., illus.

AAS, BP, BU, CU, H, HEH, LC, N, NYP, UC, UP, UVB, Y

Fourteen of these sketches were previously published, Wright (1774-1850), No. 2594. The following are new: Summer Retreat in Arkansas—Large and Small Steamers of the Mississippi—A Storm Scene on the Mississippi—Mike Fink, the Keel-Boatman—Woodcock Fire-Hunting—Opossum Hunting—A "Hoosier" in Search of Justice—Major Gasden's Story—The Great Four-Mile Day—The Way That Americans Go Down Hill.

2496 [————] The Master's House: A Tale of Southern Life. By
Logan [pseud.] . . . New York: T. L. McElrath & Co.
London: John Cassell, 1854. 391 p., illus.
AAS, BP, CU, HEH, LC, N, NYH, NYP, UC, UP, UVB, Y

2497 THE THRILLING AND EXTRAORDINARY ADVENTURES of Charles L.
Marshall and His Lost Bride, Cornelia Dunnington . . . Phila-
delphia: Barclay & Co., 602 Arch St. [cop. 1866]. 40 p., illus.
HEH

2498 THE THRILLING NARRATIVE AND EXTRAORDINARY ADVENTURES of
Miss Madelaine H. Everett, Who Was Abducted from the
Bloomington Ladies Seminary in Florida . . . Was Finally
Rescued by Her Friends at an Auction Mart in Havana,
Where She Was About to Be Sold as a Slave. Philadelphia:
Barclay & Co., 1859. 40 p., illus.   LC
LC enters under Madelaine H. (Everett) Donaldson.

2499 THRILLING NARRATIVE OF THE LIVES OF SARAH SHARP and Charles
Edwards, the Victims of Crime. Also, the Life, Trial and
Execution of Matthew Carrigan, for the Murder of David
Romer. Cincinnati: H. M. Rulison, 1853. 48 p., illus.   LC

2500 [THROOP, GEORGE HIGBY.] Bertie; or, Life in the Old Field. A
Humorous Novel. By Capt. Gregory Seaworthy [pseud.]
. . . Philadelphia: A. Hart, 1851. 242 p.   LC, NYP, UP

2501 ———— Lynde Weiss: An Autobiography . . . Philadelphia:
Lippincott, Grambo & Co., 1852. 188 p., illus.   BP, LC, UP

2502 TIDBALL, WILLIAM LINN. Mexican's Bride; or, The Ranger's
Revenge . . . New York: Frederic A. Brady, 22 Ann Street
[186-?]. 89 p. Printed in double cols.
Bancroft Library copy, University of California.

2503 ———— Olinda; or, The Mexican's Daughter. A Tale of
Love and War . . . Cincinnati: H. B. Pearson & Co. [cop.
1854]. 89 p. Printed in double cols.
Western Reserve Historical Society copy.

2504 [TIERNAN, MRS. FRANCES CHRISTINE (FISHER).] Carmen's
Inheritance. By Christian Reid [pseud.] . . . Philadelphia:
To-Day Printing and Publishing Company, 1873. 89 p., illus.
Printed in double cols.   BA, LC, LCP, NYP

2505 [————] A Daughter of Bohemia: A Novel. By Christian Reid [pseud.] . . . New York: D. Appleton and Company, 1874. 222 p., illus. Printed in double cols.

AAS, BA, BU, CU, HEH, LC, LCP, UP, UV, Y

2506 [————] Ebb-Tide, and Other Stories. By Christian Reid [pseud.] . . . New York: D. Appleton and Company, 1872. 166 p., illus. Printed in double cols.

AAS, BA, CU, H, HEH, LC, LCP, NYP, UC

Also contains: Miss Inglesby's Sister-in-Law—The Story of a Scar—A Doubt.

2507 [————] Hearts and Hands: A Story in Sixteen Chapters. By Christian Reid [pseud.] . . . New York: D. Appleton and Company, 1875. 99 p. Printed in double cols.

AAS, H, HEH, LC, LCP, NYP

2508 [————] Mabel Lee: A Novel . . . New York: D. Appleton and Company, 1872. 162 p., illus. Printed in double cols.

AAS, BA, CU, H, HEH, LCP, NYP

2509 [————] Morton House: A Novel . . . New York: D. Appleton and Company, 1872. 266 p., illus. Printed in double cols.

AAS, BA, H, HEH, LCP, UP, UV

2510 [————] Nina's Atonement, and Other Stories. By Christian Reid [pseud.] . . . New York: D. Appleton and Company, 1873. 154 p., illus. Printed in double cols.

AAS, BA, CU, H, HEH, LCP, NYP

Also contains: Hugh's Vendetta—Miss Cheriton's Rival—My Story—The Painter's Dream—Powell Vardray's Life—Bernard's Invention.

2511 [————] A Question of Honor: A Novel. By Christian Reid [pseud.] . . . New York: D. Appleton and Company, 1875. 501 p.   ° AAS, BA, HEH, LC, LCP, NYP

2512 [————] Valerie Aylmer: A Novel. By Christian Reid [pseud.] . . . New York: D. Appleton and Company, 1870. 221 p. Printed in double cols.   LC, LCP, Y

2513 TIFFANY, OSMOND. Brandon; or, A Hundred Years Ago. A Tale of the American Colonies . . . New York: Stanford & Delisser, 1858. 285 p.

AAS, BA, BU, CU, H, HEH, LC, LCP, NYP, UM, UV, Y

2514 [TILDEN, CATHERINE.] The First Patient: A Story Written in Aid of the Fair for the "Channing Home" . . . Boston: John Wilson and Son, 1859. 63, [1] p.

AAS, BP, BU, CU, H, HEH, LC, LCP, UC

2515 TILTON, THEODORE. Tempest-Tossed: A Romance . . . New York: Sheldon & Company, 1874. 606 p.

AAS, BA, BP, BU, H, HEH, LC, LCP, N, NYP, UM, UV, Y

2516 [TILTON, WARREN.] Trifleton Papers. By Trifle [pseud.] and the Editor. Boston: Whittemore, Niles and Hall. Milwaukie: A. Whittemore & Co., 1856. 310 p.

AAS, BP, BU, CU, HEH, LC, NYP, UM, UV, Y

William Augustus Crafts, Jr., jt. au.
Written in a series of letters.

2517 TIPPLETONIA and the Countries Adjacent, Considered Historically, Geographically, Politically and Morally. By One Who Has Been There. Terre Haute: Adrian Child, 1854. 121, [1] p., front. LC

A temperance tale.

2518 TITAN AGONISTES: The Story of an Outcast. New York: G. W. Carleton & Co. London: S. Low, Son & Co., 1867. 544 p.

AAS, HEH, LC, LCP, UP

2519 TODD, JOHN. Summer Gleanings; or, Sketches and Incidents of a Pastor's Vacation . . . Collected and Arranged by His Daughter. Northampton: Hopkins, Bridgman & Co., 1852. 281 p., front. AAS, CU, HEH, LC, N, NYH, NYP, UC, Y

2520 TOGETHER: A NOVEL. By the Author of "Nepenthe," "Olie," . . . New York: Carleton, 1865. 259 p. AAS, BP, CU, H, LCP

2521 [TORREY, ELIZABETH R.] Theognis: A Lamp in the Cavern of Evil. By Catius Junior [pseud.] . . . Boston: Wentworth and Company, 1856. 346 p. AAS, BP, CU, H, HEH, Y

Of ethics.

2522 TORREY, MRS. MARY (IDE). City and Country Life; or, Moderate Better Than Rapid Gains . . . Boston: Tappan & Whittemore; John P. Jewett & Co. Milwaukie: A. Whittemore & Co. Chilicothe: Whittemore & Saxton, 1853. 318 p.

AAS, BA, BP, CU, H, HEH, LC, LCP, NYP, Y

2523 [TOURGÉE, ALBION WINEGAR.] Toinette: A Novel. By Henry Churton [pseud.] ... New York: J. B. Ford and Company, 1874. 510 p.   AAS, BA, CU, HEH, LC, LCP, NYP, UV, Y
The South before and after the war.

2524 TOWLES, MRS. CATHARINE WEBB (BARBER). Stories for the American Freemason's Fireside. By Mrs. C. W. Towle [sic], of Alabama. Cincinnati: American Masonic Publishing Association, 1868. 408 p., front.   HEH
According to Appleton and others, Mrs. Towles also wrote *The Three Golden Links* (1857), but this has not been found.

2525 TOWNLEY, ARTHUR. Clifton; or, Modern Fashion, Politics and Morals. A Novel ... Philadelphia: A. Hart, 1852. 192 p. Printed in double cols.   BU, LC

2526 [TOWNSEND, FREDERIC.] Fancies of a Whimsical Man ... New York: John S. Taylor, 1852. 281 p.
    AAS, BP, H, HEH, LC, NYP, UC, UP, Y
An undertone of satirical humor in some of his writings would seem to warrant the inclusion of his works.

2527 [————] Fun and Earnest ... New York: John S. Taylor, 1853. 274 p.   AAS, H, LC, N, NYP, Y

2528 [————] Ghostly Colloquies ... New York: D. Appleton and Company, 1856. 267 p.   AAS, BU, H, HEH, LC, NYP, UC

2529 [————] Glimpses of Nineveh, B.C. 690. New York: Miller & Curtis, 1857. 236 p.   AAS, BP, BU

2530 [————] Mutterings and Musings of an Invalid. New York: John S. Taylor, 1851. 281 p.   AAS, H, LC, NYP, UV
Also published as: *Musings of an Invalid.* New York: John S. Taylor, 1852.   BP, H, LC

2531 [————] Spiritual Visitors ... New York: John S. Taylor, 1854. 346 p.   H, LC, UP
Conversations of distinguished ghosts.

2532 TOWNSEND, GEORGE ALFRED. Lost Abroad . . . Hartford, Conn.: S. M. Betts and Company. Chicago, Ill.: Gibbs & Nichols, 1870. 594 p., front.   AAS, H, LC, UM, Y

2533 [TOWNSEND, MRS. MARY ASHLEY (VAN VOORHIS).] The Brother Clerks: A Tale of New-Orleans. By Xariffa [pseud.]. New York: Derby & Jackson, 1857. 417 p. HEH

2534 TOWNSEND, VIRGINIA FRANCES. The Battle-Fields of Our Fathers . . . New York: John Bradburn, 1864. 368 p.
AAS, BP, CU, HEH, LC, LCP, NYP

2535 ———— Darryll Gap; or, Whether It Paid . . . Boston: William V. Spencer, 1866. 456 p. AAS, LC, NYP, Y

2536 ———— The Deerings of Medbury . . . Boston: Loring [cop. 1871]. 229 p., illus. AAS, BP, HEH, NYP

2537 ———— The Hollands . . . Boston: Loring [cop. 1869]. 412 p. AAS, CU, H, HEH, LC, NYP, UC, UP, Y

2538 ———— Janet Strong . . . Philadelphia: J. B. Lippincott & Co., 1865. 314 p. AAS, LC, LCP, NYP, UP

2539 ———— Living and Loving . . . Philadelphia: J. W. Bradley, 1857. 288 p., front. BU, CU, LC, NYP, UC
Discusses unsuitable marriages.

2540 ———— The Mills of Tuxbury . . . Boston: Loring, 205 Washington Street [cop. 1871]. 363 p., illus.
CU, HEH, LC, NYP

2541 ———— One Woman's Two Lovers; or, Jacqueline Thayne's Choice . . . Philadelphia: J. B. Lippincott & Co., 1875. 284 p. H, LC

2542 ———— Temptation and Triumph, with Other Stories . . . Cincinnati: Poe & Hitchcock; R. P. Thompson, printer, 1863. 389 p. LC, UC
Also contains: The Turrets of the Stone House—How One Will Was Made—After Three Years—The Heart of Mark Truman—Two Evenings, Two Years Apart—Tempted, but Not Overcome—The Old Turnpike Road—One Man's Work—The Story of Edna Randolph—Nathan! Nathan!

2543 ———— While It Was Morning . . . New York: Derby & Jackson, 1858. 374 p. AAS, HEH, UP, Y

TRAFTON, ADELINE. *See* Knox, Mrs. Adeline (Trafton)

2544 TRAMMELL, WILLIAM DUGAS. Ça Ira: A Novel . . . New York: United States Publishing Company, 1874. 358 p.

Laid in Georgia. AAS, H, LC, NYP

TRAP, TIMOTHEUS, *pseud.* *See* Reynolds, Elhanan Winchester

TRIFLE, *pseud.* *See* Tilton, Warren

2545 [TRIPP, ALONZO.] The Fisher Boy. By Willie Triton [pseud.] . . . Boston: Whittemore, Niles & Hall, 1857. 362 p.

Commercial fishing off the New England coast. AAS, NYP, Y

TRITON, WILLIE, *pseud.* *See* Tripp, Alonzo

2546 TROWBRIDGE, JOHN TOWNSEND. Coupon Bonds . . . Boston: Ticknor and Fields, 1866. 48 p. BP, LCP, NYP

2547 —————— Coupon Bonds, and Other Stories . . . Boston: James R. Osgood and Company, 1873. 411 p., illus.

AAS, H, LC, NYH, NYP, Y

Also contains: Madam Waldoborough's Carriage—Fessenden's—Archibald Blossom, Bachelor—In the Ice—Nancy Blynn's Lovers—Mr. Blazay's Experience—Preaching for Selwyn—The Romance of a Glove—The Man Who Stole a Meeting-House.

2548 [——————] The Deserted Family; or, Wanderings of an Outcast. By "Paul Creyton" [pseud.] . . . Boston: L. P. Crown and Company. Philadelphia: J. W. Bradley, 1853. 252 p., front. AAS, H, HEH, Y

2549 [——————] Father Brighthopes; or, An Old Clergyman's Vacation. By Paul Creyton [pseud.]. Boston: Phillips, Sampson & Company, 1853. 274 p., front. AAS, NYP

This was written originally for family reading. In 1875 it was included in the Bright Hope series for older juveniles.

2550 [——————] Hearts and Faces; or, Home-Life Unveiled. By Paul Creyton [pseud.] . . . Boston: Phillips, Sampson and Company, 1853. 288 p., front. AAS, BU, H, HEH, Y

Contents: The Twin Cottages—Marrying a Family—Mary Darwell's Grief—Mutton in Brambletown—The Misfortunes of Basil Gray—Mrs. Dalton's Trials—Lily Bell—The Cross Husband—The Blue Eyes—The Journey for a Wife—Edgar Edson—Mrs. Jaslitt's Spaniel.

2551 ——— Lucy Arlyn . . . Boston: Ticknor and Fields, 1866.
564 p. AAS, BA, BP, CU, H, LC, LCP, NYP, UM, UVB, Y

2552 [———] Martin Merrivale: His X Mark. By Paul Creyton [pseud.] . . . Boston: Phillips, Sampson and Company. New York: J. C. Derby, 1854. 558 p., illus.
AAS, BP, CU, H, HEH, N, UC, UM, UP, UVB, Y
Also issued with imprint: Boston: Lee and Shepard, 1854. NYP
A young writer's adventures in Boston among publishers, editors, and authors.

2553 [———] Neighbor Jackwood. By Paul Creyton [pseud.] . . . Boston: Phillips, Sampson and Company, 1857. 414 p.
Antislavery. BP, H, HEH, LC, N, Y

2554 ——— Neighbors' Wives . . . Boston: Lee and Shepard, 1867. 318 p. AAS, BA, BP, BU, H, HEH, N, NYP, UP, Y

2555 THE TRUE LIFE OF WILLIAM POOL . . . With a Full Account of the Terrible Affray at Stanwix Hall, in Which He Received a Fatal Wound . . . New York: William L. Knapp, 1855. 80 p.
LCP

2556 THE TRUE NARRATIVE of the Five Years' Suffering & Perilous Adventures by Miss Barber, Wife of "Squatting Bear," a Celebrated Sioux Chief . . . Philadelphia: Barclay & Co., No. 21 North Seventh Street [cop. 1872]. 108 p., illus. H
HEH copy with copyright date 1873 collates 107, [1] p.

2557 TRUMAN, ERNEST. Leander; or, Secrets of the Priesthood . . . Philadelphia: Claxton, Remsen and Haffelfinger, 1869. 76 p.
BA, H, LC, LCP, NYP

TRUSEDALE, PHELEG VAN, *pseud.* See Adams, Francis Colburn

TRUSTA, H., *pseud.* See Phelps, Mrs. Elizabeth (Stuart)

2558 TUCKER, ST. GEORGE. Hansford: A Tale of Bacon's Rebellion . . . Richmond, Va.: George M. West, 1857. 356 p.
AAS, BP, BU, CU, H, HEH, LCP, N, NYP, UP, UVB, Y

2559 TUCKER, MRS. WILLIAM H. Hawthorne Dale, and Miscellaneous Sketches, Chiefly Masonic . . . Chicago: Chicago Printers' Co-Operative Association, 1869. 394 p.

AAS, LC, N, UC

Also contains: Masonic Address [by William H. Tucker]—A Romance of Chicago—A Hospital Scene—My Mother's Grave—The Stricken Mother—A Masonic Funeral—Kelley's Island.

2560 TURNBULL, CHARLOTTE. The Lawrences: A Twenty Years' History . . . New York: the American News Company [cop. 1872]. 498 p.

BA, CU, LC

Also published as: *The Lawrences: New England Men and Women as They Grow Up and Develop*. New York: United States Publishing Company, 1874. Y

2561 TURNER, BESSIE A. A Woman in the Case: A Story . . . New York: G. W. Carleton & Co. London: Low, Son & Co., 1875. 288 p., front.

HEH, LC, LCP

A detective story.

2562 TURNER, WILLIAM WILBERFORCE. Jack Hopeton; or, The Adventures of a Georgian . . . New York: Derby & Jackson, 1860. 364 p.

AAS, BP, CU, HEH, LC, LCP, N, NYP, UC, UM, UP, UV, Y

2563 TURNOVER: A Tale of New Hampshire. Boston: James French; Redding and Company; Hotchkiss and Company, 1853. 86 p.

BP, LC

2564 TUTHILL, MRS. LOUISA CAROLINE (HUGGINS). Reality; or, The Millionaire's Daughter. A Book for Young Men and Young Women . . . New York: C. Scribner, 1856. 310 p.

H, HEH, LC, NYP, Y

TUTTLE, SAMUEL WATKINS. Let Those Laugh Who Win. *In* Stories and Sketches (1867), No. 2386.

———— Sam's Sermon. *In* Rougegorge (1870), No. 2130.

TWAIN, MARK, *pseud. See* Clemens, Samuel Langhorne

2565 TWELLS, MRS. JULIA HELEN (WATTS). The Mills of the Gods: A Novel . . . Philadelphia: J. B. Lippincott & Co., 1875. 366 p.

AAS, BP, HEH, LC, LCP, NYP

2566 THE TWO LOVERS; or, A Sister's Devotion. A Domestic Story
... Philadelphia: T. B. Peterson, 1857.
Title listed in Roorbach 1855-1858.

2567 TWO WAYS TO WEDLOCK: A Novellette. (Reprinted from the
New York Home Journal.) New York: Rudd & Carleton,
1859. 253 p.   AAS, BP, HEH, LCP, NYP, UP, Y
This has been attributed to Sarah S. Ellis.
New York City society in 1835.

2568 TYLER, MRS. MARTHA W. A Book without a Title; or, Thrilling
Events in the Life of Mira Dana ... Boston: printed for the
author, 1855. 260 p.   AAS, BP, HEH

2569 ——————— —————— 2d ed., with Additions. Boston: printed
for the author, 1856. 298 p.   AAS, CU
Last three chapters of 1st ed. rewritten and two more added.

2570 TYLER, MOSES COIT. The Brawnville Papers: Being Memorials
of the Brawnville Athletic Club ... Boston: Fields, Osgood
& Co., 1869. 215 p.
AAS, BP, BU, CU, H, HEH, LCP, N, NYP, UC, UP, UVB, Y

2571 TYNG, STEPHEN HIGGINSON. The Captive Orphan: Esther the
Queen of Persia ... New York: Robert Carter & Brothers,
1860. 414 p.   HEH, NYP

UMSTED, MRS. LILLIE (DEVEREUX). See Blake, Mrs. Lillie
(Devereux) Umsted

UNCLE BEN, pseud. See White, Mrs. Rhoda Elizabeth (Waterman)

2572 [UNDERHILL, EDWARD FITCH.] The History and Records of
the Elephant Club, Compiled from Authentic Documents
Now in Possession of the Zoölogical Society. By Knight
Russ Ockside, M.D. [pseud.] and Q. K. Philander Doesticks,
P.B. [pseud.]. New York: Livermore & Rudd, 1856. 321 p.,
illus.   AAS, BP, H, HEH, LC, N, NYP, UC
Mortimer Thomson, jt. au.

2573 UNDERWOOD, FRANCIS HENRY. Cloud-Pictures: 1. The Exile of Von Adelstein's Soul; 2. Topankalon; 3. Herr Regenbogen's Concert; 4. A Great-Organ Prelude . . . Boston: Lee and Shepard. New York: Lee, Shepard & Dillingham, 1872. 166 p.   AAS, BA, BP, CU, H, HEH, LC, NYP, Y

2574 ———— Lord of Himself: A Novel . . . Boston: Lee and Shepard. New York: Lee, Shepard and Dillingham, 1874. 512 p.   AAS, BA, BP, CU, H, HEH, LC, LCP, NYP
Ante bellum Kentucky.

2575 UPTON, GEORGE PUTNAM. Letters of Peregrine Pickle . . . Chicago: the Western News Company, 1869.   340 p.
BP, CU, H, HEH, LC, N, NYH, UM

2576 URBINO, MRS. LEVINA (BUONCUORE). Sunshine in the Palace and Cottage; or, Bright Extremes in Human Life . . . Boston: Heath and Graves, 1854.   239 p., illus.   AAS, BP, H, HEH, LC
Also published as: *The Home Angel*. Boston: Wentworth and Company, 1857.   AAS, HEH, N, NYP, Y

VALE, FERNA, *pseud.   See* Hallett, Miss E. V.

VALERIO, KATHERINE, *pseud.   See* Washburn, Mrs. Katharine (Sedgwick)

2577 VAN ALSTYNE, MRS. FRANCES JANE (CROSBY). A Wreath of Columbia's Flowers.   1858 . . . New York: H. Dayton, 107 Nassau Street [cop. 1858].   138 p.   AAS, BU, NYP, UM
Contains: The Mountain Chief; or, The Home of Medora—Annie Herbert—Phillip Synclave; or, The Traitor's Reward—Margerie; or, The Sybil of the Revolution.

2578 VAN NAMEE, J. WILLIAM. The Faithless Guardian; or, Out of the Darkness into the Light. A Story of Struggles, Trials, Doubts, and Triumphs. By J. William Van Namee, Author of "In the Cups," "The Unknown," "Estelle Graham," "A Prize Story," "Woman's Love," "Pride and Passion," "Adown the Tide," "Deep Waters," "Guardian Angels" . . . Boston: William White and Company. New York: the American News Company, 1870.   246 p.   AAS, LC

343

2579   ———— Hopedale Tavern and What It Wrought . . . New York: National Temperance Society, 1870. 252 p., illus.
Information from LC card for copy withdrawn from circulation.

2580 [————] Juliette Moore; or, Passion and Reality. A Tale of the South. By Willie Ware [pseud.], Author of "Driftwood," "Estella Graham," "Pride and Passion," "Woman's Revenge," "The Choice," "Deep Waters" . . . Franklin Mills, Ohio: Marsh, Dewey & Co., 1861. 54 p. Printed in double cols.   LC

2581 VAN RENSSELAER, LESLIE. Search after a Lost Heart . . .. New York: Cushing, Bardua & Co., 1873. 292 p.   AAS, CU
With this was issued his: *The Marriage Contract: A Mystery.* New York: Cushing, Bardua & Co., 1873. 152 p.

VAN TRUSEDALE, PHELEG, *pseud.* *See* Adams, Francis Colburn

2582 VANCE, SUSA A. Lois Carrol; or, Her Two Selves . . . Philadelphia: J. B. Lippincott & Co., 1874. 327 p.   LC, UV

2583 [VARNHAM, MRS. R. G.] Boston Common: Tale of Our Own Times. By a Lady . . . Boston: James French & Company, 1856. 556 p.   AAS, HEH, NYP, UC, Y
This has been attributed to a Mrs. Farren.

VERNON, CHARLIE, *pseud.* *See* Craven, Braxton

VERNON, RUTH, *pseud.* *See* Ram, Stopford James

VIATOR, *pseud.* *See* Smith, Nathan Ryno

2584 [VICTOR, MRS. METTA VICTORIA (FULLER).] The Dead Letter: An American Romance. By Seeley Regester [pseud.]. New York: Beadle and Company, 1867. 308 p., illus.
    AAS, CU, LC, NYP, Y

2585 ———— Fashionable Dissipation . . . Philadelphia: See, Peters & Co., 1854. 237 p., front.   Y
Also contains: Adela Lincoln: A Tale of the Wine Cup, by M. F. Carey, with separate title page but with continuous pagination.

2586 [————] The Figure Eight; or, The Mystery of Meredith Place. By Seeley Regester [pseud.] . . . New York: Beadle & Company, 98 William Street [cop. 1869]. 111 p., illus. Printed in double cols. BP, HEH, LC

2587 ———— Fresh Leaves from Western Woods . . . Buffalo: Geo. H. Derby and Co., 1852. 315 p., illus.

AAS, HEH, LC, N, UC, Y

Contents: The Tempter—A Sequel to the Tempter—The Silver Lute; or, The Gipsy Singer—The Lost Glove—The Living Statue—Mother and Daughter—Edith Manfred—Innocence.

2588 [————] Miss Slimmens' Window, and Other Papers. By Mrs. Mark Peabody [pseud.] . . . New York: Derby & Jackson, 1859. 312 p., illus.

AAS, BU, HEH, LC, LCP, NYH, NYP, UC, Y

Also contains: The Tallow Family in America—Lucy in the City—Mr. Fitz Foom in the Country.

2589 ———— Mormon Wives: A Narrative of Facts Stranger Than Fiction . . . New York: Derby & Jackson. Cincinnati: H. W. Derby & Co., 1856. 326 p.

AAS, BU, CU, H, HEH, LC, N, NYP, UM

Also published as: *Lives of Female Mormons*. Philadelphia: G. G. Evans, 1860. LC

2590 ———— The Senator's Son; or, The Maine Law a Last Refuge. A Story Dedicated to the Law-Makers . . . Cleveland, O.: Tooker and Gatchel, 1853. 291 p.

BP, HEH, N, UC, UM, Y

Also published as: *Parke Madison; or, Fashion the Father of Intemperance*. Auburn and Buffalo: Miller, Orton & Mulligan, 1855. LC

[————] The Skeleton at the Banquet, by Seeley Regester [pseud.]. *In* Stories and Sketches (1867), No. 2386.

2591 [————] Too True: A Story of To-Day. New York: G. P. Putnam & Son, 1868. 295 p. AAS, HEH, LC, LCP, NYP, Y

2592 ———— Who Was He? A Story of Two Lives . . . New York: Beadle and Company, 118 William Street [cop. 1866]. 83 p., front. Printed in double cols. BP, LC

VICTOR, VERITY, *pseud. See* Wright, E. M.

2593 VIDI, *pseud*. Mr. Frank, the Underground Mail-Agent. By Vidi [pseud.] . . . Philadelphia: Lippincott, Grambo & Co., 1853. 238 p., illus.　AAS, BP, CU, H, HEH, LC, N, UM, UP, UVB, Y

Proslavery.

2594 VINCENT, ELLERTON. The Artist's Dream . . . New York: G. W. Carleton & Co. London: S. Low, Son & Co., 1868. 374 p.　HEH, LC, LCP

2595 [VINGUT, MRS. GERTRUDE (FAIRFIELD).] Irene; or, The Autobiography of an Artist's Daughter. And Other Tales. Boston: Damrell and Moore, 1853. 383 p., front.

AAS, BU, CU, H, HEH, LC, N, NYP, UC, UM

Contents: The Vice President's Daughter, by Miss G. G. Fairfield—The Wife of Two Husbands, by Miss G. G. Fairfield—Irene; or, The Autobiography of an Artist's Daughter, by Miss Gertrude Fairfield.

2596 ———— Naomi Torrente: The History of a Woman . . . New York: John Bradburn, 1864. 275 p., front.

AAS, BP, H, HEH, LC, LCP, UV

2597 ———— ———— New York: John Bradburn, 1864. 326 p.

NYP

This ed. adds: "Our Unity as a Nation," and other prose and verse.

2598 A VOICE FROM THE PARSONAGE; or, Life in the Ministry. Boston: S. K. Whipple and Company, 1854. 470 p.

AAS, BA, BP, H, HEH

On the injustice of dismission.

2599 VOSE, JOHN DENISON. Fresh Leaves from the Diary of a Broadway Dandy. Edited by John D. Vose. Revised, Enlarged and Corrected by the Author . . . New York: Bunnell & Price, 1852. 123 p., illus.　AAS, H, LC, NYH, NYP

First ed. in book form.

2600 ———— Seven Nights in Gotham . . . New York: Bunnell & Price, 1852. 128 p., illus.　AAS, H, NYH, UP, Y

Also published as: *Ten Years on the Town; or, The Adventures of the Played-Out Club*. New York: Dick & Fitzgerald [cop. 1863].　LC

2601 ———— Yale College "Scrapes" . . . New York: Bunnell &
Price, 121 Fulton Street [1852?]. 114 p.   H
Copies examined of the Garrett & Co. and the Dick & Fitzgerald
imprints appear to be later reprints.
Also published as: *The Gay Boys of Old Yale: A Book of Wit and
Humor.* Hinsdale, N. H.: Hunter & Co., 1869. 98 p.   Y

2602 [VOSE, REUBEN.] Despotism; or, The Last Days of the Amer-
ican Republic. By Invisible Sam [pseud.] . . . New York:
Hall & Willson, 1856. 463 p.
Anti-Catholic.   AAS, BP, CU, HEH, LC, N, NYH, NYP, UC, UM, Y

W., A. O.   *See* Wheeler, A. O.

W., C. S.   *See* Guild, Mrs. Caroline Snowden (Whitmarsh)

W., H. LL.   *See* Williams, Henry Llewellyn

W., I.   *See* Sands, Alexander Hamilton

2603 WAISBROOKER, MRS. LOIS (NICHOLS). Alice Vale: A Story for
the Times . . . Boston: William White and Company. New
York: the American News Company, 1869. 255 p.
                                            BU, LC, NYP, Y

2604 ———— Helen Harlow's Vow . . . Boston: William White
and Company. New York: the American News Company,
1870. 290 p.   HEH, LC
An unwed mother overcomes social ostracism.

2605 ———— Mayweed Blossoms . . . Boston: William White
and Company. New York: the American News Company,
1871. 264 p.   BP, LC
Contains: Charity; Founded on Facts.

2606 ———— Nothing like It; or, Steps to the Kingdom . . . Boston: Colby & Rich, 1875. 336 p.   AAS, BP, LC
On free love.

WAITE, CHARLES E. The Chevalier Tremlet. *In* A. J. H.
Duganne, The Prince Corsair [185-?], No. 797.

347

———— A Tale of a Crusader. *In* M. M. Ballou, The Duke's Prize [185-?], No. 203.

2607 WAKEMAN, JOEL. The Mysterious Parchment; or, The Satanic License. Dedicated to Maine Law Progress . . . Boston: John P. Jewett and Company. Cleveland, Ohio: Jewett, Proctor and Worthington, 1853. 323 p., front.

AAS, CU, H, HEH, N

Also published as: *The Maine Law Triumphant; or, The Mysterious Parchment and Satanic License. Showing the Necessity of Total Abstinence and Stringent Prohibitory Laws.* Boston: Albert Colby and Company, 1859. AAS, HEH, Y

2608 [WALDO, JAMES CURTIS.] Mardi Gras: A Tale of Ante Bellum Times. By Tim Linkinwater [pseud.] . . . New Orleans: P. F. Gogarty, 1871. 131, [1] p. Printed in double cols. LC

2609 WALKER, DEMOSTHENES. Stanley; or, Playing for Amusement and Betting to Beat the Game. Scenes in the South . . . Nashville, Tenn.: printed for the author by J. B. M'Ferrin, 1860. 320 p. AAS, Y

2610 [WALKER, MRS. MARY (SPRING).] The Family Doctor; or, Mrs. Barry and Her Bourbon . . . Boston: Henry Hoyt [cop. 1868]. 384 p., illus. AAS
A temperance novel.

2611 ———— The Rev. Dr. Willoughby and His Wine . . . New York: National Temperance Society, 1869. 458 p., illus.
A temperance novel. BU, H, LC

2612 [WALL, SARAH E.] Orange Grove: A Tale of the Connecticut . . . Worcester: B. G. Howes, 1866. 420 p.

AAS, BP, BU, HEH, LC, NYP, UP, Y

2613 WALLACE, MRS. E. D. Strife: A Romance of Germany and Italy . . . Philadelphia: H. C. Rogers & Co., 1871. 335 p.

H, NYP

2614 WALLACE, LEWIS. The Fair God; or, The Last of the 'Tzins. A Tale of the Conquest of Mexico . . . Boston: James R. Osgood and Company, 1873. 586 p.

AAS, BP, CU, H, HEH, LC, LCP, N, UV, Y

2615 WALLACE, M. A. Well! Well! A Tale Founded on Fact . . . [2d ed.]. New York: D. & J. Sadlier & Co.; 31 Barclay Street, Boston; 128 Federal Street, Montreal, C. E., 1863. 312 p. LC

Date in copyright notice 1855. Roorbach 1855-1858 lists: New York: Sadlier & Co., 1856.

2616 WALSINGHAM, CHARLOTTE, *pseud.?* Annette; or, The Chronicles of Bellevue . . . Philadelphia: Claxton, Remsen & Haffelfinger, 1875. 374 p. BP, H, HEH, LC, LCP, NYP

Laid in Pennsylvania at the turn of the century.

2617 WALWORTH, MRS. JEANNETTE RITCHIE (HADERMANN). Against the World . . . Boston: Shepard and Gill, 1873. 334 p.

AAS, H, Y

2618 ———— Dead Men's Shoes: A Romance . . . Philadelphia: J. B. Lippincott & Co., 1872. 420 p. BP, HEH, LC

Laid in Louisiana.

2619 ———— Forgiven at Last . . . Philadelphia: J. B. Lippincott & Co., 1870. 333 p. LC

Laid in the South during the war.

———— How Mother Did It. *In* Not Pretty, but Precious (1872), No. 1804.

2620 WALWORTH, MANSFIELD TRACY. Beverly; or, The White Mask. A Novel . . . New York: G. W. Carleton & Co. London: S. Low, Son & Co., 1872. 422 p. AAS, HEH, NYP

2621 ———— Delaplaine; or, The Sacrifice of Irene. A Novel . . . New York: G. W. Carleton & Co. London: J. C. Hotten, 1871. 300 p. AAS, BP, BU, H, HEH, LC, N, NYH, NYP, Y

An historical novel laid in Persia.

2622 ———— Hotspur: A Tale of the Old Dutch Manor . . . New York: Carleton, 1864. 324 p.

Laid in New York. AAS, BP, H, HEH, LC, LCP, NYP, UM, UP

2623 ———— Lulu: A Tale of the National Hotel Poisoning . . . New York: Carleton, 1863. 367 p.

Laid in Washington, D. C. AAS, BP, CU, H, HEH, LC, LCP, N, NYP, UC

2624 ———— The Mission of Death: A Tale of the New York Penal Laws . . . New York: D. & J. Sadlier & Co., 1854. 281 p.

No copy found. Reviewed in *Brownson's Quarterly Rev.*, 3d ser., II (Jan. 1854), 133.

Xavier University Library has a copy dated 1855, with copyright notice dated 1853.

N has copy with imprint: New York: D. & J. Sadlier & Co.; 31 Barclay Street, Boston; 128 Federal Street, Montreal [cop. 1853].

2625 ———— Stormcliff: A Tale of the Highlands . . . New York: Carleton, 1866. 387 p. AAS, HEH

2626 ———— Warwick; or, The Lost Nationalities of America. A Novel . . . New York: G. W. Carleton. London: Low, Son & Co., 1869. 470 p. AAS, CU, H, HEH, N, NYP, UM, UP, Y

WARBLER, FOREST, *pseud.* *See* McCormick, M. R.

WARD, ARTEMUS, *pseud.* *See* Browne, Charles Farrar

2627 WARD, AUSTIN N., *pseud.?* The Husband in Utah; or, Sights and Scenes among the Mormons, with Remarks on Their Moral and Social Economy. By Austin N. Ward [pseud.?]. Edited by Maria Ward [pseud.?] . . . New York: Derby & Jackson. Cincinnati: H. W. Derby & Co. London: Sampson Low, Son & Co., 1857. 310, 130 p., illus.

The 130 p. at end on "Mormonism." CU, H, HEH, LC, LCP, NYP, UM, Y

Also published as: *Male Life among the Mormons; or, The Husband in Utah.* Philadelphia: John E. Potter and Company [cop. 1863]. 310 p.
AAS, CU, H, LC, NYH, NYP, UC, UV

WARD, MRS. BETSEY JANE, *pseud.* *See* Comstock, William

2628 WARD, MRS. ELIZABETH STUART (PHELPS). The Gates Ajar. By Elizabeth Stuart Phelps . . . Boston: Fields, Osgood & Co., 1869. 248 p.
AAS, BP, BU, CU, H, HEH, LC, LCP, N, NYP, UC, UM, UP, UV, Y

First printing probably one with "nears" in second line of dedication instead of "approaches."

2629 ———— Hedged In . . . Boston: Fields, Osgood & Co., 1870. 295 p. AAS, BA, BP, BU, H, HEH, LC, LCP, N, NYP, UC, UM, UP, Y

2630 ———— Men, Women and Ghosts . . . Boston: Fields, Osgood & Co., 1869. 334 p.

AAS, BA, BP, BU, H, HEH, LC, LCP, N, NYP, UC, UM, UP, Y

Contents: No News—The Tenth of January—Night-Watches—The Day of My Death—"Little Tommy Tucker"—One of the Elect—What Was the Matter?—In the Gray Goth—Calico—Kentucky's Ghost.

2631 ———— The Silent Partner . . . Boston: James R. Osgood and Company. London: Sampson Low & Co., 1871. 302 p.

AAS, BA, BP, BU, H, HEH, LC, LCP, N, NYP, UC, UM, UP, Y

2632 [WARD, MRS. MARIA] *pseud.?* Female Life among the Mormons: A Narrative of Many Years' Personal Experience. By the Wife of a Mormon Elder Recently from Utah. New York: J. C. Derby. Cincinnati: H. W. Derby. Buffalo: Wanzer, McKim & Co. Chicago: D. B. Cooke & Co. Detroit: Kerr, Morley & Co. St. Louis: Edwards & Bushnell, 1855. 449 p., front. AAS, BP, BU, CU, H, HEH, LC, N, NYP

Sabin 24185 attributes this to a Mrs. Benjamin G. Ferris.

Also published as: *Maria Ward's Disclosures: Female Life among the Mormons* . . . New York: Derby & Jackson, 1858. 449 p., illus. N

Also published as: *The Mormon Wife: A Life Story of the Sacrifices, Sorrows and Sufferings of Woman.* Hartford, Conn.: Hartford Publishing Company, 1872. 449 p., illus. H, NYP, UM, Y

———— *ed. See* Ward, Austin N., *pseud.?* The Husband in Utah (1857), No. 2627.

2633 WARDEN, HARMER S. Black Rolf; or, The Red Witch of Wissahickon. Being the History of the Blue Beards and Scarlet Ribbons. A Tale of Secret Crimes and Hidden Mysteries of Quakerdom . . . Philadelphia: A. Winch, 505 Chestnut Street [cop. 1856]. 96 p. Printed in double cols. AAS

WARE, WILLIE, *pseud. See* Van Namee, J. William

2634 WARFIELD, MRS. CATHERINE ANN (WARE). A Double Wedding; or, How She Was Won . . . Philadelphia: T. B. Peterson & Brothers, 306 Chestnut Street [cop. 1875]. 406 p.

AAS, H, HEH, LC, LCP, NYP, Y

2635 ———— Hester Howard's Temptation: A Soul's Story . . . Philadelphia: T. B. Peterson & Brothers, 306 Chestnut Street [cop. 1875]. 569 p. AAS, CU, H, HEH, LCP, N, NYP, UP, Y

2636 [————] The Household of Bouverie; or, The Elixir of Gold. A Romance, by a Southern Lady . . . New York: Derby & Jackson, 1860. 2 vols. (373, 413 p.)
AAS, AP, BP, BU, CU, H, HEH, LC, LCP, N, NYP, UC, UM, UP, UV, Y
Laid in Kentucky.

2637 [————] Miriam Monfort: A Novel . . . New York: D. Appleton and Company, 1873. 556 p.
AAS, BU, HEH, LC, LCP, N, UC, UV
Also contains: Life at "Lesdernier"—Sea and Shore.

2638 [————] The Romance of Beauseincourt: An Episode Extracted from the Retrospect of Miriam Monfort . . . New York: G. W. Carleton & Co. London: S. Low, Son & Co., 1867. 456 p.　AAS, CU, LC, N, NYP, UC, Y

2639 ———— The Romance of the Green Seal . . . New York: Beadle and Company, 118 William Street [cop. 1866]. 73 p., front.　BP, LC

2640 [WARNER, ANNA BARTLETT.] Dollars and Cents. By Amy Lothrop [pseud.] . . . New York: George P. Putnam, 1852. 2 vols. (515 p.)
AAS, AP, BA, BP, BU, CU, H, HEH, LC, LCP, N, NYP(v.2), UC, UP, UV, Y

2641 [————] Miss Tiller's Vegetable Garden and the Money She Made by It . . . New York: Anson D. Randolph & Company, 770 Broadway [cop. 1873]. 140 p.　AAS, BA, BP, LC, LCP

2642 ———— My Brother's Keeper . . . New York: D. Appleton & Company. London, 1855. 385 p.
AAS, HEH, LC, NYP, UC, UV

WARNER, CHARLES DUDLEY, *jt. au. See* Clemens, Samuel Langhorne. The Gilded Age (1873), No. 549.

2643 [WARNER, ELIZA A.] Our Two Lives; or, Graham and I. By A. H. K. [pseud.]. New York: Anson D. F. Randolph & Company, 770 Broadway [cop. 1873]. 233 p.
CU, H, HEH, LC, NYP, Y
On marriage.

2644 WARNER, FANNIE. Beech Bluff: A Tale of the South . . . Philadelphia: Peter F. Cunningham, 1870. 332 p.   LC, Y
Also contains: Agnes–After Many Days.

2645 [WARNER, SUSAN BOGERT.] Daisy. Continued from "Melbourne House" . . . Philadelphia: Lippincott & Company, 1868-69. 2 vols. (435, 380 p.)
AAS, CU, HEH(V.1), LC, LCP, N, NYP(V.1), UP, Y
Vol. II called "Second Series" on title page.

2646 [————] The Hills of the Shatemuc . . . New York: D. Appleton and Company, 1856. 516 p.
AAS, BA, BP, BU, CU, H, HEH, LC, LCP, N, NYP, UC, UP, UVB, Y

2647 [————] Melbourne House . . . New York: Robert Carter & Brothers, 1864. 2 vols. (300, 306 p.), front.
AAS, CU, H, HEH, LC, LCP, UC, UP, UV

2648 [————] The Old Helmet . . . New York: Robert Carter & Brothers, 1864. 2 vols. (328, 368 p.)
AAS, BA, BU, CU, H, HEH, LC, LCP, N, NYP, UC, UP, Y
Also issued with imprint: New York: Robert Carter & Brothers. Philadelphia: J. B. Lippincott & Co., 1864.   AP

2649 [————] Queechy. By Elizabeth Wetherell [pseud.] . . . New York: George P. Putnam, 1852. 2 vols. (410, 396 p.)
AAS, BU, CU, H, HEH, LC, LCP, N, NYH, NYP, UC, UP, UVB, Y

2650 [————] Say and Seal . . . Philadelphia: J. B. Lippincott & Co., 1860. 2 vols. (513, 500 p.)
AAS, AP, BU, H, HEH, LC, LCP, N, NYP, UC, UM(V.1), UP, UVB, Y

2651 [————] The Wide, Wide World. By Elizabeth Wetherell [pseud.] . . . New York: George P. Putnam, 1851. 2 vols. (360, 330 p.)   AAS, AP, BA, H, LCP, UP, UVB, Y

2652 WARREN, EBENEZER W. Nellie Norton; or, Southern Slavery and the Bible. A Scriptural Refutation of the Principal Arguments upon Which the Abolitionists Rely. A Vindication of Southern Slavery from the Old and New Testaments . . . Macon, Ga.: Burke, Boykin & Company, 1864. 208 p.
CU, LC, NYH, NYP, UVB, Y

2653 WARREN, ISRAEL PERKINS. Chauncey Judd; or, The Stolen Boy. A Story of the Revolution . . . New York: Warren and Wyman [cop. 1874]. 314 p., illus.   H, Y

2654 [WARREN, NATHAN BOUGHTON.] The Lady of Lawford, and Other Christmas Stories . . . Troy, N. Y.: H. B. Nims and Company [cop. 1874]. 346 p., illus.   AAS, BP, CU, HEH, LC, Y
Also contains: Lawford Hall; or, The Story of a Haunted House—Parson Ingram: A Tale of True Love—Hidden Treasure; or, The Good St. Nicholas.

2655 [————] Lawford Hall, and The Lady of Lawford; or, The Boughtons of Warwickshire . . . [Hartford, Conn.: M. H. Mallory & Co.] 1873. 93 p., front.   AAS, LC
These two stories are included in the above collection, but "Lawford Hall" was rewritten.

2656 [WARRINER, EDWARD AUGUSTUS.] Victor la Tourette: A Novel. By a Broad Churchman . . . Boston: Roberts Brothers, 1875. 406 p.   BP, H, HEH, LC, LCP, NYP
Religion on the Michigan frontier.

2657 [WASHBURN, CHARLES AMES.] Gomery of Montgomery: A Family History . . . New York: Carleton, 1865. 2 vols. (309, 316 p.)   AAS, BP, H, HEH, LC, LCP, NYP, UC
The period after the American Revolution.

2658 [————] Philip Thaxter: A Novel. New York: Rudd & Carleton, 1861. 350 p.
AAS, BP, HEH, LC, LCP, NYP, UC, UM, UP, UVB, Y
Life in California and at the mines.

2659 [WASHBURN, MRS. KATHARINE (SEDGWICK).] Ina. By Katherine Valerio [pseud.]. Boston: James R. Osgood and Company, 1871. 133 p. Printed in double cols.
AAS cover title dated 1872.   AAS, BP, H, HEH, LC, NYP
Laid in "Turine."

2660 ———— The Italian Girl . . . Boston: Lee and Shepard. New York: Lee, Shepard and Dillingham, 1874. 390 p.
AAS, BA, HEH, LC, NYP
Begins career as circus rider in America and later becomes famous actress in Italy.

2661   ———— Perfect Love Casteth Out Fear . . . Boston: Lee and Shepard. New York: Lee, Shepard and Dillingham, 1875. 319 p.   AAS, BA, BP, H, LC, NYP, Y
Americans in Italy.

2662   [WASHBURN, WILLIAM TUCKER.] Fair Harvard: A Story of American College Life . . . New York: G. P. Putnam & Son. London: S. Low, Son & Marston, 1869. 309 p.
AAS, BA, BU, CU, H, HEH, LC, NYP, UC, UP, UV, Y

2663   WATSON, JAMES V. Tales and Takings, Sketches and Incidents, from the Itinerant and Editorial Budget of Rev. J. V. Watson . . . New York: Carlton & Porter, 1857. 466 p.
AAS, BP, HEH, LC, N, NYH, Y
Contains: The Young Preacher—Self-Disparagement; or, Elder Blunt and Sister Scrub—The Eleventh Commandment, by T. S. Arthur—The Village Slander, by William Comstock—Charity Envieth Not, by Alice B. Neal—The New Pleasure, by T. S. Arthur—The Unmeant Rebuke, by Sylvanus Cobb—Marrying Rich, by W. B. Slaughter—The Sea-Captain's Daughters—The Texas Camp-Meeting, by Charles Summerfield—The Poor Washerwoman, by Mrs. Caroline A. Soule.

2664   WAYNE, MARION W. Marguerite Kent: A Novel . . . Philadelphia: J. B. Lippincott & Co., 1870. 511 p.   AAS, HEH, LCP

2665   WE, BY US, That Is to Say, James Yellow and John Blue. Their Travails, by Them. New York: Baker, Godwin & Co., printers, 1854. 196 p.   LC, NYP

2666   [WEBB, CHARLES HENRY.] John Paul's Book, Moral and Instructive: Consisting of Travels, Tales . . . By John Paul [pseud.] . . . Hartford, Conn. and Chicago, Ill.: Columbian Book Company, 1874. 621 p., illus.
AAS, BA, BP, BU, CU, HEH, LC, N, NYH, NYP, UM, Y

2667   ———— Liffith Lank; or, Lunacy . . . New York: Carleton, 1866. 48 p., illus.
AAS, BP, BU, CU, H, HEH, LC, LCP, NYP, UC, UM, Y
A travesty of C. Reade's *Griffith Gaunt*.

2668   ———— St. Twel'mo; or, The Cuneiform Cyclopedist of Chattanooga . . . New York: C. H. Webb, 1867. 59 p., illus.
AAS, BU, H, HEH, LC, LCP, NYP, UC, UP, Y
A travesty of Augusta Evans Wilson's *St. Elmo*.

2669 ———— The Wickedest Woman in New York . . . New York: G. W. Carleton. London: S. Low, Son & Co., 1868. 44 p., illus.   H, LCP, NYP, UC, UM

———— ed. See Clemens, Samuel Langhorne. The Celebrated Jumping Frog (1867), No. 548.

2670 [WEBBER, CHARLES WILKINS.] The Prairie Scout; or, Agatone the Renegade. A Romance of Border Life . . . New York: DeWitt & Davenport [cop. 1852]. 288 p.   HEH, LC
This is, in part, his *Gold Mines of the Gila* (1849), Wright (1774-1850), No. 2687.

2671 ———— "Sam;" or, The History of Mystery . . . Cincinnati: H. M. Rulison. Philadelphia: Quaker City Publishing House, 1855. 550 p., illus.   AAS, CU, H, HEH, LC, N, NYP, UC, Y
American history fictionalized.

2672 ———— Tales of the Southern Border . . . Philadelphia: Lippincott, Grambo & Co., 1853. 400 p., illus.
        AAS, BU, H, LC, LCP, N, NYP, UP, UV, Y
Contents: Jack Long; or, The Shot in the Eye—The Border Chase: A First Day with the Rangers—Gonzaleze Again; or, The Bravo's Stratagem—Adam Baker, the Renegade—The Texan Virago and the Tailor of Gotham—Death of Little Red-Head—Gabrielle, the White Mare of Chihuahua—The Wild Girl of the Nebraska—The Fight of the Pinto Trace—Back from the Wilderness.
Apparently issued in parts in 1852; see Nos. 2673-2674. "Jack Long" was first published in 1846, Wright (1774-1850), No. 2688.

2673 ———— The Texan Virago; or, The Tailor of Gotham, and Other Tales . . . Philadelphia: Lippincott, Grambo & Co., 1852. Cover title, 90 p.   HEH, LC
Also contains: Death of Little Red-Head—Gabrielle, the White Mare of Chihuahua.
"Tales of the Southern Border. Part II."

2674 ———— The Wild Girl of the Nebraska . . . Philadelphia: Lippincott, Grambo & Co., 1852. Cover title, 87 p.   BU, LC
"Tales of the Southern Border. Part III."

2675 ———— Yieger's Cabinet. Spiritual Vampirism: The History of Etherial Softdown and Her Friends of the "New Light" . . . Philadelphia: Lippincott, Grambo & Co., 1853. 254 p.
        AAS, CU, LC, NYH, UC, UP, Y

WEBBER, FRANK. A Saw Log Blind; or, Poker Out West. *In*
O. P. Baldwin, *comp.*, Southern and South-Western Sketches
[1855?], No. 200.

2676 WEIR, JAMES. Simon Kenton; or, The Scout's Revenge. An
Historical Novel . . . Philadelphia: Lippincott, Grambo and
Co., 1852. 195 p., illus.   BP, LC, NYP, UC

2677 ———— The Winter Lodge; or, Vow Fulfilled. An Historical Novel, the Sequel to Simon Kenton . . . Philadelphia:
Lippincott, Grambo and Co., 1854. 231 p.
                                          AAS, HEH, LC, N, NYP, UV

2678 WEISS, S. W. Jacob Weller; or, Church Intemperance. A
True Story, Illustrating the Sad Effects of Tippling among
Ministers and Members of the Church . . . New York:
printed for the author by Nelson & Phillips, 1873. 322 p.
A copy is in the possession of Roger Butterfield, New York City.

WELD, HORATIO HASTINGS. The Story of a Genius. *In* B. P.
Poore, The Mameluke (1852), No. 1928.

WELLMONT, MRS. EMMA. The Love and the Money Match.
In S. Cobb, Alice the Fisher Girl [185-?], No. 563.

2679 ———— Substance and Shadows; or, Phases of Every-Day
Life . . . Boston: John P. Jewett & Company. Cleveland,
Ohio: Jewett, Proctor & Worthington, 1854. 320 p.
                                          AAS, CU, LC, UP, Y

———— Triumph of Love and Duty. *In* O. Bounderby,
pseud.?, The Law Student [185-?], No. 321.

2680 ———— Uncle Sam's Palace; or, The Reigning King . . .
Boston: Benjamin B. Mussey and Company, 1853. 308 p.,
illus.   AAS, BU, CU, H, HEH, LC, N, NYP, UP
Also published as: *The Palace and the Hovel; or, Rich Sam Beals and
Poor Mark Brown. A Story of the Evil Reign of King Alcohol.* Boston:
Albert Colby and Company, 1859. AAS

2681 WELTY, MRS. E. A. Self-Made; or, Living for Those We Love
... New York: Sheldon and Company. Boston: Gould and
Lincoln, 1868. 280 p.   BP, LC, LCP, NYP

2682 [WENTZ, SARA A.] Amy Denbrook: A Life Drama ... New
York: James O'Kane [cop. 1867]. 482 p.   LC

2683 ———— Smiles and Frowns ... New York: D. Appleton
and Company, 1857. 376 p.   BP, H, HEH, LC, NYP

WEST, WILLA, pseud. See Slocom, Mary S. F.

2684 WESTCOTT, MARGARET JANE COOK. Bessie Wilmerton; or,
Money and What Came of It. A Novel ... New York:
G. W. Carleton & Co. London: S. Low, Son & Co., 1874.
384 p.   AAS, CU, HEH, LC, LCP, NYP, UC

2685 WESTERN BORDER LIFE; or, What Fanny Hunter Saw and
Heard in Kanzas and Missouri. New York: Derby & Jackson.
Cincinnati: H. W. Derby & Co., 1856. 408 p.
                          BP, CU, H, HEH, LC, LCP, N, NYP, UM, Y
The struggle to make Kansas a free state.

2686 WESTMORELAND, MRS. MARIA ELIZABETH (JOURDAN). Clifford
Troup: A Georgia Story ... New York: G. W. Carleton &
Co. London: S. Low, Son & Co., 1873. 338 p.
Ante bellum.   AAS, HEH, LC, NYP, Y

2687 ———— Heart-Hungry: A Novel ... New York: G. W.
Carleton & Co., 1872. 332 p.   AAS, LC
Laid in Georgia.

2688 WESTON, AMANDA. Home Scenes: A Family Story ... Syracuse: L. C. Matlack, 1853. 159 p., illus.   HEH

2689 [WESTON, MRS. MARIA D.] Bessie and Raymond; or, Incidents
Connected with the Civil War in the United States ... Bos-
ton: Edward Payson Weston, for sale by Crocker and
Brewster, 1866. 411 p.
                          AAS, CU, H, HEH, LC, N, NYH, NYP, UC, UP, UV, Y

2690 [————] Kate Felton; or, A Peep at Realities. By an American Lady . . . Boston: Edward Payson Weston, 1859. 444 p., front. AAS, BP, BU, CU, HEH, LC, UC, Y

WETHERELL, ELIZABETH, *pseud. See* Warner, Susan Bogert

2691 [WETMORE, HENRY CARMER.] Hermit's Dell. From the Diary of a Penciller . . . New York: J. C. Derby. Boston: Phillips, Sampson & Co. Cincinnati: H. W. Derby, 1854. 285 p. AAS, BP, CU, LCP, NYP, UP, Y

Also published as: *Rural Life in America; or, Summer and Winter in the Country. By Harry Penciller* [*pseud.*]. New York: J. C. Derby. Boston: Phillips, Sampson & Co. Cincinnati: H. W. Derby, 1856. AAS, CU, HEH, NYH, NYP, UP, Y

2692 [WHARTON, GEORGE M.] The New Orleans Sketch Book. By "Stahl" [pseud.] . . . Philadelphia: A. Hart, 1853. 202 p., front. HEH, LC

The T. B. Peterson reprint without date on title page records a fictitious copyright date of 1843.

2693 ———— The Portfolio of a Southern Medical Student . . . Philadelphia: Lippincott, Grambo & Co., 1851. 181 p., illus. AAS

Also published as: *A Southern Medical Student's Portfolio.* Philadelphia: Claxton, Remsen & Haffelfinger, 1872. 186 p., illus. LC

2694 [WHEELER, A. O.] Eye-Witness; or, Life Scenes in the Old North State, Depicting the Trials and Sufferings of the Unionists during the Rebellion. By A. O. W. . . . Boston: B. B. Russell and Company. Chicago: S. S. Boyden, 1865. 276 p., illus. AAS, BA, BP, HEH, LC, N, NYP, Y

WHELPLEY, JAMES DAVENPORT. The Denslow Palace. *In* Atlantic Tales (1866), No. 155.

2695 WHICH, THE RIGHT, OR THE LEFT? . . . New York: Garrett & Co., 1855. 536 p. AAS, AP, BP, H, HEH, LC, LCP, NYH, NYP, UP, Y
Of religious interest.

2696 WHITAKER, MRS. MARY SCRIMZEOUR (FURMAN). Albert Hastings: A Novel . . . New York: Blelock & Co., 1868. 461 p. AAS, HEH, LCP, UC
Ante bellum Southern life.

2697 [WHITCHER, MRS. FRANCES MIRIAM (BERRY).] The Widow Bedott Papers. With an Introduction by Alice B. Neal. New York: J. C. Derby. Boston: Phillips, Sampson & Co. Cincinnati: H. W. Derby, 1856. 403 p., illus.

AAS, CU, HEH, NYH

Verso of title page: "W. H. Tinson, stereotyper. George Russell & Co., printers."

Also issued with imprint: New York: Derby & Jackson. Cincinnati: H. W. Derby, 1856. NYP, UC

Another issue with imprint: New York: J. C. Derby. Boston: Phillips, Sampson & Co. Cincinnati: H. W. Derby, 1856. AAS, BP, CU, H, HEH, LC, LCP, NYH, UM, UP, UV, Y

This issue gives the name of the author on the title page, and verso reads: "Stereotyped by Thomas B. Smith, 82 & 84 Beekman Street. Printed by Pudney and Russell, 79 John Street."

2698 ———— Widow Spriggins, Mary Elmer, and Other Sketches . . . Edited, with a Memoir by Mrs. M. L. Ward Whitcher . . . New York: Geo. W. Carleton & Co. London: S. Low, Son & Co., 1867. 378 p., illus.

AAS, BP, CU, HEH, LC, LCP, UM, UV, Y

Also contains: Mary Elmer; or, Trials and Changes—Letters from Timberville—Aunt Magwire's Account of the Mission to Muffletegawny —Going to See the President.

2699 WHITE, AMBIE. Leander Hall; or, The Investigation of Religious Truth, Comprehending the Origin and Nature of the Church of Christ, with Its Laws and Ordinances, Embraced in a Web of Romance . . . Louisville, Ky.: Waller, Sherrill & Co., 1865. 639 p., front. UC

2700 WHITE, ANNA L. Kate Callender; or, School-Girls of '54, and the Women of To-Day . . . Boston: published by the author, 1870. 208 p. AAS, H, LC

WHITE, BLYTHE, JR., *pseud. See* Robinson, Solon

2701 WHITE, HOMER. The Norwich Cadets: A Tale of the Rebellion . . . St. Albans, Vt.: Albert Clarke, 1873. 136 p.

AAS, BP, CU, HEH, LC, N, NYH, NYP

2702 [WHITE, MRS. RHODA ELIZABETH (WATERMAN).] Jane Arlington; or, The Defrauded Heiress. A Tale of Lake Champlain. By Uncle Ben [pseud.], of Rouse's Point. Rouse's Point: D. Turner, 1853. Cover title, 48 p. Printed in double cols.

UVB

2703 [————] Mary Staunton; or, The Pupils of Marvel Hall . . . New York: D. Appleton and Company. London, 1860. 398 p.   H, LC, LCP, NYP, Y
Laid in New York City.

2704 [————] Portraits of My Married Friends; or, A Peep into Hymen's Kingdom. By Uncle Ben [pseud.]. New York: D. Appleton & Co. London, 1858. 343 p., illus.
        BP, H, HEH, LC, NYP, UP

2705 [WHITE, RICHARD GRANT.] The Adventures of Sir Lyon Bouse, Bart., in America during the Civil War. Being Extracts from His Diary. New York: the American News Company, 1867. 64 p.   AAS, BA, BP, CU, H, LC, LCP, NYP, Y
Humorous satire.

2706 [————] Book of the Prophet Stephen, Son of Douglas. Wherein Marvelous Things Are Foretold of the Reign of Abraham. New York: Feeks & Bancker, No. 26 Ann Street [cop. 1863-64]. 2 pts. (48, 48 p.)   AAS, BP, BU, HEH, LCP, NYP
"Book Second" imprint: New York: J. F. Feeks, No. 26 Ann Street.
Political satire in Biblical form.

2707 [————] The Chronicles of Gotham . . . New York: G. W. Carleton & Co. London: S. Low, Son & Co., 1871-72. 2 pts. (87 p.)   AAS, BA, BP, BU, CU, H, HEH, LC, LCP, N, NYP, UC, Y
In Biblical language.

2708 [————] The Fall of Man; or, The Loves of the Gorillas. A Popular Scientific Lecture upon the Darwinian Theory of Development by Sexual Selection. By a Learned Gorilla . . . New York: G. W. Carleton & Co. London: S. Low & Co., 1871. 48 p., illus.   AAS, BP, H, LC, LCP, NYH, UM, Y
A satire on Darwin's theory.

2709 [————] The New Gospel of Peace According to St. Benjamin. New York [cop. 1863-66]. 4 vols. (42, 48, 47, 55 p.)
    AAS, BP, BU, CU, H, HEH, LC, LCP, N, NYH, NYP, UC, UM(v.4), Y
Imprint varies: Vols. I-II, New York: Sinclair Tousey [cop. 1863]; Vol. III, New York: American News Agency [cop. 1864]; Vol. IV, New York: the American News Company [cop. 1866].
Political allegory on the Civil War.

2710 [————] Revelations: A Companion to the "New Gospel of Peace," According to Abraham. New York: M. Doolady, 1863. 36 p.

AAS, BA, BP, BU, CU, H, HEH, LC, LCP, N, NYP, UM, UP, Y

Cover imprints of the various copies vary.
Satire in Biblical form.

WHITE, THOM., *pseud. See* Elliott, Charles Wyllys

2711 [WHITING, M. H.] Faith White's Letter Book, 1620-1623, Plymouth, New England . . . Boston: Henry Hoyt, No. 9 Cornhill [cop. 1866]. 365 p., front.

AAS, BA, CU, HEH, LCP, N, NYP, Y

2712 WHITMAN, WILLIAM EDWARD SEAVER. The Ship-Carpenter's Family: A Story for the Times . . . New York: H. Long and Brother, 121 Nassau Street [cop. 1855]. 399 p.

AAS, HEH, LC, UC, UP

WHITMARSH, CAROLINE SNOWDEN. *See* Guild, Mrs. Caroline Snowden (Whitmarsh)

2713 WHITMORE, WALTER. Wilburn; or, The Heir of the Manor. A Romance of the Old Dominion. By Walter Whitmore, Esq., Author of "Ella Winston," "Ainslie," "Retribution," etc., etc. Cincinnati: R. E. Edward, 115 Main Street [cop. 1852]. 104 p. Printed in double cols.
LC

2714 [WHITNEY, MRS. ADELINE DUTTON (TRAIN).] The Gayworthys: A Story of Threads and Thrums . . . Boston: Loring, 1865. 399 p.
AAS, BA, CU, H, HEH, LC, LCP, UC, Y

2715 ———— Hitherto: A Story of Yesterdays . . . Boston: Loring, cor. Washington and Bromfield Streets [cop. 1869]. 473 p.
AAS, BA, BP, CU, H, HEH, LC, LCP, NYP, UP, UV, Y

2716 ———— Patience Strong's Outings . . . Boston: Loring, 1869. 233 p.
AAS, BA, H, HEH, LC, LCP, UC

2717 ———— Real Folks . . . Boston: James R. Osgood and Company, 1872. 308 p., illus.

AAS, BA, BP, BU, CU, H, HEH, LC, LCP, N, NYP, UC, UM, UP, Y

2718 ———— Zerub Throop's Experiment . . . Boston: Loring, cor. Bromfield and Washington Streets [cop. 1871]. 146 p.

AAS, BA, BP, CU, H, HEH, LC, LCP, NYP, UM, UP, Y

———— *jt. au. See* Hale, Edward Everett, *ed.* Six of One (1872), No. 1058.

2719 WHITSON, MRS. LORENZO DOW. Gilbert St. Maurice . . . Nash-ville: Tavel, Eastman & Howell, 1874. 331 p.   H, NYP
Also contains: Brenda Merton.
Tennessee and South Carolina during the Civil War.

2720 ———— ———— Louisville: Bradley & Gilbert, printers, 1875. 337 p., front.   CU, HEH, LC, N, NYH, UC, UV
This ed. contains a new chapter entitled: "Bravery of Col. Lawton and His Gallant Georgians."

2721 WHITTLESEY, ELSIE LEIGH. Helen Ethinger; or, Not Exactly Right . . . Philadelphia: Claxton, Remsen & Haffelfinger, 1872. 318 p.   H, LC

2722 ———— The Hemlock Swamp and a Season at the White Sulphur Springs. By Elsie Leigh Whittlesey, Author of "Helen Ethinger," "Who Was She," "Castles in Spain" . . . Philadelphia: Claxton, Remsen & Haffelfinger, 1873. 245 p.
BP, H, HEH, LC, LCP, Y

2723 [————] Who Was She? or, The Soldier's Best Glory. Philadelphia: Claxton, Remsen & Haffelfinger, 1871. 380 p.
H, HEH, LC, Y

2724 WHITTLESEY, SARAH JOHNSON COGSWELL. Bertha the Beauty: A Story of the Southern Revolution . . . Philadelphia: Clax-ton, Remsen & Haffelfinger, 1872. 382 p.   AAS, LC, NYH, NYP
Miss Whittlesey was married to a Mr. Smith for a short while.
Laid in Virginia, 1850-1865.

2725 ———— Herbert Hamilton; or, The Bas Bleu . . . Alexandria, Va.: State Journal job printing office, 1868. Cover title, 123 p. Printed in double cols.   LC
Laid in Virginia.

2726 ———— The Stranger's Stratagem; or, The Double Deceit, and Other Stories ... New York: M. W. Dodd, 1860. 405 p.

AAS, CU, HEH

Also contains: Reginald's Revenge; or, The Rod and Reproof—Italia Alman; or, The Child Heiress—Lilia Rosely; or, The Triumph of Virtue —The Drunkard's Daughter—Eva Evylin—The Gem; or, The Charm That Wins.

2727 THE WHOLE HISTORY OF ADELINE FOSBENNER, a Wealthy and Accomplished Young Lady, Who ... Was Tempted to Purloin a Pair of Gloves from a Dry-Goods Store, and Being Detected ... by a Designing Old Villain Was Compelled, Under Threats of Exposure to Do His Most Infamous Bidding ... By a Member of the New York Bar. Philadelphia: Barclay & Co., No. 21 North Seventh Street [cop. 1873]. 70 p., illus.

Cover title: "The Beautiful and Accomplished Adeline Fosbenner."

A copy is in the possession of Roger Butterfield, New York City.

Thomas M. McDade has informed me that the records in the Copyright Office show this as entered by Barclay & Co. May 3, 1866, but no copy with that date has been found.

WICKHAM, MARTHA, *pseud.* *See* Huntington, Cornelia

2728 WIGHTMAN, WILLIAM F. The Fatalist ... Athens, Ga.: power-press of Christy, Kelsea and Burke, 1851. 160 p.

Copy noted in *Georgia 1800-1900. A Series of Selections from the Georgiana Library of a Private Collector* (Atlanta Public Library, 1954), ser. 3, item 60.

2729 WILBOR, MARY H. Violet: A True Story ... Providence: George H. Whitney, 1861. 251 p. AAS, CU, HEH, Y

Author's name misspelled "Willbor" on title page.

WILBUR, ANNE T. The Concert. *In* A. J. H. Duganne, The Prince Corsair [185-?], No. 797.

———— The Forget-Me-Not. *In* O. Bounderby, *pseud.?*, The Law Student [185-?], No. 321.

2730 [WILBURN, GEORGE T.] Sam Simple's First Trip to New Orleans. By the Author of "Bob Snobs," "Mason Family," &c. Americus, Georgia: Hancock, Graham & Reilly, 1870. 106 p.

LC

2731 THE WILD PARKS FAMILY of Wyoming County, Pennsylvania: A True Narrative, Showing the Frightful Results of the Intermarriage of Own Blood Cousins . . . Philadelphia, Pa.: Old Franklin Publishing House, cop., 1874. 30 p., illus.   AAS

2732 WILEY, CALVIN HENDERSON. Life in the South: A Companion to Uncle Tom's Cabin . . . Philadelphia: T. B. Peterson, No. 98 Chestnut Street [cop. 1852]. 144 p., illus. Printed in double cols.   H, LC, NYH, UC

Also published as: *Roanoke; or, "Where Is Utopia?"* Philadelphia: T. B. Peterson & Brothers, 306 Chestnut Street [cop. 1866]. 156 p., illus. Printed in double cols.   HEH, NYH

WILL, *the Rover, pseud.   See* Prince, George

2733 WILLARD, MRS. CLARA A. Fifty Years Ago: A Story of New England Life . . . New York: Anson D. F. Randolph & Company, 770 Broadway [cop. 1871]. 323 p.   BP, H, LC, NYP, Y

2734 ———— May Chester; or, Home Light . . . New York: A. D. F. Randolph & Co., 1869. 224 p., illus.
Information from LC card for copy withdrawn from circulation.

2735 ———— Nellie Greyson . . . New York: A. D. F. Randolph & Co., 1868. 146 p., front.
Information from LC card for copy withdrawn from circulation.

WILLBOR, MARY H. *See* Wilbor, Mary H.

2736 [WILLCOX, ORLANDO BOLIVAR.] Faca: An Army Memoir. By Major March [pseud.] . . . Boston: James French & Company. Detroit: Raymond & Selleck, 1857. 338 p.
                AAS, BA, BP, BU, H, HEH, LCP, NYP, UC, Y
Action takes place on board a ship bound for Texas with an army.

2737 [————] Shoepac Recollections: A Way-Side Glimpse of American Life. By Walter March [pseud.]. New York: Bunce & Brother, 1856. 360 p.
                AAS, BP, BU, CU, H, HEH, LC, N, NYP, UC, UM, Y
Also contains: Jeptha Jumps's Speech—The Battle of Windsor—The Shoepacs.
Also published as: *Walter March; or, Shoepak Recollections. By Major March [pseud.]*. Boston: J. French and Company. Detroit: Raymond & Selleck, 1857.   LC

2738 [WILLIAMS, HENRY LLEWELLYN.] L'Africaine; or, The Maid of Madagascar. Adapted from "The Law of Java," by G. Colman, the Younger, [and] L'Africaine, by E. Scribe . . . By H. Ll. W. New York: R. M. DeWitt [1866]. 100 p.
Copy noted in BM.

2739 [————] Arrah-Na-Pogue (Arrah-of-the-Kiss); or, The Wicklow Wedding. Founded on the Same Incidents as the Celebrated Drama, by Dion Bourcicault . . . New York: Robert M. DeWitt, 13 Frankfort Street [186-?]. 96 p.
CU, NYP

2740 [————] Binnacle Jack; or, The Cavern of Death. By Mat Mizzen [pseud.] . . . New York: Robert M. DeWitt, No. 13 Frankfort Street [186-?]. 100 p.
H, NYP

2741 [————] The Black Cruiser; or, The Scourge of the Sea. By Mat Mizen [pseud.] . . . New York: Robert M. DeWitt, 13 Frankfort Street [186-?]. 100 p.
NYP

2742 [————] Black-Eyed Beauty; or, One of the Lost. A Brilliant Picture of the Follies and Frailties of Fast Life . . . New York: Robert M. DeWitt, No. 13 Frankfort Street [cop. 1868]. 100 p.
AAS

2743 [————] Bob Brierly; or, The Ticket-of-Leave Man. A Romance of the Present Day. Founded on the Great Play of the Same Title by Tom Taylor . . . New York: Robert M. DeWitt, No. 33 Rose Street [187-?]. 100 p.
AAS
Copyright notice dated 1867, but DeWitt did not move to Rose Street until 1870.

2744 [————] Delaware Dick; or, The Chase of the Wasp . . . New York: Robert M. DeWitt, 160 & 162 Nassau Street [185-?]. 100 p., illus.
H
On cover: "By Matt. Mizzen."

2745 [————] The Fenian Chief; or, The Martyr of '65. Founded on Recent Events in Ireland's Struggle for Liberty . . . New York: R. M. DeWitt [1865]. 100 p.
Copy noted in BM.

2746 [————] The Flying Arrow; or, The Pirate's Revenge. By Matt Mizzen [pseud.] ... New York: Robert M. DeWitt, 160 & 162 Nassau Street [185-?]. 100 p., illus.   NYP

2747 [————] Gay Life in New York; or, Fast Men and War Widows. By an Old Traveller. New York: R. M. DeWitt [1866].
Copy noted in BM.

2748 [————] The Icy Deep; or, True unto Death! A Story of Wild Adventures and Fearful Perils. By Mat Mizen [pseud.] ... New York: Robert M. DeWitt, No. 13 Frankfort Street, cop. 1868. 100 p.   NYP

2749 [————] Joaquin (the Claude Duval of California); or, The Marauder of the Mines. A Romance Founded on Truth. New York: Robert M. DeWitt, 33 Rose Street [187-?]. 160 p.   HEH
Copyright notice dated 1865, but DeWitt did not move to Rose Street until 1870.

2750 [————] Murty, the Rover; or, The Irish Buccaneer. Full of Wild and Thrilling Romance. By Mat. Mizen [pseud.] ... New York: Robert M. DeWitt, No. 13 Frankfort Street, cop. 1868. 100 p., front.   CU

2751 [————] Rip Van Winkle; or, The Sleep of Twenty Years. A Legend of the Kaatskills ... New York: Robert M. DeWitt, No. 13 Frankfort Street [cop. 1866]. 100 p.   NYH

2752 [————] The Serf; or, Love Levels All! ... Written upon the ... Play of That Name by Tom Taylor ... New York: R. M. DeWitt [1873?]. 100 p.
Copy noted in BM.

2753 ———— The Steel Safe; or, The Stains and Splendors of New York Life. A Story of Our Day and Night ... New York: Robert M. DeWitt, No. 13 Frankfort Street, cop. 1868. 100 p. Printed in double cols.   AAS, CU, LC, NYP

2754 [————] Susan Wylie; or, The Smuggler's Bride ... New York: Robert M. DeWitt, 13 Frankfort Street [186-?]. 100 p., illus.   NYP

2755 [————] Will Watch, the Bold Smuggler: A Stirring Tale of Wild and Desperate Adventure . . . New York: Robert M. DeWitt, 160 & 162 Nassau Street [185-?]. 100 p., illus.

NYP

WILLIAMS, JOHN R. Clara: A Story of Life in Africa. *In* A. H. T. Cudlip, Lady Lorme's Stratagem [*ca.* 1865], No. 669.

2756 WILLIAMS, T. WARSAW. Kidnapped: A Novelette . . . [Milwaukee?, cop. 1873.] Caption title, 53 p. Printed in double cols.

LC

LC copy deposited for copyright by the author; title page lacking.

2757 [WILLIAMSON, EDWARD HAND.] The Quaker Partisans: A Story of the Revolution . . . Philadelphia: J. B. Lippincott & Co., 1869. 294 p., illus.

AAS, BP, BU, H, LCP, NYH, NYP, UP, UVB

2758 WILLIS, JULIA A. What a Boy! What Shall We Do with Him? What Will He Do with Himself? Who Is to Blame for the Consequences? . . . Philadelphia: J. B. Lippincott & Co., 1875. 362 p., front. BA, BU, H, LCP

WILLIS, KATE, *pseud. See* Coolidge, Sarah E.

2759 WILLIS, NATHANIEL PARKER. Fun-Jottings; or, Laughs I Have Taken a Pen to . . . New York: Charles Scribner, 1853. 371 p.

AAS, BA, BP, BU, CU, H, HEH, LC, LCP, N, NYH, NYP, UC, UM, UP, Y

Contents: Larks in Vacation—Meena Dimity; or, Why Mr. Brown Crash Took the Tour—Mrs. Passable Trott—The Spirit-Love of "Ione S——" —The Ghost Ball at Congress Hall—Pasquali, the Tailor of Venice—The Widow by Brevet—Nora Mehidy; or, The Strange Road to the Heart of Mr. Hypolet Leathers—The Marquis in Petticoats—Tom Fane and I— The Poet and the Mandarin—The Countess of Nyschriem, and the Handsome Artist—The Inlet of Peach-Blossoms—The Belle of the Belfry; or, The Daring Lover—The Female Ward—The Pharisee and the Barber —Mabel Wynne—The Bandit of Austria—My One Adventure as a Brigand—Count Pott's Strategy—The Power of an "Injured Look"— Mrs. Flimson—From Saratoga [5 short pieces]—Miss Albina McLush— The Need of Two Loves.

Also issued with imprint: Auburn: Alden Beardsley & Co. Rochester: Wanzer, Beardsley & Co., 1853. AAS, NYP

2760 ——————— Paul Fane; or, Parts of a Life Else Untold. A Novel
. . . New York: C. Scribner. London: Sampson Low, Son
& Co., 1857. 402 p.

BA, BP, CU, H, HEH, LC, LCP, N, NYP, UC, UP, UV, Y

Also issued with imprint: New York: C. Scribner. Boston: A. Williams
& Co. London: Sampson Low, Son & Co., 1857. AAS, UM

WILLOWILL, WILL., *pseud.* The Dying Husband. *In* A. Cary,
The Adopted Daughter (1859), No. 466.

2761 [WILMER, LAMBERT A.] The Victim Bride; or, A Father's
Sacrifice. Being a True and Touching Recital of the Mental,
Moral and Physical Sufferings of the Beautiful and Accom-
plished Kate Rigby, Daughter of the Philadelphia Millionaire
. . . Philadelphia: Barclay & Co., No. 21 North Seventh
Street [cop. 1875]. 96 p., illus. HEH

At head of title: "The Modern 'Roman Father.'"

2762 WILSON, MRS. AUGUSTA JANE (EVANS). Beulah . . . New
York: Derby & Jackson, 1859. 510 p.

AAS, BU, CU, H, N, NYP, Y

2763 [———————] Inez: A Tale of the Alamo. New York: Harper &
Brothers, 1855. 298 p. AAS, H, HEH, LC, LCP, NYH, UVB, Y

2764 [———————] Macaria; or, Altars of Sacrifice . . . Richmond:
West & Johnston, 1864. 183 p. Printed in double cols.

BA, BP, N, UVB

Also issued with imprint: New York: John Bradburn, 1864. 469 p.
AAS, BU, CU, LC, LCP, NYP, UP, UVB, Y

2765 ——————— St. Elmo: A Novel . . . New York: Carleton.
London: S. Low, Son & Co., 1867. 571 p.

AAS, BU, CU, H, HEH, N, NYP, UP, UVB, Y

2766 ——————— Vashti; or, "Until Death Us Do Part." A Novel
. . . New York: Carleton. London: S. Low, Son & Co., 1869.
473 p. AAS, H, HEH, LCP, NYP, UC, Y

WILSON, EMMA T. Alice Tracey. *In* H. P. Cheever, The Rival Brothers [*ca.* 1852], No. 495.

2767 [WILSON, MRS. H. E.] Our Nig; or, Sketches from the Life of a Free Black in a Two-Story White House, North. Showing That Slavery's Shadows Fall Even There . . . Boston: printed by Geo. C. Rand & Avery, 1859. 140 p.

AAS, HEH, N, NYH, NYP, UC, Y

2768 WINDLE, MARY JANE. Life at the White Sulphur Springs; or, Pictures of a Pleasant Summer . . . Philadelphia: J. B. Lippincott & Co., 1857. 323 p.

CU, NYP, UV

2769 WINNIE AND I. New York: J. C. Derby. Boston: Phillips, Sampson & Co. Cincinnati: H. W. Derby, 1855. 351 p.

AAS, BP, HEH, NYP, UP, Y

2770 WINSTON, JAMES. Cora O'Kane; or, The Doom of the Rebel Guard. A Story of the Great Rebellion. Containing Incidents of the Campaign in Missouri under Generals Fremont and Sigel, and the Thrilling Exploits of the Unionists under Major Zagonyi . . . [Claremont, N. H.]: published by an association of disabled soldiers, 1868. 84 p.

AAS, BU, CU, H, HEH, LC, N, NYH, NYP, UM, Y

2771 WINTHROP, THEODORE. Cecil Dreeme . . . Boston: Ticknor and Fields, 1861. 360 p.

AAS, AP, BP, H, HEH, LC, LCP, NYP, UC, UP, UVB, Y

Laid in New York City.

2772 ———— Edwin Brothertoft . . . Boston: Ticknor and Fields, 1862. 369 p.

AAS, AP, BA, BU, CU, H, HEH, LC, LCP, N, UC, UM, UP, UVB, Y

Laid in New York state during the American Revolution.

2773 ———— John Brent . . . Boston: Ticknor and Fields, 1862. 359 p. AAS, AP, BA, BP, BU, CU, H, HEH, LCP, UC, UP, UVB, Y

Of Mormon interest.

2774 ———— Life in the Open Air, and Other Papers . . . Boston: Ticknor and Fields, 1863. 374 p., illus.

AAS, AP, BA, BP, BU, CU, H, HEH, LC, LCP, NYP, UM, UP, UVB, Y

Contains: Love and Skates—Brightly's Orphan: A Fragment.

——— Love and Skates. *In* Good Stories (1867-68), No. 1012.

2775 WISE, HENRY AUGUSTUS. Captain Brand, of the "Centipede." A Pirate of Eminence in the West Indies, His Loves and Exploits . . . By Harry Gringo (H. A. Wise, U.S.N.) . . . New York: Harper & Brothers, 1864. 299 p., illus.

AAS, BA, BU, CU, H, HEH, LC, LCP, NYP, UM, UP, UVB, Y

2776 [———] Tales for the Marines. By Harry Gringo [pseud.] . . . Boston: Phillips, Sampson & Company. New York: J. C. Derby, 1855. 436 p., front.

AAS, BP, BU, CU, H, HEH, LC, LCP, N, NYP, UC, UM, UP, UV, Y

2777 WISE, ISAAC MAYER. The Combat of the People; or, Hillel and Herod. A Historical Romance of the Time of Herod I . . . Cincinnati, Ohio: Bloch & Co., 1859. 151 p. Printed in double cols.

NYP

2778 ——— The First of the Maccabees . . . Cincinnati: Bloch & Co., 1860. 180 p. Printed in double cols.

Y

2779 [WISE, JOHN.] The Fate of Donaldson and Grimwood in a Balloon Voyage from Chicago . . . Philadelphia: John Wise, 1875. 23 p., illus.

LC, LCP

WOLCOTT, RICHMOND. Broken Idols. *In* Stories and Sketches (1867), No. 2386.

——— Coming from the Front. *In* Stories and Sketches (1867), No. 2386.

2780 WOLFE, HELEN JOSEPHINE. Out in the World; or, A Selfish Life . . . Cincinnati: Hitchcock & Walden, 1870. 228 p.

Information from LC card for copy withdrawn from circulation.

2781 WOLFERSBERGER, GEORGE ANDREW. Tales for All Seasons . . . Philadelphia: Crissy & Markley, printers, 1863. 240 p.

LC, LCP

Contents: The Old Arm Chair—An Unfortunate Man—The Phantom Hand—Jonas Lair's Fortune—In the Snow—The Burgess of Tumbletown—Mr. Frisby's Journey—The Goblin's Lesson—The Stranger.

2782 WOMAN'S FAITH: A Tale of Southern Life . . . New York: Derby & Jackson. Cincinnati: H. W. Derby, 1856. 310 p.
AAS, HEH

2783 WOMAN'S STRATEGY; or, The First Time I Saw Her. A Novel . . . New York: G. W. Carleton & Co. London: Hogg & Sons, 1867. 190 p., illus.　　AAS, HEH, LCP, NYP
Also contains: The Heiress of Elkington.

2784 THE WONDERFUL BUT TRUE LIFE OF ELLA CAMERON: An Extraordinary Revelation. Being the Only True Life of This Well-Known Washington Belle, and a True Picture of High Life in Washington, and Its Connection with New York Society. Philadelphia: Barclay & Co., No. 21 North Seventh Street [cop. 1875]. 72 p., illus.
Also contains: Adventures of Charles L. Marshall and His Lost Bride, Cornelia Dunnington.
A copy is in the possession of Roger Butterfield, New York City.

2785 WOOD, BENJAMIN. Fort Lafayette; or, Love and Secession. A Novel . . . New York: Carleton, 1862. 300 p.
AAS, BP, BU, CU, HEH, LC, LCP, NYH, NYP, UP, UVB, Y
On the first battle of Bull Run.

WOOD, FRANK. Shot on Sight. *In* A. H. T. Cudlip, Lady Lorme's Stratagem [*ca.* 1865], No. 669.

2786 WOOD, GEORGE. Future Life; or, Scenes in Another World . . . New York: Derby & Jackson, 1858. 359 p.
AAS, BP, BU, CU, HEH, LC, LCP, NYP, UC, UV, Y
Also published as: *The Gates Wide Open; or, Scenes in Another World*. Boston: Lee and Shepard, 1869.　　AAS, BU, H, LC, NYP, UV

2787 ——— Marrying Too Late: A Tale . . . New York: D. Appleton & Company, 1857. 432 p.
Matrimonial difficulties.　　AAS, BA, CU, H, HEH, LCP, NYP, Y

2788 ——— Modern Pilgrims: Showing the Improvements in Travel and the Newest Methods of Reaching the Celestial City . . . Boston: Phillips, Sampson & Co. New York: J. C. Derby, 1855. 2 vols. (396, 396 p.)
AAS, BA, BU, CU, H, HEH, LC, LCP, NYP, UC, UM, UP, UVB, Y

2789 [WOOD, MRS. JULIA AMANDA (SARGENT).] Hubert's Wife: A Story for You. By Minnie Mary Lee [pseud.] . . . Baltimore: Kelly, Piet & Co., 1875. 246 p.   LC, UM

2790 [WOOD, W. S.] How Bennie Did It. By Matthew Merchant [pseud.]. Portland: Hoyt, Fogg & Breed, 1869. 439 p., illus.
BP, CU, HEH

WOODLAND, RUTH, *pseud. See* Perkins, Mrs. Sue (Chestnutwood)

2791 [WOODRUFF, MRS. JULIA LOUISA MATILDA (CURTISS).] Holden with the Cords. By W. M. L. Jay [pseud.] . . . New York: E. P. Dutton & Company, 1874. 517 p.
H, HEH, LC, LCP, NYP, UV

2792 [————] Shiloh; or, Without and Within. By W. M. L. Jay [pseud.]. New York: E. P. Dutton and Company. Hartford: Church Press Co., 1870. 488 p.
New England farm and parish life.   BP, BU, H, LC, LCP, NYP, Y

2793 [WOODS, CAROLINE H.] The Diary of a Milliner. By Belle Otis [pseud.]. New York: Hurd and Houghton, 1867. 200 p.   AAS, BP, CU, HEH, LC, LCP, NYP, UV

2794 WOODS, GEORGE BRYANT. Essays, Sketches and Stories Selected from the Writings of George Bryant Woods. With a Biographical Memoir. Boston: James R. Osgood and Company, 1873. 399 p.   AAS, BA, BP, H, HEH, LC, N, NYH, NYP, UM, Y
Contains: A Freshman's Romance—The Blue River Bank Robbery—Our Breakfast at the Astor—Our Maid: How We Lost and How We Found Her—Marrying a Pickpocket.

2795 [WOODSON, MARY E.] The Way It All Ended: A Novel. Richmond, Va.: author's edition, 1859. 375 p.   UV
Laid in Virginia.

2796 WOODVILLE, FANNY. Edward Wilton; or, Early Days in Michigan. [N. p., n. d.] Caption title, 124 p.   AAS
AAS copy lacks title; preface signed and dated "Fanny Woodville, Kalamazoo, May, 1851."

WOODVILLE, JENNIE, *pseud. See* Stabler, Mrs. Jennie Latham

WOODWORTH, FRANCIS CHANNING. My Early Friend. *In* A. Cary, The Adopted Daughter (1859), No. 466.

2797 WOOLSON, CONSTANCE FENIMORE. Castle Nowhere: Lake-Country Sketches . . . Boston: James R. Osgood and Company, 1875. 386 p.   AAS, BA, BP, CU, H, HEH, LC, UP, UV, Y
Contents: Castle Nowhere—Peter the Parson—Jeannette—The Old Agency—Misery Landing—Solomon—Wilhelmina—St. Clair Flats—The Lady of Little Fishing.

WORMELEY, ELIZABETH. *See* Latimer, Mrs. Mary Elizabeth (Wormeley)

WORTH, MRS. L. L., *pseud. See* Ellsworth, Mrs. Mary Wolcott (Janvrin)

2798 WRECKS AND RESCUES. By an Early Member of the Board of Managers of the A. F. G. S. . . . New York: American Female Guardian Society, 1859. 255 p., illus.
Case histories fictionalized.   AAS, H, LC, NYP

2799 WRIGHT, CALEB EARL. Marcus Blair: A Story of Provincial Times. Written for the Young . . . Philadelphia: J. B. Lippincott & Co., 1873. 165 p., illus.   BA, BP, CU
An historical tale dealing with adults.

2800 WRIGHT, DANIEL THEW. Mrs. Armington's Ward; or, The Inferior Sex . . . Boston: Lee and Shepard. New York: Shepard and Dillingham, 1874. 332 p.   AAS, BP, LC, NYP, Y

2801 [WRIGHT, E. M.] Behind the Scenes: A Story of the Stage. By Verity Victor [pseud.]. Boston: New England News Company, 1870. 284 p.
          AAS, BP, BU, CU, H, HEH, LC, NYP, UC
Pages 281-284 set forth the virtues of insurance.

2802 WRIGHT, EDMUND, *pseud.* Narrative of Edmund Wright [pseud.]: His Adventures with and Escape from the Knights of the Golden Circle . . . Cincinnati: J. R. Hawley, 1864. 150 p., illus.   LC, LCP, N, NYH, NYP, UM

2803 WRIGHT, MRS. JULIA (MCNAIR). Almost a Priest: A Tale
That Deals in Facts . . . Philadelphia: McKinney & Martin,
1870. 432 p., illus. AAS, HEH, LC, NYP
Anti-Catholic.

2804 ———— The Best Fellow in the World: His Haps and Mishaps . . . New York: National Temperance Society, 1871.
352 p., illus. AAS
A temperance tale.

2805 ———— The Corner Stall: A New York Story . . . Boston:
Henry Hoyt [cop. 1868]. 257 p., illus. BP

2806 ———— How Could He Escape? A Temperance Tale . . .
New York: the National Temperance Society, 1870. 324 p.
LC

2807 ———— John and the Demijohn: A Temperance Tale . . .
Boston: Henry Hoyt, 9 Cornhill [cop. 1869]. 408 p., illus.
UM copy dated 1870 which may be the 1st ed. BP, LC, NYP

2808 ———— Jug-or-Not . . . New York: National Temperance
Society, 1870. 346 p., illus. H, LC
NYP copy without date on title page.

2809 ———— The Life Cruise of Capt. Bess Adams: A Temperance
Tale . . . New York: National Temperance Society, 1874.
413 p., illus.
Information from LC card for copy withdrawn from circulation.

2810 ———— A Million Too Much: A Temperance Tale . . . Philadelphia: Porter & Coates, 822 Chestnut Street [cop. 1871].
276 p. AAS, CU, LC, NYP, UM

2811 [————] Moth and Rust: A Very Plain Tale. Boston:
Henry Hoyt, No. 9 Cornhill [cop. 1870]. 394 p., illus.
AAS, BP, CU, HEH, LC, N

2812 ———— Nothing to Drink: A Temperance Sea Story . . .
New York: National Temperance Society, 1873. 399 p., illus.
LC

2813 ———— Our Chatham Street Uncle; or, The Three Golden Balls . . . Boston: Henry Hoyt, No. 9 Cornhill [cop. 1869]. 345 p., illus. LC

2814 ———— Priest and Nun . . . Philadelphia: Crittenden & McKinney, 1308 Chestnut Street [cop. 1869]. 540 p., illus. BU

The 544 p. ed. with imprint: Philadelphia: Crittenden & McKinney, 1308 Chestnut Street. Springfield, Mass.: D. E. Fish [cop. 1869], adds two newspaper accounts regarding the imprisonment of nuns. NYP, UM, UV

2815 ———— Secrets of the Convent and Confessional: An Exhibition of the Influence and Workings of Papacy upon Society and Republican Institutions . . . Cincinnati: Jones Brothers and Company, 1872. 622 p., illus. LC

2816 ———— Under the Yoke, and Other Tales . . . Cincinnati: Western Tract and Book Society, 1871. 216 p., front. LC
Also contains: Making a Proselyte—The Lay Sister.

2817 WRIGHT, MRS. SARAH ANN. The Boys in Blue; or, A Soldier's Life. A Story of the Late War . . . New York: New York Publishing Company [cop. 1869]. 100 p., front. HEH
This is her *Clara Hollinbrook* rewritten.

2818 ———— Clara Hollinbrook, the Beauty of Fairfax; or, The Life and Adventures of an Officer in the Union Army during the Present War . . . Authoress of "Scandal," "The Disguised Lawyer," etc. New York: M. Doolady, 1863. 94 p., front. BA, HEH, NYH
Rewritten as *The Boys in Blue*.

2819 ———— The Crimson Star; or, The Midnight Vision. A Romance Founded on Facts . . . New York: Masonic and Miscellaneous Publishing Co., D. Sickels & Co., managers, 1875. 226 p. AAS, UC

2820 ———— The Gem of the Lake: A Novel . . . New York: American News Company, 1868. 60 p. Printed in double cols. LC, NYP

2821 ———— The Golden Ladder; or, The Stolen Jewel ... New York: American News Company, 1871. 377 p., illus.

AAS, HEH, LC

Also issued with imprint: New York: Bible Brothers, 1871.   BU

2822 ———— The Secret Duel; or, The Soldier's Dream. A Story of the Late War ... New York: New York Publishing Company [cop. 1869]. 102 p., front.   H, LC

2823 [WYNNE, MRS. EMMA L. (MOFFETT).] Cragfont: A Novel. By a Young Southern Lady. New York: Blelock & Co., 1867. Title listed in Kelly 1866-1871. Excerpts of reviews in I. Raymond, *Southland Writers* (Philadelphia, 1870), I, 419-420.

2824 ———— Crown Jewels; or, The Dream of an Empire. An Historical Romance . . . New York: Carleton. London: S. Low & Co., 1871. 436 p.   AAS, BP, CU, LCP, NYP, UC, UM
Mexico and Maximilian.

XARIFFA, *pseud. See* Townsend, Mrs. Mary Ashley (Van Voorhis)

2825 [YALCRABB, B. L. G.] The Travellers' Library: Containing Interesting Stories, Laughable Anecdotes, and Enjoyable Reading . . . Philadelphia: Barclay & Co., No. 21 North Seventh Street [cop. 1874]. 96 p., illus.   LC
Contains: Helen Bertram: The Modern "Joan of Arc"—The Serpent's Sting: A Tale of Woman's Devotion and Self-Sacrifice.

2826 [YALE, MRS. CATHERINE (BROOKS).] Abbie Nott and Other Knots. By "Katinka" [pseud.] . . . Philadelphia: J. B. Lippincott and Co., 1856. 342 p., illus.

AAS, BP, H, LC, NYP, UP, Y

2827 THE YANKEE BOY FROM HOME ... New York: James Miller, 1864. 294 p.   AAS, BP, BU, CU

2828 THE YANKEE ENTERPRISE; or, The Two Millionaires, and Other Thrilling Tales. Boston: Wentworth & Co., 1855. 334 p., illus.   AAS, HEH, N

Contents: The Two Millionaires, by Sarah Fry [Eng. au.]—I Owe You Nothing Sir—Notes of a Journey across the Isthmus of Panama—The Two Passports—Australia and Van Diemen's Land—The Fairy Cup, by Alfred Crowquill [pseud. of Eng. au.]—The White Swallow: An Indian Tale—Fowling in Faroe and Shetland—A Fuqueer's Curse—The Deserts of Africa—Life in an Indiaman—The Dealer in Wisdom—The Key of the Street.

Also issued with imprint: Boston: Dayton and Wentworth, 1855. AAS, UVB, Y

Also published as: The Mirror of the World; or, Stories from All Climes. By Moulton Hampton [pseud.?]. Boston: Wentworth & Co., 1856. 316 p., illus.   HEH

This contains a new introduction. The text of the tales is from the same plates as Yankee Enterprise, but repaged.

Also published as: Rovings on Land and Sea by Capt. Henry E. Davenport [pseud.?]. Boston: Wentworth and Company, 1857. 316 p., illus. AAS, N, NYP

2829 THE YANKEE SLAVE-DEALER; or, An Abolitionist Down South. A Tale for the Times. By a Texan . . . Nashville, Tenn.: the author, 1860. 368 p.

AAS, BP, BU, CU, HEH, LC, N, NYH, UC, UM, Y

2830 YELLOTT, GEORGE. The Funny Philosophers; or, Wags and Sweethearts. A Novel . . . Philadelphia: J. B. Lippincott & Co., 1872. 296 p.   AAS, BP, BU, LC, LCP, UC

YELLOW BIRD, pseud.   See Ridge, John Rollin

2831 [YOUNG, WILLIAM.] Mathieu Ropars et Cetera. By an Ex-Editor. New York: G. P. Putnam & Son, 1868. 236 p.

Contains short tales, poems, etc.   BP, BU, CU, HEH, LC, NYP

2832 ZILLAH, THE CHILD MEDIUM: A Tale of Spiritualism. By the Author of "My Confession, the Story of a Woman's Life" . . . New York: Dix, Edwards & Co., 1857. 298 p.

Laid in New Jersey.   AAS, BP, H, HEH, LC, N, NYP, UC, UM

TITLE INDEX

TITLE INDEX

Initial articles are usually omitted in this index.
Numbers refer to items.
An "n" after a number refers to the notes under the item.

Abbie Nott, 2826
Abraham Page, 1251
Actress in High Life, 7
Adalaska, 297
Adela Lincoln, 2585n
Adela, the Octoroon, 1271
Adèle Dubois, 2156n
Aden Power, 1831
Adopted Daughter, 466
Adopted Daughter; or, The Trials of Sabra, 29
Adrian, 1334
Adrift with a Vengeance, 638
Adventure on a Frozen Lake, 1305
Adventures in the Apache Country, 397
Adventures in the Wilderness, 1766
Adventures of a Gentleman, 805
Adventures of a Lodger, 445
Adventures of Clarence Bolton, 2167n
Adventures of Col. Gracchus Vanderbomb, 1369
Adventures of Fudge Fumble, 441n
Adventures of Lena Rouden, 1830
Adventures of My Cousin Smooth, 9
Adventures of One Terence McGrant, 1865
Adventures of Sir Lyon Bouse, 2705
AEnone, 1482
L'Africaine, 2738
After a Shadow, 82
After the Storm, 83
Against the World, 2617
Agnes: A Novel, 1903
Agnes Farriday, 537
Agnes Graham, 776
Agnes Hilton, 1218
Agnes of Sorrento, 2389
Agnes; or, The Beautiful Milliner, 1411
Agnes Stanhope, 2012
Agnes the Beautiful, 334
Agnes Wentworth, 1838
Ah-Meek, the Beaver, 436
Aid-de-Camp, 1604
Alas, Poor Ghost, 2210n

Alban: A Tale, 1309
Albert Hastings, 2696
Aldeane, 1152
Aleck and Pete, 40
Alethe, 2063
Alexander Tardy, 1293
Alfred Moreland, 266
Alice Barber, 335
Alice Brand, 2036
Alice Granger, 55
Alice Lee, 2331n
Alice Murray, 1219
Alice the Fisher Girl, 563
Alice Tracey, 495n
Alice Tracy, 674
Alice Vale, 2603
Alice Waters, 1194
All for Love, 806
Allegories of Life, 18
Allen House, 84
Allworth Abbey, 2290
Almost a Priest, 2803
Alone, 2438
Alpine Guide, 1894
Altha, 896
Amabel, 1511
Amanda Willson, 409
Amber Gods, 2338
Ambition, 629
Ambrose Fecit, 870
American Cardinal, 1519
American Evening Entertainments, 454n
American Family in Germany, 398
American Family Robinson, 250
American Girl Abroad, 1496
American Nights' Entertainments, 1022
American Scenery, 2030n
Americans in Rome, 1533
Among the Guerillas, 1002
Among the Pines, 1003
Amorous Intrigues, 61
Amours of an American Adventurer, 62
Amy, 1278n
Amy Denbrook, 2682
Amy Lee, 1205

381

ADDITIONS AND CORRECTIONS

ADDITIONS AND CORRECTIONS

The additions follow the form of presentation in *American Fiction,
1851-1875,* but no effort has been made to locate more than one copy
of each. New entries are those in which the item number is followed
by "a" or "b." The corrections and notes are self-explanatory when
used in conjunction with the main list.

Two bibliographies referred to in the notes are cited as follows:
Bibliography of American Literature, comp. Jacob Blanck, Vols. I-IV
(New Haven, 1955-63), as BAL; and William S. Powell, ed. *North
Carolina Fiction, 1734-1957* (Chapel Hill, 1958), as W. S. Powell.

10   See No. 14 for a later ed. with a new title and preface.

14   This is a later ed. of No. 10 with a new title and preface; first
      two and last three chapters (chapter XLVIII misnumbered
      XLIX) rewritten.

27a   ADDISON, ALVIN.   Ellen Walton; or, The Villain and His Victims
      . . . Cincinnati: H. M. Rulison, Queen City Publishing House.
      Philadelphia: Quaker City Publishing House, 1855.   77 p.
      Information from Princeton University Library.

29a   AGNES ARLINGTON; or, Life, Times, Troubles, Tribulations, and
      Sad End of Agnes Arlington, the Cotton Planter's Daughter
      . . . An Autobiographical Narrative.   Edited by Rev. A. R. B.
      . . . Baltimore, Philadelphia, New York, and Buffalo: A. R.
      Orton, 1854.   46+ p.
      A copy is in the possession of Thomas McDade, New York.

52a   [ALEXANDER, O. C.]   The Hermit of Aleova; or, The Shepherd
      Girl's Triumph. By Rob. Rapler [pseud.] . . . Albany: J.
      Munsell, 1857.   380 p.   AAS

52b   ALFREDUS, *pseud.* The Needle-Woman . . . [Boston], 1871.
      155 p.   LC

63a   ANNA, LOUISA, AND NANNIE; or, The Three Victims. With Full
      . . . Statements of the Intrigue . . . and Murder, Commit-
      ted by Daniel Longrave, the Accomplished Accomplice of
      Mother Higgins. Philadelphia: M. A. Milliette, 1859.   48 p.,
      front.
      A copy is in the possession of Thomas McDade, New York.

81   Written by Joseph Holt Ingraham.

83a ARTHUR, TIMOTHY SHAY. All's for the Best . . . Philadelphia: J. B. Lippincott & Co., 1869. 219 p. LC

Contents: Faith and Patience—Is He a Christian?—"Rich and Rare Were the Gems She Wore"—Not as a Child—Angels in the Heart—Cast Down, but Not Destroyed—Into Good Ground—Giving That Doth Not Impoverish—Was It Murder, or Suicide?—The Nursery Maid—My Father—The Christian Gentleman.

93 Add note: *And*, Philadelphia: J. W. Bradley. Auburn, N.Y.: H. A. Yates. New Haven: M. Bradley, 1855. HEH

100 1st ed. imprint: Philadelphia: J. W. Bradley, 1853. HEH

101 1st ed. imprint: Philadelphia: Lippincott, Grambo & Co., 1851. HEH

103 1st ed. imprint: Philadelphia: J. W. Bradley, 1853. HEH

137 1st ed. imprint: Philadelphia: Lippincott, Grambo & Co., 1851. AAS

138 Add note: *And*, Rochester: E. Darrow & Brother, 1856. HEH

138a ARTHUR, TIMOTHY SHAY. True Riches; or, Wealth without Wings . . . Philadelphia: J. W. Bradley, 1852. 210 p., front. Y

154 Written by Mrs. Sarah Mary (Brownson) Tenney.

160a THE AUTOBIOGRAPHY OF CHARLES MOORE, Revealing the History of the Most Remarkable Robberies . . . and His Terrible Revenge in the Murder of Richard White at Marseilles, France . . . Baltimore, Philadelphia, New York, and Buffalo: A. R. Orton, 1854. 48 p. HEH

188 Title and imprint should read: The Breach of Trust; or, The Professor and Possessor of Piety . . . Boston: Andrew F. Graves, 20 Cornhill [cop. 1869]. 330 p., illus. HEH

191 1st ed. imprint: Boston: Shepard, Clark and Company, 1857. AAS

239a [BEAN, FRANCIS A.] An Allegory: Containing an Interesting Analogy between the Order for Discovering Natural Curiosi-

ties and Founding Cities, and the United States of America . . .
Philadelphia, cop. 1872. 42 p.   HEH

HEH copy autographed by author.

240a [BEAUMONT, DONNA BROOKS.] Garangula. *See* title listed anonymously, No. 974.

242 This is a later ed. of No. 2782, with a new title and a front.

292a BERLIN, ELIZA ANNIE. Earth Angels and Hidden Oppression; or, The Life of Little Annie . . . Columbus [Ohio]: Printed by Nevins & Myers, 1868. 309 p.   HEH

309a BLANCHARD, G. C. Metropolitan Tales and Sketches . . . New York, 1873. 98 p., illus. Printed in double columns.   AAS

Contents: Ravelwild—Metropolitan Sketches: Morning, Noon, Night—Haunted House—Christmas Dreams—Gold Balls—Match Girl—Hobson & Co.—My Poor Relation—People's Choice for Alderman—Policeman's Story.

Cover imprint: New York: Union Printing Co., 1873.

311a BLAND, THOMAS AUGUSTUS. Farming as a Profession; or, How Charles Loring Made It Pay . . . Boston: Loring, 1870. 87 p.   LC

318a [BOERNSTEIN, HENRY.] The Mysteries of St. Louis. *See* title listed anonymously, No. 1778.

338 Earlier imprint: New York: Garrett & Co., 18 Ann Street [1853]. Copy noted in George MacManus Sales Cat. 137, item 117.

339a BRADBURY, OSGOOD. Emily, the Beautiful Seamstress; or, The Danger of the First Step. A Story of Life in New York . . . Boston: George H. Williams, 52 Washington Street [cop. 1853]. 100 p. Printed in double columns.   HEH

344 Earlier imprint: New York: Robert M. DeWitt, 160 & 162 Nassau Street [cop. 1857].   HEH

356a BRADLEY, JAMES A. A Story of Ocean Grove . . . [Asbury Park, N.J., 1874?] Cover title, 28 p.   HEH

405 Author's name: Mrs. Sarah Mary (Brownson) Tenney.

438   Imprint date should read 1854.   N

439   Add note: Also published as: *The Oracle of Romance; or, Young Ladies' Mentor . . . By a Lady*. Boston: Phillips, Sampson & Co. [cop. 1853].   AAS

439a   BUZ, *pseud*. Dolby and Father . . . New York: P. S. Wynkoop & Son, 1868. 53 p.   HEH

464a   CARRA, EMMA, *pseud*. Edna; or, An Antique Tale . . . Boston: James French and Company, 1858. 348 p., front.   HEH

470   Add publisher's address to imprint: No. 8 Howard Street.   BU

475a   CASSY; or, Early Trials. Boston: John P. Jewett and Company. Cleveland, Ohio: Jewett, Proctor, and Worthington. New York: Sheldon, Lamport, and Blakeman, 1855. 32 p., illus.   HEH

        Evidence not sufficient to attribute *Cassy* to Harriet Beecher Stowe. But a character of the same name had appeared in *Uncle Tom's Cabin*, which was issued by the same publisher in 1852. Several of the plates in *Cassy* were used earlier in the same publisher's 1853 ed. of *Uncle Tom's Cabin*.

520   Attributed to William G. Chester by Edgar J. Hinkel, ed. *Bibliog. of Calif. Fiction* (Oakland, 1938).

522a   THE CHRONICLES of the "Great Peace Jubilo" . . . Boston: New England News Company, 41 Court Street [cop. 1860]. 23 p.   HEH

        At head of title: "Price, Ten Cents."
        Copyright date fictitious; text of satire indicates events of about 1869, the date in the cover imprint.

538   Author's name: Mrs. Caroline E. T. Clarke. Wife of General DeWitt Clarke.

541   1st ed. dated 1864.   HEH

541a   CLARKE, THOMAS. Avondale: A Story of English Life . . . Chicago: Published and for sale by the author, 1874. 415 p.   HEH

567a [COBB, SYLVANUS.] Henry la Nuit; or, The Foundling of the Castle of Estella. A Tale of Navarre in the Olden Time. By Austin C. Burdick [pseud.]. New York: Samuel French, 121 Nassau Street [185-?]. 100 p. Printed in double columns.

AAS

Also contains: The Heroine of Cumberland Valley, by Mrs. M. E. Robinson.

——— Love's Triumph. *In* G. C. Hill, Rodolpho (1853), No. 1210a.

578 1st ed. title and imprint: The Ocean Martyr; or, The Hunter Spy of Virginia. A Revolutionary Story of Sea and Shore. By Austin C. Burdick [pseud.]. New York: Samuel French, 151 Nassau, corner of Spruce Street [185-?]. HEH

586a COBB, SYLVANUS. The Yankee Champion; or, The Tory and His League. A Revolutionary Story of the Land and Sea . . . Boston: F. Gleason's Publishing Hall, 1852. 100 p. Printed in double columns. AAS

598a COLFAX, JASPER. Over the Brink; or, The Peril of Beauty. A Story of Life in a Factory Town . . . Lewiston, Maine [1869?]. 100 p. HEH

627 1st state imprint: New York: E. B. Treat & Co. Baltimore, Md.: J. S. Morrow. New Orleans, La.: J. H. Hummel. Nashville, Tenn.: A. S. Kimzey, 1867. Listed by BAL 3725.

CORINNE, *pseud. See* Tucker, Mrs. William H. (in Additions and Corrections).

645a COWAN, FRANK. Zomara: A Romance of Spain . . . Pittsburgh, Pa.: [Stevenson & Foster, printers], 1873. 70, [1] p., illus. Information from LC card.

648a COX, PALMER. Squibs of California; or, Every-Day Life Illustrated . . . Hartford, Conn.: Mutual Publishing Company. San Francisco, Cal.: A. Roman & Co., 1874. 491 p., illus.

HEH

649 DELETE. Cozzens wrote only the "Ante-Preface." The author was Sir Samuel Ferguson, according to Jacob Blanck.

654   1st ed. imprint and pagination: Ashborough [N.C.]: R. H. Brown, 1851. 32 p. Listed by W. S. Powell, No. 115. His No. 116, by the same author, is *Naomi Wise* . . . Pinnacle [N.C.]: W. C. Phillips [n.d.]. 27 p.

CREOLE, *pseud.* *See* Massena, Mrs. Agnese M. C. (in Additions and Corrections).

669a   CUMMINS, MARGARET. Leaves from My Port Folio, Original and Selected, Together with a Religious Narrative . . . St. Louis, Mo.: Wm. E. Foote, book and job printer, 1860. 181 p.

                                                             AAS

Contains: A Story of Real Life in Kentucky—Mary Bradford: A True Story—Rose Haywood's Dream—Coming Down.

674   Imprint of HEH copy includes New York.

DARGAN, CLARA VICTORIA, should read Maclean, Mrs. Clara Victoria (Dargan).

694   Imprint of ed. in note should read: Boston: Tompkins & Company, 1863.   AAS

750a   DICKENS, CHARLES. The Mystery of Edwin Drood. Complete . . . Brattleboro, Vt.: T. P. James, 1873. 488 p.   HEH
     2d title page: Part Second of the Mystery of Edwin Drood. By the Spirit-Pen of Charles Dickens, through a Medium [i.e., Thomas Power James] . . . Brattleboro, Vt.: T. P. James, 1873.

DOUGHTY, Mrs. S. P. First Impressions. *In* F. Hunter, The Heiress of Toulon (1852), No. 1306b.

790   Read "sold by" for "published by" in notes.

828   Delete note.

828a   DURIVAGE, FRANCIS ALEXANDER. Steel and Gold; or, The Heir of Glenville. A Domestic Tale of Revolutionary Days . . . New York: Samuel French, 121 Nassau Street [185-?]. 100 p. Printed in double columns.   HEH

829   This is a later ed. of No. 828, with a new title.

EARNEST, ELSIE, *pseud.* *See* Scruggs, Mrs. M. V. (in Additions and Corrections).

834a EDGERTON, WILD, *pseud?* Railroad Life in America . . . Chicago: Birney Hand & Company, 1870. 279, [1] p.   HEH
Copyrighted by Brock L. McVickar. Cushing credits the work to him.

839a EDWARDS, HENRY. Fashion and Famine: Life in New York . . . New York: Advance Publishing Company [n.d.]. 98 p. Printed in double columns.   N

864a EMERALDA, *pseud.* Myrtle Leaves in Spring Time; or, Early Friends and Friendships . . . Cincinnati: Joseph A. Hemann, 1863. 202 p.   HEH

868 Written by Mrs. Rebecca Harrington (Smith) Taylor Pollard.

869a EMMONS, L. A Prophetic Abstract from the Proceedings of the Trojan Society for the Retardation of Science . . . Troy, N.Y.: Wm. H. Young & Blake, 1870. 20 p.   HEH

870a ENGLISH, THOMAS DUNN. Zara; or, The Girl of the Period. A Novel . . . New York: Hilton and Syme, No. 128 Nassau Street [1869]. [84] p.
Listed by BAL 5525.

877 HEH copy has wrapper dated 1852.

905 Author's name: Mrs. Anna (Mariska) Fitch.

962a FROTHINGHAM, WASHINGTON. Once More: A Story of New York . . . New York: Sheldon & Co., 1875. 336 p., illus.
  HEH

965 1st ed. imprint: New York: Robert Carter and Brothers, 1872.
  HEH

974 Written by Donna Brooks Beaumont.

977 1st ed. imprint adds: London: S. Low, Son & Co.   HEH

978 1st ed. imprint adds: London: S. Low, Son & Co.   HEH

995 Bracket date in imprint.

1014a GOTT, ADA AUGUSTA. Dare Fairfax . . . New York: E. J. Hale & Son. Baltimore: W. H. H. Adkisson, 1872. 174 p.   HEH

1018a GREELEY, ROBERT F. Cedar Cliff; or, The Mystery of the Haunted Acre . . . New York: Henry L. Williams, No. 12 North William Street [1872]. 95 p. Printed in double columns. HEH

Cover imprint: New York: American News Company, 1872.

1037 Title should read: The Elm Tree Tales.

1039a GUERNSEY, CLARA FLORIDA. The Merman and the Figure-Head. *See* under Lucy Ellen Guernsey, where it was incorrectly entered, No. 1042.

1042 Written by Clara Florida Guernsey, not Lucy Ellen Guernsey.

1044 1st ed. imprint: Philadelphia: Parry and McMillan, 1857.
AAS

1073 Note should read: HEH has a 2d copy with textual variations pp. 218-223; the song "Our Lady of the Hospital" added pp. 220-222.

1078 Imprint of HEH copy includes: London: S. Low, Son & Co.

1114a HARRY GRANTHAM; or, The Robbers of Saint Louis. A Tale Designed to Show the Superior Power and Efficacy of Mild and Persuasive Treatment over That of Harsh, Tyrannical, and Debasing . . . Steubenville: Printed at the Messenger Book and Job Office, 1851. 31 p. HEH

1135 Title should read: The House of the Seven Gables.

1153a [HEAVEN, MRS. LOUISE (PALMER).] Leah's Confessions: An Autobiography . . . San Francisco: A. Roman and Company. New York, 1867. 130 p. Printed in double columns. HEH

1153b [HEBBARD, WILLIAM WALLACE.] Will It Come? A Story of Instinct, Intuition, Metaphysics, Love, and Worship. By Leland Searcher [pseud.]. Hyde Park [Mass.]: Hildreth & Getchell, printers, 1870. 355 p. HEH

1205 Add note: *Also issued with imprint:* Boston: Higgins & Bradley, 1856. HEH

1210 1st ed. date of title in note: 1856. Information from Princeton University Library.

1210a HILL, GEORGE CANNING. Rodolpho; or, The Mystery of Venice. A Romance of Venice and the Adriatic ... Boston: F. Gleason's Publishing Hall, 1853. 100 p., illus. Printed in double columns. AAS

Also contains: Love's Triumph; or, The Music Teacher's Conquest, by Sylvanus Cobb—The Arrest; or, The Daring of a Patriot Lover, by F. Clinton Barrington [i.e., A. G. Piper].

"The Arrest" printed earlier, No. 1909.

———— Tim Tilbury's Vision. *In* F. Hunter, The Heiress of Toulon (1852), No. 1306b.

1216a THE HISTORY OF A SEWING-MACHINE. New York: C. S. Westcott & Co., printers, 1867. Cover title, 16 p. HEH

As told by the machine.

1216b HISTORY OF THE MULLIGAN GUARD ... New York: Collin & Small, 1874. 31 p., illus. HEH

1234 Read "Maude" for "Maud" in title.

1253 Add note: Also published as: *Kate Sinclair; or, Home Is Home.* Cincinnati, Ohio: A. A. Kelley, 1861. HEH

1255a A HOME SCENE; or, Mr. Aston's First Evening with Grover & Baker's Celebrated Family Sewing Machine ... New York: T. Holman, printer, 1861. Cover title, 20 p., illus. HEH

Story occupies first 6 p.

HOWE, MRS. SARAH M. Ervilla. *In* F. Hunter, The Heiress of Toulon (1852), No. 1306b.

1293 1st ed. imprint: New York: H. Long & Brother, 43 Ann Street [cop. 1852]. NYP

1303 Author's name: Mrs. Rebecca Stockwell Hume.

1306a HUNTER, FRED. The Belle of Paris; or, The Wrecker of the Cliff. A Romance of England, France, and Italy ... Boston: F. Gleason, 1851. 100 p., illus. Printed in double columns.
HEH

Also contains: The Secret; or, The Gambler's Daughter—The Prisoner of Ehrenburg.

1306b ───── The Heiress of Toulon; or, A Sailor's Fortune. A Descriptive Romance of the Land and the Ocean ... Boston: Frederick Gleason, 1852. 100 p., illus. Printed in double columns. HEH

Also contains: Ervilla; or, The Patriot Captive, by Mrs. Sarah M. Howe —First Impressions, by Mrs. S. P. Doughty—Tim Tilbury's Vision; or, Raising a Salary, by Geo. Canning Hill—Oaklawn High School, by Mrs. E. C. Lovering.

1314a [INGRAHAM, JOSEPH HOLT.] The Arrow of Gold. *See* title listed anonymously, No. 81.

1317 Cf. BAL 10053 for variant imprints.

1319 Read "illus." for "front."

1319a INGRAHAM, JOSEPH HOLT. Rivingstone; or, The Young Ranger Hussar. A Romance of the Revolution . . . New York: Dewitt & Davenport, 1855. 100 p. UVB

"The Young Sculptor," by Mrs. Ellis, an English writer, occupies pp. 67-100.

1321 Add note: *And:* Philadelphia: G. G. Evans. New York: D. W. Evans and Co., 1860. Listed by BAL 10054.

JAMES, THOMAS POWER. *See* Dickens, C. The Mystery of Edwin Drood (1873), No. 750a.

1355 DELETE. Not written by Virginia Wales Johnson.

1366 Bracket: Innes & Company, printers.

1366a JONES, CLEMENTINA. The Shades of Sorrow Dispelled by the Sunshine of Love: A Story Illustrating Christian Benevolence, Gratitude, and Early Piety . . . Troy, N.Y.: Daily Times Steam Printing House, 1870. 160 p. HEH

1399a [JONES, JUSTIN.] The Smuggler King! or, The Rovers of the Antilles. An Ocean Romance. By Harry Hazel [pseud.] . . . Boston, 1855. 100 p., illus. Printed in double columns. HEH

At head of title: "An Original Story, by Harry Hazel."

1400 1st ed. title and imprint: Sweeney Todd; or, The Ruffian Barber. A Tale of the Terrors of the Seas and the Mysteries of the City. By Captain Merry [pseud.]. New York: H. Long & Brother, 121 Nassau Street [ca. 1854-57]. 110 p., illus.   HEH

1405   Add to imprint: Cincinnati: H. B. Pearson & Co., 17 East Fourth St.   AAS

1477a   KINGMAN, MRS. FRANCES. Intuition . . . Hartford: F. Kingman, 1870. 258 p.   HEH
Verso of title page: "Printed by Case, Lockwood & Brainard, Hartford, Conn."

1524   Publishers in main entry and note should be exchanged.

1549a   THE LIFE, CONFESSION, AND EXECUTION of the Jew and Jewess, Gustavus Linderhoff and Fanny Victoria Talzingler, Where [Who?] Were Hung in Asheville, North Carolina, Oct. 27, 1855, for the Triple Murder of . . . Three Orphan Children . . . Baltimore: A. R. Orton, 1856. 50 p.
Listed by W. S. Powell, No. 323.

1562   Author's name: Mrs. Elizabeth Dorcas (Abbot) Livermore.

1568a   [LOCKE, DAVID ROSS.] Inflation at the Cross Roads: Being a History of the Rise and Fall of the Onlimited Trust and Confidence Company, of Confedrit X Roads. In a Series of Five Letters. By Petroleum V. Nasby [pseud.]. New York: American News Company, 1875. Cover title, 24 p., illus.   HEH

1578a   LOGAN, THOMAS B. History of Timothy Tugg Mutton . . . St. Louis, Mo.: Printed by M. Needner, 1852. 108 p.   N

1589a   LOVE, SUICIDE, AND MURDER!! The True History of the Unfortunate Loves of Mary Caroline Austin and Edgar Worthington, with the Full Particulars of Their Awful Suicide . . . Baltimore, Philadelphia, New York, & Buffalo: Arthur R. Orton, 1856. 36 p., front.
A copy is in the possession of Thomas McDade, New York.

LOVERING, MRS. E. C. Oaklawn High School. In F. Hunter, The Heiress of Toulon (1852), No. 1306b.

1598   Written by Lydia M. Millard.

1608   Title and imprint should read: The Irish Widow's Son; or, The Pikemen of Ninety-Eight. A Story of the Irish Rebellion . . . By Con O'Leary [pseud.] . . . Boston: Patrick Donahoe, 1869. 224 p.   HEH

1609   Read "220 p." for "230 p."

1638a   McLAIN, MARY WEBSTER. Daisy Ward's Work . . . Boston: Loring, cor. Bromfield and Washington Streets [cop. 1871]. 242 p., front.   HEH

         MACLEAN, MRS. CLARA VICTORIA (DARGAN). Riverland: A Charming Story of Southern Life. *In* The Southern Field and Fireside Novelette [1863], No. 2287.

         MARCH, CHARLES, *pseud. See* Munn, B. T. (in Additions and Corrections).

1674   HEH ed. has imprint on verso of title page: Portland: Press of B. Thurston and Co.; date at end of text, "February, 1867."

1677a   [MASSENA, MRS. AGNESE M. C.] Marie's Mistake: A Woman's History. By Creole [pseud.] . . . Boston: Pratt Brothers, 1868. 357 p.
         Information from LC card.

1679   DELETE. Of English origin.

1682   Read "99 p." for "96 p." Printed in double columns.

1691a   [MEANEY, MARY L.] Elinor Johnston, Founded on Facts, and Maurice and Genevieve: Catholic Tales . . . Philadelphia, 1868. 136 p.   AAS

1708a   [MILLARD, LYDIA M.] Olie. *See* under author's initials, No. 1598.

1718a   MISS TAMAR ALLEN'S NARRATIVE of the Tientsin Massacre in China, during Which So Many Christians and Foreigners Were Ruthlessly Butchered by the Chinese . . . and Her Own Miraculous Escape . . . Philadelphia: C. W. Alexander, No. 224 South Third Street, cop. 1870. 28 p., illus.   LC

1729a THE MONK OF THE MOUNTAINS; or, A Description of the Joys of Paradise. Being the Life and Wonderful Experience of an Aged Hermit, Who Was Taken by His Deceased Friend to the First Heaven and There Shown the Beauties and Happiness of the Spirit Land . . . Indianapolis, Ind.: Downey & Brouse, printers, 1866. 256 p., front.   HEH

1733a MOORE, DAVID ALBERT. The Age of Progress; or, A Panorama of Time. In Four Visions . . . New York: Sheldon, Blakeman & Co., 1856. 321 p., illus.   LC

1763a [MUNN, B. T.] Love on the Wing: A Novel. By Charles March [pseud.] . . . Boston: Frank H. Fuller, 1871. 436 p.   HEH

1764 1st ed. imprint of title in note: Philadelphia: John E. Potter, 1865.   HEH

1778 Written by Henry Boernstein.

1784a THE NEW FARMS: A Story for Farmers. Boston: John M. Hewes, 1860. 42 p.   H

1829a OUR NOVEL. By Six Authors. Souvenir. Hand-Press Edition. Complimentary to the Authors. [Chicago?], 1874. 129 p.   HEH

Contents: How They Met, by A. L. B.—Now You See Him, by B. L.—And Now You Don't, by B. D.—Here He Is Again, by A. G. K.—A Much Needed Explanation, by M.—Finale, as Usual [unsigned].

"This work a souvenir of the Chicago conflagration . . . dedicated by the editor to rebuilt Chicago," dedication.

1850a PATTERSON, JOHN. Charles Hopewell; or, Society as It Is, and as It Should Be . . . Cincinnati: Longley & Brother, 1853. 290 p.

Information from LC card.

1860a PEASE, NETTIE M. The Golden Key; or, Mysteries beyond the Veil . . . Chicago: Northwestern Publishing Company, 1871. 391, [1] p.   HEH

1877a PETERSON, BELLE. One Word and a Tear; or, The Wounded Dove. The Story of Lenore Parolee . . . St. Louis: Published for the authoress, 1875. 248 p.

Listed by W. S. Powell, No. 476.

1886   Add note: *Also issued with imprint:* Andover: W. F. Draper, 1851.   HEH

1905a   [PINCKARD, MRS. M. E.] Bread of Heaven and Husks of Swine; or, The Curse of Jealousy. A Life History. Baltimore: Printed by John Y. Slater, 1874.   304 p.   HEH

1909   Add note: Later printed in No. 1210a.

1909a   [PIPER, A. G.] The Bel Isabel; or, The Conspirators of Cuba . . . By F. Clinton Barrington [pseud.]. Boston: F. Gleason, 1851.   100 p.   Printed in double columns.   AAS

1910a   [————] Kate Wynyard; or, The Wanderer of the Sea. A Story of River, Main, and Ocean. By F. Clinton Barrington [pseud.]. Boston: F. Gleason, 1851.   100 p.   Printed in double columns.   AAS

1911   DELETE. This is an incomplete part of No. 1912.

1915a   PLACE, EDWARD R. The Commotion in Moontown: Unique Assault on the Newspapers. A Rare Discussion . . . San Jose, Cal.: Printed at the office of the Mercury, 1874.   74 p.   HEH

1916   Add note: *Also issued with imprint:* New York: H. Dayton. Indianapolis, Ind.: Asher & Company, 1859.   HEH

1918a   [POLLARD, MRS. REBECCA HARRINGTON (SMITH) TAYLOR.] Emma Bartlett. *See* title listed anonymously, No. 868.

1949a   PRATT, MISS L. J. The Unfortunate Mountain Girl . . . Boston: Printed by W. S. Damrell and F. C. Moore, 1860.   160 p., illus.   HEH
      Contents differ in part from No. 1949.

1973   Written by Isaac Fitzgerald Shepard. This is Wright (1774-1850), No. 2380, rewritten. Contents differ in part.

1986   1st ed. imprint: Boston: Patrick Donahoe, 3 Franklin Street, 1853.   AAS

1990   DELETE. English author.

1991   DELETE. English author.

RAPLER, ROB., *pseud.* *See* Alexander, O. C. (in Additions and Corrections).

2016   See Bibliog. Soc. of America, *Papers*, LVI (1962), 488, for variant eds.

2021   Add note: *And*, Gloucester: Proctor & Brothers, 1856.   HEH

2029a   RICHARDS, MRS. MARIA (TOLMAN). The Year of Jubilee; or, Familiar Phases of Hebrew Life . . . New York: Sheldon, Blakeman & Company [cop. 1858]. 140 p., illus.   HEH

2030   1st ed. date: 1855.   HEH

2033a   [RICHMOND, JOHN M.] The Adventures of Jefferson Plum and His Daughter Nancy, in the Great City, the First Time . . . Thompsonville, Conn.: Printed for the publisher, 1866. 46 p.
        HEH

2072   1st ed. imprint: New York: Samuel French, 151 Nassau, corner of Spruce Street [185-?]. Printed in double columns. *Also contains:* The Two Mottoes, by Miss Anne T. Wilbur.
        HEH

2084a   ROBINSON, JOHN HOVEY. Sibylla Joy; or, The Mystery of the Brownstone House . . . New York: Frederic A. Brady [cop. 1864]. 82 p., illus. Printed in double columns.   AAS

ROBINSON, MRS. M. E. The Heroine of Cumberland Valley. *In* S. Cobb, Henry la Nuit [185-?], No. 567a.

2091   Title and date should read: The Enchanted Princess . . . 1872. 201 p.   AAS

2112a   ROE, AZEL STEVENS. To Love and to Be Loved, and The Minister's Story . . . New York: Carleton. London: S. Low, Son & Co., 1873. 309 p.   HEH

2120a   ROE, PETER QUIRK. Regina of Gazeran Castle; or, The Countess and the Gamekeeper. A Stirring Tale of France . . . Bos-

ton: George H. Williams, 52 Washington Street, cop. 1852.
100 p.   Printed in double columns.   HEH
Copyright notice at head of title.

2132a [RUFFIN, EDMUND.]   Anticipations of the Future, to Serve as
Lessons for the Present Time.   In the Form of Extracts of
Letters from an English Resident in the United States, to the
London Times, from 1864 to 1870.   With an Appendix on
the Causes and Consequences of the Independence of the
South . . .   Richmond, Va.: J. W. Randolph, 1860.   416 p.
HEH

2144a RUSSELL, ROBERT.   Die Russischen Schwestern: Eine Ge-
schichte von der Belagerung von Sebastopol . . .   Baltimore,
Philadelphia, New York, und Buffalo: Arthur R. Orton, 1856.
50 p., illus.   HEH

2158a SCHELE DE VERE, MAXIMILIAN.   The Great Empress: A Portrait . . .   Philadelphia: J. B. Lippincott & Co., 1870.   397 p.
HEH

2169a [SCRUGGS, MRS. M. V.]   Sketches.   By Elsie Earnest [pseud.].
Baltimore: Turnbull Brothers, 1874.   181 p.   HEH
Contains: Advertising for a Wife; or, The Love Chase of a Con-
federate Soldier—Circumstantial Evidence—Virginia and South Caro-
lina: United in Love as in War—The Wife's Temptation—Will It Pay?
A Minister's Mistake—Moral Heroism—What Novel Reading Did for
Me—Mismatched—In the Country; or, Literature vs. Housewifery—
All for the Best—That Old, Old Story—Annie Armistead—Love and
Hate.

SEARCHER, LELAND, *pseud.*   *See* Hebbard, William Wallace (in
Additions and Corrections).

2200a [SHEPARD, ISAAC FITZGERALD.]   Household Tales.   By Job
Puritan [pseud.].   *See* under pseud., No. 1973.
This is Wright (1774-1850), No. 2380, rewritten.   Contents differ in part.

2232a SINGLETON, *Col.*   Ella Marshall; or, All for Love.   A Prize
Tale . . .   Dexter, Me.: Leviathan Printing Establishment
[185-?].   47 p.   AAS

2235a SIX MONTHS among the Secessionists: A Thrilling Narrative of . . . Miss Sarah L. Palmer . . . Philadelphia: Barclay & Co., 1862. 40 p., illus. UVB

2237 Delete subtitle, which first appeared in 1854 ed., No. 2238.

2247a [SMALL, GEORGE G.] Masonry Exposed. New York: Winchell & Small, 1871. 32 p., illus. Printed in double columns. HEH

2248a [————] Odd-Fellowship Exposed . . . New York: Winchell & Small, 1872. 32 p., illus. Printed in double columns. HEH

2272a SMITH, RICHARD PENN. The Miscellaneous Works of the Late Richard Penn Smith. Collected by His Son, Horace W. Smith. Philadelphia: H. W. Smith, 1856. 326 p. HEH
"Fugitive Prose Now First Collected" occupies pp. [139]-326.

2275 Add note: Also published as: *Romance and Humor of the Rail.* New York: G. W. Carleton & Co. London: S. Low, Son & Co., 1873. This is the 1871 ed. rewritten and rearranged. HEH

2287 "Clara Victoria Dargan" in note should read "Mrs. Clara Victoria (Dargan) Maclean."

2334 DELETE. English author.

2336 In note read "Fate" for "Faith."

STOCKTON, FRANK RICHARD, preferred to Stockton, Francis Richard.

2436a TELLALL, TEMPERANCE, *pseud.* The Minister of E.; or, Evils in the Church. A True Story . . . Skowhegan [Me.]: Printed for the author, 1862. Cover title, 59 p. AAS

2437a [TENNEY, MRS. SARAH MARY (BROWNSON).] At Anchor. *See* title listed anonymously, No. 154.

2437b [————] Marian Elwood. *See* under maiden name, No. 405.

433

2454a TESTUT, CHARLES. Le Vieux Salomon; ou, Un Famille d'Esclaves au XIXe Siecle . . . Nouvelle-Orléans, 1872. 176 p.

Title listed by Donald E. Thompson, *A Bibliog. of Louisiana Books . . . in . . . the University of Alabama Library* (University, Ala., 1947), No. 1999.

2468 1st ed. date: 1872.　　HEH

2488a [THOMPSON, GEORGE.] Mysteries and Miseries of Philadelphia. By a Member of the Pennsylvania Bar. New York: Williams & Co., 21 Ann Street [185-?]. 100 p., illus.　HEH

2525a [TOWNSEND, FREDERIC.] Clouds and Sunshine . . . New York: John S. Taylor, 1853. 254 p.　　HEH

2552 Delete "Also issued" note.

2559a [TUCKER, MRS. WILLIAM H.] Idealities. By Corinne [pseud.]. Philadelphia: J. B. Lippincott & Co., 1859. 50 p., 1 l.　　AAS

2567 Add note: Also published as: *False Pride; or, Two Ways to Matrimony*. Philadelphia: T. B. Peterson & Brothers, 306 Chestnut Street [cop. 1866].　　HEH

2576a [VALENTINE, MANN SATTERWHITE.] Amadeus; or, A Night with the Spirit. By Karl Valmann [pseud.]. New York: Charles Scribner, 1853. 102 p.　　HEH

VALMANN, KARL, *pseud. See* Valentine, Mann Satterwhite (in Additions and Corrections).

2589 1st ed. date of title in note: 1859.　　HEH

2624 1st ed. imprint: New York: D. & J. Sadlier & Co., 164 William Street. Boston, 128 Federal Street. Montreal, cor. of Notre Dame and St. Francis Xavier streets, 1853.　　AAS

2701a WHITE, M. AGNES. Gordon Lodge; or, Retribution. An Autobiography . . . Baltimore: Kelly, Piet and Company, 174 W. Baltimore Street [cop. 1873]. 292 p.　　HEH

WILBUR, ANNE T. The Two Mottoes. *In* J. H. Robinson, The Maid of the Ranche [185-?], No. 2072 (in Additions and Corrections).

434

2741   Earlier imprint: New York: R. M. DeWitt (late DeWitt & Davenport), publisher, 160 and 162 Nassau Street [1858?].

                 HEH

2757a   WILLIS, F. R. The Dancing Star; or, The Smuggler of the Chesapeake. A Story of the Coast and Sea . . . Boston: F. Gleason, 1851. 100 p. Printed in double columns.   HEH

2779a   WITHBECK, TREBOR R. The Life, Adventures, and Elopement of Emily La Croix, the Poisoner. Also, an Account of Jean La Croix, Her Brother, Better Known in California as Leon Gabralli . . . Baltimore, Philadelphia, New York, and Buffalo: M. A. Milliette [cop. 1856]. 50 p., illus.   HEH

2782   See No. 242 for later ed. with a new title and a front.

2827   DELETE. Teen-age category.